The Rise of the Global Co

This is the first full account of how an influential form of commercial organization – the multinational enterprise – drove globalization and contributed to the making of the modern world. Robert Fitzgerald explores the major role of multinational enterprises in the events of world history, from the nineteenth century to the present, revealing how the growth of businesses that operated across borders contributed to an unprecedented worldwide transformation and deepening interdependence between countries. He demonstrates how international businesses shaped the economic development and competitiveness of nations, their politics and sovereignty, and the balance of power in international relations. *The Rise of the Global Company* uses the lessons of history to question prominent contemporary interpretations of multinationals and their consequences, and offers a truly wide-ranging survey of multinational enterprise, spanning two hundred years and five continents.

ROBERT FITZGERALD is a Reader in Business History and International Management at Royal Holloway, University of London. He is the author or co-author of six books, including *Doing Business in Emerging Markets: Opportunities and Challenges, Rowntree and the Marketing Revolution, 1862–1969* (Cambridge University Press, 2007 and 1995), *The Growth of Nations: Culture, Competitiveness and the Problems of Globalization*, and *British Labour Management and Industrial Welfare, 1846–1939*. He is also the editor of seven books, including *Remaking Management: Beyond Global and Local* (Cambridge University Press, 2008).

NEW APPROACHES TO ECONOMIC AND SOCIAL HISTORY

SERIES EDITORS

Nigel Goose, University of Hertfordshire
Larry Neal, University of Illinois, Urbana-Champaign

New Approaches to Economic and Social History is an important new textbook series published in association with the Economic History Society. It provides concise but authoritative surveys of major themes and issues in world economic and social history from the post-Roman recovery to the present day. Books in the series are by recognized authorities operating at the cutting edge of their field with an ability to write clearly and succinctly. The series consist principally of single-author works – academically rigorous and groundbreaking – which offer comprehensive, analytical guides at a length and level accessible to advanced school students and undergraduate historians and economists.

The Rise of the Global Company

Multinationals and the Making of the Modern World

ROBERT FITZGERALD

Royal Holloway, University of London

CAMBRIDGE
UNIVERSITY PRESS

University Printing House, Cambridge CB2 8BS, United Kingdom

Cambridge University Press is part of the University of Cambridge.

It furthers the University's mission by disseminating knowledge in the pursuit of education, learning and research at the highest international levels of excellence.

www.cambridge.org
Information on this title: www.cambridge.org/9780521849746

© Robert Fitzgerald 2015

This publication is in copyright. Subject to statutory exception and to the provisions of relevant collective licensing agreements, no reproduction of any part may take place without the written permission of Cambridge University Press.

First published 2015

Printed in the United Kingdom by TJ International Ltd. Padstow Cornwall

A catalogue record for this publication is available from the British Library

Library of Congress Cataloguing in Publication data
Fitzgerald, Robert, 1959–
The rise of the global company : multinationals and the making of the modern world / Robert Fitzgerald.
    pages   cm. – (New approaches to economic and social history)
Includes bibliographical references and index.
ISBN 978-0-521-84974-6 (hardback)
1. International business enterprises.   I. Title.
HD2755.5.F49   2015
338.8′8 – dc23   2015002847

ISBN 978-0-521-84974-6 Hardback
ISBN 978-0-521-61496-2 Paperback

Cambridge University Press has no responsibility for the persistence or accuracy of URLs for external or third-party internet websites referred to in this publication, and does not guarantee that any content on such websites is, or will remain, accurate or appropriate.

Contents

Tables

Preface and acknowledgements

I began writing this book with a number of objectives. I wanted to offer a comprehensive survey of the development and impact of modern multinational enterprise, from its origins to contemporary times. I hope that the story that emerges will appeal to any reader with an interest in history or world affairs, as well as offering insights for the specialist. I decided on a largely chronological account. There was the solid reason that such an account did not exist for a general history of multinational enterprise, and chronological narrative – describing the sequence of events, and connecting the context and the detail – is a fundamental part of an historian's toolkit. It was always apparent that it would be impossible for one book or one author to cover every aspect of multinational enterprise over the span of 200 years and more. I have focused on showing the major role of multinational enterprises in the events of world or international history. Empires, nation states, government policies, wars, and differences in economic development have been critical to the evolution of multinational enterprise, and to the ability of multinationals to exploit their competitive advantages and to fashion global networks. By the end of the book, I trust the reader will have a clearer notion of the when, where, why and how of multinational enterprises over their long history.

In so far as I have been able to achieve any of my aims, I should acknowledge a number of debts. I have to thank Cambridge University Press, Michael Watson, the History editor, for his many valuable insights and useful advice on everything, from content to structure and language, and my excellent copy-editor, Pat Harper. I received a great deal of help from companies, archives and libraries that answered my enquiries. I am grateful to several anonymous referees, who raised questions of the original proposal and the final manuscript. I owe special thanks, however, to Mira Wilkins for spending so much time reading my manuscript, and I benefited greatly from her analytical precision and acknowledged standards of scholarship. I would also like to thank specific colleagues at the School of Management of Royal Holloway, University of London, who encouraged me in my writing of such a large historical monograph, and colleagues in other departments and in the Universities and Colleges Union, whose support I had reason to greatly appreciate. Finally, for deferred holidays, and other impositions, I want to thank my wife, Maria Christina, my young daughter Izabelle who luckily absorbs so much of my attention, my son Alex, and the rest of my family, Louisa and Christopher.

Robert Fitzgerald

1 | Multinationals, states and the international economy

International business and the historian

Through tracing the rise of the global company, we can observe a major influence on the modern era: few would question the importance of multinational enterprise to the world economy, but multinationals have shaped, too, the politics and societies of individual countries, and the relations and power balance between nations. The bonds between the economic and political are too often downplayed in the accounts of international history, more concerned with states, diplomatic alliances, and wars. Yet European industrialization and rising living standards in the nineteenth century incited the search for raw materials and commodities, trade and investment overseas, and imperial expansion. Cold War divisions and the economic, technological, and military hegemony of the USA shaped the workings of the post-war international economy. With the liberalization of markets and cross-border investment from the late twentieth century onwards, it was multinationals that hastened and transformed the economic interdependence of countries.

While the governments of investing nations supported their firms abroad, host nation governments strove through their policies to gain from these investments, and, in many cases, to protect encroachments on their sovereignty; for multinationals, governments were as much part of the business challenge as trends in the global marketplace. In addition to changing the nature of individual states, the rise of the global company reminds us that national economies did not develop in isolation: cross-border interaction and the transfer of capital, technology, business practices and much else have determined the fortunes of countries and their industries. As a result, multinationals have been both a force for change and dynamism, and a magnet for criticism and concern.

Economists, during the 1960s, fashioned the idea of 'multinational enterprise', without realizing how long it had existed as a form of business. Others soon grasped that the giant international corporation, which had become such a prominent feature of the post-war world, had deep origins (Wilkins, 1970; Stopford and Wells, 1972; Stopford, 1974; Franko, 1976). Each revelation remained, nonetheless, a preamble to the main analysis. Why might we move historical study centre stage instead? One suggestion borrows heavily from leading ideas in strategic management and the theory of international business, which view the firm or the multinational as a unique bundle of organizational systems, managerial knowledge, technologies, products and skills. These 'capabilities' – held internally within the firm – are portrayed as the sources of a multinational's success against competitors, and the reason why it can overcome the liability of being in a 'foreign' market (Dunning and Lundan, 2008). The choices made within the firm, whether done consciously or unconsciously, when evolving its unique traits, occur over time, and have long-lasting effects on its performance and on the prospects of competitors. The development of internal capabilities, it follows, is a suitable candidate for the techniques of the historian (Jones and Khanna, 2006).

Another argument appears more closely linked to factors external to the firm, and more rooted in the academic traditions of (international) political economy (Stopford and Strange, 1991): multinationals have had far-reaching effects on nation states and on the structures of global commerce, just as they have been influenced in turn, and analysts can only study their complicated interactions over a lengthy period of time. Finally, history, by its very nature, has a role in questioning claims of the 'new'. How do we judge the many confident assertions that globalization began in the 1990s; that it would inevitably bring an end to the nation state; or that the world had reached an unprecedented turning point? The past can and does offer salutary, alternative perspectives on current events.

On the other hand, we run the danger of a contrary mistake, tracking continuities in international business, and failing to spot changes of long-term significance. We have to ask, too, whether history should be a testing ground for contemporary questions. If so, how far back should we reach into the past before exaggerating connections with the present, and misunderstanding or disregarding the circumstances of times gone? It is not immediately obvious how dating the origins of a firm's competencies helps an analysis of its contemporary strengths and weaknesses. In 2008, the largest multinational was General Electric. Its history is closely tied to the history of US technology, not surprising perhaps for an enterprise that grew from the laboratory of iconic innovator Thomas Edison (Whitney, 1985).

But how might this fact change any detailed explanation of the $4bn and more currently spent by GE on research across five world-wide locations? *Fortune Global 500*, in 2011, classified the modern GE as a 'diversified financial', since it had become a complex business group making multiple products; the *Forbes Global 2000* opted for 'conglomerate'. General Electric no longer concentrated on electrical engineering, and earnt nearly half of its profits from loans and services. The difficulties facing historians of business and multinationals in particular are difficulties for all historians. We might trace German nationalism to the times of Martin Luther, or link the Geneva Conventions to the chivalric codes of medieval knights, but the relevant events and circumstances in the nineteenth and twentieth centuries seem more consequential.

International business theorists have tended to focus on the strategies and internal mechanisms of firms (such as building technological competence, for example) rather than broader issues (such as the international economy's structures and trends, or the context of the nation states within which multinationals operate). Business historians, wanting to be seen as analytically rigorous, and seeking the wider acceptance of management scholars, have imitated their frameworks and concepts. The quality of the research that followed is proof of how much has been learnt, but it is fair to ask which issues have been downplayed.

One assessment of the theory of international business, in 2009, wondered if fifty years of analysis had brought much insight into 'business' but revealed nothing that was specifically 'international'. Companies may have been looking for sales and profits abroad, but their decisions and methods were not very different in essence from those of companies looking for sales and profits in domestic markets only. In both cases, the principle is the same: they need to build their internal 'competencies' over time, or decide how to contract out these activities to suppliers, sales firms, specialists, or strategic partners. The solution, it was argued, is to give more attention to what can only be international, such as differing stages of economic development between nations, or varying macro-economic, institutional and cultural environments (Pitelis, 2009).

Box 1.1 Understanding the past, interpreting the present?

What are the uses, and, it would follow, the abuses of history? The subject's origins are usually linked with the German historian Leopold von Ranke: from the 1820s, he established history as an academic discipline – separate from philosophy or literature – and revolutionized historical writing by insisting on original sources. He believed in interrogating rather than simply accepting documentary evidence. For our purposes, it is worth noting that he showed a strong preference for writing national histories – despite awareness of a broader European context – and historians after him undoubtedly followed his bias or even a tendency towards highly nationalist histories.

Critics unfairly labelled Ranke an inveterate empiricist obsessed only with facts, but he was wary of grand schemes and universal interpretations, while believing, contradictorily, that nations somehow incorporated moral and divine forces. He himself sought to judge the past and the people from the past in their own terms: they should not, in other words, be used to validate the present, or to create the very common danger of romanticizing existing political institutions (R. J. Evans, 2005; Iggers and Powell, 1973; Stern, 1973).

Can the past, with its unique set of circumstances, be left to speak for itself, or do historians inevitably impose their own priorities? The philosopher Benedetto Croce summed up the doubts of generations after Ranke: 'All history is contemporary history' (Croce, 1941). As well as being famous for his pro-Soviet views, in which Stalin's crimes became the necessary price of progress, E. H. Carr urged that history and the social sciences should move closer together, with contemporary issues, hypotheses, and generalizations being explored or tested through historical evidence (Carr, 1962). History as a subject broadened during the postwar years: economic, social, and cultural issues became as mainstream as the political, diplomatic and military (R. J. Evans, 2005). As a subject, it had to prove its theoretical credentials, or remain self-consciously inferior to more exact 'sciences' such as economics. Purely narrative history lost its good reputation. Historical writing – aimed at the specialist – claimed greater rigour, but arguably never found a large audience or wide influence.

One of the first media dons, A. J. P. Taylor, continued to say that the only point of history is history, and that the subject is worth studying simply because humans find the past interesting. He claimed that, as he matured as an historian, the more he believed that his main task was to answer the child's question 'What happened next?' He was a professional contrarian, but there is reason to think that here was his genuine belief (Taylor, 1984). He also seemed unconvinced by man's ability to learn from the past, when he summed up the career of Napoleon III, Emperor of the French: *'Like most of those who study history, he learned from the mistakes of the past how to make new ones'* (Taylor, 1963). Napoleon III is best remembered for the events of 1870, when he lost both the Franco-Prussian War and his throne, and enabled Bismarck to create a united Germany at the centre of Europe. Yet, interestingly, before his enforced retirement, he had imitated Britain's policies of free trade and overseas expansion, and associated them with the forces of modernization and national success.

Postmodernists (proportionately, literary critics and philosophers rather than historians) attacked any notion that you could substantiate any historical fact, let alone draw any meaningful lessons. They saw historians as imposing their own assumptions or ideologies over historical documents, and argued that 'truths' were merely relative or culturally determined. In this world, evidence could not show how one belief might be more soundly held than any other, and so (to take one rightly emotive and significant case) the Holocaust both happened and did not happen.

Some asserted (quite incorrectly) that historians were generally too trusting of documentary sources; historians replied that their methods were always founded on the questioning of evidence, the careful verification and cross-checking of facts, and, when proposing interpretations and generalizations, a preference for caution (R. J. Evans, 2005). Eric Hobsbawm pondered why the innocent in a murder trial would prefer judgement according to the evidence, while the postmodernist's uncertainties and relativism would appeal to the obviously guilty in desperate need of a defence (Hobsbawm, 1998).

Even during the high point of national histories, some historians were pointing out how any stretch of designated land would be affected by world events. The transnational perspective does not reject the importance of national histories, but wants to add the powerful interactions that take place at many different levels between countries (Miller, 2012). Transnational history highlights how national borders constantly change, and it focuses, therefore, on those factors or forces at work between territories or nation states, with multinationals not receiving due credit for their role in world history (Saunier, 2013). There is a view that economic history is not a separate subset of general history, but should be used to form a particular perspective on history generally. We can follow that approach by arguing that the history of the multinational should not be an historical subset, but serve as an insightful and important means of viewing world or global history.

Transnational history and global forces

This book fits securely into the category of world or transnational history, privileging cross-border forces and events over national accounts, and scrutinizing multinational enterprise as a potent vehicle of global change. Increasing attention has been paid to the links between polities, though there is a debate about whether 'international', 'transnational', or 'global' history or even 'connected' or 'shared' histories make better terms. The study of multinationals inevitably challenges the long-established historical tradition of studying the nation state as the main vehicle for understanding the political, economic and cultural life of humans. This book is, additionally, a study in international political economy, recognizing the importance of firms, nations, and their interactions.

We begin with the quickening pace of economic internationalization in the nineteenth century, and the emergence of an international economic system based on market transactions, complex transcontinental commodity chains, large-scale capital flows, technology transfer, and convergence in business practices. The analysis considers, too, the role of the multinational in these developments – how it brought about the escalating transfer of assets, goods, and ideas across borders, affected the fortunes of national states, and influenced the calculations of international politics. Global investment and trade spurred economic growth and consumption; altered the landscape through the building of infrastructure and cities, the digging of mines, and the founding of landed estates; and transformed the work and lives of those drawn into networks of cross-border finance, commerce and production.

The process was uneven, both between regions and between industries, and not smooth over time, but multinationals were at the centre of a cumulative revolution – occurring concurrently at global, regional, national, and local levels – and they were transporters and models of economic modernity. They did not make the world 'flat' in the sense of creating one single global marketplace, since the interaction between countries and territories showed disparities in economic power and outcomes. While fostering or imposing cross-border interdependence, the international economy could cause or heighten divisions between and within polities, raise awareness of vital differences and inequalities, and generate antagonism and conflict.

This book explores the workings of the 'first global economy' in the decades before 1914, and its 'retreat' during the worldwide conflict, instability, and nationalism that would be experienced in a second phase by the following generation. It compares the 'third global economy' of the 1950s and 1960s with its first incarnation, and asks if trends, starting from the 1980s, can fairly be seen as the global economy's new, 'fourth' phase. The approach lends itself to the question – 'Why have things changed?' – that is often at the forefront of the historian's mind.

Multinationals from developed economies – Europe, North America, and subsequently Japan – historically dominated foreign direct investment and cross-border commerce, and broadly reflected the mix of technological, military, diplomatic and economic advantage between nations and regions. Indeed, it has been argued, with good reason, that 'the West' has determined the main course of world history for five hundred years. One widely read contribution by Niall Ferguson reformulates well-established ideas about 'modernity' – the combining of the rule of law, market competition, property rights, science, technology, and high living standards – and reasserts the argument that they were essentially Western, and something 'the Rest' had to imitate. By ignoring what had made it successful, he adds, Western civilization is ensuring its own decline (Ferguson, 2011). An alternative view of world history, by C. A. Bayly, interprets modernity as something historically led by the West, but holds that the interactions of the West and the Rest were, if not equal, not in one direction either (Bayly, 2004).

Nations modernize by emulation of global best practice, but, through adaptations and learning, and because their contexts differ and circumstances change, they can never modernize in exactly the same way. Although the West initiated industrialization, and historically determined globalization trends, the desire for material well-being is not of course something uniquely Western, or something only achievable with Western institutions. While spread by the advanced economies, and the forces of internationalization, markets and competition proved dynamic because they could adapt to a variety of national institutions. Even if the West was first, and historically influential, other nations would inevitably close the gap, and generate their own managerial best practices for adoption or (more likely) adaptation by others. Therefore, Western companies, during the 1980s, feeling the threat of competition, attempted to imitate Japan's leading business systems. They did so often with mixed success, and they never incorporated the Japanese model wholesale.

Max Weber, in 1904, famously credited North European and North American achievements to the Protestant work ethic (Weber, 1903–4); critics stated that, even if Protestantism and capitalism emerged together, capitalism would still have occurred without Protestantism ever existing (Tawney, 1928). Less known is Weber's conclusion that it was Confucianism that explained China's failure to industrialize. Clearly, times have changed. More contemporary analysis has linked the rise of East Asia to Confucian values, including the work ethic, duty, long-termism, education, and self-improvement. Or was it economic development, competitive markets and international trade and investment that brought about modernization, entrepreneurship, and the disciplines of factory routines, by replacing or reinterpreting deep cultural traits? It is modern, best practice or effective business systems that create growth and change values, not Western or any set of values that creates growth. That is, industrialization and the international economy began with the West, but would have occurred even if the West had never existed.

Arguments about the rise and fall of the West recall, in many ways, the writings of Arnold Toynbee: he believed that great men and elites created civilizations, with each example having a definable character or 'soul', and that hardship and struggle favoured the growth of a leading civilization over effete societies (Toynbee, 1934–61). Geyl did not fall back on the traditions of gentlemanly refutation when he accused Toynbee of being a prophet, not an historian, for reducing the richness and complexity of history to 'presumptuous construction' (R. J. Evans, 2005; Geyl, 1955). We are too often guilty of generalizations that overlook political, social and economic differences within countries, while perhaps overemphasizing the depths of the differences between them (Smith, McSweeney and Fitzgerald, 2008). The arrival of Japanese multinationals, from the 1980s onwards, and the rise of emerging market multinationals, beginning a decade later, posed interesting questions about the causes of the dominance previously held by Western companies.

Meanings: globalization and multinationals

Critics are concerned by globalization's threat to local cultures and identities, and by the powerlessness of communities against large corporations in pursuit of profits. Environmentalists question an international economy founded on economic growth, and anti-capitalism campaigners chant against powerful vested interests that are perceived as both exploitative and rootless. Globalization is associated with continuous economic and social change, constant uncertainty, and cycles of crisis and rapid contagion. Others rationalize that international trade and multinational enterprise have expanded because, ultimately, the benefits have outweighed the costs. For its advocates, the international economy enables the efficient allocation of productive resources without the limits of borders, creating mutual gains for firms and nations. Its dynamism spurs the innovation in technology, business organization, management systems and markets on which the generation of wealth and the material welfare of people depend.

Globalization envisages producers adopting best practice, while consumers enjoy lower prices and improved goods and services. Increased measures of multinational investment, trade and output are automatically associated with progress, but you can also gauge globalization's impact by its ability or failure to improve education and health, most obviously in developing countries (Stiglitz, 2002). From 1979, China ended its experiment in autarky and central planning. By shifting hundreds of millions out of poverty, it achieved one of the most remarkable transformations in human history (Sachs, 2005). Yet, for decades, the inland rural provinces remained largely untouched, and factory workers continue to endure the long hours and harsh conditions that have enabled the phenomenal growth in exports. China's experience, as an industrializing country, revealed the dual nature of economic growth, and the internationalization process that has, historically, accompanied it. The effects of globalization are uneven: within countries, and

also between them. While many Asian nations became major beneficiaries of change, nations in Africa have generally not achieved equal
levels of economic and social transformation.

The term *globalization* is potentially misleading, used as a catch-
all to explain any trend. It is used, too, in a way that bestows a
sense of inevitability. Here, once again, history can offer a corrective.
The workings of the international economy are far from straightfor-
ward or easily summarized. The international economy involves nation
states, multinational enterprises, financial and commodity markets,
and supranational institutions such as the World Trade Organization
(WTO) or the International Monetary Fund (IMF). Issues of politics,
regulations, diplomatic and trade relations, levels of economic development, communications, technology, and business organization have
relevance. All of these factors impact on each other, and none can be
considered in isolation. The effects of globalization can be studied at
the level of cross-border transactions, nations, regions, and firms.

Some nation states have been more deeply involved in the international economy than others. They have differed in their policies, and
in their ability to manage trends and to maximize benefits from international trade and investment. Some localities within nations, often
home to specific industries or clusters, have been more developed and
globalized than others. Some firms have been more orientated towards
exports or foreign investments, or more engaged in joint ventures or
strategic alliances with foreign businesses. In theory, globalization has
necessitated the eventual imitation of leading firms and nations (called
convergence), but simultaneously the drive for continuous innovation
and differentiation has stopped firms and nations all becoming the
same (leading to divergence). Outlining the progress of economic internationalization or globalization is consequently tricky; disentangling
the costs and benefits is even more so.

How, then, can we describe globalization, or use the term legiti-
mately? The term first appeared in the 1960s – the same decade in
which 'multinational enterprise' became more accepted – but twenty
years later it evolved into a common label for many important worldwide trends. A rough count of books and academic papers with the
buzzwords 'global' or 'globalization' in their title shows a prominent
rise from the mid 1980s but 'take-off' after 1992 (Dicken, 2003).

It can, firstly, be considered at the level of societies. Given developments in media and communications, some have foreseen the

assimilation of cultures and values. It is possible, secondly, to consider nation states and their sovereignty. Governments, since the 1980s, have followed a trend in privatization, openness to trade and investment, and deregulation, and they have (arguably) converged towards the market-driven Anglo-American business model. National sovereignty, furthermore, has competed against supranational economic organizations such as the WTO, the IMF or the International Organization for Standardization (ISO), but also against the extending remit of the International Criminal Court, or the policies of the World Health Organization; against international political entities, such as the European Union; against trade bodies, such the North American Free Trade Association, or the ASEAN Free Trade Area; and against large multinational enterprises, in charge of essential economic assets, and, to some degree, independent of their country of origin.

Others, thirdly, tend to focus less on cultural and political considerations, and more on the levels of cross-border trade and investment. They note the increasingly free movement of products, knowledge, people and money, and the growing interdependence of national economies, fostered by the policies of governments, under international frameworks established initially by the General Agreement on Tariffs and Trade (GATT) and latterly by its successor, the WTO. The 'hyperglobalist' perspective extends this idea to predict the formation of a borderless global marketplace (Friedman, 2005; Ohmae, 1995; Ohmae, 1999; Giddens, 1999). Critics perceive the idea of a single flat 'playing field', in which local practices are irrelevant and borders frictionless, as an ideology rather than a reality. They challenge claims about the end of the nation state and its power to negotiate trade terms, enforce regulations and impose sanctions (Held et al., 1999). We might add that, despite talk of globalization, the processes of economic internationalization have remained notably regional and within the 'Triad' of North America, Europe or East Asia (Rugman, 2005), although shifts towards emerging economies generally since the meltdown of 2008–9 have been noted.

Hyperglobalization pays too little attention to the role of nation states, and the influence of localities on the organization of business. It tends to ignore the complexities of internationalization, presenting trends as a new global era, one in which polities become powerless. Historians, on the other hand, trace the origins of an interdependent international economy back several hundred years, and, in particular, to the rapid changes in industry, trade, technology and management that emerged from the mid nineteenth century onwards. Individual nation states have been important actors in the framing of the international economic system, and leading economies have been critical as providers of foreign investment, business organization, and technology. Diplomatic alliances, rivalries, and territorial control have all shaped patterns of traded natural resources and the international division of labour. What the internationalization of national economies (or globalization) shows is that its processes cannot be neatly separated from world history in general.

One further aspect of globalization, fourthly, is the role of multinational enterprise. The cross-border organization of production, technology, finance, product development, personnel and marketing within or by single businesses points to levels of international integration and interdependence even deeper than the exporting of goods and services. The strategic decision to operate in two or more national locations involved the long-term commitment of assets, and firms needed substantial advantages to balance the difficulties of establishing businesses abroad. When analysts forged the term *multinational*, in the 1960s, they were struck by the rapid international expansion of US companies during the post-war period. They wanted to explain why firms would found and own subsidiaries in foreign markets, rather than taking the organizationally simpler choice of exporting, or, alternatively, licensing local companies to act on their behalf.

These pioneer investigators – mainly evaluating the high incidence of US manufacturers investing in Western Europe – had a considerable influence on the theory of foreign direct investment (FDI), the cross-border transfer of capital and other resources directly undertaken by multinationals. As noted earlier, they perceived the multinational as having to own a competitive advantage in technology, management, products or some other corporate capability, internal to the firm, which the company could transplant from its country of origin to foreign subsidiaries, as the basis for success in host economies. Initial accounts saw multinationals as motivated by a drive to extend their monopoly to foreign markets, and, given continued barriers to trade, FDI was the most effective option for achieving their objectives. Later thinking acknowledged the power of international competition and the benefits of FDI for host economies, in terms of employment, output, technology, business expertise, consumer choice, and exports. It noted, too, how a multinational could acquire additional competitive advantages for being abroad, such as returns to scale, responsiveness to customer demands, access to technological knowledge, low wage labour or reduced transport costs, which offset the expense of investment in and operational support for a subsidiary.

It followed that, as a multinational's international business evolved, it became less dependent on sales within its home nation. It might move away from an organizational structure based on one dominant parent firm plus dependent subsidiaries to a structure in which subsidiaries take greater charge of production management, product development, or marketing. Such a company has to be increasingly transnational in strategy, and, in principle, more cosmopolitan in the appointment of its senior managers. Its competitive advantage shifts from the capabilities of the parent multinational, rooted in its home economy, and their transfer to subsidiaries towards the exploiting and coordinating of advantages subsidiaries possess in their various localities.

Since the original framers of FDI theory focused on manufacturing and the international movement of capabilities within the company, their ideas might not have been so relevant to many service industries with strategies reliant on developing external networks and capabilities locally. Nor was the multinational's long history taken into account, and the study of multinational strategies, business organization, and international political economy from the nineteenth century might have provided them with alternative perspectives (see Chapter 2). Changes in the international economy from the 1980s onwards – most notably, the rapid growth of cross-border production chains spanning many international locations to make a single good, and the rise of emerging-economy multinationals – have posed new questions about the aims and organization of multinational enterprise (see Chapter 5).

How, then, should we define the multinational enterprise? One confusion is the availability of several terms, sometimes employed to differentiate firms, but commonly used as alternatives. In addition to the multinational enterprise, or the MNE, we can find the multinational corporation (MNC), the transnational corporation (TNC), or, finally, for a business with genuinely worldwide as opposed to just international scope, the global company. One problem for any attempted definition is the need to aim at a moving target: international enterprise – its geographic scope, organization and location – has inevitably changed since its origins in the nineteenth century. Nonetheless, the multinational or the global company has sought to close and manage the distance between cross-border locations and business opportunities.

Theorists suggested, at first, that a multinational should have economic assets abroad: that this factor had to be a fundamental difference between it and the purely domestic company. But the relationships between parent firms and foreign subsidiaries were complicated, and patterns varied between industries and countries, and over time. Some subsidiaries were clearly part of a multinational; other instances were more contestable. One aspect of the relationship was whether a subsidiary was wholly or partially owned by the parent, and the percentage needed for strategic control or effective international integration by the parent. Should it be 10 per cent, or 30, or at least 51? Multinationals have, moreover, arranged international strategic alliances, and participated in networks of coordinated production and distribution involving multiple parties. The strategic influence or economic importance of a multinational, in the international economy and in individual nation states, has in practice extended beyond officially owned subsidiaries.

The emphasis in FDI theory on the ownership of businesses overseas and of capabilities internal to the firm might have downplayed key strategies of internationally contracting production, logistics and support services, as well as the skills required for building external connections and relationships with partner firms (Gereffi, 1994). International business constitutes a web of inter-firm collaboration and contracts, alongside the intra-firm organization of finance, production and marketing within multinationals. One definition of a multinational – an alternative to a firm that directly owns subsidiaries or assets abroad capable of producing its major products or services – is 'a firm that has the power to coordinate and control operations in more than one country, even if it does not own them' (Dicken, 2003). The history of multinational enterprise shows the changing complexity and variety of internal organization and external networks, but raises questions, too, about FDI theory's focus on the firm's internal and external capabilities without due weight being given to the context of the international economic system and nation states.

Firms internationalize or 'multonalize' through various stages: from exporting to appointing a sales agency abroad, to establishing their own sales firm in a foreign market, to founding a subsidiary under-taking the final stages of their main products or services, and, finally, to creating a host-country subsidiary engaged in a full or wide range of their mainline activities. A relaxed interpretation of a multinational is a firm that owns or controls value-creating assets in more than one country, and, as this book will illustrate, tight definitions do not always recognize the complexities of multinationals, their strategies and organization. Analysis and statistics do not consistently distin-guish between different types of assets associated with multinationals. Since the move from exporting to FDI is a important moment in the evolution of a multinational, this book only mentions instances of exporting and sales agencies where useful as background. It focuses, to some extent, on directly owned or controlled sales subsidiaries, and, to a much greater extent, on the strategically significant shift to producing mainline goods or services in foreign markets.

The international economic system, nations and firms

Multinationals can be said to have operated both in the international economic system and within national economies. They have had to secure their place within trade and investment flows, and in cross-border networks of production and distribution, alongside maintain-ing a role in the countries in which they have located. The idea of an international 'system' may be misleading, since it is a range of bilat-eral and multilateral relationships, operating at different levels, and not something built to a master plan. Commercial treaties between nations, state agencies, intergovernmental organizations, and the activ-ities of exporters, importers, financiers, multinationals, intermediaries, production and commodity chains, and business alliances all shaped opportunities in the international economy, and determined levels of convergence in practices and standards.

Global structural changes in finance, production, technology, and policies – since the nineteenth century, and through subsequent vary-ing stages – have pushed multinationals to centre stage of the inter-national economic system. Prominent nation states have been another determining factor over the workings of the international economy, since some economies have been well placed to set the terms of their international economic engagement. It has been the lead of a nation or region that, historically, accelerated the emergence of an international system, and determined the flows of trade, capital, technology and management practices. The statistics show the significance of Britain to the international economy of the nineteenth century; the role of the USA in the decades following the Second World War; and the continued influence of advanced economies over trade, capital and FDI flows.

The 'challenge of the West' and its allies has been portrayed as the replacement of one production system (such as peasant agriculture, feudalism, or mercantilism) with another (capitalism) (Wallerstein, 1974–2011; McNeil, 1963). The term *capitalism* can carry strong ideological dislike or approval. It is associated with free markets, entrepreneurship, high rates of capital investment, the systematic pursuit of output and profits, and enforceable legal and governance structures (now that China is the world's second-largest economy, we are increasingly less certain about the last requirement). In its expansion internationally, capitalism or its most advanced model have been linked in turn to Britain and empire, and to the USA and its hegemony.

While the history of exploitative empires goes back to ancient times, the era of capitalism and the global economy in the nineteenth century added one important element. For some, Europe did not simply occupy foreign lands, but exported a new and dynamic system of production. The international economy that emerged had systemic features that constantly undermined territorial barriers and transformed economies and societies. Yet Britain's role in the international economic system was bigger than its empire, and not simply reliant on its navy and military aggression. London was the global financial capital for the world, and its multinationals operated successfully beyond its colonies and notably in Latin America. Britain's imperial and economic advantages rested, nonetheless, on a number of conditions which it could not control, and its leadership was shattered during the twentieth century when relations with the other European great powers, the USA and Japan changed (Darwin, 2009). The material costs of the Second World War, from 1939 to 1945, and US economic interests combined to break European imperialism.

It is a difficult matter to measure, so we have to rely on numerous examples, but the hegemony of US investment, technology and management know-how on the world economy in the post-war years – without resort to formal empire – was as far-reaching as and possibly more far-reaching than British commercial leadership in the nineteenth century. Moreover, multilateral diplomatic and military relationships influenced and deepened patterns of international trade and investment between the USA, Canada, and Western Europe (even if they do not fully explain them), and Cold War tensions accounted for US technological and financial assistance to Western Europe, Japan, South Korea, Taiwan, and other allies. The relationship between levels of national economic output, living standards, trade, foreign investment, multinational enterprise, and military and diplomatic relationships has been a distinct one.

By the later part of the twentieth century, European and Japanese multinationals had finally recovered or developed enough to offer greater competition to the USA and the British. Differences of state–industry relations and business management in the Anglo-American, Japanese and Central European systems pointed not to one dominant system of production (capitalism in shorthand) but to a number of competing capitalist systems, from which to draw varying lessons and advantages. There was basic agreement on the primacy of markets, and developing and former Communist bloc countries would adopt market-based solutions, liberalize inward investment, and seek to attract multinationals. But differences in the nature of government, finance, and employment relations remained. Trends after 1980 indicated a further shift in global economic power to nations such as China, India and Brazil, and the passing of a high point for Western dominance of the international economy. Nonetheless, a minority of nations continued to gain disproportionately from the workings of the international economic system.

Multinationals looked to multi-territoriality, interdependence, cross-border integration, markets, and contractual obligations; states were founded on notions of territoriality, autonomy, unity, laws, institutions, and the monopoly use of force. Despite intrinsic differences, they have had mutually advantageous reasons for cooperation. The decisions of multinationals have affected the welfare of nations, and national economies have influenced the emergence and location of international business. Where countries achieved a lead, for example, in scientific research, education, or finance systems, they possessed the conditions for internationally competitive industrial clusters, advanced firm-level capabilities, and ultimately the rise of global companies. Differences in economic development between nations have underpinned the processes of globalization, and the control of international business has remained predominantly with developed, high-income nations, despite the recent expansion of emerging-economy multinationals (Dunning and Lundan, 2008).

There was a dynamic relationship between the development stage of a home economy and its outward FDI. To succeed in the long term, however, multinationals had additionally to achieve benefits from operating across borders and in host nations too. Through law, taxation, subsidies, regulation, and policies, the state has been a strong influence on multinational business strategy, corporate organization, and employment. Good governance has influenced investment incentives and rates of growth, and improved market efficiencies (North, 1990). In industrializing economies, government has played a central role in obtaining technologies, prioritizing limited resources, and choosing strategic industries for development (Gerschenkron, 1965). East Asia's rapid growth after the Second World War has been associated with developmental states and policies of export-orientated industrialization.

On the other hand, some firms have acquired their core capabilities mainly through cross-border activities and outside their 'national' base. Some locations rely on a trade-orientated or entrepot function (such as Singapore); small economies must look outwards for scale and expansion (such as the Netherlands); and others are fundamentally affected by proximity to a very large neighbour and its demands (such as Canada). Where states or territories have exercised sovereignty, they have had to decide between policies that keep out multinationals (to allow local firms to develop) and policies that encourage inward investment (to spur managerial, technological and competitive upgrading). The impact of inward investment has depended on several factors, including local incentive structures, innovatory capacities, and entrepreneurship, as well as government policy. For the whole period of the modern international economy, both the national origins and the destination of FDI have been highly concentrated within leading national economies.

Multinationals – key organizations in transnational economic relations – gained and offered competitive advantages through their ability to connect economies. Just as nations required the bargaining power and administrative resources to manage their relationships with multinationals effectively – and, of course, this was not always the case – multinationals had to develop the capabilities they needed to deal with governments or to form local commercial alliances. Where countries have been unable to guarantee or secure adequate infrastructure or security, multinationals have had to consider a range of activities beyond their primary business activities, and difficulties with host-country governments have had the potential to involve the home-country government of the multinational. Since the theory of the multinational has largely concerned itself with the micro-economics of the firm, it has not so far dealt extensively with matters of nation state policies, levels of economic development, and international political economy. Although they have, since the 1980s, adopted policies that acknowledge their growing reliance on the capabilities and resources controlled by multinationals, nation states are not set to disappear.

Multinationals became part of a complex transnational system of bilateral and multilateral economic and political relationships. Many questions remain about why, when and how their role in the international economy achieved its current importance; about their fundamental function; about their ability to transfer or coordinate technological, organizational, entrepreneurial, and financial resources; and about their desirability as engines of economic growth. In providing answers, therefore, we cannot just look at the internal workings of multinationals and their bundles of assets. Of course, a history of the multinational must deal with the strategic motivation and ability of wealth-producing entities to organize cross-border production and transactions, through assets they own and direct, or through the coordination of strategic alliances and business networks. But it must deal too with changes in economic, political, and diplomatic conditions, and with the international events that shaped the decisions of multinationals.

The growth in trade since the nineteenth century is linked to the first industrial revolution, and to the rising demand of advanced economies for raw materials and consumer goods unavailable at home. Differences in wealth and power established an international division of labour between manufacturing nations and commodity producers, and brought colonization to large parts of Asia and Africa. What is less well known is the role of multinational trading companies, largely from Europe, which organized much of the global trade, and played a central role in imperialist ventures. The expansion of trade explains the investments made by multinationals from industrialized nations in mines, plantations, and transport infrastructure in emerging territories.

Transformations in transport and communication – steam-powered ships, the Suez Canal, or the telegraph – supported the growth in the scale of commerce, while giving entrepreneurs further opportunities to found international businesses.

The second industrial revolution, from the late nineteenth century onwards, is associated with new technologies and products, such as electrical goods, chemicals, or automobiles. Breakthroughs in the nature of manufacturing required mass production and large-scale organization, and firms gained a competitive advantage over rivals through their ownership of scientific, financial, organizational and human resources and through the integration and systemization of processes and decision making within the firm. These manufacturers, many of whom became household names, might have proprietary rights over technology or brands, and they developed the capacity to exploit returns to scale or synergies from multiproduct operations. Deals with other firms risked loss of technological leadership, product quality or brand reputation. Competencies in production, marketing, technology and management helped firms to acquire the additional skills associated with cross-border operations. In transferring their core capabilities to foreign subsidiaries, they created mini-versions of the parent business in foreign markets.

Investments by US manufacturers in the 1950s and 1960s altered the nature of the international economy, although the delay between this surge in manufacturing FDI and mass production's invention seventy to eighty years before suggests a complex chain of causes. The giant integrated and managerial US manufacturing multinational became the model for the multinational, yet it is a viewpoint that ignores the role of trading and financial multinationals in the history of the international economy. It is an emphasis, moreover, on particular types of competitive advantage, international business strategy, and management organization over others. Instead of minimizing market transactions and contracts with buyers, suppliers, and partner firms, and following a strategy of internalizing activities inside the firm, large companies and multinationals can utilize strategic alliances and coordinated business networks. These methods were characteristic of the nineteenth-century international economy, and remained central to certain sectors and especially services throughout the twentieth century. They are, interestingly, being increasingly replicated in the global economy of the twenty-first century.

History and perspective

One key factor in transnational relations has been the multinational or global company. Diplomatic, military, and political factors moulded the fortunes of international business, but international business was frequently an active participant in international events too. The micro-economics of the firm are instructive, but by themselves they can be a limiting perspective. World or transnational historians seek to escape nationally based histories because certain forces shaping the modern period are cross-border in character. In considering big themes, complex issues, and a multitude of factors, history is especially useful. Its customary role is to analyse specific cases and their circumstances together, and to look at causes and consequences over time. It offers the authenticity of evidence, and, since we have no means of subjecting human societies to controlled laboratory experiments, long-term perspective is needed to deepen our understanding.

The historian Ferdinand Braudel stated that time does not always move at the same speed (Braudel, 1996 [1949]). He meant that many relevant factors – whether economic, social or political – do not change at the same rate or in the same way in differing locations. Global forces have been a transformative feature of the last two hundred years and more, but their effects have not been even, either across the world or within single nations. Braudel believed that long-term factors – slow-moving economic and social trends, or mentalities – were determinant, and he saw everything else as 'surface disturbances'. Nonetheless, the material in this book looks by necessity at the long-term in combination with immediate events, revealing how deep-rooted and rapid change is possible, and how multinationals have been a major global force. Studying the sequence of events is important because the past has influenced the present, and, presumably, the present will shape the future.

The historian is interested in describing the sequence of events, or the processes of time, and explaining the causes of events. Every historian knows the problem of weaving narrative and analysis together. Narrative is a powerful means of describing and explaining a complex sequence of trends and events. Even though it is not number crunching – and maybe because it is not number crunching – it can produce meaningful conclusions. The international political economy and the role of multinationals did not evolve by blind chance, but through human decisions over time, and we need to dig into the past to understand the sequence of events that have shaped their development. Historians tend to avoid one-dimensional explanations, and an adequate analysis of the rise of the global company can be no different. Since the historian has only one lifetime, he or she has to ask a limited number of questions, but, hopefully, without losing the richness and complexity of the past.

In this survey of the global company, its evolution, and its impact, a number of major themes will emerge. It emphasizes the strong link between the history of international business and international, diplomatic, military, and political history generally. Histories that integrate the economic with other themes do exist, but the rise of the global company is never prominent, and world-historical events have passing mention in the historical surveys of international business. Industrialization, globalization and colonialism occurred together in the nineteenth century; the power blocs of the Cold War era determined the geography of post-war international trade and investment; and, since the late twentieth century, both the falling away of ideological and commercial borders and competition from emergent economies have loosened the established international order, posed questions for global governance, and given multinationals new challenges.

Historians have entered the public sphere – through television, and widely read books – to offer insights into international affairs. Business historians have so far been reticent, and more concerned with the micro-economics and organizational details of the firm than with broader topics. This book looks closely at the strategies, organization, and competencies of multinationals in order to advance understanding of the international economic system and its development, and to add to our historical understanding of the relations between countries. It acknowledges that it is impossible to study the multinational without giving full attention to the nation state. They evolved together, and influenced each other's development.

Policies towards capital exports, restrictions on inward investment, legal systems and institutions, trade agreements, and diplomatic alliances all affected the structure and operation of the global economy. Governments may seek the competencies of foreign businesses – their capital, technology, management, products, supply networks, and marketing channels – but their interests cannot be exactly the same. States have the dilemma of being open to international economic forces, while seeking to protect and develop their national economies. Through their control of important human and organizational assets, multinationals have shaped the economic policies of all governments, increasingly so as nation states compete for their investment. They have had, in addition, a profound effect on the political and social development of smaller or economically weaker states, and the clash between international property rights and national sovereignty is a recurrent feature of multinational history. Some states have been more suited, institutionally or economically, to deal with the fact of multinational firms.

This book considers the impact of multinationals on the economies of host countries. Globalization has historically been a driver of change. Multinationals were and are transmitters of capital, business systems, technology, products, and services, and they have been managers of complex operations in institutionally and culturally diverse locations. They have been bringers of 'modernity' – higher living standards, consumption, competition, professionalized management, and scientific research – but they stand accused of entrenching the disadvantages of home-grown enterprise. The recent popularity of world history demonstrates a desire to escape national histories and adopt a panoramic appreciation of how the world was formed. The book is about how multinationals were centre stage in determining the nature of the modern world.

2 | Empires of business: 1870–1914

Multinationals and empire

How legitimate is it to portray the decades before 1914 as part of the age of globalization? We can quickly discover in the nineteenth century signposts to the 'modern' world, including industrialization, urbanization, electrification, motorized transport, and long-distance communication; there existed the rise of democratic (and, more latterly, anti-democratic) popular movements, a strong sense of nation, and armies equipped with deadly technologies; firms that could utilize science and undertake large-scale production; within cities, amongst much poverty, we can trace the origins of mass consumption; and a world that was dependent on flows of international trade and investment and on multinational businesses able to operate across continents.

After the First World War, the economist John Maynard Keynes attacked those victorious nations whose governments, he believed, had imposed peace terms without proper regard for global interdependence. He acknowledged what, before the catastrophe of 1914, had been a remarkable surge in transnational business, meaning that someone living in London could order by telephone the products of the whole earth, and invest in the natural resources to be found all over the world. He viewed the internationalization of social and economic life as 'nearly complete in practice', but acknowledged, too, how 'the projects and politics of militarism and imperialism, of racial and cultural rivalries, of monopolies, restrictions, and exclusion...were to play serpent to this paradise' (Keynes, 1919). Admittedly, the metropolitan figure Keynes described was more typical of his social class than the majority of London's inhabitants, but, during the nineteenth century, international trade and investment grew to have a far-reaching impact on populations throughout the globe.

As well as tracing the origins of the multinational enterprise, we are interested in its dynamism. In what ways was the international economy before 1914 distinct from later periods, and can we talk of a first global economy or International Economy I? As we shall see, multinational enterprises had become an established feature of this international economic system. Inevitably, their effect was not purely commercial, but intimately tied to developments in politics, society and diplomatic affairs. The late nineteenth century is most easily characterized as the era of empire. The scale of imperialism shaped the flow of global trade and investment, as would its later decline. The redistribution of over one quarter of the world's surface from 1865 to 1915 influenced the strategies and operations of multinational enterprises. Nations and businesses that pursued colonies were, not accidentally, prominent players in the international economy. With the exception of the USA (which gained Puerto Rico and the Philippines) and Japan (Taiwan and Korea), extensions of territorial control went to European powers (Hobsbawm, 2003).

Ultimately, in the decades after 1945, Europe lost its hold over much of the world – thanks to the great powers' costly habit of military conflict, plus colonial liberation movements, and the rival diplomatic and economic interests of the USA. 'Empire' came to be a blemish consigned to the past, with European dominance over international business simultaneously reaching its end. Did one trend explain the other? Although imperialism was never an entirely economic mission, it would be foolhardy to delete economic calculation as a motive. International businesses could and did benefit from empires, which could forcibly draw territories, their natural resources and labour forces into the international economy, and then ensure the security of multinational investments and their favourable treatment. On the other hand, generally, we have to acknowledge the specific dynamism of international trade and investment, and their power to bring about global transformation. What marked the successful international businesses of the nineteenth century, and what ultimately explained their impact, was their ability to adapt and flourish in a wide variety of international and national settings, including independent lands and colonies, and absolute monarchies and budding democracies. Their success depended on particular capabilities and commercial advantages – in managerial or product knowledge, technology, finance, or access to trade networks and consumer markets – even if the advantages of empire assisted their activities over foreign or local firms.

Imperialism had been reinvented, in the late nineteenth century, as a popular political movement at home and as an inescapably conflicted

ideal for promoting human progress overseas. The same period, moreover, devised the concept of nationalism and ethnic national identity.
Unlike imperialism, the nation state remains as a key component of
the modern world (although, supposedly, footloose and cosmopolitan
corporations at the end of the twentieth century began to assail the
reality of national sovereignty). Just as nation states and multinationals influenced each other's development, so, historically, did empires
and multinationals.

Case evidence is needed to sort out the complicated and changing
relationship between nation states, the international political economy,
and multinational enterprise, but one early general point is possible: in
the decades before 1914, the existence of two very different 'worlds'
determined the emergence of multinational investment and bolstered
the fact of imperialism. On one side were Europe and also the surging
USA, as seats of industry, applied science, capital investment, mass
consumption, and advanced business systems. These nations were the
leading economies, and explained the greater proportion of both world
trade and output. Britain, the most economically developed and urban-
ized nation, had the largest share of foreign markets, while being, in
tandem, the biggest imperial power. Yet it was, also, a country increasingly fearful of its waning supremacy. In 1850, Britain had supplied 43
per cent of all manufactured exports, and, in 1870, had nearly 32 per
cent of world manufactured production. By 1913, Britain could claim
only some 14 per cent of the world's manufacturing production, while
Germany, with 15.7 per cent, had overtaken its rival, and the USA,
with 35.8 per cent, had established its industrial primacy (Chandler,
1990; Matthews, Feinstein and Odling-Smee, 1982).

So, Ernest Edwin Williams sought in 1896 to raise alarm amongst
his fellow Britons. In writing his well-known book *Made in Germany*,
he talked through the many German products to be found in the average English home, including the pencil one might use to list them all.
In portraying Germany as 'a gigantic commercial state', which would
contend with Britain for its international trade, Williams was highlighting the perceived clash of interests that eventually ripped Europe
apart, and badly injured the first phase of the international economy
in the period before 1914 (Williams, 1896).

William Thomas Stead was a campaigning journalist, a liberal
reformer and an imperialist (in the hope that British power would help
spread liberal ideals). He detected a greater threat to British leadership

on the other side of the Atlantic. In his *Americanisation of the World*, he noted for his part the unsettling presence of US goods in England's homes. In particular, the 'average man' in England could not resist his children's enthusiasm for Quaker Oats breakfast cereal, or avoid using American-made elevators and trams. Stead went on to predict the economic, political and cultural sway of the USA, arguing that the European 'world' would be surpassed (Stead, 1902). The Germans and the Americans, by the end of the nineteenth century, had ended Britain's clear lead in advanced manufactures and management skills. With this analysis in mind, Stead was an active supporter of the international peace gatherings held at The Hague and attended by sceptical governments from 1899 onwards. Journeying to attend, in 1911, a conference called by US President Taft, he unfortunately booked passage on the *Titanic*. By the time of Stead's death, European governments were already planning for a prospective war, and protectionist tariffs and national preference had added an economic edge to diplomatic and military tensions (Schults, 1972).

The other side of the world, outside Europe and much of the USA, was mainly composed of non-industrialized – or, therefore, economically underdeveloped – regions. These were, as a result, often colonies or zones of influence. Weak states and economies proved vulnerable to imperial aggressors, and remained more prone to fluctuations in the international economy and to the actions of multinationals. Living standards in Asia and Africa were far behind those in Western Europe by 1870, and further so by 1913, although European places of settlement (with the vast resources and lands that attracted migrants) revealed early promise (see Table 2.1). Both undeveloped and developing regions were drawn into an interdependent international system with a startling capacity to effect both economic and political change.

To sustain many of its industrial processes, and lives of mass consumption, Europe required the natural resources and commodities of far-flung places. International chains of production and distribution linked the gathering of raw materials with their manufacture or final use. There were transcontinental movements of capital, labour and expertise, and a network of financial and support services. Between 1821 and 1915, maybe some 44 million Europeans emigrated, and some 1 billion acres of new land were cultivated. World food exports grew ten times from 1850 to 1914, when they reached some 40m tons. Britain imported 80 per cent of its wheat, 65 per cent of its fruit, and

Table 2.1 *Regional GDP per capita averages, 1820–1929 (1990 $US)*

	Western Europe	Western offshoots	Southern Europe	Eastern Europe	Latin America	Asia & Oceania	Africa	Average
1820	1,292	1,205	804	772	679	550	450	651
1870	2,110	2,440	1,108	1,085	760	580	480	895
1913	3,704	5,237	1,750	1,690	1,439	742	575	1,539
1929	4,385	6,653	2,153	1,732	1,832	858	660	1,806

Maddison includes the USA and the British Dominions under the category 'Western offshoots'.
Source: Maddison (1999).

40 per cent of its meat (Ponting, 2000). In response to the new possibilities, and the promise of high returns, European companies went overseas. Those engaged in trading, mining, and commodities dominated multinational business activities during the last quarter of the nineteenth century, and other multinationals brought expertise to the building of railways, harbours, and other forms of infrastructure.

Multinationals and economic transformation

It is important to emphasize – in case we exaggerate the overall economic importance of colonialism – how the total value of commerce between developed nations remained the more sizeable. Yet underdeveloped regions did become integral to the world system, within which Europe exported manufactured goods in return for imported primary products. For this period, we have to distinguish between trade and FDI in order to explain the structure of the international system and the particular relationship between Europe and its colonies. That is, empire had a larger influence on multinational enterprise compared to international commerce overall.

The industrial companies of the developed world, in this period, preferred to manufacture in their country of origin, meeting foreign demand through exports, most likely to other nations with comparatively high living standards. But undeveloped regions, especially those rich in natural resources, required a different strategic response. As there was a need to transfer European capital, management and technology, and a need to build trade routes and facilities, direct investment by companies and cross-border management (the very definitions of a multinational) followed. Natural resources may have accounted for half of all foreign direct investment from Britain and the USA by 1914; firms from France and the Netherlands were also prominent acquirers of overseas supplies; and, to serve their growing industrial output at home, German enterprises showed leadership in metal mining and trading. One third of British direct investment went into utilities, railways and financial services, many of the projects being commodity-orientated. While trade flows between the leading world economies dominated, Asia, Africa or Latin America were hosts to some 60 per cent of FDI assets, as late as the 1930s (Wilkins, 1970; Corley, 1994).

The Communist Manifesto is accurately quoted as a text that acknowledges the power of a globalizing economy, and then goes on to predict the rise of the large-scale corporation. Its authors, Karl Marx and Friedrich Engels, wrote only six years after the end of the Opium War between Britain and China. The East India Company, which still held the British government's charter to rule a subcontinent, oversaw the growing and processing of poppies, and smuggled the refined drug into China. The East India Company was joined by newer, more dynamic outfits such as Jardine Matheson, an independent trading company founded by expatriate Scotsmen. British-controlled firms brought back on their return another valued consumption good, that much milder drug tea. After decades of hesitation, the Chinese government decided to enforce its official ban on opium imports. When British bombardments forced China to recant, emphatically putting the right to trade above notions of national sovereignty, they provided Marx and Engels with a notorious example of international business out of control.

As a system based in principle on competition and markets, capitalism determined the relations between countries by promoting or, if necessary, imposing the free movement of goods and finance. It possessed, crucially, an unprecedented ability to replicate its methods of competitive markets and to spread economic, political and social change. In the words of Marx and Engels:

The bourgeoisie has through its exploitation of the world market given a cosmopolitan character to production and consumption in every country . . . In place of the old wants, satisfied by the production of the country, we find new wants, requiring for their satisfaction the products of distant lands and climes . . . we have intercourse in every direction, universal inter-dependence of nations . . . The cheap prices of its commodities are the heavy artillery with which it batters down all Chinese walls . . .

In another example of the evocative language we associate so much with Marx, we also have the following: ' . . . the bourgeoisie has drawn from under the feet of industry the national ground on which it stood' (Marx and Engels, 1848).

States and traditional systems of commerce, in this outlook, were subservient to the realities of a single, dominant economic system that was defining the times (modern observers, it seems, are merely repeating ideas about the weakening position of nation states). In Marx and Engels' class-based analysis, the rise of a universal economy could only serve the interests of business owners, who would be increasingly cosmopolitan in outlook and interests. In describing an inherently unstable system they saw as destined to collapse, they underestimated its complexity, and its ability to adapt over time and across different locations. The word 'imperialism' is not found in Marx's writings. Engels and he were writing before the high point of empire as a political, cultural and even economic force, before states sought to forge strong national identities, by extending the functions of government into the daily lives of citizens, and before the era of 'modern' mass manufacturing and consumption, in which many more than a new industrial elite would have a stake.

The global economic system of the late nineteenth century operated in a world of empires, nation states, and rising industrial production and consumer demand. The international economy offered compelling economic prospects, but (like the observers of modern globalization) contemporaries witnessed continuous change, insecurity, and severe disadvantage amongst the participants. The writer H. G. Wells (with the advantage of more hindsight) commented on the size and nature of international trade in the nineteenth century: 'Hitherto the chief commodities that had attracted the European powers into unsettled and barbaric regions had been gold or other metals, spices, ivory, or slaves. But in the latter quarter of the nineteenth century the increase of the European populations was obliging their governments to look abroad for staple foods; and the growth of scientific industrialism was creating a demand for new raw materials, fats and greases of every kind, rubber, and other hitherto disregarded substances. It was plain that Great Britain and Holland and Portugal were reaping a great and growing commercial advantage from their very considerable control of tropical and sub-tropical products' (Wells, 1920). The availability of popular commodities – such as sugar, margarine, coffee and tea – relied on a mixture of international business and imperialism. Wells differentiated scientific industrialism and mass production from earlier forms of industry, and acknowledged their greater reliance on raw materials collected from all over the world. It was a period in which the quality of life in developed countries rose markedly and in which the majority had interests in the international economy either as producers or as consumers (albeit to highly diverse degrees).

Empires were ancient in origin; 'imperialism' was a political and cultural concept new to the 1870s. It built on a heightening sense of nationalism and often on assertions of racial superiority, and it carried with it the intention to subdue and transform other lands. Nationalism and imperialism as popular movements in Europe were intertwined, involved the pursuit of economic interests, and produced a dangerous set of international rivalries. In Asia and then in Africa, commercial interests, trading posts, treaties with local rulers, and disputed juris-dictions could create unstable borders and international disputes, per-suading European states to intervene, ending in colonization. Their governments were often wary of the financial and administrative costs involved, and they had to weigh the diplomatic and military com-plexities, but, from the 1880s onwards, growing national enmities in Europe made them more easily inclined to seek the prestige of empire. The securing of raw materials overseas – as industrial competition intensified – added further justification (Fieldhouse, 1965).

The Liberal commentator J. A. Hobson associated the politics of imperialism with its economics. He argued that inequality and poverty caused 'under-consumption' at home, and so explained the intense interest of investors in foreign markets (Hobson, 1902). He provided an inspiration for Keynes's path-breaking analysis, thirty years on, which called on government spending to stimulate lagging domestic demand, whenever the business cycle took a turn for the worse (Keynes, 1936). Lenin too built on Hobson's ideas, believing that the world had entered a phase of 'monopoly capitalism': corporations had acquired such huge demands for raw materials that they needed and obtained the great powers' control of the world's lands and resources (Lenin, 1916). We do not necessarily have to accept Hobson's or Lenin's central arguments, but it is clear that the deepening integration of the world economy in the nineteenth century reinforced the relationship between national interests and cross-border commerce, and imperialism was a means of pursuing national interests and economic advantage. Late twentieth-century debates contrasted the institutions of the 'nation state' with 'global' forces, including multinationals; in looking at the earlier origins of the international system, however, we can add the third ingredient of 'empire'.

If we are to look closely at the historical record, do we have to move beyond the tradition of merely differentiating between 'domes-tic' and 'foreign' investment, and differentiate in particular the cate-gory of 'within empire' investment? There is a case to be made, since undoubtedly the nature and balance of political and economic risks when investing in an established colony or in a formally sovereign nation were different in character. Yet most of the usable available global statistics for FDI do not make the distinction. Multinationals, as we shall see, adopted similar methods of operation and organization for formally sovereign Latin America and for colonial Asia, to where the large proportion of FDI flowed during this period. They showed a bias for investing in natural resources and commodities for transportation back home, and, because they were in undeveloped or developing territories, they had to show capabilities in deal making, partnership agreements, trading, banking, manufacturing, and the building of infrastructure. It was these factors that explained the location and specific characteristics of FDI, rather than colonization, although FDI and colonization were very frequently intertwined.

The historical record from ancient times shows empires to have been exploitative, expropriating surpluses from conquered territories, while, possibly, offering opportunities for greater trade. It is surely easy to find examples of imperial exploitation in the nineteenth century. The challenge posed by the 'West' to the rest of the world in this period was military and imperialistic, but economic too. What differentiated European empires in this period was their ability to promote or to insist upon a system predicated, in theory, on competitive markets, and to spread leading business practices, capital, technology, and worldwide supply and distribution networks. Multinational businesses undertook seemingly paradoxical aims: they needed the ability both to connect different parts of the world through their exploitation of best international practice, and, chameleonlike, to operate successfully in a wide variety of political and economic conditions.

It helped, therefore, that colonial regimes could install governance rules and business systems with which European multinationals were familiar, and the guaranteed protection of property rights lowered the risks for international investors. Empires facilitated trading networks by promoting global communication and transport (for military as well as commercial reasons). In many cases, institutional bias, personal networks, and tariffs could and did unfairly favour enterprises from the imperial country. Yet, despite handicaps, non-European traders and investors continued to play a critical role in colonial economies, most obviously in the case of Asia. The world economy that emerged had global systemic features that had the potential to undermine sovereignty through internationalization and interdependence. Nonetheless, multinationals had to operate at various levels – local, national, regional, international, and possibly imperial and transcontinental. The creation of a 'world system' was driven from Europe, and subsequently the USA, but cannot be explained by looking at European and US influences alone. Outside Europe and North America, multinationals needed the cooperation of local producers and merchants, and oversaw a variety of practices and arrangements.

Mercantilism and opium

During the Bronze Age, tin mined in Cornwall travelled all over Europe and facilitated the breakthrough in technology that defined a whole era in human evolution. International trade in a wide variety of commodities was, of course, a feature of the ancient world, and it spurred the period of European seafaring and expansionism from the sixteenth century onwards. There were very obvious formative antecedents to the nineteenth-century world, but the rapid acceleration in trade, the greater scale of cross-border transactions, and, critically, changes in the structure and organization of the international economy were nonetheless marked. We can see the final ending of one type of system and its replacement by another: so, to put it very simply, mercantilism and slavery gave place to international competitive markets and (despite tragic exceptions continuing) waged labour. Mercantilism became associated with the exploitation of colonies and their resources, and with the restricting of commerce to the benefit of the imperial power.

To be exact, many of the chartered companies that had been granted overseas monopoly rights by their governments had been in long-term decline, and many of them were disbanded in the eighteenth century, including the Muscovy Company (1746), the Royal African Company (1752), the French, Danish and Dutch East Indies companies (1769, 1779, and 1800 respectively), and the French West Indies Company (1791). The Levant Company, however, continued for a while longer (1825), as did England's East India Company and the Hudson Bay Company (Gabel and Bruner, 2003). The idea that it was industrial capitalists that integrated across borders, forging raw materials and marketing channels, and killed off mercantilism is incorrect (Dunning, 1993). Historical timing makes such an interpretation unlikely, since manufacturing companies in the nineteenth century preferred, in the main, to increase exports rather than to launch into FDI. It was private trading companies that offered from the eighteenth century onwards the major challenge to chartered enterprises. They proved adept at seizing worldwide entrepreneurial opportunities – they had no charter to restrict their sphere of operations – and they demonstrated flexibility in their means of financing and organization.

The European powers abandoned a commerce based upon protectionism and government-sponsored monopolies. They embraced instead the advantages of markets, competition, and free trade, which had become associated with industrialization, scientific principles and progress (Wallerstein, 1974–2011; McNeil, 1963). What the new system offered was the mutual benefits of open trade: each country raised its living standards by specializing in the production of goods and commodities, and all participants made gains from economic interdependence and exchange. Yet both the ending of trade barriers and shared advantages remained an ideal or goal – not universal reality – since chartered firms did not completely disappear, and national objectives and protectionist tariffs began towards the end of the nineteenth century to challenge the internationalist philosophy of mutual trade.

Imperial control cut across ideas of free commerce between sovereign nations – by definition, it challenged the ideal of national sovereignty – and did not necessarily operate a level playing field for all businesses. The principles of free labour markets could be described, unemotionally, as nuanced. In order to continue supplying commodities for the 'West', including sugar, tobacco and rubber, unfree indentured labour in many cases took the place of chattel slaves. In Africa, many colonial regimes used punitive and sometimes violent measures that forced indigenous populations into producing goods for international markets. An estimated 4 million people – mostly Indian, next Chinese, but also Japanese, Malays and others – went to work in plantations and mines in the Caribbean, Latin America, the Pacific and Indian Ocean islands, and South East Asia, and they laboured in construction and railway projects in the USA and in developing territories, from 1830 to 1914 (Bayly, 2004). Japanese and then Chinese labour was needed for Peru's guano trade and agricultural estates; Tamils from south India journeyed to the tea plantations of Ceylon, and, later, made possible the rubber industry that would become associated with Malaya; Indians worked the sugar plantations of the Caribbean, and, with their practical experience gained back home, they were imported to build the railways of East Africa.

Governments had granted to investors charters bestowing monopoly rights and protective tariffs. In return, they received levies and taxes, and the chartered companies were a means of privatizing the management of colonies and even the conduct of warfare. Policy sought to exploit overseas territories, to limit imports, and to maximize the inward flow of gold or silver; it was in principle based on advantaging and strengthening wherever possible only the imperial homeland. One of the best-known examples of the old system had been Britain's Royal African Company. Europeans bartered merchandise for African spices, ivory, and slaves, which they then sold in the West Indies. On their return home, they completed history's most notorious trade 'triangle'. They brought sugar, which was continental America's most important slave crop, but tobacco, cotton, coffee, and mining claimed their share of victims too (Carlos and Kruse, 1996). Of the 11 million Africans forcibly transported across the Atlantic, British merchants probably accounted for 3 million captives.

When it first lost its monopoly, the Royal African Company continued with slaving, but eventually came to depend on ivory and gold. The Dutch West Indies Company was a strong competitor: it took the place of the French West Indies Company and Portuguese shippers, delivered its human traffic to France's American colonies, and became also the leading importer to Brazil, the world's biggest slave market. European nations looked east as well as west for profit and plunder. There were East Indies companies from France, Denmark and Sweden, but it was those from England and Holland that ultimately acquired reputations as both commercial and fighting units. The Dutch United East Indies Company (Vereenigde Oostindische Compagnie, or VOC) drove out the Portuguese from numerous trading outposts, and then established commercial relations as far as Japan. Its seizure of Batavia (today's Jakarta) began a series of developments with long-term implications for both Dutch colonial history and overseas investment (Gabel and Bruner, 2003).

It was Britain that gained both recognition and notoriety for the reach of its imperial and economic interests (Bowen, Lincoln and Rigby, 2002; Jones, 2000). The defeat of the French East Indies Company by its English rival during the Seven Years' War (1756–63) was a turning point. By 1818, much of the Indian subcontinent had fallen under the control of the East India Company, and, after the loss of the North American territories, it constituted the core of a new imperial economy. Trade had drawn India into Europe's ambit, and the wars fought between British and French trading companies on behalf of their governments settled its fate. The triumphant East India Company had deep origins (back to 1600), and by the eighteenth century it was the most prominent example of the 'mercantile system', and, consequently, a target of Adam Smith's condemnation (Smith, 1776). When, in 1765, the Mughal Empire granted the East India Company revenue collection rights in Bengal, it opened its gates wide to an opportunistic and ruthless operator. As the power of the Mughals continued to disintegrate, the company obtained further territories through political intrigue and conquest. It sought expansion and security for its commercial interests, but could not always profitably administer its new responsibilities (Chaudhari, 1978; Bowen, Lincoln and Rigby, 2002; Carlos and Nicholas, 1988).

More dynamic independent merchants competed with and ultimately replaced the mercantilists, and commercial monopoly became, first, unenforceable, and, second, undesirable. The East India Company persisted, but in 1813 a revised royal charter ended its control of Indian trade, with the notable exception of the tea trade and dealings with China. Glasgow's James Finlay (cotton traders in Europe and the US) was amongst those that quickly set up offices in India. Liverpool's John Gladstone, previously a corn, cotton, and sugar trader in the Americas, and an owner of West Indies slave plantations, followed. As was the usual practice, he asked a relative to go overseas and establish an associate firm (Jones, 1986; James Finlay, 1951). Sir John Gladstone later became better remembered as father of the British prime minister William Ewart Gladstone.

In the space of forty years, by assuming monopoly rights over the opium crop in Bengal, the East India Company made India the world's leading supplier of narcotics, and in effect brought mass addiction to China. Opium and raw cotton went from India, Chinese tea was sent to Britain, and, finally, textiles and machinery went from Britain to India: a new trading triangle had replaced the one that had swapped slaves and goods across the Atlantic. Opium was so lucrative that British and Indian traders ignored the East India Company's official control, helped by the availability of new, independent sources from the princely states of western India. Drug profits were big enough to attract 'Yankee traders', who found it worthwhile to carry the drug from Turkey around Cape Horn, and on to China. Private companies, with the British to the forefront, also conducted highly profitable and clandestine activities in indigo, sugar, cotton, and spices.

By the 1820s, the East India Company probably accounted for only one third of opium exports from India. Jardine Matheson, formally registered in 1832, emerged to control one third of the foreign trade at Canton (modern Guangzhou), the main entry port to China. It was the first firm to send Chinese tea to Britain. One of the founders, William Jardine, had been employed by the East India Company as a surgeon; James Matheson had worked for his uncle's trading firm in Calcutta, before seeking his fortune in China. J. S. Dent & Co. was Jardine Matheson's biggest competitor for the opium business. Under pressure from independent merchants, the British government in 1833 ended the East India Company's hollow monopoly over the China trade. When China's imperial government banned opium imports, and gave the British a formal reason to open hostilities, it generated an international debate about the rights of international traders and sovereign nations. During the First Opium War, from 1839 to 1842, Jardine Matheson was determined to beat any embargo on its business. It simply operated under a Danish flag of convenience, and James Matheson assumed the post of Denmark's consul in Canton.

The 1842 Treaty of Nanjing forced the Chinese to make compensation, cede Hong Kong in perpetuity, and establish four further entry ports. Two years later, in 1844, Jardine Matheson transferred its main office to Hong Kong, where it could now enjoy British rule, plus easy access to the mainland.[1] During the Second Opium War, 1856–60, British and French forces occupied Beijing and Canton. In ending the first phase of the conflict, the 'unequal' Treaty of Tianjin in 1858 opened ten further ports and allowed foreign ships on to the Yangtze River (Cheong, 1979; Lange, 1971; Allen and Donnithorne, 1954; Keswick, 1982; Harcourt, 1981; Fairbank, 1980). Illicit imports to China probably doubled in the years between 1842 and 1858. Amongst the 95 clippers running between the auction houses of Calcutta and the Chinese coast, the Cowasjee family, Parsis from India, owned 6; Russell & Company 8; and Dent and Jardine a combined total of 27.[2] Travelling across the Pacific, US traders could be found in Honolulu and Manila in the 1820s, and Russell, founded in 1824, would establish a long presence in nineteenth-century Asia, as would Olyphant & Co., with an office in Canton from 1848 to 1878 (Wilkins, 1970).

The new international system

The flow of commerce between India and China brought change to South East Asia. Britain had administered Java during the Napoleonic Wars, and its governor, and one-time East India Company officer, Stamford Raffles, having fought for the territory, deeply resented its return to the Netherlands (Wutzberg, 1986). So, with the cooperation of a local sultan, Raffles received the natural port of Singapore in 1819 as a replacement, and so reinforced Britain's presence in the Malay Peninsula. Guthries (1821) and Edward Boustead (1830) founded agencies in this new free trade port. They transacted through region-wide commercial networks with both European and Asian businesses, and they dealt with Chinese merchants, in particular, as the most established players throughout South East Asia. The East India Company extended its control to the coast of Burma in 1826 (the naval lessons learnt by British steam-powered gunboats along the Irrawaddy were later used in the Opium Wars) (Myint-U, 2001; Ponting, 2000). Siam (now Thailand) looked at the course of international events, and, under the Bowring Treaty of 1855, reluctantly accepted more open commercial relationships. Around the trading and military hub of Singapore, in the southern part of the peninsula, investments in sugar, coffee, nutmeg and cloves were highlighting the potential of the whole region (Wyatt, 2003; Jones, 2000; Allen and Donnithorne, 1957; Chew and Lee, 1991).

Both Jardine Matheson and J. S. Dent had shareholdings in the P&O Steam Navigation Company, which dominated Bombay–China opium shipping, by the 1850s. The two firms effectively controlled the import price, but their good times could not last forever. After the Second Opium War, China legalized the drug, and local producers drove prices downwards. David Sassoon & Sons, Iraqi Jews that had settled in Bombay to trade in cotton, challenged the Jardine–Dent opium duopoly by buying crops directly from Indian farmers. Jardine Matheson survived because it was able to diversify its activities and expand trade routes. The biggest business group, however, came to be Mackinnon, Mackenzie & Co. It founded an office in Calcutta in 1847, importing finished textiles from Britain, and exporting tea, sugar and rice. India was at the centre of its profitable trading route, which stretched east towards China and eventually Japan and Australia, and west towards Africa and Europe.[3] Mackinnon, Mackenzie was another example from that long list of expatriate Scots firms – including James Finlay, Jardine Matheson, Guthries, Wallace Brothers, T.D. Findlay, Grahams, and the Borneo Company – that became commercial forces across Asia and much of the world. Others, such as Yule (located in Manchester), or Gladstone and Balfour Williamson (both Liverpool) were Scottish in origin (Jones, 2000).

It was the First War of Independence (Britain's 'Indian Mutiny') that ended the East India Company as a proxy political power, and the subcontinent was converted into a crown colony in the following year, 1858. Nevertheless, until its final dissolution in 1874, the East India Company continued to manage the Indian tea trade on behalf of the British government. The chartered Hudson's Bay Company (founded in 1670) proved even more resilient. It discovered new and profitable commercial avenues, and converted itself into a business that could compete in the nineteenth century's international system. Having lost its monopoly rights in western Canada, it was bought, in 1863, by London merchant bankers, and it was reborn as a general trading company and retailer (Hudson's Bay Company, 1934; Taylor and Baskerville, 1994).[4] Defined by the terms of their charter, and formally without competitors, mercantilist firms did not have the adaptability of commercial rivals. Independent traders could transfer their operations and skills from one part of the world to Asia, and eventually undermined the economic foundations of the formal East India Company monopoly. They were better suited to the greater scale and highly transformative character of an international system based on competitive trade.

While the colonization of Asia and Africa was associated with the expansion of the world economy, it was paradoxically the end of imperialism that generated new opportunities in Latin America, most obviously for the British. The French had invaded Spain during the Napoleonic Wars, and by stages Spain's authority across its American colonies fell away. A wave of revolutions created nation states that ultimately sought trade and investment. Governing elites in Latin America looked to Europe for models of progress, and over time acquired a strong belief in free trade and in foreign firms as bringers of modernization (Abel and Lewis, 1985; Williamson, 1992). Commission merchants and intermediaries grew into multinational businesses with an aptitude for cosmopolitan cooperation (Platt, 1972; C. Jones, 1987). The importance of trade and commodities opens up debates about the involvement of foreign multinationals in Latin America accelerating or holding back the region's development. We can say, with more certainty, that the boom in Latin American trade, covering the long span of the nineteenth century until 1930, brought an increasing perception of economic reconquest in a region that had liberated itself from formal or political imperialism (Topik and Wells, 1998).

It was international trade that turned unappealing piles of birds' droppings into a commodity. Anthony Gibbs & Sons, originally founded in 1808, had lost its textile export business in Spain thanks to the conflict with France. It had to secure business elsewhere, and one big decision it made was to go to Latin America. The firm is a good example of an international business adapting its commercial skills and trading connections to suit the nineteenth-century world economy. It did so, additionally, in markets where it had no imperial advantages. Gibbs arrived in Lima, Peru, in 1822, and in Valparaíso and Santiago, Chile, in 1826. The government of Peru became dependent on guano revenues, and it relied at first on native capitalists connected to a trading firm from Liverpool. In 1842, Peru offered the guano concession to Anthony Gibbs & Sons, recognizing its organizational skills, as well as its ability to commercialize the commodity in foreign markets. The firm also knew how to win favours, and financed the government and its officials. As demand grew, Peru encouraged the entry of Chinese indentured labour to undertake the arduous and dirty task of collecting the guano by shovel, which in turn helped reformers in the country abolish black slavery and the enforced labour of indigenous Americans. By 1861, local feeling and agitation against Gibbs were so strong that the contract could not be renewed (Platt, 1977; Pike, 1967; Williamson, 1992). The firm had to learn during these years how to deal with Peruvian governments – indebted, unstable, and often arbitrary in their actions – and it was not especially concerned by the end of its monopoly. There were other commercial opportunities to be seized, and the company was suffering from 'guano weariness'. Gibbs turned to the production of nitrate in Peru and Bolivia, selling the product throughout the Pacific Coast, California and Europe. The firm succeeded, latterly, as London merchant bankers, illustrating how easily

Table 2.2 *Value of world exports, 1820–1929 (1990 $USm)*

	World exports	World GDP	Exports/ GDP (%)
1820	7,255	694,772	1.0
1870	56,247	1,127,876	5.0
1913	236,592	2,726,065	8.7
1929	334,408	3,696,156	9.0

Source: Maddison (1999).

the frontiers between trading and financial services dissolved (Maude, 1958).[5]

Trade patterns

There is a stack of statistics to show how the rise in economic growth, manufacturing and trade coincided, and how much Europe was at the centre of developments (Kuznets, 1966; Miller, 2012). Global trade accelerated by some 1 per cent per year between 1500 and 1800, but the nineteenth century seems a turning point. World output per head appears to have grown by an average of 7.3 per cent per decade between 1800 and 1913, but per capita world trade in merchandise expanded at an average of 33 per cent. So, output per head was 2.2 times larger in 1913 in comparison to 1800, while trade was a remarkable 25 times larger. International commerce may have quadrupled between 1850 and 1880, and then grew three times larger again between 1880 and 1913 (Kenwood and Lougheed, 1992; Maddison, 1999). The figures reveal that trade was, throughout the nineteenth century, a catalyst of growth; they show, too, since exports grew in relation to world GDP throughout the nineteenth century on to 1914, that many nations became economically more interdependent (Table 2.2).

Although Europeans conducted the bulk of trade with other Europeans or with places of European settlement, their dealings with the rest of the world were significant. Europe's industries and people relied on internationally sourced raw materials and commodities. British FDI assets alone were worth over 57 per cent of national income in 1913, but only 9 per cent in the case of the USA in 1914. For E. E. Williams, interestingly, the issue was not the strength Britain had gained through the international economy, but its vulnerability: 'we are at the mercy of foreign nations, not only for our food and clothes, but for our huge invested capital' (Williams, 1896). While Americans built a massive transcontinental and resource-rich economy, Europe leant more heavily on its international commerce. In 1850, it accounted for some 70 per cent of total global trade; by 1913, it still held 62 per cent. Its reliance on the rest of the world particularly grew in the decades after 1870, the period of high imperialism, when contemporaries were similarly conscious of the growth in population, consumption, urbanization and 'scientific industrialism' (to borrow H. G. Wells's phrase). Next to Europe's hold over world trade, in 1913 other regions were demonstrably more inward-looking: North America with 13 per cent of the total; Asia, 11 per cent; Latin America, 8 per cent; and Africa and Oceania together, 6 per cent (Maddison, 1999; Lewis, 1978).

The North Atlantic was a major crossing point for commerce. Despite the growth of other markets, especially in Latin America, 60 per cent of US exports in 1913 still went to Europe, and 50 per cent of its imports originated from there. These trading relationships were powered by the USA's economic development and the abundance of its natural resources. As a result, large-scale European investment flowed to the USA. The British share of US imports fell from a peak of approximately 46 per cent in 1853 to 17 per cent by 1913, by which time other European countries had increased their share to some 33 per cent. Germany was successfully competing for international markets: the value of its manufactured exports was equal to one third of Britain's in 1873, but it overtook its prime competitor by 1913. Half of the exports from Asia, Africa and Latin America went to Britain in 1860. As other nations industrialized, trading patterns changed: the figure was 25 per cent in 1900, compared to the 31 per cent headed for the rest of Western Europe (Pollard, 1985; Hobsbawm, 1989; Topik and Wells, 1998).

Some 66 per cent of Latin America's trade was still with Europe in 1904–5 (24 per cent was with the USA). It was only from the turn of the century that the USA began significantly to curb the influence of European and notably British enterprises in its designated 'backyard', giving commercial substance to the Monroe Doctrine, by which the USA declared its opposition to European imperialism in the Americas. One further set of statistics is indicative. In 1876–80, primary products comprised 62 per cent of all exports, and manufactured items 38 per cent; by 1913, the figures were still 62 and 38 per cent respectively. The underdeveloped territories' share of all exports, 27 per cent in 1876–80, was 28 per cent in 1913 (although, of course, the actual level of trade had risen dramatically). The figures themselves hide much that did alter in the character of international business, but there was a remarkably stable relationship between a system of 'two worlds': on the one side, Europe and places of European settlement; on the other, the vast ranges of Asia, Latin America, Africa and Oceania (Kenwood and Lougheed, 1992).

It is estimated that 22.5 per cent of Britain's imports came from its colonies (1892–6 average), and that 33.2 per cent of its exports went in return. The British Empire (as the largest) contained a market of some 325 million people (in locations, nonetheless, highly diverse in their wealth), while that of the French (as number two) could claim only 36.2 million. Portugal obtained 15.8 per cent and the Netherlands 14.5 per cent of their imports from colonies; and Spain sent a substantial 24 per cent of its exports to controlled territories; but, for most European countries, both the import and the export figures were below 10 per cent.

Overall, imperialism had a greater effect on colonial economies than the ruling power. As a result, 49 per cent of the exports from British colonies went to Britain, and some 55 per cent of imports to British colonies originated from Britain. Similarly, 61 per cent of French colonial trade was connected to France (Foreman-Peck, 1994; Fieldhouse, 1965). Imperialism had an impact on trade patterns, and European markets in particular provided demand and growth opportunities. Colonies needed capital, technology and business organization, and, consequently, the services of multinational enterprise as well as trade. Greater open competition was possible in Latin America or China, but elsewhere the bias towards the imperial nation in most colonies was apparent. Prospects in developing lands had an especially important bearing on the development of multinational enterprise, whose strategies and organization were, not surprisingly, frequently trade related.

National policies and tariffs

The dynamism of the international economy has been closely associated with the policy changes that saw the decline of mercantilism and the rise of free trade. For political as well as economic reasons, the switch was stuttering rather than smooth. From 1842, Britain began the process of ending tariff protection and imperial preference, leaving by 1860 the small total of 48 goods subject to duties. Britain's colonial governments generally followed. The power of free economics reorientated Canada away from the imperial power, and it signed, in 1855, a commercial treaty with the USA. It was principally Britain that forced the weakened Chinese government to open its ports; Siam too yielded; the USA, looking closely at the British presence in Singapore and Hong Kong, forced Japan, from 1854, to establish diplomatic and external commercial relations. On the other hand, most European countries never committed themselves as fully as Britain to the tenets of free trade.

British policy could call on a persuasive set of abstract principles, philosophical as well as economic, but there was also calculated advantage. The rest of the world had reasons to fear Britain's lead in products, services and management methods, and, therefore, its potential to crush their own budding industries. The bilateral agreements that materialized from the 1860s saw the reduction of duties, not their abolition. In any case, it was difficult in practice to distinguish between levies that protected domestic businesses (wholly unjustified) and those that raised public revenue (quite legitimate). When open markets did not suit its interests, Britain too could overlook policy principles: preferential tariffs retained India as a market for its cotton goods (Kenwood and Lougheed, 1992; Ashworth, 1964). The resurrection of the government-sponsored chartered company in Africa, after 1885, was an attempt to justify economically the development of territories with highly unlikely returns or huge risks. While necessary to fulfil their imperialist aims, the grant of monopoly jarred with free market principles (Fieldhouse, 1965).

The years 1850–80 came to be regarded as the high point of world free trade, but reversals were already apparent. Fashioned by an act of revolutionary war, and a rejection of Britain's mercantilist controls, the USA was inclined toward manufacturing self-sufficiency and protectionism. It was a view most famously expressed in a report by Alexander Hamilton, a former Secretary of the Treasury (*Report on Manufactures*, 1791). Hamilton shaped the ideas of Frederich List, the German economist, who attacked the idea of one commercial policy fit for all, arguing instead that the industries of less advanced nations required state protection (*The National System of Political Economy*, 1841). Although tariffs were gradually reduced in the USA after 1833, they were increased in 1861. The measure was seen as favouring Northern manufacturers and, by increasing the threat of retaliatory action overseas against cotton and tobacco exports from the South, it widened the country's fault-lines. Greater government expenditure during the American Civil War of 1861–5 soon led to the return of high custom duties. Having recently liberated its serfs, and therefore its labour market, Russia was concerned with stabilizing its troubled domestic scene, and so it introduced, in 1868, measures designed to shield its emerging industries.

Before long, most independent nations were committed to curtailing free trade. The Great Depression, dated from 1873 and formally lasting till 1896, witnessed a fall in prices and profits, and encouraged European governments to protect both their farming and manufacturing. Cheapening grain from the USA threatened powerful agricultural interests and landed estates in Europe, and hastened peasant populations on to ships headed for New York (Hatton and Williamson, 1998). One European country could disadvantage any nation with which it had no commercial treaty, and renegotiations brought an upward trend to duty levels. The legacy was a highly confusing structure of differential rates. Over the whole period 1880–1913, only Britain, the Netherlands and Denmark held true to the practice of open commerce. The best ideals of free trade were vulnerable to the realities of national self-interest and imperialism. From 1879, and especially after 1902, Germany penalized finished manufactures and agricultural products, but tariffs on semi-finished goods were low and raw materials entered unhindered. Italy acted from 1878, although France was more uncertain until 1892. In the USA, in 1890, the McKinley tariff increased the average rate to some 50 per cent, notably affecting textiles, steel, glass, tinplate, and agriculture, and the Dingley Act of 1897 established a figure of 57 per cent.

Trade expansion

Why, however, did the partial abandoning of free trade principles not halt the expansion of trade? The industrial transformation of economies beyond Britain, the spread of new technologies, more efficient management methods, and therefore improved living standards were all relevant. The greater demand for goods of all types stoked the cross-border transfer of commodities, minerals, raw materials, finance, services, and labour. Tariff increases were not a determining hindrance to the rising tide of economic internationalization and interdependence. As the statistics reveal, those nations that took a larger share of world output in the last quarter of the nineteenth century were also a bigger presence in the world's markets. The Gold Standard, by which governments linked currencies to the value of their reserves, had been widely adopted during the nineteenth century. It was seen as a bulwark against inflation, and created confidence in international business and in the stability of exchange rates. The Gold Standard was not abandoned during the Great Depression of 1873–97.

The motives behind protectionism and state intervention were complex, as were the consequences. Landowners and manufacturers did safeguard their vested interests, and growing nationalism was easily inclined towards the protection of vital or developing industries. If the political and pragmatic benefits of trade restrictions could be accepted, so could other acts of state intervention. Governments sponsored the infrastructure that facilitated both industry and trade. With the notable exception of Britain, financial subsidies or grants of land encouraged the laying of railways, and, in some instances, lines were state-owned. Railway tariffs were often biased towards domestic goods or exports, but, interestingly, businessmen in Britain complained that its domestic railways actually favoured foreign products. State bounties sped the expansion of indigenous merchant fleets. More government expenditure on armaments was ominous proof of intensifying international rivalry, and pushed the growth of domestic engineering and shipbuilding companies. Enlarged commercial consular services highlighted the importance of economic competition, and they were a visible statement by nation states of their determination to increase export shares. Universal education systems had national as well as social and economic purposes. Schools offered lessons on national history and identity, and basic literacy and arithmetic prepared populations for work in factories, trade and services.

Nations achieved growth and higher living standards through economic specialization – whether German electricals, US machinery, or Netherlands margarine – which was only possible where a nation traded for the goods or raw materials it did not produce or make so efficiently. Industrialization beyond Britain ended its supremacy, and, as other nations closed the gap, they drove the competition for international markets and resources. The quest for new and alternative sources of growth is identified with imperialism generally but, in particular, with the Berlin Conference of 1884–5, during which the European great powers divided Africa. The symbolism of this agreement and its impact on the political and social development of a continent, however, were initially more powerful than its economic consequences (Shillington, 2005). Africa's trade and investment opportunities on a world scale remained comparatively small. By the turn of the century, the continent accounted for less than one twentieth of total global trade. Yet British exports headed there did grow from 5–6 per cent of the country's total in 1880–4 to some 12 per cent by 1900. By 1913, Europe took nearly 85 per cent of all imported primary products, obtained increasingly from tropical or far-off locations (Kenwood and Lougheed, 1992: 60–73; Ashworth, 1964).

Despite worldwide deflation, and the tendency towards protectionism, there were enough countervailing tendencies to ensure that the expansion of trade and business continued. If exports such as woollen products or steel to certain countries were disadvantaged, the proportion of semi-finished goods and commodities grew at the expense of final manufactures. Overall trends did not drastically diminish the operations of leading multinationals in trade, commodities and minerals. While merchandise exports had grown by 4.2 per cent per annum between 1820 and 1870, they still averaged 3.4 per cent between 1870 and 1913 (and from a larger base) (Maddison, 1999). The needs of humanity – and their rising expectations – had to be met. In the 1880s, the world population was some 1.5 billion, probably twice the number it had been one hundred years before, and some 1.7 billion by 1914, half of whom were in Asia, and over one quarter in Europe. By 1890, there were 103 cities with populations of over 600,000 needing food and commodities (Hobsbawm, 2003). The fall in prices that so defined the Great Depression drove up the real wages of consumers (or those located in the world's industrialized countries), and their greater spending power multiplied the consumption of essential foods, packaged household goods, and semi-luxuries.

New demands required appropriate infrastructure. Railway mileage in 1840 totalled 4,772 miles, but 130,361 in 1870 and 490,974 in 1900. The train in Central America turned the once exotic banana into an item of mass production, and opened up the US Midwest and the Argentine pampas to the grain and meat business. Technological improvements altered the nature of shipping too: after 1865, companies out of Liverpool, such as Holt or Booth, began to introduce non-stop steam services to Mauritius, Brazil, India and China. The world's merchant fleet (20m net tons in 1880, and 34.6m in 1910) supplied the demand for goods and passenger travel, and it was supported by investments in ports, warehousing, waterways, coal stops, and supply stations, often financed by multinationals, and all, potentially, with imperial and naval implications. The first refrigerated ship sailed from Buenos Aires to France in 1877. The Suez Canal opened in 1869, the Panama Canal in 1912. Rotterdam's link to the North Sea was improved in 1872, and the Manchester Shipping Canal (connecting 'Cottonopolis' through the port of Liverpool with the rest of the globe) was constructed by 1894.

The telegraph put London in touch with Calcutta in 1866, and with Australia in 1872, and it was operational across the North Atlantic by 1866. Firms such as the German-owned Siemens, which manufactured and laid cables,[6] or the British operator Eastern Telegraph Company converted an innovation into practical reality,[7] and they were (by obvious necessity) global in their strategies. They were assisted by the International Office of Telegraphy (1869), which, like the Universal Postal Union (1874), and the Berne Convention on international copyright protection (1886), facilitated the foundation of common standards and practices (Ashworth, 1964). Finally, bilateral commercial treaties between nations had established a tradition of international law, affirming property and full compensation rights for investors and traders. Before 1914, there were no large-scale sequestrations of foreign-owned property, and the international system offered practical security to its participating businesses.

Foreign direct investment

Trade was one indicator of the international system's vitality. Overseas investment was another. But, for the nineteenth century, we have unfortunately only very approximate measures of its importance. Calculations of the world stock of foreign investment by 1914 hover around a figure of $40–45bn. The majority was undoubtedly portfolio, meaning that numerous governments borrowed money in the world's financial capitals, or projectors raised funds for enterprises,

Table 2.3 *Location of British overseas assets in 1914 (%)*

USA	21
Latin America	19
Europe	5
Asia (not British colonies)	5
British colonies	44

Source: Crouzet (1982).

Table 2.4 *Sectoral distribution of total British assets in 1914 (%)*

Railway companies	40
Government securities and municipal loans	30
Raw material production, especially mining	10
Banks and financial companies	8
Public utilities	5

Source: Ashworth (1964).

often infrastructure schemes, which were owned and controlled over-seas. London was the globe's pivotal money market, and Britain the biggest source of international investment. A large part of these funds had gone to the USA, and also Latin America, but by far the biggest share was for the colonies (Table 2.3). British capital exports accel-erated from the 1850s onwards, and assets grew twenty times by the eve of the First World War. The majority went to railway companies, and to government securities and municipal loans, mostly therefore as portfolio investments (tables 2.4 and 2.5).

France's capital exports increased significantly from the 1850s, and trebled in the thirty-four years after 1880. Once the Franco-Russian Alliance was signed, in 1894, French money poured into Russian rail-ways, industry, and government bonds. In contrast to the British case, 70 per cent of France's assets, by 1914, were in Europe, and included one third of Russia's total joint-stock capital. The 1880s were a turn-ing point for German overseas investments, especially in the USA and Latin America. As for US investors, their lending surged after 1897,

Table 2.5 *Sectoral distribution of British FDI in 1910 (%)*

Resource-based	
Mining	21.0
Plantations	2.6
Oil	1.9
Total	27.2
Market-based	
Food and brewing	1.7
Metals, including manufacturing	7.6
Total	9.3
Railways	28.9
Banking and insurance	4.8
Utilities	
Electric power	1.1
Gas and water	1.9
Tramways	4.4
Telegraph	3.1
Shipping and docks	0.3
Total	10.8
Land and property	17.1

Source: Corley (1994).

and they looked primarily to Canada and Mexico, with Europe in general, the West Indies, and the remainder of Latin America following, ahead of Asia, Africa and Oceania. The priorities (in order) were mining, petroleum, manufacturing, agriculture, railroads, other utilities, and sales organizations (Wilkins, 1970). Britain, by 1914, owned some 40 per cent of world overseas assets; the French approximately 18 per cent, Germany 12 per cent and the USA 5 per cent (Gabel and Bruner, 2003). Britain continued to be the greatest source of international capital until the Second World War.

There is great uncertainty over exactly how much of the $40–45bn in overseas assets by 1914 could be classified as portfolio investment. It follows that the remainder – the foreign direct investment (FDI) undertaken by multinationals headquartered in one country and operating in another – lacks a precise figure. There is an unresolved debate both on the total and on the composition of FDI statistics. While analysts had once favoured a tenth of all overseas investment being FDI, that is some $4–4.5bn, more recent scholarship recalculated the figure to be one third or some $14.6bn (Platt, 1980; Platt, 1986; Feinstein, 1990; Dunning, 1993), while the latest analysis takes $14.5bn as the lowest total and leans towards some $18bn (Dunning and Lundan, 2008). In which case, FDI stock was equal to a sum between 9.0 and 11.1 per cent of global GDP by 1914, above the situation in 1960 (4.4 per cent), and not matched until 1990 (9.4 per cent) (see chapters 4 and 5). It is worth noting, in addition, that the merchandise export level in 1913 (8.7 per cent of global GDP) did not recover from the Wall Street Crash of 1929 and the Second World War until 1964 (when it measured 8.8 per cent). Given the paucity of data sources on FDI for this period, we would be right to exercise caution on several aspects. Nonetheless, FDI and trade figures suggest historically high levels of international economic integration in the global economy before the First World War, and indicate that multinationals had a role in the world economy that was not surpassed for nearly eighty years.

The large flow of FDI from Europe across the North Atlantic and to the South was apparent. In 1914, it is estimated, Britain owned 45 per cent of world FDI assets, with Germany at 14 per cent, France at 10 per cent, the Netherlands at 5 per cent, and the rest of Western Europe at 5 per cent. The USA with 15 per cent accounted for much of the remainder (Dunning and Lundan, 2008; Sluyterman, 2003) (tables 2.6 and 2.7). According to one source, the percentage of British FDI located in the dominions and colonies was at 66 per cent in 1910; in 1914, total overseas investment in the dominions and colonies, both portfolio and FDI, stood at 44 per cent of the total. Portfolio investment opportunities came from all over the world, whereas multinational enterprise was more focused on the empire, where capital and managerial expertise were needed, and political circumstances were favourable (Davis and Huttenback, 1986). South Africa with its capital-intensive mining interests, followed by Australia and New Zealand, were especially prominent as locales for British FDI (by 1910). Latin America and the USA had the lead amongst the remaining 44 per cent to be found in foreign (that is, non-imperial) territories (Corley, 1994). In 1938, Britain still owned nearly 40 per cent of world FDI stock, and the USA, closing the gap fast, held close to 28 per cent (Dunning and Lundan, 2008) (Table 2.7).

Table 2.6 *Location of British FDI assets in 1910 (%)*

Empire and Dominions	
South Africa	25.1
Rest of Africa	2.3
Australia and New Zealand	12.6
Canada	6.3
India and Ceylon (Sri Lanka)	5.1
Malaya	1.6
Others	2.9
Total	55.9
Foreign locations	
Latin America	16.3
USA	10.8
Europe	10.0
China, Japan and Thailand	7.0
Total	44.1

Source: Corley (1994).

If we look at the location of world FDI assets in 1914, the USA at over 10 per cent, China at nearly 8 per cent, Russia at just over 7 per cent, and Canada at near to 6 per cent are shown as the largest host nations, with Britain indicating a figure of 1.4 per cent. The USA prohibited foreign nationals being directors of domestic banks, and multinationals found the barriers to investing in banking prohibitive. Similarly, only US citizens or companies could own mineral rights. On the other hand, most parts of the insurance industry were open to inward FDI, as was mining and oil extraction. Some states prevented the foreign ownership of land, and these provisions blocked investments in ranching and agriculture. But, overall, the size of the US economy, its rich resources, and rapid growth were all major attractions for foreign investors (Wilkins, 1989).

Crucially, the majority of inward FDI (some 60 per cent) was to be found in the developing regions of Latin America, Asia and, to a much lesser extent, Africa. If we take all territories beyond Western Europe and the USA, then the figure rises to over 80 per cent (Dunning and Lundan, 2008) (Table 2.7). India and China were the principal destinations in Asia; in Latin America, Brazil, Argentina and Mexico

Table 2.7 *Estimated stock of accumulated FDI by country of origin, 1914–38*

	1914		1938	
	$m	%	$m	%
Developed economies	18,029	100.0	26,350	100
North America				
USA	2,652	14.7	7,300	27.7
Canada	150	0.8	700	2.7
Western Europe				
UK	8,172	45.3	10,500	39.8
Germany	2,600	14.4	350	1.3
France	1,750	9.7	2,500	9.5
Belgium, Italy, Netherlands, Sweden, Switzerland	1,925	10.7	3,500	13.3
Other European or European offshoot economies				
Russia	300	1.7	450	1.7
Japan	300	1.7	750	2.8
Australia, New Zealand				
South Africa	180	1.0	300	1.1
Other	neg.	neg.	neg.	neg.
Developing economies	neg.	neg.	neg.	neg.
Total	18,029	100.0	26,350	100.0

Source: Dunning and Lundan (2008).

were notable (Dunning, 1993) (Table 2.8). A majority of British FDI, some 56 per cent, was destined for the colonies, and, even allowing for manufacturing being under-reported, a larger percentage went to undeveloped or developing economies (Table 2.6). German FDI was important in Europe and global in its reach: not only in the usually known areas of manufacturing, but additionally in mining, banking, trading, and insurance. We seem to know less about the details behind the very large amounts of French FDI, but investments and businesses from France were especially important in Russia and Spain (Wilkins, 1993). From 1880 to 1913, approximately 50 per cent of all capital

Table 2.8 *Estimated stock of accumulated FDI by recipient economy or area, 1914–38*

	1914		1938	
	$m	%	$m	%
Developed economies	5,235	37.2	8,346	34.3
USA	1,450	10.3	1,800	7.4
Canada	800	5.7	2,296	9.4
Western Europe	1,100	7.8	1,800	7.4
UK	200	1.4	700	2.9
Other Europe	1,400	9.9	400	1.6
Russia	1,000	7.1		
Australia, New Zealand, South Africa	450	3.2	1,950	8.0
Japan	35	0.2	100	0.4
Developing economies	8,850	63.8	15,969	65.7
Latin America	4,600	32.7	7,481	30.8
Africa	900	6.4	1,799	7.4
Asia	2,950	20.9	6,068	25.0
China	1,100	7.8	1,400	5.8
India and Ceylon	450	3.2	1,359	5.6
Southern Europe	n/a	n/a	n/a	n/a
International and unallocated	neg.	neg.	n/a	n/a
Total	14,085	100.0	24,315	100.0

Source: Dunning and Lundan (2008).

invested in industrial corporations in Russia was of foreign origin (McKay, 1970).

The bulk of Britain's outward FDI was, moreover, directed towards railways and natural resources (Corley, 1994), although the available figures may underestimate to some degree the levels of overseas manufacturing FDI (Table 2.5). Perhaps 55 per cent of world total FDI stock was invested in natural resources (renewable and non-renewable); 20 per cent in railways; 10 per cent in trade, distribution, public utilities, and banking; and about 15 per cent in manufacturing, the last being almost entirely located in Western Europe and North America (Dunning and Lundan, 2008). There was a strong link, during the nineteenth century, between the search for natural resources, infrastructure investment, trading, the need for FDI in developing and colonial lands, and the rise of multinational enterprise.

Multinational organization and activities

In order to appreciate the full significance of FDI, and its effects, we need to look beyond measures of capital stock towards the ways in which it was controlled and organized. In Siemens and Singer, we can see pioneers of overseas manufacturing investment: companies that transferred managerial skills, production systems and technological knowledge from their home base to overseas subsidiaries. They were replicating mini-versions of themselves, founding subsidiaries in foreign markets, transplanting the organizational capabilities and systems intrinsic and internal to a manufacturing firm. This form of FDI was more pronounced in the interwar decades, especially prevalent in the decades after the Second World War, and (for both of those periods) normally directed towards the more developed economies. What is striking about multinational enterprise in the nineteenth century is the free-standing company (FSC), whose home nation base was essentially a source of capital investment and the formal place of registration. From the outset, however, operations were conducted only in an overseas market, and not first established in the home nation. Other than key managerial personnel, the transfer of capabilities (such as technology, or marketing) to permanent overseas subsidiaries was not conspicuous.

FSCs were investment vehicles designed to exploit the opportunities of a booming world economy and imperial expansion. Britain and the Netherlands, as the two most internationalized economies, led their formation. Nor is it a coincidence that 75 per cent of those formed in the Netherlands operated in the colonial Dutch East Indies (modern-day Indonesia). FSCs tended to focus on a single core activity, commodity, or service, but could overcome any lack of scope or size through strategic alliances, cross-directorships, and business groups linked by equity. Given the locale of their operations, in colonies and developing economies, they were frequently involved in trading, or in the exploitation of natural resources (Wilkins, 1988a; Corley, 1994; Sluyterman, 1994; Hennart, 1994a; Jones, 1998; Wilkins and Schroter, 1998).

Despite the conclusions of some historians, there is little evidence that a failure to adopt more complex, integrated organizational structures (associated with mass manufacturing and US corporations) disadvantaged FSCs. Trading, banking and financing in distant locations suited the FSC form, allowing for on-the-spot entrepreneurship and flexible deal-making. Europe was a source of capital and possibly management, but commercial opportunities and consequently operational decisions were elsewhere. When economists 'discovered' the 'multinational enterprise' in the 1960s, they used concepts that helped explain the then dominance of US manufacturers. The FSCs, when they were revealed and examined at a later date, seemed an oddity. FSCs could, nonetheless, evolve international management structures and headquarters functions, many doing so by the end of the nineteenth century. If not on a par with systems of multinational manufacturers in the twentieth century, we should not assume that they had to be comparable, and they were often suited or appropriate to the nature of the businesses linked to FSCs.

Seven types of multinational business became prominent in the period before 1914, with all of them, with the exception of manufacturing, producing notable examples of the FSC form. However, what their descriptions demonstrate is the fluidity of business activities between different types of firms, and the difficulties of fitting any one firm into a distinct category; they highlight, too, the limits of statistics that adopt the three classifications of service, natural resource or industry. The scale and scope of international commerce, firstly, rested heavily on the competencies of large trading companies. Often – while Europe was the source of their founding capital and top management – their competitive success rested on local commercial knowledge and their overseas networks of business associates. As entrepreneurial opportunism and product diversity were characteristic of trading companies, they easily branched out into agriculture, ranching, mining and industry. It was a small step from profitable middleman to investing in the harvesting or manufacturing of products, and as a result trading companies gained security of supply. It was an equally small step to move from investment to the providing of other financial services, including banking and insurance, and merchants were naturally drawn to shipping and transport businesses. Trading companies acquired economies from their varied mix of commercial activities, and, whenever they evolved into conglomerates, they exercised an importance in Asia, Latin America and Africa rarely matched at the time by multinationals in other parts of the world.

Imperialism offered traders a favourable investment climate (so shaping the histories of Guthries in Malaysia, or Borsunij in the Dutch East Indies), yet they needed the market knowledge or organizational skills to succeed across the globe (as demonstrated by Britain's Balfour Williamson in North and South America, or the Swiss-owned Volkart in Siam). In Latin America, Asia, and Africa, Western trading companies gained from their global or regional reach. Vitally, they had access to the European capital markets that financed trade and shipping, and used the flow of funds to invest in trade-related plantations, mining, and industry (on noted occasions, with local business interests). Because of their strategic and operational advantages as large, diversified and international businesses, the European trading company stimulated colonial imitators (such as Tata from India, which moved from trading into textiles, steel production, coal mining and electricity generation by 1914), and ultimately competitive challengers (prominently, Mitsubishi and Mitsui from Japan).

Traders within Europe did not, in general, have the same opportunities to evolve into international businesses undertaking substantial acts of FDI. One known exception was W.H. Hubbard, a cotton merchant, which opened a spinning mill in Russia, and established a diverse range of banking interests and investments (Jones and Schroter, 1993). Another was John Hughes, who had supplied the Russian government with the iron it needed to build a battleship. Thanks to his connections, and insider market knowledge, he won a coal and iron ore concession in the Donetz basin, and formed his New Russian Company in 1871. The settlement that formed around the mine was for a short while named Yuzovka after its owner (Milward and Saul, 1978). However, although a large market, with abundant lands and resources, Russia was a technologically laggard and capital-hungry country. As we shall see, the bulk of overseas investment there, during the nineteenth century, went into railways, utilities and oil, not manufacturing. Large traders could form significant enterprises, and participate in complicated chains of commerce.

By the 1860s, we know that Van Stolk, from the Netherlands, had built a distribution network in Germany that brought grain from southern Russia, the Danube Basin and the USA. Yet foreign merchants later lost their prominent role in Russian trade, as producers forged their own links with the rich urban markets of Western Europe (Minoglou, 1998; McCabe, Harlaftis and Minoglou, 2005). The Greek Ralli family became associated with some fifteen partnerships: the office in Liverpool traded in textiles, another in Odessa dealt in grain, while the Calcutta branch revealed the scope of its international reach. The business later relocated to London and diversified into banking (Minoglou and Louri, 1997; Minoglou, 1998; Harlaftis, 1996).[8]

There was, secondly, finance, an intermediary service like trading. Closely associated with trading companies, banks emerged as important examples of multinational enterprise. From the 1830s, British overseas banks established themselves in colonies, and then developed businesses throughout Latin America and Asia, where they were highly influential. At first, they followed the trade and offered loan and exchange facilities to British customers, but they evolved by building an overseas client base. Ownership of these banks was usually held in London, but their businesses did not depend on large amounts of FDI. European banks and financial groups were concentrated in colonial territories and in Latin America, but frequently needed representation too in London, as the world's leading financial centre. International finance across North America and Europe, unlike that in developing regions, continued to rely on correspondent banks, in effect partner institutions based in the world's financial centres (Jones, 1993; Hertner and Jones, 1986). Insurers, too, had substantial global interests with companies from Britain, Germany, France, the USA and Canada generating large revenues overseas. There were strong connections between international insurance and banking, and in addition, as noted above, between international trading, banking and insurance (Borscheid and Haueter, 2012; Wilkins, 2009; Borscheid and Pearson, 2007; Pearson, 2010).

There were, thirdly, infrastructure and transport projects, which attracted construction and engineering multinationals with the specialist skills and technologies to build railways, harbours, tunnels, canals and bridges (Linder, 1994). As well as British firms like S. Pearson & Son, there were German rivals such as Holzman, or the Danish Christiani & Nielsen. They operated globally, but had greater competitive advantages in undeveloped territories. Military as well as economic interests could follow: the French and British governments could not overlook the strategic importance of the Suez Canal (initiated by the Compagnie Universelle du Canal Maritime de Suez),[9] and the Baghdad Railway was a source of diplomatic tension between the Ottoman Empire, Germany and Britain.[10] Capital flows, most notably from London, funded construction and engineering projects, which, in turn, often facilitated the supply of traded commodities.

There was, fourthly, the worldwide phenomenon of urbanization, which created an international demand for the financing, building and operation of public utilities, from tramways, gas, electricity, sanitation, and water to telephones. The British-owned Lucas & Aird was a leading builder of gas and water systems, while the overseas successes of German electrical engineering firms such as AEG and Siemens posed mounting questions about Britain's industrial and technological future (Linder, 1994). Governments and cities usually had responsibility for and ownership of these large-scale projects, the promoters bringing both the capital and expertise not always available locally.

There was, fifthly, the fact that geology determined the places where precious stones, metals and minerals were to be extracted. To meet the developed world's need for natural resources, it was international mining companies (such as Rio Tinto, or Metallgesellschaft) that possessed the specialist technological, managerial, and financial capabilities required in large-scale, complex and capital-intensive ventures. In Africa, Asia and Latin America, the economic and political implications could be profound: diamonds and gold, for example, changed the history of Southern Africa (Harvey and Press, 1990). Free-standing companies (financed and headquartered in one nation, and operating in another) were a common organizational means of connecting capital markets with exploration projects overseas. Mines were risky investments in non-transferable assets bearing substantial (and literal) sunk-costs. They were, furthermore, technically and organizationally complex, and involved the international transfer of equipment, expertise and management (Hennart, 1982; Hennart, 1986). In obtaining land and concession rights, companies had to be reasonably confident that their investments would be safeguarded or protected. In several cases, colonization was the catalyst for investment, and free-standing companies were formed to take advantage of the unfolding opportunities. In other cases, investments were the catalyst for colonization.

Essential raw materials were not simply issues of commerce but matters of national security.

There were, sixthly, the activities of international enterprises involved in renewable natural resources, which were as location-bound as the extractive industries or the demand for utilities. Larger and wealthier populations relied on basic goods that had become global in origin (including wheat, beef, tea, soap and rubber), and, with their new purchasing power, they came to demand more exotic items (cocoa, bananas and tropical hardwoods). Secure and expanding supplies were the flip side to mass manufacturing. They protected major investments in production facilities, which remained in the developed world, and brought greater certainty and control to the management and control of international supply and production chains. Some manufacturers, such as Lever Brothers (needing palm oil for margarine and soap) or Dunlop (needing rubber for its tyres), copied trading conglomerates and overseas investment companies by acquiring big landed estates overseas. Natural resource multinationals had access to international capital, marketing channels, and the final consumer, and often overwhelmed the endeavours of peasant farmers (Fitzgerald, 1995; Wilkins, 1970; Wilkins, 1974; French, 1991; Bucheli, 2005; Fieldhouse, 1994).

Lastly, at seventh, there were the earliest examples of manufacturing FDI. The aim was usually market seeking, and, unlike the other six multinational types, they looked in the main to other developed economies, Canada and Europe, where there was demand for their products. The USA may have been exceptional in the extent to which its manufacturers founded subsidiaries abroad (Wilkins, 1970), although Britain offered, too, a range of prominent examples, as did Germany and France. Through the leadership of a few dominant enterprises, smaller economies such as Switzerland, the Netherlands and Sweden revealed high levels of manufacturing FDI in relation to their GDP. In many cases – as in Ford, International Harvester, Courtaulds, Siemens, Bayer, or Nestlé – firm-level, home-country capabilities in production, technology or brands underpinned their decision to invest and their ability to prosper abroad. The management of their national-based subsidiaries tended to operate independently, but did receive the help of expatriate executives and technical assistance. Manufacturing multinationals created fully controlled subsidiaries to supervise transferred proprietary assets, but they were willing to form joint ventures with local interests whose local knowledge was valued, or when to do so facilitated the awarding of contracts from host-country governments.

Box 2.1 Multinational theory and competitive advantage

It is Hymer who is credited as the originator of International Business (IB) theory. He argued that an enterprise must possess an advantage to offset the disadvantage of conducting commercial activities overseas. He claimed that the advantages 'owned' by the company – such as those in innovation, costs, finance, or marketing – were transferred 'intra-firm', that is from the main company in the home country to an overseas subsidiary in a host country. FDI was not just a transfer of capital funds but the transfer of various company resources. It followed that the investing firm needed to exercise cross-border control, or, in other words, learn the lessons of international management. Hymer interpreted the strategies of multinationals as monopolistic: large firms sought to extend their lead in a home market to overseas economies (Hymer, 1960).

Vernon elaborated the work of Hymer with his international product life cycle. When an innovative product is at an early stage of its life cycle, development costs are high, and market awareness, returns to scale, sales, and profits are low. Overseas demand justifies exports, but not FDI. At the second stage in the life cycle, market awareness and returns to scale enable FDI, and the firm seeks first-mover advantages for its product over potential competitors and imitators in host economies. At the third, mature stage, subsidiaries may achieve breakthroughs in exports. But rival and substitute products reduce profits, and the firm needs another innovation to begin the life cycle once more. It can simultaneously license its original product to cheaper producers, or invest in countries where labour and other inputs cost less (Vernon, 1966).

One criticism of Hymer and Vernon is that they paid little attention to the management aspects of multinationals, and there are limited insights on business organization, backwards or forwards integration, cross-border coordination, or industry-specific differences. Utilizing the work of Coase (1937), Buckley and Casson use transaction cost theory, and state that contracts with outside parties can be too risky, uncertain, and ineffective, and that multinationals internalize operations within their own organization. Technological investment and its implementation in new products and processes, for example, are lengthy projects, requiring long-term appraisal and intensive managerial coordination. Uncertainty over the motivations, honesty and capabilities of contracted firms brings its own costs, and only the multinational itself can effectively integrate assets in technology, plant, systems, and human resources dedicated to specific products or services.

Integration brings returns to scale and scope, and internalization offers gains that can be offset against local competitors and their competitive advantages (Buckley and Casson, 1976). Although transaction cost theory does address the internal dimensions of the firm, it does not look in detail at the relationship between parent multinationals and subsidiaries, nor at the characteristics of multinational operations as they evolve over time and after the initial act of FDI. But the theory can be applied to address levels of backwards and forwards integration within multinationals, and to explain matters of multinational strategy and organization over a period of time (Hennart, 1982; Hennart, 1986; Hennart, 1994).

The writings of Williamson on transaction costs more generally – on the growth of firms, the internalization of business activities, and the replacement of market mechanisms – have also been influential (see Williamson, 1975). Business historians have widely adopted the insights of Penrose (1959) into management resources (as being key to firm growth), and those of Chandler (1962, 1977, 1990) on the phenomenon of managerial enterprise (as a device for the coordination of finance, supplies, production, technology, and marketing within firms that compete through scale and scope). Their ideas can be extended to multinational business because management personnel and the internal structures of departments and divisions are needed to coordinate finance, supplies, production, technology and marketing between parent firms and their subsidiaries and across borders (Chandler, 1980; Chandler and Mazlish, 1997).

The most influential thinker on the multinational is Dunning. He developed the 'eclectic paradigm' to argue that no one factor can adequately explain the complexities of multinational enterprise, and that a broad comprehensive approach is needed. His OLI framework attempts, therefore, to include the full range of factors. He builds on Hymer's theory to state that a successful multinational must have ownership (O) advantages, or internal capabilities in technology, management, human resources, finance, production, and marketing. It can then transfer its competitive advantages from the home market to overseas.

In his later writings, Dunning specifies three types of O advantage: innovatory capacity, and experience in management and organization (Ownership asset, or Oa); the ability to govern its organization, and efficiently configure capital, labour and resources (Ownership transaction, or Ot); and the supportive political, institutional and social context within which multinationals develop (Ownership institutional, or Oi).

Dunning extends transaction cost analysis to highlight internalization (I) advantages, in which multinationals achieve efficiencies through the coordination of cross-border production, marketing, research, and human resources. The stronger the O advantages, the greater is the incentive to internalize activities, found cross-border managerial hierarchies, and reduce the risks of market-based contracts.

Dunning adds the notion of locational (L) advantages to those of ownership and internalization. From being based in differing national locations, multinationals can acquire advantages such as R&D networks, lower costs, human skills, intermediate inputs, infrastructure, nearness to markets, cheaper finance, or government assistance. In international business, firms can choose between exporting, licensing and FDI, and, where all three OLI advantages can be found, a firm will decide on FDI. Dunning takes the view of the transaction cost theorists that O advantages will not by themselves explain FDI, as a successful firm can continue to exploit these advantages in the home economy through exports and licensing. Locational factors that reduce the costs or increase the benefits of FDI compared to exporting and licensing are necessary, and it is the existence of locational differences between nations that allows multinationals to maximize advantages through internalization and cross-border coordination (Dunning and Lundan, 2008).

The relative importance of the three OLI factors will vary between firms and industries, and, crucially, will alter over time. The focus remains on the parent multinational and on its creation and transfer of ownership advantages, and on the parent multinational's strategic use of locational and internalization advantages through the coordination of home and host operations. The role of subsidiaries, knowledge and business networks, and governments is relatively passive.

We can see that the multinational history of the nineteenth century – with European trading firms and those from the USA operating in undeveloped territories to obtain and market natural resources having a prominent role – do not fit quite so neatly into the OLI approach. The trading multinationals did not develop O advantages in their home economies – although they were typically where financial resources were raised – and their operations were begun and almost entirely carried out abroad. As a result, other than sending chief personnel for service overseas, there was no transfer of O advantages to the so-termed host economies. Nor do ideas about the internalization of management decision making or growing control of capabilities explain the much looser network structures so evident in this important case of multinational history. While accepting much of the OLI model, we may need to look elsewhere for a fuller explanation.

The Raj and multinational investors

Trade has been important to developing economies, since their home markets can be characterized by their low total demand and per capita consumption. In most cases, developing economies offered their natural resources for export, and needed international investment in transport, machinery and landed estates. Trade, as a result, became associated with economic growth and modernization; it remained a high proportion of output until or unless further internal developments or industrialization followed; and it brought, too, the threat of colonization. If industrial firms, notably from the late 1950s onwards, set the pace in FDI, it was the trading, mining and service sectors that led initiatives before 1914, and the flow of that investment was predominantly towards developing lands in Latin America, Asia and Africa.

To succeed, traders relied on business networks, and built trust relationships with clients. Individual entrepreneurship, reputation, contacts and market knowledge fostered and secured deals. Traders thrived by connecting international demand to supply, and they were prepared to deal in a highly varied range of goods and services. Personal connections, private partnerships and flexible methods of working amounted to competitive and necessary strengths. On the other hand, trading firms that grew in scale or those that became highly diverse in their activities did become more organizationally complex, and their transcontinental interests required the coordination of administrative teams with experience and expert knowledge. Yet they still differed from mass manufacturing companies, whose success fundamentally rested on internal production routines or an applied technology. Manufacturers, for the most part exporting to the more developed nations, could rely on established sales agents and local distributors. The benefits from transferring and managing complicated production systems overseas were not evident, and the size and nature of their export markets did not justify the investment. But trends in the nineteenth-century world economy, both commercial and imperial, amounted to weighty and lucrative incentives for multinational traders.

When the Indian economy accelerated in the 1860s, it was a natural lure for British merchants, most of whom settled in the trading centre of Calcutta. They brought their experience of dealing in textiles, but enjoyed favourable political and institutional advantages. The British

Governor General ruled India as a sovereign, and, outside the princely states that continued under imperial aegis, there was a united system of civil service, law courts, police, and military (Fieldhouse, 1965). Lancashire, in England, was the world's leading centre for making thread and cloth, but, when the American Civil War disrupted raw cotton supplies, many of its mills had to cut production or close. India was an alternative place to grow cotton, and the opening of the Suez Canal in 1869 sped transcontinental commerce and shipping between Asia and Europe.

Andrew Yule & Co., for example, arrived in 1863, Bird & Co. in 1864, and Shaw Wallace followed in 1868. Prominent amongst non-British traders in India was Volkart Brothers Winterthur, with offices in Switzerland and Bombay, for the purpose of trading in cotton and industrial goods, but soon venturing into coffee (Guex, 1998; Jones, 1998).[11] Both expatriate and local Indian businessmen quickly diversified from trading. Records show that they acquired plantations in jute, tea, coffee and sugar, as well as cotton; they dug and extended coal, copper, and tin mines; and held assets in flour milling, oil, trams, light railways, and coastal shipping. Binny's, at Madras, founded two cotton mills. Both Greaves Cotton and Killick, Nixon built factories in Bombay, the centre of Indian cotton manufacture, where, normally, native Indian firms supplied the entrepreneurial initiative. As for cotton manufacturers in Lancashire, they showed no interest in establishing or buying Indian subsidiaries.

British trading firms preferred to found legally separate mining, plantation or industrial enterprises, usually registered locally, and they then frequently provided highly profitable management agency services to these newly founded partner enterprises. Informal Indian capital markets and business networks produced much of the investment, but the City of London was a vital source too. By 1911, seven agency houses controlled nearly half to two thirds of India's jute, tea and coal companies. Bird & Co. and Andrew Yule grew into the largest business groups in India. Bird, which originated from a service contract with the East Indian Railway, became a substantial holder of jute and coal interests; Andrew Yule was the most diverse of the Calcutta agencies, with four jute mills, a cotton factory, fifteen tea companies, four coal enterprises, two flour mills, a railway, and an oil distribution business. Shaw Wallace restructured into R. G. Shaw in London and Shaw Wallace in Calcutta in 1886, moving from cotton and tea trading into coal mining. After 1891, its most valuable business was its distribution of kerosene for the British-owned Burmah Oil (Ray, 1979, Bagchi, 1972). In Ceylon (now Sri Lanka), Boustead Brothers owned tea estates, and organized tramways and electricity generation.

Leading trading companies evolved into diversified international business groups, and, in order to raise capital for their expanding operations, several founded headquarters in London. David Sassoon formally transferred its head office from Bombay in 1872, and Dalgety incorporated in 1884 as a means of funding its enterprises in Australia and New Zealand (Daunton, 1989; Vaughn-Thomas, 1984). When Dodwell, Carlill was founded, in 1891, to take control of a business with interests in India and North America, it located its head office in London.[12] From the 1890s, Harrisons & Crosfield, well established in the Indian and Chinese tea trade, founded offices and engaged in a miscellaneous range of merchandise in Australasia and North America. In addition, from 1899 to 1914, it invested in Indian and Ceylonese tea estates, rubber in Malaya, and tea and tobacco in the Dutch East Indies (Brown, 1994; Allen and Donnithorne, 1957). Its London head-quarters controlled branches overseeing commodity trading, insurance and finance, shipping services, and plantation management and advice. Harrisons & Crosfield placed plantation and timber ventures into separate firms, in which it held equity, and appointed board members to each of these concerns. It floated some forty rubber plantation companies on the London market between 1903 and 1914.

The largest shipping and trading firm of them all, Mackinnon, Mackenzie, had acted for the British India Steam Navigation Company (BI), when established in 1865. Trader Gray Dawes was deeply integrated into the Mackinnon complex, and it was BI's passenger agent in London. It had offices in the Arabian Gulf, where it could organize the shipping line's extensive freight, passenger and mail services, and imported goods from textiles to opium. In London, Mackinnon, Mackenzie founded, and registered, Indian tea and jute companies; in Australia, it took on the role of meat processer; in India, the task of cotton spinning. The firm grew quickly under the stewardship of Sir William Mackenzie, from his return to London in 1873 until his death in 1893. James Lyle McKay, who had served nineteen years in the Calcutta office, then became the company's leading figure, extending its activities through new partnerships and joint ventures. In 1914, as Lord Inchcape and chairman of BI, he arranged a merger with P&O to establish the world's largest shipping group, dominating passenger and commercial traffic from Britain to Asia and Australia (Munro, 1987). As in the case of Jardine, Matheson and Swire, the leading figures of the Mackinnon, Mackenzie group based themselves in the imperial capital of London, from where they could coordinate their complex network of enterprises (Jones, 1998; Jones, 2000; Roy, 2006; Allen and Donnithorne, 1957).

China and the trading imperative

China in the nineteenth century demonstrated, as Japan did, a capacity for political and industrial renewal, but internal strife left it vulnerable to the incursions of Western powers and their business interests. The Taiping Rebellion against the Qing dynasty, still distrusted for its foreign Manchu heritage, came to an end in 1864, but not before exacting a heavy death toll and widespread economic dislocation. The Yangtze Delta, China's most developed region, especially felt the effects of devastation. One of the first firms to seek commercial possibilities there was the US shipper Russell & Co., founded in 1824. Having once profited from the opium trade, it had established itself in Shanghai as a commission agent. The new initiative came from an employee, Edward Cunningham, who used his contacts with Chinese financiers and merchants to found jointly the Shanghai Steam Navigation Company in 1862.[13] Russell dominated trade in the Yangtze Delta, acting for many US and other traders, for nearly twenty years (Wilkins, 1970). The river was an excellent waterway for the side-wheel steamer previously tested along the length of the Mississippi.

As China in 1870 was a country with 350 million potential customers (28 per cent of the world's population), even larger than India's 212 million (19 per cent), foreign traders were so excited by the scale of commercial possibilities that they grossly exaggerated the market for Western goods. One manufacturer in the UK mistakenly envisaged his pianos in China's fashionably wealthy but also countless homes. In Shanghai, British firms between 1867 and 1881 followed Russell's example, establishing the Union Steam Navigation Company (traders Glover & Co.) and the China Navigation Company (Butterfield and Swire), while Jardine Matheson alone founded three shipping lines. Another important player, the North-China Steamer

Company, belonged to the German-owned Trautmann & Co. For a time, Russell competed successfully with US rivals Augustine, Heard & Co., but first Jardine Matheson and then Butterfield & Swire emerged as the most important international firms in China, thanks to the depth of the networks they cultivated with local merchants (Liu, 1962).

Jardine Matheson's branches throughout China, most prominently those in Shanghai and Hong Kong, invested in railways, silk, sugar, harbours, shipping, insurance, and banking, also building China's first cotton mill in 1895 (Borscheid and Haueter, 2012). Once the US Navy had forced Japan to open its trade, Jardine Matheson was the first foreign business to establish itself, in 1858, in Yokohama. It then set up offices in Kobe and in Nagasaki, where the Japanese had once allowed only the Dutch to trade from the tiny, man-made island of Dejima. Jardine Matheson had global ambitions, often using agencies connected through ownership and shared partners: it ran an office in New York; it worked in tandem with Jardine Skinner & Co. in Calcutta; and it was represented in London by Matheson & Company, a merchant bank with Spanish and Californian copper mines, banking interests in Iran, and its own trading house in Calcutta. Not everything of course was a success: Jardine Matheson's mining ventures in Russia and oil exploration in Peru did not go well. From 1886, a relative of the Mathesons, William Keswick, gradually assumed control, directing a worldwide business group from a headquarters in London. When Jardine Matheson and Matheson & Company were merged and incorporated in 1906, he was the natural choice as managing director.[14] The Dent trading firm officially went bankrupt in 1866 – a victim of the international credit crisis caused by the collapse of Overend, Gurney, the respected and cautious English bank turned risky railway stock speculator – but the Dent family continued to have substantial and influential business interests throughout Asia (King, King and King, 1987–8, vol. III).[15]

By the mid nineteenth century, Liverpool was replacing Glasgow as the leading source of merchant enterprise. Examples were Harrisons & Crosfield, Booker Brothers, and Balfour Williamson. The city's trading firms and shipping lines benefited from the several partnerships they formed, and Liverpool became an international hub of commercial intelligence and deal making. One major force out of Liverpool was the shipping line Alfred Holt & Company. In 1865, it evolved from selling cotton goods to founding the Ocean Steamship Company, better known, due to its notable insignia, as the Blue Funnel line. Another shareholder in the venture was John Swire & Sons, similarly a Liverpool-based firm with trade interests in cotton and the USA. In 1867, on establishing Butterfield & Swire in Shanghai, it began its long rivalry with Russell and Jardine Matheson. Cargoes from its regional China Navigation Company (founded in 1872) were networked with the transcontinental Blue Funnel line and therefore the world's markets. Holt was associated additionally with Mansfield & Company in Singapore. As freight agents, Mansfield bought goods – including sugar, spices and rice – throughout South East Asia for a both regional and transcontinental trade. Swire and Holt opened the Taikoo Sugar Refinery in Hong Kong in 1881, processing produce from Java and the Philippines. By the beginning of the 1890s, Swire had abandoned direct involvement in cotton, tea and other merchandise to focus on its more profitable shipping and agency work.

There were various means to protect revenues and profits. In 1879, Swire had been instrumental in forming the China Conference, a collusive agreement between major shipping lines, freight agents and traders, intended to stabilize rates.[16] It was a successful formula, which Swire replicated in 1897 with the Straits Conference. Adamson, Bell – a major competitor to Jardine, Matheson and Swire in the tea trade – was transformed after 1887 by contracts with Canadian and then US railways into one of the Pacific's major shipping lines. Its leading figure, George Dodwell, created Dodwell, Carlill to take over the business, in 1891; he had reconstituted and registered the enterprise as a private limited firm called Dodwell & Co. by 1899. As well as exporting tea to Britain, the USA and Russia, by 1914 it owned tea and coconut estates in Ceylon, salmon canneries in Vancouver, flour mills in Tacoma and Seattle, and branches in China, Japan and New York. George Dodwell acted, also, as chairman of the Malacca Plantation Company.[17]

Commodities and colonizing South East Asia

As in the case of India, Burma became a British colony by stages. Border tensions gave place to the First Anglo-Burmese War (1823–6), through which Britain extended India's frontier and gained a foothold in the south, at Tenasserim (today's Taninthayi). Using a pretext, the British provoked the Second Anglo-Burmese War (1852–3), annexed what became known as Lower Burmah, and took control of the Lower Irrawaddy. Inside this new frontier, by no coincidence, were rich teak forests and other valuable resources. A family of traders from Glasgow created T. D. Findlay & Son in 1839 to manage its Burmah operations. Its Irrawaddy Flotilla Company began in 1865 with four steamers and three barges. Scottish officers commanded the boats, built in Dumbarton, while Indians supplied the crew. Contractors, employing hundreds of elephants, floated the timber down waterways, from where it was eventually collected by what became one of the world's largest river fleets.[18]

Wallace Brothers, in 1863, founded, with a group of Indian merchants, the Bombay Burmah Trading Corporation for felling and dealing in teak. When, in 1885, the Burmese fined Bombay Burmah for illegal logging and tax avoidance, it provided an eagerly accepted reason for a Third War (1885). The Burmese king could be portrayed as a tyrant, and British commercial interests had long eyed the resources of the Upper Irrawaddy Valley and a possible new trade route to China. There were, too, calculations of diplomatic rivalry: Britain was reacting to the threat of westwards expansion by the French, who had just beaten China in a conflict (1884–5) for rule over Tonkin (in modern Vietnam). Having left its former base in Penang, T. D. Findlay & Son created in Rangoon a complex of local shipping lines, and an international route to Glasgow, Liverpool and elsewhere.[19] After Burmah's incorporation into the British Raj, in 1886, British companies invested in rice fields, and imported large numbers of labourers from India. While they transformed the Burmese economy, they did not generally benefit indigenous villagers, many of whom were displaced from their lands. To manage its new rice business, Wallace Brothers founded the Arracan Company. Steel Brothers built rice mills in Burmah and as far away as Germany, and invested in teak, oil and elephants (Myint-U, 2001).

The policy of the East India Company and then the British government towards the Malay Peninsula had parallels: the objectives were to secure the coastal bases, stabilize borders, protect business interests, and finally expand trade. After the Anglo-Dutch Treaty of 1824, the

British were responsible for administering the Straits Settlements of Singapore, Malacca and Penang. Between 1874 and 1910, the Malay sultanates accepted 'residents' to represent the British government. The arrangement allowed the formality of independence, but (with the ultimate backing of the Indian army) it led to effective colonization. British investors, whose main concern was tin mining, and to a lesser extent gold, saw intervention as a means of safeguarding their assets. From 1877, they introduced the rubber tree, native to the Amazon, for development as an export crop (Huff, 1994).

The Federated Malay States, formed under British direction in 1896, streamlined the administration of Selangor, Perak, Negeri Sembilan and Pahang, and increased British power in the peninsula's most developed regions. Guthrie, an established Straits trader and an agent for British insurers in Singapore, arrived in the same year, opting to invest in coffee, and, in partnership with a local Chinese businessman, rubber. Dealings between British firms and Chinese entrepreneurs and financiers were common. The sizeable Chinese community, moreover, supplied the labour which worked in Malaya's mines, mills and docks. By 1891, towns such as Singapore, Penang, Ipoh and Kuala Lumpur and the states of Perak and Selangor had Chinese majorities. Yap Ah Loy, called the Kapitan China of Kuala Lumpur, was by the 1890s the Malay Peninsula's richest individual through his ownership of mines, plantations and shops. It was the Chinese who controlled the local banking and insurance industries that financed the Malay sultans whenever they fell, as they frequently did, into debt (Chew and Lee, 1991; Andaya and Andaya, 1982).

It was the bicycle's mass appeal and the motor car's arrival in the last decade of the nineteenth century that transformed rubber into a mass international commodity. As in Burmah's rice plantations, British firms displaced native villagers and marginalized the local population. They likewise imported indentured labour from India, this time from the Tamil-speaking south. Harrisons & Crosfield, which had grown into a global business and transferred its headquarters from Liverpool to London, invested in rubber from 1903, and two years later began its long association with the Golden Horn Rubber Estate. Between 1903 and 1914, it floated on the London market some forty rubber plantations located throughout South East Asia. In Malaya, Edward Boustead and Boustead Brothers controlled numerous rubber-producing companies, as well as other enterprises, by the time of the First World War.

The Wallace Brothers' Arracan Company acquired rubber plantations in both Malaya and the Dutch East Indies from 1906 onwards.

The British tyre manufacturer Dunlop viewed rubber growing in Malaya as a strategically vital investment in a key raw material, establishing plantations there in 1910, and US Rubber went to the Dutch East Indies for the same reason. In less than twenty years, South East Asia accounted for two thirds of the world's rubber supplies.[20] Palm oil, native to West Africa, had been successfully cultivated in the Dutch East Indies (from 1848). In 1902, a Scottish entrepreneur, William Sime, and an English banker, Henry Darby, founded a trading firm in Malacca, with the active participation of local Chinese entrepreneurs. Sime-Darby brought the palm oil tree to Malaya in 1910, and began an enterprise that would have a major and long-term impact on its landscape and economy.[21]

The common mix of established trading interests, border instability, treaty disputes with local rulers, and national rivalries brought about French colonization of South East Asia. Merchants in Saigon wanted to extend control over the Mekong Delta, and to operate in Tonkin, where France and China competed for influence and territory. The threat of further British expansion in Burmah and Malaya (later realized, as we have seen) was another, very strong motive. Between 1858 and 1884, in steps, France founded protectorates or colonies in Cochin-China (centred around Saigon), Annam (the middle of modern Vietnam), Tonkin (the north) and Cambodia, creating the Union Indo-Chinoise in 1887. It contemplated taking Siam, but, wary of provoking the British too much, restricted itself to occupying Laos (Karnow, 1994). Britain formally guaranteed the independence of Siam in 1896, and the kingdom continued its open trade policy (Fieldhouse, 1965).

Andersen & Co., established in Bangkok by a Danish mariner, Hans Niels Andersen – who had served on Siamese vessels – exported teak from 1886 onwards. It began by building strong commercial interests in Siam, one of the few Asian nations to remain independent, and it was a forerunner to the East Asiatic Company, registered in Copenhagen, a free port, in 1897. Den Danske Landmandsbank (latterly, Danske Bank) supported the venture, and provided the EAC with its first chairman. The EAC ran both freight and passenger lines. It expanded its shipping lines to the Baltic, the Black Sea, Asia, the North Pacific and London; in 1907, it created the Siam Steam

Navigation Company to operate throughout the kingdom; and by 1914 it had set up trading offices in St Petersburg, Paris, South Africa, China, Singapore, and Malaya, where it also purchased rubber plantations. Once its ships were emptied of the vegetable fats, soap, foods, and other Asian commodities they imported to and processed in Denmark, the EAC filled them with the products of its cement and soy cake factories for the return journey (Guex, 1998; Eggers-Lurat, 1993; G. Jones, 1996).[22]

British business rule in South East Asia

Despite having no formal medical education, the American Josiah Harlan had served as a military surgeon for the East India Company in the First Burmah War. His adventurous personality soon tired of taking orders. Instead, in Afghanistan, he led an expedition on behalf of a local ruler, and in 1840 he ended up as Prince of Ghor. Harlan was the probable inspiration for Rudyard Kipling's quest novel *The Man Who Would Be King* (published in 1888). In Borneo, equally spectacular private adventure had a lasting impact. Here, Britain's imperial government had preferred to avoid policing actions, so long as native governments did not discriminate against British businesses. In 1839, yet another former East India Company officer, James Brooke, used an inheritance to purchase a ship, and his mercenaries helped to quell a rebellion in Sarawak. The territory was formally but precariously ruled by the Sultan of Brunei, who in 1841 appointed Brooke as Rajah of Sarawak with mixed feelings (thanks and fear). Brooke could not be contained inside his Kuching base, pushed outwards, and, in the process, founded a dynasty (which, after invasion by the Japanese, was not formally replaced until 1946). On a trip to London, in 1847, he was appointed Britain's consul-general in Borneo, and, when he was knighted by Queen Victoria, he gained formal public acceptance.

The Borneo Company Ltd, which was founded in 1856 and based in Singapore, was established by a group of Glasgow merchants associated with the Brookes, who consequently granted the enterprise special trading privileges. Since Thailand had just opened to international trade, the Borneo Company immediately set up a Bangkok office; it decided, additionally, to establish jute and sugar mills near Calcutta. R. & J. Henderson – based in Glasgow, London and Calcutta – became the largest shareholders, and BCL evolved into an operational sub-sidiary, while remaining a limited liability enterprise in its own right (Longhurst, 1956). From 1879, it was allowed to buy out the Burmese gold mines owned by Chinese investors, and after 1884 it became Thailand's largest teak company after the Bombay Burmah Trading Company. Although it later manufactured bricks in Singapore and grew tea in the Dutch East Indies, gold and teak were its commercial mainstays. The third-largest teak producer in Thailand was the Anglo-Siam Corporation, established in 1884 by British merchants based in Bombay.

The Sultan of Brunei had long since lost control of western Borneo, too, where Chinese Hakka immigrants had arrived to work in its gold and tin mines. Chinese merchants dominated the trade between their homeland and the Lanfang Republic, which lasted (from 1777) until its overthrow by the Dutch in 1884. In Sabah, in north-east Borneo, several powers contended for the right to rule, and the Sultan needed outside help to deal with rebellions and piracy. In 1865, the US consul for Brunei, Claude Lee Moses, obtained a ten-year lease, which he passed to the American Trading Company of Borneo, owned by a group of American and Chinese investors. Taking the precedent of Sarawak, the Sultan of Brunei appointed the company's leading figure, Joseph W. Torrey, as the Rajah of Ambong and Maudu, and as the Maharajah of North Borneo.

American Trading failed to make headway, and a businessman and Austrian consul to Hong Kong, Baron Gustavus de Overbeck, took over the North Borneo lease. He was speculating: he hoped to sell North Borneo to Germany as quickly as possible and at a profit; he then put his hopes on Austria-Hungary, and finally Italy; to his disappointment, however, they all turned down his offer. In 1877, he went into business with Alfred Dent, his former employer in the Dent trading company, who persuaded him that any investor would need guarantees of British military and diplomatic support. Overbeck agreed, moreover, to settle the counterclaims of the Sultan of Sulu, who found the remainder of his territory occupied by Spain. In London, Alfred Dent's brother Edward could call on the support of a China lobby that linked important business interests, politicians and government officials. They had to fight off opposition from Sarawak's 'White Rajah', Charles Brooke, who could similarly claim powerful associates in Britain's Parliament. Fortunately for Dent, Brooke was known for his unpleasant personality and bullying manner, and could not match the strength of his rival's connections. Yet the British government was not easily persuaded, and it was driven to action only by fear of Spanish and even German intervention in the contested territory (Turnbull, 1989).

The Economist saw the granting of a royal company charter in 1882 as anachronistic and unintelligible. The Liberal prime minister, William Gladstone, was suspicious of imperial adventures, and one of the founders of Britain's free trade policy. On the other hand, unlike the mercantilist past, the British North Borneo Company was not formally granted monopoly rights, or administrative responsibilities (though, in fact, it had both). The Colonial Office, which had opposed the charter, had an official on the BNBC board. Finally, the company had to commit itself to the protection of indigenous rights, and promised not to use forced labour or slavery. As the Dent brothers knew, the charter signalled British support for their business project against the possibility of local and external threats, and the BNBC was finally in a prime position to exploit the region's bountiful timber resources. In 1888, both North Borneo and the Brunei Sultanate became British protectorates, although North Borneo continued to be administered by the company (until the arrival of Japanese forces in 1942).[23] The China lobby that helped win the charter reconstituted itself as the China Association in 1889. Sir Alfred Dent was its first president, and other participants included Swire, Jardine Matheson, Paton and Baldwins, and eventually Shell Petroleum, plus members of Britain's political and civil service establishment (Jones, 1998; Jones, 2000; Allen and Donnithorne, 1957; King, King and King, 1987–8, vol. III).[24]

Netherlands and German business in Asia

For much of the nineteenth century, the Nederlandsche Handel-Maatschappij took responsibility for the rule and economic development of the East Indies. When occupied by the French during the Napoleonic Wars, the Netherlands had fought and lost colonial possessions to Britain, but the 1824 Treaty formally resolved territorial disputes and established British Malaya and the Dutch East Indies respectively. As we have seen, it created areas of instability in the middle, resulting finally in one privately owned dynasty, a British protectorate, and openings for the Borneo and British North Borneo companies. The Dutch colonial administration was based at Batavia, and it had reconquered much of Java by 1830 and West Sumatra by 1837. Elsewhere in the East Indies, it exercised control through trading outposts and agreements with local rulers. In founding the NHM, in 1824, the Netherlands looked at first to the chartered VOC – the United East Indies Company – as its model, although the royal decree did not bestow public powers or official monopoly, and the new enterprise was to contract and use private businesses, whenever possible. Charged with building ships and commissioning merchants in the Netherlands, its purpose was to revitalize the Dutch economy, not primarily to develop the colonies. Its over-generous freight rates and the fixed division of trade between Netherlands ports discouraged competition and innovation.

The company lost large sums on ventures in the Americas and in China, before limiting its ambitions to investments in the Dutch East Indies. The colonial government introduced the Cultivation System during the 1830s, which forced the local population to grow commodities on one fifth of their land, in lieu of taxes and servitude, and repeated epidemics and famine led to the deaths of hundreds of thousands. The NHM exported the coffee, sugar, and indigo grown under compulsion for sales in auction houses throughout the Netherlands. It fostered sugar, rice and cotton companies back in the imperial homeland, and exported processing machinery to the Dutch East Indies. By 1850, some 50–60 per cent of imports to the Netherlands were colonial products. As Sumatra and other islands became colonized, in the years after 1856, and frequently through military action, commercial agencies, banks, and shipping lines, most prominently the NHM and the Javasche Bank, extended their reach. But the trading firm's accounts continued to deteriorate, and many of the industries it helped to found in the Netherlands did not last long after the lifting of protective tariffs in 1870. As a result, four years later, NHM decided to abandon many of its commercial projects and to focus on banking.

Trade and shipping restrictions were lifted in the Dutch East Indies in 1861; the oppressive Cultivation System and local tariffs went in 1870. Without the NHM awarding contracts, private enterprise took the initiative in growing and exporting commodities, and in extending shipping and infrastructure across the archipelago, often in the wake of brutal military campaigns. As industrialization gathered speed in the Netherlands during the last quarter of the nineteenth century, large-scale trading companies and specialists in single commodities responded to the challenge. With the opening of the Suez Canal, the Stoomvaart Maatschappij 'Nederland' (SMN) began regular steam services to Batavia (1870), followed by Rotterdamsche Lloyd (1872). Deli-Maatschappij and Tabaksmaatschappij 'Arendsberg' developed tobacco estates in East Sumatra; Deli also had cinchona, copra, and light railway interests, and pioneered the cultivation of rubber; throughout Java, Sumatra, and Kalimantan in Borneo, enterprises opened tin and coal mines. The Handels-Vereniging Amsterdam (HVA), created in 1879, invested from 1900 in a broad range of crops and plantations, building a sugar refinery in Java, and establishing sales offices in Manchester and Singapore. The Koninklijke Paketvaart Maatschappij (KPM) was founded by the SMN and Rotterdam Lloyd lines in 1891 to undertake government contracts and organize shipping throughout East Asia. The newer products of oil, rubber and copra accounted for a third of East Indies exports by 1914, the demand for kerosene being a phenomenon, and famous Dutch manufacturers, like Jurgens and Van Den Bergh, used copra in their branded margarine and soap.

East Indies exports were increasingly orientated, moreover, towards world markets, becoming less dependent therefore on the Netherlands. The reborn NHM emerged as an influential overseas bank in the Dutch East Indies, with branches in Saudi Arabia and Surinam. The Nederlandsche-Indische Handelsbank, Rotterdamsche Bank, and others similarly grew to provide the banking services needed by colonial businesses and plantations. From 1870 to 1913, there were over 4,000 incorporations in the Netherlands seeking commercial success in the Dutch East Indies, and most of them were free-standing companies dealing in agricultural products and other commodities. Investment by the Netherlands in the Dutch East Indies doubled between 1900 and 1914, accounting for some 70 per cent of the total investment in the colony, divided between plantations (45 per cent), mining (20 per cent), and the processing industries (most of the remainder).

From 1870, Batavia could communicate by telegraph with Europe via Singapore, and, as a result, between 1888 and 1902, futures markets dealing in coffee, pepper, copra, tin, cloves and sugar were founded in the Netherlands. Java producers, which had to sell their sugar in the bigger trading centre of London, established representation there. Borneo-Sumatra Handelsmaatschappij (Borsumij) first sold by telegraph in 1905, and it was one of the big five Netherlands colonial houses that emerged, led by Internatio, and including also George Wehry, Lindeteves, and Jacobson & Van Den Bergh. Borsumij was formally created in 1894, by J. W. Schlimmer & Co. and other major businesses. It owned river and local shipping, traded in gum and rattan, and branched into coal mining, rubber plantations, coffee exports (sold directly to the USA), and paraffin (for the Royal Dutch company). By 1912, with its headquarters moved to The Hague, the directors travelled regularly to monitor the activities of its company and general manager, and its agents submitted quarterly reports. Rotterdam businessmen had founded the Internationale Crediet- en Handelsvereeniging (Internatio) in 1863 as a limited company and commission agent, but it transformed itself through the acquisition of existing firms. It traded with India, China and Japan, and, in 1878, Rotterdam Lloyd appointed it as their commercial representative in the East Indies. It was the general manager in Asia that supervised the international network of agents, while the Rotterdam headquarters gave directions through correspondence.

The Dutch had a long-established claim over the western half of New Guinea. Because the British colony of Queensland had annexed the south-east portion of the island, the German chancellor, Otto von Bismarck, encouraged businessmen in Berlin to found the New Guinea Company, in 1884, and to claim the remaining north-easterly region. He wanted commercial interests to take on the task of colonial administration (which he viewed as peripheral to imperial affairs), but could not in practice make good his preference. The NGC's objective was to carve out German New Guinea or, as it was also called, Kaiser-Wilhelmsland, and to exploit its resources. The chartered company gave up its extensive administrative powers and responsibilities, in 1889–92, and more fully so by 1899; it kept its monopoly, but, verifying Bismarck's scepticism, failed to realize any profits. Spain sold the Spanish East Indies (later called the Marshall Islands) to Germany, which incorporated its acquisitions into German New Guinea in 1886. Trading companies there, Hemsheim & Co. and the Deutsche Handels- und Plantagengesellschaft (DHPG), merged into the Jaluit Company:

this new business was free of administrative duties, but it did have a monopoly, and it did, from its hub of cross-Pacific commerce, generate profits (Fieldhouse, 1965). Norddeutscher Lloyd (based in Bremen, and dating back to 1857) was primarily a major presence in North Atlantic shipping, but, from 1885, the German government commissioned the line to provide postal services to Australia and its territories in the Asia Pacific region. It became one of the world's largest shipping companies, second only to Britain's P&O. It bought out the Scottish Oriental Steamship Company and the Holt East Indian Ocean Steamship Company, in 1899, to establish its freight, passenger and mail services in Asia and the Pacific, simultaneously stirring up public controversy in Britain about commercial concerns ignoring the national interest (Jonker and Sluyterman, 2000; Sluyterman, 2003; Dick, 2002; Vickers, 2005).

Indian and Chinese traders

Western firms involved in trade, shipping and finance and operating in Asia had numerous advantages. Having increased the scale and distances of transcontinental commerce, they controlled access to the rich markets of Europe and North America; they could call on international sources of finance; they had a lead in technologies, including those associated with the steamship, mining, or crop diseases; and they often had support and concessions from imperial authorities (whenever necessary, with the force of arms). Western firms transformed transcontinental commerce, and they had an impact on intra-regional commerce too, but they formed only part of the Asian international system. Indian, Chinese and Arab merchants had already pioneered the region's trade routes. Their pivotal role in Asia's economy did not disappear: indeed, economic growth and trade expansion gave them new opportunities. While Western firms in Asia might compete against local businesses, they equally needed their cooperation, partnership, commercial expertise, market knowledge and, as recorded in prominent cases, their finance. Through diaspora and family relationships, cross-border networks cemented trust levels between traders, strengthened the capacity for striking and managing deals, and quickly transferred commercial information.

Indian growers and shippers had been deeply involved in the opium trade, and the Cowasjee family had connections and resources that rivalled those of Jardine Matheson, Dent, or Russell. They worked through trading and finance agencies located around the Indian Ocean, historically a large-scale arena for South Asian enterprise (Lombard and Aubin, 2000). Calcutta remained the subcontinent's trading centre, and the Raj's economy depended on the raising of local as well as international capital to fund the development of mining and plantations (Bagchi, 1972). Western traders transacted with Indian businessmen to gain entry into their markets and commerce, and learnt from their experience. Indian merchants were able to mobilize investment networks, which shared directorships, partners, or management contracts, connected operatively flexible and formally independent enterprises, dispersed commercial information, and spread commercial risks. Across the subcontinent, large Western companies, such as Birds and Yule, simply imitated or slipped easily into the established practice of business networks and alliances. As well as providing essential capital for India's plantations, mines, commodity trade, transport, and infrastructure, Indian merchants were major investors and partners in the Bombay Burmah Trading Corporation, the National Bank of India, the Hongkong Bank, and the Indo-Burma Petroleum Company.

Dealings between British partners and the Chinese business diaspora in Malacca were the starting point for Sime Darby. In Malaya, as we have seen, industrial sectors came to depend on the activities of Chinese as well as British businesses, most crucially in the case of tin mining. The Straits Steamship Company had its origins in an 1890 agreement between Mansfield & Co. and wealthy Singaporean tycoons Tan Jiak Kim, Tan Keong Saik and Lee Cheng Yan. It focused at first on carrying tin ore, but took substantial cargoes in coffee, pepper, rice, rubber and tobacco, and brought Chinese labourers to work in the tin mines and rubber estates along the Malay Peninsula. In China, Western traders relied on local partners, investors, buyers, sales agents, and managers for their success. We know that ownership of the Shanghai Navigation Company was divided equally between a US shipping line, British financiers, and Chinese business interests in possession of essential commercial knowledge and connections.

The success of Jardine Matheson and Butterfield and Swire in importing to and exporting from mainland China rested on indigenous agents. When the Chinese government, from 1842, confirmed rights of extraterritoriality for Western powers, it was forced to end the system of appointing official merchants with exclusive rights to deal with foreign traders. To trade deep in China, multinationals evolved a network of 'compradors' to supply finance and make deals. In time, many compradors gained enough experience and resources to establish themselves as independent commission agents. As their control over business transactions increased, profits for Western businesses declined. Jardine Matheson eventually withdrew from trading inside China, turning instead to financial and shipping services, as did Butterfield and Swire later, in 1902.[25] Although their approach was not typical, a few multinational importers responded with directly owned distribution networks, storage facilities, and transport, in their attempt to reach some 400 million Chinese customers: notable were the British chemicals firm ICI; Standard Oil's highly promoted kerosene, for use as lamp oil; and British American Tobacco, which formed the Union Trading Company with a Chinese partner, in 1911, and created an impressive marketing organization to sell its brands of rolled cigarettes (Cox, 2000).

From 1861, the Qing government initiated the Self-Strengthening Movement, a series of educational, administrative and military reforms. It sponsored, as a result, the China Merchants' Steam Navigation Company (CMSNC), from 1872, just as the Kaiping Coal Mines, the Shanghai Cotton Mill and the Imperial Telegraph formed other attempts at modernization, as did, later, the Kweichow Ironworks (1891) and the Hupeh Textile Company (1894). The Qing government wanted to halt the Western penetration of its coastal trade, and the CMSNC, as China's first joint-stock enterprise, was a watershed in national business practice. Its founder, Li Hung Zhang, utilized his trading links with the overseas Chinese, and the company benefited from its monopoly of the grain tax tribute to Beijing.

From 1873, CMSNC was managed by Tong King Sing, a former Jardine Matheson comprador, and he bought the Shanghai Steam Navigation Company from Russell & Co. and other partners in 1877, a move that led to a welcome decline in the US share of the China trade. CMSNC made gains against multinational competition until 1885, as a private firm within the state ministry, but increasing government control and bureaucratic mismanagement undermined its later performance (Lai, 1994). The Ministry of Agriculture, Industry and Commerce – to finance China's modernization – sought to raise international capital through its people's diaspora. The tin magnate Foo Chee Chun supported projects in Kwangtung and Fujian, and an overseas consortium funded the Teochew–Swatow Railway, but, however notable, such cases were rare.

Chang Pi-Sheh, who emigrated to the Dutch East Indies in 1856, founded a steamship line between Penang and north Sumatra, and later gained fame as one of the world's richest Chinese. He had a contract from the Dutch navy, flew the Dutch flag, and his three steamers competed effectively against Western lines (Yen, 1982). Fujian was a particularly rich source of emigrant merchant enterprises, and its entrepreneurs built Chinese trading networks throughout East Asia. Zhang Baojing, for example, left Xiamen to trade in the Dutch East Indies when aged sixteen, and founded the Yiho tea firm. Guo Chun-yang joined his uncle's firm in Samrang, in the Dutch East Indies, in 1872. By 1914, he had founded trading enterprises in Taiwan, Hong Kong, Xiamen, Zhangzhou, Shanghai and Tianjin. He owned sugar plantations in China, and refined the commodity in Hong Kong. Politically, he was pragmatic. He had good relations with both the imperial Qing government and its republican successor after 1911. He was involved with the Taiwan Oolong tea trade, from 1888, exporting the Baozhong scented variety to the Chinese populations to be found throughout the Dutch East Indies and Thailand.

When China lost the Sino-Japanese War of 1894–5, and Japanese forces occupied Taiwan, Guo claimed residency of the island and took Japanese nationality. Thanks to this decision, his Taiwanese enterprises received greater legal protection and reduced taxation; anti-Chinese sentiment in the Dutch East Indies was another motive. Many owners of large Taiwanese firms were from the Fujian ports of Fuzhou, Xiamen and Quanzhou, and, due to the pressure from the Japanese authorities, the majority changed their citizenship. Guo's younger brother first encountered Mitsui as a comprador for Jardine Matheson, and this major Japanese trading company began selling Guo's Oolong tea in the USA from 1898 (Lin, 2001).

Because British companies had been slow to invest in tin mining in Malaya, they had left the initiative to others. It is estimated that, before 1912, some 80 per cent of the capital employed in the industry in Malaya was Chinese (there were, however, no Chinese-owned tin mines in the Dutch East Indies). The fact that Malayan tin was near the surface and easy to mine reduced the capital costs involved. As it contained few impurities, it could be used by most smelters, who had small incentive to integrate backwards and buy up Malayan mines (Hennart, 1982; Hennart, 1986). Many of the medium-to-small rubber estates in

Malaya, the Dutch East Indies, and Siam were Chinese-owned. Leading Chinese groups operated between Malaya, Siam and the Dutch East Indies, involved in shipping, docks, insurance, and banking, as well as commodity trading. Khaw Soo Cheang and his family became major figures in the mining, smelting and exporting of Siamese tin. For this, they established close relations with the government: they collected taxes, took up appointments as regional governors, imported Chinese labour, and harshly re-established royal authority in Ranong province when the workers revolted against their conditions. In Siam, leading Chinese business groups also dominated the export of rice and teak, much of it going to Singapore and Hong Kong. Thio Thiau Siat in Sumatra received contracts from the Netherlands colonial authorities, developed shipping enterprises, and participated in the founding of the Deli Bank at Medan and the Batavian Bank. Throughout South-East Asia, Chinese merchants were pivotal in financing, procuring, processing and distributing rice and fish, and they were influential in fruit, vegetables, poultry, pigs, tea, hemp and timber. In Singapore, the regional centre for processing and trading, small Chinese factories produced beer, aerated waters, ice, food, furniture, and building materials (Barnett, 1943).

On the other hand, as the Dutch increased their political and economic control of the East Indies, investments in plantations and steamship lines created a scale of operations that disadvantaged the Chinese merchants as producers and middlemen (Lasker, 1946). Political and diplomatic events had their impact elsewhere too. Japanese gunboat diplomacy in Korea (copying the examples of Western empires) had led to the Japan–Korea Treaty in 1876, and opened up the peninsula to more trade. Despite growing Japanese influence in Korea, the trading skills of Chinese merchants at first maintained their large presence there, exporting goods such as ginseng and specie, and importing Chinese silks and medicines, as well as Western matches, kerosene, soap and cotton textiles. Only Japan's full occupation of Korea in 1905 and the later annexation in 1910 ended their success (Larsen, 2000).

The Americas and non-colonial investments

The British trading firm of Gibbs, an early arrival to Latin America, had been well placed to benefit from rapid growth of the international commodity trade from the 1860s onwards. Since Britain had no formal rule over the region, the firm needed political connections, but possessed, too, commercial expertise, shipping networks, and global scope. As well as its nitrate, copper, mining and flour interests in Chile and Peru, Gibbs built businesses in freight agency, coastal shipping, sheep and cattle ranching, and mining; it had interests in Australia; and organized securities and loans in London for overseas projects (Platt, 1977). Balfour Williamson (founded in 1851) emerged from Liverpool to open a business in Valparaíso, Chile. By 1869 it had arrived in San Francisco, where its associated office of Balfour, Guthrie exported grain and farm produce, and imported British chemicals and Australian coal. Balfour, Guthrie's list of activities grew in length: it included marine insurance, warehousing, lumber, coal mining, salmon fishing, flour milling, vineyards, fruit growing and packing, and mortgage loans across California and Oregon. In Chile and Peru, there were investments in nitrate, railroads, water companies, coastal shipping, flour milling, and the smelting of silver, lead and copper; there was also a flirtation, with little financial return, in the 1900s, with the Peruvian and Californian oil industry (Hunt, 1951; Rothstein, 1963). Alfred Booth & Company, closely associated with the Holt-Swire group, diversified from its US interests with a steamship service to Brazil in 1865. It subsequently owned port and transport facilities there that met the needs of the rubber trade, plus having tanneries in London and New York. By the 1870s, E. Johnston & Sons was the second-largest exporter of coffee in Brazil, ultimately investing in related support and financial services. It sent the commodity to the USA, picked up timber destined for Liverpool, and returned to Brazil with a variety of manufactured goods (Platt, 1977; Topik and Wells, 1998).

Not surprisingly, US traders were active at an early point in Latin America: Alsop & Co. in Valparaíso (from 1824), Alsop, Wetmore & Co. in Lima, Augustus Hemenway in Chile (both by 1828), and S. B. Hale & Co. in Buenos Aires (1833). Hemenway additionally entered copper mining and smelting. Providing an early indication of international business's influence on emerging countries, Alsop & Co. bought a percentage of Bolivia's custom revenues, notably those generated from the trade in silver, and it acquired future concession rights when it helped the government with its debt obligations. Traders such as Ladd & Co. led the building of sugar estates in Hawaii from the

1830s onwards, and Drake Brothers had acquired sugar plantations in Cuba by the late 1840s (Wilkins, 1970).

William Russell Grace began his remarkable personal story when he left Ireland, like so many of his starving and impoverished compatriots, to escape the potato famine, and worked in Peru as a ship's chandler for US traders Bryce & Co., engaged in the harvesting and shipping of guano for final use as fertilizer and gunpowder. He set up his own business, W. R. Grace & Co., in Peru in 1854, exporting sugar and guano, and founded his own merchant steamship line in 1860. The firm transferred its main office to New York in 1865 in order to expand its import business in the USA, and to promote a triangular trade with Europe. Grace & Co. opened its Chile office in 1880 and one in Argentina twenty years later. It was involved in the region's economic development during the 1880s, managing cotton spinning, woollen manufacturing, and sugar refining in Peru, and vegetable oil and paper industries in Chile and Colombia. Twice mayor of New York City, in 1885 Grace accepted the Statue of Liberty as a gift from the people of France. The three flexibly organized firms in Peru, Chile and New York were consolidated and incorporated by 1899, when the global reach of the company's activities required a higher measure of coordination. Grace & Co. had the honour of sending the first commercial vehicle through the Panama Canal, in 1914, and expanded its commercial portfolio with the Grace National Bank (forerunner of Marine Midland).[26]

The firm of Gunther controlled Liebig's Extract of Meat Company, maker of the well-known consumer brand, and it founded the Forestal Land, Timber and Railway Co. in 1906. It was Belgian in origin, but preferred to run its business from the global business centre of London (De Guevara and Miller, 1999).[27] W. H. Muller & Co., from the Netherlands, owned iron ore mines in Latin America, from where it took its products to Europe, most famously up the Rhine to the Krupp steel and armaments factory at Essen (Jonker and Sluyterman, 2000). There were, too, firms such as the Peruvian Amazon Company, which was locally owned but registered in London in order to raise finance. Its task was to collect rubber from forest areas, but, by 1910, its abuse of native labour drew the anti-slavery campaigner Sir Roger Casement to Peru. By this date, he had attracted international acclaim for exposing widespread barbarism in the Belgian Congo, again on behalf of rubber production. The dominance of trading firms in Latin

America did decline: responsible for 27 per cent of Chile's exports in 1870, Gibbs held (albeit a still very lucrative) 4 per cent in 1907 (Platt, 1977). In Argentina, which was Latin America's most important economy, leading meat, grain and wool firms became big enough to employ their own overseas sales representatives.

One of the largest international businesses in Latin America was the St John d'el Rey Mining Company, founded in London in 1830 as a free-standing company, to operate and lease mines in southern Minas Gerais in Brazil. The majority of the managers were British expatriates, but many who laboured in its mines were slaves. Long after the Royal Navy had enforced Britain's ban on the transatlantic trade in people, a British-registered company had continued to own slaves overseas. Abolition came late to Brazil, in 1882: after that date, coffee growers and other vested interests turned to free rural labour, and to Portuguese and Italian immigrants. By 1913, St John d'el Rey had the world's deepest mine, employed 150 Europeans and 2,500 others, produced most of Brazil's gold, and controlled railways, hydroelectric generation facilities, and a complex of houses and buildings (Eakin, 1989).

Dozens of US mining and processing companies – such as the Batopilas Mining Company in the extraction of silver, or the Consolidated Kansas City Smelting and Refining Company, in lead and silver – could be found in Mexico by the 1880s. The country was nearby and, under the rule of Porfirio Díaz, stable; there were few labour problems, and firms could negotiate on duties, levies, taxes and other concession terms. Over later decades, the 'Robber Baron' families so intimately tied to American industrialization and big business set the pace of investment. The Guggenheims, who had imported lead and silver ore from Mexico for processing in its own smelters, built two plants across the border in 1890. The motives of US mining concerns in Mexico and in America more generally usually differed from those of trading enterprises, since securing supplies for operations back home and vertical integration were primary goals, alongside the gain from cheaper labour costs.

M. Guggenheim's Sons bought a Mexican copper mine, in 1893, and the firm was operating a silver smelter in Bolivia by 1898.[28] The Pittsburgh Reduction Company, with the financial assistance of the Mellons, owned a bauxite mine in Puerto Rico, a territory annexed from the Spanish (the firm, in 1907, became the Aluminum Company of America, or Alcoa). Mexican Coal and Coke Co., by 1899, established self-government at its Coahuila township, where it owned a machine shop, hospital, drugstore, schools, jail, post office and telegraph office. A group of leading businessmen, including some linked to the Rocke-fellers and Standard Oil, formed one the USA's biggest trusts, the Amalgamated Copper Mining Company, in 1899. Their new busi-ness acquired a majority in the Anaconda Copper Company, buy-ing out both the London and the Paris Rothschilds, then controlling some 40 per cent of world copper production.[29] Amalgamated Copper entered Mexico, in a small way, in 1906 (Meyer and Sherman, 1987; Williamson, 1992).

Founded by the Guggenheim banking family in 1901, with the sup-port of J. P. Morgan, the Kennecott Mines Corporation bought copper mines in Chile, amongst them the Braden Copper Company, whose El Teniente, in the Andes, was the world's largest underground mine.[30] Standard Oil associates created too the American Smelting and Refin-ing Company (ASARCO), in 1899, as a device for dominating the processing of non-ferrous metal in the USA. Aggressive tactics enabled the Guggenheims to take over two years later, and ASARCO under-went a period of rapid expansion, including the purchase of five Mex-ican mines. Due to ASARCO, the Guggenheims emerged as Mexico's largest investors, with sixty-four known properties in 1904, and they ran company towns in many of these locations.[31] US firms were early investors to the south (some $302m of investment by 1914), and also went north (a smaller figure of $159m). We know about the Anglo-American Iron Company, and the Bethlehem Iron Ore Company, by 1900, plus, supplying most of the world's nickel, the Canadian Cop-per Company.[32] American capital, by 1910, dominated the asbestos business centred around Quebec (Wilkins, 1970). The US chemicals firm Du Pont in 1912 became an early example of an industrial firm seeking security of supply through vertical integration, by investing in a Chilean nitrate mine, but the capital commitment was small-scale.[33]

The case of the New York and Bermúdez Asphalt Company was a reminder of the political risks that investors ran in Latin America. The three-times President of Venezuela Antonio Leocadio Guzmán Blanco had the habit of offering 'exclusive' concessions several times over in return for the associated kickbacks. The deal signed with the International Telephone Company, in 1883, was followed by a further 'monopoly' for another US enterprise. Guzmán granted rights that included the Guanaco asphalt lake to an Irish-American,

Horatio Hamilton, who had associated himself with his regime, during the same year. Hamilton founded New York and Bermúdez to oversee the project in 1885, but, due to incompetent management, the concession was sold to the Barber Asphalt and Paving Company in 1892. Venezuela was in dispute over territory along the border with British Guyana, and in 1895, when Britain agreed to US intervention and to international arbitration, it in effect acknowledged the principles of the Monroe Doctrine. The court, sitting in Paris, finally ruled in Britain's favour, inevitably stirred resentment and nationalist feelings in Venezuela. During 1898, Joaquín Sinforiano de Jesús Crespo, who succeeded Guzmán, settled a legal dispute over the rights to Guanaco's asphalt in favour of local business interests (Ewell, 1999; Wilkins, 1970).

Banana republics

One of the first importers of bananas grown on its own plantation was Frank Brothers & Co., founded by Carl Franc, once a steward on the Pacific Mail Company, and, from 1866, transporting the fruit from Panama (then a province of Colombia) to New Orleans. United Fruit – a union of trading, railway and plantation projects – became so associated with the economies and politics of Central America that it earned the nickname 'el pulpo' (the octopus). Its origins were complex. Lorenzo Dow Baker founded Boston Fruit Company in 1885 to ship and sell Jamaican bananas, soon from its own estates. When European beet began to supplant tropical cane in the 1870s, Jamaica had looked for alternative means to earn a living, and welcomed US investors. Sugar accounted for only 11 per cent of Jamaica's exports by 1896, and bananas had taken up some of the decline with a 20 per cent share (almost entirely handled by the BFC). There were 114 US importers of bananas by 1899, and 22 of them owned overseas plantations. At this point, however, firms were securing better and cheaper bananas from Central America and Colombia, and BFC attempted to cope by diversifying into sugar plantations and other commodities in Cuba.

In Costa Rica, Minor Cooper Keith was an entrepreneur adventurer, who began by building railroads and ports, and ended with a personal grip on the economy and politics of a country. Coffee exports to Europe formed the mainstay of the Costa Rican economy, but the commodity had to be taken by ox cart from the central region, where it was grown, to Puntarenas, inconveniently located on the Pacific coast (Topik and Wells, 1998). Aiming to link the capital San José with Limón on the Caribbean, the government commissioned a railroad in 1871, with the finance being raised from London banks. As the line lacked sufficient revenues, Keith decided in 1873 to plant bananas along the route. The government of President Prospero Fernandez Oreamuno defaulted on its payments in 1882, forcing Keith to refinance the project, for which he received in return 3,200 square kilometres of land, or 5 per cent of the national territory, and a 99-year lease to run the new railroad. It was said that, to complete his great project in 1890, Keith lost one uncle and two brothers, and married into the Costa Rican ruling family. It is estimated, too, that more than 4,000 people lost their lives to jungle conditions and disease, and replacement labour had to be imported from Jamaica, China and Italy. Keith then developed banana plantations in Panama and Colombia, and came to dominate the fruit's production in Latin America. He also founded his own shipping line, as well as using Britain's Hoadley & Company.

Financial difficulties drove Keith into a merger with BFC in 1899, to create the United Fruit Company: it controlled a quarter of a million acres in Central America; it operated 112 miles of railroad; it owned 11 steamships, and ran 11 charters; it possessed a wholesale and sales network throughout the USA; and it had controlling interests in 9 other importers. For a delicate perishable, such as the banana, the case for vertical integration – linking cultivation, shipping and distribution – was persuasive. The new business's ships carried a wide range of goods, and Guatemala hired the firm to manage its postal services to the USA in 1901. Keith signed a contract with its President, Manuel Estrada Cabrera, three years later, to construct and control railroads, ports and telegraph services on the Atlantic side of the country, in return for land grants, tax exemptions and the chance to lay out banana plantations. It provoked, nonetheless, opposition from Guatemala's coffee growers, who wanted a greater say over the rates and the operations of railways and ports. After 1912, Keith completed his International Railways of Central America (IRCA) but failed in his ambition to build a system from Guatemala to the Panama Canal. Along the Caribbean coast, the UFC installed warehouses, hospitals, trams and commissaries – sometimes small towns – to serve the needs of its plantations and their workers. By 1914, the company provided two thirds of all bananas eaten in North America.

In El Salvador, where bananas did not replace the commercial importance of coffee, the UFC had a rival in the British-owned Salvador Railway Company (Topik and Wells, 1998). But it was Samuel Zemurray, an immigrant from Bessarabia, who became United Fruit's biggest rival and a man that surpassed even Keith's reputation for ruthlessness. Without a formal education, Zemurray made himself one of New Orleans's leading banana traders, making a fortune by the age of twenty-one. He bought a ship in order to trade in Honduras, whose government, in 1903, looking to attract foreign capital, decided to sell land concessions. Another New Orleans firm, the Vaccaro Brothers – Joseph, Luca and Felix were originally from Sicily – had been importing bananas since 1899, and took up the offer. With the help of United Fruit, they built a railway from the port of La Ceiba to its new plantation (their firm later evolved into Standard Fruit and subsequently the Dole Food Company). Zemurray established banana estates in Honduras, during 1910–11. This time, United Fruit reacted by sending a business associate – called, threateningly, 'Machine Gun' Maloney – to build a railroad and establish banana growing. The location of plantations determined the route of this line, which looped around mountains to reach flat jungle plains.

The politics of the region and US foreign policy were inextricably mixed up with business manoeuvres. Both the Honduran and the Nicaraguan governments were seeking international loans, despite having defaulted on previous agreements. The US bank J. P. Morgan, which took on the role of underwriter, secured Honduras's debts in return for directly managing the collection of customs revenues and trade concessions. Zemurray, by nature suspicious, believed that Cuyamel Fruit was being gradually excluded from the political influence it needed. The US Secretary of State, Philander Knox, did not want Honduras destabilized, and warned him against interfering. In response, Zemurray returned to New Orleans, secretly met the former Honduran president, Manuel Bonilla Chirinos, and funded the mercenaries that Bonilla hired to return to power during 1912–13 (Topik and Wells, 1998).

Cuyamel and United Fruit preferred – pragmatically and generally – to cooperate until events came to a crisis in 1913. UFC had even invested in the Hubbard-Zemurray shipping line, but, with the prospect of a Department of Justice investigation into Cuyamel, it divested its interest. But, since bananas quickly exhausted the land on which they grew, Cuyamel and UFC kept moving further inland until they clashed at the Motagua river valley. Zemurray had the backing of Banillo and his successor, Francisco Bertrand, and the argument between the two companies exacerbated an outstanding border dispute between Honduras and Guatemala. United Fruit and the associated IRCA, by 1914, had an uneasy relationship with the Guatemalan dictator, Estrada Cabrera. The two Central American states asked their giant neighbour, in 1917, to mediate in their disputes over borders and bananas. As the USA had just entered the European war, its main concern was to avoid any interruption to food supplies, and, in January 1918, under pressure, Zemurray secretly agreed to UFC buying up Cuyamel Fruit's stock, so long as he remained in effective control of his business (Wilkins, 1970; Casson, 1983; Dosal, 1993; McCann, 1976; Davies, 1990; Wilkins, 1970; MacCameron, 1983; Walker, 2011; Leonard, 2011).[34] William Sydney Potter – a one-time convicted fraudster and the humorist better known as O. Henry – used Honduras, in his 1904 collection *Cabbages and Kings*, as his model for Anchuria, the original 'banana republic'.

The presence of US banana firms in Jamaica posed an unsolvable dilemma for one prominent British politician, who had linked his ambitions to the imperial project. The island's bishop approached Britain's Colonial Secretary, Joseph Chamberlain, over his concerns that United Fruit might entirely exit Jamaica as a result of recent events in the region. Insurrection in Cuba had drawn the USA into open warfare with Spain in 1898, and ended with its occupation of the island. The protection of economic interests was a strong motive behind the intervention, and there was every prospect of US investment increasingly gravitating towards Cuba. Washington, in fact, would fail to find a viable political settlement: they returned Cuba to independence in 1902, reoccupied the island in 1906–9, and again intervened in 1912 (E. Williamson, 1992). Chamberlain, from a family of Birmingham steel makers, had split Britain's Liberal Party over its policy of Home Rule for Ireland, and surprised contemporaries by asking the Unionist-Conservative prime minister, Lord Salisbury, for the job of Colonial Secretary. He wanted to be the architect of a commercially and politically united empire, based on preferential tariffs and common interests. Jamaica became a test-case project for this ambitious and energetic politician.

Chamberlain's first step was to convince the Jamaica Produce Company to contract and operate three steamers that would carry fruit from Jamaica to Britain. The firm was keen so long as it received an annual subsidy of £20,000 from the public purse. Despite what seemed generous terms, the enterprise was soon in trouble, and Chamberlain's next step was to consult Alfred Jones, from Elder Dempster & Company, a trading and shipping line with interests in West Africa, and (since 1892) an importer of bananas from the Canaries to Britain. Elder Dempster had begun as a coaling agent, but took over the British and African Steam Navigation Company and the African Steamship Company to gain a near monopoly of commercial shipping between Britain and West Africa. Jones sent an investigator to Jamaica, who reported that Chamberlain's proposal was not viable. Britain's Colonial Secretary continued to pressure, and so Jones requested a yearly £60,000 subsidy. They agreed to £40,000, so long as the government of Jamaica paid half, and the Imperial Direct West India Mail Service Company was operating by 1900.

Jones soon offered a partnership to Fyffe, Hudson & Company, through which they could merge and reorganize the British banana trade. For a model of such a large integrated operation, they could look to the recently formed United Fruit (which continued to dominate banana growing in Jamaica). Elders & Fyffes (Shipping) Ltd was established in 1901, but by 1903 United Fruit had a 50 per cent interest, and by 1910 it had full control. Therefore, Jones personally profited from a political and imperial failure, and the former cabin boy on the way picked up a knighthood (Davies, 1990; Beaver, 1976). In this instance, the realities of the international economy – the gravitational pull of the USA on Jamaica, the competitive lead of the UFC giant, and the business participants' unsentimental capacity for cosmopolitan deal-making – overwhelmed the calculations of the empire builders.[35]

International rivalry and business in Africa

Africa became the most conspicuous example of late nineteenth-century imperialism when European powers divided the continent into spheres of interest. Until the Berlin Conference of 1884–5, some 80 per cent of Africa had remained uncolonized; after that date, the continent fell under imperial occupation. To make good the hoped-for economic gains, Belgium, Germany, and even free-trading Britain resurrected the charter company, a policy Germany extended, as we have already noted, to New Guinea and the Pacific islands. They contravened the accepted nostrums of the day, but, clearly, European investors saw free markets as unsuited or as too risky for ventures in undeveloped and untried lands. It was Leopold II, the Belgian king, who instigated the transformation of a whole continent and its people. Portugal had long claimed but never effectively controlled the Congo, and the Belgian government would not support their own king's bid for the territory. Leopold founded, therefore, in 1876, an organization for exploration, and it reformed, three years later, as the International Association of the Congo or the Congo Society, initially with private capital, but soon entirely owned by Leopold. His front organization sent Henry Morton Stanley (the man who had presumed to find Dr Livingstone) to the Congo in 1879–84. In the belief he was working for a philanthropic organization rather than a commercial one, he bribed chieftains south of the Congo river, and formalized treaties that granted political authority and commercial rights (constituting eventually the future Congo Free State).

Yet Leopold also provoked the French into sending Pierre de Brazza, a naval officer, to establish Brazzaville (setting the parameters for the Republic of the Congo), and he brought, too, protests from the Portuguese, who had British support. He had fired the starting gun for an international rivalry with widespread repercussions (in brief, military action, protectorates or colonization in Tunisia, Guinea, Egypt, Sudan and Somaliland), and Bismarck (calculating the effects on European diplomatic relationships) took the initiative in calling the 1884–5 meeting, better known to the Germans as the *Kongokonferenz*. The agreement it forged sought popular support by insisting on the end of slavery in all areas of European control, and the Congo Free State was given to the Congo Society (Leopold's private property) in return for it being open to all European investment. The agreement also designated the lands where European nations might sign treaties with African leaders, as the first step in control of their lands. Therefore, the meeting at Berlin did not, as became commonly believed, resolve all areas of dispute: failure actively to enter a territory, or to create an effective administration or police force, or, critically, to use or develop lands economically, all could lead in principle to the rejection of any claim (Chamberlain, 1999).

Both business and governments lobbied at the Berlin Conference, jostling to secure and extend their established interests. George Taubman Goldie, who was introduced to Africa while serving with the

Royal Engineers, was the principal figure in converting Britain's trading posts in the Niger Delta into a colony. He arrived there in 1877, and spent twenty years arguing that the territory could be added to the British Empire if the idea of the chartered company were revived. European traders operated through trading posts dotted along the West African coast, and bought commodities grown or harvested by locals. There were overlapping networks of British and French interests across Western African, generating tensions, and Germany was beginning to establish its presence. At this stage, traders did not own or seek plantations, and, as they required the cooperation of African rulers, they were ready and willing to sign treaties. At this point, European governments were wary of costly entanglements and their implications, rather than seeing Africa as part of some imperial project (Fieldhouse, 1965).

As a first step to achieving his personal ambition, Goldie, in 1879, combined the four companies that controlled British commercial interests in the Niger into the United African Company. When the British government refused it a charter in 1881, Goldie was not deterred. The business was renamed the National African Company, and re-established with a larger capital and more trading stations. When the talks in Berlin designated the Niger Delta as a British sphere of influence, the danger of a diplomatic or military clash with France was averted. By buying out French traders along the lower part of the river, and attending the conference as a Niger expert, Goldie had facilitated the decision in his favour. No longer wary of international disputes, the British government was willing to reconsider the advantages of a charter. By the latter part of the nineteenth century, however, it had to weigh public concern for native rights. Once Goldie had signed 400 agreements with local chiefs, the necessary legislation was passed in 1886 to convert NAC into the Royal Niger Company, with prominent positions in palm oil, palm kernels, groundnuts, tin, hide and rubber. The ability of RNC to make advantageous treaties with local chieftains ultimately determined the size of the colony of Nigeria. For his service to business and his homeland, Goldie was soon knighted (Fieldhouse, 1965).

The RNC's first governor was Henry Austin Bruce, 1st Baron Aberdare: he was a coal and steel magnate, but, as a former Home Secretary and Lord President of the Council, he offered political connections back in London. The RNC's main problem in Africa was Germany.

Until his dismissal as Chancellor by the Kaiser in 1890, Bismarck continuously sought to extend the colony of Cameroon, and German commercial agents acted in Nigeria without permission from RNC. Legal action provoked compensation claims from the German consul, who was Bismarck's nephew. In July 1890, the British prime minister, Salisbury, concluded the Heligoland–Zanzibar Treaty with Germany, and, with Goldie more concerned with the French threat from the north, it was decided to settle the Nigeria–Cameroon frontier in 1893. There were internal difficulties too, and Goldie personally led an expedition to quell native resistance. He succeeded Aberdare as governor in 1895. With the chartered territories surrounded by French and German protectorates, the British government became more and more concerned at leaving a hotspot of international relations with the RNC. In 1900, territorial control was transferred, for the sum of £865,000, and Nigeria reappeared as a formal part of the British Empire one year later (Heaton, 2008).[36]

The fact no German company wanted to invest in Cameroon or Togoland was a disappointing setback for Bismarck, and his government had to assume direct rule. The principal figure in the founding of Germany's East Africa colony (later Tanganyika, and today's Tanzania) was Karl Peters. He formed the Society for German Colonization, and concluded treaties with local inland chiefs, returning home, in 1885, to form his East African Company and to lobby the Berlin Conference. Bismarck, uninterested in some unknown territory of unproven value, had greater concern for relations with Britain, obsessed with its India trade and the route to Suez. Peters countered by threatening to sell his concessions to Leopold II, and pressure from imperially minded allies in the Reichstag made it politic for the chancellor to give 'the stupid guy' his charter, bestowing colonial powers, but no commercial monopoly.

Nonetheless, Bismarck was careful to sign a treaty with Britain during the following year, allowing a temporary solution to competing claims. Peters struck his own deal, in 1888, with the Sultan of Zanzibar, Khalifa bin Said, to develop the nearby coastal regions on the African mainland, and then went into the interior without German government sanction to the kingdom of Buganda (in modern Uganda), where he completed a treaty with its ruler, Mwanga II. When a larger expedition from the Imperial British East Africa Company arrived,

Peters was forced to flee. Britain had just granted the IBEAC, part of the Mackinnon conglomerate, administration of the lands between the Indian Ocean and Lake Victoria, an historical trade route, with further links to the Congo.

In the 1890 Heligoland–Zanzibar Treaty, Germany traded Zanzibar and the area west of the Mombasa coast to the central lakes (later, Kenya and Uganda) for a British-owned island near to the Kiel Canal and some strategic harbours. It additionally gained British confirmation of German rights to South West Africa (Namibia), and to its settlements along the Cameroon–Nigeria and Togoland–Gold Coast (Ghana) borders. The East Africa Company was left with the uneconomic territories inland from Dar es Salaam, which would later constitute German East Africa. With the Abushiri people in revolt against Peters's harsh rule, the German government was forced to send troops, who acted brutally, and it revoked the East African Company's responsibilities for colonial administration.[37] Over time, the enterprise dominated the colony's mining activities, and it took revenues from customs duties, land deals and banking (Fieldhouse, 1965).

During a stint as German East Africa's governor, 'Hangman' Peters committed further crimes against the indigenous people, for which he was found guilty back home in 1897. So, he left for London to run a gold mining company with projects in Rhodesia (Zimbabwe) and Portuguese East Africa (Mozambique). (Peters would be welcomed back to Germany in 1914, and he was formally pardoned of his crimes, after his death, by Adolf Hitler) (Perras, 2004). As for IBEAC, it too met armed resistance, and the crown similarly took over its colonial rule, in 1893. Mackinnon and its fellow investors felt that the promise of subsidies had not been kept, and lost interest in IBEAC.[38] Smith McKenzie continued, nonetheless, to act as the McKinnon group's trade agents in the region, and invested in coffee and rubber in Zanzibar (Munro, 1987). It was left to the colonial government to fund the building of a railway between the port of Mombasa and Kisumu on Lake Victoria, from 1896 to 1901, and it imported the workers it needed from India, many of whom settled permanently. By connecting the fertile highland plains to the coast, the railway instigated European investment in tea and coffee estates. The Germans built a parallel line from Dar es Salaam to Kigoma on the banks of Lake Tanganyika (Wolmar, 2009; Shillington, 2005).

International outrage and Africa

Kerdijk and Pincoffs, from Rotterdam, had established trading posts along and around the Congo River from 1857 onwards, often carrying goods to Britain, and it evolved, in 1869, into the Afrikaansche Handels-Vennootscap (AHV). It was the first company to sponsor Stanley's explorations – some time before his association with King Leopold – and he publicly praised AHV's operations, its medical facilities, housing, and the abundant food it provided to labourers. When Louis Pincoff fled to New York, to escape accusations of fraud, the business was reincorporated as the Nieuwe AHV, in 1879. Henrik Muller, from 1861, founded the biggest West African trader from the Netherlands, renamed the Oost-Afrikaansche Compagnie (OAC), in 1883. The Dutch government, fully focused on the East Indies, did not actively support its African traders, handing over Muller's fortified posts in Ghana to Britain in 1872. Nor did it make much mark on the Berlin Conference, merely arguing for free trade in the Niger basin and in the Congo too, where NAHV had fifty trading posts, with some 200 European employees and 2,000 Africans.

Without strong backing from its government, in the age of high imperialism, NAHV was gradually eased out of the Congo. The territories were now Leopold II's personal property and fiefdom, and he viewed them as a financial investment. Lacking the capital to invest in mining, he concentrated instead on ivory, wild rubber, and palm oil. In contravention of the Berlin agreement, which prohibited monopoly, he designated two thirds of the Congo Free State – the Domaine Privé – to his own agents or to concessionaries in which he had a share. His other device for extracting gain was forced labour, in lieu of a personal tax, copying the now-defunct Cultivation System of the Dutch East Indies.

Initially, Leopold had only debts to show for his seizure of the Congo, and it was the sudden demand for rubber in the 1890s that rescued his business venture economically, but it ended with international outrage over the barbarity of his rule. Within the Domaine Privé, the pay of district officials relied on commission, and locals had to meet ivory or rubber quotas at prices fixed by the state. Punishments included death, maiming, the macabre chopping-off of hands, and the burning of villages. Starvation and disease drove up the widespread and considerable loss of life, estimated by some to be in the millions, although it is impossible to give exact figures.

E. D. Morel – a shipping office clerk who became an investigative journalist – wondered why ships laden with rubber returned to the Congo with guns and ammunition, and he attracted the support of campaigners and merchants hoping to break Leopold's monopoly system in the colony. The British parliament demanded an enquiry, and a consul, Roger Casement, won fame for an intrepid investigation which revealed the depth of the human tragedy to the world. The literary talents of Joseph Conrad (*The Heart of Darkness*), Arthur Conan Doyle (*The Crime of the Congo*), and Mark Twain (*King Leopold's Soliloquy*) all maintained popular concern and anger.

European nations and the USA demanded reforms, and the Belgian government, reluctantly, assumed control of the Congo from its king in 1908. Since rubber prices had fallen, and South East Asian sources were now more competitive, it was in effect bailing out Leopold. The governor-general began to report to Brussels, but forced labour to pay for the head tax continued, as did widespread brutality and arduous working conditions. With revenues from rubber falling, the colony looked to palm concessions, and demanded that local communities surrender lands and forests (Fieldhouse, 1965, Hochschild, 1998; Davidson, 1969). Lever Brothers – founded by William Lever, later called Lord Leverhulme – was a mass manufacturer of soap and margarine, and needed secure supplies of palm oil. The company established plantations in the colony in 1911, and, since it relied on the colony's system of forced labour, its name was inevitably mixed up with continued reports of atrocities (Fieldhouse, 1965).[39]

Punitive punishment and forced labour were part of Africa's colonial story. The scale of the atrocities and their notoriety especially distinguished the Belgian Congo, yet Portugal's policies attracted international outrage too. News of forced labour, imported from Angola to the islands of São Tomé and Príncipe, and their harsh working conditions emerged in 1904. It is worth recalling that Portugal's colonial trade remained less valuable than its trade with independent Brazil. Imperial commerce and tariffs did benefit Lisbon merchants, who oversaw the lucrative re-export of commodities, and the Empresa Nacional de Navegação line, with its monopoly and government contracts. Cocoa was worth twice as much as the other main commodities, rubber and coffee, and São Tomé and Príncipe was at the time the world's main source of cocoa, and, therefore, the pearl of the Portuguese empire.

Accounts of slavery particularly embarrassed the Cadbury chocolate enterprise in Britain. The owning family, as pacifist Quakers, were historically associated with the abolition of the transatlantic slave trade, and they had more recently campaigned against the Congo abuses and the use of indentured Chinese labour in South Africa's mining industry. Like its fellow Quaker enterprise, and competitor, Rowntree, the Cadbury company depended on supplies from São Tomé and Príncipe. Both companies had bought plantations in the West Indies (Cadbury in 1897 and Rowntree in 1899), but neither investment fulfilled the ambitions placed on them. By 1909, Cadbury had managed to switch to the Gold Coast for most of its cocoa. Crucially, in the interim, the family had instructed the popular *Daily News*, which it owned, not to mention the accusations of cocoa plantation slavery, while they investigated and lobbied the Portuguese authorities. As seems the rule, it was the decision to sue – over claims that the company profited from slavery – that dragged the family into controversy and public suspicion. They won the court case, but received damages of one farthing (Fitzgerald, 1995).

Settler capital funded developments in São Tomé, Príncipe, and Portuguese South West Africa, although Belgium's Banque d'Outremer also is known to have bought land for cultivation in São Tomé and Príncipe.[40] In Portugal's empire, the Banco Nacional Ultramarino continued to enjoy numerous monopolistic advantages in banking transactions. Whenever lenders defaulted, it also acquired cocoa estates, river navigation companies, and tobacco factories, and in 1900 it formed the Companhia Agrícola de Cazengo to take over from bankrupted South West African coffee planters.[41] Foreign firms frequently rescued failed enterprises, too: in the Zambezi delta, the Sena Sugar Estates, exporting to Portugal and the Transvaal, became British-owned, and French investors took control of the Boror and Madal copra enterprises. The Companhia de Moçambique had received a royal charter in 1891, with monopoly and sovereign rights in the area between the Zambezi and Save rivers, and the power to use forced labour (Neil-Tomlinson, 1998).[42] Within a short period, it was controlled by France's Banque Imperiale Ottomane. The company's gold mine and railway projects did not generate positive revenues, and it relied on land leases and on an African head tax instead (G. Jones, 1990).[43] The South African miners Lewis and Marks owned the chartered Niassa Company in northern Mozambique, importing labour, until its own government banned the practice in 1912. There were accusations, moreover, that the Niassa Company profited from trafficking slaves to the Middle East.[44]

In Southern Africa, it was the adventurer-capitalist Cecil Rhodes who most prominently and personally identified international mining with empire building. By 1887, the De Beers Company dominated the Kimberley diamond fields. Rhodes had been the architect of this, but he relied on his connections with Lord Nathaniel Rothschild, the head of the London bank, who became the company's largest share-holder. Within a year, Rhodes was drawn by the possibility of gold deposits north of the Limpopo River. Once granted a concession by the chief of the Matabele, he hoped to end local control, and, on behalf of the British Empire, to sweep onwards into central Africa. In 1889, the chartered British South Africa Company was formed, with the commercial tasks of establishing trade and making treaties with Africans, distributing and managing lands, and organizing a police force. Rhodes referred to his enterprise as 'another East India Company'. For the British government, it was a manoeuvre by proxy that blocked German and Portuguese plans to own territories running coast to coast across central Africa (Fieldhouse, 1965). BSAC sent a force of 700 men to settle a dispute with the Matabele over a mining conces-sion, and, helped by the Maxim gun, it wiped out any resistance at the Battle of Shangani River. Interestingly, Rothschild was also a director of the Maxim Gun Company, whose deadly effectiveness had now so clearly been revealed.

Eventually, BSAC carved out a territory, named Zambezia, and then Rhodesia (covering modern Zambia and Zimbabwe); the two Boer republics, the Transvaal and the Orange Free State, emerged as the main opposition to British rule in Southern Africa. Rhodes was elected Prime Minister of the Cape Colony in 1890, and covertly used his office to organize the Jameson Raid on the Transvaal, hoping to de-stabilize its government. The incursion was a debacle, and Rhodes left office in 1896. He was motivated by a belief that the whole world could gain from British rule, and seriously talked of the USA's return to the British Empire.[45] But conflict with the Boers was principally economic: the Transvaal produced one quarter of the world's gold supplies, and mining operations were largely financed through British capital.

Salisbury, the British prime minister, did not share Rhodes's notion of maximum expansion across the continent, preferring to calculate the advantages of each acquisition. He thought that the line of British territories from the Cape to Cairo (as was being considered) would be strategically vulnerable. But his colonial secretary, Chamberlain, was more visionary. In 1899, he provoked the Boer War on the bogus demand of votes for *uitlanders*. Early success by Boer farmers against a global empire brought humiliation, and one cost of the British Empire's final victory, in 1902, was an international reputation for brutality against a small population of farmers and their families. The Union of South Africa in 1910 was, nevertheless, a remarkable example of rapid reconciliation between enemies, and offered security to those interested in economic pursuits. Two fifths of world capital invested in mining by 1914 went into the digging of South African gold (Harvey and Press, 1990; Shillington, 2005).

Trade and multinational banking

If we look closely at the origins of merchants and bankers, it is hard to distinguish between them. Foreign merchant houses, such as the Rothschilds and Schroders, settled in London, and evolved into merchant banks. Traders and agents collected and settled bills of exchange for customers; they dealt in foreign currency; they took deposits; and gave credit and commercial guarantees. Merchant banks came into contact with overseas governments and firms through trade finance, and came to issue securities for them on the London Stock Exchange. Over time, bankers and traders tended to specialize, but Anthony Gibbs, Wallace Brothers, and Matheson & Co. continued in both types of business. Traders collaborated in the founding of overseas banks, and they gained and needed access to financial resources. The majority of British overseas banks were registered in London, and took the form of free-standing companies; all were unconnected to banking firms operating in Britain. Their Dutch counterparts, too, were formally based at home and separated from domestic firms. But French and German overseas banks tended to be the subsidiaries of domestic firms or linked to a business syndicate. The USA, during this period, was wary of foreign entanglements, placed strict limits on its banks becoming multinationals, and stated that the directors of domestic banks had to be Americans (Wilkins, 1989).

Within Western Europe and the USA, international businesses could rely on a network of corresponding banks, many based in well-developed financial capitals, including London, Paris, New York,

Table 2.9 *Number of overseas banks and branches, 1912*

	Banks	%	Branches	%
Britain	46	28.8	1,525	64.4
Netherlands	7	4.8	73	3.1
France	28	19.2	419	17.7
Germany	26	17.8	169	7.1

Source: Battilossi and Cassis (2002).

Brussels, Hamburg, Zurich or Berlin. Cooperative arrangements were a well-established means of transferring funds, gaining credit, or obtaining exchange. Banks might, too, have representatives and agents in foreign capitals to negotiate on government loans and securities. The Rothschilds in London operated through family members to be found throughout Europe, all running formally independent firms. In the case of overseas banks, registration and ownership were usually based in Europe, while management and operations took place on other continents.

One estimate suggests that there were 56 overseas banks with 653 branches in 1880. Of these, 34 banks (60.7 per cent) and 600 branches (91.9 per cent) were British-owned. By 1912, there were 146 identifiable overseas banks with 2,369 branches active in 85 sovereign or colonial entities. Even by this date, Britain's multinational banks and branches remained the international leaders, although they had lost ground to competitors (see Table 2.9). Large banking networks in Australia, New Zealand, South Africa and Canada explain why Britain controlled nearly two thirds of overseas branches. As measured by value, over half of the assets held by British multinational banks were in Asia. Colonial policy and expanding commerce in the East Indies heavily influenced the emergence of Dutch overseas banks. Those from France were especially prominent in the Mediterranean and the Middle East, and Germany's could often be found within its economic sphere of influence, south-east Europe, while before the First World War it made impressive incursions on traditionally British commercial spheres in Latin America and Asia.

British multinational banking can be dated from the 1830s: at this juncture, individual royal charters stipulated reserve and asset levels, or entitlements to issue local currency; they were used to enforce

Colonial Banking Regulations; they might bestow the especially profitable right to handle government funds; and, with each bank restricted
to particular territories, they recalled the mercantilist principles of the
past, even if the absence of a monopoly did not. With the changes in
corporate law in 1856–62, banks were allowed to form joint stock
companies without the need of a charter. British investors founded the
Ionian Bank in 1839, after the islands had been turned into a protectorate. The Oriental Bank Corporation, established in Bombay, in
1842, was confident enough of the regulatory regime in British India
not to seek a charter. On the other hand, the Anglo-Egyptian Bank and
the Imperial Bank of Persia operated in territories only latterly drawn
into Britain's imperial orbit.

As with trading companies, the growth of the international economy
from the 1860s was a turning point. So, it was traders who created the
London and River Plate Bank, and the London and Brazilian Bank.
In Argentina, Uruguay, Brazil and Chile, British banks had major economic roles, and funded developments in railways, mining and utilities.
John Thomas North controlled much of Chile's nitrate industry and its
associated railways, and was responsible for the Bank of Tarapaca and
London. Both Indian and expatriate British businessmen founded the
National Bank of India, in Calcutta, during 1866, but they registered
the company in London. The British Bank of West Africa, brought
into existence in 1894, was directly associated with the Elder, Dempster steamship line, and was instrumental in the expansion of Britain's
commercial and imperial interests in Africa (Cameron and Bovykin,
1991; Jones, 1990; Jones, 1993; Cassis, 2006).

Trading firms were closely associated with the most important overseas bank of the period, certainly in Asia: the Hongkong Bank (and
predecessor to the Hong Kong and Shanghai Bank, or HSBC). Its
objective was to finance regional trade and to service the needs of its
founding companies. British firms supplied six of the fourteen board
members: these were Dent & Co., which supplied John Dent as its
first chairman; Gilmans; and the Borneo Company. There were, in
addition, German and US companies, and three Bombay merchants
(including two Parsis, and the David Sassoon enterprise of Iraqi Jewish origin). As Dent and Sassoon were its biggest competitors for the
opium trade, Jardine Matheson refused to join the Hongkong Bank's
board until 1877; its participation, in turn, excluded Swire until 1912.
Thomas Sutherland, a future chairman of the P&O Steam Navigation

Company, founded and ran the bank on 'Scottish principles'. The business was unusual for being registered in Hong Kong, as opposed to London, but much of its ownership and management were British, and, by 1888, 36 per cent of its deposits came from the imperial capital.[46]

Overseas service was the main source of management for multinational banks, as for trading companies, in the same way as educated Britons left their homeland to staff colonial administrations. In Australia, on the other hand, British overseas banks eventually employed large numbers of local managerial personnel. By the First World War, competition from domestic firms had begun to erode the dominance of British firms in the dominions of Canada, Australia and New Zealand. Following the Baring bank crisis of 1890, the result of excessive lending and risk-taking in Argentina, Latin American firms offered greater competition. The credit crunch in London triggered in Australia, during 1893, the collapse of the 'land-finance companies' that had lent money to settlers, and exposed the imprudent policies of banks (Jones, 1990; Jones, 1993).

As we have seen, NHM, the Nederlandsche-Indische Handelsbank, and Rotterdamsche Bank were amongst the overseas concerns from the Netherlands that were mostly active in the colonial Dutch East Indies (Jonker and Sluyterman, 2000). Belgium's Société Générale, in 1902, incorporated the Banque Sino-Belge, beginning in Shanghai, and later opening branches in Tientsing and Beijing. Société Générale became formally the Société Générale de Belgique in 1905, and, four years later, and one year after Belgium as a state had taken responsibility for the Congo, it joined other major Belgian banks to found the Banque de Congo-Belge, with a monopoly for note issuance and government contracts. SGB was soon the dominant owner, and the main force behind the Banque Italo-Belge, which did business in Latin America. When Banque Sino-Belge changed into the Banque Belge pour l'Etranger, in 1913, it assumed a role throughout Europe, the Middle East and Asia.[47]

Two domestic banks founded the Banque d'Indochine in 1875: it helped the French government manage its assets in South East Asia, and dominated business and investment in these territories. From 1900, it transacted trade between France and China, and acted as France's representative in the collection of the indemnity imposed on China after the Boxer Rebellion against foreign incursions. Outside South East Asia, the Banque d'Indochine could be found in Shanghai (where it would finance the Shanghai Power Company and the Shanghai Tramways), and in Bangkok, Hong Kong, and Djibouti, possessing nineteen branches in all by 1914 (Meuleau, 1990). The Compagnie Lyonnaise l'Indo-Chinoise, by 1900, was active in Yunnan, where the French, much to the concern of the Chinese government, had territorial ambitions.[48] The French domestic banks that backed the Banque de l'Afrique Occidentale, from 1901, raised much of its finance through its London office (Brunschwig, 1970). Crédit Lyonnais managed twenty overseas branches, excluding colonial locations, by 1914 (Cassis, 2006).

The Paris Rothschilds were significant players in the world of international business: they had oilfields and processing facilities in Russia, and, by 1914, extensive interests in Spanish railways, plus a large metal processing and marketing business (McKay, 1970). The USA's International Banking Corporation owned seventeen foreign branches, in 1914, spread across East Asia, Panama and Mexico. It was a consortium of New York businesses, which, by not doing business across state lines in the USA, did not breach federal laws prohibiting domestic banks from owning foreign branches (the law was changed in 1913) (Wilkins, 1970; Cassis, 2006). To meet the needs of its clients in the USA, the National City Bank of New York opened a Buenos Aires office.

In response to its country's growing international trade, the Japanese government founded the Yokohama Specie Bank, in 1880, and it first went abroad in 1892 to the booming commercial centre and port of Shanghai. It had twenty overseas branches by 1914, throughout China, the USA and Europe, and could claim to be an effective rival to the Hongkong Bank and to other European-owned banks. The Bank of Taiwan was opened in 1899, after the island's colonization, to invest in its commodities trade and infrastructure. It was used to found branches in mainland China – because its name hid its ownership and did not provoke anti-Japanese sentiments. The colonial government in Korea established the Bank of Chosen in 1910, and assisted with transactions in Manchuria (Jones, 1990).

German banks were mainly occupied with the development of their home economy. But Disconto-Gesellschaft, thirty years after its establishment in 1851, began to develop a network of branches in Europe, Latin America and Asia, and it organized, amongst others, state loans for Russia, Romania, Japan and China. It financed the Great Venezuela

Railway, built by Krupp between 1888 and 1892, which would end with one more example of gunboat diplomacy, in 1902, this time by the German navy responding to Venezuela defaulting on its debt. Disconto-Gesellschaft raised the funds needed to lay railways in colonial Cameroon before 1914. By this point, it had long lost its leadership of German finance to Deutsche Bank, founded in 1870 to stop British houses taking all the international short-term credit and loan business. Deutsche Bank created branches in Shanghai and Yokohama, therefore, as quickly as 1872, and it followed this by setting up offices in London, Brussels and Istanbul. It purchased the Deutsch-Belgische La Plata-Bank, with its operations in Buenos Aires and Montevideo, which it eventually liquidated in order to establish the Deutsche Übersee Bank, in 1886. DUB was soon doing business in Chile and, principally, Argentina (perceived as a place of great prospects). The company was refounded as the Deutsche Überseeische Bank in 1893, another repercussion of the Argentine crisis, and it could be found in Bolivia, Uruguay, Brazil, Peru, Spain, Mexico (with Speyer & Co.) and Central America (with Credit Suisse) by 1914.

In partnership with Disconto-Gesellschaft and Bleichröder, in 1889 Deutsche Bank established Deutsch-Asiatische Bank (Cassis, 2006), for which Hongkong Bank's opening of a Hamburg branch was a blatant retaliation. Moreover, Jardine Matheson had just funded China's purchase of cannons from Krupp, just as the traders had proved willing to act for Krupp's competitors, Armstrong and Schneider. Consequently, government pressure was important in helping the German banks to overcome their rivalry and to found DAB. Their new subsidiary fruitfully cooperated with the Hongkong Bank in financing Chinese government loans and its railway projects. Deutsche Bank, from 1888, was associated with the Ottoman Empire by its financing of the Baghdad Railway, a troubled and uncompleted project that threatened British interests in the Persian Gulf. There was an Istanbul office by 1909. Opportunities for trade-related finance, government loans, and overseas railway projects were expanding in the 1880s, the same decade that German banks could adopt the universal bank model and the joint-stock form, as devices for maximizing their scale and resources.

Disconto-Gesellschaft and the Nord-Deutsche Bank created the Brasilianische Bank für Deutschland in 1887, and the Bank für Chile und Deutschland in 1895. German banks, by 1914, controlled approximately one third of Brazil's deposits, and over one quarter of those in Argentina and Chile (Gall et al., 1995). The most important place for German investment was the USA, including its railways, and shared German personal and family connections solidified links with American banks. One case was the Warburgs of Hamburg and Kuhn, Loeb & Co. in New York, and a Deutsche Bank director was related to members of Speyer & Co., which became DUB's agent in Chile. Overall, Deutsche Bank evolved into Germany's largest provider of FDI, with overseas assets of $73m in 1914.

Close bank–industry ties in Germany converted into overseas enterprises providing the finance that could win large-scale engineering projects, increase the scale and price competitiveness of German manufacturers, and boost exports. The most significant, and one of Germany's most important multinationals, was the Deutsche-Überseeische Elektrizitäts-Gesellschaft (DUEG), founded in 1895 by a bank consortium led by Deutsche Bank and Allgemeine Elektrizitäts-Gesellschaft (AEG). Deutsche Bank provided loans to the Austro-Hungarian government, but German companies penetrated little into eastern Europe (Hennart, 1982; Hertner and Jones, 1986; Jones, 1990; Jones and Schroter, 1993). One exception was Deutsche Bank's purchase of Steaua Romana, the oil concern, in 1902. Half of Romania's oil assets were German-owned by 1914, and Deutsche Bank was in addition a major distributor of oil throughout Europe (McKay, 1970).

Cosmopolitan financiers

Colonial advantage gave rise to a prominent strand of overseas banking, but it is apparent, too, that the business of international finance dissolved national identities and loyalties. Both local and expatriate businessmen founded the National Bank of India. The cosmopolitan Sassoons had shares and board representation in the Eastern Bank (founded in London in 1909), as did the Société Générale of Paris and the Banque d'Outremer. The Imperial Ottoman Bank was officially Anglo-French, with board meetings in London and Paris, and its management in Constantinople. While the officers of the Hongkong Bank were predominantly British, its founders included German, US and Indian firms. Colonial rivalries inevitably affected the Hongkong Bank and the Imperial Bank of Persia, but, as commercial organizations, with cosmopolitan interests, they sought to keep their distance.

When it became involved in the Baghdad Railway, and found itself in the middle of diplomatic power play, Deutsche Bank sought to involve British and French investors. At one point, it tried to sell its shareholding to the Russian government. Although a good means of exit for the bank, the threat of Russian involvement would probably have angered Britain even more than the German connection.

Within Europe, banks showed a preference for consortia that spread commercial risks, maximized the capital available, and allowed access to cross-border and local networks, both commercial and political. French investment in overseas banks grew tenfold between 1891 and 1914, much of it establishing minority interests rather than full control. Partly motivated by a desire to exclude British influence in eastern Europe, Russia and the Ottoman Empire, the French government encouraged cooperation with German and other banks. Paribas formed a long-standing alliance with Deutsche Bank and Wiener Bankverein. The Banque de l'Union Parisienne (BUP) was itself a *haute banque* consortium, which gave birth to the Banque Commerciale Roumaine in 1906, in cooperation with the Anglo-Austrian Bank, Wiener Bankverein and the Trieste-based Greco-Romanian Economos. France's Société Générale worked with the Austrian Länderbank and the Anglo-Austrian Bank to do business in south-east Europe and the Ottoman Empire. In 1910, in partnership with the Länderbank, it bought the Ungarische Escompte und Wechslerbank. On the other hand, Paribas founded the Banque de Bulgarie by itself in 1906, and Société Générale and BUP bought out the Banque Balkanique by 1910.

These investments hinted at a change of approach amongst French banks: in place of agencies offering credit to governments, they began to establish branches with local roots and contacts to develop a variety of business routes. Before 1914, however, the foreign penetration of domestic banking in Britain, Europe or the USA remained small in scale or nonexistent. French, Belgian, German and Swiss firms frequently participated in the international financial holding companies that built utilities and transport systems throughout Europe and Latin America (of which DUEG was one example). On other hand, while German banks were motivated to finance engineering contracts and export orders abroad in the interests of German companies, critics accused French bankers of being like their British counterparts, looking only to the deal's profit potential.

To fulfil their role of international financers, banks needed a presence in the world's leading centres of capital. Money raised in London funded domestic and foreign ventures all over the world. Leading US houses – J. P. Morgan, Lazard, and Speyer – had to be in Europe, all of them locating in London and Paris, if they wanted to attract foreign money and market bonds. From 1870, to assist its business in Turkey and Egypt, Crédit Lyonnais had a London office; its lead was followed by Deutsche Bank (1873), Dresdner (1895), Disconto-Gesellschaft (1899), and numerous others. In some instances, correspondent relations between banks became ill suited to changing commercial needs. As its interests in the silk trade grew, in 1881 the Hongkong Bank replaced Crédit Lyonnais as its representative, setting up its own Lyon office. By establishing itself in Paris, in 1895, the London and River Plate Bank no longer needed the services of the French Rothschild family. Two British domestic banks – Lloyds, and London County & Westminister – were drawn to Paris between 1911 and 1913. The Hongkong, the London and Brazilian, the Standard Bank of South Africa, and the British Bank of West Africa were amongst the eleven British firms to be found in New York by 1913, and there was a total of five British banks in Hamburg, a shipping and financial centre (Jones, 1990; Cassis, 2006; Cameron and Bovykin, 1991).

Within finance and services, the insurance industry demonstrated a significant level of international activity, mostly involving the appointment of overseas agents, but supplying instances of true FDI through branches or affiliates abroad. British companies led the way: Royal Insurance and the Liverpool and London set up New York branches, in 1851, and British, German and Canadian firms established themselves more fully in the USA after the Civil War. By 1914, Royal Insurance was operating in Britain, its colonies (notably Canada), Belgium, Denmark, France, Holland, and Spain, and Phoenix Insurance, too, had a worldwide network of businesses. New York Life – in Canada, England, France, Germany, Scotland, Belgium, Russia, Ireland, Switzerland, Italy and Austria – could match British firms, and the other big US life companies, Equitable and Mutual, were substantial international players. We know that there were Asian enterprises: Tokio Marine Insurance and Yang-tze carried out international transactions in marine insurance. There were, furthermore, the Bulgarian National Insurance Company, with a New York branch, and the First Bulgarian Insurance Company, which sold policies in England, Germany, Belgium, France, the Netherlands, Spain, Greece, and Turkey.

The arrival of the steamship and the telegraph, and the expansion of trade generally developed the market for marine, fire and reinsurance business, although life policies, in part because of regulations, tended to remain domestic. The Employers' Liability Assurance Corporation, founded in London, and Zurich General Accident and Liability Company Ltd catered to casualty cover. The Allianz Insurance Company, from 1890, embarked on international business in France, Switzerland, Belgium, and the USA. As in the cases of the Aachen and Munich Fire Insurance Company, and the Prussian National Insurance Company, Allianz was highly international, and, by the time of the First World War, some 14 German firms had sold 2 million policies in the USA. One estimate, for 1901, states that 90 per cent of all life insurance in China was provided by New York companies; some two thirds of Spain's life cover, in 1912, was in foreign hands; German firms provided, by 1914, nearly 50 per cent of life cover in Switzerland; a total of 30 firms, predominantly British, took one third of Argentina's insurance premiums in 1914, mainly from the fire and marine sector; and in Uruguay by 1911, foreign firms accounted for two thirds of all fire insurance (Borscheid and Haueter, 2012; Wilkins, 2009; Borscheid and Pearson, 2007; Pearson, 2010; Wilkins, 1970; Wilkins, 1986a; Wilkins, 1988; Wilkins, 1993).

Japan's industrialization and international business

Commander Matthew Perry became famous because the US government sent him to Japan, in 1852 and 1854, to force the opening of the country to trade. A series of 'unequal' treaties were signed in 1858, and international trading firms were quick to respond to the prospects. William Keswick of Jardine Matheson arrived in Yokohama almost as soon as the treaties were ratified, followed by the Comptoir d'Escompte de Paris (1867), the Hongkong Bank and the Oriental Bank(1870), the Deutsch-Asiatische Bank (1905), and the Banque Franco-Japonaise, a joint venture (1912). As a result of his visit, in 1859 Keswick sent a 21-year-old employee, Thomas Blake Glover, to Nagasaki. In 1861, he founded his own firm, Glover & Co., which specialized in exporting

students and people of connection, and in importing the weapons that
the local rulers of Japan's south-west provinces needed to depose the
shogun and restore the Meiji emperor.

With the cooperation of Jardine Matheson, Glover smuggled the
'Choshu Five' out of Japan in 1863, and, in Britain, they were assisted
by James Matheson, the leading partner of the trading firm. At the
time, Japanese citizens were not allowed to visit foreign countries, but
the travellers were determined to go to Britain to be educated and to
work. They wanted to modernize and arm their part of south-western
Japan, ruled by the Choshu clan, in order to resist the rule of the Tokugawa shogun. Amongst the five were future cabinet ministers, and Ito
Hirobumi, four times Japanese prime minister between 1885 and 1901,
who remained Glover's lifelong friend. Another was Yamao Yozo,
who went to Anderson's College (now the University of Strathclyde),
where he studied with the engineer Henry Dyer. Hirobumi returned
to Britain as part of the worldwide Iwakura Mission, in 1871–3, and
asked Dyer to be the new principal of the Imperial College of Engineering in Tokyo. Yamao, as the minister of public works, had supervision
of the college (he is additionally credited with introducing the tune of
'Auld Lang Syne' to Japan where, as 'The Light of the Fireflies', it is
sung at high school graduations). Dyer left Japan in 1882, and helped
form the tireless pro-Japanese lobby rife amongst the business classes
and informed opinion of Scotland (Miyoshi, 2004). He saw Japan as
the 'Britain of the East', arguing that his country should follow Japan
'for a truly national spirit for the achievement of great ends' (Dyer,
1904).

Alongside trading in food and commodities, Glover made a fortune selling armaments to the Choshu and Satsuma clans, and also
arranged for fifteen officials from Satsuma to visit Britain in 1865.
The two clans, traditional enemies, finally joined forces and played a
vital role in the Meiji Restoration in 1868. Glover was active, too,
in bringing machinery and engineers to Japan, and undertook a role
in many commercial projects, from docks, shipbuilding, coal mining
and railways to lighthouses. They were not all successful, and Glover
was bankrupt by 1870. He found other openings, and in 1877 the Mitsubishi company (one of Japan's newest but fastest-expanding zaibatsu
conglomerates) restored his fortunes when they made him their consultant. Glover received the 2nd Order of the Rising Sun, unprecedented
for a foreigner, and died in Japan in 1911.[49]

In reforming its economy and staving off colonization, the first aim of the Japanese government was not industrialization but to take control of its trade. Foreign trading firms and shipping lines oversaw some nine tenths of its external trade by the 1880s. As well as taking away Japan's right to set its own tariffs, the five 'unequal' Ansei Treaties of 1858, signed with the USA, Britain, the Netherlands, Russia and France, forced the opening of key ports. At these designated locations, Japanese merchants had to deal with foreign trading firms, which maintained their grip on this trade through their international shipping line contacts, insurance facilities, and access to finance. W. R. Adamson & Company, in the early 1860s, was reputedly the first British merchant house to enter Japan, opening in Yokohama, and becoming Adamson, Bell, in 1867. The first firm to export Japanese rice was the USA's Walsh, Hall & Co., in 1872, and E. Fischer & Co. organized much of the coal trade out of Yokohama (fuel for American ships had been one motive for Perry's gunboat diplomacy with Japan) (Kawabe, 1989).

Amongst the specialists in trade with Japan was Marcus Samuel & Co., importing machinery, and especially textile looms, and exporting boxes made of sea shells, ornaments, rice, coal, and anything else that might make a profit. It created Samuel Samuel and Company – it was established by Marcus's brother – which operated originally from Yokohama and then from Kobe. Later, M. Samuel distributed Russian and Dutch East Indies oil throughout Asia (Henriques). From 1875, the Japanese government sought to establish its own trading firms, assisting them through the founding of the Tokyo Marine Insurance Company (in 1879), and the Yokohama Specie Bank (1880), which provided exchange and credit. One consequence was the international boycotting in 1881 of the government's silk office, which supervised the country's most important export at that time, and similar threats held back Japan's commercial development. Growing economic strength and victory in the Sino-Japanese War of 1894–5 empowered Japan to fix its own tariffs and to abolish the port settlements, in 1899. By 1911, the country directly controlled 51 per cent of its exports and 64 per cent of its imports.

Leading general trading companies (*sogo shosha*) were often arms of business conglomerates (zaibatsu), and government sponsorship and contacts had been and continued to be vital to their progress. As general trading companies, they developed and provided the overseas expertise and knowledge much of Japanese business lacked, and, by dealing in many products and acting for many clients, their scale became one source of advantage against international competitors that remained at this point more experienced and better connected (Yonekawa and Yoshihara, 1987; Fruin, 1992; Yonekawa, 1990). The size and diversity of the *sogo shosha* have been seen as unique, but (as we have seen) many British and European traders operated as multiproduct global enterprises by 1914. What did distinguish the *sogo shosha* was their importance to the Japanese economy and its development, while their British and European counterparts were only formally registered in their home economies, while largely conducting business elsewhere. Another distinguishing factor was the existence of management teams, with firms investing in their recruitment and skills. While a managerial cadre coordinated and directed transborder business deals, within a single formal enterprise, British trading companies oversaw a loosely knit network of agency houses, partnerships and cross-shareholdings (Yonekawa and Yoshihara, 1987; Yamazaki, 1987). The *sogo shosha* as a result annually hired graduates, often from specialized commercial schools (Yonekawa, 1990).

Mitsui Bussan, established in 1876, was descended from one of Japan's most ancient merchant houses. A former finance minister, just before his return to politics Inoue Kaorun had asked Masuda Takeshi to establish the trading company. Masuda had recently founded Senshu Kaisha, and Inoue was president of its most important customer, Okada & Company, both cotton producer and Japan's largest manufacturer. Senshu was merged into Mitsui Bussan. The new *sogo shosha* was closely associated with the Japanese government, and in a position to respond entrepreneurially to national development aims. Inoue had been one of the 'Choshu Five', and became one of Japan's most important politicians and modernizers.

From 1876 onwards, Mitsui Bussan challenged Walsh, Hall for the rice trade, although, to achieve its aims, it had to rely on the cooperation of another set of foreign traders, E. B. Watson (Kawabe, 1987). In Japan, it acted as representatives for Carnegie Steel, the American Locomotive Company, and the world leader in cotton textile machinery, Britain's Platt Brothers (a contract secured through the good offices of the Okada cotton company). As well as gradually extending Japanese control over the export trade, the *sogo shosha* obtained the raw materials and machinery needed to industrialize. Mitsui Bussan accounted, by 1912, for 80 per cent of the nation's machinery imports.

In this period, it was as a prominent agent for the state that Mitsui Bussan was able to build its organization, providing woollens to the army, and collecting and selling the land tax rice on behalf of the finance ministry. In 1878, using its experience chartering ships for the government, it founded its own shipping department, and, having exported state-owned coal, it bought the privatized and very profitable Miike Mine in 1888. It supplied fuel coal to Norddeutscher Lloyd, P&O, and Messageries Maritimes, which was expanding in the region, catapulted by France's colonization of South East Asia, and building, in Saigon, its second most important port. Mitsui Bussan then bought out Japan's silk production in 1893, as the government privatized the companies it had founded in order to initiate industrialization and national renewal. Since the USA was its largest market, Mitsui Bussan founded a New York office in 1896. It did so in cooperation with traders R. W. Irwin, who had already helped them to establish a London cotton agency (in 1873) (Kawabe, 1987).

In extending contacts and markets overseas, therefore, the firm relied on links with established foreign partners. It bought raw cotton from India, and owned, from 1893, a Bombay office, where it cooperated with Ralli Brothers. Between 1893 and 1908, Mitsui Bussan established offices throughout Asia (especially China), Siberia, the USA, Australia and Germany. Its growth was assisted by its close relations with Mitsui Bank, another part of its parent conglomerate, as well as the Yokohama Specie Bank. Mitsui Bussan, like other Japanese traders, was instrumental to the economic development and integration of the colonies, through their investing in manufacturing and natural resources.

The Sino-Japanese War in 1894–5 decided the control and future of Korea, its iron and coal deposits, and other commercial assets. China lost the battle, formally acknowledged the independence of Korea, and ceded the Liaodong Peninsula, Taiwan, and the Penghu Islands. Mitsui Bussan emerged as a major investor in Taiwanese sugar plantations and in the island's sugar exports. Taiwan was during this period the principal destination for Japanese overseas investment, and the joint-stock companies founded to grow sugar there dominated, as measured by capital, the list of Japan's largest businesses (Suzuki, 1990). Diplomatic complications followed from the exacting terms that the Japanese imposed on China, however. Concerned Western powers – Russia, Germany and France – forced Japan to relinquish some of its gains.

The Liaodong Peninsula was transferred to Russia, which proceeded to construct its Port Arthur naval base, adjacent to Dalian. Russia built, in addition, a spur of the Trans-Siberian Railway, south-east from Chita, linking, via Harbin, with Dalian and Port Arthur (Lushun), and creating in addition a short cut to Vladivostock (the line would be called the Chinese Eastern Railway). Nearly 200,000 troops and mining and forestry concessions across the Korean border heightened Japanese anxiety about further Russian expansionism. A confident czarist government refused to reach an agreement, and, after Ito Hirobumi had failed to secure guarantees over Korea, the result was the Russo-Japanese War of 1904–5 and the adamant defeat of Russia by the Japanese. Interestingly, during the fighting, Dodwell & Company acted as the Japanese government's exclusive agent for chartering ships, and, in the years that followed, increased its trade in Japanese commodities, such as coal, porcelain, and straw-braid manufactures, to Asia.[50]

In the peace treaty that followed the 1904–5 war, most of Manchuria was demilitarized and returned to China, but Japan obtained the lease on the Liaodong Peninsula (with Dalian and Port Arthur) and on the Russian-built railway in southern Manchuria, with its access to the region's economic resources. It acquired, too, the southern part of Sakhalin island. Korea was turned into a Japanese protectorate in 1905, and into a full colony in 1910. Japan established the South Manchuria Railway, in 1906 and its viability depended heavily at the time on the trade in soy beans and products. Mitsui Bussan took a lead in developing the South Manchuria territory, and it formed the Sentai Oil Mills Ltd, as a joint venture in Dalian, for the production of soya cakes (Patrikeff and Shukman, 2007).

In China, Mitsui Bussan was established in Asia's commercial hub of Shanghai, where it owned cotton and flour mills, and it merged its textile interests into Shanghai Cotton Manufacturing Ltd. During years in which British and European traders were losing control over their trade in inland China, Mitsui Bussan replaced its network of independent agents with its own directly owned distribution organization, run by Japanese managers who spoke Chinese (Yonekawa, 1990). By 1910, the trading company moved about half of Japan's fabric exports, while being pivotal in importing raw cotton and textile machinery. By 1914, with its thirty overseas branches, it was responsible for some 20 per cent of the country's trade.

Mitsui Bussan's great competitor was Yataro Iwasaki. Through his contacts with government ministers, especially Shigenobu Okuma, Inoue's great rival, and his purchase of state-owned businesses, he built a zaibatsu. He began in 1870 with the shipping company Tsukumo Shokai, which he renamed Mitsubishi three years later. Iwasaki's business aim was to make his trading business competitive with foreign lines, and he was associated with Japan's largest shipping business, the Nippon Yusen Company (NYK), founded under government sponsorship in 1885. Mitsubishi Shoji was, later, formally established as a separate *sogo shosha* (in 1918).[51] Nihon Menka (Nichimen) was in origin a cotton spinner that engaged in active third-country trading, setting up offices in Liverpool, London, Milan and Bremen.[52] Most merchants began by dealing in what became Japan's most important export, cotton, before becoming general traders, although there were exceptions like Marubeni (which started in woollens and rayon), Ataka and Co. (steel, chemicals and machinery, as well as textiles), and Maruzen (originating in 1869 as an importer of books and fancy goods) (Allen and Donnithorne, 1957; Beasley, 1972; Beasley, 1963; Gordon, 2003).

Canals, railways and sovereignty

Two canals were the most famous engineering projects of their time; additionally they had important geopolitical implications, and they were both foreign-owned multinationals. Said Pasha, the ruler of Egypt, had awarded the concession to build the Suez Canal in 1854, with a ninety-nine-year operating lease, to Ferdinand de Lesseps. French support for his rule had been a factor, as had been the personal relations de Lesseps and his family had forged as diplomats in Egypt. The original concept was for an internationally owned company, but the Suez Canal Company, formed in 1858, came to be owned by French investors and Said Pasha. Very wary of the implications for trade with India, Britain had opposed the project, condemning successfully the use of forced labour, and stoking local rebellion. Britain ensured, too, that the formal if not the actual ruler of Egypt, the Ottoman Sultan, withheld his agreement to the waterway's construction.

The Suez Canal was completed in 1869, but revenues at first caused disappointment. Said Pasha, now the Khedive, had his own financial difficulties, owing vast sums to European banks, and British and French supervisory appointees in his cabinet were in effect in charge of his government. He sold his shares to the British government in 1875, without the formal approval of its parliament but with the assistance of financing from the Rothschilds. Britain moved from opposition to the canal to, in a short time, majority owners. When nationalists gained the upper hand, in 1882, Britain and France intervened militarily, and created a British protectorate over Egypt. Three British representatives sat on the Suez Canal Company board, and they were joined, in 1884, by seven shipping merchants and businessmen.[53] The main artery of the Egyptian economy was a foreign-owned multinational, and Britain and France retained formal sovereign control of the Suez Canal Zone (Hall, 2012; Barnett Smith, 1893).

By the time Egypt dealt with the Suez Canal and its fateful consequences for its history, de Lesseps had transferred his energies elsewhere. He assumed presidency of the front organization established by Leopold II of Belgium to colonize the Congo, and helped de Brazza found what would become the French Congo colony. By 1879, he had raised the money to create the Panama Canal Company, following the route of the foreign-owned Panama Railway. By no coincidence, he took on leadership of the Franco-American Union, which presented the Statue of Liberty to the USA in 1886. This time, with the Panama project, he failed, with maybe 23,000 dying in the attempt. The business was liquidated in 1889. There was predictable anger amongst investors back home. One repercussion was a trial for bribery, in 1892, involving 150 French parliamentary deputies who had voted financial support for the Panama Canal (Piquet, 2004).

After the Spanish war of 1898, the USA expanded its navy, and, having taken supervision of territories as far away as the Philippines, it sought to establish its influence across the Pacific. There was a deeply ingrained resolve to exclude European influence in the Americas, and a determination to protect regional economic interests. In 1902, the USA took up the cause of a strategic waterway across the Central American isthmus, and in 1903, under the presidency of Theodore Roosevelt, it helped Panama achieve its independence from Colombia (Kinzer, 2006). The USA bought out France's Panama Company in 1904, completing the waterway by 1914 with the assistance of its Army Corps of Engineers (McCullough, 1977; Wilkins, 1970).

Foreign capital fed the nineteenth-century railway boom, although most of the investment was portfolio in nature, not FDI. Railways were a central component of economic development, and they required large amounts of capital, not all of it available locally. In Europe, generally speaking, the state had taken the lead in funding and developing new technology, although in the early stages there was sustained demand for British consulting engineers, and most prominently Thomas Brassey. The Russian and Indian systems – government-built – were part-financed by bonds issued overseas, and US lines – privately constructed – were the largest cause of inward investment to the country between 1875 and 1914 (Wilkins, 1989).

The Trans-Siberian Railway was a military and political project, less a commercial venture, stamping Russian authority on the recently acquired territories of the Far East, and encouraging 'russification' through migration. It did, as we have seen, act as a main cause of war with Japan, which ended in the unexpected and ignominious defeat of Russia. In Africa, railway building had everything to do with the exploitation of commodities and exports. It depended mostly on the initiative of colonial governments, or, in some cases, their chartered company surrogates, although private enterprises, local and multinational, were active too in British-controlled territories.

A Cape-to-Cairo railway was Cecil Rhodes's imperialist vision, as was linking the interior of Africa with the coast. He worked in tandem with the Cape Government, which, under his urging, in 1885, laid a railway to Kimberley and Rhodes's mining operations. Within four days of receiving its charter, in 1889, the British South Africa Company began building a line north from Kimberley, completing the route to Vryburg, in Bechuanaland, in just over a year. The Cape Government Railway then purchased the new line, which was extended, in 1897, to Bulawayo. Rhodes was chairman of the Bechuanaland Railway, established in London in 1893 and rebranded, in 1899, as the Rhodesia Railway. He formed, in addition, the Beira Railway in London, in 1892, running through Portuguese East Africa to Salisbury, in Mashonaland (Salisbury was renamed Harare by an independent Zimbabwe). A mix of financial and construction problems led to its refounding as the Beira Junction Railway in 1895, combining BSAC and Portuguese investment. A connecting line to Umtali (Mutari) on the border with the Portuguese was finally completed in 1898, and its operation was contracted out to its constructors, Pauling & Company.[54]

As well as being associates of Rhodes, George Pauling, his brother Harry and cousin Harold were pivotal and energetic figures in the

building, operating and even financing of railways in southern and
central Africa. Their company put down and ran the Mashonaland
Railway, founded, in 1897, to connect Umtali and Salisbury in 1899.
They took the permanent way north from Bulawayo to the Wankie
coalfield and on to the Victoria Falls by 1904. As the link with the
government-constructed southern Sudan and Egyptian railway was
never made, however, the imperialist Cape-to-Cairo railway envisaged
by Rhodes and the Paulings never materialized. With the discovery
of copper in Katanga, in the Congo, the Belgian colonial government
depended on the Pauling company to build its railway network to
the coast, establishing a company town with brick houses, school and
hospital around its hub, Huambo. Since copper had also been located
in adjacent Bwana Mkumba (in north-western Rhodesia, and later
Zambia), the Rhodesia Railway, in league with the BSAC and the
Paulings, extended its network, and joined with the Chemins de Fer
Katanga at Elizabethville.[55] The uncovering of the Copper Belt would
transform central Africa, its economy and society over the following
decades (Wolmar, 2009; Raphael, 1973).

In Latin America, FDI was a common driver of railway building,
although generally ownership gradually passed to local interests. A US
company was responsible for the Panama Railway Company, founded
in 1851 and completed in 1855. Its project could claim to be the first
large-scale US overseas investment, but the completion of the transcontinental railway back at home in the USA, in 1869, undermined much
of its commercial rationale (Gabel and Bruner, 2003). In the case of
Cuba, the fall in sugar prices hurt the local planters who had built the
island's railways, and British and US investors bought up much of the
network. Venezuela needed both infrastructure and foreign engineering expertise, and, in 1883, President Guzmán used US investors to
build the railway from Guaira to Caracas (Ewell, 1999).

A shortage of cash and a conflict with Chile halted railway building
in Peru, and the British-controlled Peruvian Corporation took over
the country's rail system, in 1890. British finance and multinationals
greatly influenced Argentina. William Bragge won the first railway
concession in Argentina, and completed the line from Buenos Aires to
Flores in 1857, but, within three years, through financial difficulties, it
passed to the Buenos Aires government (the system would become the
Buenos Aires Western Railway). British capital owned and operated the
Central Argentine Railway, established in 1870, and the Buenos Aires

& Pacific, opened in 1888 (Lewis, 1983; Regalsky, 1989; Wolmar, 2009). By 1914, out of a total of 142 British-owned overseas railways, 75 were located in Latin America (G. Jones, 1996; Williamson, 1992).

Deutsche Bank's most spectacular and controversial overseas venture was the Baghdad Railway. The Sultan, Abdul Hamid II, wanted to develop Anatolia through creation of a railway link with Constantinople, but the further extension of the line was more a political gesture, a means of stamping authority on distant territories. With the Banque Impériale Ottomane administering his government's finances and debts, the Sultan did not want to pass more power to French financiers, and looked for alternative sources. Once it had secured its own government's diplomatic support, in 1888, Deutsche Bank agreed to head a German consortium to build the Anatolian Railway. The company asked British banks to participate, hoping to attract international support for railways within the Ottoman empire, but they declined.

After Bismarck had been dismissed as chancellor in 1890, the Kaiser was increasingly attracted by the possibilities of extending German influence through a Baghdad railway, and pushed a hesitant Deutsche Bank into leading the project. A concession was given to the Baghdad Railway Company in 1903, and involved Deutsche Bank (40 per cent of the shares), the Banque Impériale Ottomane (with 30 per cent), and the Anatolian Railway Company (10 per cent), in partnership with Wiener Bankverein, Credit Suisse, Banca Commerciale Italiana and several Turkish banks. Plans for a line from Baghdad to Basra threatened a British-owned river navigation company, and Britain's interests generally in the Middle East and India. Deutsche Bank was willing to trade the concession granted by the Constantinople government in the Mosul oilfield, if the British would agree to the Basra route, yet no agreement emerged (Gall et al., 1995).

China, fearful of foreign influence, had once opposed the building of all railways within its borders. The first line, organized by Jardine Fleming, was built between Shanghai and the port of Woosun in 1876, but without official permission. British pressure forced the Chinese government to buy the line before it could enforce its sovereign decision to dismantle it. A policy from 1881 that relied on domestic capital – or on overseas Chinese finance, which was not forthcoming – meant that railway building proceeded at a very slow pace. The complex created around the Kaiping coal mines accounted for a larger portion of the national railway system, and so much of the country remained untouched by the transport technology that defined the era. Military defeat by the Japanese, in 1896, sparked a national reappraisal, and railways came to be a principal instrument of the modernization China sought in order to resist foreign incursions.

But success – paradoxically – rested on overseas capital and participation. China immediately signed a treaty of alliance with Russia. The overseas Russo-Chinese Bank (founded in St Petersburg in 1895) was busy issuing Chinese government bonds to fund the indemnity imposed after its military defeat by Japan, and it, in turn, relied on raising French capital. By taking a minority interest in the Russo-Chinese Bank, China's government had the links it needed to fund the Chinese Eastern Railway, work beginning in 1897. The CER was Russian-owned and -built, but had China's consent to enter its territory, the project being completed in 1903. The fortunes of the railway, of course, were inextricably tied to disputes between Russia, China and Japan over the sovereignty of Manchuria. The Russo-Chinese Bank evolved into China's second-largest bank, and, through a merger, became the Russo-Asiatic Bank (in 1910).

China's agreement with Russia was a pointer for the international business community, and, out of the scramble for Chinese concessions that followed, 29 lines were to be built by 1914 (with a further 45 from 1915 to 1936). The Hongkong Bank cooperated closely with Jardine Matheson in obtaining railway concessions, and the Banque de l'Indochine, Banque Belge pour l'Etranger, Banque Sino-Belge (from 1910, the Société Financière et Industrielle Belge en Chine), the Deutsch-Asiatische, and the International Banking Corporation (IBC, established in 1901 and fully acquired by one partner, the National City Bank of New York, in 1915) were all involved. They employed British or European construction firms, and projects commonly supported trade around controlled territories, such as British-ruled Kowloon-Canton, or Germany's Tsingtao. Foreign banks soon began to cooperate and allocate the deals, in order to secure better terms from the Chinese government (Lin, 1937).

China's emperor was deposed in 1911, and the republican administration that replaced him asked Deutsch-Asiatische, Hongkong, Banque de l'Indochine, the Russo-Asiatic, and Yokohama Specie to provide a Reorganization Loan, in 1913, but the US government ensured that the IBC did not participate. The new Chinese government was committed to modernization, and, to that end, sought to establish an industrial bank. It was unable to form a broadly based international consortium – there were too few takers – but the Banque Industrielle de Chine was registered in France in 1913. Paris investors formally put up two thirds of the capital, but actually loaned China the funds it used to purchase the remaining one third. The French government actively encouraged the arrangement, hoping to extend its diplomatic influence in a reformed China. The Banque de l'Indochine had decided not to participate in the Banque Industrielle de Chine, and, as the venture over the next decade produced more financial scandal than profits, it took the right commercial decision (Patrikeff and Shukman, 2007).

Engineering, construction and utilities

Railways had stimulated the demand for international engineering services. Having participated in the laying of Britain's railway network in the 1840s, Brassey and Peto & Betts had accepted operational and support contracts in continental Europe, India, Canada, and Latin America (Linder, 1994). Britain had been a pioneer of gas lighting, too: the Imperial Continental Gas Company, indeed, was an historical prodigy, formed, in 1825, as a free-standing firm in Ghent, and overseeing, by 1900, ten municipal concerns, including that of Berlin. British companies, notably the Eastern Telegraph Company, began laying submarine cables from the 1850s onwards. As a result, Britain became a global communications hub for transatlantic telegraph traffic, and its firms came to control routes throughout Asia and Latin America. The Mexican Cable (later Telegraph) Company (established in 1878), and the Central and South American Cable (later Telegraph) Company (1879) were US-owned, and the American Union Telegraph Co. set up business in Canada (1879) (Wilkins, 1970). Other prominent engineers were Britain's Lucas & Aird (water and gas works in Europe, India, Argentina, Brazil, and the Aswan Dam on the River Nile), Germany's Holzman (railways in Mesopotamia and German East Africa, and harbours in Morocco and Russia), and Denmark's Christiani & Nielsen (bridges and concrete structures in Scandinavia, Russia, Germany and Britain) (Linder, 1994). French firms, which had gained their expertise building harbours and tunnels in Europe and the wider Mediterranean area, arrived in Latin America in the 1900s, engaged in railways, sanitation and ports (Barjot, 1988).

Internationally, Pearson & Son, from Britain, first made its mark in New York, and forged close links with the government of Porfirio Díaz in Mexico, in power for most of the years between 1876 and 1911. It drained the Valley of Mexico, reconstructed the Tehuantepec Railroad, and established electricity supply for a number of important cities. The company used its experience in Mexico to run utilities in Chile, and notably built Santiago's hydroelectric capacity. One problem was the almost inevitable tension between the foreign ownership and management of public utilities, and public pressure for local control and regulation. Throughout Latin America, political uncertainties and a downward pressure on prices challenged the profitability and security of investments in utilities. Over time, multinationals tended to divest.

By the eve of the First World War, British-owned gas, electricity, tramway, bus, and dockyard companies were located in Argentina, Brazil, Chile, Uruguay and other parts of Latin America (Rippy, 1959; Finch, 1985). Canadian multinationals were also substantial players in the region. The Montreal-based Mexican Light and Power Company organized, from 1902, hydroelectricity and tramways in Mexico City. The São Paulo Tramway, Light and Power Company (formed 1898) and the Rio de Janeiro Tramway, Light and Power Company (1904) were Canadian free-standing companies, which managed, in addition, gas and telephone services in these cities. In 1912, the Toronto-based Brazilian Traction, Light and Power Company Limited acquired both businesses. The Canadian utility multinationals were truly international: to support operations in Mexico and Brazil, financiers in Canada raised funds in London and other European cities, the engineering expertise was American, and the purchasing function was located in New York (McDowell, 1988; Armstrong and Nelles, 1988). The Belgian electrical group Empain in 1904 created the Compagnie Générale de Chemins de Fer et Électricité, which subsequently acquired electrical and tramway assets across Europe and Russia.

The telephone was a US invention, and the country contained two thirds of all the world's telephones by 1912. Boosted by this home advantage, Edison founded the Edison Telephone Company, in London, in 1880, later merged with American Bell into the United Telephone Company. American Bell and Edison invested in municipal companies throughout Europe, although they often took minority interests only, with governments and cities leaning towards monopoly or licence arrangements. Bell Company of Canada, furthermore, was the industry leader in Canada (Wilkins, 1970). The honour for having the highest concentration of telephones, however, belonged to Stockholm (19 instruments per 1,000 inhabitants, next to London's 2.8). Stockholms Allmana Telefon (SAT) had the technical expertise to run telephone systems in Warsaw and Moscow, and, with its competitor Ericsson, in more distant Mexico (Lundstrom, 1986b). Marconi, founded by an Italian who had emigrated to Britain, specialized in radio communication: it established a US affiliate in 1899, and later began transatlantic transmissions (Wilkins, 1989).

From the closing decades of the nineteenth century, multinationals were at the centre of worldwide electrification. They had a complicated and evolving relationship with governments and municipalities, as the granters of concession rights, and as bodies accountable to the public for the regulation of a life-transforming service. In many cases, portfolio investment met requirements, but developing countries would hire contracting engineers to construct or run systems of generation or transmission. In other cases, multinationals could use the freestanding-company form to raise money for a specific business overseas, and transfer the technical and management skills. Ownership and financing were cross-border, whereas operations were not. There are, during these years, therefore, no known examples of a power company transforming itself into a multinational (Hausman, Hertner and Wilkins, 2008).

The regulatory framework for electricity generation in Britain proved a major failure, and multiple suppliers created low levels of standardization amongst the manufacturers of electrical goods, which consequently lacked efficiencies of scale, financial resources, and research expertise. It was German companies that took the lead in electrical engineering projects in Europe and Latin America. A policy of *Unternehmergeschäft* – in this case, financing construction contracts and overseas utility concessions, in return for equipment orders – meant the creation of a worldwide market for German electrical plant and products (Schroter and Jones, 1993; Lanthier, 1989). British companies accused their rivals of unfair practices: the giant concerns of AEG and Siemens were associated with German banks, which could provide foreign governments and municipalities with the loans that financed their projects. Siemens, indeed, had the surety of Deutsche Bank as its house bank, and the two firms shared board membership. It was doubly irksome when German companies obtained funds for their overseas schemes from the City of London's international markets. The Victoria Falls & Transvaal Power Co. Ltd, although registered in Britain and operating in British-controlled territory, was German-owned, and a symbol of national failure.

AEG and Siemens formed *Finanzierungsgesellschäften* with banks to float and sell equities in utilities, and these financial holding companies were typically headquartered in Belgium or Switzerland, as a means of masking German control. AEG promoted, for example, the Società per lo Sviluppo delle Impresse Elettriche in Italia. Deutsche Bank and AEG had a controlling share in Compañía Barcelonesa de Electricidad. For Latin America, AEG and Deutsche Bank had Deutsch Überseeische-Elektrizitäts Gesellschaft (DUEG). They both owned 16 per cent of the shares, and the rest was divided between eight German and Swiss banks. This multinational began with the construction of power stations, lighting and tramways in Buenos Aires, and established a strong presence in Argentina, Uruguay and Chile. With $73m of assets overseas, it was the biggest example of German FDI by 1914.

Financing could be cosmopolitan: Deutsche Bank, AEG and Credit Suisse were the major shareholders in the Gesellschaft für Elektrische Unternehmungen (Elektrobank), founded in 1895, in Zurich, and Siemens was a minority participant in Schweizerische Gesellschaft für Elektrische Industrie (or Indelec, established in 1896) (Hausman, Hertner and Wilkins, 2008; Cameron and Bovykin, 1991). The French engineers Schneider saw the benefits of extensive, Europe-wide finance, and, with the Banque de Paris et des Pays-Bas, the Union Financière de Genève, and the Union Bank of Switzerland, formed the Société Franco-Suisse (Jones, 1990). The Société Générale des Chemins de Fer Economiques, owned by a consortium of Belgian banks, possessed tramways worldwide by 1914, and we know that a total of 23 Belgian companies were running tramway systems in Russia (McKay, 1970).

The industrialized countries and manufacturing

Early examples of manufacturing FDI concerned companies from small countries locating in nearby larger national markets, but did not prove long-lasting: Swiss cotton firms, in the 1830s, had appeared across the border in southern Germany, taking advantage of evolving customs union arrangements (Schroter, 1993). By 1914, there were major cases in chemicals, pharmaceuticals, electrical equipment, machinery, autos, tyres, branded foods, and cigarettes. Market seeking, often with the added incentive of tariffs and host government pressure, was the major reason for West and North European enterprises investing in each other's national markets, and Britain was the leading venue, as the world's most developed and most globally connected economy.

Firms with advantages in technology, products, or management grew into mass manufacturers, making competitive gains in scale, price and distribution. They were drawn to exploiting their commercial leads abroad, wherever commercial conditions or import restrictions made exports unsuited for growing a large business abroad. Britain, until the last quarter of the nineteenth century, might have claimed primacy in almost every sector of industry, but then fell behind German and US competitors in chemicals, electrical equipment, machinery and autos. By the time of the First World War, the technological advantages of German and US companies in many industries was widely recognized. The origins and successes of manufacturing multinationals reflected the shifting balance of national economic power.

Although artificial dyestuffs had been a British scientific break-through in 1856, it was German firms that spearheaded further research, and, commercially, grabbed the first-mover advantage. They diversified, moreover, into other chemicals and pharmaceuticals. Bayer, in 1865, only two years after its founding, had bought a share of a dye factory in Albany, New York, and established subsidiaries in Russia, France, Belgium and Britain by 1913, with some 1,000 of its 10,000 employees working outside Germany.[56] Badische Anilin und Soda-Fabrik (BASF) and Hoechst joined Bayer's overseas expansion from the 1870s onwards. On the other hand, the preferred strategic inclination of German chemicals companies continued to be exports, not FDI, and the raising of tariff walls largely explained decisions to multinationalize.[57] So, although six factories belonging to five German manufacturers did account for 80 per cent of the Russian market by about 1900, the Hoechst and BASF plants in Liverpool, in free-market Britain, employed only 94 people between them before the First World War.

One figure shows the scale of Germany's domination within a new industry: eight of its companies, including foreign subsidiaries, made

75 per cent of world dyestuffs output at the beginning of the twentieth century (Wilkins, 1989). It is known that Deutsche Gold und Silber Scheideanstaldt (Degussa) produced cyanides, bleaching agents, sodium and chloroform in the USA before 1914 (Wilkins, 1989; Chandler, 1990). E. Merck, a specialist maker of pharmaceuticals, started to develop a site in New Jersey in 1899, beginning the production of morphine, codeine and cocaine four years later; it could be found in France from 1912 (Hertner and Jones, 1986).

Siemens & Halske, at its founding in Berlin from 1847 onwards, focused on equipping and building telegraph systems. The Russian government awarded it a large contract, in 1853, eventually bringing about a communications link stretching from Finland to the Crimea. Siemens & Halske set up its first foreign subsidiary in St Petersburg in 1855, to serve an underdeveloped market with commercial potential. Once it had produced the first deep sea cable, during 1857 the company established an independent, locally registered but associated business in Britain, where it could best exploit its new technology. Despite failing in so many areas of electrical engineering, Britain remained the international leader in the making and laying of cables, and Siemens & Halske was drawn there to take advantages from its opportunities. The contract to construct and operate the Indo-European Telegraph Line – from London to Calcutta – was an early reward for investing in Britain. Siemens & Halske accepted engineering projects abroad, building electrical plant in Beijing, and installing its street lighting and tramways, by 1899. Part of the firm was merged with Schuckert & Company to form Siemens-Schuckert in 1903, founding an associated or subsidiary seeking a global position in power technology. Siemens & Halske owned ten factories in five foreign countries, accounting for one fifth of all its employees, by 1914. The various branches of the Siemens family received titles and honours from the Kaiser, the Czar, and Britain's King-Emperor.[58]

From the time Thomas Edison invented the first commercially practical light bulb, in 1878, Siemens was in dispute over patent rights. Its legal action stalled commercial developments at home, and family relatives at Deutsche Bank blocked the financing of projects based on Edison's technology, including initiatives by the industrialist Emile Rathenau. By 1883, with ownership of the US inventor's patents in France, and having added the German rights, the Compagnie Continentale helped Rathenau form Deutsche Edison Gesellschaft (DEG).

The French firm took two seats on DEG's board, but the German management, who wanted US assistance and know-how, showed a strong and nationalist suspicion of its involvement. Business difficulties in France, in 1887, led to DEG acquiring the Edison patents and assuming what would become the famed trading name of AEG. The new company ensured cooperative relations with its great rival by giving Siemens membership on its board.

AEG – as well as undertaking engineering contracts and utilities through DUEG – bought businesses in Russia and Austria-Hungary, formed a joint venture with Siemens in Russia, and went into partnership with General Electric of America in Italy (Feldenkirchen, 2000; Weiher and Goetzeler, 1984; Hertner and Jones, 1986; G. Jones, 1996). Deutsche Bank, Siemens and AEG created Accumulatoren-Fabrik (AFA) with the maker of industrial and transport accumulators Busch & Muller in 1899. It bought up eleven German battery firms within ten years, and by 1914 it was manufacturing in Austria-Hungary, Spain, Russia, Switzerland, Romania, Sweden and Norway.[59] Mannesmann's breakthroughs in the rolling of steel tubes offered it a competitive advantage, from its founding in 1890, and it acquired a tube mill in Landore, Wales, and an electric steelworks and tube mill in Dalmine, Italy (Wessel, 1997).[60] The auto manufacturer Daimler licensed company promoter and fraudster Harry Lawson, who set up a separate British enterprise in Coventry in 1896. It did, on the other hand, initiate directly owned manufacturing in Austria, in 1902 (Laux, 1992).

A key trio of German mining multinationals supported the demands of industrialization at home: these were Aron Hirsch & Sohn; Sondheimer & Company; and the biggest, Metallgesellschaft, which, founded as a metal trader in 1881, moved into the mining, processing and distribution of copper, lead and zinc. Metallgesellschaft invested in the USA, Mexico and Europe, and its subsidiary, the American Metal Company, was by 1887 involved in coal mining, smelting and refining. In 1912, Metallgesellschaft's Belgian refinery, which processed colonial ore from the Congo, was the largest in Europe. German metal businesses were noted for internationally integrating the mining, smelting, refining, manufacturing and marketing of non-ferrous metals (Däbritz, 1931).[61] By cooperating with each other, they were known, too, for controlling the world prices of lead, zinc, copper and nickel (Jones, 1998). The Rio Tinto Company was established in 1873 to acquire copper mines from the Spanish government, and, within ten years, it controlled a vast infrastructure and complex that supported its core business (Harvey, 1981). Since mining was a capital-intensive enterprise, banks and investment houses were active participants in an expanding international business. By 1905, the London Rothschilds held one third of the Rio Tinto Company's ordinary capital (Wilkins, 1989), and, as we have seen, the Guggenheim banking family, pre-eminently, and, additionally, J. P. Morgan invested extensively in US miners (Bosson and Varon, 1977).

Undoubtedly, many large-scale US manufacturers – especially in machinery, autos, electrical equipment and branded goods – held advantages in technology and management, although the increasing vastness of their home market acted as a distraction, before the First World War, from expansion abroad. We can find early examples of industrial firms testing their fortunes abroad, but the gun maker Colt, in 1853, and the rubber footwear producer J. R. Ford, in 1856, both having invested in Britain, were not durable success stories. As a result, Singer Sewing Machines is usually quoted as the USA's first multinational manufacturer, its subsidiary being in Glasgow, Scotland, from 1867 onwards. What distinguished Singer was a sophisticated marketing strategy. The company had to prove the uses of its domestic sewing machine, then a novelty, to potential customers, and achieve high visibility for its product. Existing distributors could not offer the needed practical and technical advice, and each product was a comparatively expensive consumer durable. Singer accordingly created a dedicated force of door-to-door sellers, set up its own retail outlets, and supplied hire purchase credit. By 1914, the company owned factories in Canada, Austria, Germany and Russia (where it had 4,000 depots and shops, and 27,000 people), and it was responsible for 90 per cent of all sewing machines sold worldwide (Davies, 1976; Carstensen, 1984).

Thomas Edison registered his Edison Illuminating Company in order to commercialize his light bulb in 1878. To avoid conflicting patent claims with fellow inventor Joseph Swan in Britain, he established the joint Edison and Swan United Electric Company in 1883, but the Canadian Edison Electric subsidiary was fully owned. Edison preferred to license his patents in Europe, and to establish collaborative relationships with Compagnie Continentale and, by proxy, DEG. Tariffs and the right to protection under German patent laws made a local factory a necessity, and encouraged FDI. Question marks over the viability of patents in foreign jurisdictions and rival claims, however, made the raising of investment capital problematic, and directed Edison towards licensing and joint ventures with potential rivals. He employed agents throughout the world to market his technology rights, but the collapse of Kendall and Company, in Valparaíso in 1885, unearthed a swindle conducted in his name.

A syndicate reformulated Edison General Electric in 1889, and this business merged with US rival Thomson-Houston to become the General Electric Company in 1892. It established, too, a GEC in Canada, and the Thomson-Houston International Electric Company. It was Charles A. Coffin, from Thomson-Houston, who masterminded GE's growth into a large conglomerate. The new company expanded abroad by taking controlling and minority stakes in foreign companies, mostly through Thomson-Houston International. Compagnie Française Thomson-Houston (CFTH) was formed in 1893, as, in 1894, was British Thomson-Houston (BTH, almost wholly US-owned during its existence). GE preferred fully controlled enterprises in Mexico (founded 1897), South Africa (1898) and Australia (1898). What it initiated was an intricate – and clandestine – set of corporate relationships in the world's electrical industry. Secrecy avoided nationalist protests about a vital modern industry being owned by foreigners, and governments were amongst the industry's most important customers. GE's strategy was based on transferring patents and know-how in return for market-sharing and price agreements.

In 1903, GE had sold to French investors any control and rights over CFTH (which evolved, over forty years later, into Thomson-CSF, and, in the 1990s, into Thales). It also came to terms with AEG: GE accepted a small stake in the German company and sold in exchange its interest in Union Elektrizitäts Gesellschaft.[62] Japan, following its victory over China in 1898, during which it had proved its military strength and industrial progress, carried out commercial treaty revisions that abolished the imposed system of extraterritoriality and recovered control of its tariffs. GE multinational acquired the Tokyo Electric Company in 1905, and achieved a patent-sharing and minority stake in the Shibaura Engineering Works, a business associated with the Mitsui conglomerate, during 1909–10 (in later decades, Shibaura was given the nickname Toshiba).[63]

The internationalization of Westinghouse, GE's great rival, was a contrast. George Westinghouse preferred wholly owned subsidiaries to joint venture and licensing strategies. He built a massive factory complex at Old Trafford, in Manchester, England, in 1899, to be run by engineering personnel transferred from the USA. He raised the capital by selling preference stock to British investors, while retaining the controlling shares for his own parent business. BTH, British Westinghouse and the British and wholly independent version of the General Electric Company (founded by German émigrés) straddled electrical production in Britain and its colonial markets. By 1914, Westinghouse plants existed in France, Germany, Canada and Russia (where the government was the sole customer). While GE's complicated web of foreign businesses generated profits, Westinghouse's directly controlled subsidiaries were a drag-weight on its commercial prospects (Wilkins, 1970).

Technology and brands

The American Bell Telephone Company's manufacturing subsidiary, Western Electric, opened an assembly plant in Antwerp in 1882, in response to a Belgian government contract. It founded its British subsidiary, the Standard Telephone Company, in 1883, largely importing from Antwerp until 1898, when Western Electric bought the Fowler-Waring Cables Company. Its largest customer, the National Telephone Company – operating under a licence from the government-owned Post Office – had indicated its commercial preference for home-made supplies. Other assembly plants in France and Germany were similarly needed for the winning of local contracts (Wilkins, 1970).[64] Western Electric also took a controlling interest in Nippon Electric Company in 1899, as soon as the Japanese government had allowed foreign FDI. The US company had failed to come to terms with a large local manufacturer: therefore, it established the new NEC joint venture with Japanese investors, and appointed Kunihiko Iwadare, an engineer with knowledge of the business in the USA and Japan, as managing director. There was no direction from the USA, and a local subsidiary guaranteed government orders, the bulk of Japan's telecommunications market at this point. NEC purchased a site for another factory from Mitsui in 1900, and grew the business from the assembling of imported components to increasing levels of self-manufacture. The Ministry of Communications was engaged in a national project to link Japan's islands, then to entrench imperial expansion into Korea and Manchuria, and NEC opened offices in Seoul (1908) and Port

Arthur (1909). Western Electric could offer its technology; it brought the factory machinery, engineers and foremen, and sent key Japanese employees to the USA for training in production systems and accounting.[65]

The international strategy of Western Electric's Swedish competitor had the same principal motives. Lar Magnus Ericsson had founded his firm in 1876, and, by studying and improving on the equipment made by Bell and Siemens in particular, made his first telephones three years later. Given Bell's domination of telephony in Stockholm, Ericsson had to rely on provincial and export markets, until the founding of a competitor to the US company, in the form of Stockholms Allma-a Telefonaktiebolag, in 1883 gave him a new and important opportunity. A St Petersburg factory, its first overseas, ensured continuity of supply from 1899 onwards; it ensured, in addition, local orders, as did the plants that appeared in Britain, the USA, France and Austria-Hungary, supplying telephone exchanges and equipment. Ericsson, furthermore, exported 95 per cent of its Swedish output by about 1900.[66] While Ericsson transformed itself into Sweden's most successful multinational, there was, in addition, ASEA, an engineering company and a specialist in electrical transmission, which bought a British firm in 1898.

Ford Motor Company formed a joint venture with local investors in Canada in 1904, and the subsidiary had the marketing rights, Britain exempted, to the British Empire, so providing a production location on the right side of imperial tariff walls. The US company founded its plant in Britain in 1909, and its Old Trafford factory was producing cars within two years, using imported components. Ford owned a small assembly unit in France also (Wilkins, 1970). The motive was market seeking, and, by 1914, the Old Trafford subsidiary had a version of Henry Ford's moving assembly line. International Harvester transformed itself into a multinational in 1909 by investing in Russia. To avoid the government minister who had encouraged the decision being accused of fostering foreign firms, International Harvester agreed to act as a Russian enterprise. Tariffs also explained the existence of its four more plants in Canada, Sweden, France and Germany, in 1911, by which time foreign subsidiaries accounted for 40 per cent of company sales.

Otis Elevator emerged as the first international maker of elevators by building, between 1902 and 1914, factories in Britain, Germany, France and Canada.[67] American Radiator arrived in Britain, during

1891, in order to exploit its lead in cast iron equipment and to fulfil a market-seeking strategy; it located, from 1898 to 1911, in Canada, France, Germany, Italy and Austria-Hungary in order to surmount tariff barriers.[68] Eastman Kodak began manufacturing in Harrow, near London, in 1891, exporting both US equipment and management teams; [69] National Cash Register, an industry first mover, owned factories in Germany and Canada by 1914;[70] and Du Pont formed Canadian Explosives as a joint venture with Britain's Nobel Company in 1910.[71]

Three brothers who had emigrated from Scotland to Virginia founded tobacco makers Cameron Brothers, and they built four factories in the various colonies of Australia, between 1873 and 1889, in order to overcome tariff walls.[72] The American Tobacco Company followed, to protect its export markets, and to respond to high import duties, and it organized the formation of joint ventures in New South Wales, South Australia, and Victoria (in 1894). It next formed ATC of New Zealand (1895), utilizing a business it had recently acquired; it repeated this entry strategy with ATC of Canada (1895). The US company, experienced in the automated and profitable mass production of rolled cigarettes, sought to use its resources through the tactic of buying foreign businesses (Wilkins, 1970). It acquired a majority shareholding in Murai Brothers, in Japan, in 1899, a base from which to develop a regional Asian market, and soon afterwards began a factory in Europe's largest market, Germany.

When ATC purchased Ogden, in 1901, in response thirteen firms united under a holding company – called Imperial Tobacco – and fought back with discounts for wholesalers and ownership of a tobacco retailing chain. W. D. & H. O. Wills, the most important firm behind Imperial, set up a joint venture in Australia in 1901, and bought a US-owned factory in Shanghai, so taking the fight overseas. Fierce competition had high costs. American and Imperial came to terms, in the following year, with Ogden passing to the British conglomerate, and the former rivals agreeing not to trade in their respective home markets. For the rest of the world, they jointly formed British American Tobacco (BAT), and this company emerged as a truly worldwide multinational. It inherited ATC's and Imperial's overseas factories. As a result, it refounded the Canadian operations as the Imperial Tobacco Company of Canada, under local management; BAT (Australia) consolidated the varied interests of Wills, ATC and the Cameron Brothers;

and the company established a Shanghai-based manufacturer, in 1905, in a joint venture with the Wing Tai Vo Corporation. BAT, in addition, reorganized and extended a global distribution network, through which it advertised its high-profile brands. Antitrust action in the USA, in 1911, forced ATC to divest from BAT, which over time transformed into a British-owned but highly internationalized multinational (Cochran, 1980; Cox, 2000).

The British thread company J. & P. Coats was a vigorous and well-managed business, and, through a subsidiary, emerged as formidable international marketers. It ran factories in the USA, Canada, Russia, Austria-Hungary, Spain, Belgium, Italy, Switzerland, Portugal, Brazil and Japan by 1914.[73] H. G. Tetley, in his determination to modernize Samuel Courtauld & Company, made it a world leader in the manufacture of artificial silk, or rayon. To take advantage of a technological lead but inevitably to surmount tariffs, in 1910 Courtauld founded the American Viscose Company, which in a few years was earning more money than its parent, and was one of Britain's most successful multinational subsidiaries (Coleman, 1969). The Dunlop tyre company, from 1892 onwards, established factories in France, Germany, the USA, Australia and Canada, although the US and Australian enterprises were sold in 1898 and 1899 respectively. Subsequently, in 1909, Dunlop built a factory in Kobe, in Japan (McMillan, 1989; Mason, 1990; Udagawa, 1990; Wilkins, 1990).[74] Similarly, Italy's Pirelli made tyres in Britain, France and Argentina, and, in 1914, formed a joint venture with Britain's GEC to manufacture electrical cables.[75] Lever Brothers, after 1890, emerged as a formidable multinational. It began with a small factory in Cambridge, Massachusetts, in 1890, and expanded with another in Philadelphia in 1892, eventually achieving nationwide sales of its Lifebuoy and Lux brands. Other subsidiaries followed, by 1914, in Canada, Germany, Switzerland, Belgium, France, Japan, Australia and South Africa, seeking to be responsive to differing national consumer markets (Wilson, 1954; Wilkins, 1989; Wilkins, 2004).

French companies offered examples of manufacturing FDI. Having existed for nearly two hundred years, the glass and chemical producer St Gobain leased a works in Stolberg, in Germany, in 1857, and, through a merger with competitor St Quirin, it acquired another in Mannheim during the following year. The company was seeking to secure its position against growing Belgian competition. The same calculation motivated the building or buying of further production sites in Italy (1889), Belgium (1900), the Netherlands, Spain, Austria-Hungary and Germany (by 1914), making St Gobain into Europe's largest glassmaker, with nearly 27 per cent of the market. Michelin founded its first foreign factory, in Turin, in 1906, followed by the second, in Milltown, New Jersey, in 1907. Renault was an auto pioneer: by 1913, it had 31 dealers throughout the world, including Russia and China, and small assembly plants in Italy, Spain, Britain and the USA. We know that Société Schneider et Cie, before 1914, was active in Britain, Italy, Chile and Russia, and, in addition to its Lorraine iron mines, it acquired coal pits in Belgium. The company owned diversified interests in mining, electricity and gas in Morocco, and made major investments in a wide range of firms in Argentina. Its principal aim was to attract business orders, and it favoured joint ventures, but many of its ventures proved fragile (Laux, 1992; Wilkins, 1988; Wilkins, 1993; Wilkins, 2009).

Smaller countries – relative to the size of their economies – produced a disproportionate number of FDI cases. Solvay & Cie, a maker of caustic soda from Belgium, came to Britain in 1872 and could be found in the USA (two factories), Russia (three plants), Austria, Hungary and Germany by 1900, expanding to Spain and Italy by 1914 (Bolle, 1968). The Netherlands margarine and food enterprises Van den Bergh and Jurgens, which merged in 1908, produced in Germany and Belgium, and bought a retailer in Britain, by 1914, in order to further sales of its goods there (Sluyterman, 2003). The Swiss chemicals maker Geigy began manufacturing in Russia in 1888 and acquired a small enterprise in Lyon, France, in 1892, supplying the local textile industry. By the First World War, Geigy, Ciba and Sandoz could be found in the USA, Britain, France and Germany, and the pharmaceutical maker Hoffman La Roche established a factory in Britain in 1909 (Schroter, 1993; Wilkins, 1970). Suchard had a chocolate plant in Lorrach, Germany, in 1880, and a plant in Austria by 1888; it launched its Milka brand in 1901, and established manufacturing in France (in 1903) and Spain (1909) (Edlin, 1992).[76]

By 1872, the Anglo-Swiss Condensed Milk Company was manufacturing in Britain in order to be present in the world's biggest consumer market; it acquired the English Condensed Milk Company two years later, and bought a factory in New York, in 1881 (sold to US rivals Borden in 1902). Nestlé, a producer of baby food and milk chocolate, was determined to stay in Switzerland but, despite intentions, from 1898 onwards had operations in Norway, the USA, Britain, Germany and Spain. Anglo-Swiss and Nestlé merged in 1905. One of the company's first acts, in 1906, was to buy Cressbrook Dairy in Brisbane – again for the familiar reason of tariffs – and, by 1914, Nestlé owned seven factories in Switzerland, six in Britain, three in Norway, and one each for the USA, Spain, Australia and Germany (Wilkins, 1989; Gabel and Bruner, 2003).

International oil

In 1914, Winston Churchill was a rising British politician and First Lord of the Admiralty. Since oil-powered turbines meant faster and more mobile ships, he decided that the Royal Navy's battle fleet would adopt the new fuel. In doing so, he gave up the secure supplies of the Welsh valleys (which contained the world's best steam coal) for the vulnerable fields of Persia and their like. The decision encapsulated how, from the outset, oil was an international business with unsettling strategic and economic implications. Like mining, it was technologically and organizationally demanding. It required large-scale investments in both production and distribution, and companies had to be global in their reach.

The modern oil industry began in the flatlands of Pennsylvania, in the USA, where the first well was drilled in 1859. Its main product was kerosene, used for heating and lighting, but there was a substantial market in lubricants, paraffin, fuel oil, and the petroleum increasingly needed for internal combustion engines. Through his control over refining and marketing, John D. Rockefeller squeezed producers and came to dominate the US oil industry, formally establishing Standard Oil in 1870. Half of the USA's kerosene output went overseas, mostly destined for Europe, and Standard Oil alone was responsible for 90 per cent of this trade.

Successful exploration of the Caucasus Mountains in imperial Russia brought the first major challenge to Standard Oil's near monopoly. Once the czarist government had opened up the region to competitive tendering, companies began drilling in 1871. The refineries coalesced around Baku, recently annexed by Russia from the Ottoman Empire, and the oily smoke they produced was responsible for its nickname 'Black Town'. The Nobel Brothers Petroleum Producing Company was founded by the brothers Ludwig and Robert Nobel, and it opened its Baku refinery in 1873. Ludwig was a Swede with several armaments enterprises in Russia, and was in possession, consequently, of high-powered connections. They had another sibling, Alfred, famed for his dynamite and nitroglycerine business. Nobel Brothers Petroleum grew to produce half of all Russian kerosene, owning a complex of refiner-ies, depots and railways, and employing a multinational workforce. To expand his business, Ludwig needed international finance, and France's Crédit Lyonnais was a prominent lender, willing to accept future production as collateral.

Home production forced American imports out of the Russian mar-ket, but heavy transport costs hindered the development of an export trade. Refined oil from Baku could be taken across the Caspian Sea, but it was a further 2,000 miles by river and land to the Baltic. Since waterways were frozen in the winter months, when the demand for heating and lighting peaked, transport and as a result refining opera-tions ceased. The Nobels largely controlled the route northwards, and another producer, Bunge and Palashkovsky, began to consider alter-natives. The government granted permission to build a railway from Baku to Batum on the Black Sea soon after that port had been annexed from Turkey in 1877. When the enterprise encountered financial dif-ficulties, it was rescued by the Paris branch of the Rothschild family. Unlike the Nobels, they were more interested in Russian exports than the Russian home market.

The Paris Rothschilds had been importing US oil into France since the 1870s. As it owned a refinery at Fiume, within the Austro-Hungarian Empire, it was now in search of low-priced Russian crude. When the railway was completed in 1883, it turned Batum into one of the world's most important oil ports. The Rothschilds established the Société Commerciale de Naphte Caspienne et de la Mer Noire (called, by its Cyrillic acronym, Bnito) – in 1886 – to manage all their Russian oil assets at Batum. With supplies of Russian oil, they then built a distri-bution network throughout Europe. The Nobels quickly followed the Rothschilds to the Black Sea, and similarly founded an international marketing subsidiary. Family connections gave them reliable supplies of dynamite, which they used to blast parts of the Caucasus mountains and to lay pipelines. The big players – Standard Oil, Rothschild and Nobel – made several unsuccessful attempts between 1892 and 1895 to share world markets and control prices, and so fierce competition continued.

When establishing their European distribution network, the Rothschilds had relied on the help of Fred Lane, a member of the London-based ship brokers Lane and Macandrew. His firm sold Batum oil to ports in the Mediterranean, and it had been the first, in 1884, to charter tankers carrying bulk oil to Britain, ending its reliance on the pervasive Standard Oil tins. When, in 1888, the Rothschilds and then the Nobels had set up their importing and distributing businesses in Britain, Standard Oil followed. Called the Anglo-American Oil Company, it was Standard Oil's first foreign subsidiary (by 1907, it owned fifty-five refining and distribution businesses outside the USA). Ludwig Nobel died that same year, in 1888, but some European newspapers mistakenly reported the death of Alfred, describing him, accurately, as a munitions manufacturer. Having brooded over his reputation, Alfred rewrote his will, so funding the prizes honouring human progress in science, economics, literature and, ironically, peace-making.

In distributing oil across Asia, the Scottish trading companies became pivotal. The first movers were the Wallace Brothers, who sold Standard Oil products to India from 1878, switching ten years later to selling the Rothschild's Bnito. Wallace Brothers in turn commissioned other trading houses, such as Jardine Matheson in China and Japan, and dealt with the firm of M. Samuel & Company (wholly London in origin, it was not Scottish) (Sluyterman et al., 2007). When the Wallaces lost the Bnito contract in 1891, they switched back to Standard Oil. During the following year, the traders won a concession in the Dutch East Indies and formed the Netherlands-registered Sumatra Petroleum Company (the firm later added rubber estates to its assets in the colony).

Lane assisted in building relations between the Rothschilds and Marcus Samuel, whose connections with numerous British trading houses throughout East Asia the bankers valued. Marcus journeyed to the Caucasus and noted the existence of the bulk tankers pioneered by the Nobels. Marcus grasped the idea of an ocean-going tanker fleet, and persuaded traders from Calcutta to Japan to join the project. He had to commission new giant ships (having overcome the technological difficulties), to secure access through the Suez Canal (where there were safety concerns), and to create an intercontinental network of storage depots. He was wary of a self-defeating price war with Standard Oil, but Lane persuaded him to pursue the project. The Samuel brothers, plus Lane and Macandrew and key British trading firms, including the Graham partnership in India, and Boustead in Malaya, formed the Tank Syndicate in 1892. Tankers took oil eastwards from Batum to Asia, and, once cleaned, they brought imports to Europe. The strength of the Shell brand they promoted soon bestowed market power on Samuel and the Syndicate, even though they owned few oil wells of their own (Jones, 1981; Jones, 2000).

There was, in fact, only one source of oil under British control: after ten years attempting to develop a business in Rangoon, it was the well-known trading enterprise of Finlay, Fleming & Company that was behind the formation of Burmah Oil in 1886. It was the year that brought the final annexation of Burma, ending for traders and investors difficulties of royal monopoly, bribes and extortion. Burmah Oil, floated on the Glasgow stock exchange, continued to have its headquarters located in Scotland. The colonial authorities had pledged not to allow foreign exploration, as an incentive for Burmah Oil, and they were as a result to reject future applications from Standard Oil (1902) and Royal Dutch (1904). The British company erected a refinery in Rangoon, and sold largely to India, where it enjoyed a tariff advantage, ultimately replacing Russian and US imports.

To handle its marketing, from 1891 Burmah Oil commissioned another Scottish trader, Shaw Wallace, based in Calcutta, and oil rapidly became the mainstay of Shaw Wallace's business. The biggest local rival, by 1908, was Scotland's Steel Brothers, which had many long-established Burmese businesses. They formed the Indo-Burma Petroleum Company, in partnership with Indian merchants (Jones, 1981). Burmah Oil began supplying the British Admiralty from 1903, but could not meet the quantities needed from its already depleting resources. The Admiralty used the terms of its contract with Burmah Oil to achieve an even better deal from Royal Dutch, Shell and Standard Oil. The British-owned producer was soon making losses, but the British government secured the chance to explore the promising Persian oilfields as compensation. The company, from 1904, established a London office, transferring decision-making powers from Scotland, and imitating Royal Dutch in the employment of university graduates. American drillers and managers continued, nonetheless, to be in charge of its oilfields (Corley, 1983; Corley, 1986).

Back in 1880, Aeilko Jans Zijker, a manager for the East Sumatra Tobacco Company, had spotted the presence of kerosene in local marshland. Sumatra was at the time only nominally under Netherlands control, but, with the backing of a consortium based in Batavia (modern Jakarta), Zijker won a concession from the Sultan of Langkat, and the first successful well was drilled in 1885. When the Royal Dutch Company was founded in 1890, its title reflected the economic value of oil and the officially recognized importance of colonial trade to the Netherlands. Zijker died in the same year, and leadership passed to Baptiste August Kessler, an East Indies trader, who began the process of building a strong internal organization. Oil began to flow, in 1892, down ten kilometres of pipeline to a refinery on the north-east coast of Sumatra, where a small camp with a fort, prison and sleeping quarters accommodated the mix of US drillers and refinery workers, European engineers, and Chinese and other Asian labourers. In this remote jungle region, the death rate was high, and malfunctions and accidents plagued the operation of the refinery (Sluyterman et al., 2007).

Royal Dutch founded the Crown brand of tinned kerosene in an effort to compete with Standard Oil's Devoes. Its fleet was soon too small to cope with its own output, but could not call on the Tank Syndicate which was excluded from the Dutch East Indies. Samuel, because he knew that his Tank Syndicate depended for its supplies on others, had bought exploration rights in Kutei in east Borneo. The field's first gusher was poor in kerosene but high in fuel oil, so turning Samuel into a prominent advocate of oil-powered ships. Given their matching needs, Royal Dutch and Samuel began talks in 1896. While they looked for agreement, a recently knighted Sir Marcus Samuel was anxious to ensure the loyalty of those trading houses involved in the Tank Syndicate. He made them, in 1897, shareholders in the Shell Transport and Trading Company, which incorporated the tanker fleet and oil interests as well as the storage depots (Jones, 1981; Sluyterman et al., 2007).

In China, the Boxer Rebellion disrupted one of Shell's promising markets, and many of the company's facilities were pillaged or damaged. Ruthless capitalism and lawlessness had long been characteristic of the Caucasus, and, from 1903, discontent led to continuous strikes amongst oil workers. Following Russia's defeat in the Russo-Japanese War, the Revolution of 1905 nearly ended the czarist regime, and it was around Baku that Stalin – part gangster, part insurgent – first made his mark (Sebag-Montefiore, 2007). Ethnic violence between the Tatars and the Armenians destroyed some two thirds of the region's oil wells. For several reasons, between 1904 and 1913 Russia's share of world exports fell from 31 to 9 per cent. The impact on Shell, which was so dependent on Russian supplies, was immediate.

Samuel had displayed a talent for deal making, but had little inclination for tireless administration, and was willing to sell. Shell's failure to build a strong administrative structure was another weakness. In Sumatra, Royal Dutch's wells were drying. It looked northwards for a new site at Perlak, where rebels had declared holy war against the local rajah. Royal Dutch sent Hugo Loudon – an engineer, and the son of a former Dutch East Indies governor – to the principality. He was able to negotiate with both warring parties, and the discovery of high-quality oil in 1899 would transform a territory once linked with the pepper trade, and boosted Royal Dutch's commercial prospects and bargaining power. Henri Wilhelm Deterding became Royal Dutch's manager in Asia in 1900. He had originally ventured east to Malaya with Nederlandsche Handel-Maatschappij (the Netherlands Trading Society), a famous banking concern, before agreeing to establish Royal Dutch's international marketing system.

Thanks yet again to the intermediary skills of Fred 'Shady' Lane, Samuel agreed to the union with Royal Dutch, and a hurried deal was agreed in December 1901. Using his potential link with Shell as leverage, Deterding had persuaded other producers in the Dutch East Indies to join his combination. Given Shell's depleted finances, and once Samuel had rejected yet another offer of alliance from Standard Oil, Deterding held the stronger hand. He was appointed chief executive, while Samuel took the chairmanship. Semi-retired, Samuel could spend more time on another role, as the City of London's lord mayor. The Shell Transport Royal Dutch Petroleum Company was formed. The Rothschilds asked for a merger of the distribution businesses in Asia, and 'British Dutch' was replaced in June 1902 by the Asiatic Petroleum Company.

To Deterding, the connection with Shell offered marketing channels and greater price stability, but he recognized lucidly the advantages of Britain's imperial, diplomatic and trading power in building a global enterprise. He saw the Netherlands as too small for Royal Dutch; he showed, outwardly, few hints of nationalism or patriotism; and he was primarily motivated by the intrigues of international commerce and very large profits. Indeed, he perceived the commercial value of residence in London, and embraced the habits of the English landed gentry. The Royal Dutch Shell headquarters were cosmopolitan in character, and German managers and accountants, it was noted, staffed the London office.

As Shell's financial position deteriorated, Deterding was able to substitute Dutch direction for control. During 1907, he converted Royal Dutch and Shell into holding companies, 60 per cent owned by Royal Dutch and 40 per cent by Shell. They were legally independent, and enabled a Dutch-controlled company to present itself as British or, at least, as substantially British. The Group, as it was called, had three major operating companies: the Bataafsche Petroleum Maatschappij (BPM) oversaw production and refining from The Hague, while the Anglo-Saxon Petroleum Company (transportation) and the Asiatic Petroleum Company (in which the Rothschilds continued to have an interest) were based in the British imperial capital (Beaton, 1957; Garretson, 1958; Jones, 1981).

Standard Oil had aggressively gained a near monopoly in the USA, and, deep down, preferred control over partnership in its international dealings. But Batu's nearness to Europe and to Suez put Standard Oil at some disadvantage. One strategic solution was to find oil sources in Asia, and, from 1897, it considered a deal with the Royal Dutch Petroleum Company. But the US company remained blocked in the Dutch East Indies, as well as Burma (Reed, 1958; Wilkins, 1970; Jones, 1981). In 1904, it owned a company in Romania, now producing commercial quantities of oil, and Royal Dutch Shell and Deutsche Bank were the other two major investors. Deutsche Bank's subsidiary, Steaua Romana, bought with the assistance of Paribas, contracted Shell to market its products in Europe from 1903.

Yet price competition in West European markets was intense. In 1906, the Rothschilds, the Nobels and Deutsche Bank formed a cartel called the European Petroleum Union (EPU), which later branched out into tanker shipping and creosote. In Britain, Fred Lane negotiated the formation of the British Petrolem Company (BP), which united the kerosene brands of Consolidated Petroleum (Rothschilds and Nobels), General Petroleum (Deutsche Bank and Shell) and Homelight Oil (independent Russian producers). In 1911, in a significant move, Royal

Dutch Shell took over the Rothschild operations in Russia, which it bought with its own shares. Two concerns – the Shell group and Standard – had come to dominate the world oil industry.

However, a trust action, begun by President Theodore Roosevelt, forced Standard Oil to dissolve itself during 1911, so shaping the modern US and global oil industry. Standard Oil of New Jersey (later Esso, and then Exxon) retained the greater share of the original business, and amongst the others were Standard Oil of New York (Mobil), Standard Oil of California (Chevron), and Standard Oil of Indiana (Amoco). Standard Oil (New Jersey) received most of the foreign assets, including the oilfields in Romania and Canada, and refineries in Romania, Canada, Western Europe and Latin America. Standard Oil (New York) took control of the East Asian distribution operations. Alongside these was another business, the Texas Company (later named Texaco), which by 1913 had developed sales operations in Europe, Latin America and Asia.

Despite Deterding's deep-rooted preference for cooperation, Standard (NJ) and Shell continued to invade each other's backyard. Standard Oil founded a Dutch subsidiary by 1912 to explore southern Sumatra, and, in the following year, RDS bought assets in California and Oklahoma (Wilkins, 1970; Jones, 1981). It also entered the Canadian market. Standard Oil, which had bought Imperial Oil in 1898, had established itself as a strong commercial entity there. It viewed Canada as an extension of its US operations, closing Imperial's refineries, and managing marketing from its New York headquarters. Standard Oil of New Jersey, as the successor enterprise, returned control to Toronto, and used Imperial to develop South American fields out of the sight of US antitrust authorities (Taylor and Baskerville, 1994). In China, Jersey Standard, by 1914, had replaced networks of indigenous merchants with its own distribution organization (Cochran, 2000; Sluyterman et al., 2007; Tarbell, 2009).

Petro-diplomacy

One of the companies bought by Shell in 1913 was California Oilfields Limited. This firm had been established by the British trader Balfour Williamson in 1901, and it had emerged as the West Coast's largest producer. It followed a pattern seen in Asia, where trading companies had been formative in the history of the original Shell (Marcus Samuel) and Burmah (Finlay, Fleming). Balfour Williamson, from 1901, had interests in Peru, and founded Lobitos Oil in 1908. Jardine Matheson was a key investor in another Peru-based business, the London and Pacific Petroleum Company, created in 1889 and sold to Jersey Standard in 1913 (Jones, 1981). On the other hand, S. Pearson & Son was a famous firm of international construction engineers. One of its tunnels lay under the river Thames in London; another linked New York with Long Island. As we have seen, it owned railways in Mexico, and had a big part in the development of Mexico City. Weetman Pearson used his influence with the Mexican dictator Porfirio Díaz to begin drilling in 1902. He thought it would be politic to register his interests as La Compañía de Petróleo (Mexican Eagle) in 1909, but he retained a majority or controlling holding.

Big discoveries from 1910 quickly turned Mexico into the world's third-largest oil producer, and justified for Pearson the title of Baron Cowdray. Eagle's largest competitor was an importer, Walters, Pierce Oil Company, closely associated with Jersey Standard, and a fierce competitor. Revolution replaced Díaz with Francisco Madero, who had the support of US President Woodrow Wilson. Madero died at the hands of Victoriano Huerta, whom the British government recognized. Wilson, mistakenly, detected in Huerta the influence of Pearson, and the US government used its weighty diplomatic influence to block Mexican Eagle's commercial activities throughout the rest of Latin America (Spender, 1930; Jones, 1981; Meyer, 1977; Williamson, 1992).

Despite its anxiety over strategic oil supplies, the British government instinctively preferred to avoid the entanglements of international commerce and diplomacy. But it found itself gradually drawn into the Middle East. In 1900, an agent of the Persian government approached the British entrepreneur William Knox D'Arcy to buy an oil concession. The Shah needed funds to continue his prodigal lifestyle. D'Arcy had made his fortune in Australian gold mining before returning to Britain, and was in search of new opportunities. Persia, however, was problematic. Many of its regions lacked infrastructure and transport, and the authority of central government was not necessarily recognized. Persia was a buffer territory between an expanding imperial Russia and the British Raj, and their power play and competitive economic diplomacy had left it increasingly defenceless. Russia was especially interested in a naval and maritime base on the Persian Gulf, viewed by the British government as a wholly unacceptable threat to India

and Suez. Imperial Russia was Persia's most important trading destination, but the British government hoped that an oil concession would
gradually draw Persia into its orbit.

Despite the very apparent practical and commercial difficulties of
the project, D'Arcy remained inspired by patriotic duty, the backing
of the British government, and, of course, the allure of big profits.
In May 1901, he bought rights for 60 years over some 75 per cent
of the country. He excluded the northern territories, hoping not to
provoke Russia, which, immediately and unsuccessfully, demanded
the right to build an oil pipeline from Baku to the Gulf. Inhospitable
terrain, climate, and local tribes hindered exploration at Chiah Surkh
in north-west Persia, and all the heavy equipment had to travel from
Basra via the Tigris River and over mountains by mule. This risky and
speculative venture had cost £200,000, by 1903. D'Arcy had official
contacts: his consultant, and an influential figure in the global oil
industry, Thomas Boverton Redwood, sat on the British Admiralty's
Fuel Oil Committee; furthermore, at a spa in Bohemia, D'Arcy met the
fleet reformer Admiral Jack Fisher, who supported the Royal Navy's
conversion to fuel oil (he was, moreover, soon to be First Sea Lord). He
was therefore able to approach the Admiralty for a loan. Although the
Royal Navy and the Foreign Office saw the project as in the national
interest, the Treasury refused.

When a second well began to produce, D'Arcy lobbied cigar
importers and caterers Joseph Lyons & Company for an investment,
and, less patriotically, Standard Oil and the Paris Rothschilds. They,
too, were wary. Eventually, the Admiralty persuaded a syndicate led
by the millionaire Lord Strathcona, highly influenced by the imperial
point of view, to offer financial support. Amongst his many consultancies, Redwood offered his expertise to Burmah Oil, which in 1904
had its tentative Admiralty contract to supply fuel oil from Britain's
only secure source. On the other hand, outside India, Burmah Oil
needed the downstream support of Shell, with whom it signed a distribution deal in 1905, to make good its supplies. With each passing year,
moreover, it needed oilfields outside Burma. Finlay, Fleming – Burmah
Oil's owners – wanted to know if the government viewed Persia as
a protectorate. Once assured, it purchased D'Arcy's Persian venture,
establishing the Concessions Syndicate Ltd in 1905.

Exploration shifted southwards to Masjid-i-Suleiman, where
regional rulers once more caused problems, and, when the Shah was

deposed in July 1906, the new Majlis questioned the terms of the oil concession. In response, the British government dispatched a token troupe of Indian troops to guard the company's facilities. While the difficulties in Persia seemed to intensify, the global situation eased. Revolution and defeat by Japan had weakened Russia. Yet, to Britain's alarm, German influence within the Ottoman Empire had grown. The Anglo-Russian Convention of 1907 settled spheres of influence in Persia, Tibet and Afghanistan, in time for a large oil strike in Persia in May 1908. When, in 1909, the Anglo-Persian Oil Company was refloated on the Glasgow stock exchange as a free-standing enterprise, there was frenzy amongst shareholders.

A pipeline took the oil to Abadan, on the Gulf, and Indian workers were transferred from Rangoon to operate the new refinery there. By 1910, APOC employed some 2,500 people. The British Admiralty regarded the flow of Persian oil as a strategic asset, but it continued to hesitate over the crucial decision to convert its main battle fleet. The Agadir Crisis in 1911 – in which Germany threatened to annex the Mediterranean port as compensation for a French protectorate over Morocco – galvanized Churchill as First Lord of the Admiralty. Despite accepting the need to convert its fleet, the British government had not solved its supply problems, and by 1912 APOC had run out of working capital. The company tried to use the threat of acquisition by Shell to obtain government finance and contracts. In the meantime, the formation of the Turkish Petroleum Company to explore Mesopotamia seemingly underlined APOC's patriotic cause, as did German support for the new enterprise. Amongst TPC's financial backers were the British-owned National Bank of Turkey, Deutsche Bank and the Shell Group.

When APOC signed a needed distribution deal with Shell's Asiatic Petroleum in 1912, it excluded fuel oil. APOC's managing director was Charles Greenway, a one-time Bombay trader and an old Burmah Oil hand. He continually argued that Shell, as a Dutch firm, was susceptible to German pressure, and highlighted Samuel's Jewishness. The Netherlands remained strategically suspect. Yet Burmah-APOC could not supply all Britain's defence needs. While it kept a distance from Shell, the Royal Navy had been buying fuel from two Jersey Standard subsidiaries, Anglo-American and Romano-Americana in Romania, for six years. By need, it also dealt with British Petroleum, owned jointly by Germany's Deutsche Bank, the Paris Rothschilds and the

Russo-Swedish Nobels, which marketed the oil produced by the Steaua Romana Company, entirely controlled by Deutsche Bank.

Marcus Samuel offered his government a fuel contract in return for its international diplomatic support. The Admiralty did not purse the proposal, but it did, in 1913, sign an agreement with Mexican Eagle, seen through its association with Weetman Pearson as friendly. Finally, in 1914, the British parliament agreed to a 51 per cent stake in APOC, and acquired the right to appoint directors. During the debates, to make his claim for official intervention, Churchill attacked the Shell giant as a foreign company. Marcus Samuel was incensed, as was his brother Samuel Samuel, a Member of Parliament; Deterding preferred worldly cynicism. The British Foreign Office in addition negotiated a deal with the TPC, by which APOC became the largest shareholder in partnership with Shell and Deutsche Bank. Through Admiral Fisher, in charge of fuel oil policy, Deterding communicated to Churchill that Shell tankers would supply Britain in the circumstances of war, demonstrating, he argued, the group's freedom from German influence (Jones, 1981; Ferrier, 1982; Sluyterman et al., 2007; Tarbell, 2009).

Multinationals: 1870 to 1914

The transnational history perspective offers much to our understanding of the world in the nineteenth century, and, even more pertinently, in the period 1870–1914. In some cases, histories taking the nation state as the centre of their analysis, as the objective to be explained, have accepted the nation state as the natural structure for organizing human communities. In the worst cases, they have used the story of its development to justify or increase a sense of nationhood or to promote a feeling of national pride and achievement (history curricula if devised by governments for public schools too often have this uncritical acceptance). The history of this period shows that the borders of polities underwent dramatic changes, as did their composition and nature – in Europe, in the expansive cases of the USA, Canada and the Russian Empire, across the length of Latin America, throughout Asia, and, finally, in the conquest of Africa. If we seek explanations of the events of this period, the impact of external forces is obvious. Transnational history cannot replace the legitimate focus on a particular nation, but asks that the interpretation be broadened.

One dynamic component of nineteenth-century transnational history is the rapid growth of the international economy. The advance in trade had large consequences for production, consumption and living standards globally, but most obviously for the industrialized nations. The multinational added an extra element to cross-border business interactions, because it required the ownership and possibly even the control of management, personnel, technology and assets in a host location. It demanded that companies operate in host economies with potentially very different expectations about business methods, legal mechanisms and political favours.

When companies acquired assets overseas, they sought, not surprisingly, to protect their property interests and to minimize risks to their investments. The emerging international context in which they did so – the age of imperialism – involved the undermining or loss of sovereignty for host nations, and so provided multinationals with solutions. The framework set held, despite growing challenges, until the mid 1950s, and the consequences persist in the trade and investment policies of once-colonized countries. We can conclude, as many have, that there was a strong connection between trade, multinational enterprise, finance and colonization for the years 1870 to 1914, but, in fact, the repercussions of imperialism for the strategies of and responses to multinational enterprise lasted much longer. The legacy presents a specific reason why the study of business should be historical as well as transnational.

From ancient times, military conquest had determined the relationship between peoples, and frequently involved economic exploitation of the losing power, including enslaved labour. Nonetheless, more endurable empires might over time offer some security from violence, as well as political stability, systems of law and administration, and the deepening of trade routes. The combined drivers of trade expansion and military conquest, led by European merchants and adventurers, brought about global transformation from the fifteenth century onwards. In South America, the conquerors came looking for precious metals, and the flow of minerals and natural resources across the Atlantic boosted the economies of Spain and Portugal; in Asia, incorporated businesses acting under charters from their governments, and with their own militia forces, began by establishing coastal trading forts, and, as in the case of Britain's East India Company, ended up as rulers. Mercantilism and slavery were the twin characteristics of the international political economy prevailing by the eighteenth century. The rise of European nations and the exploitation of undeveloped territories for their resources showed a shift in global power relations, although, in the case of India, military power brought the subjugation of regions that were arguably equal to or more advanced than Europe.

What differentiated the international system that emerged in the nineteenth century, therefore? The period saw the emergence of multinationals that – admittedly more slowly than is sometimes thought – replaced the chartered concerns of the mercantilist era. These independent multinationals, after 1820 and more emphatically after 1840, brought about an unprecedented boom in exports and imports. Without the grants of monopoly, they evolved competitive capabilities in management, technology, finance, international logistics, or market access, and they had the freedom to operate anywhere and in any sphere of business. They invested in mines, plantations, ports, railways, trams, water and electricity. They laid the basis for the integration of the world economy and its expansion. Many emerging markets continue to rely, even today, on the infrastructure built by multinationals in Global Economy I.

We can see, moreover, in the period before 1914 the arrival of every type of multinational – in services, natural resources, finance and manufacturing. While their ways of functioning would evolve – as would the role of different sectors in the world economy, and the political circumstances in which companies operated – the multinational in its various forms would have been familiar to the generations that followed. As well as transferring capital, management and technology, multinationals fostered the capitalist system of competitive markets, although, as we have seen, the policies or character of governments and administrations worldwide and the realities of inter-firm links and collusion frequently cut across the principles of economic theory. The positive and negative aspects of the 'creative destruction' brought by competitive markets were visible.

FDI flowed mainly from Europe, and went mostly to the politically independent Latin America and to an Asia that was increasingly colonized. Africa, later divided between European powers, received small amounts of FDI in global terms, but the investment would have significant impact on a continent. The trading and investment imperative in many instances encouraged colonization, and, from 1870 onward, the cause of imperialism gathered impetus. Multinational organization was frequently based on international networks of producers, shippers, buyers, suppliers and partnerships, and reflected the trade-related nature of FDI and an international division of labour between the developed and commodity producers. Imperial guarantees bolstered a system of finance and ownership for companies operating entirely overseas in what might have constituted prohibitively risky locations. As trading and mining firms grew in size, they created examples of organizational centralization that could assist capital raising in their 'home' economy and the cross-border coordination of assets overseas.

By 1914, much of the production or marketing of the world's resources outside the USA was controlled by multinationals. While natural endowments decided the location of trade, mining and plantations, investments in utilities, construction or civil engineering were market seeking, and linked often to the pockets of development and urbanization created by export industries. The emergence of mass production and multi-plant firms led also to early examples of market-seeking manufacturing FDI in industrialized host nations, involving the transfer of proprietary technologies, products and management skills (an early sign of a stronger and significant trend in the 1920s). Overall, their strategies were to replace exports rather than to gain from the cross-border coordination of production and distribution, with subsidiaries serving their host markets as minor versions of the parent company. Total manufacturing FDI flows and assets remained smaller than resource-seeking and trade-related investments in commodities, mining, banking and services. Industrial companies that became multinationals showed clear examples of capabilities and technologies being transferred internationally, and in this period usually they did this by investing in industrialized economies.

Nonetheless, the transfer of capabilities and management to Latin America, Asia and Africa was visible through investments in shipping lines, ports, railway and tram lines, and electricity, and through the investments in mines, oil, plantations, infrastructure, processing and manufacturing made by a large number of trading and extractive multinationals. These enterprises transformed the nature of international trade, finance, and the acquisition of natural resources, so that by 1914 the world economy had evolved into a complex and interdependent system. The span of international investment would be more global than in any decade before the 1990s.

From a nineteenth-century viewpoint, three key elements are missing from established, modern-day FDI theory. The nature of multinationals in this period counters, first, the idea that they exist to control and coordinate vital capabilities and resources internationally within an organizational hierarchy. It demonstrates that looser network structures have historically been perfectly viable and highly effective (as we shall see, it is an approach now with an echo in the international economy after 1990). FDI theory underplays, second, the calculation of risks in developing markets, and risks include dangers from political instability, weak legal protection, macroeconomic instability, bribery and corruption, civil unrest, and violence. Local business partners helped to provide some enhanced security, and influence with or over the local ruling elite, as in much of Latin America, brought or bought protection in the period before the First World War (but not, increasingly, in the decades that followed). It is commonplace to say that, after 1914, the volatility of international politics forced the multinational into a retreat that lasted until the 1950s. In our review of the interwar period (Chapter 3), we will question the accuracy of such statements, and look, in particular, at trends in manufacturing investment.

FDI theory, third, does not give appropriate acknowledgement to the importance of governments or to the relationships between states, or to the dominant trend in the relations between states (or the international political economy). It has evolved through its emphasis on the internal workings and capabilities of firms, and added the broader context as an afterthought. A number of factors can determine the economic and power relationship between a multinational and its host economy. There is the scale of resources and capabilities in finance, management, technology and market access at the command of the multinational, and the extent to which the host country needs these resources and capabilities or any ruling elite might benefit from them. Institutional weakness or the small size of a host economy can increase the bargaining power of the multinational. A third party, the home country government, might also be involved.

The age of high imperialism, between 1870 and 1914, shows example after example of European governments undertaking colonization to protect the property and interests of multinationals and traders. In doing so, they transformed the risk calculations of investors. They did so by advocating the prevailing ideology of mutually beneficial free trade, in which foreign companies should receive equal treatment with indigenous firms. But imperialism biased trading relationships and the flow of commerce, and, in practice, gave a favoured if not monopoly status to businesses from the ruling power. The ideological dispute between the West and the Soviet Union during the Cold War, some fifty years later, was the main cause of military and diplomatic intervention in the designated Third World. The defence of multinational investments was a secondary motive, and, paradoxically, the global battle for democracy required support for repressive or authoritarian regimes (Chapter 4).

The history of the nineteenth century shows that multinationals were not passive responders to the international scenario in which they operated, but formative to its development. Their activities could be a cause of political, social or economic instability overseas, and they sometimes drew their imperial governments into a reluctant extension of their control and responsibilities. Military action or intervention offered a solution to persistent or increasing risks. The change brought across South East Asia – in Burma, Malaya, Borneo, the Dutch East Indies, or German New Guinea – provided such instances. France, feeling that it was losing the imperial race, took on the rule of Indochina more enthusiastically. In the carve-up of Africa, governments wanted to resolve the dangerous jostling for territorial control. Belgium's king saw the Congo as a place that could be rapaciously pillaged, although the 'returns' did not meet the high expectations placed on this infamous example of exploitation. Commercial interests or unsubstantiated claims of commercial interests led the British and German governments into East Africa. To give substance to their reluctant decisions, they resurrected the anachronism of the chartered company. Their monopoly rights failed to generate commercial success, and, when they could not fulfil their governing responsibilities, the territories were formally passed to the imperial power.

Where colonization did not occur, as in Siam, military and diplomatic pressure ensured commercial treaties that protected foreign firms. Iran was another example. China supplies the most prominent example of extraterritoriality, which undermined its sovereignty and affected its politics long into more modern times. Japan was the sole case of an Asian country, after 1899, and more so after 1905, that loosened foreign control of its trading policies and commercial laws, but continued to have its search for colonies and foreign economic

interests curtailed. In Latin America, the terms of the land and mineral concessions won showed the influence with local elites of foreign multinationals and governments. Governments of later generations would challenge the terms and rights of these concessions. In
Peru, British interests gave way to those from the USA. There were
late examples of gunboat diplomacy, and, in Central America, the
USA began what would be constant interventions. Where diplomatic
pressure did not work, the actions of the US Navy and the Marines
secured regional stability or protected multinational property rights.
It is impossible to understand the history of Honduras and Guatemala
without accounting for one multinational (United Fruit) that dominated their economies. There are no recorded instances of governments
expropriating multinational business assets (though we can find examples in the interwar decades, and, with growing frequency, from the
1960s onwards).

In other words, in an international political economy greatly set on
political imperialism in Asia and Africa, and on economic imperialism
in Latin America, the risks of international investments were minimized. Multinationals were a central influence on the international
history of the late nineteenth century and greatly influenced by the
course of events. While multinationals cannot fully explain imperialism, and nor can imperialism fully explain multinationals, the growth
in international business and the spread of colonization occurred in
parallel and not by accident. For all countries needing external supplies
of oil, and for those territories with resources, international events disinterred what would be an unbreakable link between business and governments. The evident miscalculations made in the capitals of Europe
in the summer of 1914 suggest complex causes for the First World War,
but the competition for world markets and international investment
added significantly to Great Power rivalry.

The needs of multinational enterprise undoubtedly complicated the
foreign policies of the USA in Central America, and those of European
powers across Asia and Africa. Yet, as stressed previously, the influences of multinationals on states varied from case to case. Britain and
the USA were the most important locales for FDI, but the economic
impact of inward investment on these large developed economies and
others would in practice be less marked. Similarly – despite the USA's
limited curtailing of foreign involvement in banking, insurance and
land ownership – there are during this period no discernible major

effects on the politics of the USA, Britain, Germany and France. For Russia and Japan, inward FDI was favoured as a device for transferring technological and managerial knowledge, and their governments did apply pressure for local involvement in foreign-owned firms. Although there were examples of concession rights falling into dispute or being revoked, there seem to be no recorded instances of the property of multinational enterprises being expropriated during Global Economy I. Latin America was a politically complex arena for investors, but, during this period, the ruling elites favoured and benefited from open commerce. After 1914, the First World War and the Russian Revolution brought about the first examples of the sequestration of multinational subsidiaries. In the international politics of the interwar years, matters of multinational enterprise and imperialism continued to be deeply entangled throughout Asia and Africa. What changed was the relationship between multinationals and governments in Latin America, which became much more problematic; the greater leverage industrializing or developing economies were prepared to exert on foreign investors; and, by the 1930s, the reduced inclination on the part of both developed and developing states to accept the idea of international commerce having precedence over national sovereignty.

3 | *The reverse gear?: 1914–1948*

Ending the first global economy?

Before 1914, Europe seemed the secure pivot of world trade and multinational business; after that date, global power discernibly shifted. Through two world wars, Europeans left behind an earlier era of peace and rising prosperity, and fought themselves into exhaustion. Their wars within Europe, for much of the nineteenth century, had been comparatively short, and, indeed, after 1871 no one great European power found a reason to fight another. Rival states, from the 1880s onwards, colonized Africa by reaching diplomatic solutions to territorial disputes: no imperial gain there was worth the cost of a major conflict back home. In Asia, the governments of Britain, France, Russia, Germany, the USA and Japan settled disputes over the control of China's ports; meanwhile, Britain, France and the Netherlands gradually divided the lands and resources of South East Asia by reserving military action for the people being colonized. Tibet, Afghanistan and Persia were all dangerous flashpoints, but did not pull Russia and Britain into war with each other; quite the contrary, as the Treaty of 1907 was a breakthrough resolution of their imperial contests, and the agreement over Persia, in particular, secured Britain's oil interests there and safeguarded its trade routes to India.

On the other hand, Russia had fought an economically and militarily emergent Japan in 1904–5, and decisively lost, bringing about the handover of a railway at the heart of South Manchuria's commercial development. Anglo-Russian rapprochement, in turn, facilitated the founding of the Triple Entente – between Britain, France and Russia – which lined up against a Germany that gave support to an Austria-Hungary destabilized by nationalist forces in the Balkans. International tussles over Morocco, Bosnia-Herzegovina and Tunisia – between 1905 and 1911 – issued early warnings of how obscure disputes overseas might threaten the long period of peace. Historians continue to debate the causes of the Great War: nonetheless, while most accept that conflict was hardly inevitable, the dangers of diplomatic miscalculation in a Europe divided by two opposed military blocs were ultimately proven. Every one of the combatants, in 1914, had its own strategic and ideological reasons for escalating a local conflict into a worldwide catastrophe, and, consequently, all of them should receive, if not equal shares, some portion of the blame (Clark, 2012).

Commercial rivalries added to the perception that nations were direct competitors for power and success. To protect their domestic agriculture or to further industrialization at home, states had increasingly resorted to tariffs and other trade barriers, so that only Britain, the Netherlands and Denmark had held to the orthodoxy of open and mutually beneficial trade. Cross-border investment and business frequently went in search of raw materials in developing territories, and imperial rivalry overseas further heightened European tensions. However, on the other side of the balance sheet, nations had continued to meet their commercial obligations, maintaining exchange stability, settling payments, and ensuring the legal rights of overseas investors. The global economy was becoming increasingly integrated (and, as events turned out, increasingly vulnerable). The long-term trajectory was upwards: for trade between Europeans and industrialized countries; for capital flows, as well as manufactured exports, from Europe to the rest of the world; and for commodity supplies from the Americas, Asia and Africa, most likely destined for industrialized countries. High levels of migration, opening up new lands, had helped to sustain the demand for international capital and trade, as did improvements in production technology, engineering, and agricultural science, in combination with population increases, greater urbanization and rising living standards, and, also, better transport and communications (Ashworth, 1964).

The European War, beginning in August 1914, inevitably prevented or disrupted cross-border trade and investment, reversing decades-long growth. The scale and length of the conflict forced combatant nations to restructure their economies, and to divert resources and personnel away from commercial objectives into munitions production and the expansion of armed services. The conflict did spill out from Europe to the Middle East, and there were clashes around Germany's colonies in Africa, Asia and the Pacific, in addition to naval engagements in the

Atlantic. Britain and France recruited forces throughout their empires, and the USA would join the Allies in 1917. Nonetheless, Europe was the principal site of the war and its devastation, and so, overall, it was industry and trade in other parts of the world that advanced. The First World War was distinguished by the total number of combatants and by its death toll, even if the infamous influenza epidemic of 1919–20 in all likelihood inflicted even bigger fatalities.

It was the first 'total' war, requiring the reorganization of political systems and national economies, as well as the marshalling of troops in unprecedented numbers. Across Europe, the conversion of factories into makers of munitions, plus state controls on industrial production, shipping and manpower, and, finally, consumer rationing had profound social, political and economic repercussions. The old faith in the free flow of goods, people and capital now clashed obviously with the need for national security, because trade dependence had brought the experience of submarine warfare, blockades and shortages. Europe had been at the centre of international trade, importing foodstuffs and resources, and exporting manufactured goods, and it had served as the source of cross-border capital. By the end of the First World War, Europe was increasingly reliant on transatlantic imports, and the USA had replaced Europe as the main provider of overseas finance, at this point covering the war debts of governments rather than expanding the productive capacity of the global economy.

The victor nations permanently expropriated the assets of leading German multinationals, and many businesses lost property to the Russian Revolution, in itself an evident consequence of the European conflict. Following the post-war slump of 1920–1, France's unwavering insistence on war reparations and the continued weakness of Germany all slowed the recovery of the global economy, but that recovery did occur. In the upswing after 1924, world exports had nearly reached in real terms the totals achieved in 1913 (Table 3.1). Governments remained publicly committed to the return of normal conditions – that is, the international system of 1914, one founded on open trade and fixed exchange rates – although emerging economies became determined to protect the tariffs they had introduced as a tool for encouraging inward investment and industrialization.

In the interwar period as a whole, the export of primary products grew faster than trade in general. Colonial policies and the investments of trading companies focused on cash crops such as rubber and palm

Table 3.1 *World output and exports, US$bn (1990 = 100), 1913–50*

	World GDP	World exports	Ratio
1913	2726.1	236.6	8.7
1924		253.8	
1929	3696.2	334.4	9.0
1938		303.0	
1950	5372.3	375.8	7.0

Source: Maddison (1999).

oil, and brought about a situation of overproduction. Falling prices helped consumers in the developed world, but hurt the producers of primary goods and numerous international trading and shipping companies. Everywhere, mechanization, fertilizers, pesticides and selective breeding had increased the productivity of agriculture. In Europe, new crops such as sugar beet brought self-sufficiency, but damaged tropical cane producers. There was a shift from wheat consumption to more expensive foods. Advances in mining technology enabled economic access to low-grade ore, such as Chilean copper, and oil and rubber output were in the 1920s boom sectors. The expansion of artificial fibres such as rayon, on the other hand, increased self-sufficiency amongst developed nations. Half of all long-term overseas investment was direct, during the 1920s, and much of it went into rubber, coffee, oil, and metal smelting. But there were flows, too, into railways, utilities and public finance. Over half of Britain's long-term investment was direct by 1930: Australia, India, Canada, South Africa, Argentina and Brazil were amongst the largest recipients, and 59 per cent of the total could be found in Empire locations (Ashworth, 1964; Kenwood and Lougheed, 1992).

World economic breakdown after 1929 swept aside any plans to restore the trade principles of the nineteenth century. Unlike the First World War, the Wall Street Crash impacted negatively upon every part of the globe, and, as the shock waves spread outwards, it threatened the stability of nation states and the existence of capitalism. It caused bankruptcies and cut deeply into demand; it disrupted trade flows and cross-border investment; and it inflicted unemployment, falling incomes, and impoverishment on much of the world. The Great Depression drove the malcontent countries of Japan, Italy and

Table 3.2 *Shares of world trade, 1913–37 (%)*

	Industrial Europe	Other Europe	USA and Canada	Oceania, South Africa, Japan	Rest of the world
1913	54.4	5.7	14.5	5.4	20.0
1928	43.1	7.9	18.8	6.9	23.3
1937	43.8	6.3	16.5	9.5	23.9

Source: Kenwood and Lougheed (1992).

Germany into the unravelling of post-war border and territorial settlements, and, ultimately, they reverted to belligerence. In Latin America, hardship and inequality radicalized governments and turned countries against multinational companies and foreign influence. During the 1930s, developed and developing countries alike set higher tariffs for a longer list of goods and services, and, for some, such as Germany or Spain, autarky became the desired, if elusive, aim. Nation states exerted their sovereign legal and political authority over international enterprises, becoming exercised by an enterprise's origins, and sought from the subsidiaries of manufacturing multinationals greater control over technology and skills. Governments abandoned their formal attachment to free trade, and, one by one, they committed themselves to the principles of protectionism and import substitution.

From 1929 to 1938, the real value of world exports declined by 9.4 per cent (Table 3.1), and it did not recover until after the Second World War. The interdependence of the global economy went into reverse. Since exports as a percentage of world output had grown from a figure of 5.0 to one of 8.7 between 1870 and 1913, the sum of 9.0 per cent for 1929 shows the ability of the international economy to recover rapidly during the mid 1920s. But the figure of 7.0 per cent for 1950 – itself an outcome of some years of recovery – can reveal to some extent the combined and unprecedented effects of the Great Depression and the Second World War on the role of international trade in the global economy (tables 2.2 and 3.1). For the interwar decades, compared to 1914, Europe had lost some of the dominance it had over world trade, in part as a consequence of the First World War, and in part because industrializing nations were able to retain their gains (Table 3.2). Changes in the composition of exports by sector remained fairly

Table 3.3 *Export shares of commodities, by value, 1913–37 (%)*

	Food	Agriculture	Minerals	Subtotal	Manufactures	Total
1913	27.0	22.7	14.0	63.7	36.3	100
1927	24.3	21.5	15.8	61.6	38.4	100
1937	23.0	21.0	19.5	63.5	36.5	100

Source: Foreman-Peck (1994).

stable during the same period, excepting a shift from food to mineral commodities (Table 3.3).

There is a problem in securing clear or comparable data on FDI trends during the interwar decades. Measured in current terms, the total amount of overseas assets for 1914 was $18.2bn; by 1938, it equalled $26.4bn (tables 2.8 and 3.4). Despite the difficult economic conditions with which the interwar years are associated, multinationals found a number of reasons to establish foreign subsidiaries. Amongst these was an expansion in manufacturing FDI, most obviously by US enterprises, adopting strategies of market seeking, and the significant growth of oil exploration. In order to further the aims of industrialization, and to discourage imports, governments used tariffs and quotas, and multinationals overall proved willing to invest (although policies adopted by certain countries in the latter part of the 1930s would have a negative effect). Britain remained the largest holder of FDI assets, but by 1938 the USA was on its way to closing the gap. Expropriations as a result of the First World War and continued economic difficulties at home brought the near disappearance of German FDI during the 1920s, but France held its share of world totals at 9–10 per cent between 1914 and 1938.

By the time of the Second World War, the developed economies and predominantly those of Western Europe and North America still accounted for all recordable outward FDI assets, and their dominance was still clearly visible in 1960. As in 1914, some two thirds of FDI assets were located in developing countries. It was, therefore, the postwar period that brought about the transformation in the locale of multinationals, explicable from the collapse of European imperialism, the growth of manufacturing FDI, and the scale of the investment made by the USA, in the era of the Cold War, in Western Europe (tables 2.7, 2.8, 3.4, and 3.5). We can, nevertheless, detect the roots of

Table 3.4 *Estimated stock of accumulated FDI by country of origin,*
1938–60

	1938		1960	
	$m	%	$bn	%
Developed economies	26350	100	65.4	99.0
North America				
USA	7300	27.7	31.9	48.3
Canada	700	2.7	2.5	3.8
Western Europe				
UK	10500	39.8	10.8	16.3
Germany	350	1.3	0.8	1.2
France	2500	9.5	4.1	6.2
Belgium, Italy, the Netherlands				
Sweden, Switzerland	3500	13.3	12.1	18.4
Other developed economies				
Russia	450	1.7	neg.	neg.
Japan	750	2.8	0.5	0.8
Australia			0.2	0.3
New Zealand	300	1.1	neg.	neg.
Other	neg.	neg.	2.5	3.8
Developing economies	neg.	neg.	0.7	1.0
Total	26350	100.0	66.1	100.0

Source: Dunning and Lundan (2008).

the trend in large manufacturers with competitive capabilities in products, production, technology, and marketing undertaking FDI in the
interwar decades. These investments were from economically advanced
economies and towards industrialized or industrializing countries.

First setback: the Great War

When trading with the enemy became a criminal offence, major
exporters automatically lost overseas markets. In the era of total war,
victory rested on the mass mobilization of materials and labour, and,
therefore, armaments output took priority over both consumption and
trade, with the soaring levels of demand inevitably causing widespread
profiteering and price inflation. Governments introduced controls on

Table 3.5 *Estimated stock of accumulated FDI by recipient country or area, 1938–60*

	1938		1960	
	$m	%	$bn	%
Developed economies	8346	34.3	36.7	67.3
North America				
USA	1800	7.4	7.6	13.9
Canada	2296	9.4	12.9	23.7
Western Europe	1800	7.4	12.5	22.9
UK	700	2.9	5.0	9.2
Other Europe	400	1.6	neg.	neg.
Australasia and South Africa	1950	8.0	3.6	6.6
Japan	100	0.4	0.1	0.2
Developing economies	15969	65.7	17.6	32.3
Latin America	7481	30.8	8.5	15.6
Africa	1799	7.4	3.0	5.5
Asia	6068	25.0	4.1	7.5
China	1400	5.8	neg.	neg.
India and Ceylon	1359	5.6	1.1	2.0
Southern Europe	n.a.	n.a.	0.5	0.9
Middle East	621	2.6	1.5	2.8
Total	24315	100.0	54.5	100.0

Source: Dunning and Lundan (2008).

imports and shipping space, and the conversion of factories to war production disrupted 'normal' commercial activities. After almost a century of seemingly unstoppable growth, international business stumbled, and the challenges to European leadership in cross-border trade and investment grew markedly.

The industrialized nations of Europe, with over 54 per cent of world trade in 1913, began to lose to the USA and industrializing countries in general; by 1928, industrialized Europe held a 43 per cent share (Table 3.2). The value of Britain's foreign investments fell some 15 per cent between 1914 and 1918, but those belonging to France (given its especially substantial losses during the Russian Revolution) plummeted by 55 per cent. Germany's overseas assets, many of them sequestrated, were worth a mere fraction of their pre-war value when the armistice was signed in November 1918 (Foreman-Peck, 1994). Capital flows from Europe dried, and, to pay for their war, European nations were transformed into net debtors, with US loans going to Britain, and US and British loans being supplied to their European allies. Unlike overseas investments before the Great War, these credits did not expand the potential of trade, but allowed belligerent nations to sustain their costly military efforts.

There were clear examples of economic warfare. The Royal Navy imposed its planned blockade on Germany. When the Ottoman Empire entered the conflict, it closed the Dardanelles and halted some 90 per cent of Russia's trade, mostly in oil, grain and other vital commodities. For Britain, the move posed a threat to the Suez Canal and British trade routes along the Persian Gulf. The redirection of essential raw materials to meet the limitless demands of war affected diplomatic relations between countries. In Malaya and Ceylon at the end of 1914, Britain imposed an embargo on commercial rubber exports, but drew protests from US tyre manufacturers, who, to ensure their supplies, had to promise that none would reach Germany. The First World War created amongst the leaders of this emerging US industry deep suspicion of British-controlled rubber supplies, and fears that their overall reliance on international market purchases would mean escalating prices. In 1916, Goodyear thought that buying plantation land in Sumatra, in the Dutch East Indies, would be prudent (although it could not produce for another seven years).[1] For the US government, secure – that is, non-British – sources of rubber became an object of commercial policy (French, 1991).

During the war, Lever Brothers further developed its palm oil estates, and the Huileries du Congo Belge continued to absorb capital rather than generate profits. On the other hand, supply shortages and shipping controls made many of Lever's trading enterprises along the western coastline of Africa highly lucrative, despite palm oil piling up in its reopened mills for want of available shipping space. Three more businesses – John Walkden's, Bathurst Trading, and King's of Bristol – were absorbed into Lever's trading operations but, even consolidated, they remained smaller than the regional giants, the Niger Company and the West African and Eastern Trade Corporation. Other West African merchants continued to be dependent on the near monopoly of the Elder Dempster shipping line, and Lever Brothers decided, during 1916, to buy a fleet of ships in order to create a competitor (Wilson, 1954; Gondola, 2002).[2]

Australia, New Zealand and Japan had seized Germany's territorial possessions in the Pacific by the end of 1914; since their commercial value was comparatively small, the main motivation was military. Japan, in addition, replaced Germany in China's Tsingtao enclave, which contained a German-owned brewery and other commercial assets, and the territorial gains it made overall during the war reinforced its position as an important regional power. With the exception of Tanganyika, Germany's colonies in Africa went, by 1916, to France, Belgium, Britain and South Africa. Both the naval blockade of the Central Powers and Germany's submarine campaign formed a very powerful illustration of economic warfare and its consequences. As trade lifelines across the North Atlantic became hazardous, cargo space was controlled and reserved for vital materials and foodstuffs, with governments forced to underwrite marine insurance for those shipping lines risking their vessels. The mounting death toll of its citizens aboard passenger ships was one major reason for the USA's entry into the war in 1917, and the naval blockade, ultimately, sapped Germany's ability to fight. Control of the world's mineral and oil resources – in their own territories, or across Latin America, Asia and Africa – made an indispensable contribution to eventual Allied victory.

There was no historical parallel to the number of men in uniform, or the scale of munitions needed. Governments had to acquire, through repeated emergencies, the administrative ability to muster their nation's resources; they imposed planning and controls over consumption, transport, finance, raw materials, and labour; and they interfered directly in the running of businesses, setting levels of output, or redirecting production into armaments and ammunition. When orders for civilian electrical equipment slowed, Siemens & Halske looked instead to communication devices and military orders, and made, amongst much else, aircraft engines and explosives. Its gunnery control system would give the German Navy its superior firing power in the Battle of Jutland, in 1916, so helping to sink two Royal Navy ships.[3] As motor vehicles, airplanes, and then the tank had such vital military roles, automobile manufacturers and engineering companies switched production, by necessity scaled up their operations, and accordingly learnt lessons in the standardization of output. Manufacturers, with the encouragement of government departments, and the research they sponsored, finessed their management techniques.

For André-Gustave Citroën, war demand was an opportunity to construct a large factory, finished by 1915 and situated in Paris (Gallard, 2004; Reynolds, 1997); similarly, Giovanni Agnelli introduced the latest techniques from the USA when building his new five-storey plant at Lingotto, Turin, between 1917 and 1919.[4] Military orders reinforced the strength of the tyre-producing cluster in Akron, Ohio, and Goodyear, B. F. Goodrich, and Firestone achieved competitive advantages in production and products that would sustain their subsequent international expansion. Amongst other war projects, Goodyear, from 1917, built airships for the US Navy; thereafter, it became associated with the gimmick of advertising its name on a blimp (French, 1991).[5] Michelin turned its factory over to the making of war equipment, most notably the manufacturing of airplanes: in a very public patriotic gesture, it presented the first 100 airplanes free of charge to the French government, and would sell those produced afterwards at cost. Its worksite served as a military hospital.[6] In Germany, Daimler lost its independence, in March 1918, when the War Ministry took direct charge of its business, having become angered by the company's dodgy accounts and exaggerated payment claims for munitions (Laux, 1992).

Tariff duties, introduced in once free-trade Britain during 1915 – and intended to protect much-needed shipping space and exchange currency during wartime – would take on a permanent status. The Safeguarding of Industries Act, passed in 1921, placed a 33.3 per cent protective duty on industries – from fine chemicals to optics and dynamos – designated as strategically and militarily important. In one act of significant social engineering, again originally passed as temporary, government, troubled by the thought that drunkenness was slowing munitions output, cut the opening hours of public houses. For fifty years, it would hold the drinking establishments scattered around the munitions factories of the Lea Valley and Carlisle under national ownership. In Britain, the USA and other countries, reformers gained the impetus after the war to ban or restrict the well-established and once legitimate international sale of cocaine and heroin products. The religious lobby in the USA used wartime emergency arguments to impose prohibition on the manufacture, sale and transportation of alcohol for fourteen years, creating an illegal cross-border trade, much of it south from Canada.

In Australia, both the traumas of conflict and a growing sense of nationhood had political and economic resonance. The Labour prime minister, Billy Hughes, while on a visit to Britain during 1916, and to the surprise of his cabinet colleagues, purchased a fleet of some twenty-five freighters, mostly requisitioned from German firms, and formed the government-owned Commonwealth Shipping Line.[7] As a founder of the Waterside Workers Federation and as an Australian, he resented the monopoly grip that British shipowners had long exercised over his country's trade (Meredith and Dyster, 1999). In the USA, as a measure of national security, legislation was passed in 1916 that restricted the foreign ownership of shipping lines (Jones, 2005).

At the outbreak of war, the Allies had cut enemy transatlantic telegraph cables, and Germany had to turn to communicating through neutral countries such as the Netherlands, or rely on the growing potential of radio. The US Navy, in 1917, took and retained control of international cable networks, and the Federal government acquired ownership of all radio patents, recognizing that the new technology had significant strategic as well as commercial implications. It then allocated the production of radio equipment between the army, navy, marines, and coastguard. The War and Navy departments lobbied hard, but could not, in 1918, convince Congress to renew this state monopoly, but they were able to influence the development of the radio industry domestically and internationally. They were determined to prevent control of this new technology in the USA going to a foreign company: the British-owned Marconi Wireless Telegraph Company of America was the most successful operator in the USA, and it also managed the Pan-American Telegraph and its chain of radio stations throughout Latin America. The Army and Navy asked General Electric to lead the creation of a US-owned company, in return for which the new enterprise would handle all of their long-distance radio communications; next, they pressed General Electric, Westinghouse, AT&T and United Fruit into pooling their varied radio patents within, in effect, a cartel.

General Electric founded the Radio Corporation of America in 1919, and Marconi, acknowledging political realities, sold up. RCA was to be instrumental in the development of US broadcasting, including the establishment of the National Broadcasting Company (NBC), and in 1929 it bought phonograph maker Victor Talking Machine, which was the main owner of the Victor Company of Japan (JVC). An antitrust action by the Department of Justice in 1930 would force General Electric and Westinghouse to divest, but after the restructuring RCA was allowed to continue both as a manufacturer of radios and communications equipment and as a broadcaster (Baker, 1988; 'Radio Company of America', 2010).[8]

War and sequestration

As we have seen (Chapter 2), in the two decades or so leading up to the First World War, European and US businesses owned significant investments in one another's territories, even if the bulk of FDI had gone south to developing territories. These companies – amongst them, to name just a few, J. & P. Coats, Dunlop, the Gramophone Company, Lever Brothers, Bayer, Merck, Degussa, AFA, Mannesman, St Gobain, Solvay et Cie, Singer, NCR, International Harvester, Otis, Westinghouse, and American Radiator – all invested in nations that became enemy combatants, at different stages, between 1914 and 1917. Interestingly, in the case of Dunlop, it lost its share of a German joint venture during 1915, but remained in friendly contact with its former partners through a Netherlands intermediary (Jones, 1986).

The most common result was sequestration and loss of control, and, for the defeated Germany, there was the permanent loss of assets, under the terms of the Versailles Treaty. The Tsingtao Brewery, some 70 per cent German-owned, was one small example of the virtual disappearance of German multinational enterprise during the war and its aftermath. As we have seen, Britain's ally Japan seized control of the Tsingtao Brewery, on the Kiaochou peninsula in China, and, while the Anglo-German Brewery Company, located in Shanghai, formally remained as the parent firm, it sold the assets to Dai-Nippon Brewery during 1916 (both the peninsula and the brewery would be handed over to China four years later).[9]

In Britain, the government seized the subsidiaries of German multinationals: some of them were essential to the war effort because companies such as BASF controlled the dyes needed for military uniforms,[10] and Bosch provided the magnetos that started almost every motor vehicle and aeroplane.[11] No less than 90 per cent of the dyes used in Britain came from Germany, and the 10 per cent made domestically relied to some extent on German involvement; furthermore, dye factories produced as by-products the raw materials for explosives. British Dyes Ltd was formed in 1915 through the state takeover of Read Holliday & Sons, based in Huddersfield, England, and one of the few companies, despite once being almost driven to bankruptcy, that had shown a level of competitive innovation against German firms. The British government, contributing £1.7m of the capital, was the major shareholder and loaned £100,000 for research projects, creating employment for some one hundred chemists (though half of them would be sacked almost as soon as the armistice had been signed in 1918). During 1919, British Dyes and Levinstein Ltd merged to establish the British Dyestuffs Corporation, in control of 75 per cent of British dye production, so achieving the economies of scale pioneered by German chemical firms, and manufacturing 16,000 tons of dyes in Britain during 1920, or eight times the whole national output before the war (Morgan Rees, 1922; Garfield, 2001; Reader, 1975).[12]

In 1915, the Custodian of Enemy Property acquired formal control of Siemens Brothers and Siemens Dynamo, whose heavy engineering plant and know-how were deemed vital for the war effort. As a matter of policy, in order to strengthen Britain's position within new growth industries, the government sold sequestrated companies only to domestic interests. In the interwar years, nonetheless, Siemens Brothers felt it was commercially useful to re-establish cooperative relations with its one-time parent, Siemens & Halske, overcoming the anger felt back in Germany about Britain's theft of the family name.[13] Deutsche Bank lost substantial assets: in Britain, a state-owned business, the Anglo-Persian Oil Company, acquired its distribution enterprise, the highly profitable British Petroleum Company, in 1915, and a subsidiary, Deutsche-Asiatische Bank, lost a commercial network stretching across India, China and Japan.[14] In Bolivia, the miner and metal trader Metallgesellschaft handed over its tin smelter, bought ultimately by Balfour Williamson (Jones, 2000). When Romania entered the war, in August 1916, on the side of the Allies, Deutsche Bank no longer had management of its major oil producer, Steaua Romana. After the war, however, unlike the story of German assets seized in Britain and elsewhere, it was allowed formally to sell the company, on this occasion to an international banking consortium.[15] Germany was home to the greatest international rivals in rayon – all now barred from Allied markets – and Vereinigte Glanzstoff Fabriken (VGF), via the Custodian of Enemy Property, fell under the control of Courtaulds in early 1917. The British company saw its output and profits soar during the war, in large part because of the achievements of its subsidiary the American Viscose Company (AVC), which was reincorporated as The Viscose Company in 1915. At this most successful of overseas investments, rises in the cost of living brought strikes and wage increases, despite attempts to use a welfare policy based on an industrial village and sick benefits to assuage dissent (Coleman, 1969).

Chemical companies emerged as essential cogs of an industrialized nation's war machine: they manufactured explosives and poisonous gases, and synthetic substitutes that could counter the effects of trade blockades. Britain, France and the USA all found themselves at a technological disadvantage against Germany, and governments intervened actively to create viable indigenous producers. Pharmaceuticals confronted the Allies with the same problem, now they were separated from German suppliers. Once the USA had entered the war, in 1917, it assumed control of Bayer's pharmaceutical and dyestuffs subsidiaries.[16] George Merck – having lived in the USA on behalf of the German parent firm, E. Merck, for more than twenty years – decided to hand over his family's share of Merck & Co. to the Custodian of Alien Property. His 'patriotic' action was rewarded in 1919: after a $3m flotation, Merck & Co. was fully privatized, and George Merck was back in charge. But the US business remained wholly separate from its German corporate origins.[17] Metallgesellschaft's American Metal, similarly seized, passed into US ownership and management (Wilkins, 2004).

During 1918 and 1919, the US Custodian auctioned the assets and patents of American Bayer's pharmaceutical and chemicals businesses, and sold the Bayer brand to Sterling Drug, and its Synthetic Patents Company, with its dyestuffs rights, to the Grasselli Chemical Company. Bayer lost 'aspirin' and 'heroin' as registered trademarks in the USA, Britain, France and Russia, as was required by the Versailles Treaty. As early as 1920, however, Bayer had made an agreement with Sterling because, before the USA entered the war, American Bayer had added oversight of the Latin American trademarks to its North American business. So, attempts to export aspirin to Cuba and Latin America from Germany provoked costly legal action from Sterling, and both companies concluded that commercial competition in the region was simply pointless. In return for Sterling being able to market under the Bayer label, the German company obtained an attractive deal: it would receive 75 per cent of the profits from aspirin sales, and the return of its other trademarks in Latin America. In the supplementary agreement of 1923, between Bayer and Sterling's holding company Winthrop Laboratories, the Americans kept control of American Bayer and aspirin, and acquired access to the Germans' scientific data, while Bayer gained a 50 per cent profit share in Winthrop, where its former patents, with the exception of aspirin, were housed. Back home, in a Germany experiencing economic turmoil and hyperinflation, the flow of dollar revenues was welcome. Both Bayer and Sterling agreed to avoid any further insoluble legal disputes over international trademarks.[18]

Almost as soon as it had purchased the bundle of Bayer assets sequestered by the US government, Grasselli had offered the German company cooperation, recognizing its need for access to a superior technological know-how. Bayer was powerless to reverse the sequestration, or to restore the loss of its trademarks in the USA, but it was wary of the proposal: its technological lead still provided a long-term competitive advantage in overseas markets. Tariffs, introduced in 1921–2, placing prohibitive duties on German chemicals, were meant to shore up the weak position of US producers, and US legislators accused Bayer, Hoechst and BASF of dumping chemicals below cost, with the aim of eliminating local competition. In 1923, when war reparations set out in the Versailles Treaty did not materialize, French and Belgian forces occupied the Ruhr and its coalfields, and accelerated Germany's economic meltdown. Severe domestic difficulties renewed Bayer's interest in the US market, and it opened talks with Grasselli. They formed a 50–50 joint venture, in the following year, called the Grasselli Dyestuffs Corporation, charged with manufacturing for the USA and Canada only. With its joint venture, Bayer overcame US tariff barriers, secured access to the world's most important market, and eliminated a competitor in North America and other export markets (Wilkins, 1989; Glaser-Smith, 1994; Jeffreys, 2008).[19]

For France, one way of supporting its ally Russia was to build factories there. Renault opened a truck assembly and shell fuse works in St Petersburg in 1914, and in 1916 it erected an auto and aircraft parts factory at Rybinsk, although revolutionary upheavals would prevent it ever moving into production.[20] Russia, nonetheless, still needed to import some 40,000 army trucks during the First World War (Laux, 1992). Combatant nations struggled to match an insatiable demand for munitions and military equipment, and it followed that there were commercial opportunities for multinational enterprises from neutral countries. The experience for Sweden's SKF, already manufacturing in Britain before 1914, was rapid cross-border expansion and investment. As it was a ball-bearing business, both the Allied and Central Powers needed its products, and it was able to grow its market worldwide – forming a sales network across Europe, North America, Latin America, China, Japan, India and South Africa – at the expense of competitors forced to focus on home production. Its Moscow factory, set up in 1914, grew quickly over the next three years, profiting from the war, but it was ultimately nationalized by the Bolsheviks.

During 1916, in a move to avoid the costs and hazards of transatlantic shipping, SKF established a works at Hartford, Connecticut, to supply the US motor vehicle and armaments industries, and, over two years, it made two acquisitions in Philadelphia, with which it formed SKF Industries Inc. In 1917, it had opened a factory just outside Paris (Fritz and Karlsson, 2007). Significant increases in research and development testified to a strategy of innovation as the foundation of its competitiveness, a commercial approach that became closely identified with Swedish manufacturing generally (Lundstrum, 1986). On the other hand, with wartime governments in control of telecommunications, Ericsson found little room for overseas growth, and, due to submarines and other shipping difficulties, exports from Sweden were limited to neutral countries and even to Russia.[21]

Rather than running their Swiss competitors out of business, before 1914 German chemical producers had preferred to cooperate, with each agreeing to focus on a market niche, and, in some instances, they had concluded profit-sharing and cartel arrangements. Swiss manufacturers had gained exclusive rights to import into Germany, and had relied on German suppliers for nearly 80 per cent of their raw materials. War needs, however, destroyed these arrangements. Ciba and Sandoz lost control of their factories in Baden, but they were in a position to sell in markets now closed to the Germans.[22] They and Geigy – that is, nearly the entire Swiss industry – obtained raw materials from the British, and sold dyes to them in return. Ciba expanded its production in France, and founded factories in Russia (Enri, 1979).[23] Hoffman La Roche – whose largest factory was at Grenzach, in Germany – faced accusations of supplying the enemy in Britain and France, but, ironically, in Germany too, to the damage of its commercial operations in all three places.[24]

As the war progressed, and despite large military orders for dairy products, supply shortages hindered Nestlé's factories throughout

Europe, and the company looked to acquire and succeed in locations such as the USA. As a result, its output worldwide, by 1918, was double what it had been before the outbreak of hostilities. By 1920, it had a controlling interest in three Australian manufacturers, and a plant in Brazil that was to be the first of many in Latin America; by the following year, Nestlé owned eighty factories across the globe (Harrison and George, 1983; Heer, 1991).[25] As margarine makers from the Netherlands, Jurgens and Van den Bergh had long operated in strategic alliance, and Germany, since they owned there some seven companies between them, was their biggest market and their most important wartime problem. When they lost much of their sales in Britain, due to supply and shipping problems, they decided that their best strategic response was to establish factories, during 1917, but they could not halt the commercial decline. The war allowed Lever Brothers, prompted by a British government anxious to secure supplies of a dietary staple, to diversify successfully from soap to margarine, with the launch of its Planters brand (Wilson, 1954).[26]

War and empires

While the closing of the Dardanelles to Allied shipping in 1914 halted the strategically vital flow of oil from Baku, via Batum, the Allies controlled all world supplies, excepting those extracted in Romania. German energy and chemical companies, such as Deutsche Erdöl-Aktiengesellschaft (DEA), had to rely on their scientific capabilities instead, and made breakthroughs in the manufacture of synthetic oil and explosives from coal. The Allies, in a move to cut Germany off from its one remaining source of natural oil, forced a neutral Romania to join the war in 1916. So, the Romanian government nationalized the fields and facilities controlled by DEA – which was largely financed by Diskonto-Gesellschaft – and the German company also lost its majority stakes in Concordia Rumänische Petroleum-Industrie-Aktien-Gesellschaft and Vega Rumänische Petroleum Raffinerie.[27]

The conflict similarly affected Steaua Romana, which was owned by Deutsche Petroleum Aktiengesellschaft (DPAG) and, therefore, ultimately by Deutsche Bank. Romania additionally placed Astra Romana under a sequestrator, despite it being only one fifth German-owned: for, with good reason, Britain suspected that the majority owner, Royal Dutch Shell, was trading with its enemy (Feldenkirchen, 2000). In response, Germany attacked and occupied Romania, and the oil was flowing again by 1917, though the fuel shortage continued to hinder German war efforts.[28] While the Ludendorff offensive on the Western Front, in the spring of 1918, brought initial success, poor supplies contributed to a loss of momentum, giving the initiative back to the Allies, being strengthened by the arrival of US forces.

At the outset of the First World War, British and Indian troops had moved into the Mosul region – in Mesopotamia, in modern Iraq – to secure what was suspected to be a new source of oil. The Ottoman Empire had just granted the Turkish Petroleum Company (TPC) a sole concession in Mosul, thanks to Calouste Gulbenkian, the influential international deal-maker. TPC was an archetypal example of cosmopolitan business interests – a cross-current to the rise in international tensions – as the Anglo-Persian Oil Company (APOC), Royal Dutch Shell, and Deutsche Bank had emerged as the main shareholders. The outbreak of war, including Turkey's decision to align with the Central Powers, brought an unwelcome halt to all plans for exploration. For the British government, the securing of oil sources, especially in the Middle East, was imperial policy, and it had territorial ambitions in the countries that emerged from the break-up of the Ottoman Empire. In 1916, the secret Sykes–Picot agreement divided the Arab territories outside of the Arabian Peninsula, handing over a future Iraq to Britain, and allocating what would be Syria and Lebanon to France.

Deutsche Bank controlled only 25 per cent of TPC, but Britain's public trustee sequestrated the whole of the oil company, declaring that enemy involvement had made its concession agreement in Mesopotamia invalid. The decision initiated a complicated series of diplomatic manoeuvres involving both governments and business. RDS's chairman, Henri Deterding, contacted Gulbenkian, who persuaded the French government to take up Deutsche Bank's portion of TPC, and to support proposals that would hand over stewardship to the RDS group. In 1919, an Anglo-French memorandum aligned the two countries' oil policies, and divided TPC into 70 per cent British ownership and 20 per cent French. Half the British share, some third of the whole company, was with the Anglo-Saxon Petroleum Company, a Shell subsidiary. The French government agreed, too, that RDS would create the Société pour l'Exploration des Pétroles in order to manage its interest in TPC, and the multinational could count on Gulbenkian's

5 per cent share. So, RDS controlled 58 per cent of TPC (Sluyterman et al., 2007).[29]

Britain's public trustee, in 1917, transferred the British Petroleum Company, the marketing arm of the Europäische Petroleum Union (EPU), to the state-controlled APOC. EPU was the consortium that had overseen the export of Russian and Romanian oil to Europe, and by the time of the Great War its main owners were Naftaproduktions-bolaget Bröderna Nobel (Branobel), Shell and Deutsche Bank. German interests were a minority but Shell, as noted above, remained suspect: the common perception was that 'un-British' interests had supervision of an economically and militarily vital business. The assets included 520 depots, 535 railway tank wagons, 102 lorries and 4 barges, giving APOC what it needed commercially, a major distribution system for its oil flows, plus, for a time, a near monopoly of oil and kerosene sales in the UK. The British government did not, at this juncture, see APOC as a viable flag-carrier for its imperial oil policy, even with its substantial assets in Persia and Iraq.[30]

In negotiations, Deterding seriously considered schemes to merge much of RDS with British commercial interests, thereby creating the mainly British-owned major oil business that the imperial government in London desired. The multinational, for its part, calculated that it needed the diplomatic support that Britain could offer during the difficult conditions of the war and, it might be assumed, its complicated aftermath. The nationalist-minded government that ruled a greater Romania justified the thinking at Shell: it wanted to exclude foreign ownership of the oil industry, and favoured the new local oil concerns – created out of former German and Austrian subsidiaries – against RDS's Astra Romana and Jersey Standard's Romana-Americana (Sluyterman et al., 2007).[31]

The era of total war – involving the mobilization of a nation's population and industry – exposed some major states as ill suited to surviving the upheaval caused. Conscription helped to fuel rebellion in Ireland, in 1916, and the strength of nationalist feeling revealed a permanent fracture to the United Kingdom. Internal dissent in Germany forced an unwilling Kaiser, in his Easter statement of 1917, to accept the principles of parliamentary democracy. Imperial Russia was the first great power regime to fall, and the defeated empires of Germany, Austria-Hungary, and the Ottomans would all formally disappear within four years of the conflict's ending. Defeat by the Japanese, before the Great War, had already revealed the shaky authority of Russia's unreformed monarchy, and war weariness, mutinies and shortages had entirely broken its legitimacy by February 1917, the month the Czar abdicated. The Provisional Government failed to establish itself, and the Bolsheviks, with their power bases in Petrograd and Moscow, and within the army soviets, carried out their coup in the following October. They still had to fight for control of much of Russia during the ensuing civil war, but they were intent on being a catalyst for domestic and world revolution.

The Bolsheviks declared the founding of a socialist soviet republic, and took foreign companies into state ownership. Amongst those permanently sequestrated was Siemens & Halske and its heavy engineering arm, Siemens-Schukert, based in the centre of St Petersburg's industrial district; Germany could also count AEG, AFA and dye makers such as BASF as lost assets. Amongst the Allies, Singer, Westinghouse, and International Harvester, from the USA, were prominent sequestrations as were, all from Belgium, a significant number of tram companies and the chemical enterprise Solvay et Cie. Some 90 per cent of light and power supply had been foreign owned. Britain's J. & P. Coats and Vickers had invested heavily in Russia (McKay, 1970). Sweden's Ericsson and SKF were amongst the companies whose neutral status in the war counted little in the new era of ideological conflict begun by the Bolshevik revolution. Ciba, from neutral Switzerland, was another example of a multinational that lost assets.

An especially well-known casualty was Royal Dutch Shell. First law and order broke down in Baku, making production impossible, and then, in June 1918, the Bolshevik government nationalized the oil industry. RDS lost one third of its oil supplies – particularly consequential as investments in Mexico, Venezuela, Egypt and the USA had all proved disappointing – and the nationalization stopped the company in its ambition to be an equal of Jersey Standard. Deterding became obsessed with recovering the Russian assets, and, when British troops occupied Baku later in 1918, the military governor returned the oil companies to private enterprise and their controlling multinationals. For a longer-term solution, Deterding had to rest his hopes on the Russian White Army, but the Bolsheviks had defeated the forces advancing on Moscow, led by General Anton Ivanovich Denikin, by the end of 1919. Deterding lost faith in the White Army – refusing to support plans by Gulbenkian and the Baku producers to finance Denikin's successor, General Baron Pyotr Nikolayevich Wrangel – and he banked on the Bolshevik regime simply collapsing. Jersey Standard was even more optimistic: it purchased title to half of the Nobel holdings in Baku in 1920, by which point the Bolsheviks had been in occupation of the region for several months.

Russia's new government responded to the countrywide commercial chaos with its New Economic Policy, declaring a partial return to private enterprise and concessions for Western firms, and RDS went into secret session with the Russian Trade Delegation, in London, about acquiring or reacquiring production rights in the Soviet Union. When the Russians considered instead a sale to APOC, RDS protested to the British government about a business it owned agreeing to buy stolen property. Jersey Standard did manage to come to terms,[32] but, before they could be effected, Lenin brought the period of the NEP and any prospect of foreign oil companies returning to an end. Britain and the Soviet Union did, however, sign a trade agreement, which included the principle of compensation for nationalized assets. RDS immediately transferred nominal ownership of the Russian business from its Bataafsche subsidiary, registered in the Netherlands, to Anglo-Saxon, registered in London, in the hope that the British government would fight its case, and, less likely, secure a concession from Lenin and his comrades (Service, 1997; Sluyterman et al., 2007).[33]

Geology was the main cause of RDS's disappointing performance in Mexico, where its La Corona subsidiary operated. While the country was far away from the events overwhelming Europe, it was torn by political dissent and internal conflict. A fraudulent election had been the immediate cause of the Mexican Revolution, but the underlying issue was the tight grip held by a social and ethnic elite on the country's government and wealth. Half the rural population worked on the ruling class's landed estates, and in the years leading up to 1914, foreign multinationals had become targets of protest too. Having lost large expanses of territory to its powerful northern neighbour during the nineteenth century, and with General J. J. Pershing leading an expeditionary force against the revolutionary Pancho Villa in an effort to protect numerous investments in oil, mining and land, anti-American feelings were strong. The problem was that Mexico, a major base of operations for Jersey Standard, supplied some 20 per cent of US domestic demand.

On becoming head of the government in 1915, Venustiano Carranza was able to introduce legal and land reforms that met many of the radicals' demands. The new constitution of 1917, which gave ownership of the subsoil and minerals to the state, challenged the established ownership rights of foreign oil and mining companies. It effectively declared all existing concessions to be void, but frequent changes of government meant that exact policy outcomes remained uncertain, although taxation on the production and export of oil did rise. The Zimmerman Telegraph – sent in secret by the German Foreign Secretary during 1917 but intercepted and revealed by British intelligence – had hoped for a military alliance with Mexico if the USA ever joined the Allies. It stirred anger in the USA, already mounting over the loss of American lives in the German submarine campaign (Topik and Wells, 1998).

In the middle of highly difficult political circumstances, the British-owned Pearson chose to sell its Mexican Eagle oil business to Royal Dutch Shell in 1919, instantly doubling that group's crude output. Compared to its major competitors, the multinational lacked the volume primary supplies that could meet demand pressures, but, in an unexpected turn of circumstances, it was dwindling flows from Mexican Eagle's wells and not political events that damaged its global commercial strategy (Garretson, 1958; Jones, 1981; Sluyterman et al., 2007; Meyer, 1977; Meyer and Sherman, 1987).[34]

US leadership and automobiles

The interwar period self-evidently gains its name from the two defining conflicts of the period: therefore, many historians justifiably see the years from 1914 to 1945 as a connected series of events, or as the twentieth century's version of a Thirty Years War, in the middle of which was an economic depression of devastating political and international consequences. From an economic perspective, within many Allied countries, and with the major exception of Russia, the First World War had boosted industrialization and average living standards, the USA and many non-European nations making especially notable gains. After the post-war slump, the 1920s showed the capacity for both global production and international trade to recover, despite persistently high levels of unemployment in industrialized countries; trends in the 1930s, due to the Great Depression, proved less certain, and international trade as a proportion of global GDP moved downwards.

The political and economic turmoil of the interwar years might suggest caution or withdrawal by multinationals contemplating overseas investment. But there were cross-currents, many of them positive: the long-term growth in living standards, despite lack of employment and poverty for a substantial minority; continued innovation in commodities, products, management and transport, and the spreading application of mass production and selling techniques; the rise of new technologically driven or consumer-orientated sectors, associated with electricity, motor vehicles, or branded packaged goods; and, critically, the introduction or raising of tariffs, which tipped the choice of business strategies away from exports and in favour of FDI, so long as host government policies on currency controls, remittances, or nationalization did not look too risky.

The break in trade and investment with Europe – as occurred during the First World War – provided space for other countries to expand their industrial and technological capacity and to be less dependent on European goods. Its vast natural resources made the USA comparatively independent of commodity imports, barring its attachment to the banana and other tropical products, and greater self-sufficiency in manufactures notably reduced the world trade–GDP ratio. Arguably, therefore, the Fordney–McCumber tariffs of 1922 did not have the economic impact for which they have been credited, even if the political signals were strong. New artificial textiles, such as rayon, could be produced near or in their final markets, just as breakthroughs in the synthesizing of fuel and rubber reduced the need for international trade, and created further opportunities for FDI. On the other side of the equation, the fast expansion of natural oil supplies and rubber plantations gave momentum to cross-border commerce. For the USA and territories of recent European settlement, the 1920s were a relatively prosperous period.

The motor vehicle industry demonstrated an early liking for FDI after the First World War. US producers had established, by the 1920s, a competitive lead in production management and operational scale. Along with the bulkiness of vehicles favouring at least final assembly in destined markets, tariffs were the main reason for creating subsidiaries overseas. Host governments viewed an indigenous automobile industry, with its spin-offs in supply chains and engineering know-how, as an integral component of industrialization. US companies undertook overseas vehicle production where markets justified the outlay and management commitment – as in Britain and Germany. Generally, however, international subsidiaries were assembly operations of parts that needed the cost and quality advantages to be found in the USA. The key point, often, was that some measure of final assembly allowed multinational automobile importers to escape protective duties.

The output of American car firms abroad, mostly from assembly plants, would reach some 309,000 vehicles, more than production in any one nation outside the USA. In the interwar years, only two automobile companies, General Motors and Ford – by no coincidence, both from the USA – would build full production factories overseas. GM based its decisions on which overseas markets offered the best growth prospects, on whether local production was preferable to export, and to what extent acquisition or a greenfield option had the greater advantages. Once an investment plan was agreed, the company considered operational questions about restrictive regulations and tariffs, and if the particular market or other local circumstances required a business organization different to that of the parent business. GM, after the First World War, usually made choices between full export, involving only very minor model customization abroad, and assembly operations, including 'completely knocked down' kits or CKDs, with full production being the exception.

Before the First World War, the McLaughlin Motor Company, based in Oshawa, had made Buicks under licence from the firm that would form General Motors. After considering whether to create his own Chevrolet plant in Canada, during 1915 William P. Durant decided to offer the McLaughlins the chance to manufacture for him. The Canadian entrepreneurs would agree, in 1918, to sell up, but remained as a key part of GM of Canada's management. Holden & Frost was a sixty-year-old firm, based in Adelaide, South Australia, that evolved first from a saddler into a repairer of automobile upholstery, and then into a manufacturer of motorcycle components. In 1917, the Australian government announced restrictions on the import of fully manufactured cars, with the set aim of developing its indigenous bodybuilding industry. General Motors sought out Holden to make and fit bodies to imported chassis, just as Chrysler would link up with T. J. Richards & Sons, also based in Adelaide. In 1919, Edward Holden founded Holden's Motor Body Builders, which from 1923, having gained its exclusive deal with GM, built a new factory at Woodville installing best-practice production and management techniques. Within three years, GM (Australia) had similar plants fitting Holden bodies to imported chassis in each of Australia's five states.

The US parent considered founding its first large-scale overseas venture in France, and, in 1919, it had sent a study team to report on buying a half share in Citroën. The visitors discovered too many negatives: the local management, the size of any further future investment in what, to GM executives, was a poorly equipped works, and French government opposition to an enterprise that had made such a large contribution to its war effort passing into foreign control. But the strategic imperative for GM remained: having become reliant during the war on US spare parts and machine tools, and having seen their commercial sales fall, European car firms had lobbied their governments to introduce protective tariffs on imported cars, and to impose discriminatory taxes on the higher-cylinder-capacity vehicles that came out of Detroit.

GM, in any case, during the 1920s recognized the costs of transporting complete autos and generally opened small-scale, final-stage assembly plants. The one in Copenhagen – established during 1923 – was the first outside North America, and it, in turn, re-exported the Chevrolet to other Scandinavian countries, the Baltic nations, Germany, Poland, Czechoslovakia, Austria, Hungary and the Soviet Union. In Europe, it followed this initiative with a CKD operation for Buicks in Spain (1925), and a truck and auto assembly plant in Warsaw (1928). But FDI in Britain and Germany signalled a major shift in its international commitments.

During the First World War, Vauxhall Motors had halted the production of cars in order to meet government demand for munitions, and it never recovered its reputation for well-designed, high-powered vehicles. The McKenna duties, imposed as a wartime measure, became permanent for autos, and erected a big barrier in the way of importing cars into Britain. Road licence fees were based on horsepower, and insurance costs were related to the licence, therefore doubly and then trebly prejudicing the import of US cars. The existence of too many British producers that lacked scale operations made the British market highly competitive, yet the situation did present a US company with an opening. GM, in 1924, made the attempt to buy Austin despite, as in the case of Citroën, questioning its poor plant and weak management, but the two sides could not come to agreement over the valuation. The company instead bought Vauxhall, based in Luton, England, during 1925, but had to give immediate attention to the market and regulatory conditions in Britain as they were so ill-suited to its existing model designs.

A. P. Sloan, the executive who forged the modern General Motors, writes that the company had been conscious of 'economic nationalism' as a new problem facing multinationals in the 1920s, and that it recognized why dollar-poor nations felt it necessary to impose tariffs and import quotas. The building of assembly plants, satisfying the demands of host governments, and lowering of the level of duties, was his preferred strategic response. GM, over time, strove to use locally produced tyres, glass, upholstery, and other components. Sloan gained fame for building his company's corporate organization, and its model range and marketing policies, in the 1920s, the foundations on which GM developed into the USA's dominant domestic producer. He fixed, too, the export and overseas investment strategy for the next three decades. GM secured from JWT – Madison Avenue's number one advertising agency – a promise that it would open an office in every country in which the auto firm founded an assembly operation or a full factory. At that point, beyond North America the agency had only its business in London, and Sloan remained sceptical about investing more in Britain, doubting the returns from installing the most up-to-date plant at Vauxhall. The peak year for GM exports from North America – at 290,000 vehicles – was 1928. After that date, through the commercial and political impact of the Great Depression, there was a firmer commitment to production overseas.

Cautious over full-scale FDI in general, but willing to be persuaded by his management team, Sloan came to believe more in the potential of Germany than in that of Britain. The market in Germany was large, and the local auto market was at a formative stage of development. Having operated a basic assembly plant, in Berlin, from 1926, GM was already Germany's second-largest producer. Sloan and his senior team visited the Opel factory, the country's largest auto producer and exporter, and bought the majority of the business in 1929 (gaining total ownership within two years). They noted good production facilities at the Rüsselheim works in Hesse, where some 70 per cent of the equipment had been bought during the previous ten years; Opel had been the first German auto manufacturer to employ mass production, assembly-line techniques. Other assets were a highly skilled labour force and the country's largest dealer network.

GM saw Germany as a country that would develop its domestic economy and its auto industry through low-cost manufacturing and high export volumes. It expressed concern about Opel's management – a point it made time and again about firms overseas – and knew that it had to achieve scale economies to secure long-term success. It sent an Oldsmobile executive, I. J. Reuter – a man of German descent, and with an ability to speak basic German – to take up the duties of managing director of its new subsidiary. One change was the making of interchangeable spare parts for distribution to dealers, which had expensively, and with mixed results, carried out customer servicing by fashioning their own. In buying Opel, GM committed itself to a European-designed car and accepted that large-scale cross-border investment would be needed if big established export markets were to be further developed.

Having been decisive over Germany, GM had to resolve what type of subsidiary it wanted Vauxhall to be. It decided against giving oversight to Opel, since only British-controlled production allowed preferential tariff access to the rest of the Empire, which accounted for 39 per cent of all car sales outside North America. The multinational ultimately opted to invest in a full-scale plant, and began to produce vehicles such as the Vauxhall Cadet and the Bedford truck, essentially variants of US models, by locally applying its know-how in production management and cost control. One motoring magazine, carefully noting the Cadet's American origins, thought it was a car 'meant to be driven by lazy people with a long way to go', meaning, presumably, it was easy to drive. Latin America, too, was significant in GM's international calculations. General Motors Argentina began in 1925, in Buenos Aires, assembling components shipped from North America, and by 1929 another works was needed to meet the demand for a very full range of GM, Opel and Vauxhall models. Within the same four years, GM founded three plants in Brazil, which in time assembled models from the parent company and the German Opel subsidiary. The Bombay (that is, Mumbai) operation for cars, trucks and buses, from 1928, was one further example of the multinational's strategy of export and final assembly.

In Australia, by 1929 HMBB had emerged as the dominant maker and, with its 3,400 workers, as the largest automotive bodybuilder in the British Empire. With its plant closed at the beginning of the Great Depression and workers being laid off, it asked GM (Australia) to form a joint venture, and the multinational financed the deal with cash it was unable to repatriate because of currency restrictions. In 1931, GM had effective control of the new GM Holden Ltd, while being careful to retain its outwardly Australian identity. By the time of the Second World War, there was a Holden body plant at Port Melbourne, Victoria, and one being built in Pagewood, New South Wales. In Japan, each of the Big Three – GM, Ford and Chrysler – established assembly plants, either in 1925 or 1926, and they very quickly dominated the Japanese market. Yet imports reached nearly 16,000 cars and trucks by 1929, and it would be another four years before domestic production went above 1,000 (Wilkins, 1970; Sloan, 1964; Shimokawa, 1994).[35]

Management transfer and automobiles

In Australia, T. J. Richards, one-time coach builder, had taken up the distribution of imported automobiles just before the First World War, and, once refounded as T. J. Richards & Sons, from 1917 it began to make the bodies put on the chassis imported by Dodge Brothers from the USA. The Dodge firm eventually ended up as part of the Chrysler Corporation, with whom Richards continued their long relationship (until it was formally absorbed, in 1947, by Chrysler (Australia) Ltd). In Ontario, and on its formation in 1925, Chrysler Corporation formed Chrysler Canada to take over the plant of two antecedent firms, now united as Maxwell-Chalmers.[36] HMBB – Holden's Motor Body Builders – was one of the several bodybuilders and small assemblers that worked with Ford Australia after the First World War, but, from 1925 onwards, the US multinational converted a former wool-store into an auto works, at Geelong, in Victoria. Ford had created Ford Canada before the First World War, because, amongst other reasons, it wanted to evade import duties in the rest of the British Empire. One New York trading firm had positioned itself across East Asia as selling agents for US manufacturers, and, following reorganization, in 1916, it had adopted the name of Dodge and Seymour. It owned, by the 1920s, representative offices from Tokyo and Harbin, in Manchuria, to Shanghai, Hong Kong, India, Persia and Mesopotamia, and on to New Zealand, Australia and South Africa. Dodge and Seymour sold

Ford Canada cars directly in India, but, until 1924, it had used a succession of partner agencies in Malaya.

Ford Motor Company of Malaya was founded during 1926 as a sales company for much of Asia, and technically as a subsidiary of Ford Canada, and it gradually replaced the parent company's reliance on Dodge and Seymour. In Singapore, the new business took on all of the agency's employees at the main office, and a small workshop undertaking wheel fitting and some finishing processes. It acquired, too, an established network of 250 dealers nurtured along the length of the Malay Peninsula, and it assumed responsibility for distributing cars in Burma, India, Thailand and the Dutch East Indies. Elsewhere, and also from 1926, the US multinational established Ford India Private Ltd as an assembly operation (where production lasted for some twenty-eight years), and by 1930 the Singapore workshop was assembling semi-knocked-down Ford autos brought, with the help of a preferential tariff, from Canada and England. In South and South East Asia, Ford's imported mass-produced vehicles dislodged those from Britain, and by the time of the Second World War, some 50 per cent of Ford Canada's sales were, revealingly, exports to its two plants in Malaya and India.

Ford founded an Irish subsidiary, Henry Ford & Son Ltd, during 1917 in Cork – choosing the place where his father had been born – and the directors included Henry himself, his son Edsel, and Percival Perry, head of his British business. The factory was making the Fordson tractor from 1919, and cars two years later, using components carried from England until, in 1922, the Irish Free State seceded bloodily from the UK. Tariffs and political animosities meant that tractor production ceased and, despite a brief resumption between 1929 and 1932, the factory concentrated on the assembling of motor cars. By 1930, in a city of 80,000 people, Ford claimed to employ some 7,000.

Whatever the sentimental draw of manufacturing in Ireland for Ford personally, Germany was the big commercial goal for an international auto maker, but, in 1920, its government had placed an embargo on all automobile imports. Ford decided to register Ford AG in Berlin, during 1925, in the knowledge that Germany, within a year, would end the import ban, and replace it with a prohibitive tariff that would fall significantly in the space of a further two years. By 1926, Ford AG had converted a warehouse into a plant assembling, from imported parts, the Model T and then the Model A. Because sales of cars produced by foreign companies did so well, taking 28 per cent of the national market, the government settled on a 30 per cent tariff for both assembled and complete vehicles, more or less matching policy in Britain. Once Henry Ford had heard how GM had bought Opel, he was determined on a complete German factory, and, in 1929, his firm bought land in Cologne (negotiated with the mayor and future post-war chancellor Konrad Adenauer). The ambitions of the project overrode the poor timing created by the Depression, and, with the Berlin plant now closed, the Cologne works began production in May 1931. While Ford in the UK enjoyed notable success in the decade that followed, in Germany it had no answer to the price competition from GM-Opel. Yet by 1938 it had climbed enough to be the country's fourth-largest auto maker, behind the number one Opel, Mercedes-Benz, and the Auto Union (containing DKW, that is, Dampf-Kraft-Wagen, and Audi), reorganizing itself as Ford-Werke in the year war broke out across Europe for the second time in a generation.

Ford had opened his first factory outside North America, before the First World War, in Britain, to where it had exported its techniques of the moving assembly line. With the resumption of peace, the company restored and extended the Trafford factory, claiming over 40 per cent of the British car market by 1919. With Henry Ford now determined to run his European operations from Detroit, his long-time collaborator and head of his British subsidiary, Percival Perry, decided it was time to resign. The single-minded entrepreneur Ford was intent on building a larger factory, modelled on the recent manufacturing breakthroughs evident in the USA, and one that would have a deep-water port. Henry Ford founded the Ford Motor Company Ltd during 1928 in London, and, with his US parent business taking a 60 per cent share, the remainder was made available to public subscription. Concluding that his American managers in Britain had failed him, he made the dramatic move of bringing back Perry as chairman, and gave him supervision of all the European and Middle East subsidiaries.

At Dagenham, east of London, Ford constructed its modern overseas automobile factory – then Europe's biggest – but the factory was too large for its market, a point made even truer by the onset of the Great Depression (Church, 1986). A global plan, drawn up in 1928, stated that Canada, taking advantage of preferential tariffs, would manufacture components for assembly plants within the British Empire; Dagenham would do the same for Europe. In Britain, customers found the

Model A too expensive to tax and run. The first Ford car designed out-side North America – the Model Y – appeared in 1932, some 157,000 being produced out of Dagenham or assembled at Cork over the next five years. National policy responses to the Great Depression put an end to the continent-wide role envisaged within Ford's global plan for Dagenham: during 1932, both France and Germany announced the introduction of heavy tariffs on imported components. All foreign subsidiaries, as a result, would have to operate with a higher degree of independence. Automobiles Ford Société Anonyme Française (SAF) – whose antecedent company, founded by Percival Perry (in 1916), dur-ing his first stint in charge, had begun by assembling components at Bordeaux – had moved to Asnières-sur-Seine, near Paris, in 1927. Led by Maurice Dollfus, it initially made the Model A, before switching to the Model Y in 1932 (Bonin, Lung and Tolliday, 2003; Wilkins and Hill, 1964; Wilkins, 1974; Laux, 1992).[37]

Henry Ford's most intriguing international deal of the interwar period was with the Soviet Union, ideologically opposed to every-thing one of the world's best-known capitalists might represent. With world revolution slow to materialize after 1917, and consequently facing international isolation, the Bolsheviks attempted to re-establish lost trading relationships as early as 1920. They showed themselves willing to discuss – if not in the end to pay – compensation for assets seized from multinational enterprises. In Germany, the constitutional Weimar republic had replaced the monarchy, but, through the Ver-sailles Treaty, it had accepted responsibility for the war and agreed to pay punitive reparations payments. It was soon working to under-mine the terms and impact of the treaty. It bartered manufactures and economic assistance for the Soviet Union's vast natural resources. On diplomatic issues, both countries treated the re-established Poland with suspicion, and Germany manoeuvred to ensure that a Franco-Soviet rapprochement never occurred. Through military cooperation, the Weimar Republic could undermine those clauses of the Versailles Treaty limiting the size of its armed forces and prohibiting rearmament. The nationalist-minded German foreign minister, Walther Rathenau – incidentally the son of AEI's founder – signed the Treaty of Rapallo with the newly formed Union of Soviet Socialist Republics (USSR) at the end of 1922.

As an armaments manufacturer and a leading engineering firm, Krupps was at the forefront in providing economic assistance, and hired out its underemployed engineers to the Soviet Union. Despite being an ardent monarchist, Gustav Krupps was prepared to cooperate with the Weimar Republic in overcoming the terms of the Versailles Treaty. Since Germany was prohibited from making armaments, and because French and Belgian occupation of the Ruhr in the early 1920s disrupted its main Essen works, Krupps bought an interest in Bofors, in Sweden, and established the firm of Suderius, in the Netherlands.[38] Siemens & Halske, or its power engineering arm Siemens-Schuckert, was involved in building a hydroelectric plant, on the Dnieper River, in the Ukraine, for the five years after 1927.[39] German support was central to the modernizing of the tractor and locomotive factories at Leningrad and in the Ukraine, from 1928, where tanks for the Red Army would also be made (a fact laden with future historical irony). With only a single dilapidated truck factory, the Soviet Union sought out Ford's production engineering capabilities. During the 1920s, it had no choice but to import the vehicles it needed: it purchased, for example, about 1,400 Ford cars and trucks, all assembled at the Copenhagen works, and it bought some 20,000 Fordson tractors, which the Leningrad Putilov factory ultimately copied.

Practical realities wore down the Soviet Union's ideological objections to enlisting the help of Ford or any other capitalist company; for Ford, and many others, the speed and the scale of industrialization in the Soviet Union meant obvious opportunities for profit. In 1929, after two years of talks, Henry Ford signed a deal, explaining, 'No matter where industry prospers, whether in India or China, or Russia, all the world is bound to catch some good from it.' His company agreed to supervise the construction of an assembly plant near Moscow making Model A cars and AA trucks, but, for the longer term, it would erect a full-scale works at Nizhni-Novgorod (soon to be renamed Gorky). In return, with the old capitalist demanding a highly profitable bargain, the Soviet Union committed itself to buying components for some 72,000 cars, worth some $30m, and to paying for the services of the engineers and executives sent by Ford (White, 1986).[40] Amerikanskaya Torgovlye – or American Trading, known as Amtorg – had brokered the contract. An entrepreneur influenced by his Russian descent and socialist leanings, Armand Hammer had founded the business five years previously, but the Soviet Union controlled Amtorg for much of the interwar period in order to conduct its trade and technology purchases in the USA, and to organize technical assistance agreements with other firms as well as Ford. (Hammer ended up, post-war, as chief executive and chairman of Occidental Petroleum, and as a prominent Republican) (Nevins and Hill, 1962).[41]

While Ford was overseeing the building of Soviet factories, Stalin was consolidating his power, and the forced collectivization of agriculture was the cause of widespread famine and death. Over the decade that followed, centrally planned and accelerated industrialization began the transformation of the Soviet Union, and the much-needed production of Ford-designed vehicles arrived in 1932, at the renamed Gorkovsky Avtomobilny Zavod, or GAZ. Stalin's policy of revolution in one country reduced international tensions, and, with US companies building commercial links, Washington formally established diplomatic relations in 1933 (Service, 1997). The GAZ plant, by 1935, when it achieved an output of 100,000 vehicles, largely ceased its reliance on Ford parts, although this breakthrough created a decline in quality (Nevins and Hill, 1962).[42] By 1938, and in contrast to the Great Depression and its aftermath in the capitalist world, the Soviet Union's share of global manufactured production had moved from 5 to 10 per cent (Hobsbawm, 2003).

In Italy, Fabbrica Italiana Automobili Torino – better known as Fiat – had expanded rapidly during the First World War. By 1923, under the leadership of Giovanni Agnelli and the production engineer he hired, Vittorio Valletta, it had constructed the soon to be well-known mass production factory at Lingotto, with the aim of controlling and owning all the stages of manufacture. Within two years, Fiat supplied nearly 90 per cent of the Italian car market. With tariffs on components set to fall in Germany, in 1926 it joined GM, Ford, Chrysler and Citroën in founding assembly plants.[43] Henri-Théodore Pigozzi, from 1922, had set up the Société Anonyme Française des Automobiles FIAT, or SAFAF, to sell the Italian company's cars in France, and in 1928 he created a small assembly operation, which made some 30,000 cars over the next six years. He founded Simca during 1934, and the following year bought an auto factory in the Nanterre suburb of Paris, from where it made Fiat models, emerging as France's fourth-largest producer after Citroën, Renault and Peugeot (Gallard, 2004; Reynolds, 1997).[44]

André Citroën, inspired by his hero Henry Ford, had introduced mass production methods during the high demand of the First World War, and, by 1919, at the Paris factory, his firm was able to produce the Type A, the first low-cost car designed in Europe. Citroën followed this initiative with a credit sales scheme to support a growing dealer network and to stimulate demand for a popular vehicle in France. In 1926, as well as exporting through sales offices in Europe and North Africa, Citroën established four assembly factories in Germany, Britain, Belgium and Italy, reducing transport costs and tariffs, and allowing some local customization to the bodywork. Renault's development was more leisurely, but it followed Citroën to Belgium, in 1926, and to Britain, in 1927 (Laux, 1992; Gallard, 2004; Reynolds, 1997). British firms showed themselves, overall, to be less adept at international expansion. Morris bought an auto factory in Le Mans in 1925, but withdrew six years later, having failed to break through into the French market. Austin decided on an international licensing strategy: it sold rights in Germany, France and the USA, with small success, while in Japan the company that became Nissan made a version of the Austin Seven car.[45]

National policies and industrialization

During the First World War, developing nations could no longer rely on the flow of capital and manufactures from Europe, and the conflict showed shipping routes to be highly vulnerable. Brazil was one example of the economic and political consequences: being so dependent on coffee exports, it watched its national debt climb upwards, and industrialists voiced their anger at the resources given to support the growers of São Paulo. Expanding home production and higher tariffs in the USA significantly strengthened the downward pressure on European exports, while waning British and European competition created more space for Japanese industrialization and its growing textile sector in particular. German dyestuffs and chemicals producers automatically lost their access to Japan, which joined the war on the side of the Allies, and Japanese firms supplied much of East Asia as well as their domestic market.

Sponsored and protected by their government, Mitsui Mining and Nihon Senryo Seizo Kabushiki Kaisha Senryo – or the Japan Dyestuff Manufacturing Company, and Nihon Senryo for short – kick-started Japan's modern chemicals industry. As with other Allied nations, the government seized ownership of German patents, and sold them to local firms (Kudo, 1994). Industrial development spread to the colonial territories, too. From 1916 to 1918, the South Manchurian Railway established the Anshan Iron and Steel Works in Fengtian province (modern Liaoning), and near to the Takushan iron ore deposits and the Mukden railway works, becoming part of an industrial complex making ceramics, oil, fats, flour, sugar, chemicals, shale oil and electricity (Matsusaka, 2003; Young, 1999).[46] In India, military orders presented industrialists and large business groups with an unprecedented opportunity, and the supply crisis and local pressure forced the colonial government to alter its previous indifference to local entrepreneurship. Steel, jute and cotton production made gains, for the period of the war, and in 1919 a convention formally accepted India's protective tariffs, although actual measures were not immediately forthcoming (Tomlinson, 1989).

Through manufacturing spin-offs from its mining and wood pulp industries, and US investment in automobiles, metals and farm equipment, before 1914, Canada's emerging industries could make a contribution to the Allied effort. The Canadian economy experienced a long period of expansion from the beginning of the First World War until the Wall Street Crash of 1929, which, demonstrating its continued vulnerability to commodity price falls, induced a contraction of one third of national income in four years (Pomfret, 1993). Manufacturing in South Africa before the war – in cement, engineering and explosives – had been associated almost entirely with the mining sector, but, thereafter, textiles, leather goods, furniture, dairy goods, and foods generally expanded rapidly (Feinstein, 2005). Australia's low population and small mining sector put limitations on the size of its industrial sector. Despite government assistance, the country lost export markets for dairy, dried fruit, sugar, and other consumables, during the course of the conflict, although, as we have seen, Nestlé formed the view that an investment was justified. In the British Dominions, notably Australia and South Africa, the circumstances of the war combined with other factors to induce changes of policy: there was a growing sense of nationhood, with economic interests increasingly differentiating from those of the imperial power; and local labour party and trade union suspicion of private and foreign business control pointed to future revisions of fiscal and commercial policy (Meredith and Dyster, 1999).

As shown by the example of automobile components, governments used tariffs and other measures to protect their newly expanded industries. They wanted to ensure that wartime gains in manufacturing were not lost, and the fall in commodity prices during the 1920s would give urgency to any broadening of the economic base. The Australian government introduced steep tariffs for its steel, machinery, cotton, paper, textile and chemicals industries, from 1921, and the Council for Scientific and Industrial Research that it established, in 1926, was similarly intended to foster national industrialization (Meredith and Dyster, 1999). India, fearful of dumping by producers facing low demand in Europe, adopted protection for many industries including heavy chemicals, steel, and cotton textiles, after 1923. British firms went on, during the interwar period, to establish factories for soap, tyres, chemicals, and tin containers (Roy, 2006; Tomlinson, 1989).

The Pact Government – formed in South Africa during 1925 by the National and Labour parties – had to respond to fears of an import influx and lost jobs. Nonetheless, despite the appearance of manufacturers, South Africa remained reliant on its mining industry and gold exports (Feinstein, 2005). Industrialized countries such as Britain continued to protect those industries revealed as strategically vulnerable, and dollar shortages and trade imbalances gave France, Germany, Italy, Spain, Belgium and the Netherlands additional reasons for introducing or increasing tariffs. Governments acknowledged the risks of competitive tariffs and currency devaluations, and, from 1925, leading economies re-committed themselves to trading principles espoused before the Great War. The first World Economic Conference, organized by the League of Nations, in 1927, was called to halt the introduction of new tariffs or quotas, but the strains in the international system were showing well before the onset of the Great Depression in 1929.

The majority of manufacturing FDI, in the 1920s, went from developed economies to other developed economies. Some 80 per cent of the US total, as measured in 1929, by assets, was located in Canada or Western Europe. While showing a tendency to found small operations in overseas colonies, European manufacturers made larger commitments in other European countries or in the USA (Jones, 1986). Whenever governments imposed tariffs or quotas, multinationals were reluctant to lose sales in overseas markets. While each nation raised its own very specific issues, companies proved in successive cases willing to invest overseas in component operations or, in larger markets, full manufacture. There is plentiful evidence that the adoption or increasing of tariffs by a growing number of countries persuaded firms to engage in FDI. Governments brought in tariffs and other measures to secure inward investment and to advance the cause of local industrialization, and, looking at the cases, there is confirmation that their aims brought success. Tariffs help to explain the overall rise in FDI, led by the USA, Britain, Italy and Sweden, while, notably, the lack of capital limited the horizons of German firms. Competitive advantages in available capital, products, technology or production management contributed to the doubling of FDI from the USA during the 1920s. Generally, moreover, governments showed themselves as chiefly concerned about the location of production, and, before the Great Depression of 1929–32, did not raise objections to foreign ownership.

US tyre firms followed the same strategies as automobile companies in securing export markets, and the existence of a major client, such as Ford or GM, overseas provided a double justification for FDI. Firestone decided to found Firestone Tire and Rubber Company of Canada, in Ontario, during 1919, with production taking place three years later. It identified Britain as its next important market, and erected a factory at Brentford, in west London.[47] Having only a plant in France, B. F. Goodrich began cautiously in the emerging market of Japan, by taking a joint venture shareholding in Yokohama Rubber during 1917, in partnership with Yokohama Cable Manufacturing, an arm of the Furukawa zaibatsu; in 1920, it repeated the partnership approach in Germany by acquiring 20 per cent of Continental AG. But it entered the more mature markets of Canada (1923) and Britain (1924) with fully owned factories.[48]

By 1926, Goodyear could claim to be the world's largest maker of tyres, and, as an ambitious multinational, it was entering a new phase in its history. Adding to the factory it had established in Canada before the First World War, it opened manufacturing plants in Australia and England (both during 1927), and in Argentina (during 1931). In order to make rigid airships, utilizing Zeppelin's know-how, Goodyear had struck a deal, in 1924, to form a joint venture, called the Goodyear-Zeppelin Corporation. Having founded an aeronautical division, by 1928, it built the world's largest aircraft hangar in its home town of Akron. Tariffs were the key to the timing and location of Goodyear's manufacturing investments in the interwar period, and its British factory enjoyed additionally preference in imperial markets and a transport cost advantage over the USA in selling throughout Europe.[49]

There were three significant multinational competitors in rubber from Europe. Having produced in Spain and Britain before the First World War, Pirelli established tyre, rubber and cable factories in Argentina, Brazil, Greece, Turkey, Germany and Britain over the course of the 1920s, placing them all under the Brussels-registered Compagnie Internationale Pirelli. This consolidated subsidiary evolved into the most internationalized of all tyre businesses, until Goodyear overseas overtook it in size following the Great Depression.[50] Michelin would open factories in Stoke-on-Trent, in England, and in Trente, Italy, both in 1927, but it was forced to close its operation in New Jersey during 1931, with the slump capping its failure to make a competitive breakthrough in the USA.[51] Dunlop had gone to France, Germany, the USA, and Japan, before the war, in search of markets, and, in France and Germany, it had sought local production in order to safeguard its patent rights. The company had tried to minimize its risks by forming joint ventures, which, within a short period, proved unviable, or, at a minimum, highly problematic to manage.

The Sumitomo zaibatsu, which had invested in Dunlop Japan before the First World War, founded Sumitomo Rubber in 1917, using and deepening its commercial relationship with the British multinational. Dunlop set out, after the war, to expand its rubber estates in Malaya, and it entered the world's biggest tyre market, the USA, in 1918, beginning a factory at Buffalo, although it would find the competition far too strong. After the war, Dunlop reorganized its French business, and, having remarkably maintained relations with managers at its German subsidiary during the conflict, it reacquired these sequestrated assets by 1921. It re-entered the world's biggest tyre market, the USA, in 1923, but would again find the competition far too strong. It concentrated, next, on Empire markets, beginning manufacture in Australia in 1927, and in South Africa in 1928.[52] Shojiro Ishibashi – whose name in English translates as 'stone bridge' – built a successful footwear business in Japan, adding rubber soles to the traditional *tabi* his firm made. At Kurume, in 1931, he founded the Bridgestone tyre factory, with the technical assistance of Dunlop engineers (Mason, 1990; Udagawa, 1990). Tariffs similarly explained Dunlop's founding of new factories or the expansion of existing plants overseas, and the board was determined not to fall behind its US, Italian and French rivals in the battle for international markets. Dunlop took over previously independent companies using its name in Canada (in 1927) and Australia (in 1928) (Jones, 1986).

In both autos and tyres, therefore, the imposition of tariffs and other trade barriers frequently explained the move from export-led strategies in favour of FDI. For so long as there was no protective duty on tyres in Britain, Dunlop remained the only local producer, but within two years of a 33.3 per cent charge on imports being imposed in 1927, Goodyear, Firestone, Goodrich, Michelin and Pirelli had all established factories.[53] Vickers, the British armaments and engineering group, extended its already complex network of joint ventures and equity holdings in local companies, throughout Europe, in the 1920s. In Italy, Switzerland, Romania, Poland, Spain, Estonia and Yugoslavia, the approach surmounted tariff barriers and overcame local sensitivities to national security being dependent on foreign-owned interests (Jones, 1986).

As we have seen, Ford, from 1929, had a major input into the expansion and modernization of the Soviet Union's automobile industry, but the help of other Western capitalists was sought too. US, Swiss and German firms assisted with the design and construction of automobile glass, lighting, and electrical equipment factories. In most cases, Soviet engineers travelled to the USA to acquire the necessary training. Frank A. Seiberling – the 'little Napoleon' of the rubber industry – had resigned as president of the business he had co-founded, Goodyear, in 1921, and subsequently transformed the newly founded Seiberling Rubber Company into the industry's seventh-largest business. He additionally took an active interest in creating a tyre factory in the Soviet Union.[54] We know that its Communist government obtained technical and practical support from Du Pont and RCA (Gallard, 2004; Reynolds, 1997).[55]

Similarly, International Harvester was commissioned to develop Stalingrad's tractor plant, whose systems were then replicated at Kharkov (Wendell, 1992),[56] and Caterpillar built another tractor works at Chelyabinsk, east of the Urals.[57] The government hired technical advice on the damming of the Dnieper River, and on the construction of its hydroelectric plant. Eight of the water turbines and five generators were designed and manufactured in the USA, but the Electrosila factory, at Leningrad, having gained valuable experience, was able to produce the next three generators. The power fed two giant newly built facilities: the Zaporizhia Steel Plant (Zaporizstahl) and the Dnieper Aluminium Plant (DAZ) (Dunn, 1995). In constructing the Dnieper industrial complex around the once-unnoticed provincial town of Zaporizhia, the State Institute for the Design of Metallurgical Plants (GIPROMEZ) consulted Freyn Engineering Company, from Chicago, on blast furnaces; the United Engineering and Foundry Company, another US enterprise, built a hot and cold rolling strip mill.[58] Siemens-Schuckert was another multinational that worked on the Dnieper hydroelectric scheme, at the same time as another Siemens subsidiary transformed the flow of the River Shannon, in the Irish Free State. Having fought a bitter war to be independent of the British, the Irish government was amenable to commissioning Siemens-Bauunion, in 1925, to provide the new nation's electricity; it took four years to build the Ardnacrusha hydroelectric plant. Absorbing a huge proportion of the government's budget, the project was internationally lauded as a feat of engineering, until the Hoover Dam claimed the world's attention.[59]

While industry in the Soviet Union aimed to emulate the mass production methods identified with the USA, it imposed from the top its own employment practices. Remuneration was based on piecework, but there was no guarantee of any minimum payment. Wages were directly related to measures of individual effort, and the full weight of Stakhanovite propaganda, fuelled by falsified accounts of a proletarian hero, demanded high personal commitment from the workforce. Food ration cards, company housing, and employment passports kept experienced workers in place for the vital task of industrialization, and with full equality declared to be contrary to Marxist socialism, the most skilled and essential workers received the most pay (Laux, 1992; Service, 1997).

Japan and the multinationals

Having just lost their overseas assets and trademarks, German companies in the 1920s were cautious about FDI, and did not have the capital for overseas investment. Still drawn to protecting and exploiting their technological and product advantage, many of them were reluctant to pursue licensing as an alternative international business strategy, relying instead on exports. German manufacturers, therefore, had to renew their commercial relationships with trading companies.

The war had excluded C. Illies & Co. from its main Japanese market, and from much of East Asia, but it quickly reforged its network of overseas offices. It began selling Bosch's automobile and engine components in Japan as early as 1920, and found itself involved in meeting the huge demand for construction materials, steel, and machinery in the aftermath of the Great Kanto earthquake of 1923. C. Illies grew, too, because German manufacturers provided equipment and components for Japan's heavy industry and its chemicals sector – which grew rapidly in the 1920s – and the traders supplied armaments to both an army and a navy growing in size and capability.[60]

Although the USA had long established itself as an industrial nation and a Pacific power, Japan's tradition of admiring and imitating technology and organization from Germany continued to benefit its exporters, and more than counterbalanced any legacies of animosity left over from the recent conflict. The Krupp works at Essen would play host to members of the Japanese imperial family, and – with the company widely respected in Japan – its heavy machinery, munitions, and engineering expertise made an important impact on an emerging industrializer.[61] Technological leaders from the Ruhr – notably Dr C. Otto & Company, and Heinrich Koppers – built and sold the machinery Japanese enterprises, including Mitsui Mining, and Mitsubishi Mining, needed to process coal and its by-products, such as tar, ammonia and gas.[62] After the First World War, Japan maintained or reaffirmed its openness to inward FDI, but, as an industrializing country, its government used import licensing, tariffs and quotas to foster domestic manufacturing. It especially encouraged joint ventures with foreign investors in the expectation that they would promote the transfer of technology and management. By the end of the 1920s, therefore, and before the Great Depression put trends into reverse, mining and manufacture emerged as accounting for 23 per cent of Japan's GDP. The country's commercial and industrial policy fits a common international pattern for this decade, in which governments welcomed multinationals, before the Great Depression put trends into reverse.

Siemens & Halske had sound reasons for creating a Tokyo subsidiary in 1923. The German company was impressed by the speed of Japan's industrialization and did not want to concede the market to General Electric or Westinghouse. It perceived international engagement as vital to its long-term viability, and, in Germany, simultaneously initiated a programme of product diversification,

standardization, and assembly line manufacturing. The Japanese subsidiary was called Fuji Denki Seizo, or, in later years, simply Fuji
Electric. To maximize the chances of it succeeding and, a factor important to German businesses at this time, to minimize its capital outlay,
Siemens & Halske formed a partnership with Furukawa Electric, itself
part of a large zaibatsu. The name Fuji was chosen as a compos-
ite of 'Furukawa' and 'jiimensu', the Romanized Japanese version of
'Siemens'. By making turbines and heavy machinery from its Kawazaki
factory, by 1924 the company became a classic example of transferred
technological and managerial capabilities (Kudo, 1994; Yuzawa and
Udagawa, 1990).[63]

Interessengemeinschaft (IG) Farben attempted for many years to
block Japan's policy of cross-border cooperation and borrowed know-
how. Dyestuff and nitrogenous fertilizer exports to Japan resumed,
after the First World War, because German producers continued to
own a significant product and production advantage over domestic
producers. The government did want to protect the nascent chemicals sector that had emerged during the war, but it knew that its
large textile industry and the nation's agriculture needed a low tariff. It did encourage foreign multinationals to invest in joint ventures,
so long as they assumed a non-controlling share; on the other hand,
a 1921 law designating chemicals as ineligible for patent protection
made foreign multinationals very wary of cooperation with Japanese
manufacturers. From 1924, Japan introduced an import licensing system intended to curtail imports in favour of multinational investment.
BASF, Hoechst, Bayer, Agfa and Griesheim-Elektron responded by
merging their Japanese sales organizations, but they ruled out manufacturing investments that might weaken their control of product
and production knowledge. These four firms and others were, during 1925, principals in the formation of the IG Farben conglomerate, a new and highly competitive giant within the world chemicals
industry.

The Haber-Bosch process – used in the production of artificial fertiliser and explosives – provides one example of a clash between the
Japanese government and indigenous producers, on one side, and IG
Farben, on the other. Japan had sequestrated the technology from
enemy German businesses during the First World War, and leading
zaibatsu had formed the Toyo Chisso Kumiai, or Oriental Nitrogen
Association, to buy the rights from the Japanese government. But Toyo

Chisso Kumiai found itself unable to utilize the very technology it had purchased, and the Japanese government decided it would pay IG Farben for technical assistance in order to exploit the patents that the German firm regarded as stolen. So, IG Farben, at first, reacted warily and negatively, and it was able to block Japanese attempts to strike an alternative deal with French manufacturers, which looked to their own cooperative arrangements with the German conglomerate. IG Farben did persuade the Japanese government to end import licences for German dyes, in 1925, for which it agreed to limit imports of any products that could be made in Japan. Once done, the agreement enabled the signing of the Japanese-German Commerce and Navigation Treaty between the two governments to take place, although IG Farben's relations with the Japanese government would remain uneasy (Kudo, 1994).

For their significant impact on Japanese industrialization, German companies shared the credit with US multinationals. During and after the First World War, General Electric kept its stake in the Shibaura Engineering Works (Shibaura Seisakusho), which, in turn, was linked to the Mitsui Bank, and, therefore, the Mitsui zaibatsu. It maintained, furthermore, its participation in the Tokyo Electric Company (Tokyo Denki). These two Japanese companies – though both engaged in light and heavy electrical equipment – had complementary product lines (Odagiri, 1996). In 1917, in an effort to cope with its wartime spurt in growth, the Mitsubishi zaibatsu reorganized its management and organization, and, over the course of four years, founded or refounded several of its divisions as separate companies: amongst the enterprises created, all of them bearing the Mitsubishi name, were those involved in trading, shipbuilding and heavy industries, oil, and internal combustion engines. One other, Mitsubishi Electric, was incorporated, during 1921, with Westinghouse as a shareholder.

By investing in the Miyoshi Electrical Manufacturing Company, before the First World War, and turning it into the Nippon Electric Company, Western Electric had previously founded Japan's first joint venture with foreign capital, in this case as the majority partner. In addition to producing communications equipment, using its highly modern plant, NEC had built a telephone system under government contract along the length of the Japanese archipelago. It had connected the colonies of Korea and Manchuria with the imperial homeland, and accepted telegraph projects in China. When telephone commissions slowed, from 1913, the company switched to importing and selling electric fans, kitchen appliances, and vacuum cleaners, all largely unknown to the Japanese at the time. But another phase of communication infrastructure building began in 1916. On its founding, during 1918, International Western Electric assumed responsibility for its Japanese subsidiary, just as its big rival in the USA, General Electric, consolidated its international holdings into a separate international division called International General Electric, during 1919. NEC's management believed it lacked the industrial capacity to be an equal partner with IWE in a venture to make electric cables, and brought in Sumitomo Densen Seizosho, the cable-manufacturing division of the Sumitomo group, in 1919, setting up a three-way venture. As part of the deal, all cable-making machinery and all cable production were placed with Sumitomo.

NEC lost four of its factories in the Great Kanto Earthquake of 1923, but the reconstruction after the disaster brought projects and a surge in orders. The company also re-equipped its Mita plant as an imitation of Western Electric's famous Hawthorne Works, and, in the 1920s, it made its own breakthroughs in the development and manufacture of switching gear and other technologies. On the back of a government commission, and using broadcasting equipment made by its US partner, NEC introduced radio to Japan between 1924 and 1930. It was during this period – in 1925 – that Western Electric sold IWE to the newly arrived and hastily growing communications giant International Telephone & Telegraph (ITT), which renamed its acquisition International Standard Electric (ISE).

When pro-military groups took control of the Japanese Diet, in 1930, they initiated a change in both domestic politics and foreign policy that led, in the following year, to the invasion of Manchuria. A nationalist-militarist government instinctively sought to reduce the influence of overseas capital: so, it wanted Sumitomo to exercise control over NEC's affairs and to invest more in its own technology and manufacturing capabilities. It forced ISE to transfer 15 per cent of its controlling shares to the zaibatsu. With increased tariff protection, in combination with high domestic demand, NEC sales would multiply seven times over the following five years. It was, clearly, the Great Depression that brought the nationalist-military faction to power in Japan, and it would show its opposition to the foreign ownership of industry. In 1938, one year after the Japanese attack on China, and given the importance of long-distance communications to modern warfare, the Japanese military took control of NEC's Mita and Tamagawa factories. It then forced ISE to sell a second bloc of shares to Sumitomo. After the bombing of Pearl Harbor in December 1941 and the Japanese invasion of South East Asia, NEC assumed direct control of its affiliate China Electric, and acquired a radio research facility belonging to the Post, Telegraph and Telephone Service in the Dutch East Indies.[64]

Multinational investment strategies

Ericsson turned its strategic alliance with SAT into a full merger during 1918, and strengthened itself against its two major rivals, AT&T's Western Electric and Siemens & Halske.[65] These three firms tried and failed to found an international cartel in 1921, and spent the next decade as a result battling each other for world markets. They had to contend, too, with ITT, which became a remarkable example of brisk international business success. The company was founded, in 1920, to consolidate the various activities of Sosthenes Behn, who had been building his sugar business in Puerto Rico until fully comprehending the vast potential of the telephone. Having become a US citizen, Behn served in the Signal Corps in Western Europe, and he conceived the idea of an international telephone system. He and his brother, Hemand, began by consolidating the various Caribbean operations they had acquired – the Puerto Rico Telephone Company, the Cuban-American Telephone and Telegraph Company and the Cuban Telephone Company – and set out to use their new holding company as a vehicle for purchasing further foreign concerns.

ITT made an entrepreneurially bold and opportunistic move, by 1924, when it took control of Spain's telephone service and established a model for future acquisitions and growth. With its consistent earnings, and financial backing from the National City Bank, ITT overcame doubts about the value of the securities it had floated on Wall Street, and Behn, having personally won the support of the Spanish government, appointed locals to the board of his new subsidiary, Compañía Telefónica Nacional de España, or CTNE (the roots of modern-day Telefónica). Perturbed by the quality of telephone equipment available to him while in Europe, Behn began the search for an equipment manufacturer, and, fortuitously, through an antitrust suit filed by the US government, AT&T was looking to divest its overseas operations, amongst which was the International Western Electric Company. National City Bank arranged the meeting between Behn and AT&T, and the deal was completed, with temporary use of key patents, by 1925.

ITT emerged as the owner of the Bell Telephone Manufacturing Company (BTMC), the equipment manufacturer based in Antwerp, Belgium; a British subsidiary, which it renamed Standard Telephone and Cables; and various German interests it merged into Standard Elektrizitätsgesellschaft, or SEG, which itself would go on to purchase, within five years, the electronics companies C. Lorenz and Mix & Genest. The company transformed itself into an internationalized conglomerate with manufacturing businesses and operating concessions in France, Germany, Britain and much of Latin America, working on the basis that local boards of directors, not the corporate headquarters in New York, would be responsible for their management. Overnight, ITT's had become amongst one of the hottest stocks, in what, during this period, was a bull market on Wall Street. As we shall see, however, changes in the economic and political landscape, after 1929, could only expose its highly leveraged debt financing. In the 1930s, the Great Depression and the weight of its debts would critically undermine ITT's profitability, but it was especially vulnerable, given the scale and location of its investments, to the Spanish Civil War that began in 1936 (Wilkins, 1974).[66]

Since the armed forces needed a means of preserving food, and feeding mass numbers of troops, the First World War had been a boom time for the canning industry. To cope with the restrictions on tin supplies, and to cooperate over ever larger government orders, British canning companies had formed a federation. From 1921, four of its leading members decided to reinforce their market sharing arrangements, forming what would soon be called Metal Box & Printing Industries. However, it was threatened by American Can, with its superior automated production technology, when it bought a small local producer, renamed the British Can Company, and quickly made a bid for Metal Box itself. For its salvation, Metal Box looked to American Can's rival, Continental Can: it agreed to exchange shares, and gained rights to the US firm's machinery, technical advice, training and patents. The deal eliminated the effectiveness of all other British competition, and Metal Box agreed to buy up British Can so long as its

US parent stayed out of Britain for the next twenty-one years. Robert Barlow had been the master of the new strategy, and he imposed central control on the founding company directors, who were alienated by his aggressive management style. Overseas, the plan was to divide up the world's markets, focusing on Europe and British colonies, so as to leave any remaining countries to Continental Can. Barlow established partnerships or subsidiaries in France, the Netherlands, Belgium, India and South Africa. Metal Box India, for example, was incorporated in Calcutta, during 1933, in order to manufacture a wide range of containers and packages (Reader, 1976).[67]

The three Swiss chemical majors established a cartel, Basle AG, in 1918, in effect ending all competition between themselves and pooling their profits and technical knowledge. After the First World War, the USA had imposed tariffs on imported dyes and chemical intermediates, in an explicit attempt to encourage domestic production, and Basle AG decided that only an overseas subsidiary could maintain its presence in the world's fastest-growing market. During 1920, it bought Ault and Wiburg Company and founded the Cincinnati Chemical Works: these two businesses manufactured for all three Swiss companies, which, nonetheless, kept their public identities and separate New York sales offices. Another indication of intercompany cooperation, in this sector, was the fact that the Swiss companies licensed Dow Chemical to produce many of their dyes, and the fact that Dow provided Cincinnati Chemical's raw materials.

Ciba, Geigy and Sandoz in 1925 showed themselves mindful of the traditions and the value of Swiss neutrality by refusing to join German firms such as Hoechst, BASF, Bayer and Agfa in the creation of IG Farben. By 1929, in different economic circumstances, they were prepared to join a Dual Cartel with the German giant, which was designed to protect market shares and profit levels. When French companies allied, they created the Tripartite Cartel, which grew into the Quadrapartite Cartel by 1932, when Britain's ICI accepted it could no longer remain outside such an influential grouping. The pan-European cartel these companies founded lasted until the outbreak of war, in 1939 (Enri, 1979).[68] Joseph Nathan & Co. had a very distinctive story: it was a food company from New Zealand, with operations in Australia, before it entered pharmaceuticals, in 1923, and then established Glaxo Laboratories, in 1935, as a separate firm in Britain (Jones, 1986; Davenport-Hines and Slinn, 1992).

The munitions demands of its government had left the German chemical industry, by the end of the First World War, in a deplorable condition, and companies had lost overseas markets and their control over international patents. As the USA had emerged as a competitor, in terms of both technology and production processes, they had been attracted to rationalization schemes that could reverse their loss of position. It was this basic consideration that culminated in the formation of IG Farben, in 1925 (Chandler, Amatori and Hikino, 1997). The initial response of Britain's two leading chemicals firms – Nobel Industries and Brunner, Mond – had been to join, but they were unable to agree terms. The second response was to merge – in combination with the United Alkali Company and the British Dyestuffs Corporation – and to establish Imperial Chemical Industries, in 1926. These firms especially feared the competition which the new German grouping could make in key export markets, and they hoped that ICI would be only one step in the rationalization of the world chemicals industry in partnership with IG Farben, Du Pont, and Allied Chemical. ICI gambled its whole future on the fertilizer business, investing heavily in its Billingham plant, but by 1929 it had to agree production quotas with IG Farben. It signed up for the Quadrapartite Cartel, as we have seen, and tried unsuccessfully to keep the floundering Billingham plant open with another secret agreement.

During 1935, ICI would allow IG Farben to exclusively sell nitrogen in most of Europe and throughout South and Central America, while ICI would control markets in the UK, Spain, Portugal, Indonesia and the Canary Islands, with, furthermore, both sharing the business in much of Asia. International cartels had existed before the First World War, but their coverage and impact both became significantly more pronounced during the interwar period. They were a distinct strategic option, additional to the choices between competitive exporting, licensing, or FDI (Reader, 1970, 1975).[69] With sales in decline after the First World War, and more dramatically so after the shock of the Great Depression in 1929, cartels that set production quotas and divided up markets offered the relief of increased price stability and capacity rationalization. On the whole, they maintained exports and, potentially, encouraged the sharing of technological knowledge, but thereby minimized the case for FDI. Local producers, with an agreed monopoly over their own home market, suited the policies of tariffs, indigenous ownership, and rising hostility to foreign multinationals.

IG Farben, for the twenty or so years of its existence, did not establish overseas operations; ICI made no moves abroad until after the Second World War; and Du Pont limited its investments to Latin America.

Rayon firms rode the 1920s boom in the international demand for their products, and, generally, significantly deepened their multi-national entanglements. In 1922, as soon as the USA had raised its tariff on rayon, Courtaulds decided it had to expand its output there. It consolidated The Viscose Company with a new enterprise, the American Viscose Corporation (AVC), whose carefully concealed and highly rich stream of profits buoyed the less successful parts of the business. The British parent firm had the resources to fund a series of international investments, notably in the period 1924–7: it built a plant in Canada, once again as the result of a rayon tariff; established Courtaulds (India) Ltd, located in Bombay; opened factories in Copenhagen and Barcelona; and set up a French business, La Soie Artificielle de Calais (which took on the new name of Les Filés de Calais by 1934). Courtaulds allied with VGF to take control of Italy's largest rayon maker, Snia Viscosa, and Courtaulds and VGF created a joint venture, Glanzstoff-Courtaulds, based in Cologne. The formation of Glanzstoff-Courtaulds additionally enabled the British and German parent firms to resolve disputes over patents, and to sign marketing and production agreements that set limits on their competition. Moreover, Courtaulds, in the course of the next few years, took a substantial stake in VGF itself, spinning a highly complex web of cross-border governance arrangements. It incorporated subsidiaries in Lichenstein to formally own a number of European factories and patent rights, and to minimize its exposure to local taxation.

Du Pont, in the USA, cooperated closely with Comptoir des Textiles Artificiels, and the Netherlands manufacturer Enka, having created its own plant in Britain during 1925. It would establish a joint venture with the VGF, incorporated as Algemeene Kunstzijde Unie (AKU), in 1929, which emerged as a market leader in the manufacture of artificial fibres. Cartelization of the rayon industry worked in partnership with the boom in foreign direct investment amongst European producers, during the 1920s. Global collusion principally sought to safeguard and agree on the use of proprietary technologies, but inevitably helped to maintain prices and profits. When markets contracted in the 1930s, collusion acquired even greater importance. During that decade, AVC's performance – and, therefore, that of Courtaulds –

dwindled steeply. While the British firm could point to the troubled economic conditions, its record in research and product development contrasted unfavourably with its surging rival, Du Pont (Coleman, 1969; Cerretano, 2012).

Internationalizing brands

Germany's economic difficulties of the 1920s, including hyperinflation, inexorably created operating problems for the margarine makers Jurgen and Van den Bergh, although they did gain from the expansion of the market for margarine over more expensive butter and other animal fats. With their leadership in production, branding and marketing, the companies emerged as Germany's leading margarine manufacturers in the 1920s, and they finally joined into Margarine Unie in 1927, which itself became the basis for further acquisitions. Margarine Unie expanded internationally, in 1928, with purchase of the French-Netherlands Calvé foods company, which owned factories in the Netherlands, France, Belgium, and Czechoslovakia. From 1919 to 1925, Lever Brothers set up factories in Norway, Sweden, Denmark, and Finland to gain from their rising living standards, but each investment was small in scale. With his knowledge of local marketing in the USA, Francis A. Countway continued to guide the Lever Brothers business there, and, in 1919 he reorganized his subsidiary. He wanted to expand its soap sales beyond New England: he divided the USA into ten sales territories, and focused on selling brands such as Lux, Rinso, Welcome, and Lifebuoy, until 1925, when he also introduced Lux as a toilet soap. Lever Brothers sought an alliance with wholesalers as a way to win orders from retailers, and promotional gifts, special displays, demonstrations, and door-to-door visits pushed the business into third place in the USA, behind only Procter & Gamble and Colgate-Palmolive-Peet, by 1929.

Lever Brothers during 1923 had decided favourably on the prospects of China's market, and built a factory in Shanghai. After years of prolonged negotiation, ending in 1929, Lever Brothers finalized the deal with Margarine Unie that created Unilever, in reality two legally separate firms, one based in London, the other in The Hague, but crucially with one shared board of directors. Lever Brothers was mainly a maker of soaps, while Margarine Unie was better known for edible fats. Unilever could, therefore, look for synergies in raw materials, distribution and marketing. Its biggest markets were Britain and the Netherlands, but third was Germany, where it oversaw 70 per cent of margarine sales, supplied by its 25 factories there, and, with these investments valued at £20m, by 1933, it could claim to be the largest foreign-owned company there (Osterhammel, 1989; Cochran, 2000). The new Unilever conglomerate bought an Indian subsidiary in 1931, calling it the Hindustan Vanaspati Manufacturing Company, but, within four years, there was also Lever Brothers India Ltd and United Traders Ltd. It created, too, new factories in Thailand, Indonesia, Argentina and Brazil (Wilson, 1954).[70]

Distillers, between 1925 and 1927, reached a secret agreement with a bootlegger, Sam Bronfman, to distribute liquor in the USA during the time of Prohibition, and they formed Distillers Corporation-Seagram Ltd, in Montreal, to make whiskey and other products for the journey south across the border. Their partnership ended with the repeal of the Volstead Act in 1933.[71]

Already a substantial multinational, as a major firm from a small economy, Nestlé responded to the recession after the First World War by attempting to bring its operations more in line with sales. The company closed factories in the USA, Britain, Australia and Norway, and even in its Swiss base. When the reconstruction was completed, and as economic conditions improved, it expanded production facilities in France, Belgium, Italy, Germany and South Africa. When Nestlé merged, during 1928, with Peter, Cailler, Kohler, and Chocolats Suisses, it added thirteen plants in Europe, South America and Australia to its growing international operations (Harrison and George, 1983; Heer, 1991).[72]

The three large British Quaker-owned cocoa and chocolate firms internationalized in the interwar period, usually through joint ventures: Fry and Rowntree went to Canada (in 1919 and 1927 respectively), Rowntree to South Africa (1926), Cadbury and Rowntree to Australia (1921 and 1934), and Cadbury-Fry, now associated, to New Zealand (1930). With the raising of tariff walls, there was a strong desire to protect export trades and expand sales. The smaller and more scattered populations of the Dominions, and their lower per capita incomes were not automatically receptive to brands transferred from Britain, and adjustments, with the help of local partners and their lines, proved necessary. The Dominions suffered from collapsing commodity prices, and their economic prospects gave Rowntree and Cadbury-Fry poor returns throughout the interwar decades (Fitzgerald, 1995).

One pronounced feature of FDI flows in the interwar years was investment in Europe by the US manufacturers of branded household goods, and their willingness to employ American marketing methods on the other side of the Atlantic. Their investments tended towards Britain, Canada, and Australia for sales locally or regionally (Wilkins, 2004; Feldman, 1989). Procter & Gamble's purchase of soap maker Thomas Hedley, in Newcastle, during 1930 announced its arrival in Britain and issued a major challenge to Unilever in its European heartland (Wilkins, 1974). Howard Heinz – who had succeeded his father Henry as president of H. J. Heinz in 1919 – at home expanded the business into ready-to-eat soups and baby food, during the 1920s, and he sent his son, 'Jack' H. J. Heinz Jnr, to establish, in 1935, what became Australia's biggest food processing plant.[73] The Quaker Oats Company had operated mills in Europe before the First World War, and sold its products throughout Asia and Latin America. Emerging from its first reported loss, caused by buying up grain prior to a fall in prices, the company had to reorganize, and, by 1922, it had consolidated all its overseas activities, about a quarter of its total sales, into a single corporate division.[74] Corn Products Refining Company – with its refineries throughout Europe and Latin America – decided to buy the German maker of soups and bouillon Knorr in 1926.

US cereal makers made their international mark in the interwar years.[75] The Kellogg Company – which had begun its expansion abroad in Canada just before the First World War – opened an overseas plant in Sydney, Australia, in 1924, and sent an executive to institute a marketing programme grounded on the approach of the US parent. It opened its new plant, in 1928, at Botany, where a train line took its products to wharves for shipping throughout Australia, New Zealand and the Asia-Pacific region. It built at factory at Old Trafford, Manchester in 1938 – having identified the local population as a ready source of labour and consumers – and it brought in grain along the complex system of local canals.[76] Shredded Wheat – with two plants having long utilized the hydroelectric power available on both sides of the Niagara Falls in the USA and Canada – opened its landmark modernist factory at Welwyn Garden City, in Hertfordshire, England, in 1926. Nabisco or the National Biscuit Company – which had founded its first foreign subsidiary, during 1925, in Canada – went on to buy the Shredded Wheat business in 1928 (Harrison and George, 1983; Heer, 1991).[77]

James Buchanan 'Buck' Duke remained chairman of BAT – British American Tobacco – even though it no longer had formal links with his firm American Tobacco. The First World War had greatly shifted sales from pipe tobacco towards the more convenient rolled cigarettes, and BAT, now employing greater numbers of women workers, concentrated on distributing cigarettes to troops all over the world. The company decided, in the 1920s, to expand beyond the government coastal trading stations and to sell directly to the populous Chinese market. In Tianjin, in 1922, BAT owned a local paper company, and had just built a new cigarette factory that used the most advanced machinery available. Its Western managers enjoyed a privileged émigré life, and they were entitled to bouts of home leave and secure pensions. Some local shopkeepers had been stocking their brands for decades, but the largest part of BAT's business in Tianjin was done by street hawkers selling rolled cigarettes one at a time from trays. The company prided itself on delegating to Chinese employees and associates, and employed Chinese accountants and clerks. In Shanghai, where BAT had its largest factory and based its advertising department, it ran schools for its employees (Williams, 2005).

Sir Hugo Cunliffe-Owen replaced Duke in 1923: his main worry for the next two decades was to protect sales in China, over a period in which central government was disintegrating, and he decided to restructure BAT China Ltd into regional units which could operate locally and independently. He applied the principles of decentralization in other international operations, with the aim of improving decision making and financial performance, but arguably with very mixed results. Cunliffe-Owen broke any last vestige of the historical association with American Tobacco when he opened up direct competition with the US company through acquisition of Brown and Williamson, in North Carolina, during 1927 (Cox, 2000).

Having inherited his father's business, Ivar Kreuger employed misrepresentations and ingenious schemes of financial engineering to unite the Scandinavian match industry, finally buying up the largest producer, and assuming a monopoly, in 1917. With the ending of the war, Kreuger hoped that his Swedish Match Company, a holding enterprise, could exploit Europe-wide opportunities, and he initiated an aggressive series of takeovers and joint ventures throughout the Netherlands, France, and Eastern Europe. Swedish Match joined with Lee, Higginson & Co., during 1923, to establish the International Match Corporation, formally registered in New York, which had scrutiny of all their South and North American operations. IMG formed, from 1926, the British Match Corporation with Bryant & May, which was itself owned by the USA's Diamond Match; Kreuger, illegally employing front companies in an attempt to avoid an antitrust action, was in turn the ultimate owner of Diamond Match.

A willingness to provide governments with loans often helped to secure favourable operating terms, and Kreuger and his companies held a vast array of investments in many firms and industries throughout the world. By 1930, those firms in which Kreuger could exercise more than half of the controlling shares were manufacturing some 40 per cent of the world's matches, and he had assumed a virtual monopoly in Germany. In Sweden – as well as having interests in mining, pulp, paper and banking – he was a major shareholder in SKF, and controlled the telephone firm L. M. Ericsson. SKF extended its global sales network and, back home, established Volvo cars in 1926 (a business, albeit, that became independent within the space of nine years).[78] During 1929, it was able to purchase seven German competitors, concentrated around Schweinfurt and Cannstatt, which it merged into Vereinigte Kugellagerfabriken (Lundstrom, 1986). SKF would be an early gainer from German rearmament, opening its Berlin factory in 1938, when it also made an acquisition in France (Osterhammel, 1989; Cochran, 2000).

Trade, services and utilities

In the 1920s, weakening prices and new sources of global supply led to control schemes in rubber, coffee, sugar, petroleum and tin. In addition to being producers and distributors of commodities, British trading companies were important movers of capital, but the economic conditions prevailing in the interwar period undermined both these business activities. Many of these traders found themselves unable to restore the profitable enterprises they had created before the Great War. In India, moreover, British trading companies lost market share to new competitors from Japan, and they were on a rapid retreat in Latin America, with the exception of Argentina. Ralli decided that its best option was to form a Japanese majority-owned firm – Showa Menka – to sell Indian cotton in Japan. In 1920, Lever Brothers could not pass up the opportunity to buy the Niger Company, since it would secure essential raw material supplies, and, additionally, block the Elder Dempster shipping line from extending its grip along the western African coast. Falling profits led the African and Eastern Trade Corporation, in 1929, to sell to Unilever, recently formed by the merger of Lever Brothers and Margarine Unie.

Unilever joined the two giant traders it had acquired into United Africa Company, which tended to operate separately from its parent business. To keep UAC afloat, after huge losses, in 1931–2 Unilever pumped in some £3m, but the collapse of rivals eventually gave it greater leverage as a purchaser of produce in Africa. In the hope of stabilizing falling prices, UAC organized pools of commodity buyers with Cadbury-Rowntree-Fry, which concentrated on West African cocoa, and with shippers John Holt. In the 1930s, with trading so unprofitable, it diversified into commodity processing and the distribution of automobiles and gasoline. Across West Africa, it set up manufacturing in soap, leather, timber, shirts and bacon, but these too brought poor returns (Jones, 1998; Jones, 2000). The Inchcape group showed some ability to adjust by discovering synergies within its highly diverse activities, but it was forced to pour too many resources into the troubled P&O line. When Inchcape's founder died, in 1932, the company's strategic direction faltered. Balfour Williamson's attempts to diversify in Latin America and California resulted in a string of failures. The firm sought out new opportunities in chemicals, automobiles and branded goods such as whiskey, yet the opportunities for growth in unsettled markets were few.

Axel Johnson turned to oil trading, and to investing at home, in Sweden, with a refinery, an asphalt business, and a construction firm, all in the 1920s. It bought an iron works and engineering concerns during the decade that followed (Jones, 1998). W. R. Grace – with its shipping, trade, agricultural, mining, and industry interests in Latin America – was quick to seize one new initiative. It joined with Pan American Airways, in 1929, to found the first international air service, Panagra, which operated along the west coast of South America.[79] From Switzerland, Diethelm-Keller was able to expand by acquiring interests in machinery, chemicals, pharmaceuticals and automobiles, and extending its operations to Malaya and Hong Kong. The Union

Trading Company, tainted by its association with German business during the First World War, had lost its assets in Ghana and India, but from 1921 it managed to restore its commercial connections in West Africa (Jones, 1998).

In 1919, a French textile group established Optorg – meaning 'wholesale' in Russian – to increase its sales in Russia and Asia, and by the end of the 1930s it had evolved into one of the five largest businesses in Indochina.[80] Over the course of the interwar decades, Compagnie Française de l'Afrique Occidentale (CFAO) opened subsidiaries in Cameroon, Gabon, Togo, the Congo and other, largely Francophone territories.[81] The Royal Navy had strongly curtailed the operations of Netherlands trading firms during the First World War, treating their connections with German companies as suspicious, and, economically, 1920–2 were further crisis years. The largest concerns, Internatio and Borsumij, seemed better able to cope with these major difficulties, and Hagemeyer responded by improving its administration and cost control. Trade barriers in the 1930s inevitably affected revenues, but cartel agreements with manufacturing industry in the Netherlands helped, and traders and shippers diversified by investing in plantations, mines, manufacturing and utilities in the Dutch East Indies (Jonker and Sluyterman, 2000).

The First World War had allowed Japanese companies, especially in textiles, to expand sales throughout Asia, but, lacking information and networks overseas, they became highly reliant on the *sogo shosha*, or general trading companies. Specialist suppliers and distributors provided, too, economies of scope, and maximized the country's competitive advantage. The government was set, moreover, on a policy of promoting the *sogo shosha* – including those such as Mitsui, Mitsubishi and Sumitomo that were part of highly diverse zaibatsu – in its determination to end reliance on foreign traders. On the other hand, after several years of fast growth and industrial expansion, in which it faced only limited competition in its major Asian markets, Japan would be badly affected by the post-war recession. Suzuki Shoten was bankrupt by 1927, and Mitsui Bussan went through a period of retrenchment and cost-cutting. Japan's growth and industrial expansion after the Great Depression, however, were export-led. While European dependence on trade fell, the presence of the *sogo shosha* in world markets increased, and notably so in Latin America, the Middle East and the Soviet Union (Kawabe, 1987; Sakamoto, 1990; Kawabe, 1987).

Lloyds Bank expanded internationally, buying up almost all of the London and River Plate Bank in 1918, in the expectation of providing its customers with a retail branch service, having concluded that its long-established correspondence arrangements were in the long term uncompetitive. London and River Plate merged with London and Brazilian, in 1923, to create the Bank of London and South America (BOLSA). Through acquisitions, Lloyds obtained an influence over almost all of the British-owned banking sector in Latin America, and developed extensive networks in India, Egypt and Europe. Yet it made no attempt to create a coherent international management structure that could provide adequate oversight of its now substantial overseas interests. Barclays bought three banks in the West Indies, West Africa, Egypt and South Africa, during 1925, to create a more tightly organized multiregional banking group, Barclays DCO, which, unlike that of Lloyds, generated profits. In Australia, New Zealand and South Africa, British banks maintained their competitive advantages, although in this achievement they had the benefit of cartels that blocked the threat of new entrants (Jones, 2000).

Paribas, involved in oil exploration in Africa and Asia, participated in the formation of Compagnie des Français Petroles in 1924. It was during the 1920s that it became a major competitor of Banque de l'Indochine, France's leading colonial bank. Paribas, Banque de l'Indochine, Banque Lazard and the Chinese government established, in 1925, the Banque Franco-Chinoise pour le Commerce et l'Industrie (BFCCI) to take over the assets of the Banque Industrielle de Chine: it founded offices in Beijing, Shanghai and Tientsin, plus eight in Indochina, including Saigon, Hanoi and Phnom Penh, and three in France.[82] As a result of the First World War, Deutsche Bank lost its role as one of the great multinationals. Despite its extensive business network in Latin America, it was forced to sell DUEG in 1920, with its giant Argentine utility Compañia Alemana Transatlàntica de Electricidad (CATE), to a consortium called Compañia Hispano-Americana de Electricidad (CHADE) (Gall et al., 1995).

Although they had limited exposure internationally before 1914, US banks owned 107 overseas branches by 1925, and Citibank, which opened its first foreign branch in Buenos Aires during 1914, had one hundred branches overseas, some two thirds of them in Latin America (Wilkins, 1993; Cleveland and Huertas, 1985). A firm with future global significance was founded in unusual circumstances in 1919 in

Shanghai, by a US businessman, Cornelius Vander Starr, who gave it the name American Asiatic Underwriters (AAU). He acted as an underwriter for other US insurers, but, from 1921, began a process of reverse internationalization by buying insurers back home. He founded his New York office in 1926, giving it the title American International Underwriters (AIU), and acquired a network of insurance offices throughout the Caribbean and Central America.[83]

The First World War had ended Germany's role as a pioneer of global electrification, and affected the involvement of companies such as AEG and Siemens in complex, Europe-wide banking consortia. With Germany becoming a net importer of capital, Elektrobank and Indelec ceased to be German-dominated, and the Belgian-based Sofina gained in international importance. But it was the USA that brought the greatest change. American & Foreign Power was founded in 1923, initially as a General Electric business, and by 1929 its overseas subsidiaries could boast some 47,000 employees. It dominated supply in Latin America, while making giant investments in the Shanghai Power Company and smaller-scale commitments in the Calcutta Power Electric Supply Corporation (Hausman, Hertner and Wilkins, 2008).

During the 1920s, more FDI went into utilities than into any other sector. In the subsequent decade, multinationals struggled against governments, national and local, which responded to popular suspicion of profiteering and price increases (Wilkins, 1974). As we have seen, with ITT leading the way, telephone services were a new aspect of internationalized utilities. Another innovative feature of multinational business was the commercial airline. Motivated by concerns of military security, as well as national economic advantage, governments supported airline adventures overseas, and placed restrictions on landing rights and on the foreign ownership of domestic enterprises. Pan Am – or Pan-American – began operating out of Los Angeles, in 1927, before taking on the Atlantic crossing, and buying up enough Latin American rivals to ensure it became the big regional player. Like European airlines, Pan Am was in receipt of a government subsidy.[84] Imperial Airways was a commercial operation, founded in 1924, and, while connecting parts of Europe, it concentrated mostly on Empire routes to South Africa, India, Malaya, and Hong Kong. It operated in partnership with the Queensland and Northern Territory Aerial Services (or Qantas) and with Tasman Empire Airways (TEAL). It merged, in 1939, into the British Overseas Airways Corporation (BOAC), an entirely state-owned business.[85] Koninklijke Luchtvaart Maatschappij (KLM) could trace its origins to 1919, as one of the world's oldest airlines, and it developed routes throughout Europe and to colonial Dutch East Indies (Wilkins, 1974; Dierikx, 1991; Sluyterman, 2003).

One other development in international services was notable. The rapid growth in mass consumption and marketing, in the 1920s, opened up possibilities for advertising agencies. US firms led with new ideas on survey research, branding, consumer psychology, and advertising, and firms such as J. Walter Thompson, once it had agreed to follow its client General Motors to wherever it sold its vehicles, transferred its skills internationally (Fitzgerald, 1995; Kipping and Engwall, 2003). Both Lord and Thomas and Paul E. Derrick similarly internationalized, at first to service the needs of important domestic clients, before seeking out clients abroad (G. Jones, 1996).

Controlling natural resources

The arrival of peace, in 1918, brought about a sudden decline in the demand for rubber, and, as markets should, conditions of oversupply exerted a strong downward pressure on the commodity price. The British Rubber Growers Association, by 1920, had persuaded the Secretary of State for the Colonies, Winston Churchill, to hold a commission of enquiry. When the Stevenson Plan was published, two years later, with a proposal to cut output, the colonial administrations of Malaya and Ceylon declared their support, and the recommendations passed into law. British commercial interests continued to control some 75 per cent of all natural rubber production, while, on the other hand, US manufacturers consumed some 75 per cent of all the rubber produced. Especially as Britain owed war debts to the USA, the trade was a vital source of dollar earnings, yet the US Secretary of Commerce, Herbert Hoover, perceived the Stevenson Plan as a very unpalatable mix of monopoly and old world imperialism.

Empowered with coordinating Federal economic affairs, Hoover was determined to build a powerful department at the heart of Washington, DC, and to transform thirty years of markedly fractious relations with US big business and its 'robber barons'. In 1925, he informed Britain that the USA would be protecting itself against artificially high prices (Andaya and Andaya, 1982). Du Pont took the lead in developing synthetic rubber, and the Federal government, without admittedly much success, sponsored research into rubber plants that could be cultivated domestically.[86]

Another outcome of the tension between the two commercially important countries of Britain and the USA was the decision made by Harvey Firestone – founder of the Firestone Tire and Rubber Company – to establish the world's largest rubber plantation in Liberia. This country was, at the time, the only independent state in Africa, and the dominance of former slaves from the USA or their descendants over the local tribes dominated its politics. The USA saw itself as supporting a small fellow republic surrounded by threatening colonial powers, and one with which it was historically, but also tragically, linked; the Liberian government, for its part, welcomed the prospect of investment. Firestone agreed, too, that it would build a port – not for commercial reasons, but to provide a station for the US Navy. With negotiations almost finalized, Firestone insisted on the Liberian government accepting a $5m loan from the USA. As a result, Liberia could pay off its $1m debt owed to British-owned banks, reducing Britain's influence overall, but Liberia would lose an even larger portion of sovereignty to Firestone and the USA.

The agreement between Liberia and Firestone, reached in 1926, included a million-acre land concession, on a 99-year lease, that added up to some 10 per cent of the country's arable territory. To safeguard its $5m loan, the USA appointed a Financial Advisor to control Liberia's revenues and expenditure, and converted the country into what was, in effect, a protectorate. The government was obliged to provide the plantation labour, and the ruling Americo-Liberian elite resorted to forcing the inland populations to work for cash, a commodity that was by tradition of no value to them. The League of Nations, by 1930, would publicly condemn the treatment of these native peoples, and the President, Charles King, who had been fraudulently elected, resigned as a result, raising hopes for reforms that ultimately were not forthcoming. The League's report revealed that Firestone, with its 10,000 labourers, was the only employer of any significance in Liberia, and that its army was camped on the multinational's estates to ensure the compliance of its workforce (Dalton, 1965; Cassell, 1970; Smith, 1987).[87]

Goodyear, as we have seen, invested in the Dutch East Indies during the First World War as a strategy for circumventing the British Empire's grip on rubber supplies. The small scale and low productivity of its plantation, which began production in 1923, kept the company reliant on world market transactions and unstable prices. Goodyear, unsurprisingly, viewed the Stevenson Act with deep suspicion, and decided to establish a plantation in the Philippines, from 1928, and to extend its Sumatran operations, in 1930. Yet these investments would bring it only limited supply chain advantage. Britain repealed the Act, in the same year, because British producers in Malaya were losing sales to growers in the Dutch East Indies, and because the unpredicted growth of the US automobile industry, in the 1920s, had made the whole idea of limiting output entirely pointless.[88]

The story of Fordlândia – Henry Ford's attempt to grow rubber in the forests of Brazil – offers cautionary lessons for ambitious business projects in difficult locations. By 1928, the famed entrepreneur had brokered a deal with the government of Brazil to grow the rubber his company needed, and his Companhia Industrial do Brasil gained a concession of 10,000 square kilometres, near the city of Santarém, in return for handing over 9 per cent of any future profits. The land was wholly unsuited to the cultivation of rubber. There was the additional problem that Ford's managers had small knowledge of tropical agriculture, and plants brought from Asia with no resistance to local diseases and insects were a serious miscalculation. Soon after the Brazilian army arrived, in 1930, with orders to suppress a labour revolt, it was decided to leave the Fordlândia site. Ford did not, however, abandon his idea, and he re-established the plantation and settlement in central Brazil, along with all its fundamental failings (this version of the project was shut down in 1945) (Galey, 1979; Grandin, 2009).[89]

Unlike the US tyre manufacturers, Michelin had ease of entry to French-controlled Indochina. The colonial government there allocated, in 1920, large stretches of land for cultivation, and stimulated an investment boom in France to pay for forest clearances, roads, saplings, buildings, and equipment. Some twenty-five plantations appeared along a band of territory in the southern part of the colony, leading down to the Mekong River, but more than 30,000 labourers were recruited from the more populous Tonkin, in the north. Michelin created, in 1925, the largest of the rubber plantations, at Dautieng and Thuan Loi, in Biên Hoà province (later called Phú Riềng), and began an operation that became more famous for its slavelike conditions than for its product. In 1930, some 5,000 rubber workers led by a Communist, Trần Tử Bình, formed Phú Riềng Đỏ (that is Red Phú

Riềng), taking its name from the Phú Riềng Rubber Plantation. It was the first instance of the Vietnamese Communists directing a labour protest.

Phú Riềng Dỏ occupied the plantation for four days, and forced the supervisor to accept their demands, after which they protested against the colonial administration itself. The Foreign Legion quickly suppressed the growing revolt (and Michelin would persevere with ownership of their rubber plantation until 1975, when the Vietcong forced out the US forces that had replaced the French military presence). While, in 1909–13, the Amazonian basin, Central America and central Africa had supplied the world with 80 per cent of its rubber needs, almost all of it would come from South East Asia by the 1930s, mostly grown on European-owned plantations in Malaya, the Dutch East Indies and Indochina. Separate from the 40,000 Europeans living in the colony, native labourers in French Indochina worked in harsh conditions and during long hours to supply an export trade in rice, tin, tea and, above all, rubber.[90]

United Fruit played its part in the US war effort, during 1917–18: with its fleet of 90 ships, it could bring essential supplies to its home country and ship food aid to Europe. The largest grower in the Americas owned or leased 1,25 million acres of land and operated over 1,000 miles of railroad. It built and ran towns, social and medical amenities, utilities, and infrastructure throughout the region, and invested in botanical research. By 1923, thanks to its long-term investments in Panama and Costa Rica, United Fruit had become the world's largest single producer of cocoa, another commodity added to its commercial empire in bananas, fruit, sugar and timber. Victor MacComber Cutter, who was appointed the company president in 1924, acknowledged that a business of the scale of United Fruit needed better internal procedures and more sophisticated advertising and publicity, and began to put more complex organizational structures in place (May and Plaza, 1958; McCann, 1976; Wilson, 1947).

As we have seen (Chapter 2), under pressure from the US State Department, United Fruit had bought up Cuyamel Fruit's stock as a means of resolving their disputes in Honduras and Guatemala, and Samuel Zemurray had agreed so long as he remained in charge of the company he had founded. The State Department proved willing to intervene in the affairs of its neighbours, and restored order in Honduras in 1919 and in 1924. Although it refused to act on United

Fruit's behalf, in 1920, in Honduras, it was instrumental in the return of railway concessions taken from the International Railway of Central America, a part of the United Fruit octopus, and it helped win Pacific port concessions for the business in 1929. The IRCA was, nonetheless, prepared to resist the State Department's wish, during the years of the Great Depression, that it should not carry imported goods from Europe. As for Guatemala, it entered an eleven-year phase of more radical, liberal policies after 1920, in which the interests of local growers against powerful foreign interests received better representation than under dictatorship.

It was in this period, during the 1920s, that John Foster Dulles, senior partner in the US law firm Sullivan and Cromwell, and a future post-war Secretary of State, began to act for IRCA, arranging government concessions, interfirm links and corporate restructuring, while his brother and fellow lawyer in the same firm, Allen Dulles (who would become a CIA director) worked for United Fruit. With their connections to the bankers J. Henry Schroder, John Foster Dulles could facilitate land purchases and, by arranging government loans, he was able to squeeze out competitors. Despite the exchange of shares between United Fruit and Cuyamel, the capacity for dangerous commercial disputes over banana plantations along an undetermined international border remained. Zemurray usually fared worse, and so he sought allies in a distribution war across the USA's East Coast against United Fruit, a business that was supposedly his ally. The complications for regional foreign policy drew in the State Department once again, and Secretary Francis White opened negotiations in 1929. Under pressure from the Federal government, Zemurray accepted a full merger, and United Fruit added Cuyamel's 13 per cent share of the US home market in bananas to its existing 53 per cent. Cuyamel withdrew from running a railway in Honduras, whose government could now no longer call on a sizeable counterweight to United Fruit, although there was one remaining option in Atlantic Fruit (renamed Standard Fruit in 1931).

The restructuring occurred as the Great Depression took hold, and, for United Fruit, infestation on its plantations greatly intensified the difficulties of falling demand. Zemurray, bought out before the collapse in the company's share price, could now afford to take up a controlling interest in the firm and to vote out the board of directors. Zemurray's notorious approach to business soon overrode the corporate style being developed at United Fruit by MacComber Cutter. In charge by 1933, and for the next twenty-eight years, Zemurray was the bandit leader of one of the world's most important multinationals. With the help of John Foster Dulles, Zemurray would acquire a controlling percentage of IRCA. Much to the displeasure of minority shareholders, the railroad's dividends were suppressed by the cheapness of its freight charges, which benefited a large customer such as United Fruit. At Tiquisate and Bananera, in Guatemala, the government ceded monopoly control of the ports and infrastructure to IRCA because the railroad enjoyed the support of the local caudillos, and it gained a similarly tight control over the economies of Panama and Colombia. In Nicaragua and Colombia, United Fruit continued to buy from local producers rather than relying on its own plantations, but it monopolized all the exports and marketing. With so few economies of scale in the growing of bananas, the coordination of distribution and investment in facilities and refrigeration were critical, and the vulnerability of such a perishable product required closely coordinated vertical integration from the point of harvesting to delivery to the consumer (Bucheli, 2005). In El Salvador, with no banana industry, the British-owned Salvador Railway Company still offered competition to IRCA for the country's coffee trade (Dosal, 1993; McCann, 1976; Walker, 2011; MacCameron, 1983).

In the interwar period, a wholly owned subsidiary of United Fruit, Elders and Fyffes, dominated banana sales in Britain. It began to set up sales subsidiaries in continental Europe in the 1920s, and, through a deal signed in 1936, and lasting five years, it agreed to ship the bananas of every grower in Jamaica (Davies, 1990; MacCameron, 1983). In the Congo, by 1923 the Huileries du Congo Belge (HCB) was finally making profits for Lever Brothers, despite recent falls in commodity prices, and secured the palm oil the company needed for its soap, margarine, and much else. Despite the reforms introduced by the Belgian colonial government, Lever Brothers could not evade being tainted by the use of compulsory labour, which continued to occur into the 1930s (Gondola, 2002).[91] Mostly controlled by the Société Générale de Belgique, Belgium's largest financial holding company, and in partnership with the colonial government and the British-controlled Tanganyika Concessions Ltd, the Union Minière du Haut-Katanga (UMHK) worked the African copper belt and engaged in a wide range of commercial activities. Like Lever Brothers, it could claim to be providing employment and wealth generation, and it built workers' villages with accommodation and amenities. But, in the Congo of the time, it was implicated in notorious accounts of harsh treatment and enforced labour.[92] The plantation phase of the palm oil industry began in 1917, in Malaya, with the founding of the Tennamaram Estate, and, during the 1920s the trading firms Harrisons & Crosfield, Guthrie, and Sime Darby emerged as the largest investors in a commodity originally native to West Africa.[93] In the cultivation of tea, there was no equivalent to a multinational the size of United Fruit, but James Finlay, by the early 1940s, could lay claim to some 90,000 acres and 130,000 plantation workers, producing a commodity the firm marketed mostly to Britain and the USA but also all over the world (Jones, 2000).

During the 1920s, international investment achieved economies of scale in the dredging of tin held in Malayan alluvia deposits, and British-owned production finally overtook that of the Chinese operators. Tin companies, like their rubber counterparts, used the freestanding-company form to raise capital in London and to operate overseas. The tin obtained from South East Asia, being homogenous in its composition, was easy for smelters to process, and it created small incentive, therefore, for vertical integration. Bolivian lode deposits, with more impurities and varying compositions, required asset-specific smelters, and did result in vertical integration, forcing firms to operate across borders (Hennart, 1982; Hennart, 1986). The London Tin Company was formed, in 1925, to acquire the many freestanding companies investing in Malaya, and it would, through Anglo-Oriental, control about a third of the colony's output by 1937. Its two smelters processed almost all of Malaya's tin, and LTC had, furthermore, established businesses in Thailand, Burma and Nigeria (Lyttleton, 1962).[94] Simón Iturri Patiño had acquired all Bolivia's foreign-owned tin mines before the First World War, and, in cooperation with the USA's National Lead, he founded a smelter. He created one of Latin America's first multinational enterprises. His business went international in 1929 when, to raise capital, it registered as Patino Mines and Enterprises Consolidated in New York. Patiño also bought a smelter in Malaya. He was rumoured to be one of the five wealthiest men in the world, and he certainly gained the soubriquet of 'The Andean Rockefeller' (Thoburn, 1981; Hennart, 1986; Klein, 1965; Wilkins, 1993; Hillman, 1990).

It was US mining companies that had both the capital and the technology to expand into Latin America, plus access to the world's largest and most dynamic market. They were especially prominent in Chilean nitrates and copper, in Peruvian copper, lead and zinc, and in Bolivian tin. They expanded rapidly in response to new developments in Newfoundland, Canada, and they had arrived in Queensland, Australia, by 1925 in order to exploit very recent discoveries of lead, silver, zinc and copper. The American Smelting and Refining Company (ASARCO), Kennecott, American Metal, Anaconda, Alcoa and Phelps Dodge all emerged as giant enterprises (Wilkins, 1970; Wilkins, 1974; Navin, 1978). As in the case of United Fruit, they were granted remarkably favourable concessions when they went overseas, and, with their first-mover advantages, they would show themselves to be well entrenched in host economies and hard to dislodge (Smith and Wells, 1975).

ASARCO arrived in Peru in 1922, and moved next into Canada, Mexico and Australia. The First World War had stimulated new applications for aluminium, and demand boomed in the 1920s.[95] Alcoa's Northern Aluminium subsidiary, in Canada, was a major supplier, and in 1928 it was spun off as Alcan Aluminium, with the same management running both Alcoa to the south and Alcan to the north. To avoid complications from US antitrust laws, the Canadian company took supervision of mining and power concerns in Norway, Italy, France and Spain, with the exception of the Dutch Guyana bauxite mines, and there was the hope that Alcan could make faster progress in British Empire territories. From 1933, the USA-based St Lawrence Corporation of Newfoundland began to extract vast deposits of fluorspar and asbestos in the easterly Canadian island, and an Alcan subsidiary, the Newfoundland Fluorspar Company, joined as a partner in 1939.[96] Controlled from its founding in South Africa, during 1917, by the Oppenheimer family, the Anglo-American Corporation used cross-holdings to determine the world market in gold and diamonds. It took ownership of De Beers in 1929, and founded its Central Selling Organisation, in London in 1934, as a device to set prices (Spar, 1994; Schmitz, 1986; Navin, 1978).

Controlling oil

In 1920, the Anglo-Persian Oil Company formed Commonwealth Oil Industries in a joint venture with the Australian government, intent on fostering local industrial capabilities, and it built the country's first refinery. Back in its home market, it was ironic that the APOC decided, in 1921, that it would use the BP (British Petroleum) trademark, acquired from a sequestrated German subsidiary, in order to re-inforce its national identity and to advertise its 'British-ness'. APOC set out to build its own capabilities: it ended an agreement with Royal Dutch Shell, during 1922, so that it could foster its own distribution network in Asia and Africa, and, one year later, due to its intensive lobbying of the British government with a case that mixed commercial considerations and claims of increased national economic security, it received exclusive rights to Persia's oil resources (Ferrier, 1982).

In Europe, on the other hand, its interwar activities depended on buying stakes in local refineries and companies. The merger with and ultimate acquisition of the Corporation for Austrian and Hungar-ian Mineral Oil Products (OLEX) was amongst its most important deals. Originally founded to oversee production from the Austro-Hungarian Empire's territories in Hungary, Romania, and Galicia, and called OLEX from its telegraph address of Petrolexport, the com-pany had established itself in the major market of Germany, taking the precaution to register this business, OLEX-Petroleum-Gesellschaft, in Berlin. OLEX had formed part of the Europäische Petroleum Union (EPU) – before the Great War – and had evolved into a subsidiary and sales organization for the Deutsche Erdol Aktiengesellschaft (DEA). In 1926, having begun a chain of petrol stations across Germany, OLEX joined Deutsche Petroleum-Verkaufsgesellschaft (DPVG) in a merger, and it was agreed that APOC, in command of overseas oil supplies, would take a 40 per cent interest in the new venture. APOC owned the company fully within a further five years, buying up the rest of EPU's interest and gaining the strategic and operational freedom to push its BP brand throughout Germany.[97]

Following the terms of the secret Sykes–Picot agreement concluded during the First World War, Britain and France secured, in 1920, a League of Nations mandate that awarded them rule over much of the Middle East. The San Remo conference, with Britain, France, Italy, and Japan in attendance, made initial decisions on the carving up of the Ottoman Empire. The great powers, long drawn to the region by military calculations and the security of trade routes, now had the additional attractions of oil, and had, in effect, excluded US firms from the Middle East region. There was, very quickly, a revolt in Iraq against the prospects of a new and non-Islamic imperial ruler replacing the recently defeated Ottomans. British forces brutally suppressed the uprising, and the ruthless bombing tactics of the Royal Air Force would later become infamous. Abandoning the League of Nations mandate, Britain felt it politic to legitimize its rule by creating a Kingdom of Iraq, during 1921. It imposed a monarchy from the Hashemite clan, which, as well as claiming descent from the family of the Prophet Mohammed and providing the custodians to the holy places at Mecca and Medina, could claim nationalist credentials for leading the Arab rebellion against the Ottoman Empire (Fieldhouse, 2006; Sluglett, 2007).

After the war, in 1919, the French had ceded their claim under the Sykes–Picot agreement to Mosul in return for a 25 per cent share in the Turkish Petroleum Company (TPC). During 1923, after acrimonious negotiations, Iraq abandoned its claim to the once-promised 20 per cent equity participation in TPC because it wanted to secure British support at the League of Nations against Mosul being transferred to the very recently established Republic of Turkey. The US oil companies, not surprisingly, resented the terms of the Anglo-French deal over TPC, because it excluded them from exploration and production in Iraq. Jersey Standard responded by forming a consortium of seven US companies, and, with heavy support from the State Department, with its policy of opposing commercial discrimination by European empires, TPC was forced to restructure. The company re-emerged in 1924 as the Iraq Petroleum Company (IPC), and its owners were APOC, Royal Dutch Shell, Compagnie Francaise des Petroles (CFP), and the US consortium, each with 25 per cent of the shares. The French government was the prime mover behind the founding of CFP, during that year, in order to push an enterprise of a size that would clinch its stake. In 1925, IPC signed a deal with the Iraqi government that granted a sole concession for 75 years (Jones, 1981; Ferrier, 1982; Sluyterman et al., 2007).[98]

Two critical, related factors account for the rise of the oil majors that would almost entirely dominate production, processing and distribution well into the post-war decades. One, as we have seen, was the support of governments that wanted secure energy resources, as clearly shown in the emergence of APOC and CFP. The other was gaining access to oil supplies in what might be politically difficult conditions. To win the right to a concession that offered control over foreign assets, European companies had an immediate advantage where their home country exercised imperial control, and, in the case of the USA, the State Department was never far away in the dealings with host governments. In the 1920s, with oil in short supply, access to this vital commodity had evolved into a matter of international diplomacy and tension, but by the end of the decade, with new discoveries on stream, shortage had turned into a surplus. At that point, the fixing of prices and output through international cartels became the strategic objective of the oil majors. In entering into an alliance with IPC, the major oil companies had signed a clause committing them to act in concert when exploiting the mineral resources of ex-Ottoman territories, a vast area which included the Arabian Peninsula. Kuwait on the other hand was, in principle, preserved for the British, while Saudi Arabia and Bahrain became reserved for US companies. IPC made large discoveries of oil during 1927, and fully proved the commercial potential of Middle East oil. The companies owning IPC rushed to terms, settling their region-wide disputes, and, threatening legal action, Gulbenkian got the 5 per cent he demanded in the company. Under the Red Line Agreement of 1928, the oil companies participating in IPC agreed to act in concert or in agreement on any proposals within the territories of the former Ottoman Empire (Sluyterman et al., 2007).[99]

Mexico, in the violence and political turmoil that followed its revolution, provided, as we have seen, the first example of a developing country challenging the role of foreign multinationals in the exploitation of its natural resources. Resistance to the old ruling elite came from the rural poor, still the vast part of the population, and from the growing numbers of middle and working classes, located in the cities. Both these groups formed parties with reform agenda. The constitution of 1917 had given all minerals to the state and annulled all oil concessions, but the practical policy implications changed with each government that came to power. Finally, a new law, in 1925, required the confirmation of all oil concessions. The US companies threatened to withdraw their capital and halve production. Shell was more sanguine about the principle of the constitutional clause over mineral deposits, if only because the colonial administration of the Dutch East Indies claimed a similar right (Sluyterman et al., 2007; Meyer, 1977; Meyer and Sherman, 1987).

In Argentina, during 1922 President Hipólito Yrigoyen ordered the establishment of the world's first fully state-owned oil company outside the Soviet Union, called Yacimientos Petrolíferos Fiscales (YPF). The second was the Compagnie Française des Pétroles (or CFP, in 1924); during the interwar period, Uruguay's Administración Nacional de

Combustibles, Alcoholes y Portland (ANCAP) in 1931, Yacimientos Petrolíferos Fiscales Bolivianos (YPFB) in 1936, and Petróleos Mexicanos (Pemex) in 1938 would follow. YPF's first director, Enrique Mosconi, was an advocate of national economic independence and oil nationalization, and Yrigoyen campaigned for these policies in the election of 1928. Preparing for a strong reaction from Jersey Standard, Mosconi signed a barter deal with the Soviet Union's Amtorg, but the army coup of 1930, led by General José Félix Uriburu, ended any prospect of nationalization (Alejandro, 1970; Scobie, 1971).[100] The military strongman and ruler of Venezuela, Juan Vicente Gómez Chacón, reduced the national debt by selling concessions to the oil multinationals, after discoveries had been made, in 1928. Although the revenues funded public works and infrastructure, a large part of the country's new wealth went to Gómez and his supporters.

It is said that the largest oil companies in Venezuela, Jersey Standard and Royal Dutch Shell, appeased the dictator in return for exploration and operational rights. Gómez was quick to exploit the rivalry of the multinationals, and reduced Shell's position to the benefit of US companies. When it bought the Creole Petroleum Company in 1928, Jersey Standard was confirmed as Venezuela's most important oil concern. Gómez's subsequent decision to increase oil taxes was a response to persuasive nationalist criticism that he had handed over control of the economy to foreign interests, but, otherwise, the companies in this period enjoyed a large degree of operational freedom in Venzuela (Dosal, 1993; Sluyterman et al., 2007; Topik and Wells, 1998).[101]

Second setback: the Great Depression

In an attempt to halt the rise in tariffs, the League of Nations organized the first World Economic Conference, in 1927. It was accepted that the aim was discussion rather than decision making, but the conference did declare against the trend towards trade barriers, including tariffs, quotas, export duties, and discriminatory taxation and treatment. The conference acknowledged the problems of economic disruption, trade imbalances and government debt, as a result of the war, but viewed these difficulties as serious but temporary. Delegates knew that the return of the pre-war position would not by itself give Europe back its prosperity, due to the growth of industry elsewhere in the world (Colijn, 1927). Latin American countries in particular opposed proposals that would have limited the ability of sovereign nations to pass special measures on foreign-owned enterprises (Lipson, 1985).

When the Economic Committee of the League of Nations drafted the relevant provision, in 1929, it gave precedence to the rights of individual member states, and argued that foreign investors should receive a commensurate 'national compensation' in cases of dispute, and not 'fair compensation', as wanted by the British delegation (Sigmund, 1980). The debates highlighted the importance of the calculations made by nation states on the gains and losses from fully and openly engaging in the existing international economy and its prevailing advantages. They showed how recent events had spread doubts about restoring the pre-war system, even if there was little clarity on what would replace it. In amongst this debate was another more specifically about multinationals, and their intrinsic rights to property and non-discrimination, versus an absolute view of national sovereignty. Newly industrializing countries perceived advantages in protectionism – bad for trade, but not always for FDI if governments did not also impose discriminatory taxes or currency controls.

There are justifiable reasons for seeing the years from 1914 to 1948 as a distinct period: the issues unresolved by the peace treaties signed after the First World War undoubtedly contributed to the Second World War, and, with the takeover of Eastern Europe by local Communist parties and the Soviet Union in 1947–8, the post-war structure of Cold War rivalry was set. On the other hand, the world economy did recover during the mid 1920s, and contemporaries were planning how to bring back the pre-war stability to global affairs. Historians, overall, take the view that the Nazis would not have come to office and seized power, in Germany, from 1933 onwards, but for the economic, political and social consequences of the Great Depression. From a purely economic history perspective, if we trace the trends in trade and overseas investment, it is 1929 that is the turning point (Hobsbawm, 2003; Miller, 2012; Jones, 2005). As well as inflicting unemployment and poverty, the series of economic catastrophes that followed from the Wall Street Crash transformed the policies of governments, inclining them towards protective measures, state controls, collusive arrangements, and greater self-sufficiency. At worst, states rejected liberal democracy as well as the soundness of capitalism and free markets. During the 1930s, the combination of economic conditions and national policies curtailed the investment opportunities of multinationals, and the greater hostility of host governments and a preference for indigenous enterprise directly affected the multinationals' operations and subsidiary management.

The USA raised its tariffs, in 1930, and brought immediate retaliation from Canada. When Britain, France, Germany, Australia, India and others introduced tariffs or quotas in 1931–2, they were part of a world trend that confirmed the reversal of the free trade policy identified with the nineteenth century. The Imperial Economic Conference, which put forward proposals in 1932 in Ottawa, set up a system of reciprocal tariffs to encourage trade within the British Empire at the cost of non-imperial business. One flaw in the plan was that Britain's Dominions and colonies were taking a decreasing percentage of British trade, with Canada in particular being drawn by force of economic realities into greater levels of commerce with its southern neighbour. France's exports to its overseas possessions, however, would marginally grow. Britain left the gold standard in 1931, abandoning the idea of fixed exchange rates, and the USA did likewise in 1933, the year in which the World Economic Conference failed to find a solution to the breakdown of the international system. France and other West European nations held on to the Gold Standard, but by 1936 conceded the defeat of a once-guiding principle.

As we have seen, world trade values, higher in real terms in 1924 than in 1913, fell away again from 1929 to 1933. Between 1927 and 1933, international lending fell by 90 per cent, largely the result of changed government policies and the economic downturn. Primary producers were notably hit by the Great Depression. Rice and silk prices collapsed, hurting economies such as Japan, which sent 90 per cent of its silk production to the USA. The American economy, having boomed in the 1920s, was especially affected by the slump, and lost share of world export markets to the advantage of countries like Japan and the slight gain of industrial Europe (Table 3.2). By the end of the 1930s, half of world trade was affected by tariff duties (Kenwood and Lougheed, 1999; Ashworth, 1964).

International cartels were not new to the interwar years, and had undoubtedly extended their reach in the 1920s, due to unstable or falling prices, overcapacity, or new sources of supply in raw materials. Collusion and market sharing had obvious implications for business strategies, putting limits on the need for exports, FDI, and overseas subsidiary operations. Networks of share ownership and management relationships, as we have seen, restrained competition in the world electrical industry. From 1924, a convention involving, amongst others, General Electric of America, Philips, AEG, Compagnie des Lampes, Britain's General Electric Company, and Toshiba Electric controlled the production, prices and patents of electric lamps, and appointed a court of arbitration to hear disputes. Anglo-American's acquisition of De Beers, in 1929, strengthened international collusion over diamond supplies, and the company's prominent position in gold allowed it to control much of the mineral's global production outside the Soviet Union.

In 1928, the world's three largest oil companies – Jersey Standard, Shell and APOC – signed the Achnacarry Agreement, named after the Scottish castle chosen to host the meeting of the companies' top executives. The overall objective was to bring capacity and demand more into line with each other, and to fix existing market shares. Only an increase in demand would justify the building of new facilities. To avoid the threat of an antitrust suit, the 1928 agreement did not apply to the USA. This factor and the companies' lack of control over Russian and Romanian supplies meant that the agreement was only partially effective (Bamberg, 1994). On the other hand, the cartelization of the tin industry, with the formation of the Tin Producers Association, in 1929, did put in place effective voluntary restraints on production. Within a year, the governments of British Malaya, the Dutch East Indies, Nigeria and Bolivia had made its terms compulsory, and ensured its terms held (Hennart, 1986).

The Aluminium Alliance, formed in 1931, was a renewed attempt at price and market stabilization, and, with US laws in mind, Alcoa colluded through its Canadian subsidiary, Alcan, run by the same management as the parent business. Statutory backing for the rubber cartel, as discussed earlier, was a fundamental part of its success. During the 1930s, chemicals producers signed up to a succession of agreements to increase restraints on competition, and some 80 per cent of dyestuffs output was covered by 1938 (Schroter, 1990). The International Tea Agreement, in 1933, was able to stabilize prices, again due to legislative backing and the involvement of each dominant producer in India, Ceylon and the Dutch East Indies (Gupta, 1997). It was the support of governments that made the impact of three commodity cartels – in tin, rubber and tea – far-reaching.

Manufacturers and the Depression

By 1930, the financier and fraudster Ivar Kreuger had acquired majority control of Ericsson's stock. During the following year, as the Great
Depression threatened the collapse of his dubious business dealings,
he offered to sell his interest in Ericsson to ITT. The US multinational,
as its doubts about Kreuger's solvency grew, sought to withdraw from
the deal, and there was the discovery, too, that Swedish law at the
time prohibited the foreign ownership of indigenous companies. As
his personal and business world collapsed, Kreuger decided to commit suicide. Three banks – Skandinaviska Kredit, Stockholms Enskilda
Bank and Svenska Handelsbanken – moved to restructure Ericsson, by
1933, and negotiated with ITT to acquire a large share of the company. Cartel arrangements helped to support Ericsson overseas during
the 1930s, and, at home, it benefited from Sweden's military buildup,
by manufacturing aircraft instruments, machine guns and ammunition, as well as telephones (Partnoy, 2008). The debt burden that ITT
had acquired in the 1920s to fund its rapid international expansion
endangered the future of the company over the next decade. The purchase of the Romanian telephone industry, in 1930, and the later addition of businesses in Hungary, Germany and Sweden further stretched
the company's resources. As a holding company, ITT earned money
through dividends and profits remitted by its subsidiaries, and most
of its clients were either governments or quasi-nationalized telephone
operating companies. In the restrictive trade atmosphere of the period,
many foreign nations blocked the repatriation of earnings, and ITT
sought instead to develop its US operations rather than to expand
overseas (Wilkins, 1974).[102]

Dunlop continued its internationalization in 1935–6, establishing
factories in the Irish Republic, South Africa and India, because tariffs, in the view of the company, had made imports no longer viable.
Although rubber was a new growth industry, the 1930s were a difficult
decade for Dunlop, which found itself with overcapacity. Exchange
controls, when introduced in Germany and Japan, complicated its
operations in these two countries, and prevented the repatriation
of profits. Pilkington, the British glass maker, established its Australian factories during 1935–6 (Jones, 1986). By founding factories in
Java (1934), South Africa (1935), Ireland (1935), India (1936), Brazil

(1938) and Sweden (1939), Goodyear made itself the tyre industry's most prominent multinational, and the Goodyear Foreign Operations department had, in total, oversight of seven overseas manufacturing plants and seven rubber plantations. Dunlop and Goodyear had reciprocal arrangements to manufacture each other's products in selected countries overseas. Never able satisfactorily to break into the US market,[103] Michelin closed its New Jersey plant in 1931, but did establish production elsewhere, in Germany (1931), Argentina (1933), Spain (1934), Czechoslovakia (1934) and Belgium (1937).[104]

Despite France's introduction of tariffs, most US automobile firms continued to judge demand in its home market as suited to a policy of export or assembly production, rather than FDI. The exception was Ford, which decided to take a large commercial risk. After protracted negotiations, Ford's SAF subsidiary formed a joint venture with the Alsatian manufacturer Mathis, called Matford SA, in 1934, but the union was an uneasy one. Having agreed to pull out of the joint venture, in 1937, Ford commissioned a new plant at Poissy, west of Paris, but German troops would occupy the factory in 1940, before a single car had been produced (Laux, 1992).[105] Citroën continued its programme of ambitious expansion after the Great Depression, and it received plaudits for the performance and design of the Traction Avant, when it was launched in 1934. But it made itself bankrupt, and the French government asked the largest creditor, Michelin, to become the owner, which it did in 1935, the year that André Citroën died. The tyre and rubber firm appointed a decorated aviator, Pierre-Jules Boulanger, as Citroën president and then as the Michelin joint managing director, in 1937 and 1938.[106] Henri-Théodore Pigozzi founded the Société Industrielle de Mécanique et Carrosserie Automobile, or Simca for short, in 1934, replacing the small assembly plant he managed in order to make Fiat cars on a larger scale at Nanterre, Paris.[107]

Fiat itself began the construction of its modern Mirafiori plant in 1937, although the factory did not achieve full-scale production until the Second World War (Estapé-Triay, 1999; Tortella, 2000; Harrison, 1978).[108] General Motors expanded its international network of assembly operations after the worst of the Great Depression had passed: it opened a plant in Mexico (1935), a second facility at Warsaw (1937), and, having decided against buying Citroën some twenty years previously, and never making a breakthrough in France, a CKD works for cars and trucks at Gennevilliers (1939). By the time General Motors was able to open its third assembly line in Argentina, in 1940, it was facing problems of wartime shortages, and decided that the factory should make refrigerators, batteries and suspension components instead. GM Brazil similarly switched production, and cars did not roll off its assembly line again, on a large scale, until 1948, at its São Paulo plant.[109]

Despite a difficult economic climate, after 1929 Lever Brothers in the USA was able to make progress commercially with its Lifebuoy soap brand and with Rinso, which could be used in the new electric washing machines increasingly being sold in the world's largest consumer market. Imitating Procter & Gamble's success with Crisco shortening, Lever Brothers launched Spry as a rival product during 1936, and a cross-country campaign pushed up sales so successfully that they reached three quarters of those of the well-established Crisco brand. Growth throughout the depressed 1930s revealed that soap had become a popular necessity rather than a luxury.[110] By 1936, Nestlé had established new subsidiaries in Denmark, Czechoslovakia, Chile and Mexico, and it supervised some twenty companies over five continents. At the request of the Brazilian Coffee Institute, concerned about its country's unused stocks, Nestlé successfully developed an instant soluble powder, which it called Nescafé. Originally intending to manufacture in Brazil, it found the administrative barriers problematic, and it settled on initially producing in Switzerland instead, but it was in the key market of the USA that it gained immediate appeal. Nestlé could claim ownership of some 105 factories overseas by 1938 (Harrison and George, 1983; Heer, 1966, 1991).[111] Coca-Cola created its overseas arm, the Coca-Cola Export Corporation, in 1930, to manage all its assets outside the USA, Canada and Cuba, and, within ten years its brand was sold in some seventy nations, typically through franchises that bought its 'secret' syrup formula (Giebelhaus, 1994).

Industry and politics

Tariffs might potentially encourage manufacturers, concerned to protect their export markets, to undertake FDI and overseas subsidiaries. Before 1929, the growth in per capita incomes and consumption helped to validate these decisions, but the falling away of demand as a result of the Great Depression altered the balance of considerations and endangered the viability of existing investments. In addition to the more risky economic climate, governments in Europe, Japan, and Latin America showed themselves to be increasingly hostile to foreign-owned multinationals. In a reaction to the Great Depression, and to the seemingly ubiquitous presence of US automobile assembly plants, European governments introduced import restrictions on components, and pushed US multinationals, in the 1930s, to the next step of full production plants. They calculated, too, that local producers had developed enough to compete on price and quality.

Having introduced exchange controls in 1931, Germany imposed import quotas on automobile components, and, within four years, Ford at Cologne had ceased to use any parts imported from Dagenham.[112] The acquisition of Opel constituted General Motors's boldest and most expensive strategic decision overseas, its value being thirteen times that of Vauxhall at the time of purchase. The introduction of best-practice production methods, through the transfer of US techniques, had given Opel a price advantage in the German market. In 1935, Opel became the first German-based car maker to make over 100,000 vehicles, and sold small-weight, aerodynamic, and fuel-efficient vehicles. Output reached, by 1937, over 130,000 units, and the Russelheim factory was Europe's largest and the seventh-biggest worldwide. Because of their relationship with Opel, and their understandable wish to safeguard and develop their investment, GM executives came into contact with Nazi politicians at the highest levels, and the German government was a large customer. The Nazis, despite their preference for autarky, saw a multinational such as GM as useful: it was the largest and most efficient automobile business, could transfer technology and finance, and use its worldwide networks to acquire raw materials such as rubber.

GM-Opel made a bid to make the people's car, but lost out to Frederick Porsche's 'beetle' design, which had the support of Hitler and the National Socialist Labour Front. Deep down, the Nazis wanted Volkswagen to be a state-owned factory. With the support of the Wehrmacht, GM-Opel warded off the 'Germanization' of its management and personnel during 1938, but only by undertaking more arms production and coming more under the influence of the military. GM's technological and organizational capabilities continued to give it some bargaining power, even as a US firm operating in a nationalistic dictatorship. Sloan's strategy was to portray and, as much as possible, run Opel as a German business, and to ignore the way in which the Nazis ruled Germany outside the factory gates. To protect their interests, and to fulfil their executive duties, GM's leading figures were tempted into one compromise after another, yet, on the other side of the balance sheet, they retained enough influence to prevent the imposition of 'Germanization' policies on its subsidiary. In 1938, the leading GM executive, in charge of overseas operations, was awarded the Grand Cross of the German Eagle for his distinguished service to the Third Reich. He carried a letter, in 1939, from President Franklin D. Roosevelt, which urged European leaders to avert war, and he visited Führer Adolf Hitler, Hermann Goering, who was in charge of economic planning and rearmament, Joseph Kennedy, as the US ambassador in London, Robert Vansittart, in his role as chief diplomatic advisor to the British government, and the British Foreign Secretary, Lord Halifax (Turner, 2005).[113]

Because of their large investments in Germany, US multinationals Ford, Jersey Standard Oil, Chase Bank, Sterling Drug and ITT are all on record as having had contacts with the Nazi hierarchy.[114] Jersey Standard's chairman strived to protect his firm's assets and business, and his company had close links with IG Farben (which would later be implicated in war crimes and the Holocaust).[115] Thomas Watson, head of IBM, was determined to protect his company's interests and to appease the Nazi government (Black, 2012). We know that Hitler received ITT's chief executive, Sosthenes Behn, in 1933. The multinational, through its subsidiary C. Lorenz AG, owned 25 per cent of the aircraft manufacturer Focke-Wulf from 1938 onwards (it later also gained radio and radar parts maker Signalbau AH Huth).[116] Germany publicly honoured Henry Ford for his advice on the building of the Volkswagen works, in 1939, and critics pointed out how the businessman shared with the Nazis a most extreme and loathsome form of anti-Semitism.[117] Coca-Cola – which had established its subsidiary in 1929 – adopted an advertising strategy that suggested its brand was German, and it was a major sponsor of the 1936 Olympic Games in Berlin. But when Goering introduced the Four Year Plan of rearmament, stockpiling and autarky, Coca-Cola could not convince the authorities that it was an essentially German enterprise entitled to an import licence. It agreed to begin manufacturing its secret syrup locally, as a result, but followed its usual international strategy of contracting out bottling, storage and distribution.[118]

From the time, in 1933, when the Nazis came to power, Unilever's position in Germany was made insecure. The company's directors were generally unsympathetic to the regime, with many of its directors, including the Van den Berghs, being Jewish, but over time the company made accommodations with policies of indigenous control and 'Aryanization', with the aim of protecting its major commercial interests. D'Arcy Cooper, the chairman, and Paul Rijkens, the fellow director who would eventually replace him, met the new German Chancellor, Adolf Hitler. Having obtained office, Hitler seems to have forgotten previous Nazi rhetoric, and stated that he had no objections to private business and that foreign multinationals would be treated equally. But currency rationing and exchange controls would hinder a business that imported its raw materials.

Unilever found itself ultimately negotiating with Hermann Goering, who wanted to limit imports. Specifically, he hoped to develop a German commercial oil seed, and to make a synthetic soap (which, in fact, would be produced). The Nazis were committed to the goal of autarky; large stockpiles were preparation for a future blockade, and IG Farben's research into synthetic fuel and rubber had a strategic military importance. Unilever's representatives declined to provide raw materials on credit, on the grounds that its shareholders would never sanction such a policy, but it re-emphasized its commitment to cooperative relations with the regime. They stressed that the company was amongst the largest corporate sponsors of the Anglo-German Fellowship, which included other manufacturers such as Firth-Vickers Stainless Steels and Dunlop, the oil giant Shell, financial institutions Schröder, Lazard and the Midland Bank, accountants Price Waterhouse, and travel agent Thomas Cook & Sons (Forbes, 2000; Kershaw, 2004; Pugh, 2006).

Unable to remit its profits, Unilever resorted to a number of unrelated investments in Germany, although it was allowed to buy and then export ships built in German yards as a way of releasing blocked Reichsmarks. Alongside price controls, the government's limiting of margarine production in favour of locally made butter and fats especially hurt Unilever. The cheaper price of its margarine was well suited to the prevailing economic conditions, including official restraints on incomes, but economics was not the principal driver of Nazi policy. Unilever, with its blocked and accumulating Reichsmarks, bought into Neue Norddeutsche und Vereinigte Elbeschiffahrt, a fishing fleet and fish distribution business, stretching from France, Germany, Austria, Czechoslovakia and Poland up to Norway, and down to Turkey. With this acquisition, in 1937, there were very obvious commercial synergies, but the Nazi administration refused Unilever, as a foreign business, permission to buy more than 49 per cent of the ownership. Unilever was involved in an – ultimately unfulfilled – attempt to create a major German whaling fleet, although D'Arcy Cooper, Rijkens, and Viscount Hugh Trenchard attended the launch of the first processing ship, held in Bremen. Trenchard was the founder of the Royal Air Force, and a former Commissioner of the Metropolitan Police, who had been appointed chairman of Unilever's United Africa Company because of his experience of Africa during the Boer War and his role in suppressing Ibo tribesmen in Nigeria.

During 1938, the year of the Kristallnacht pogrom, which so visibly exposed the racist and brutal nature of the Nazi regime to the rest of the world, the 'Aryanization' of the German economy and its professions was extended to large businesses. Unilever seems to have made fair settlements with the Jewish owners compelled but eager to sell (although the company would not be free of post-war legal disputes on this sensitive issue). In the midst of this human tragedy was the irony that Unilever was classified as a 'non-Aryan' – that is, a Jewish – firm. While helping to extricate its Jewish managers from the Third Reich, the company provided assurances to the Nazi government that its Jewish shareholding was a very minor percentage, and that Jewish directors were not involved in oversight of its German operations. Georg Schicht, a director, conveyed the official line to Goering that, 'as businessmen doing business in all countries of the world they stood completely aloof from politics'. Still preferring to work with the conglomerate, applying the 'bizarre' logic of the Nazis, Goering confirmed that Unilever, although officially registered as 'non-Aryan', would be treated as if it were 'Aryan'. Mounting trading difficulties in Europe meant that profits from the Netherlands operation, formerly two thirds of the total, and from the British-controlled business, one third, were exactly reversed by 1937 (Gondola, 2002).[119]

With so many economic and political difficulties in Europe, in the 1930s, and the fall in advertising revenues, the J. Walter Thompson agency withdrew most of its offices, although it did establish itself for the first time in Rio de Janeiro (1931) and in Calcutta (1935) (Jones, 2005). During 1939, Credit Suisse concluded it was an opportune time to establish its first overseas branch, the Swiss-American Corporation, in New York, far from the tensions in Europe.[120]

Before the annexation of Manchuria in 1931, Japan had welcomed foreign capital, if not wholly foreign-controlled businesses, but, as nationalist and military factions took control of the functions of government, they sought to exclude or scale back foreign capital. The Japanese automobile industry had emerged through cooperation with foreign multinationals, but by the end of the 1930s foreign companies would be forced to withdraw. As for Nihon Sangyo Company, it decided to manufacture the Austin Seven under licence from the British company. In 1931, Tobata Imaon Company, an automotive parts manufacturer, purchased a controlling interest in Dat Jidosha Seizo Company (whose predecessor company had built the original Datsun model during the First World War). It had the high ambition of making mass-produced vehicles that could compete with foreign models in both quality and price. The subsidiaries of General Motors and Ford – and to some extent, Chrysler – dominated automobiles sales in Japan's home market. To make the vision into a reality, Imaon agreed to Jidosha Seizo forming a joint venture with the Nihon Sangyo Company, to be located, from 1933, in Yokohama, where in future the Datsun would be manufactured. By utilizing its experience as a parts supplier to Ford, Nihon Sangyo wanted to diversify forwards into full vehicle production.

With its new name, acquired in 1934, the Nissan Motor Company owned an integrated automobile factory, which it operated under the technical guidance of American industrial engineers. But with US multinationals still dominating the Japanese market, Nissan could not make a commercial success out of the Datsun or the Austin Seven. While established zaibatsu like Mitsui and Mitsubishi were too cautious to enter the auto industry, an emergent new zaibatsu, Nissan, and other companies accepted the challenge. In time, Austin would regard its arrangement with Nissan as its most profitable licensing deal.[121] Ishikawajima Automobile Manufacturing, incorporated in 1929, could trace its beginnings to the Tokyo Ishikawajima Shipbuilding and Engineering Company, which, having made trucks during the First World War, produced cars in the 1920s under licence from Britain's Wolseley Motors.[122] Once he had travelled, during 1933, to the USA to study its production management, Kiichiro Toyoda used the revenues of his family's textile machinery firm to establish an automobile division. His father had made a critical technological breakthrough in cotton textile weaving: the automatic loom transformed a key process stage in the making of cloth, encouraged the integration of spinning and weaving within larger enterprises, and reinforced Japanese competitive advantage within a major global industry.[123]

In 1936, the Japanese government acted, and passed the Automobile Manufacturing Industries Act, which was designed to break the US monopoly of Japan's home market. The other part of the policy was for the government to select local companies for direct state support and volume military orders. Given this encouragement, Toyoda Loom formally founded the Toyota Motor Corporation, during 1937, the name adjusted slightly from that of the family's because the new one, in Japanese script, looked more streamlined and dynamic.[124] Ishikawa-jima Automobile became Tokyo Motors, producing its first ever Isuzu truck in the next year.[125] Once exchange controls had been introduced, when Japan started the Pacific War against China in 1937, the three US producers GM, Ford, and Chrysler closed their assembly plants. Another outcome of war was that the military increasingly exercised direct control over automobile factories and their production plans.

The Japanese government had long promoted joint ventures with foreign multinationals as a means for organizational and technological learning, but the final objective, more actively pursued in the 1930s, was to secure industrialization of the economy and indigenously owned enterprises. Jointly owned by Siemens & Halske and Furukawa, Fuji Electric spun off its telephone department, in 1935, as Fuji Tsushinki, which continued to be in receipt of state contracts (later becoming known as Fujitsu).[126] In Japan, Siemens had opted for engaging with Japanese companies through licensing and direct investment, and transferred knowledge of their management and production technology to partner companies. General Electric remained linked to Tokyo Electric and the Shibaura Engineering Works, since cartel arrangements and shared ownership in the global electrical industry supported market sharing, price control, and patent transfers, and countered the nationalist desire for full indigenous control. The two firms were merged, in 1939, into the Tokyo Shibaura Electric Company (soon widely known as Toshiba), in which General Electric had a 24 per cent shareholding (Odagiri, 1996; Wilkins, 1990).[127]

From 1929, due to the Great Depression, the falling value of the yen, and strong protectionist tariffs, imports of chemicals declined sharply.

IG Farben had small minority holdings in two manufacturing plants, making rayon and pesticides. In 1935, six members of the international dyestuffs cartel – including IG Farben, Du Pont and ICI – signed a deal to assign the Japanese company 85 per cent of the sales in its 'home' territory of Japan, Manchuria, Dalian, and Taiwan. It also fixed prices for China, as well as Japanese-controlled territories. Further agreements involving the cartel and Mitsui Mining followed, covering several aspects of chemical production. By this point, in a significant reversal of its overseas trading policy, IG Farben had to acknowledge that Japanese companies dominated their home and regional markets. With inward investment effectively prohibited, the company had to opt for licensing if it was to exploit to some extent its technological competitive advantage. It gave assistance to five companies in fertilizers, including the Taki Fertiliser Works, necessitating an exchange of personnel and the building of new plant. IG Farben approached the South Metropolitan Railway and Mitsubishi Mining over synthetic oil, but, wary of embedding reliance on a foreign company, the Japanese Navy blocked the proposal. By the end of the 1930s, Japanese firms accounted for over 3 per cent of worldwide sales of dyestuffs, and Mitsui Mining, Nihon Senryo and Mitsubishi Chemical Industries controlled some 90 per cent of the market in Japan. Import licensing helped too with the expansion of fertilizers and pharmaceuticals.

How did Japanese multinationals perform in the decade before the Second World War? In this period, it is impossible to separate the commercial capabilities of firms from Japanese military and imperial policy. By 1930, the South Manchurian Railway (Mantetsu) was Japan's largest single corporation, and its most profitable, generating over one quarter of the country's tax revenues. Freight secured some 75 per cent of South Manchurian revenues, and Manchukuo, the puppet state with the former Chinese Emperor Aisin-Gioro Puyi as its titular ruler, produced about half of the world's soya beans for use as food, animal feed and fertilizer. The colony was a classic example of an imperial power exploiting the natural resources of other territories. The South Manchurian Railway changed the name of its primary mill, in Liaoning, to Showa Steel Works, in 1933, and, by the end of the decade, nearly 800 Japanese-owned industrial and mining enterprises had been founded in Fengtian province, producing and processing steel, digging and liquefying coal, making cement and bricks, and carrying out a diversity of engineering activities (Young, 1999).[128]

Under the direction of the Kwangtung Army, which effectively ran
Manchukuo, the businessman Yoshisuke Aikawa formed a holding
company that controlled his major business, the Nissan Konzerne,
and in 1937 it took a major interest in Mantetsu. He moved Nissan's headquarters to Manchukuo, and his company established the
Manchurian Industrial Development Company, equally owned with
the Manchukuo government, in return for overseeing the planned
industrialization of Japan's colony. Aikawa argued that the colony was
too underdeveloped for free market capitalism. To deliver his expansionary plans, Showa Steel licensed technology from Krupp, and the
training of Japanese engineers in Germany began in 1937 (Kudo, 1994;
Matsusaka, 2003).[129] As domestic coal stocks in Hokkaido depleted
in the 1930s, Mitsui Mining established mines and refineries in China
and South East Asia, and the company evolved into Japan's largest producer of coal, non-ferrous metals, explosives, chemical weapons and
synthetic oil. In 1938, wharf workers at Port Kembla in New South
Wales boycotted ships loading pig iron en route to Japan, protesting
against the attack on China, and at reports of massacres.[130]

Resources and sovereignty

The Great Depression caused the price of rubber to plummet. In the
previous decade, attempts to control output and prices within the
British Empire had provoked opposition from the rest of the world.
By 1934, however, the major producers had signed an International
Rubber Regulation Agreement (IRRA): Britain (meaning, in the main,
Malaya), India, the Netherlands (including the Dutch East Indies),
France (that is, Indochina), and Thailand formed a cartel. In their
actions, the signatories showed themselves as sensitive to the needs
of US tyre and rubber manufacturers. Goodyear, however, objected
to its Sumatran estates falling under the IRRA, and it invested in
experimental sites in Panama (1935) and Costa Rica (1936), which
lay outside the control of the scheme.[131] The rubber cartel caused
resentment in Japan, and stoked support for imperial expansion in
South East Asia, to ensure control of its own raw materials.

Since Jamaica was the British Empire's only producer of bananas,
the imperial preferential tariff policy was a boost to the transatlantic
trade conducted by Elder and Dempster (admittedly, a United Fruit
subsidiary), and German planters in the Cameroons would transfer

their business to a British-owned shipping line, in 1939, to obtain the lower duty (Davies, 1990).

The main problem for APOC in the 1930s was the rise in Iranian nationalism. A military coup had brought the new Shah, Reza Khan, to power in 1925, and there was a determination to end foreign dominance of the country. APOC was by far the biggest symbol of economic imperialism in Persia, and there was additional local resentment at falling royalty payments during the Great Depression. The Persian government cancelled its concession in 1932, although, thanks to arbitration by the League of Nations, a new agreement was signed in the following year. Royalty payments were increased, and the concession area was significantly reduced. In reality, however, with the British government backing the company, Iran gained little from the dispute. The business was renamed the Anglo-Iranian Oil Company in 1935, with the formal founding of Iran (Bamberg, 1994). In 1937, AIOC and Royal Dutch Shell established the Shell-D'Arcy Exploration Partners in Nigeria.[132]

The US government actively supported an open-door policy in the Middle East in order to allow its oil companies the right to operate in the region, especially as they resented their exclusion from the Dutch East Indies and Burma. The Standard Oil Company of California (Socal), through its subsidiary the Bahrain Petroleum Company (BAPCO), struck oil in 1932, and made everyone aware of the Arabian Peninsula's potential. The House of Saud achieved control of much of the Arabian Peninsula, in the same year, with the support of the fundamentalist Islamic Wahhabi sect. In 1933, Socal signed a deal with King Ibn Saud that gave it exclusive rights to survey much of central and southern Saudi Arabia, having beaten off a rival bid from IPC. The fixer was Harry St John Bridger Philby, a British adventurer and close friend of the king (and whose son, Kim Philby, would be exposed as probably the most successful double agent to betray Britain's Secret Intelligence Service, on behalf of the Soviet Union). There was no guarantee that the explorations by the newly formed subsidiary, California-Arabian Standard Oil Company (CASOC) would bring success, and, when none was forthcoming, Socal felt it necessary to sell half of the concession to the Texas Oil Company (the future Texaco).

The breakthrough arrived in 1938 with a big discovery. The original concession had contained a clause that showed sensitivity to local concerns about foreign influences on a nation responsible for the holy places at Mecca and Medina and the very origins of Islam. But it is apparent that the terms set by the Saudi government and the supervision were light, with the regime bolstered by the flow of oil funds, and that the four companies operated in the 1930s without facing strong social or political resistance (the company would be renamed the Arabian American Oil Company (Aramco) in 1944, and, to meet the expanding flows, Standard (Exxon), and Socony-Vacuum (Mobil) would become partners, four years later (Wilkins, 1974; Venn, 1986).[133] APOC/AIOC and Gulf Oil established the Kuwait Oil Company, in 1934, once more with the grant of favourable exploration and concession terms (Ferrier, 1982).

In Latin America, although the goals of independence had long been fulfilled, and the region was an important participant in the international economy, the vast land holdings and tied labour of the hacienda remained, and politics were essentially matters of patronage and bargaining between the power holders and their clients. The ruling elites accrued vast profits from their privileges, and had little incentive to innovate or compete. Societies were rigidly patriarchal and stratified along racial and economic lines. Much of the investment, as we have seen, was left to foreign capitalists. Only a handful of states – Argentina, Brazil, Uruguay, Chile and Costa Rica – had constitutions that allowed some orderly transfer of government. Export trades had, however, brought some changes: cities had expanded; roads, railways and ports had been built; and a secondary economy in light manufactures was visible. Wealth from trade had strengthened central governments, and funded improvements in education, health and housing. In the sizeable urban populations that had emerged, middle-class professionals, white-collar employees and an industrial working class, as a group, generated tensions between city and country and, between themselves, class friction. After 1918, instability in the international economy hurt Latin American trade, caused dissent, and weakened the grip of the ruling white elites.

The Great Depression, whose impact was released after 1929, brought the several urban classes into national politics. Whenever they achieved power, they attempted to replace oligarchic liberalism with some form of corporate state and state-led industrial development. The earliest changes came to Chile, Argentina, Uruguay, Brazil and Mexico, due to their more open and dynamic economies, and their more liberal elites. Radical liberal parties representing the middle classes wanted a new politics. Social legislation and political changes, from the 1920s, were meant to improve working-class conditions, assuage labour unrest, and incorporate organized labour into the state. Yet military coups and authoritarian regimes were another common characteristic of the region. The wish to build up local industries was an expected response to the decline in commodity exports during the 1930s, and appealed to nationalist forces that wanted economic progress and less dependence on the outside world (Williamson, 1992; Topik and Wells, 1998).

US commercial interests had steadily dislodged those of British businesses in Latin America, in the interwar period, with the very notable exception of Argentina. US investment, however, would not match the fall in the flow of British capital to the region during the interwar period. The Great Depression especially hurt the price of commodities, and endangered Argentina's export business. The government implemented exchange controls and devalued the currency, in 1931, and affected the ability of multinationals to repatriate their profits. The Roca–Runciman Treaty of 1933 was designed to guarantee Argentina a quota of the British market for Argentina's commodity exports, but discriminatory imperial tariffs and deflation in fact induced a small decline in its trade. The Depression ruined the profitability of the largely British-owned railways in Argentina, but the government forbade job dismissals or wage cuts. As the traditional agricultural sector stagnated, migration to the cities was a source of political instability.

The Argentine government did embark on an industrialization drive, based, with the imposition of tariffs and quotas, on a policy of import substitution. Argentina created some of the earliest known examples of Latin American multinationals, just after Bolivia's Patiño mines internationalized. Torcuato di Tella's friendship with Enrique Mosconi, the director of the newly established oil concern YPF, secured a contract to build fuel dispensers, and converted Sección Industrial Amasadoras Mecánicas (SIAM) di Tella into a leading manufacturer. From its factory south of Buenos Aires, SIAM di Tella made industrial machinery and home appliances, and, in the 1930s, it evolved into Latin America's biggest domestic industrial conglomerate, producing also in neighbouring countries. The agricultural and food trader Bunge and Born could be found in Brazil by this decade (Alejandro, 1970; Scobie, 1971).

Tin had replaced silver as the main source of wealth for Bolivia, and a small number of very wealthy businessmen had come to control its mines. Indigenous peoples made up the workforce, and they laboured underground for long periods in highly primitive conditions, denied access to education and participation in the political process. Through its victory in the Chaco War of 1932–5, Paraguay took large chunks of territory and Bolivia's access to the sea. Defeat discredited the Bolivian ruling classes, and allowed competing groups to vie for control of the country for the next sixteen years. Jersey Standard was accused of duplicitously supplying Argentina, an ally of Paraguay, at the time of the Chaco War, and popular feeling against the US multinational was strong. A military junta seized power during 1934, bringing an end to the Oligarchic Republic and decades of civilian rule; within two years, Colonel José David Toro Ruilova was de facto President. The new Bolivian government established Yacimientos Petroliferos Fiscales Bolivianos (YPFB), in 1936, half owned by private investors and half owned by the state. Then, in 1937, to popular rejoicing, Toro ordered the nationalization of Jersey Standard and the transfer of assets to YPFB. Lieutenant Colonel Germán Busch Becarra, who was of German extraction, soon replaced Toro, and, associating himself with European fascism, he introduced his ever more bizarre if brief experiment in 'Military Socialism', portraying the interests of the army and the working classes as mutual. More generally, the nationalization of Jersey Standard inaugurated a period of statism, a clear difference from the previous economic and political liberalism (the statist economic policy would last until the 1952 National Revolution) (Williamson, 1992).

Mexico, as we noted earlier, had been the first Latin American country to nationalize its mineral assets, in 1917, but turnover in the composition and objectives of government meant that the oil multinationals were not significantly affected. This outcome seems to have repeated itself with the 1925 law requiring all oil concessions to be confirmed. Advantaged in part by the level of anti-American feelings, Shell's Mexican Eagle was able to expand, but it could not escape the consequences of nationalist and trade union agitation. The government began to refuse new concessions and threaten nationalization, and, by 1934, Shell was contemplating withdrawal. Demonstrating a renewed radical path for Mexico, the President, Lázaro Cárdenas del Rio, distributed land to the peasants and granted union rights and wage increases to workers. Although Shell controlled some two thirds of the country's oil output, by 1936 reserves were failing and the country, disappointingly for the company, accounted for a dwindling proportion of global production.

Cárdenas, in 1938, nationalized the Ferrocarriles Nacionales de Mexico, while he waited for a report from a commission he had appointed on acquiring the remaining oil industry from the foreign multinationals on agreed terms. He attempted negotiation with Shell and Jersey Standard, but the companies rejected all of his proposals. So, in 1938, the assets of the oil industry were compulsorily transferred to the newly established Petróleos Mexicanos (Pemex). Britain and the USA declared a boycott of Mexican goods, and, by the time of the Second World War, the nation's oil was being sent to Nazi Germany instead. Mexico remained prepared to pay compensation (finally agreeing a price with Shell in 1945), and its nationalization of the oil industry would serve as a model for governments worldwide in the post-war period (Sluyterman et al., 2007; Meyer, 1997; Meyer and Sherman, 1987; Topik and Wells, 1998).

Third setback: the Second World War

The First World War has been seen as the first 'total' war, one that needed important changes in government policy, the economy and society, in addition to putting men in uniform. The lessons of 1914–18 were well understood in 1939: governments implemented controls on industrial output, finance, shipping, trade, raw materials, labour, and personal consumption more quickly and more comprehensively, and economies shifted from peacetime to wartime production. States once more sequestrated enemy property, and were likely to turn the subsidiaries of even an allied power away from their commercial activities to meet the national emergency. As well as having their international transactions curtailed, trading companies and other investors would lose control of their assets in Asia: the Japanese takeover of French Indochina, in 1940–1, and then the invasion of British-controlled South East Asia and the Dutch East Indies, in 1941, were transformative for several reasons. The sudden collapse of the British and Netherlands empires had transferred vital raw materials to Japan, and showed nationalist movements that the period of European imperialism was nearing its end. While Europe was bankrupted by the Second

World War, and its economies and infrastructure were devastated, the USA emerged as the clear winner, economically speaking, with an unmatched leadership in capital resources, management, technology, scale of output, and productive efficiency.

As its industry responded to the needs of war, under Federal government direction, the USA took on the role of equipping its British ally, and sent essential supplies to the Soviet Union. The loans it provided to allied governments frequently maintained their ability to stay the distance in history's most destructive conflict. Planners in Britain created a highly efficient war machine compared to those in Germany, applying the *Führerprinzip* through the creation of rival ministries and agencies. There are debates on how equally sacrifices during the war years were shared, but Britain introduced a system of food rationing that overall arguably improved the diet of its population.The populations of Canada, Australia, and New Zealand, like those of the USA, escaped privation. The Soviet Union, at one point near defeat, was able remarkably to mobilize an army that would inflict defeat on Nazi Germany, and simultaneously create a vast armaments industry. The cost could be seen in a decimated, starving population and in widespread physical destruction. Britain drained resources from its colonies – most pointedly in the case of India, where there were also outbreaks of famine – and the peoples of Asia directly experienced very high human and economic costs of world war.

As nations became belligerents, companies had to break established commercial relations and alliances. Siemens Brothers, for example, could no longer cooperate with Siemens & Halske, and APOC lost its extensive distribution network in Germany. Unilever was divided, and the Netherlands government went into exile in London. In the USA, it could continue as a commercial organization, and, during the war, it fully acquired T. J. Lipton, the largest tea firm in the country, and it bought Birds Eye frozen foods from General Foods (Wilson, 1954; G. Jones, 2005).[134] For the period of the Second World War, Nestlé directors transferred to the USA, from where they could more easily run the company's activities in the Americas, the British Empire and worldwide. Nescafé became part of the familiar rations pack given to US troops, who, after 1942, spread knowledge of and demand for instant coffee to Europe (Harrison, 1983; Heer, 1991).[135] Coca-Cola followed US forces wherever they were sent, laying distribution channels and organizing bottling plants for military personnel, and helping to create a global brand icon.[136] On the other hand, during negotiations over the lend-lease, by which President Roosevelt hoped to equip Britain in its war against Germany, members of Congress asked why a country with impressive assets needed assistance. Attention especially focused on the American Viscose Corporation, arguably at the time the most successful overseas subsidiary of any British multinational. The debate was overlaid with accusations of collusion under antitrust regulations levelled at the company. Courtaulds was forced, in 1941, to sell almost half of its most profitable enterprise at a knock-down price, although a tribunal would soon award compensation (Coleman, 1969).

After the attack on Pearl Harbor, the involvement of General Electric and Dunlop in Japanese industry was terminated. There was a long list of US multinationals in Germany – General Motors, Ford, Jersey Standard, IBM, BF Goodrich, and ITT amongst them – which were sequestrated. Sterling Drug ended the relationship it had forged with IG Farben, in order to overcome substantial legal and competitive difficulties, during the interwar years. Very nearly the subject of Federal action on doing business with the enemy, two Sterling subsidiaries in Latin America, Winthrop Products, and the Sydney Ross Co., accepted the logic of their situation and became the USA's advance guard in an economic and technological war against IG Farben.[137] ITT's many interests in Mexico, Uruguay and Argentina involved companies from Germany, and the US government set up a commission to rid the American hemisphere of enemy influence in the telecommunications industry. ITT additionally owned part of Ericsson, which also had links with German businesses, and ITT's great rival RCA continued to participate covertly in ventures with German, Italian and Vichy French communications firms.[138]

It is impossible to prove or fully contradict many of the claims made against multinationals putting their commercial interests before that of the war effort or their home nation. After 1939, and while the USA was not officially at war, Coca-Cola personnel in Germany advised the Nazi regime after the forced taking over of soft drink plants in occupied territories. When relations between the parent multinational and the subsidiary were severed, and the base syrup and other supplies were no longer available, the local management in Germany produced Fanta as a replacement.[139] At the beginning of the Second World War, ITT's holdings were in danger of being taken from the company by governments sympathetic to Germany, most obviously in Argentina, and it became impossible to repatriate profits. From 1939, Behn's business acumen enabled him to sell some of ITT's holdings in Romania. His willingness to employ local managers and his contacts in Germany managed to hold up interference in his subsidiary when other US companies did not fare so well (Wilkins, 1974). It was rumoured that ITT's Sosthenes Behn talked to the management of the German subsidiary in 1942, when visiting Madrid, although there exists no solid proof.[140] Jersey Standard was accused of supplying aviation fuel to the Nazi regime, due to the legacy of complex and probably confused commercial commitments with German companies such as IG Farben.[141]

Swiss banks, such as Credit Suisse and UBS, have been implicated in receiving funds and trading in gold and securities, as a result of loot stolen by the Nazis across Europe.[142] The Bank of International Settlements had been founded, in Basle, in the year after the Wall Street Crash, to foster cooperation between the central banks of national states, and to ensure they met their obligations to each other. The board of directors included two Nazi officials, who would be found guilty at the war crimes trial at Nuremberg, as well as several prominent German businessmen. There were accusations that to maintain the workings of the international banking system as much as was possible, the BIS during the war maintained contacts between formal enemies, and that it assisted in the 'laundering' of assets stolen from occupied Europe.[143]

Through administrative edicts and contracts, governments set about putting their economies on a wartime footing, and included the assets of home-country firms and multinational subsidiaries alike in their plans. Siemens & Halske entirely converted to munitions production.[144] In a conflict associated with blitzkrieg and mobilized forces, Daimler Benz, General Motors' Opel, and Ford made an essential contribution to the German war effort. Ford had erected a plant in Berlin, during 1939, to manufacture trucks for the Wehrmacht. German nationals managed the works at Russelheim and Cologne for the production of trucks and military vehicles, and they would later face accusations of war crimes for the use of slave labour. Interestingly, the Nazi government never entrusted either company, because of their suspicious foreign origins, with the production of tanks, although, contradictorily, Opel would make bombers and munitions, mostly at the Brandenburg factory, and Ford's Cologne works produced turbines for

V-2 rockets, the Nazi's secret weapon (Turner, 2005; Bonin, Lung and Tolliday, 2003).[145] Its extensive use of slave labour was one reason why IG Farben was particularly associated with the Nazi war crimes, but its principal role in the making of the zyklon B gas used in the Holocaust made its record amongst the most heinous in German industry (for these reasons, the Allies would break up the conglomerate into its former constituent firms). IBM became separated from its German subsidiary as a result of the war, and its business in Germany came under local and increasingly Nazi management. Deutsche Hollerith-Maschinen Gesellschaft mbH (Dehomag, for short) provided technical solutions, with its punch-card technology, to recording the asset confiscation, ghettoization, and, finally, the annihilation of Europe's Jews and other minorities (Black, 2001).

Britain integrated Vauxhall, the General Motors subsidiary, and Ford at Dagenham into its war machine, and sequestrated the Bosch and Fiat assembly plants. It contracted Ford and the Packard Motor Company, during 1941, to establish Merlin aircraft factories. The government added Morris and Vauxhall as tank producers, since it could not rely on Vickers alone. Vauxhall, having ceased car production, would make 5,600 Churchill tanks and some 250,000 military trucks (Sloan, 1964).[146] Over time, however, the British Army would depend on the Sherman tanks being made in and sent from the USA. Amongst the contributions Firestone made to the Allied military effort, from 1942 onwards, was the doubling of rubber exports from Liberia. Indeed, in that year, the government of Liberia signed a Defense Pact, which assured the USA and their allies that supplies of its vital war good would be forthcoming. It agreed, too, that the USA could establish military bases in its territory. As well as building the Roberts Field airport, the Americans financed the free port of Monrovia and roads pushing into the interior. The bases had an important role in Operation Torch, in 1942, in which US and British forces landed in North Africa behind the Afrika Korps and other Axis contingents being pushed westwards by the British and Empire 8th Army. The USA agreed that it would hand over the infrastructure it had funded to the Liberian government, with the proviso that any revenues would be used to pay back any remaining debt.[147] Washington ordered Goodyear, General Tire, Firestone, and Goodrich to build synthetic rubber factories, which became commercially viable in 1943 (French, 1991). Goodyear increased its productive capacity by founding a works in Mexico in 1941, and made munitions and aircraft, with its aeronautical section, at its main plant in the USA. Having lost its rubber plantations in the Philippines and Sumatra to the Japanese invasion, it would establish another in Peru, by 1945.[148]

At the instigation of its government, General Motors built two assembly plants in Iran, during 1942, to make trucks for the Red Army. Of the 467,000 vehicles received from the USA, some 184,000 were assembled in Iran, and the plant was moved to the Soviet Union in 1945. During the war, General Motors abandoned smaller overseas factories, such as the one in Lima, and, from 1942, a shortage of parts forced its Argentine operation to replace automobile production with refrigerators and car accessories. With war declared in 1939, in Australia GM-Holden's bodybuilding plants began the switch to war production.[149] Normally with the support of the federal government, and notably the Labour Party and trades unions, the elected Liberal and Country League in South Australia implemented policies of industrialization, stirred to action because the country was cut off from suppliers of manufactures overseas. It promoted the development of local munitions factories, infrastructure and shipyards, and British Tube Mills opened a plant. By 1946, South Australia had nationalized Adelaide's electricity supply, as another means of encouraging industrialization, and as part of its efforts to close the gap with more developed states in its emerging nation. But GM-Holden and Chrysler-Richards continued to dominate the making of automobile components. During the war, the federal government asked GM and Ford to present proposals for an Australian-designed and mostly locally manufactured car, and decided to back GM's plans when it was clear they needed less government assistance.[150]

Economics were a major cause of Japan's decision to start a conflict with the USA. Australia had already banned iron ore exports because of the atrocities in Nanjing and elsewhere in China. The control of rubber supplies, through government-backed cartels, had caused resentment in Japan, which believed that the restrictions had been unfairly imposed on its producers. In 1940, President Roosevelt ended the USA's commercial treaty with Japan, and threatened to embargo oil when Japan partially occupied French Indochina. He held back for fear of provoking an attack on the Dutch East Indies, but, in 1941, the whole of France's colony was occupied. With its oil set to run out in six months, Japan attacked the Pearl Harbor naval base; during 1942, it quickly defeated the British and the Dutch in their colonies in South East Asia. In Japan, under its Enemy Property Control Law, passed at the end of 1941, the government seized the remaining 20 per cent or so of shares held by International Standard Electric, and, under the Munitions Company Law, in 1943 the military forcibly gave the whole of NEC to the Sumitomo zaibatsu, which founded Sumitomo Communications Industries. When the zaibatsu were dissolved by the US occupying forces after the war, NEC was refounded.

The Japanese southward invasion ended the control of Western enterprises over a vast network of trading, mining, oil, plantation, infrastructure, and processing investments. The Japanese expropriated British American Tobacco's factories in China during 1941, when its war with the Allies began (Cochran, 1980; Cox, 2000). The Japanese invasion of South East Asia, undoubtedly, surprised the Ford automobile company. With deliveries from Europe disrupted, and having some four fifths of the market in the peninsula, Ford Malaya established the first and at the time the only body assembly plant in South East Asia, at Bukit Timah, in 1941. Its new factory assembled aircraft for the RAF, and, when the British were pushed to the Indian border, it became the Japanese army's headquarters in Malaya. Contemporaries, including Winston Churchill, saw surrender of the 'impregnable' Singapore, in February 1942, as one of the most disastrous defeats in British military history, with 80,000 Allied troops added to the 50,000 prisoners already in the hands of the Japanese. Such signal public humiliation particularly undermined the credibility of the European imperial regimes in Asia. Lieutenant-General Tomoyuki Yamashita forced his adversary, Lieutenant Arthur Percival, to go to the boardroom at the Ford Malaya factory to sign the surrender document, giving the plant its main reason for fame. Within a short period, the plant was manufacturing Nissan trucks for the Japanese army, before coming under British military administration after the war, and being returned to Ford in 1946 (the factory was finally closed in 1980, and converted into a museum twenty-six years later) (Wilkins & Hill, 1964; Yacob, 2003).[151] It is said that the Dunlop warehouse in Shanghai kept open during the war because it provided the Japanese military commander with his favourite golf balls (McMillan, 1989).

The Nazi occupation of Europe created opportunities of internationalization for German companies, because they were given control of assets in conquered territories. It led to the rounding up of slave labour, usually Slav or Jewish in ethnicity, for exploitation by German industry. Auschwitz is especially identified with the Holocaust, as the Third Reich's largest extermination camp, and it was the centre of a brutal industrial complex. IG Farben was awarded dyeworks located in Czechoslovakia. Gustav Krupp had been chair of the Reich Federation of German Industry, and his successor, Alfred, was a committed Nazi. During the Second World War, his company was allowed to take over companies in occupied nations, including a tractor factory and a mechanical construction firm in France and, crucially, the Skoda works in Czechoslovakia, used to make munitions. Krupp exploited slave labour, and, in 1942, it supervised the Molotov steel works at Kharkov and Kramatorsk in eastern Ukraine and the mines supplying the iron, manganese, and chrome vital for steel production. Having bombed Krupp's Essen works out of production, the British dismantled it after the war as a reparations payment.[152] When Italy joined the Allied side, in 1943, the Germans seized the Fiat facilities in Turin.

In France, Maurice Dollfus, the head of Ford SAF (Société Anonyme Française), was a willing accomplice of the occupation, and turned over the Poissy factory to the manufacture of munitions for German armed forces. He assisted in setting up another branch of Ford SAF in Vichy Algiers, from where it could build armoured cars and trucks for Erwin Rommel's Afrika Korps.[153] In a clear contrast to the wartime record of Dollfus, his collaborationist counterpart at SAF, Citroën's president Pierre-Jules Boulanger refused to cooperate with the German occupying authorities, or their Vichy satellite regime. He would communicate only through intermediaries, and would not meet the famous engineer Ferdinand Porsche, who was organizing the production of armoured and amphibious vehicles at the Wolfsburg plant built, in partnership with the Auto Union, to design the 'people's car' commissioned by Hitler before the war. Boulanger organized a 'go-slow' and encouraged sabotage at the Citroën works ordered to make Wehrmacht trucks, and he was listed as an enemy of the Third Reich to be arrested if the Allies ever invaded France. Contravening the orders of the Germans, the firm's researchers continued to work on a popular car that would eventually be made as the 2CV (Gallard, 2004; Reynolds, 1997). The Allies would later remove Porsche as chairman of the Wolfsburg plant, and they imprisoned, but never tried, him for war crimes related to the use of slave labour. It was he and his son who founded the Porsche company and its famous luxury models in the immediate post-war years.

As a maker of planes, trucks and armoured vehicles, the Fiat factory at Turin became a target for Allied bombers from 1943, and Valletta, named as president and managing director in 1945, would begin planning and rebuilding the damaged plant with the help of secret loans from the USA.[154] During the Second World War, Deutsche Bank expanded aggressively throughout occupied Europe with new branches and acquisitions, including in the Czech territories, Slovakia, Yugoslavia, the Netherlands, Greece, Austria, Hungary, Bulgaria and Romania. It purchased, during 1942–3, large amounts of gold from the Reichsbank for sale to the Turkish government, through its Istanbul branch, although there is no firm documentary evidence that it knew that some of the gold had been taken from Holocaust victims. It can be countered, of course, that the perpetrators, right to the top of the Nazi hierarchy, showed themselves to be reluctant about putting details of the Holocaust on record, and they were cautious even to talk about their industrialized organization of genocide (Evans, 2001). But Deutsche Bank could not deny that it financed the construction firms that built the concentration camp and the IG Farben factory at Auschwitz.[155]

Multinationals: 1914 to 1948

It became commonplace to portray the period of the two world wars of the twentieth century and the decades in between as the systematic unwinding of a successful international system of trade and investment. As we have seen, the commitment to the free movement of exports and imports had been nuanced at best, and, with the exceptions of Britain, the Netherlands, and Denmark, nation states in Europe and North America willingly used tariffs to protect vital or powerful sectional interests or to encourage industrialization at home. They were already retreating from the principles of free trade. In any case, while the preponderance of trade was conducted between industrialized nations, it was developing territories that had taken the greater proportion of FDI to finance and organize the infrastructure, mines and plantations that gave them entry, as commodity exporters, into the international economy. Underpinning the activities of multinationals – while governments might have argued for the benefits of open competitive markets – was the reality of imperial control and influence.

The disruption caused by the First World War – new or increased tariffs, trade and currency controls, the termination of commercial relations with enemy nations, shortages, the redirection of economies in the cause of 'total war' and munitions manufacture, the loss of shipping, the falling away of cross-border and productive investment – was far-reaching. Few would have predicted the length of that emergency, over four years, or the depth of the post-war slump and other economic consequences of the peace, such as the scale of the indemnity imposed on Germany. The impact was strongly political, too: the First World War ended the existence of empires and transformed the political structures of Europe, the Middle East and, to a lesser extent, Africa and Asia. The movement of borders turned companies overnight into unexpected multinationals. Sequestrations in Russia reduced the international reach of leading companies, and, for many prominent German enterprises, sequestrations reduced once-important multinationals to the status of domestic businesses.

The assumption, nonetheless, was that broken commercial relations, new tariffs, and greater intervention by the state in economic affairs would be temporary responses to a particular emergency, and, by the mid 1920s, increases in output and trade were reasons for optimism. The question was how far the pre-1914 system could or should be resurrected. For example, with Europe's great powers engaged in conflict, with unclear causes but obvious catastrophic results, industrializing economies elsewhere had gained, and came to see tariff barriers as permanent and as beneficial for inward investment, technology transfer, and domestic processing and manufacturing. They perceived free trade as hurting the industries they were striving to develop by various measures of government support. There were long-standing precedents for international cartels, but their incidence grew in the interwar period. Cross-border collusion was a means of coping with unstable trade conditions, falling prices, and oversupply, and raised more doubts about the advantages of fully competitive open markets, even if cartels mostly protected the interests of producers.

Behind the policies of many governments in the 1920s, there was the assumption that the rise in international transactions and living standards under the pre-1914 system of free trade – but, actually, a system of qualified free trade – had fulfilled its underlying principle of mutual advantage. The power of the international economy and the multinational investor to transform was not in doubt, and there were enough pockets of development in Latin America, Asia and even Africa to perceive the internationality and connectivity of the world economy. But the gains of the revitalized 'old' system for the industrialized countries of Europe and North America would be markedly more pronounced. They reflected continued advantages in capital, organization, technology, and market access.

Developments in the international economy provided further examples of multinationals gaining control of raw material sources with land rights and concession terms that would themselves grow into political issues. There were the palm oil estates of Africa and South East Asia; the rubber plantations of South East Asia; US mining companies and telecommunications firms in Latin America, where they joined the United Fruit 'octopus'; European miners throughout Africa and Asia; and, manifestly, the expansive and organizationally complex oil majors, whose commercial objectives were overlaid with imperial or diplomatic policies in the Middle East and Latin America. The international division of labour between industrialized nations and primary producers remained, although manufacturing did spread to Japan and to territories associated with commodity exports such as Canada and Australia. Trading firms, which had prospered so effectively in the pre-1914 years, saw their revenues and profits squeezed, and they rationally looked to increase their investments in raw materials or processing, albeit with mixed results. Because host economies in developing territories faced difficult economic circumstances, and as local resentment of foreign-owned power, transport or water firms and their price increases grew, utility multinationals began a long sequence of withdrawals.

Far from tariffs and other trade barriers holding back FDI, the evidence indicates that they encouraged multinationalization, most notably by manufacturers. There were, of course, numerous examples of industrial enterprises setting up overseas subsidiaries, usually in developed countries, before the First World War. The 1920s saw an important increase. US automobile companies invested because they had a lead in production management, technology and products. Their objectives were market seeking, and, where the size and wealth of the host economy justified the decision, they moved to full-scale production and their preferred option of full ownership. Control facilitated the transfer of management techniques, and protection of proprietary knowledge. Where markets did not support full-scale production, companies opted for assembly operations. Rubber producers proved themselves to be enthusiastic multinationals, followed by branded food, drink and household product companies. As exampled by oil, manufacturers had to tackle the management complexities of multi-nationalization. The experience of these two sectors contrasts with that of trading firms and utilities, and demonstrates that the interwar period was not consistently negative for all forms of multinational enterprise. Oil was transnational in its operations, coordinating extraction and marketing across continents, while the subsidiaries of manufacturers were created in the main to provide for their host market economies and so did not seek cross-border efficiencies. In utilities, there was the fast expansion of multinational telephone companies.

The important turning point was not, therefore, 1914, but 1929. In the economic collapse that followed, governments would finally reject any return to the international system associated with the period before the First World War, and formally ended policies of free trade, capital mobility, and currency convertibility. They looked more to national economic development, and away from reliance on trading relationships. While they had previously been interested in the location of industry, governments became more exercised about its ownership and control. Tariffs were, as we have seen, likely to be an incentive for manufacturing FDI, where the host market circumstances could validate an investment. The increases in protective duties were not the key issue for multinationals, whereas the passing of exchange and capital controls, by preventing the repatriation of investments and profits, was more fundamental.

In Germany, the Nazis extolled the state over markets and private enterprise, and sought autarky rather than participation in the international economy. By the end of the 1930s, multinationals were forced to make uncomfortable compromises to maintain their commercial interests, which they could not, in effect, sell. The Nazis brutally enforced anti-Semitic policies on businesses, and, while they pressured multinational subsidiaries to undertake 'Germanization', they did make compromises with those they saw as useful to their plans. As well as industrialization, Japan had shown a preference for Japanese control of businesses, using joint ventures as a means of acquiring technological and managerial know-how. As the power of the military and the nationalists increased during the 1930s, they forced multinationals to divest, except where the capabilities of the foreign firm remained vital. The period generated numerous conspiracy theories of multinationals cooperating with dictatorships and enemy nations, some no doubt exaggerated, and, in the nature of conspiracies, most are hard to validate. It does show companies reaching accommodations principally to protect their investments, but, in some cases, multinationals could use their bargaining power to protect employees and others.

In Latin America, radical and nationalist movements began to view the grip of multinationals on utilities, infrastructure, land ownership and the export trades with suspicion, and questioned in particular the foreign ownership of minerals and the concession terms given to mining and oil companies. So, in 1937 Bolivia and then Mexico in 1938 provided the first examples of nationalization since the Russian Revolution, when both countries took the oil industry into public control. In doing so, they set the policies for Third World countries in the post-war period, whenever they renegotiated concession terms or nationalized foreign-owned assets.

The impact of the Great Depression had been global and, for that reason, shattered the very basis of capitalism, free markets, and the international economy. The Second World War, in 1939–45, followed its 1914–18 predecessor by breaking up trading relationships, and it led to property sequestrations and government controls on a scale even greater than during the previous generation. Europe remained at the centre of the world economy during the interwar period, and the First World War did not destroy the imperial system territorially or economically. The Second World War did, and confirmed the USA as the main provider of overseas investment, technology and multinational enterprise. What the period of Global Economy II – that between 1914 and 1929, and more so from 1929 to 1948 – especially illustrated was the influence of home and host country governments on the activities of multinationals, and it revealed the power that nation states, even those in the developing economies of Latin America, could impose on foreign-owned businesses, many with assets in management and technology. These decades showed, too, how state intervention became associated with the control of natural resources and the achievement of industrialization, and how assertions of national sovereignty could strongly clash with the multinational's assertion of private property rights and preference for open cross-border trade.

4 | Cold War and the new international economic order: 1948–1980

Superpowers and the international system

By the end of the Second World War, having transformed its economy and then gone on to defeat Nazi Germany, the Soviet Union appeared a country of power and significant achievements. The USA had grown in industrial and armed strength, too, and it had assumed a complex mix of global influence and interests. Both democracies and autocracies had participated in the first international economy, prior to 1914, founded on a political economy of private enterprises and of markets open to investment and trade, albeit with increasing deviation from the conventional wisdom and its principles. From 1945, and by 1948, former allies had become military and diplomatic opponents. The incompatible systems of the Soviet Union and the USA represented sharp alternatives to human progress and modernity: was it the communist or the capitalist model – and ties with either of the two superpowers – that offered the greater benefits? In contrast to the nineteenth century, there was a struggle over the fused issues of ideology, international politics, and economics.

The two new superpowers pursued a Cold War of diplomatic suspicion and espionage within the critical European theatre, but elsewhere in the world the rivalry was too frequently more bloody. In 1959, boosted by the Sputnik satellite's triumphant launch, the Soviet leader, Nikita Khrushchev, told the US Vice-President, Richard Nixon, then on a trade mission to Moscow: 'if you want capitalism you can live that way ... We can still feel sorry for you.' In reality, having already condemned Stalin's terror, Khrushchev knew that socialism in the Soviet Union had brought systematic repression, and failed to meet the material needs of its citizens. The war had placed Eastern Europe in the grip of its powerful neighbour, but this new political and military bloc was unable to match the West for cross-border commerce, investment and economic growth (Gaddis, 1998).

Perceiving President John Kennedy's response to the building of the Berlin Wall as weak, Khrushchev decided, in 1962, to test the USA by placing nuclear missiles in Cuba, and provoked the most dangerous and potentially apocalyptic international crisis.

Within a decade of Khrushchev's boast, the USA had surpassed its global rival in space exploration, and, outside the Communist world, the post-war decades had acquired the label of a 'Golden Age' characterized by long-term rises in output, demand, trade and productivity. After the hiatus of the war period, multinational enterprise resumed its progress, and US firms led and stimulated advances in technology and management worldwide. Prestige space projects and military expenditure were proof of superpower status, but hid the peacetime weaknesses of the Soviet economy. Nixon's reply to Khrushchev – there 'may be some instances in which we are ahead of you – in colour television, for instance' – hinted at the better or consumer-focused life which Americans enjoyed and other nations envied. US capital and know-how had helped to secure, to the envy of those to the East, the prosperity of Western Europe.

Having experienced colonization, many countries in the so-called Third World were unsurprisingly wary of 'economic imperialism', or dependency and exploitation by foreign businesses, and they associated progress and national sovereignty with central planning and import controls. But trade and the investment leverage of advanced industrial countries could win diplomatic links, and (where ideology was not an insuperable bar) they could overcome autarchic or nationalist tendencies. The Communist bloc remained separate from the international system of trade and investment which the West and its allies established. With the end of the Cold War, in which a decaying Cuba and despotic North Korea became the last examples of Communism in practice, the outcome of ideological and military rivalry seems in retrospect to have been inevitable. But the 'victory' of an international system of open, competitive markets had been far from certain.

From 1948, the international economy gradually re-emerged from the Second World War and its immediate aftermath. There was a further shift away from Britain to the USA as the global hub for capital and multinational enterprise; the investments of international businesses flowed more towards the richer nations, and the proportion of FDI stock in the less advanced fell; there was a long-term trend towards multinational manufacturing, as well as mining and oil, and the international expansion of these sectors and important changes in management aided the cross-border transfer of technologies, practices, and products; another associated feature was a noteworthy rise in transatlantic trade and investment, involving the USA, Canada, and Western Europe. One reason behind these developments, amongst many, was the impact of the Second World War on American policy, meaning that the new superpower supported a new international economic framework, and found the determination to support Europe and halt the spread of Communism. The allied combatants – and successive Washington administrations especially – could see that the conflict had been the tragic result of a political and economic order that had failed.

In the democracies of Britain and the USA, promises of a better future had justified the sacrifice required to defeat Germany and Japan. It had been a 'people's war' because it had mobilized whole societies in the military or in industry (and, moreover, because civilian populations across Europe, Asia and Africa had suffered tragically). Those affected looked for guarantees that the experiences of previous decades – the unemployment and poverty that had inflicted personal humiliation and feelings of helplessness – would not recur. The shock delivered in the interwar years to the market and capitalist system had been global, and economic nationalism, by replacing free trade and ending fixed exchange rates, had overturned established international business and commercial relations. Social and political disorder had fired the aggressive fascism and militarism that the allies decided, belatedly, to resist. If governments were to ensure economic security and progress at home, they had to devise economic security overseas. But agreeing a plan on how this was to be done was tricky. To inflict defeat on Germany, the Allies had by necessity a common purpose, and they had formally supported the founding of the United Nations. But they had diverged on the terms of a new international economic settlement, and over the partition of Europe and East Asia. Ultimately, events showed that the Soviet Union, on one hand, and the USA and Britain, on the other, had been expedient military partners only.

The division of East and West exposed underlying diplomatic and ideological tensions, and erected a barrier to international trade and investment. Both the USA and the Soviet Union avoided open warfare with each other. The author George Orwell used the term 'cold war', in 1945, to describe a world partitioned by hostile totalitarian 'super-states', in which fear of nuclear annihilation would permanently create a 'peace that is no peace'. It was an early glimpse into the nightmare vision of his novel *1984*. During 1947, the Truman Doctrine committed the USA to halting the growth of Communism outside those spheres of influence agreed during the Second World War and mainly determined by the presence of the Red Army. The publication of a book edited by columnist Walter Lippman and called *The Cold War* helped to popularize the term (Lippman, 1947). Former allies accepted that, for the foreseeable future, two systems would have to coexist, yet spill-overs in the developing world frequently threw up direct contests that could be economic, political and, at worst, military. The accelerating force of international trade and direct investment would, to an important degree, influence the policies of Third World governments, which looked to foreign capital and know-how to transform their economies.

The USA, unlike other combatants, had not been deeply damaged by the war, and commanded unequalled resources in finance, technology and skills. It produced half the world's manufactures in 1946 (compared to 32 per cent in 1936–8). While it had become the leading investor in the western hemisphere, and additionally in Saudi Arabia and Liberia, by the 1930s, the USA in the post-war era assumed global economic leadership. Britain (needing finance, raw materials and equipment) had reluctantly relinquished assets in the Middle East, and the unwinding of European empires transformed world politics and reshaped patterns of investment across Asia and Africa (Wilkins, 1974). South East Europe, in the Soviet sphere, ceased to be a region of German economic influence, and the pre-war flow of supplies and commodities from East to West Europe dwindled. By contrast, US influence grew in Latin America, the Caribbean, Australia, New Zealand and East Asia, as well as in Western Europe.

The Iron Curtain lowered across Europe between 1945 and 1948 marked an uneasy zone of military and diplomatic rivalry, and high-lighted the ideologically competing systems of markets and private capital versus those of state control. West European governments were anxious that the Iron Curtain should not move in their direction, and accepted US loans and technical assistance. Prosperity was viewed as the best antidote to Communism, which enjoyed popular support in

Italy and France. Marshall Aid – more formally the European Recovery Program – combined US largesse with self-interest, and was at its high point from its beginning in 1948 till 1952. Policy makers in Washington believed that the stabilizing of democracy, containing the Soviet Union, and ensuring economic revival amongst its allies were all linked.

Alongside finance and loans, the USA promoted a productivity mission amongst European industry, offering advice on advanced technology and organizational methods. Paul G. Hoffman, who had been president of the Studebaker auto company, was director of the Economic Cooperation Administration that supervised Marshall Aid: they were engaged, he said, in a battle between the 'American assembly line' and the 'communist party line' (Schroter, 2005). US multinationals benefited from their technological and managerial lead in autos, oil and chemicals during the 1950s, and, in the 1960s, investment moved sharply upwards across many sectors. Most European nations welcomed American firms, which in their turn became attracted by Europe's high growth rates and rising levels of wealth. The writer and politician Jean-Jacques Servan-Schreiber described trends rather dramatically, reflecting in addition French wariness of transatlantic influences: 'the world's third greatest industrial power, just after the United States and Russia, will not be Europe, but American industry in Europe' (Servan-Schreiber, 1968).

The Second World War elevated the USA and the Soviet Union to superpower status, and the decades that followed confirmed the ending of an imperialist and more Europe-centred international system, in which manufactures had been traded for colonial commodities, and the bulk of FDI had once gone to developing territories. The British prime minister, Winston Churchill, had fought to end Nazism, liberate continental Europe, and preserve his country's empire and worldwide influence. He achieved the first of his war aims, the second (given Soviet control of Eastern Europe) was a very partial success, and the combat-exhausted British Empire would, bit by bit, be in retreat. The USA, for one, was opposed to colonialism and remained deeply suspicious of imperial trade systems, which, it argued, disadvantaged its multinationals. Defeats inflicted by the Japanese had ended the certainties of British, French and Netherlands rule, and liberated territories in Asia and Africa unpicked the privileges once granted to European-owned firms.

The Pax Britannica – once associated with fixed exchange rates, currency convertibility, and open trade and investment – had rested on capital exports, imperialist trading relations, and the easy availability of sterling. The Roosevelt–Truman administrations which devised the Pax Americana sought to restore the principles of open trade and investment lost in the 1930s and 1940s, but argued that a new international institutional framework was needed for their successful return. Economic principle, based on open competitive markets, fitted well with the USA's unrivalled position for exporting capital, goods and influence. Within this new international system, nonetheless, 'declining' Britain and the Netherlands continued to be highly successful international players, and, once their post-war domestic recovery had been secured, other nations such as Germany, France and Japan emerged again as major foreign investors.

Overall, multinational firms from industrialized nations invested in other industrialized nations. With the greater growth opportunities available in advanced countries, and Communist bloc suspicions of an American-led world order, US visions of a global free market economy were abandoned for a largely Western free market economy with a strong North Atlantic dimension. FDI patterns in the developing world differed in character for several reasons. Political and economic instability, local insurgency, disagreements with host governments, and the threat of nationalization made international investors uneasy. Parties might resolve disputes by referring to the rules of international business as set by the World Bank or the International Chamber of Commerce, but clashes over national sovereignty and the rights of multinationals were not in practice well regulated or resolved. During the high point of US power, and rising European prosperity, in the 1950s, multinationals were generally able to resist threats to their operations. As well as receiving the support of their own governments, they controlled the technologies, organizational skills, or market access that host governments needed.

International economic institutions

The economic strength and international policies of the USA enabled the world to escape post-war disintegration. Although the Bretton Woods Agreement of 1944 had been a British proposal, it was the USA that decided the details, as finally signed by 44 nations. The new international economic order had been conceived as a partner to the new political and diplomatic order of the United Nations. While the Soviet Union had attended the diplomatic gathering, ultimately Stalin ordered withdrawal from a system that his country could not aspire to lead. The agreement between those that remained affirmed domestic objectives such as full employment and rising incomes, but rejected exchange rate manipulation to achieve these favourable outcomes, and the Bretton Woods institutions were operational by 1947. The International Monetary Fund, instead, held a currency pool from which members could finance temporary balance of payments deficits. For nations facing more entrenched difficulties, the IMF would agree on an orderly adjustment of exchange rates. Signatories pledged not to extend existing exchange restrictions, and to avoid discrimination against any one currency. Bretton Woods founded, additionally, the International Bank for Reconstruction and Development, or, more popularly, the World Bank, to finance post-war reconstruction. The IMF had limited reserves and tight lending rules, and, during the disturbed conditions prevalent in the immediate post-war years, resources could not meet its defined policy prescriptions. Member governments could not expose their weakened economies and currencies to international competition.

How should we assess the system founded at Bretton Woods against the underlying economic realities? Inevitably, the IMF granted more exchange rate adjustments than had been originally envisaged, and the USA accepted that the IMF rules, if applied too rigorously, might bring ruin to some economies and halt world economic recovery. It was American aid and credit that prevented world economic collapse, and the international availability of the dollar, after a period of reconstruction in Europe and elsewhere, turned commitments to open trade and currency convertibility into a reality. There was, therefore, no instantaneous return to the liberal capital regimes of 1913, or even 1929. From Washington, there was genuine assistance for allies, and enlightened calculation. Europeans had to repair the physical damage of war, and escalating debts and dollar shortages would have stopped them buying the supplies that kept American factories at full capacity. The long view was that the USA needed wealthy trade partners.

Not until 1958 did most European economies substantially ease exchange restrictions, with the immediate effect of stimulating FDI by the USA and other countries (Wilkins, 1974). The Bretton Woods exchange rate arrangements, based on parity with the dollar, had no relevance for most major European currencies, since they were not convertible until January 1959, coincident with the founding of the European Common Market. Elsewhere, developing economies tended to operate currency restrictions in some form. Then, the USA's balance of payments deficits and the glut of dollars on the international market over the next decade destabilized the system of stable exchange rates: the dollar was devalued in 1971, and currencies were in effect allowed to float from March 1973 onwards (Kenwood and Lougheed, 1992).

The restoration of non-discriminatory trade proved even more elusive than fixed exchange rates: unfettered commerce unnerved governments concerned with building and protecting their domestic economies. The Bretton Woods conference had agreed that a system of multilateral free trade would partner currency convertibility and set exchange parities, since import controls (a feature of the 1930s, and then the war years) could simply replace any commitments to end restrictions on international payments. In 1947–8, the UN organized a meeting of the International Trade Organization, in Havana, and aimed to extend to trade the same philosophy inspiring the IMF in the monetary field. But European countries (feeling they were economically threatened) resisted the end of import duties and preferential treatment. American companies, conscious of their competitive advantage, lobbied hard but unsuccessfully on the charter's neglect of property rights and restrictive practices (Wilkins, 1974). So, critically, the US Congress refused to ratify the ITO treaty.

In the meantime, Washington had announced it would directly discuss the relaxing of import controls with other governments, using current legislation and presidential powers. At Geneva in 1947, 123 bilateral agreements involving 23 nations, called the General Agreement on Tariffs and Trade (GATT), emerged. There were clauses on future tariff reductions for any country being granted to all member countries, on automatic reciprocity for any country lowering duties on another's goods, and on the founding of a regulatory secretariat. Waivers enabled the Europeans to maintain quotas on American and Canadian goods, in return for tariff reductions, and the USA retained import restrictions and support prices for its agricultural sector. Although dollar shortages placed limits on international commerce and growth amongst the nations of Europe and elsewhere, GATT provided a framework for liberalizing trade as conditions improved, and, between 1947 and 1967, six meetings took place. The last of these, the Kennedy Round, initiated substantial and across-the-board reductions on import duties. The term 'free trade', therefore, is an inaccurate or incomplete description of the post-war international system. It ignores the separation of the Soviet bloc from the West; other nations outside GATT; the varying and pragmatic arrangements between GATT signatories; and the fact that commercial barriers were only removed piecemeal after lengthy and arduous negotiation.

The USA's Economic Cooperation Administration was a prime mover, during 1948, in establishing the Organisation for European Economic Cooperation (OEEC), and, during 1950, the European Payments Union (EPU). Being steps in regional commercial and monetary cooperation, they met to some extent US belief in large integrated markets as the needed counterpart to mass production (the OEEC, with the creation of the European Economic Community, evolved into the Organization for Economic Cooperation and Development, or OECD, a club for all advanced economies). Each participating government founded its own recovery agency, and set up national production centres and productivity teams to learn the secrets of US industrial efficiency. The Usinor steel mills and the Genissiat hydroelectric project in France, the Finsider and Falck steel plants in Italy, the Margram rolling mill in Britain, and the Donawitz and Linz steel mills in Austria were all prominent examples of US assistance.

But the Marshall Aid administrators recognized that European recovery must ultimately come from within Europe itself (Van der Wee, 1991; Kenwood and Lougheed, 1992; Pollard, 1997). Its US Technical Assistance and Productivity Mission sought to improve European industry and administration, and government-appointed agencies in Britain, Germany and Austria responded to its initiatives. Yet not every country was receptive, and the USA forced the European Productivity Agency on the OEEC in 1953 (Schroter, 2005). Inside the Communist bloc, there was the Council for Mutual Economic Assistance, or Comecon. As the Cold War intensified, from 1947, Stalin ordered the East European countries to leave the Marshall Aid discussions, fearing the renewal of their economic ties with the West. Comecon, established in 1949 for the multilateral coordination and integration of state plans, was an alternative system, but in reality no replacement. As Cold War enmities eased, in the 1960s, East European trade with West Europe

Table 4.1 *World merchandise exports and GDP,*
1820–1992 (1990 $US)

	World exports	World GDP	Exports/GDP
1929	334,408	3,696,156	9.0
1950	375,765	5,372,330	7.0
1960	700,956	8,448,637	8.3
1964	907,368	10,215,338	8.8
1973	1,797,199	16,064,474	11.2
1980	2,049,411	20,029,995	10.2
1990	3,432,253	27,359,022	12.5
1992	3,785,619	27,994,920	13.5

Source: Maddison (1999).

grew faster than its commerce with the Soviet Union (Bideleux and
Jeffries, 1998).

Trade, output and foreign direct investment

Trade volumes had stagnated during the Second World War (increasingly by barely 3 per cent in the ten years between 1938 and 1948);
from 1948 to 1971, they grew by over 500 per cent. The value of
world exports rose by 7 per cent per year over the period 1950 to
1973, compared to world GDP at 4.9 per cent. Many reasons explain
this upward trend: new international institutions encouraging cooperation, US leadership and resources, expansionary domestic policies,
post-war reconstruction, and advances in technology and business
organization. The decline in trade barriers improved productivity, as
nations increasingly specialized in those goods they could produce
more efficiently. Commodities whose consumption grew in line with
higher living standards, and goods whose production was complex and
capital-intensive (such as machinery, cars or chemicals) showed the
greatest advances in cross-border commerce. The total value of merchandise exports from non-Communist countries grew by an average
6 per cent every year for 1948–60, and accelerated to 8 per cent for
1960–73 (Table 4.1).

Much of the gain went to a small number of rich market economies,
which received about 63 per cent of world imports, by value, in 1960.

These industrialized countries in North America and Western Europe accounted, in addition, for 64 per cent of world exports, while developing countries produced 21 per cent, leaving 3 per cent to Australia and South Africa, and 12 per cent to the centrally planned Communist economies. Some 70 per cent of exports from developed economies were destined for other developed economies. By 1973, the industrialized nations had made further ground: the value of manufactures increased, as a proportion of world exports, from 43 per cent in 1950 to 62 per cent. During this period, a 'Big Six' – the USA, Canada, France, Germany, Italy and Britain – accounted for much of global output, with 46 per cent of world GDP in 1950, and approximately 44 per cent in 1973. The USA alone had responsibility for 27 per cent of world GDP in 1950, despite having only 6 per cent of the world's population. Worldwide recovery allowed its competitors to close the gap by 1973, but the USA still had a remarkable 22 per cent of world GDP, and its economy was two and half times bigger than in 1950 (Maddison, 1999).

Living standards in 1950 were $9,573 in the USA and an average $5,513 in ten West European nations. By 1973, they had risen to $16,607 in the USA (a 73 per cent increase) and to $11,694 in West Europe (129 per cent), when the world average was $1,332 (based on 1990 values). Did economic growth and unprecedented levels of wealth become more reliant on the opportunities for trade? In 1960, the relationship between exports and world GDP reached 8.3 per cent; by 1973, the figure was 11.2, and, therefore, higher than for 1914 (8.7 per cent) and for 1929 (9.0 per cent); by 1980, it was 11.4 per cent (Kenwood & Lougheed, 1992; Maizels, 1963; Maddison, 1999). The world economy had reached new levels of interdependence, and demonstrated a clear recovery from the effects of the Great Depression and world war.

Just as the international economy expanded in relation to world output, so the role of multinationals in international business and within national economies grew too. The world stock of outward FDI stood at $66bn in 1960 (using contemporary currency values); at $211bn in 1973; and at $524bn in 1980. Total outward FDI stock grew to 4.0 per cent of world GDP in 1967, to 4.2 per cent in 1973, and 5.0 per cent by 1980 (admittedly, these figures still remained well below those created in the first wave of globalization by 1913). That the vast majority of FDI assets in 1960 were owned by ten countries reflected the great international disparities in technology, management know-how, and finance. A top ten still dominated in 1980, and developing nations were responsible for between 1.1 and 3.1 per cent of all outward FDI for the whole of this period. Of the increase in world FDI in the 1950s, the major economic and industrial power, the USA, supplied two thirds, and nearly half of the growth between 1960 and 1978. At its peak, in 1960, US businesses owned some 48.3 per cent of outward FDI stock, nearly four times the share of its nearest rival, the UK; their 40.0 per cent in 1980 was still nearly two and half times larger. Britain and the Netherlands were successful as homes to multinationals, and the three largest international investors had approximately three quarters of outward FDI stocks in 1960 and 1973. The 1960s showed a peak in world FDI flows, which tailed off during the economic turmoil of the next decade, before beginning to recover in the 1980s, and surging more dramatically in the 1990s (tables 4.2 and 4.4).

To where did the investment go? While we should admit the poor quality of FDI statistics before the Second World War, we can more confidently track general shifts in post-war investment flows. It is estimated that some 66 per cent of world stock was located in developing territories in 1914, and 55 per cent by 1938 (Dunning in Casson, 1983). In direct contrast, approximately 67.3 per cent was, by 1960, in developed nations, compared to 32.3 per cent in developing countries (tables 4.3 and 4.4), thanks to a rise in manufacturing FDI, to multinationals increasingly adopting market-seeking strategies (inevitably, in the richer economies), and to US firms in particular leading with large-scale investments in Western Europe and Canada. The rise in manufacturing FDI undoubtedly had important antecedents back to the 1920s, but reached a new scale after 1945, or, more exactly, from the late 1950s onwards. The trend appears to have peaked by 1973. A total of 73.8 per cent of the FDI stock owned by the seven leading countries could be found in developed economies and the remaining 26.2 per cent elsewhere by 1978. Forced divestments from the 1960s onwards had made investments in developing countries – and consequently in their extractive industries and agriculture – more risky. For multinationals in manufacturing and services, the richer developed nations were more attractive as avenues of investment.

Unlike the flow of funds from industrialized to commodity-producing colonies during the nineteenth century, post-war FDI occurred more often between nations with capital of their own.

Table 4.2 *Outward stock of FDI by major home countries and regions, 1960–80 ($bn)*

	1960	1967	1973	1980
Developed economies	65.4	109.3	205.0	507.4
European Union				213.0
UK	10.8	15.8	15.8	80.4
France	4.1	6.0	8.8	23.6
Germany	0.8	3.0	11.9	43.1
Belgium	1.3			
Belgium and Luxembourg				6.0
Netherlands	7.0	11.0	15.8	42.1
Spain				1.9
Italy	1.1	2.1	3.2	7.3
Sweden	0.4	1.7	3.0	3.7
Other Western Europe				22.1
Switzerland	2.3	2.5	7.1	21.5
Norway				0.6
North America				244.0
USA	31.9	56.6	101.3	220.2
Canada	2.5	3.7	7.8	23.8
Other developed economies				28.3
Japan	0.5	1.5	10.3	19.6
Australia	0.2			2.3
Other	2.5			
Developing economies	0.7	3.0	6.1	16.5
Asia				
Hong Kong, China				0.1
Singapore				3.7
Taiwan, China				0.1
Malaysia				0.2
Republic of Korea				0.1
India				0.2
Africa				
South Africa				0.6
Latin America				
Brazil				0.6
Mexico				0.2
Argentina				6.1
World	66.1	112.3	211.1	523.9

Source: Dunning and Lundan (2008); UNCTAD (2001).

Table 4.3 *Inward stock of FDI by major home countries and regions, 1960–80 ($bn)*

	1960	1967	1973	1980
Developed economies	36.7	73.2	153.7	374.9
Western Europe	12.5			
European Union				185.7
UK	5.0	7.9	24.1	63.0
France				22.9
Germany		3.6	13.1	36.6
Belgium and Luxembourg				7.3
Netherlands				19.2
Spain				5.1
Italy				8.9
Ireland				3.7
Other Western Europe				15.1
Switzerland		2.1	4.3	8.5
North America				137.2
USA	7.6	9.9	20.6	83.0
Canada	12.9			54.2
Other developed economies				37.0
Japan	0.1	0.6	1.6	3.3
Australia				13.2
Australasia and South Africa	3.6			
Developing economies	17.6	32.4	54.7	240.7
Asia	4.1			
Asia and the Pacific		8.3	15.3	174.5
Hong Kong, China				138.8
Singapore				6.2
Taiwan, China				2.4
China				6.3
Malaysia				5.2
Republic of Korea				1.1
Indonesia				10.3
India				1.2
India and Ceylon	1.1			
Turkey				0.1
Africa	3.0	5.6	10.2	16.2
Nigeria				2.4
Egypt				2.3

(*cont.*)

Table 4.3 (*cont.*)

	1960	1967	1973	1980
Latin America	8.5			
Latin America and Caribbean		18.5	28.9	50.0
Brazil				17.5
Mexico				9.0
Argentina				5.3
Chile				0.9
Southern Europe	0.5			
Middle East	1.5			
World	54.3	105.6	208.4	615.8

Source: Adjusted from Dunning and Lundan (2008).

Multinationals were transferring their know-how, management, technologies or products across borders, having first mastered these competencies in their home markets. Approximately 41 per cent of world FDI stock was found in Western Europe by 1975, and 33 per cent in other developed nations. Investment in the Soviet Union and Eastern Europe was negligible. Western Europe, the USA and Canada remained, in 1980, the locations for nearly two thirds of FDI assets. Lastly, it follows that some 80 per cent of US manufacturing FDI flowed to developed countries between 1950 and 1979. The economic interests of the USA became more transatlantic and more geographically diverse: while in 1946 the value of US assets in Latin America was three times greater than those in Europe, they were by 1967 about half of the European total. Europe's significance as a host to US FDI doubled between 1950 and 1970 (tables 4.5 and 4.6) (Dunning, 1993; Dunning and Lundan, 2008).

Foreign direct investment (FDI) was 80 per cent of all long-term foreign investment undertaken between 1951 and 1964, highlighting the importance of multinationals in the conduct of international economic transactions. The operational scale of leading individual enterprises likewise grew. In 1970, multinational enterprises (MNEs) controlled nearly 75 per cent of all foreign assets, and their foreign subsidiaries employed some 40m people, by 1975. Manufacturing was responsible for 32.5 per cent of all US FDI stock in 1950; that proportion – as

Table 4.4 *Outward stock of FDI by home countries (%), 1960–80, and inward stock of FDI by host countries (%), 1960–80*

Outward stock of FDI by home countries (%), 1960–80

	1960	1973	1980
France	6.2	4.2	5.2
West Germany	1.2	5.7	7.0
Italy	1.7	1.5	1.7
Netherlands	10.6	7.5	6.4
Switzerland	3.5	3.4	3.5
Belgium	2.0	1.0	1.2
Sweden	0.6	1.4	1.8
Total Western Europe	25.8	24.7	26.8
USA	48.3	48.1	39.6
UK	16.3	12.8	16.7
Japan	0.8	4.9	5.6
Other	8.8	9.5	11.3
Top 10	94.4	97.1	93.1
Developed economies	98.9	97.1	96.9

Inward stock of FDI by host countries (%), 1960–80

	1960	1973	1980
USA	13.9	9.8	13.5
Britain	9.2	11.6	10.2
France			3.7
Germany		6.3	5.9
Canada	23.7		8.8
Developed economies	67.3	73.8	61.0
Developing economies	32.3	26.2	39.1

Source: Schroter (1993).

Table 4.5 *Outward stock of developed economies in the USA and Western Europe (%), 1960–80*

1960	1970	1980
32	38	47

Source: Dunning in Casson (1983).

Table 4.6 *Percentage of US FDI in Europe, 1950–70*

1950	1960	1970
14.7	21.0	31.4

Source: Schroter (2005).

Table 4.7 *Distribution of world outward FDI stock by sector (%), 1978*

Manufacturing	52
Services	26
Natural resources	22

Source: Dunning in Casson (1983).

in the case of Britain – had risen to about 35 per cent by 1960; and, with the easing of currency controls and rising prosperity, some 44 per cent of the FDI assets owned by US firms in 1971 were in industrial facilities. Manufacturing still accounted for over half of world FDI stock in 1978. Investments in oil and mining were by this stage taking a greater share, as was the service sector, but those in agriculture and public utilities continued their decline (Table 4.7). Public utilities, for example, constituted only 4 per cent of US multinational investments, by 1970 (Dunning and Lundan, 2008; Stopford and Dunning, 1983; Casson, 1983; Wilkins, 1974).

Assembly line and party line

Soon after the USA had entered the Second World War, in December 1941, Alfred P. Sloan as President of General Motors appointed a policy group to reflect on future international events. Edward Riley, as Vice-President and General Manager of the Overseas Operating Division, offered his views in February 1943, arguing how the USA must never again retreat into isolationism. International problems and activities would require 'American guidance, intervention and support', in case they turned once more 'in directions wholly opposed to our interests'. Riley repeated the established US view that European empires were essentially an unfair means of excluding US business. He welcomed Britain's willingness to abandon imperial protection and industrial cartels in return for closer collaboration with the USA, and noted optimistically the 'English determination' to compete instead on the basis of 'low costs through efficient production'.

Lower trade barriers, Riley insightfully recognized, would have immediate implications for business management, since other nations would seek to imitate US 'best practice'. He was prescient on the topic of Russia, accurately predicting that it would avoid warlike expansion, but instead engage in a battle of economic and political philosophies. By showing the material benefits of their 'system of life' to the mass of people in Europe and Asia, the USA and Britain could successfully combat Communism. He concluded, in what should be dry understatement, that those areas under Russian influence 'will probably not present a fertile field for our type of business'. In its report of June 1943, the Overseas Policy Group identified how GM could gain from the long-term worldwide trend towards greater industrialization. To do so, it would have to think 'multi-nationally'. For the time being, only Canada, Europe and Australia (all places where the company had operated before the war) could support full-scale manufacturing plants (Sloan, 1964).

The giant General Motors came to epitomize the power of US business, and its cars the opportunities of a modern, American existence. Its post-war international policies reflected US hostility to the British Empire, associated with discriminatory tariffs and restrictive practices, and acknowledged the impact of Cold War politics. They expressed a strong belief in the superiority of American management and technology, and noted how the spread of industrialization outside the USA would need a more proactive multinational business strategy. American FDI had barely grown between 1940 (when it was valued at $7.0bn) and 1946 (worth some $7.2bn), and strategic control and ownership of oil, rubber, metals and other raw materials had been the pressing wartime concern.

Charles Wilson, GM president throughout the Second World War, had been closely involved with the Federal government and its munitions drive. In 1953, offered the post of Secretary of Defense, he became famous for a remark he never made. Rather than the very questionable 'What's good for General Motors is good for the USA', he told a Congressional appointments committee 'for years I thought what was good for the country was good for General Motors and vice versa'.[1]

President Eisenhower, although elected on a platform critical of US military weakness, gave Wilson the task of cutting defence expenditure and reforming the Pentagon. The result was greater dependence on the nuclear deterrent. Wilson (fairly or unfairly) was perceived as part of the 'military-industrial complex', which President Eisenhower criticized in his valedictory speech. It is interesting, too, that Robert McNamara – a Ford executive, and, for a few weeks, president of the company – was made Defense Secretary in 1961. An architect of US policy in Vietnam, he left in 1968 to head the World Bank for over thirteen years (Gaddis, 1998; Blight and Lang, 2004).

Post-1945 American administrations – providing international loans and raw materials, and later organizing technology, management and productivity programmes for its allies – saw the investment of multinationals as an extension of the national interest. One component of Marshall Aid, under the Economic Cooperation Act of 1948, was the Investment Guaranty Program. This insured American businesses against the risks of war and the non-convertibility of currency, both very real dangers in the Europe of the time, and, from 1950, there was cover for expropriation. The US government, moreover, negotiated treaties that prohibited double taxation and discriminatory policies; gave credits for any tax paid abroad; and improved the lending capabilities of the Export-Import Bank (Sigmund, 1980). The International Development Act of 1950 sponsored scientific advances and industry in developing nations, and, over the next decade, US financial support switched away from Western Europe. The Mutual Security Agency, which took over indemnity cover in 1951, was similarly more focused on investments in the Third World, where the risks and the threat of Soviet influence were greater.

Although US policy supported outward FDI, it did not entirely or immediately coincide with the strategic calculations and actions of multinationals. The take-up of government investment guarantees in Western Europe (mainly available during 1948–51) was small. While the oil, mining, and commodity sectors had to venture abroad, manufacturers remained cautious about foreign investment, given the experiences of the 1930s and 1940s, uncertain world economic conditions, and host government restrictions on taxes, profit repatriation, or local ownership. There was the danger of East–West military tension, and concerns about the high levels of Communist support in Italy and France. For many years after the Second World War, only Canada, highly integrated with the US economy, offered a familiar and secure location (Wilkins, 1974). Manufacturers seeking profitable returns in foreign markets through FDI looked for reassurance that European recovery was under way. Each individual national market had to justify the substantial transfer of financial, technological, organizational and human resources.

The majority of US companies waited, as we have noted, until the late 1950s and the 1960s, when the economic and political signals were clearer, before making big commitments in Europe. Very soon, as outward investment peaked, US governments became concerned about a declining balance of payments and more sensitive to criticisms about American businesses exporting production and jobs (Chapman, 1991). Washington, in 1965, asked multinationals to limit FDI and to repatriate profits. Restrictions on outward FDI, imposed in 1968, were quickly lifted for Canada and developing countries generally, but remained in place for Europe, Australia, Japan and the Middle East until 1970, when they were removed by President Nixon. The USA ran its first deficit for over a hundred years in 1971, and the devaluation of the dollar marked the weakening – but not the ending – of its hegemony. As the pressure to devalue spread, throughout the decade, and fixed exchange rates were abandoned, it undermined the IMF, which had to rewrite its rules (Van der Wee, 1991; Safarian, 1993; Wilkins, 1974).

American autos and Europe

General Motors had lost its Opel subsidiary soon after Germany declared war on the United States. The Soviet Union came to control the Brandenburg factory in 1945, and demanded the rest of Opel as war reparations. The US military government in southern Germany accordingly handed over equipment from the Russelheim plant, before switching policy completely to promoting West German reconstruction and resisting the Soviet threat. GM was wary about resuming control, however, fearing it might have to pay back $35m of tax concessions – received from the US government for property lost to the enemy – and it lacked confidence in German recovery. Although the company president, Charles Erwin Wilson, favoured renewing operations, his view within the company was the minority one. It was General Lucius D. Clay – Allied Commander Dwight D. Eisenhower's successor as military governor and US High Commissioner – who resumed production at Russelheim, and, in 1947, as Cold War enmities intensified, he threatened permanent takeover unless the US auto giant returned to take charge.

GM formally did so in November 1948, on a two-year trial, but did not send any new capital or personnel, and international instability during the 1948 Berlin blockade seemingly justified its commercial caution. Opel's output, in the year that followed, was only 40,000 vehicles. The dismantling of hundreds of factories, reparations payments, and the confiscation of scientific patents had all weakened Germany, as did the loss of the Saarland coalfields to French occupation for a decade. Nonetheless, the *Wirtschaftswunder* was under way. With West Germany on the front line of the Cold War, US policy changed from wariness of a resurrected German state and economy to wanting and needing a strong ally (Gimbel, 1990). In 1954, Opel made 165,000 vehicles, surpassing the 131,000 produced at the UK Vauxhall subsidiary (Sloan, 1964), and by 1972 Opel had become bigger in West Germany than its main rival, Volkswagen (Cray, 1980; Dassbach, 1989).[2]

General Motors and Ford were far ahead of their foreign competitors in production, output and financial resources, and they were, before the 1960s, the only car makers to own 'complete' foreign subsidiaries, as opposed to minor assembly plants or foreign sales firms. To exploit their lead, they pursued the complete ownership of their subsidiaries, control facilitating the transfer of capabilities to overseas plants, and the adoption of more competitive production methods. The US auto makers abandoned interwar strategies of joint ventures with local companies, undertaken as a means of gaining entry to established distribution networks, or of overcoming their low brand recognition. Post-war, their strength in design, manufacturing, and marketing led logically to wholly owned subsidiaries.

GM, which took tight control of management and car design in its foreign businesses, made 1.1m of the 8m cars sold worldwide outside the USA and Canada in 1963, and the Overseas Operating Division supervised sales of $2.3bn generated by some 135,000 employees.[3] But the pressure for internal reform mounted, and it was not forthcoming: overcentralized decision making was hindering its domestic and international operations, and standardized models were failing to meet emerging consumer trends in diverse national markets (Cray, 1980).

For many British customers, Vauxhall had a tin-can image; Germans liked air-cooled cars that did not freeze up during winter; and, generally, Europeans bought smaller models than Americans. With tariffs on auto imports – including duties in the USA (10 per cent), Germany (20–22 per cent), Britain (25 per cent), and Japan at the high end (35 per cent) – distinct national car markets would remain a reality. In 1973, Opel's declaration that it was, primarily, a German company and, secondarily, a multinational indicated a desire for more independence in operations and design.[4]

Ford, the pioneer of mass manufacturing, had been an early pioneer of manufacturing FDI too. Back in the USA during the interwar period, the firm nonetheless had lost ground to GM (Sloan, 1964). Henry Ford, the company's creator, was a brilliant if idiosyncratic engineer and entrepreneur, but his individualistic methods were ultimately no match for GM's managerial and marketing sophistication. He had been forced out of retirement by his son's death, but he was finally replaced by his namesake and grandson, Henry Ford II. It was succession to a new generation, in 1945, that triggered Ford's revival. When the Allies crossed the Rhine, during the previous year, they had arrested forty-four Ford Werke officials for their Nazi party links. The Cologne factory was largely intact, and the British military government (unlike its US counterpart at GM's Russelheim plant) wanted it returned quickly to production. A British team from Ford's Dagenham works, near London, was soon on the scene, while the Dearborn headquarters was too distracted by difficulties of managerial succession. Henry Ford II crossed the Atlantic in 1948, the first year of Marshall Aid and European economic revival, when GM confirmed (albeit tentatively) its multinational re-engagement. Ford Werke was soon making passenger vehicles again. Dagenham had been one the best-equipped production lines in Europe, but relentless war production had inevitably done its damage. In the past, other European subsidiaries had reported to Dagenham. In the new era of reconstruction, only the parent factory, at Detroit, had the technical expertise as well as the resources to rebuild the businesses in Germany or elsewhere, and it founded an International Division for the task.

Of Ford Werke, Henry Ford II was adamant about the new international strategy: 'This is an American company and it is going to be run from America.' Once the USA and British had begun to dilute policies of de-Nazification, Robert Schmidt was one of six Ford Werke executives to return, despite being accused of using slave labour at the Cologne factory during the war. When the third US High Commissioner of Germany, a lawyer and former Assistant Secretary for War, John J. McCloy, released a number of convicted industrialists – amongst them, Friedrich Flick and Alfred Krupp – in 1951, he was implementing the Cold War policy of restoring West Germany as a strong front line against Communism. For others, the decision hid the past and obscured the guilt during the Nazi period of leading German businessmen, many of whom re-entered commercial life in the 1950s, although less prominent figures were to face trial under the Federal Republic.[5]

The reasons why Ford turned down the opportunity to acquire Volkswagen are disputed, but VW's manager, Heinrich Nordoff, saw Ford's executives during their visit to Europe and urged them to make an offer. Henry Ford II and the head of the International Division saw the idea as demonstrating 'practical interest on the part of American private capital in Germany, so necessary to its revival'. They had the support of William Draper, Undersecretary of State for War, who, as a former partner in the merchant bank Dillon, Read, was well acquainted with German business. Operational synergies and the small Beetle car were pluses, but Ford preferred a minority holding so that VW could keep its German identity. The proposal fizzled out, during complicated negotiations with both British and US governments, and from fear of adverse reaction in Germany to foreign ownership.

Ford's strategic priorities at home had greater pull, and, overseas, the UK had the first claim on resources. It was as late as 1958 before Ford made a major investment at Cologne, leading in 1960 to the launch of its first car designed in Germany. In France, a shortage of trucks and experienced managers persuaded the authorities to overlook the wartime record of Maurice Dollfus, chairman of Ford SAF, whose Poissy factory, in the west of Paris, had assisted the Nazi war effort. He persuaded Dearborn into a misconceived recapitalization in 1945, but the subsidiary turned into an embarrassment, with its poor management, old equipment, and labour disputes, and no car suited to the tastes and incomes of France's national market ever appeared. The French government's opposition to foreign control was further reason against investment. Dollfus, an opportunist, persuaded France's economic planning agency to view Ford SAF as a French company, so it was included in plans to revitalize the national auto industry. In 1954,

Simca (Société Industrielle et Carrosserie Automobile) bought most of Ford SAF.[6]

Dearborn had rejected the Dagenham team's post-war plans for a small car, and, in 1950, it sent US prototypes for 'productionizing' and introduced new machinery and production techniques. Decision making from Dearborn took no account of Britain's supply shortages, and USA-style mechanization and large-scale output were not as efficient in Britain's much smaller economy, or in any of Europe's national markets. The consumer appeal and price competitiveness of its large model range generated sound profits for Ford UK throughout the 1950s, but it remained less successful in developing the small cars that most British customers preferred. As a result, while it was well ahead of GM Vauxhall's 9 per cent market share, in 1954, its 27 per cent lagged behind that of 38 per cent for the British Motor Corporation (the merged Morris and Austin enterprises). Top management and engineers at Dearborn kept a direct grip on product and investment policy, but British management, led by a stubborn Patrick Hennessy, did gradually build up independent product development capacities. Ford now viewed local minority shareholders as barriers to the adoption of US best practices, and by 1961 it had gained full ownership. Furthermore, UK exchange controls (since 1947) had formally favoured local participation, but, over time, British governments concluded that they had instead to compete for inward investment. There was a fear that, if Ford were frustrated in its ownership and strategic aims, then its capital and other resources would head for Germany (Hodges, 1974). By the 1960s, with the European mainland's economies growing faster than Britain, Germany was best placed to benefit.

The statist and autarkic policies of the fascist dictator General Francisco Franco insisted on investing multinationals involving indigenous capital and management, whereas full ownership and control were now core tenets of Ford's international strategy. Spain began to build its 'economic Gibraltar', and, since the Barcelona factory was in poor condition, and Spain's home market was stagnating, Ford sold its share to local interests in 1954. International Telegraph and Telephone (ITT) and Rio Tinto also exited at this time (Estape-Triay, 1998). Despite reversals in France and Spain, Ford employed, by 1960, some 100,000 people outside the USA.

Although the multinational's subsidiaries became dependent on product design, technology and finance from Dearborn, the

International Division had only formal supervision of national subsidiaries which, in the main, operated separately. In production and marketing, Ford was (in the jargon) a 'multi-domestic' enterprise rather than a true 'multinational'. It opened research and development centres in Britain and Germany during the 1960s, but they showed little instinct for cross-border coordination between national subsidiaries. Dagenham and Cologne were evolving their own capabilities, but it made little sense for them to conceive and produce rival cars. Ford, as an alternative, put forward a pan-European strategy. The result was Ford Europe, founded in 1967: operating across borders would bring synergies and economies of scale in research, production and marketing, and the USA and Canada were already a model of 'two nations but one integrated economy'. It followed that Dearborn had to transfer large measures of managerial autonomy to a new regional headquarters more alive to the needs of the European customer. Integrated design, development and operations implied truly European cars, and, by 1980, Ford Europe's eleven regional factories had obtained a clear cost lead over GM in Europe (Nevins and Hill, 1954; Bonin, Lung and Tolliday, 2003; Wilkins and Hill, 1964).[7]

The establishment of Ford Europe highlighted the firm's commitment to multinational growth, and by 1972 Europe accounted for some 27 per cent of the multinational's output (compared with North America's 66 per cent). The expansion of the European Economic Community, in 1973, from six to nine nations seemed to justify its decision, and the company was able to return to Spain. Impending national bankruptcy, in 1959, combined with US and IMF pressure, had forced a reluctant Franco on to a path of economic liberalization, and technocratically minded administrators took over from the statist ideologues. They facilitated the 'Spanish Miracle' of the 1960s, when only Japan achieved a higher growth performance. Opportunities brought multinational investors back, as did the advantages of low taxes, low wages, no strikes, and minimal regulations. The Authi car company signed a deal with the British Leyland Motor Corporation, in 1965, under which it would make the totemic Mini, and SEAT and Citroën-Hispania became equal partners in auto parts maker Industrias Mecánicas de Galicia (Indugasa) in 1973. The dilution of ownership restrictions on foreign companies, whenever nine tenths of production went for export, was another needed concession for multinational investors. Since Ford wanted to make the Fiesta small car for the European market, the condition was easily accepted. By the time the Valencia factory made its first vehicle, in 1976, Spain's dictator had died, and the country had begun its transformation to democracy (Nevins and Hill, 1954; Bonin, Lung and Tolliday, 2003; Wilkins and Hill, 1964).[8]

Unlike General Motors or Ford, Chrysler first ventured abroad in the post-war period. Rising incomes, expanding markets, and import barriers were all reasons for its quick internationalization through acquisition. Simca came under Chrysler's control between 1958 and 1964. The original idea was to maintain the Simca name, mixing American ownership with French-style management, but in 1970 the subsidiary was re-christened Chrysler France. In the UK, the government allowed the US firm, in 1964, to buy Rootes, a maker of outmoded family cars, so long as ownership and management remained part local. With a threat of closure, three years later, it had to surrender to the multinational and agreed to full foreign ownership. Hastily, Britain embarked on an industrial strategy of protecting what was left of its vehicle industry, overseeing its consolidation, by 1968, into the British Leyland Motor Corporation. Another Chrysler acquisition was Spain's Barreiros Diesel SA, in 1969, building on its six-year-old licensing deal (Hodges, 1974); the company, overall, came to control 7.5 per cent of the European vehicle market. But its foreign ventures foundered through a combination of poor vehicle design and a confused brand identity, and, in the USA, the parent firm fell during the troubled 1970s into financial crisis. The new chief executive, Lee Iacocca, did not hesitate, and, in 1978, he sold Chrysler Europe to PSA Peugeot Citroën for one US dollar (Maxcy, 1981; Gallard, 2004).[9]

US oil and chemicals in Europe

After the Second World War, Europe had, inevitably, a badly damaged infrastructure, and urgent shortages in fuel and raw materials. During the period 1945 to 1950, oil multinationals, rather than manufacturers, had led FDI initiatives. Marshall Aid prioritized both oil and oil-based products, and US firms, which had recently extended their control over Middle East supplies, were able to meet the demand. They had, additionally, to build or rebuild refineries, and re-establish distribution networks. Governments insisted on refining imported crude locally, in the interests of economic reconstruction, and because dollars were in short supply. For multinationals, rising profits justified the large-scale capital costs involved, and output at Jersey Standard's French refinery, for example, matched pre-war levels as early as 1948. The company refounded its Hamburg plant, and opened the giant Fawley complex near Southampton in 1951.[10] Socony-Vacuum moved forward on multiple fronts: it returned to France and Italy, bought plants in Germany and Austria, by 1950, and formed a joint venture (with Powell Duffryn Company) at Coryton on the Thames estuary in 1953. The company changed its name to Mobil in 1966.[11] Caltex – dually owned by Standard Oil of California and Texaco – engaged in a burst of activity in 1947–9, erecting new refineries in the Netherlands, Spain, Italy and France.[12] Europe was home to approximately 14 per cent of US FDI oil assets in 1950, and this figure had almost doubled (to 27 per cent) by 1970. Canada showed a similar increase (13 to 24 per cent), but the relative importance of Latin America and Asia declined (Wilkins, 1974).

Of the 'Seven Sisters' that dominated the post-war oil industry, five – Jersey Standard, Gulf Oil, Texaco, Standard Oil of California (Socal), and Mobil – were American; BP was British; and Shell was Anglo-Dutch. Between them, in the 1950s, they were responsible for 85 per cent of the crude produced outside North America and the Communist bloc, and they traded some 90 per cent of the world's oil; they still extracted 75 per cent of the crude in 1968, and, given more competition from independents, the Soviet Union, and state-owned enterprises, they marketed about 50 per cent of it. All of the Seven Sisters, in 1956, led by Jersey Standard, were amongst the world's 25 largest businesses (as measured in sales). US firms such as Mobil and Jersey Standard began, during the 1960s, to unify global operations, while simultaneously establishing regional subsidiaries and forming what became a familiar form of organization amongst the oil majors. Jersey Standard changed its name to Exxon Corporation in 1972 (Wilkins, 1974).

Alongside exploration, shipping, refining and distribution, the Seven Sisters were involved in the making of chemicals (Penrose, 1968). Before 1939, IG Farben had been the technological leader in turning coal into petrol, and other processes, and US firms recruited scientists and engineers from a defeated Germany. The Americans were best placed to trigger the post-war transformation of industrial chemistry, most obviously in petrochemicals (Chapman, 1991). The most-produced organic compound was ethylene, turned mostly into plastics, but also into detergents, lubricants and polystyrene. Some 98 per cent of ethylene output, in 1950, was located in the USA, but thereafter firms adopted strategies of production transfer. By 1970, world capacity was 26 times greater, and production was distributed between the USA (48 per cent) and Western Europe (33 per cent). Outside the USA, if we discount Japan, where inward investment was effectively barred, American and other multinational companies came to control one third of output.

FDI and not cross-border trade was the main instrument of international competition, and most ethylene was produced to be sold locally by 1980. Alongside the well-known oil businesses, Dow and Union Carbide were major players. From 1958, Dow opened ethylene plants in the Netherlands, Germany and Spain, as did Union Carbide in Britain and the Netherlands. Dow Chemical International, founded in 1959, was reluctant to license its technology and name, and preferred instead to own foreign subsidiaries and gain the advantages of operating internationally at scale.[13] Standard Jersey and Texaco – as well as BP, Shell, Compagnie Française des Petroles, and Compagnie de Raffinage – had subsidiaries making a wide range of petrochemicals in France, West Germany and the UK (Chapman, 1991).

As with autos, US oil and chemical firms sought to exploit their inbuilt managerial and technological know-how abroad, and the transferring of capabilities from the parent firm and the safeguarding of competitive expertise were simplified when subsidiaries were fully owned. Ownership guaranteed managerial control, and managerial control helped firms impose their strategy and methods. In the USA, total chemical sales had tripled between 1939 and 1946, propelled by military demand and by scientific advances in polymerized fibres, plastics, insecticides, pesticides and synthetic rubber. Amongst the big chemical corporations, Allied Chemicals lagged technologically (its management, in addition, ultimately resisted the pull of foreign markets).[14] For others, the pursuit of competitive leadership and new international ambitions made collusive agreements, alliances and joint ventures abroad less attractive. Legal judgements in the Federal courts (under antitrust legislation) were an extra reason, because they forced companies to abandon long-standing arrangements with foreign businesses. The remaining alternative strategy to the collusive sharing of national markets was to found foreign subsidiaries that competed for those markets. The international dollar shortage and trade restrictions, finally, put limits on exports, and pushed the choice in the direction of FDI. Although antitrust codes did not technically prohibit joint ventures with foreigners, firms feared expensive and lengthy legal entanglements with the Department of Justice. Proceedings in 1947, for example, persuaded National Lead to acquire, fully, its businesses in Canada and Germany, and to sell its joint ventures in Britain and Japan.[15]

Another ruling in 1952 ended Du Pont and ICI's international cartel, but, at first, the managerial old guard in Delaware preferred to cultivate an expanding home market. Unsettled by government policies in Brazil and Argentina, where they had subsidiaries, they resisted further entanglement outside the USA. But a mix of economic and legal issues, from 1957 onwards, changed their minds. A downturn in demand brought price reductions, and the industry's high-riding stock prices fell. When the Supreme Court ordered Du Pont to divest its General Motors holdings, deeming the link uncompetitive, the firm lost a large part of its revenues and became dependent on its own declining profits. One response was to develop new lines, gradually disengaging from rayon and dyestuffs and investing more in high-resistant metals. Another response was to look abroad, where there were bigger commercial opportunities, cheaper labour costs, and, because there were import tariffs, a need for FDI. The courts had decided that ICI could no longer be a collusive international partner, but the British company's decision to buy a US dye plant turned it into a rival. Infuriated, Du Pont abandoned its deep-set suspicion of multinational investments, starting in Londonderry in Northern Ireland in 1958, and following with others in the Netherlands, France and Germany.

The Foreign Relations Department at Du Pont was converted into the International Department, in charge of exports, multinational subsidiaries, and international patent management, though one hitch in the plan was the US-based manufacturing departments, which, in an internal tussle for control, withheld technical support. The new company president, Lammot du Pont Copeland, representative of the new management outlook, talked of a choice between 'rapidly expanding markets abroad' versus 'economic isolation'. Exports and foreign operations – which had been 6 per cent of total sales in 1944, and 18 per cent in 1963 – accounted for 31 per cent in 1978.[16] Compared to Du Pont, Dow was an earlier and more enthusiastic internationalizer (achieving 45 per cent of sales in foreign markets by 1963), tracked by Hercules (40 per cent), and American Cynamid and Union Carbide (each in the 33–35 per cent range). Across the US chemical industry, production by foreign subsidiaries was twice as large as exports by 1963, and the $13bn invested abroad by 1970 (equal to one third of the industry's capital expenditure at home) signalled a very high degree of 'multinational-ity' (Chapman, 1991; Taylor and Sudnik, 1984; Wilkins, 1974).

US industry and national markets

Over the post-war decades, the automobile and transportation equipment sector was, amongst US industries generally, the largest foreign investor, followed by chemicals and oil. After these came machinery, foods and metals, and household branded products, office equipment and computers achieved prominence. US companies in these sectors owned global competitive leadership in technology, products or management. The turning-point year of 1966 – when the value of US manufacturing FDI assets overtook the oil sector – confirmed major trends in international competitive advantage. This was the same year, moreover, that US FDI, at 7.3 per cent of GDP, equalled the levels of 1929; by 1970, the figure was 8 per cent (Wilkins, 1974). In 1957 there were 2,800 US businesses with 10,000 foreign subsidiaries, and, in 1970, 3,350 businesses with 15,000 foreign operations. The value of the assets held by US manufacturers in Europe overtook those in Canada in 1970, highlighting how international, transatlantic business strategies had come to replace regional ambitions. Similarly, while Latin America's commodities had once attracted a majority of the USA's total FDI, industrial investment in Europe soared ahead.

The modern corporation had originated in the USA from breakthroughs in technologies and operations, the sheer size of its domestic demand, and high per capita incomes, with success resting on an ability to operate on a huge scale. As we saw in the interwar decades (Chapter 3), such firms put together complex multi-departmental organizations, run by teams of professional managers, with experience and expertise in mass production and marketing, and they were able to invest significant sums on research and development. US businesses with their lead in products, know-how and personnel had the resources and capabilities to establish foreign subsidiaries that could succeed against local competition. In business machines, electronics, computers and aerospace, Federal-sponsored research and huge government orders, most obviously in the defence sector, continued into the post-war years, and enabled leading US firms to gain critical mass in technology and output. While Britain had arguably once been in the vanguard of computing and jet engine technology, their American competitors pushed ahead with mass manufacture and commercialization, and, ultimately, in innovative capabilities.

Alongside home-based push factors in the USA (such as leadership in technology, scale and price) making successful internationalization possible, there were pull factors justifying cross-border investments (rather than exports). The wealthy markets of Western Europe, once reconstructed, were a logical and natural location for multinationals making consumer and advanced capital goods: export distances were large; labour, relative to the USA, was cheap; and, despite early concerns about the spread of Communism, the region became a politically secure location for valuable assets. Canada, Australia and other developed economies were other choice destinations for the creation or expansion of foreign subsidiaries. US manufacturers adopted market-seeking strategies. Generally, foreign subsidiaries were mini-versions of the parent, receiving technological and managerial support, but operating independently to serve distinct and separated national markets. Companies faced practical limits to their day-to-day control and coordination of their foreign outposts, and governments, to retain the benefits of inward investment, placed restrictions on investing businesses: as a result, by 1968, some 89 per cent of the industrial output of US multinationals was sold in the host country where production had occurred (Wilkins, 1974).

Planning for a sharp decline in military spending following the end of the Second World War, IBM's president, Thomas J. Watson Sr, looked beyond the USA for options, and in 1949 created the IBM World Trade Corporation: within twelve years, the company employed 33,000 people in 86 countries, and, after another nine years, its foreign businesses generated 40 per cent of total revenues and 50 per cent of profits. Control of the firm passed to Thomas J. Watson Jr, between 1952 and 1956, and, far from Federal spending falling away, IBM gained from the Cold War and the Department of Defense's realization that digital computing had big military applications. Political support for isolationism effectively ended with the Korean War (1950–3), when

Communist-ruled North Korea, with the support of the Soviet Union and the People's Republic of China, attacked the USA's ally to the south. It was the overriding competitive lead that IBM had in business machines that provided the strategic rationale behind internationalization. Overtaking Remington Rand, IBM had, by 1958, some 80 per cent of the US computer market, and it reinforced its first place with the famed System 360 in 1964.

IBM was by far the largest of eight US computer enterprises at this time, provoking people in the business to refer to 'Snow White and the Seven Dwarfs'. It decided against licensing its products to international partners, fearing a loss of its technological secrets, and opted for direct control of international operations. New factories appeared in the Netherlands, Scotland, France, Italy and England, from 1952 to 1966, and IBM France alone had 16 branches located in 13 cities. Some 90 per cent of IBM machines sold in foreign markets came to be made outside the USA. With the introduction of the System 360, IBM had two regional production networks, one in North America, the other in Europe, where it founded laboratories that could provide local technical services more effectively and efficiently (Hodges, 1974; Dassbach, 1989).[17]

Minneapolis-Honeywell's investment in a British factory, from 1948, was defensive, not the outcome of a well-conceived international strategy. Import licence restrictions hurting sales provided the motive, but the company minimized its investment in Britain for so long as restrictions on currency exchange and the repatriation of profits remained.[18] From 1950, as an incentive, and in desperate need of capital, the British government eased controls over remittances for approved US subsidiaries (Wilkins, 1974). Minneapolis-Honeywell's subsidiaries in Britain, Canada, Japan, and the Netherlands grew from almost nothing to 23 per cent of the multinational's sales and to 20 per cent of total employees, by 1965, when there were 17 overseas operations staffed by 12,000 people.[19] NCR re-established itself in Britain, West Germany and Japan from 1946 to 1949, and built new plants in Australia and Canada over the following decades.[20] Hewlett-Packard, having made its first corporate acquisition in the USA, set up a marketing office in Geneva and a manufacturing facility in Boeblingen, in West Germany, in 1959. It followed this international breakthrough with a joint venture in Japan in 1963, in partnership with the Yokogawa Electric Works.[21]

ITT – whose main customers were government-owned utilities – had subsidiaries that actively promoted a local national identity. Brussels, nonetheless, did act as its European headquarters, but it suffered a setback, as we have noted, in 1954, when it was forced out of Franco's Spain as a foreign-owned enterprise. Yet half of ITT's revenues, ten years later, originated in Europe, where it was responsible for 30 per cent of all the telephones manufactured (Schoenberg, 1985; Sobel, 2003). Governments' post-war preference for publicly owned communications, transport and energy left few opportunities for utility FDI, and ITT diversified at home and overseas with acquisitions that included Avis car rental (in 1965) and Sheraton hotels (1968).[22]

Bell Laboratories, owned by ATT, produced the first semiconductors in 1948; Texas Instruments had developed silicon chips by 1954; and Fairchild Semiconductor made a successful integrated circuit in 1959. In the post-war decades, the USA evolved a national innovation system connecting the Federal government, the military, universities, and business, which other countries could only envy. In 1960, spurred by links with the military and the aerospace sector, the US home market accounted for 75 per cent of all semiconductors sold. Texas Instrument's British plant was, in 1957, the first example of semiconductor FDI, and within three years the multinational had established a French subsidiary that could supply the local IBM factory (Wilkins, 1974). Overall, US firms had 19 wholly owned semiconductor factories and 3 joint ventures in Europe by 1974, plus 24 component assembly plants (Langlois, 1989). They constituted a clear example of corporate technological and organizational advantage breeding overseas investment.

Goodyear tyre and the Caterpillar construction equipment company moved quickly after 1945 to expand internationally. Goodyear had established itself throughout Latin America by the late 1940s, and moved into Europe's key markets after 1959.[23] Caterpillar benefited from the rebuilding of Europe and Japan, initially with the assistance of Marshall Aid and other US funding. It announced its first subsidiary abroad in Britain, in 1950, and continued with others in Brazil, Australia, Scotland (1954–6), Japan (1962), and Belgium (1972).[24] Haloid Company formed a joint venture in Britain with the Rank Organisation, in 1956. It became, in another four years, the Xerox Corporation, and by 1969 it had effective control of its British investment, one more demonstration of the preference multinationals displayed in this period for wholly owned subsidiaries, and their drive to protect technological and managerial knowledge.[25] Rank Xerox and the Fuji Photo Film Company formed Fuji Xerox, originally as a fifty-fifty partnership, in 1962, initially just importing and distributing in Japan, but moving into research and production.[26]

Not every US firm, of course, opted for FDI. RCA, for one, preferred, in the 1950s, to license its technology to Philips for the production and sale of products in Europe (Jones, 2005). The mighty General Electric of America turned its back on an internationalizing world economy: it responded to an unfavourable antitrust decision by selling its secretive and complex network of minority interests in leading British, French, Netherlands, and Swedish enterprises during the course of the 1960s. It did retain its Latin American subsidiaries, kept its links with AEG and Toshiba, and bought a French computing company, but GE saved its strategic energies for its US and Canadian businesses, where it exercised majority control.[27]

Alongside the high-tech sectors, US manufacturers made an international impact in branded household goods. Coca-Cola, in the post-war decades, became a global icon, and a potent symbol of Americana. In the USA, it had learnt how to make an appealing mass product at the right price; it had mastered the techniques of brand creation and advertising; it licensed and coordinated local processors of its secret-formula syrup; and it ran an efficient distribution network across a populous, transcontinental economy. It was able to extend these techniques in marketing, licensing, and distribution to other national markets, and it did so after the attack on Pearl Harbor, when the company had followed the GIs on campaign. By 1946, Coca-Cola owned 155 bottling operations abroad (Giebelhaus, 1994). During the 1950s, it opened 15–20 plants every year, and made its red-and-white logo known throughout the world.

Coca-Cola began to diversify its product line, in 1960, with the reintroduction of Fanta, originally developed by its German subsidiary during wartime, and followed this initiative with Sprite, Tab, Fresca and diet versions of its drinks. One inspiration for this change of policy – and its comparative advertising campaign fronted by the slogan 'It's the Real Thing' – was the rise of a major competitor.[28] Pepsico established foreign subsidiaries, from 1954, through Pepsi-Cola International. The marriage of film actress Joan Crawford to a company executive and future chairman boosted the challenger's profile: she even promoted the brand during a European and African tour, and later became a board member. In 1959, at the Moscow Trade Fair, where Nixon and Khrushchev debated the relative merits of capitalism and Communism, the head of Pepsi-Cola International staged another publicity coup: he persuaded the Vice-President to stop at the Pepsi booth, where the Soviet leader was promptly photographed, by an eager world press, happily quenching his thirst.[29]

Heinz's food products, also, could claim a measure of iconic status amongst world shoppers. When H. J. Heinz II (known as 'Jack') took over the company and its famous brands during the Second World War, he inherited manufacturing subsidiaries in Britain, Canada and Australia, but expanded internationally in the Netherlands, Venezuela, Japan, Italy and Portugal. Kellogg – already in Canada and Britain – built a factory in South Africa in 1948, and another in Mexico in 1951. Rapidly succeeding at home, the Campbell Soup Company formed an international division in 1957, and created firms in Italy, Mexico and Australia.[30] Having taken on the role of US distributor for Godiva Chocolatier, in 1966, Campbell acquired full ownership of the Belgian company in 1974, an example of international backwards integration.[31] General Foods – whose brands Maxwell House coffee, Birds Eye frozen foods, Jell-O and others had high recognition – began a series of international acquisitions after 1956: amongst its purchases was La India Company, Venezuela's biggest chocolate business; Hostess snack foods, in Canada; Brazil's Kibon ice cream; and French coffee roaster Établissements Pierre Lemonnier. It was, by the 1960s, an established food industry giant, with twelve major subsidiaries in Canada, Latin America, Western Europe, and Australia.[32]

Other US food companies had a low corporate profile, but a truly international presence. Better known, during this period, through its Mazola cooking oil and Hellmann's mayonnaise brands, the Corn Products Refining Company (CP) processed corn and starch all over the world. In 1958, it added the C. H. Knorr Company in West Germany, a maker of bouillon, dehydrated soups, and convenience foods, to a long series of domestic acquisitions. The firm built a Knorr plant in Japan five years later, transforming itself into CPC International from 1969 (the branded grocery business was to be spun off as Bestfoods in 1997, prior to its merger into Unilever in 2000, with the remaining food ingredient business becoming Ingredion in 2012).[33]

S. C. Johnson – the maker of Johnson's Wax, with long-established businesses in Britain, Canada and Australia – founded a German subsidiary in 1953, and another in Italy in 1959, its success buoyed by the introduction of Glade air freshener and the first ever spray polish, Pledge. Thereafter, deciding that exporting was not profitable, and working with a philosophy of manufacturing with local materials for local markets, the firm opened, by 1968, some twenty overseas firms in Latin America, Europe, Africa, Japan and South East Asia.[34] Transaction costs and locational advantages, in other words, had determined international strategy at S. C. Johnson. Kimberly-Clark – the maker of Scotts and Kleenex tissues – first moved outside the USA and Canada during 1955–7: buying La Aurora paper company, which was refounded as Kimberly-Clark de Mexico; creating the Bowater-Scott joint venture in Britain; and buying Peter J. Schweitzer, Inc., a world supplier of thin papers, with mills in the USA and France. It launched Huggies in 1978, a disposable diaper designed to challenge the established leader, Procter & Gamble's Pampers, by this date on sale for seventeen years.[35]

Host governments and US multinationals

The US occupying administration wanted to upgrade Japan's archaic communications system, utilizing American technology, and effectively deprived Fujitsu of its main business, government contracts. When Japan surrendered in 1945, it had accepted the military rule of the Supreme Commander of the Allied Powers (SCAP), Douglas MacArthur – soon nicknamed the 'Gaijin Shogun', or, loosely, the 'Foreign Generalissimo'. His General Headquarters (GHQ), situated in the requisitioned Dai Ichi Life Insurance building in Tokyo, transformed Japan's constitution, politics, and land ownership before power was handed back in 1949 (the occupation formally ending three years later). When the state-owned Nippon Telephone and Telegraph was formed, in 1952, it evolved into Japan's leading investor in electronics research, and made Fujitsu once more the beneficiary of state-controlled telephony contracts. After years of experimentation, Fujitsu produced Japan's first commercial computer, but the Japanese government realized that, to avoid falling further and further behind in the international technology race, it would need access to US patents. In

1961, it made an agreement with IBM, in return for the US company being allowed by the government to manufacture locally as IBM Japan. In parallel, Japan restricted imports, subsidized native producers, and curtailed needless competition in the interests of stimulating innovation.

After a period, the government forced Fujitsu to devote itself to mainframes and integrated circuits. Product successes were forthcoming, but could not match those from IBM Japan. The Ministry of International Trade and Industry (MITI) decided to reorganize the nation's computing sector, and paired Fujitsu with the computing division of a major rival, Hitachi. In 1972, a small investment in the USA's Amdahl Corporation, founded by an former IBM engineer, gave access to the new firm's technological insights, and Fujitsu traded limitless capital from the Japanese government and NTT's captive sales market. The Fujitsu-Hitachi M-series was the result, and, by 1980, it was outselling IBM in the Japanese home market. By this point, back in the USA, Amdahl was struggling from a counter-attack from IBM, armed with a new line of computers.[36]

For policy makers, the Fujitsu-IBM story was a clear case of how engagement in the international economy could be combined with government-led industrial strategy, if a developing country wanted to close the gap with global leaders rather than just exposing itself to advanced competition. Once its economic miracle was under way and Japan had joined the group of developed countries, it was another logical destination for overseas manufacturing investment. But the government maintained regulations curtailing imports, and the Foreign Investment Law (passed in 1950) forbade outward and inward FDI, with the aim of keeping all capital for the industrialization of the Japanese home economy by Japanese companies, and preventing a foreign industrial invasion. Despite the policy imbalance, the USA continued to allow the sale of patents and technology to Japan, and left its markets freely open to Japanese exports. Aside from restrictions on coastal shipping, broadcast media, nuclear power plants, aviation, and defence-related companies, where there were restrictions on foreign ownership and influence, the US borders were open to business (Safarian, 1993). Washington supported the building of a strong ally in the troubled East Asia region, a focus for Cold War tensions with the Soviet Union, Communist China and their satellites, culminating in insurgency and civil war in Vietnam. Later, balance of payments difficulties and deindustrialization in the USA and Western Europe brought new pressures, and Japan felt obliged to ease its inward FDI regulations in 1971, although abolition did not come until 1980; outward FDI was allowed too, but, interestingly, Japanese companies did not rush to become multinationals, preferring instead to maintain their highly successful policies of export.

In Western Europe, the presence of US multinational manufacturing – and the technology, management, and operational scale at their command – raised concerns about economic sovereignty and the region's future. Japan's industrial strategy was based on acquiring technology and imitating best practice, and the prohibition of inward FDI fitted neatly with the official selection and development of indigenous companies. Policy focused on the 'sunshine' industries, reducing the dependence on textiles and moving the economy, in turn, into steel, autos, electronics, and, with less success, oil and chemicals. The entry of IBM Japan is worth noting for being an exception: in this case, the desire to access a leading technology overrode considerations of foreign ownership. In Britain, events in the aluminium industry seemingly provided good evidence for national decline. US companies had been unable to meet the high levels of demand created by the Second World War, and the Federal government had stepped in to finance plants run by Alcoa. After 1945, as the structures of wartime industrial strategy were unravelled, the government decided to carry out antitrust rulings held in abeyance, which had sought to loosen the company's monopolistic grip: as a result, within five years Alcoa had 50.9 per cent of production capacity, with 30.9 per cent going to Reynolds Metals Company and 18.2 per cent to the Kaiser Aluminum & Chemical Corporation.

A US court ruled for the first time, in 1950, on the ownership of an overseas subsidiary, and decided that Alcoa and Canadian affiliate Alcan could not be owned by the same nine shareholders. Alcoa, in a device to avoid antitrust actions, had formally separated from Alcan and placed its overseas subsidiaries under its control. During the 1950s, the four North American businesses – Alcoa, Alcan, Reynolds and Kaiser – formed with France's Pechiney and Switzerland's Alusuisse the 'big six' of the world aluminium industry. Unlike steel makers, these enterprises vertically integrated mining with production and controlled the world's bauxite and alumina trade outside the Communist bloc (Rodrik, 1982; Cobbe, 1979). As well as securing the supply of raw materials, with its many political dimensions, internalizing supply chains and processing within a single management control provided the main motive behind international business strategies in aluminium. During the short 1957–8 recession, Alcoa realized it would have to internationalize and diversify, and became embroiled in what, during 1958, was Britain's largest corporate takeover. British Aluminium's chairman, Lord Portal of Hungerford, a former Marshal of the Royal Air Force, had approached Alcoa about the acquisition, but forgot to consult his shareholders. Reynolds and its British ally, Tube Investments, then launched Britain's first ever hostile bid for a public company, and battled through to victory in what was called the 'Great Aluminium War'. To do so, they enlisted the help of merchant bank S. G. Warburg, a newcomer to the City of London that was prepared to fight fiercely, and it outmanoeuvred the more established houses of Hambros and Cazenove.[37] The hostile bid exposed the 'old boy network' in Britain's corporate management, and amounted to a breach of expected business etiquette by Reynolds, TI and Warburg. British public opinion judged, too, the public spectacle of powerful foreign interests vying for control of one of its major industries.

Post-war British governments had exacted promises from investing multinationals, mostly over employment, capital investment and exports, although policy remained liberal. With the lifting of currency and exchange controls in Europe from 1958, the surge in inward FDI intensified debates about economic sovereignty and the promoting of indigenous industry. The failure to close the technology gap with the USA encouraged governments, in the 1960s and 1970s, to adopt the cause of industrial policy. Rationalization schemes in steel, textiles, coal and shipbuilding were responses to low-wage competition from industrializing countries, and industrial policy, consequently, came to mean the hopeless of task of breathing life into 'dead ducks'. US multinationals, with their technological and managerial advantages, on the other hand, had an impact on industries which should have been part of a host nation's future. Where the British government did exact promises from investors, it never monitored outcomes, and assurances could be at best only temporary, and at worst worthless from the outset.

Chrysler's broken promise after its takeover of Rootes, in 1967, had exposed Britain's fragile FDI regulations and forced the Labour government to look more anxiously for answers from industrial policy. With three US auto multinationals now inside the national redoubt, it set out to shore up what remained of the British-owned industry; specifically, it persuaded Leyland Motor Corporation to add the weakening British Motor Holdings (with its Morris, Austin, Jaguar and Daimler marques) to its existing operations (the founding commercial vehicle firm, plus the Standard Triumph and Rover acquisitions) (Gallard, 2004).[38] By 1975, British Leyland was bankrupt and effectively nationalized (later transmuting into the state-owned BL, and then Rover). Ultimately, US competition also pulled reluctant governments into owning the computing industry. British Tabulating Machine (BTM), from 1949, had ended its reliance on IBM's technology, and, by the 1950s, its local rival Powers-Samas (formally, the Accounting and Tabulating Corporation of Great Britain) had spun off from its US founder. Struggling to find a competitive response to IBM, they merged in 1959; their successor, International Computers and Tabulators (ICT) bought up much of the British computing industry, but in 1968 it joined with English Electric, Plessey and the British government to establish International Computers Ltd (ICL). Scale was seen as the answer to developing and marketing new products, and ICL was in the year of its creation the largest non-US computer business. To help the company achieve critical mass, the government granted preferred status in public sector purchase orders, but, plagued by soaring research costs and incompatible technologies, and struggling with the semiconductor revolution, ICL was financially holed as early as 1971. Margaret Thatcher's Conservative administration stuck to its free market principles, and, in 1980, ended ICL's favoured company status (the business eventually being sold, ten years later, to Japan's Fujitsu) (Campbell-Kelly, 1990; Hodges, 1974).

The computing divisions of AEG-Telefunken, Siemens, Philips, Olivetti and Machines Bull similarly received support from their governments. Compared to Britain, France was more committed to economic planning and putting the required administrative mechanisms in place. The country had set out, in 1945, with a policy of nationalizing and rebuilding its coal, electricity and gas industries, and took over much of the banking sector to support developments in aviation, defence equipment and electronics. Like Britain, France failed to close the technology gap with the USA, and the formation of the Common Market, in 1957, brought an additional cross-border threat. Charles de Gaulle became the first President of the Fifth Republic in 1959: he was committed to reasserting France as a world power, putting an end to political instability and generating long-term industrial growth. The state, as well as boosting investments in innovation, drove reform of France's comparatively small, family-controlled manufacturers, and established large-scale national champions for selected industries.

France was suspicious of US FDI and any reliance on American technology, and it had not considered computing as a strategic priority until General Electric of America acquired, by 1964, a majority stake in Compagnie des Machines Bull. The French government failed to block the takeover: instead, it formed a rival, Compagnie Internationale pour l'Informatique (CII). Then, looking at the lessons of the Machines Bull case, the government effectively blocked all foreign acquisitions for nearly ten years, when it allowed takeovers only if the acquirer had a technological lead, and placed limits on its national champions investing outside the EEC. The clash of Gaullist economic nationalism and global competition continued to produce complex and ironic twists to this story of transnational engagement. Unable to compete against IBM, GE sold its computing division to Honeywell, and, in 1975, government pressure on Honeywell won back majority local ownership of its French operations, through the founding of CII-Honeywell-Bull. West Germany, open to FDI, did not use screening procedures for multinationals, but felt it necessary to protect strategic economic assets from the control of foreign governments or their state-owned enterprises. Unlike France, however, Germany and the Netherlands never developed any sense of a US invasion. Belgian governments, too, were generally welcoming to all investors, offering tax concessions and subsidies. Yet they did support the objectives of the European Economic Community, and public contracts for computing products and services favoured Philips and Siemens over a prospective IBM monopoly (Wilkins, 1974). Italy was prepared to use exchange controls to influence inward FDI, but, it was judged, they had no significant impact on inward investment (Safarian, 1993; Gillespie, 1972).

Discovering and organizing the multinational

The impact of FDI by the 1960s, and US companies in particular, gave birth to the idea of the multinational as a business with characteristics distinct from purely domestic firms. Once the 'multinational enterprise' had been discovered and given its new name, analysts could consider what strategies and organizational capabilities brought success in foreign markets, and how firms might transfer their activities across borders. The post-war decades had witnessed changes in the scale and nature of multinational enterprise, and there was a growing political and popular awareness that multinationals were a force in the world economy and within individual nation states. Post-war multinational enterprise was not, as we have seen, the coming of the new, but the greater perception of its presence (especially in the form of US manufacturers in Europe) made it seem so. Debates in developed countries about the growing impact of FDI on ownership, technology, employment and exports were a feature of the times, even though the long history of multinationals in developing territories raised, in principle, and with much more marked consequences, very similar questions about the costs and benefits of their activities. Unsurprisingly, former colonies and newly independent nation states increasingly questioned the role of foreign investors, many linked to an imperialist past, and sought to limit their influence.

The common international strategy of post-war manufacturers was market-seeking in developed economies, with firms seeking overseas customers for goods in which they had acquired, in their home economies, an international leadership in price, product, production, or marketing. Given that much of Europe had been devastated by the Second World War, the gap in wealth, output and resources between the USA and its major competitors had never been greater. The wartime stimulus of the US economy had intensified longer-term trends in business organization, as well as capabilities. American corporations had made breakthroughs in mass manufacturing and marketing, and built teams of managers and technicians to deal with their increasingly large, complex operations. They evolved organizational hierarchies with a strategic headquarters at the top, but devolved major responsibility for products or areas of operation to a layer of divisional management (or the multidivisional or M-form), which, in their turn, oversaw departments in charge of business functions such as production, purchasing or distribution. Giant US enterprises, by allocating levels of responsibility and establishing and promulgating procedures and routines, enabled the effective coordination of finance, technology and personnel, and supported competitive advantages in products, price or sales. The emergence of large firms (notable from the 1920s onwards) had created businesses with resources and capabilities, and increased the likelihood of FDI (Schroter, 2005).

In the post-war decades, they had the clear competitive leadership to begin or to extend their presence overseas, and worldwide economic recovery and the lifting of currency controls created, over time, the local conditions that favoured foreign production over exports. Whenever the size of host market sales provided the justification for FDI, US manufacturing multinationals preferred wholly owned subsidiaries because, as we have seen in case after case, control safeguarded and better utilized technical-managerial know-how transferred from the parent company. They moved, as a result, away from joint ventures, contract arrangements and licensing. In planning their expansion overseas, some large US companies could call on the multi-divisional model of devolved management, and, as a result, they frequently formed an overseas or international division to oversee their national subsidiaries (Stopford and Wells, 1972). The Goodyear tyre company falls into the category of a good example: having invested in Latin America and South Africa after 1945, in response to the termination of government wartime contracts, it created its Goodyear International Corporation (GIC), in 1957, as a prelude to establishing, by 1967, factories in the three major European markets of France, Italy and Germany.[39]

Although US companies were experienced in establishing systems of monitoring and coordination, they had to learn new skills to operate across borders, and they had to reconsider the use of the parent's technology and methods in very different national markets. As multinationals expanding in overseas markets, companies could make further increases in scale, reduce labour and supply costs, or be more responsive to host-country customers, and they could, accordingly, extend their competitive and, some might say, oligopolistic advantages beyond their country of origin. Large-scale corporations dominated the organizational and technologically complex industries which provided the largest rises in growth and productivity. Approximately 6 per cent of the 2,800 US businesses owning overseas operations accounted for some 80 per cent of the total in foreign assets and sales (Dassbach, 1989).

An immediate strategic objective of US multinationals, from the 1950s onward, was to build a cross-border organization that would facilitate the flow of superior resources and capabilities from parent to subsidiary. The second strategic objective was to allow the subsidiary adequate operational freedom, whereby it could meet the specific needs of its host market. The obvious clash between the need for headquarters control, on the one hand, and decentralization, on the other, increased as the subsidiary itself grew in size and relative importance. In determining the relationship between parent and subsidiary, and facilitating the development of local products suited to host markets, the international transfer or appointment of senior management and technical staff was axiomatically important. In many cases, direct control, monitoring and reporting mechanisms by the headquarters or its international division had limitations, and coordination rested on having subsidiary managers familiar with and loyal to the parent company. The sharing of senior personnel consequently counterbalanced the low levels of control over daily operations, and assisted the transfer of technological, product and managerial know-how. But the cross-border integration of production remained minimal, and parent and subsidiaries tended to serve their national markets, coordinating where necessary in areas of general management or product development as opposed to operations. While the parent headquarters could transfer and establish global best practice in production management at its subsidiaries, control was critically more distant than might be experienced in the home economy (Wilkins, 1974; Humes, 1993; Child, Faulkner and Pitkethly, 2000).

The increase in the number of all US multinational subsidiaries – from 7,500 in 1950 to 23,000 in 1966 – was a measure of the organizational challenge. While, in 1950, we can locate 3 manufacturing multinationals with subsidiaries in twenty or more countries, we know, by 1975, there were at least 44 manufacturers from the USA alone that had achieved an international scope of having subsidiaries in twenty-plus countries. Mining and oil firms, too, transferred management, technology or capital, although host government policies, the advantages of local support and participation, and risk sharing meant that joint ventures were more commonly sought in the extractive industries. Their strategies were, obviously, resource-seeking, and geology decided the location of their production. Distribution subsidiaries, predominantly marketing to developed economies, were more likely to be wholly owned. Levels of integration varied between industries and mineral types, yet effective competitors had to master the cross-border coordination of extraction, processing and marketing. Mining and oil multinationals – unlike manufacturers – were less likely to produce and sell in the same national economy (Spero and Hart, 1997).

Developed economies – although we can count France as more equivocal – welcomed FDI on the assumption that the most advanced practices located in one nation would flow to a nation less advanced in that industry. Europe gained from the US Technical Assistance and Productivity Mission, from 1948, as part of the Economic Recovery Agency. There were 145 productivity teams by 1951: the Anglo-American Council on Productivity, which reported resistance amongst managerial traditionalists, was one such example, and participating nations later worked through the OEEC to launch an intra-European technical assistance programme. Europe's nation states provided subsidies and tax breaks for multinationals on the assumption that they would bring their technology and methods with them, and generate spin-offs amongst local suppliers and competitors. Volkswagen had transformed production methods by the mid 1960s. However, low skill levels and trade union opposition undermined efforts at Fiat, and the recognized advantages of high skills and management–employee cooperation meant that American mass production methods were abandoned at Volvo by 1970 (Schroter, 2005; McCreary, 1964).

One study in Britain in the 1950s showed that US subsidiaries had a higher productivity than local producers (Dunning, 1958). Royalties on licences and patents paid by US subsidiaries flowing back to parent companies indicated a transfer of technological know-how – rising from 43 per cent of total receipts in 1957 to 70 per cent by 1965 – but did not conclusively prove spin-offs for the competitive upgrading of local economies. One motive behind wholly-owned subsidiaries was to retain competitive advantage and to make knowledge transfer sticky, and internal accounting practices and the reduction of tax liabilities in part explained the scale of royalties and other remittances. Any rise in growth, employment, exports or technology could be portrayed as a crowding out of indigenous efforts, and the payment of remittances could be seen as rent and as a drain on national resources. Some multinationals did establish local research and development facilities, even though they might focus only on the national market customization of products originating with the parent company.

As overseas markets grew in importance, the rationale for technological capability at the subsidiary level increased, and the aptness of transferring products for exact or close imitation declined. One study, in 1980, showed that 15 per cent of US corporate research and development (R&D) was spent abroad, mostly by large corporations. There was, amongst multinationals generally, an equal division between the international centralization and decentralization of research and development: centralization made subsidiaries less nimble in meeting the demands of consumers, and responsible for the costs of altering parent business lines, while decentralization ran the risk of duplication and redundancy (Behrman and Fischer, 1980; Alfaro and Rodriguez-Clare, 2004).

While US multinationals demonstrated their advanced capabilities in production management and in technology, there is evidence that the British makers of branded goods and household products had already adopted advanced marketing techniques. But US multinationals did bring leading practices in advertising and sales to continental Europe, where national consumer markets during the post-war decades were less developed (Fitzgerald, 2009). In personnel management, firms such as General Motors or General Electric were well acquainted with trades unions, but companies such as IBM and Mars imported, with only partial success, their policies of non-recognition to Europe. US multinationals did, on the other hand, transfer plant or productivity bargaining, which from the late 1960s challenged the premise of national pay settlements in Britain as negotiated by employers' associations and trades unions. The US multinationals remained uneasy with officially recognized and institutionalized national pay bargaining and works councils in Germany and the Netherlands – an idea taken up by the EEC – but had to accept them as a reality. On the whole, national government policies, legal frameworks and entrenched practices greatly limited the transfer and international standardization of human resource management by multinationals (Edwards and Ferner, 2002; Fenton-O'Creevy, Gooderham and Nordhaug, 2005).

Further reductions in trade barriers (bilaterally, or through negotiations in successive GATT rounds), the growing integration of the EEC, and falling transport costs all pointed to increasing gains from cross-border interaction, and worked against autonomous national subsidiaries (Stopford and Wells, 1972). The EEC largely achieved internal free trade by 1968, and the European Free Trade Area (EFTA) similarly encouraged integration (Wilkins, 1974). The removal of trade barriers between the USA and Canada, beginning with the automobile sector in 1965, offered up a model of 'continentalism', and Ford created Ford Europe, in 1967, as a company in search of regional production networks and greater economies of scale. Such cross-border efficiency-seeking could support the established market-seeking strategies of manufacturing multinationals. A flip side to the reduced autonomy of national subsidiaries was a reduction in the international role of the US parent and the granting of greater decision-making authority to its cadre of regional managers.

As the 1970s progressed, other US firms began to replace their international divisions with regional companies or headquarters, although some preferred to found instead worldwide product divisions, usually headquartered at the parent business and managing one product type, model, brand, or service. Over time, regional and product divisions might evolve into matrix structures, appropriately incorporating and delineating cross-border lines of responsibility for two distinct organizational requirements; in addition, in some cases, the functional imperatives of purchasing, production and marketing or support services in accounting or personnel might be included in a three-way organizational matrix. But these structures remained rarer than the clearer choices made between adopting international, regional or product divisions, associated, by some, with slow decision-making, obscure lines of authority, and unneeded internal conflicts (Stopford and Wells, 1972).

Taking the US grain trader Cargill-Tradax as an example, it is clear that its attempt to bring geographical, product and functional aims into harmony by means of an organizational matrix contributed to uncertainty in decision making (Broehl, 1998). In mining and oil, companies tended to retain a centralized functional organization, finding less value in separated international divisions. Overseas upstream extraction and processing required the cross-border transfer, support and close coordinaton of capital, personnel, production methods and technology, often in developing or politically troubled locations; downstream distribution, contracting and sales often took place in different locations to production, and relied accordingly on another range of cross-border skills in distribution and contracting. The position initially differed from manufacturing, where the production and sales of foreign subsidiaries commonly took place in the same national market, but international manufacturing was beginning to undergo a process of change by the 1970s.

British multinationals, like their US rivals, tended towards parent–subsidiary structures and international divisions, although, less subject to formal monitoring, their national-based subsidiaries most likely had even greater operational autonomy (Channon, 1973). Multinationals from continental Europe were more inclined to form holding companies that incorporated the main business and overseas subsidiaries, and the holding company and the parent business exercised minimal direct control or monitoring of operations. While US manufacturers sought greater control over their technology and products, European multinationals were generally content to remain more decentralized. Legal traditions in the USA would have directed its companies away from holding-company structures (and even joint ventures), in case the Department of Justice interpreted them as examples of anti-competitive market sharing. But their large lead in technology, price, product, production, or marketing, where it existed, explained overall US preference for more formal control and for subsidiaries wholly owned by the parent.

In European firms, there was a greater tendency for the head of a parent company to exercise control or coordination through a personal relationship with the head of a subsidiary (Franko, 1976; Egelhof, 1984). The Anglo-Dutch Unilever and the Swiss-registered Nestlé viewed national markets as distinct, with their own products and brands, and cross-border integration seemingly brought few returns to scale (Channon, 1973; Heer, 1966; Schroter, 2005; Maljers, 1992). While Unilever's operations and structure were multi-domestic, that is, based on distinct national consumer markets, its competitor Procter & Gamble was more international and cross-border in its strategy and organization, and had stronger control over its subsidiaries. With the economic troubles of the 1970s, and under pressure from P&G, Unilever began with mixed results the process of product standardization across Europe (Jones, 2005).

Ciba and Philips record how managers returning from their US subsidiaries brought ideas about product divisions with them. As US management was more individual and less collegiate, Ciba adapted the M-form by appointing divisional boards. Its successor, the merged Ciba-Geigy, was noted for its matrix structure in which overseas subsidiaries reported to both product and area heads. Philips's matrix plotted the links between product divisions and national firms, and between line and technical-support managers. An assessment of

Table 4.8 *FDI in the USA, 1950, 1970 ($USbn)*

	1950	1970
UK	1,168	4,127
Canada	1,029	3,117
Switzerland	348	1,545
the Netherlands	334	2,151
Other European nations	377	1,731
Rest of world	134	599
Total	3,391	13,270

Source: Wilkins (2005).

continental European multinationals, from 1971, shows that only 11 had international divisions, but 26 relied on personal relationships between executives in different parts of the multinational, which substituted for formal reporting mechanisms. Others had gone past an organization founded on one large parent and satellite subsidiaries, and adopted global organizational models, based on worldwide product divisions (24), worldwide functions such as production or research (3), or a matrix that combined product, function or geography (6). Continental multinationals were more diversified in their product lines than those from the USA, and, consequently, and unsurprisingly, they showed a greater inclination for holding-company structures and organizational matrices that could accommodate their internal diversity (Franko, 1976; Schroter, 2005).

British and Netherlands multinationals

With its well-developed consumer markets and highly stable political environment, Britain was the favoured European destination for US multinationals. Their substantial presence was one marker of British decline, as opposed to accelerating US ascendancy, yet the continued achievements of British multinationals overseas indicated entrepreneurial vigour in an economically internationalizing world. British outward FDI equalled 16.3 per cent of the global total in 1960, and held its position at 16.7 per cent in 1980 (Table 4.4). Britain's companies owned an impressive one third of all inward FDI assets in the biggest and highly competitive home market of the USA (Table 4.8).

They showed an initial preference for investing in the Commonwealth countries of Canada, South Africa and Australia, with familiarity, calculations of low political risk, and growth opportunities being three main motives. As worldwide post-war recovery took hold, and with the founding of the EEC, priorities changed; between 1962 and 1978, the share of British FDI stock located in West Europe grew from 13 to 31 per cent, during which time investments in developing lands fell from 37 to 20 per cent. Decolonization meant that many of its overseas banks struggled, but others did successfully transform themselves; the realities for trading houses in newly independent states were more consistently bleak. Britain did remain the registered home of major mining and oil multinationals, and, by 1960, about 35 per cent of British FDI was concentrated in manufacturing (Casson, 1983), with the branded food, drinks and tobacco sectors and also chemicals at the forefront (Gales and Sluyterman, 1991).

BAT, the global tobacco giant, had lost markets during the turmoil of the Second World War. It re-entered China, once the jewel of its operations, by agreement with Chiang Kai-shek's Nationalist government, but Communist victory in 1949 led to price and wage controls that bankrupted its subsidiary. BAT struck a deal, in 1953, in which it secured the release of its leading foreign managers, held as hostages, and in return surrendered its assets. American & Foreign Power's attempts to re-establish Shanghai Power were similarly thwarted, and the Communist government took control of its business and some smaller British- and French-owned utilities during 1949–50. As medical evidence began to undermine the ethics of its business, BAT concentrated, during the 1960s and 1970s, on diversification into paper, packaging, cosmetics, food, perfume and retailing in the UK, and, between them, its subsidiaries in the USA, South Africa, Australia, Germany, Brazil and Portugal too made acquisitions in food, retailing, home improvement, juice and pulp businesses. Yet it remained dependent on tobacco sales, and, by 1970, the multinational, with its 140 factories, was manufacturing in some fifty countries. It ended its seventy-year-old collaboration with Imperial Tobacco two years later, and, through competition, could claim to be the world's largest tobacco manufacturer outside the Communist bloc, by 1978.[40]

The Rowntree and Cadbury-Fry chocolate and confectionery enterprises responded to the recently founded EEC by buying firms in West Germany, the Netherlands and France, from 1961 onwards, but they failed to make major commercial breakthroughs. The Schweppes tonic water company – which invested in independent India in 1947, in the hope of protecting sales there – merged with Cadbury in 1969, and Cadbury-Schweppes launched its ultimately unsuccessful attempt on the US market in 1978, when it acquired the Peter Paul candy business, in Connecticut. British chocolate companies proved unable to break into the USA, but Hershey eventually turned the Rowntree and Cadbury brands, under licence, into major sellers. Guinness, on the other hand, went where its exports had already won brand loyalty: it built, after 1962, four breweries in Nigeria, its largest national market outside Britain, and began to make its distinctive stout beer in Malaysia, Cameroon, Ghana and Jamaica (Fitzgerald, 1995).

ICI, seen as having an old-fashioned management that had lost its colonial monopoly, sought, after 1965, to revitalize the business with new operations in the USA and Germany, and it made the crucial decision to buy a major US rival, Atlas Chemical, during 1971. The company could not, however, shake off the perception that it was losing competitiveness, and underwent a major restructuring in the 1980s.[41] The British Oxygen Company made the post-war period one of international expansion: it acquired refrigeration firms in Germany and Ireland; formed joint ventures in Jamaica, the Netherlands, South Africa, Sweden and Spain; and, to avoid an antitrust action, in the USA it took complete control of Airco during 1978.[42] The conglomerate BTR was a master of unrelated diversification and financial engineering, and, by the mid 1970s, it had bought up businesses in Europe and Australia (Monopolies and Mergers Commission, 1982). Bowater, instead, exploited its specific skills in pulp and newsprint to build businesses, after 1954, in North America, Western Europe and New Zealand. Then, between 1962 and 1972, overstretched, it underwent a period of retrenchment, which included the sale of overseas subsidiaries. Its acquisition of trader Ralli Brothers was an admission that it should diversify away from the processing of paper.[43]

When GKN lost the British steel-making parts of its business to nationalization in 1951, it looked for further opportunities abroad. The company bought an auto parts manufacturer in West Germany and added two more, later, between 1977 and 1979, in the USA, where the subsidiary instantly became the industry's fourth-largest competitor. It worked with the rapidly expanding miner BHP in Australia to construct a steel factory, by 1969, albeit selling its share to its partner within ten years.[44] South African government pressure to promote local industry forced a reluctant Pilkington to set up a subsidiary, in 1951, and the same considerations led to the 1954 investments with local capital in Canada and India. It was the invention of the float-glass process, which came into production in 1960 and transformed the industry, which inspired a change in international business policy at Pilkington. Seeking quickly to exploit its technical advantage, it founded eight overseas subsidiaries over the next twenty years in Europe, the USA, Latin America and Australia.[45]

General Franco's troops had occupied the Rio Tinto mines in Spain since the Spanish Civil War, and the company had long since lost control of its production and employees. In 1954, RTC finally sold two thirds of its shares to local buyers, and, to its relief, exited. The company at this point needed to reinvent itself, and a new executive team led by managing director Val Duncan set out to create a broad-based natural resource company, with investments in politically stable locations, and in the Commonwealth in particular. It had already acquired a range of assets – tin and tungsten mines in Portugal, diamonds in South Africa and copper in Uganda – when, during 1955, it entered the uranium business by buying a majority interest in Canada's Algom group and a controlling share in Australia's Mary Kathleen mine. It owned, by 1960, the highly promising Hammersley iron ore deposits in Western Australia, and had the Palabora copper rights in South Africa.

Merger was a quick means of creating a diverse global mining business. Consolidated Zinc Corporation, based in London, but with its assets in Australia, aimed to internationalize, and needed capital to exploit bauxite seams in northern Queensland. Rio Tinto Zinc was established, in 1962, and Duncan became its chairman and chief executive during the following year, with the newly created Consolidated Riotinto of Australia (CRA) taking oversight of the Australian businesses. RTZ purchased a high-grade steel maker in Canada, an industrial materials firm in the USA, and a tin refiner and aluminium fabricator in Britain. Its investments in exploration yielded large-scale mines in Canada (Lornex Copper) and Namibia (Rossing Uranium), as well as, through CRA, its momentous commitments in Australia and Papua New Guinea. RTZ overcame organizational limits to its growth by devolving responsibility for commercial developments to nationally based companies. In practice, the Australian end of the operation and the worldwide assets monitored by the London office acted independently, and, by the early 1970s, the parent headquarters restricted itself to group services, major strategic and financial decisions, and the appointment of top personnel. RTZ perceived itself as a geographically and geologically diverse international enterprise, with technological expertise, and experience in raising finance for long-term capital-intensive ventures.[46]

When Iran's democratically elected prime minister, Mohammed Mossadegh, nationalized the Anglo-Iranian Oil Company, the British and US governments, in 1953, orchestrated a successful coup against him. Nonetheless, AIOC lost its control of the country's oil assets to an international consortium, and had to refound itself as British Petroleum in the following year. It began to look worldwide for sources of crude; it built refineries in Europe, Australia and Aden; and it grew into Britain's second-largest chemicals company. It put in place highly centralized and integrated international operations, coordinating upstream production in the Middle East with its main downstream markets in Western Europe.[47] A lack of presence in the USA was its primary strategic weakness. As well as discovering gas in the North Sea, the company located oil in 1969 in Prudhoe Bay in Alaska, the USA's biggest oilfield, and, as a result, bought the refining and distribution business of Atlantic Richfield Company on the east coast as a prelude to expanding across the country. Next, it handed over the Prudhoe Bay leases and Atlantic Richfield to Standard Oil Company of Ohio, which needed crude oil sources, in return for a 25 per cent stake in the US firm. As Prudhoe Bay's flows grew, BP was able to take the majority share in Sohio by 1978, a move that avoided antitrust implications and the risk of legal action by minority shareholders on conflicts of interest.

During the 1970s, overshadowed by oil crises, BP moved into coal mining in the USA, Australia and South Africa (all later sold), and bought the assets of Union Carbide and Monsanto in Europe to strengthen its place in the chemicals industry (worldwide economic conditions did not make these acquisitions profitable either) (Bamberg, 1994). As with AIOP/BP in Iran, Burmah Oil lost its original and principal base of operations to international events. It had destroyed its facilities in Burma during the Second World War, as Japanese invaders advanced, but final Allied victory allowed the company to return. However, the country achieved independence in 1948 and looked to indigenize its economy, and Burmah Oil began a process of gradual withdrawal, fully completed by 1963. It had little choice but to undertake exploration elsewhere, including the USA, Canada and Australia. Another outcome was diversification, during the 1960s, through the acquisition of British retail chains, and through the key purchase of the Castrol oil brand, in 1965 (Corley, 1986; Myint-U, 2001).

The two famous Anglo-Dutch enterprises Shell and Unilever both continued with dual headquarters in London and the Netherlands. The Second World War – with Japanese conquest of the Dutch East Indies and German occupation of the Netherlands and much of Europe – had razed Shell's commercial foundations. Its US subsidiary Shell Oil had continued as a commercial operation, exploring for reserves in Latin America and gaining recognition as a technological leader in aviation fuel, synthetic rubber and catalytic cracking. Shell Oil had operated with the highest levels of local autonomy, and, in 1949, the parent multinational placed all its large operations in the USA under its control. The subsidiary eagerly promoted itself as American, increasingly managed by locals, financing its own investments, and building its own research capability. Acceptance of its Americanness helped to overcome state-level prohibitions on alien land holdings, which were barriers to building refineries and other plant, and sidestepped Federal rules on the foreign ownership of shipping lines. Royal Dutch Shell shares were floated on the New York stock exchange in 1954, and Shell Oil, in which the parent had a 65 per cent interest, began to produce some 25–33 per cent of group profits.

The multinational reorganized, in 1959, by decentralizing control of geographic regions, and allowing operating companies in each country a large measure of autonomy. It did, however, establish four global central service companies to support line management in companies outside the USA. The 1950s and 1960s were golden decades for Shell, and it made big discoveries in the North Sea, offshore from Groningen, and in Australia. In addition to the exploration and distribution businesses, there was Shell Chemical Corporation, which owned plants in Canada, France, Germany and the USA, in addition to the two home bases of the Netherlands and Britain (Sluyterman, Jonker, Howarth and Van Zanden, 2007; Vickers, 2005).[48]

As president of Unilever, the branded household goods company whose markets had been greatly disrupted by the Second World War, Paul Rijkens's immediate task was to reunite and rebuild his huge business, although operations in Eastern Europe and China were to be lost permanently. The US authorities returned control of Lipton Inc., in 1946, but its operations remained independent from Unilever. In the USA, the multinational added a cosmetics and shampoo firm, but competition from Procter & Gamble was too high a barrier against success. Later attempts by Unilever to introduce its brands there were – except in the cases of margarine, maple syrup and vegetable shortening – unsuccessful. Lipton, in the 1950s and 1960s, would resort to acquisitions in pet food, salad dressing and ice cream as a device for growth. By 1948, Unilever owned some 400 companies to be found in 50 countries. National managements were able, generally, to resist attempts to coordinate over products or to stem brand proliferation during the 1950s. The company benefited from post-war growth and the rapid rise in consumption, but falling profit returns and growing competition from about 1955 presented a new set of problems.

Rijkens had spent the war years in London, where, as well as managing what was left of his company, he had chaired a reconstruction commission appointed by the free Netherlands government. Its report emphasized the advantages of close USA–Netherlands ties and supported the liberalization of world trade. It envisaged, too, the reopening of the German market, which occurred in 1949, and argued for closer European political union. Rijkens was instrumental in creating the Bilderberg Group, along with Prince Bernhard of the Netherlands and the Belgian prime minister Paul Van Zeeland. Its founding aims were notably Atlanticist. The post-war international ideals of free trade and convertible currencies integration had been temporarily abandoned, to cope with post-war realities, and there was a perception that US attention had shifted away from Europe to domestic concerns and to the Communist threat in Asia. With the help of CIA director Walter Bedell Smith, Prince Bernhard gained the tacit support of the Eisenhower administration, and subsequently of businessmen such as John S. Colman of the Burroughs Corporation. The original conference was held in 1954 – at the Hotel de Bilderberg, near Arnhem, from which it took its name – and included a mix of leaders from politics and commerce. Later meetings were funded by the Ford Foundation, stirring allegations about the influence of multinational companies on elected politicians. Participants believed that closed sessions enabled open discussion between themselves, but the insistence on secrecy produced good material for conspiracy theorists fearful of a hidden world government run by business and other secretive interests.

By 1955, Europe accounted for some 60 per cent of Unilever's sales, and, in 1959, with competition rising and profits falling, the company embarked on a strategy of acquisition. It bought firms in both Europe and North America, mostly in food and chemicals – becoming a conglomerate with 500 companies across 60 countries by 1968 – but, when many of the new acquisitions underperformed, they had to be resold. Another means of improved performance was investment in science, and by 1970 Unilever had founded 11 research establishments worldwide, each with its own speciality, with most of them in Europe, with the exception of the New Jersey and Mumbai laboratories. Yet the perception that its soap and detergents failed to match rival products from Procter & Gamble lingered. Unilever's nationally orientated subsidiaries were well placed to meet local consumer tastes and attitudes, yet the structure looked in the era of the European Common Market like an historical legacy. A report by consultants McKinsey, in 1971, brought European-wide rationalization, but at a very slow pace, and, in the USA, where the business overall was unprofitable, the parent company exercised little control. Unilever's reliance on Europe grew, reaching 70 per cent of its profits by 1980 (Jones, 2005).[49]

In 1947, nearly half of Netherlands FDI was located in what would soon become Indonesia, and these assets were nationalized in 1957. From this point, the bulk of outward investment went to the European Community, with the USA accounting for a rising proportion. As a small economy with high savings, the Netherlands looked outwards for investment and trade, and FDI assets in 1967 were worth a remarkable 33 per cent of GDP, compared to the UK's 15 per cent and the USA's 7 per cent, or compared to rival small economies Switzerland (10 per cent) and Sweden (6 per cent). Netherlands multinationals, by 1975, employed some 75 per cent of their personnel overseas. With Shell being one of the world's largest enterprises, a high percentage of the country's multinational efforts were in the extractive industries, about 47 per cent of national FDI by assets, by 1975, compared to 26–27 per cent for the USA and Britain.

The Netherlands could claim to be home to four significant multinationals, the two Anglo-Dutch companies of Royal Dutch Shell and Unilever, plus Philips and the chemicals firm AKU (latterly, AKSO). By 1974, the top three overseas investors – Shell, Unilever and Philips – held 69 per cent of the country's outward FDI; the top six controlled 83 per cent (Wilkins, 2005). The country's share of inward FDI assets in the USA grew from 11 to 16 per cent between 1950 and 1970, with Shell and AKU taking the lead, and oil and chemicals were, by 1980, 51 per cent of all Netherlands FDI (Gales and Sluyterman, 1993). By 1980, much of the country's FDI was within the European Community (48 per cent), relative to the USA (19 per cent), other developed economies and Japan (17 per cent), and developing territories (16 per cent) (Sluyterman, 2003; Schroter, 2005).

Philips needed to rebuild the international business it had created before the war. General Electric divested from Philips, but Philips in North America continued to avoid direct competition with GE and RCA by focusing on non-core products. The Eindhoven headquarters took control of research, product development and global distribution, but allowed the various national companies more autonomy over production. The company invested extensively in new products, including successes such as the compact audio cassette (launched in 1963) and video recorders (introduced in 1972, although its product failed to become the industry standard). The arrival of the EEC cut across autonomous overseas subsidiaries, and an International Production Centre attempted, during the 1960s, to introduce greater cross-border integration. Research and development separated itself from the headquarters, and Philips established eight laboratories throughout Europe and the USA. The company placed about one third of its R&D abroad (about the same share as other major multinationals from small economies, including Nestlé from Switzerland and SKF from Sweden).[50] Philips could not, however, find a complete answer to Japanese imports, with their mix of lower price and rising quality, and it embarked on factory closures and restructuring in the 1970s (Schroter, 2005).

With its dual Netherlands-German origins, AKU had to deal with complicated legal proceedings in the USA over which parts of its business, as potentially enemy property, were subject to compensation claims. It did regain control of Enka in both the USA and UK, but it lost those subsidiaries associated with former partner Vereinigte Glanzstoff. AKU diversified into synthetic fibres and built subsidiaries, some wholly owned, others joint ventures, in Europe, the USA, Australia, Latin America and India. Organon ended its joint venture with Hoffman La Roche in New Jersey, in 1948, to create its own subsidiary, and the parent company, in 1953, became KZO, which went on to buy International Salt, a major US business. AKU merged with chemicals, drugs, soap and detergent maker KZO in 1969, founding AKZO. The new company preferred to maintain distinct national companies because it saw a strong national identity as important to

Table 4.9 *Outward FDI stock by sector: France,*
Germany and the Netherlands (%)

	Primary	Secondary	Tertiary
France, 1975	22.1	38.2	39.7
Germany, 1976	4.5	48.3	53.7
Netherlands, 1975	46.8	38.6	14.6

Source: Schroter (2005).

Table 4.10 *FDI assets held by Swedish*
multinationals (%), 1960–74

	1960	1974
Europe	68	77
EEC	46	44
North America	12	8
Australia, Africa, Latin America	17	20

Source: Schroter (2005).

its products. From 1972 – facing intensifying competition within the Common Market, rising oil prices, and new challengers from East Asia – AKZO announced factory closures in the Netherlands, stirring local and trade union opposition.

Oce van der Grinten abandoned a policy of licensing its copy paper technology, created its first overseas subsidiary in Germany, in 1958, and repeated the approach in Norway, Italy and Denmark (Sluyter-man, 2003). Heineken laid a trail for Guinness in Nigeria by establishing four breweries there, from 1949 onwards, till 1962, and began production in eight other African countries between 1958 and 1972. Having already bought another important Netherlands producer, Amstel, it acquired James J. Murphy, the maker of stout, based in Cork, Ireland, in 1970.[51]

Europe and the small economies

Overall, and without counting Britain, Western European nations could claim about one quarter of all FDI stocks by 1960, and still held that position in 1980 (tables 4.4, 4.9 and 4.10). European multinationals were more intraregional in their investments and operations, less global than their US rivals, and leading firms, drawn from a narrower range of industries, accounted for a significantly high percentage of total European FDI. Netherlands multinationals, like the British, could claim to be more international in scope than other European companies, while progressively orientating from South East Asia towards Europe. As small economies that were not members of the EEC, both Switzerland and Sweden were large investors in the region, and, in 1960, founding members of EFTA. Ambitious companies with their origins in small economies tended to be outward-looking – in a phrase, 'born international' – and outward investment from small nations was especially clustered within a few industries in which they had a competitive lead. The Netherlands – with the 'giants' of Shell, Unilever and Philips – was a classic case of an economy demonstrating high levels of internationality, as were Switzerland and Sweden (Schroter, 1993).

With Western European consumers enjoying rising living standards, Nestlé began, in 1960, a period of expansion by buying Crosse & Blackwell, a UK food manufacturer. At first, it planned the worldwide development of this established brand, but the British business continued to perform badly against the US multinational H. J. Heinz. Nestlé bought Findus in 1963, again with disappointing results, and sold its frozen food operations in Germany, Italy and Australia to Unilever. It set out to diversify away from foods by swapping shares with French heiress Liliane Bettencourt, and taking dual control of L'Oréal, in 1974. Europe provided about 40 per cent of Nestlé's sales in 1970, compared to North America at 24 per cent, and, from 1971 to 1979, Nestlé looked to acquisition opportunities in the USA: these included Libby, with its tinned fruit and vegetables and juices; Stouffer frozen foods; National Starch, in speciality chemicals; and ophthalmic product makers Alcon Laboratories and Burton, Parsons. For all its commercial activities, Nestlé became in the public mind inextricably linked with one controversy that evoked images of an unethical multinational corporation operating from the secret regulatory environment of Switzerland: its promotion of baby formula in developing countries, where water supplies might be tainted, brought stories of unnecessary infant deaths and health problems, and provoked a worldwide boycott of all its products (Heer, 1966, 1991; Harrison and George, 1983).[52] Tobler chocolate went to the big markets of

Germany (1951) and Britain (1967), and formed Interfood with Jacobs Suchard in 1970, after which it acquired firms in Denmark, France and Canada.[53]

The chemical firms of Ciba, Geigy and Sandoz – sensing US legal pressure – ended their three-way cartel in 1950, and resorted instead to competitive FDI. Both Geigy and Ciba were highly diversified – manufacturing pharmaceuticals, dyes, petrochemicals, plastics, and agricultural chemicals – and still believed that cooperation would provide the answer to returning German production and the emergent petrochemical industries of the Persian Gulf. They began with a joint factory in New Jersey. Geigy had leadership in agricultural chemicals and a modern approach to marketing and management, while Ciba had the advantage in synthetic resins, petrochemicals and research capabilities. To win over the US federal prosecutors to any merger, Geigy sold its American dyeworks, and Ciba sold its pharmaceutical production. The formalities were finally settled in 1970, and the new enterprise commanded large-scale manufacturing assets throughout Europe, North America and Brazil (Enri, 1979; Taylor and Sudnik, 1984).[54] Operating mainly from Switzerland and Britain, Sandoz struggled to keep pace with the growth in post-war demand, but, in 1964, it reorganized its business into three divisions for dyes, pharmaceuticals and chemicals. It made important breakthroughs in hallucinogens for use in psychotherapy, but cut this research when LSD began to be made illegally. Despite this decision, it remained the company that invented 'acid'. As well as merging with competitors in Switzerland and diversifying its product range, it embarked in 1977 on a hospital supply business through a joint venture with Rhone-Poulenc.[55]

By 1960, Sweden's multinationals controlled three quarters of the country's manufacturing, organized half of its exports, and supervised half the domestic workforce. Machinery production accounted for 50 per cent of FDI assets, and electrical machinery another 18 per cent, success in both industries being grounded on engineering know-how, supportive universities, high labour skills, and access to local ferrous ore. Swedish multinationals tended to seek rapid expansion, beyond their small domestic economy, through acquisitions, and their subsidiaries existed to operate behind Europe's tariff walls. During the 1960s, while their presence in the USA fell, their position within Europe strengthened, but Swedish FDI largely dried up in 1972, when EFTA and EEC members established a free trade zone. While SAAB held back from founding manufacturing facilities abroad, Volvo, in 1963, opened a plant in Halifax, Nova Scotia, to supply the North American market. There, customers did not respond warmly to the car's size (small compared to US autos) and its plain appearance. When the Swedish government decided not to join the EEC, the company could not wait any longer and built a truck assembly plant and another for cars in Belgium, consequently avoiding import duties.

To maintain its fast growth overseas, Volvo took a share in DAF, the Netherlands firm, in 1972, and it formed a strategic alliance with Renault, which took a 9.9 per cent interest in Volvo, during 1979 (Dymock, 1997).[56] Ericsson owned 21 overseas subsidiaries by 1970, mostly in Europe, but it manufactured telephone equipment also in Brazil, Mexico and Australia. It preferred full control of these businesses to the risks of licensing and the leaking of its technological knowledge, but, with the national subsidiaries operating autonomously, international coordination with the parent business depended on individual relations and the rotation of personnel.[57] Electrolux resumed its policy of international growth as an essential strategy of competing against the larger AEG and Philips. In the 1960s, it bought at first nearby – the Elektra stove manufacturer in Norway and Atlas white goods in Denmark – but subsequently it gained the Flymo lawnmower business in Britain, in 1969, and Eureka vacuum cleaners in the USA, in 1974. It combined acquisitions at home, made to access technologies and skills, with acquisitions overseas, made to gain market share and expansion. Its takeover of Kreft & Siegas in Sweden was a foundation for evolving into an international brand leader in refrigerators.[58]

Before the Second World War, AB Separator had been a worldwide producer of dairy machinery and associated technologies, but the conflict had in effect separated the company from its foreign operations. The US government, for one, had compelled its subsidiary, Lavalco, to build oil separators for its navy. In the 1950s, ABS pioneered developments in plate heat exchangers, and made breakthroughs in food and drink manufacturing, cellulose and, later, the chemicals and marine businesses. Technological advances partnered the rapid international expansion of the company (which changed its name to Alfa-Laval in 1963): so, it established new subsidiaries in France (1947), Italy (1950), Belgium (1952), Switzerland (1960) and the Netherlands (1974); it grew and diversified in Spain (1966) and in Germany (1978), with a meat manufacturing project; it acquired a separator maker in

Melbourne (1968); in the USA, through Lavalco, it bought six firms and built a plant in New Jersey (1963–70); it grew, too, in Latin America, and located itself throughout Asia.[59]

SKF, too, utilized its technological advantage, including advances in high-precision engineering, in 1953. It had to rebuild its factories and businesses in Germany and France, and expanded in Spain, Canada and the Netherlands. It built plants in Brazil and India, at the insistence of their governments, to supply growing textile and automobile sectors. The EEC–EFTA deal, in 1972, usefully cut SKF's costs, a vital concern as it faced rising imports and competition from Japanese auto bearings. To achieve economies of scale, the company concentrated the production of particular products in separate plants, and treated Europe as a single marketplace. It broke up a structure of national subsidiaries and replaced them with divisions: the lead bearings and precision tools division came to supply France's revitalized aerospace sector; the cutting and machines tools division grew quickly and bought up rival firms in Sweden and Britain; there were, too, steel and engineering products divisions, SKF Industries Ltd (responsible for the USA, Canada and Mexico), and an overseas division (in charge of subsidiaries outside North America).

Unlike Alfa-Laval, which concentrated its R&D in Britain, SKF built its Engineering and Research Centre in Sweden, with the objective of integrating research, production and marketing internationally and keeping the company ahead of Japanese competitors with their lower production costs. AB Atlas merged, in 1955, with its Belgian subsidiary into Atlas Copco (Compagnie Pneumatique Commerciale), and, by the early 1980s it had 46 factories in Europe, Latin America, and India, due to its technological expertise in compressors, mining and construction equipment and automated industrial tools (Fritz and Karlsson, 2007). There were few examples of FDI by Norwegian companies during this period: nevertheless, Dyno Industrier made acquisitions in Britain, Denmark and Finland, in glues, plastics and paints, during 1971–2, and Borregaard opened a pulp mill in Brazil.[60]

The Swiss-registered Elektrobank (in partnership with AEG) and Indelec (with Siemens) withdrew from the funding and running of overseas electric utilities during 1945–7, transferring their financial operations, respectively, to Credit Suisse and the Swiss Bank Corporation, before ultimately dissolving in 1951. Sofina – which had decamped to New York during the war – moved away from its involvement in international utilities but remained as an investment holding company. The Swiss and Belgian groups sought compensation when France nationalized its electricity sector in 1946, and, throughout the post-war decades, public sector enterprise increasingly excluded FDI in utilities. Sofina, in 1945, owned Barcelona Traction, Light and Power Ltd (BTLP), and, with Credit Suisse and other Swiss investors, Compañìa Hispano-Americana de Electricidad (CHADE), which did business in Spain and Argentina. Sofina, concerned by government pressure on CHADE, moved its registration from Spain to a Luxembourg business controlled by Sofina and Credit Suisse. CHADE was then formally liquidated. Moreover, a friend of General Franco, Juan March, had been buying up BTLP and its subsidiary Ebro Irrigation and Power cheaply, and, in 1948–52, he engineered a hostile bid in a tussle for over 20 per cent of Spain's electricity generation. The courts declared BTLP bankrupt, for technical reasons, and protests came from Belgium, where BTLP was formally registered, and the USA, where since the war Sofina was still registered. The company went in addition to the International Court of Justice at The Hague, but effective redress was not easily obtained.[61]

ARBED kept its formative influence over the Luxembourg economy in the post-war decades, known locally as 'Les Trentes Glorieuses'. It was a major partner in a maritime steel making project in Belgium after 1962, and in the 1970s entered into mining and steel projects in Brazil, the USA and Korea. By the end of the 1970s, the company accounted for approximately one quarter of Luxembourg's GDP. ARBED worked on some big projects with the Société Générale de Belgique (SGB) finance house and conglomerate, which had ownership in four Luxembourg and Belgian enterprises with overseas subsidiaries, and it remained a domineering force in Congo's economy until its mining assets were nationalized, in 1966 (Franko, 1976).

Return of the European multinational

The central concern for European governments after the Second World War was to repair their continent, and businesses were focused on recovery, not international expansion. Their long-term challenge was to exploit and match the technical and organizational innovations of US companies, which had created such a large gap in productivity. Out of necessity, and then as policy, governments frequently supported those industries perceived as foundational to their economies. France, in 1945, nationalized steel, coal and electricity, and it acquired banks

Table 4.11 *FDI assets held by German industries (%),*
1961–75

	1961	1975
Chemicals	18.0	15.0
Electronics and electricals	14.0	10.6
Automobiles and transportation equipment	7.5	6.7
Machinery	6.2	7.4

Source: Schroter (2005).

to assist in the planning and backing of designated high-growth and technology sectors, including electronics and aviation. The only car maker to be taken into public control was Renault, punishment for the owner's collaboration with the Nazi occupation regime. Both French and German manufacturers undertook little FDI before the 1960s, relying on exports to take advantage of growing world trade and European economic integration (Jones, 1996).

With economic recovery well under way, and once currency restrictions had been lifted, companies looked to invest in the EEC and in Europe more generally. The international growth of companies from continental Europe, in the 1960s, was striking, and multinationals from France, Germany, the Netherlands and Belgium all doubled the number of their foreign subsidiaries. Only Japan could claim a parallel success. Through a survey of 85 firms, in 1970, we know of 69 from the EEC Six that, between them, had 600 subsidiaries within the EEC. On the whole, European governments welcomed investment from fellow European nations: their attitude fitted comfortably with the spirit of economic and regional union, but US multinationals with their competitive lead and global concerns were, in addition, more threatening than their European counterparts. Of the 85 multinationals headquartered in continental Europe in 1970, 29 were German and 21 French. Outward FDI remained, nonetheless, a small percentage of Germany's GDP, being only 1.6 per cent in 1967, while France's 7.0 per cent was higher than Sweden's, with its small domestic economy and outward-looking companies, if lower than Switzerland's (Schroter, 2005).

Both France and Germany were the most important locations for each other's multinationals (Franko, 1976). Unlike German multinationals, with their strong manufacturing bias (Table 4.11), outward FDI from France, as in the case of the Netherlands, went in large part to natural resources (Jones, 1996). The increase in French FDI, likewise, tracked that from the Netherlands, and exceeded its pre-1939 level by 1960 (Casson, 1983). France, over the following decade, embarked on a state-led industrial policy, intended to reform its comparatively small, family-controlled businesses and to establish national champions employing advanced technologies and methods. It halted General Electric's acquisition of Machines Bull, in 1965, and effectively prohibited all foreign takeovers with monitoring procedures that enforced delays and allowed a search for local purchasers (Gillespie, 1972). France feared the dominance of US multinationals, as well as the prospect of foreign takeovers causing redundancies and popular discontent, and it set out to transform its electronics, computers, aerospace and nuclear power sectors. It prohibited foreign ownership in defence firms, agriculture, road and maritime transport, aircraft manufacture, insurance and publishing, although these rules were to be relaxed for European Union investors by 1980 (Safarian, 1993).

Renault began its search for opportunities abroad in 1951, when it took a minority holding in Fabricacion de Automoviles Sociedad Anonima de Valladolid, and FASA made the French firm's models under licence. Later, when Renault gained 49.9 per cent of the shares, in 1965, it changed the name of the Spanish concern to FASA-Renault, acquiring majority control eleven years later. It started, in 1979, to build a substantial stake in Mack Trucks Ltd in Pennsylvania, but a poor record in production and after-sales service pointed to the need for urgent action back home (Jones and Galvez-Munoz, 2001).[62] Generally, while French car manufacturers had export successes in the USA, they failed to turn these into successful FDI enterprises. Citroën had one significant selling point in international markets: its legendary low-priced Deux Cheveaux (or 2CV), the distinctively designed 'four wheels under an umbrella'. In order to make headway in a market protected by import duties, Citroën opened Société Citroën-Hispania at Vigo, in 1958, to manufacture 2CV vans, and repeated this strategy with the 2CV car in Portugal in 1964. The company established assembly plants for its unique car in various locations between 1960 and 1964, including an agreement with the Tomos concern in Yugoslavia, a joint venture in Madagascar and wholly-owned plant in Chile. It bought luxury car maker Maserati in 1968, and hoped to gain from exchanges of design and technology.

But, in 1974, at the height of the oil crisis, Citroën was bankrupt, and the French government persuaded its owners, Michelin, to sell to Peugeot; PSA Peugeot Citroën was founded by 1976. The new business took over Chrysler Europe within two years, instantaneously extending its international operations to Britain and Spain, but mistakenly and temporarily revived the Talbot brand for its new acquisition. On the other hand, Peugeot Citroën saw no point in holding on to Maserati, and sold it to De Tomaso Industries, a racing car company founded by a former Argentinian Formula One driver, the whole arrangement needing to be propped up by Italian government funds (until Fiat bought Maserati in 1989) (Gallard, 2004). Armed with the radial tyre and the technological lead it offered, the family-controlled Michelin re-established and built factories in Italy, Germany, Britain and elsewhere throughout Europe after 1945, and by the 1960s it was ready to expand into Nigeria, Algeria and Vietnam. During the next decade, the scale of its exports in the highly competitive market of the USA justified the building of a plant in South Carolina, and others followed in Canada and Brazil, allowing Michelin to grow into the world's second-largest tyre maker, after Goodyear, by 1980.[63]

St Gobain – engaged in glass, paper and chemicals – positioned itself across western and northern Europe, sometimes through stakes in existing companies, and sometimes by building its own plants. It created American St Gobain in 1954, but Pilkington's float glass process eventually killed off its investment in factories that used older technologies and polishing processes. The overseas division, St Gobain International, was located in Fribourg, Switzerland, and, by 1969, the company had charge of 143 plants in 12 nations (L. Turner, 1970). Boussois Soucha Neuvesel (BSN) Groupe founded a flat-glass factory in Germany in 1970 and another in Belgium in 1972. Intriguingly, it merged with a yoghurt and cheese producer, Gervais Danone, during the following year, and the new company expanded with acquisitions in a Spanish spring water firm and breweries in the Netherlands, Spain and Italy.[64]

AFC took stakes in aluminium fabrication plants in Argentina and Brazil during 1947–8, and formally became Pechiney in 1950, two years after reorganizing itself into four divisions covering aluminium, electro-thermics, chemicals and mining products. It embarked on a strategy of finding new sources of energy and raw materials abroad and integrating its non-ferrous activities. It evolved into a highly important if growingly troubled multinational. Pechiney put up an aluminium plant in Cameroon, in 1954, and another in Guinea, in 1960. It developed as an international provider of technical assistance, and sold its services in Non-Aligned Yugoslavia and India, and in the Soviet Union. Alongside its activities in developing countries and behind the Iron Curtain, it bought aluminium producer Howe Sound Inc. in the USA, in 1962, which was eventually split into its aluminium and turbine businesses; it also purchased an Australian alumina factory, owned by Gladstone; the company built an integrated alumina-aluminium plant in Greece, in 1966; and, in another five years, opened an aluminium factory in the Netherlands. Pechiney merged with Ugine-Kuhlmann, forming PUK, in 1971, as part of a government-sponsored merger wave, intended to meet the challenges of US competition and greater European integration by creating huge conglomerates with complementary activities. PUK – involved in mining, chemicals, nuclear energy, pharmaceuticals and trading – took the position of France's first industrial group, yet, despite factory closures, the financial losses continued into the 1970s (Franko, 1976).[65]

In one more instance of inter-European integration, Schneider formed a holding company with another family enterprise, Empain, from Belgium, in 1969. The result was one of the world's most important heavy industry, engineering and infrastructure businesses, which, additionally, had control of the large equipment and specialist steel maker Creusot-Loire. Its CEO, Baron Édouard-Jean Empain, was famously kidnapped from his Paris home by self-proclaimed left-wing guerrillas in 1978, and, by 1980 his family had sold up its interest in the industrial group. With its business fragmented by the war, Schlumberger formally registered in the Netherlands Antilles in 1956 for tax purposes, and continued with its operational headquarters in Houston. Thanks to its technical lead, it was able to restore its fortunes in the USA, with Dowell Schlumberger (a joint venture with Dow that offered services and advice to oilfield firms) and Daystrom (the purchase of a business twice its own size supplying electronic equipment to the Department of Defense). Schlumberger diversified, too, by buying Forages et Exploitations Petrolières, a drilling company, plus French and British electronics firms. Its decision to purchase Fairchild Semiconductor, in 1979, was a marker for its high-tech ambitions, both as a manufacturer and as a service company, although its involvement would be short-lived.[66]

Perhaps the most publicized example of European integration was the Airbus Industrie consortium; it was, fundamentally, an example of pooling interests against the highly organized and profitable US aeronautical industry that had emerged, led by Boeing, McDonnell Douglas and Lockheed, out of the Second World War. Airbus Industrie, created in 1970 after lengthy negotiations, was led by France's government-owned Aérospatiale and by Deutsche Airbus (itself composed of five German firms and subsequently part of the Daimler Benz group); Hawker-Siddeley (later part of British Aerospace) was another major shareholder; and Fokker VFW from the Netherlands and Construcciones Aerospatiale (CASA) were the remaining participants. Like other multinationals, it was characterized by operations in different nation states, but it was more unusual for its complex mix of public–private partnership, and for being, as aircraft production was divided between member companies, an early example of highly integrated cross-border production.[67]

The Second World War hurt German chemical and pharmaceutical companies, which lost their foreign subsidiaries and control over their patent rights. In the USA, Sterling Drug gained the Bayer trademark and the ability to sell aspirin. Other consequences of historical legacy from the Second World War were antitrust legislation to prevent the reformation of cartels, and an open, market-led economy, albeit one with extensive welfare systems and inclusive institutions. Although the West German government did not aspire to French levels of industrial planning, it did, in the 1950s, deem oil to be a strategic industry, reflecting post-war concerns for energy security. Next in line were the automobile and electronics industries, as they were linked with the recovery and future of the economy. The German government allowed Texaco to acquire Deutsche Erdöl, in 1966, but used antitrust laws to block CFP's attempted takeover of Gelsenberg Benzin, two years later.

Founded by the Gelsenkirchener Bergwerks (GBAG), the steel and coal group, to use IG Farben's process for liquefying coal, Gelsenberg had suffered extensive war damage, but in 1950, once the Allies had decided not to dismantle the business, it resumed production but with imported crude oil in place of coal as its base material. CFP had commissioned Dresdner Bank to buy up German energy concerns, and the fact that it was itself 35%-owned by the French government was one key element behind the controversy, as was the fact that Gelsenberg was a vital national asset that met one quarter of West Germany's oil needs. Dresdner had in addition gained a stake in GBAG, whose Libyan oilfields were an attractive source of supply for CFP. What was, for the French company, very arguably a sound strategic business case ran up against different perspectives of national policy and energy security.[68] Vereinigte Elektrizitäts und Bergwerks Aktiengesellschaft (VEBA), which had been privatized in 1965, was the German energy business that – with the encouragement of the government – finally bought Gelsenberg, in 1975.

In response to the Iranian monarchy increasing its 25 per cent holding in Krupp steel, and Kuwait's expanding interest in Daimler Benz, the German government established administrative procedures to monitor the sale of shares to overseas owners and, mindful of OPEC countries awash with oil dollars, to discourage their sale to foreign governments in particular (Gillespie, 1972; Safarian, 1993). Since domestic reconstruction absorbed the bulk of capital and managerial concerns, and as German firms were rich in technological know-how but short in capital, joint ventures were in the two decades after the war very frequently their chosen means for overseas investment. As with Swedish multinationals and prominent Swiss companies, R&D tended to be an important component of German FDI strategies. As the home market experienced its *Wirtschaftswunder*, companies looked to build on their export success. Chemical and electronics firms initially took the lead, as measured in capital amounts, as, subsequently, did transportation equipment and automobiles. German FDI stock, zero in 1950, was measured as $5,784m by 1970, some 60 per cent of this gained in manufacturing. German FDI soared to $43,105m between 1975 and 1980, overtaking the totals of France and the Netherlands.

The restrictions of a wartime economy had especially hurt makers of non-essentials, such as Villeroy & Boch. After 1945, its East German factories, where not destroyed by bombing, were shipped off as reparations to the Soviet Union. Its original works and headquarters were in the Saarland, which was occupied by French troops, from 1947, for nine years, while the region's nationality and ownership of its coal deposits were in dispute. Luitwin von Boch led efforts at conciliation with the French, arguing for the Europeanization of the Saarland, separate from both France and Germany. His company, having resumed the production of tiles, tableware and bathroom fixtures, was quick and able to found its first foreign facilities in Argentina, in 1951, and in Canada, in 1959.[69]

The break-up of IG Farben by the occupying administrations brought about the re-creation of BASF, Hoechst and Bayer. By the 1950s, these 'big three' of the German chemicals industry, as well as focusing on R&D, were considering how to re-establish their presence in overseas markets. They took early opportunities in Latin America, often repurchasing their lost assets. Bayer bought Quimicas Unidas, in Mexico, during 1952, and thereafter bought back Allianca Commerciale de Anilinas in Brazil.[70] Rolf Sammet, Hoechst's chairman, in 1970 publicly stated that, 'the German chemical industry . . . should foster the industrial development of young industrial states to enlist them as training partners of tomorrow'; despite the instability of its political and economic environment, it was prominently placed in Brazil. The industry then looked to Europe and North America for expansion, and it controlled, by 1965, a total of some 150 overseas production centres, France holding the largest number of these subsidiaries, with the USA in second place (Schroter, 2005). In 1977–8, Bayer bought Allied Chemicals's organic pigments division and Miles Laboratories, maker of Alka Seltzer.[71] Of the big three, Hoechst was the most determined as a multinational, and by 1979 it had invested $55m in the USA, where its sales were equal to 40 per cent of those made by Du Pont.[72] As BASF and Bayer switched from coal technologies to petrochemicals, they became important partners of oil firms, including Shell and BP (Chapman, 1991).

Mannesmann lost its Czechoslovakian steel mills in 1945, and the Allies, in 1952, true to their policies, split the company into three. Mannesmann AG turned out to be the most successful – more or less absorbing its two siblings by 1955 – and, by 1959, very ironically, it had a majority stake in the French business that had taken over its Bous factory. Before the future of the company had even been settled, it established steel and tube mills in Brazil, Canada and Turkey, securing its place in important regional markets. Companhia Siderurgica Mannesmann evolved into a group of companies, active throughout Latin America and engaged in high-grade steels, industrial machinery, compressors, excavators, control systems, mining and trading. Back at home, Mannesmann became the world's largest maker of steel tubes during the 1970s, but, as wage costs and foreign competition grew, it began the process of diversification into machinery, automotive components and services, perceived as safeguarding the company's long-term future (ultimately entering, after 1995, cellular telecommunications).[73]

Hermann von Siemens – who had been interned by the Americans for his family company's use of slave labour during wartime – was back in charge in 1948. Siemens & Halske, which had lost its factories in the USA, Japan and Communist East Germany, moved its headquarters from Berlin to Munich. The company was able to sell its engineering expertise internationally, and built Latin America's first nuclear power station, in Atucha, Argentina. The main business was refounded as Siemens AG in 1966 and, within a decade, became responsible for one eighth of German R&D. It formed a turbine generator joint venture in the USA with Allis, and replaced Westinghouse as GE's main challenger in global markets (Feldenkirchen, 2000).[74] On the other hand, AEG – in which General Electric retained a 12 per cent share into the 1960s – put greater emphasis on developing the home market, and avoided FDI. The publishing and media company Bertelsmann first went overseas, in 1962, after Germany's recovery from the war, and in 1977 it invested in RCA's music division.[75]

The most prominent case of multinational investment by a German multinational was Volkswagen. British forces controlled the company until 1949 in order to make needed military vehicles, and saved VW from dismantling under the reparations clauses of the Potsdam Agreement. Numerous foreign owners, as well as Ford, declined the chance to buy the business. Citroën preferred, naturally, to develop the 2CV, just as Fiat wanted to make its Fiat 500 model into a success. Ownership of VW passed from the British military to a number of stakeholders, and one of the largest was the local Saxony government. It instinctively preferred investment at home to production overseas, and had an ally amongst the German trade union movement which was also represented on VW's supervisory board. Prospective foreign buyers had once doubted the viability of the company and the German automobile market, but had particularly attacked the one car it made as commercially worthless. Yet with its low price, high reliability and very visible distinctiveness, the Beetle proved itself to be VW's greatest post-war asset, both at home and, very notably, in export markets. The company soon began the move overseas, and, as result of pressure from governments, built assembly plants in South Africa (1950), Brazil (1953), Australia (1954) and Mexico (1954).

VW's one-car policy continued largely unaltered until 1968, and by 1971 some 58 per cent of total output was exported. VW itself was transformed into a symbol of German recovery, and, thanks to a creative advertising campaign masterminded by New York's Doyle Dane Bernbach, the Beetle broke through in the USA. To capitalize on this export success, VW bought a factory in Pennsylvania, in 1978, and, as the Beetle risked looking dated, it manufactured the Rabbit, an early but localized version of the Golf. With employees at Wolfsburg on short time, the trade unions campaigned against production in the USA, and the Federal government responded by saying it would look at the allowed numbers of foreign guest workers. VW's manufacturing in the USA enjoyed initial success, but the new reality of Japanese competition would bring closure within ten years.[76] Continental Tire grew in tandem with the German car industry: it built on its export success with a French factory in 1964, and, when it bought the European operations of Uniroyal, a US company, in 1979, it acquired its plants in Belgium, Scotland and France.[77] Maschinenfabrik Augsburg-Nürnberg (MAN) was a conglomerate, Germany's biggest multinational in machinery manufacture, and – after VW, Daimler Benz and BMW – the country's fourth-largest producer in the automotive sector. It and its parent, Gutehoffnungshütte Aktienverein, or GHH, lost its overseas subsidiaries in 1945, and, when the Allies forced GHH out of the steel and coal industry, its subsidiary emerged as the larger business. MAN's commercial vehicle division became its most important division, but it retained an important place in engineering too, and by 1980 it was manufacturing in Turkey, from where it supplied the Middle East, and in North Carolina, where it owned a bus plant.[78]

In the post-war decades, Fiat proved to be a major, and adaptive, multinational, and its strategy was deliberately global rather than European in its ambition. Like other Italian multinationals, it preferred not to compete directly against US and West European companies, but looked instead to the Communist bloc, developing economies, and the closed market of Fascist Spain, where, comparatively speaking, it had clear competitive advantages. The success of Fiat's car business was pivotal to the Italian economy and to the viability of Italy as a nation state, and the company had, in addition, interests in many industrial sectors. It believed, consequently, that it was entitled to special help: from 1945 onwards, it received US government loans, used to modernize and re-equip the company, plus lucrative NATO contracts. Spain's state holding company, Instituto Nacional de Industria (INI), needed a foreign company if it was to realize long-held plans to mass-produce a Spanish car. With the participation of a local bank consortium, in 1948 it chose Fiat rather than Volkswagen because the Italian firm in the interwar period had developed Simca in France and owned a subsidiary in Spain during the same period, as well as being viewed, appreciatively, as operating from a protected home market. INI established Sociedad Española de Automóviles de Turismo (SEAT), in 1950, allowing Fiat about one third of the ownership, and offering key tax and tariff exemptions. SEAT was manufacturing Fiat-based models by 1953. FASA-Renault (in 1954) and Citroën Hispania (1957) followed this initiative, but Ford (withdrawing in 1954) found operating in Spain too problematic (the Fiat–SEAT relationship lasted until 1982, after which, in order to provide needed investment, and with historical irony, Volkswagen became the owner).

In Italy, Fiat was geared for full production by 1948, but domestic demand in the years after the war remained inadequate. One response was to reduce its costs, and it did so by establishing a factory in Yugoslavia, from where it would import yearly some 40,000 cars. Fiat signed, in 1954, a long-lasting technical assistance and licensing agreement with Zastava Automobiles of Kragujevac, Serbia, which began making variations of the Italian company's cars during the following year, moving eventually from an assembly operation to fuller production (its well-known Yugo brand was to appear commercially in 1981, and Fiat subsequently acquired Zastava). Investment in Yugoslavia and the transfer of production had brought in Italy workforce protests – ironically often Communist-led – with the company president, Vittorio Valletta, on one occasion being held prisoner. By the mid 1950s, the USA included anti-Communist clauses to its contracts and purchases with Fiat, and continued investment and expansion, firings, political re-education and an extensive welfare programme gradually transformed the business in Italy and won over the largest trade union. Fiat's sales, by 1959, equalled about one tenth of the country's entire industrial output. It revived its assembly plants in Germany and Austria, and built others in India, Morocco, Egypt, South Africa and Latin America. It signed a deal, in 1965, with the Soviet Union to establish a turnkey operation, and used this experience to build another factory in Poland (Estapé-Triay, 1999; Tortella, 2000; Harrison, 1978).[79]

Fiat, by 1969, constituted a conglomerate with, amongst others, an airline, an office machinery maker, a construction company, newspapers and electrical firms. Large losses, the threat of nationalization by the Socialist government, wage and price controls, and widespread strikes turned the 1970s into a decade of difficulty at home. But Fiat did thrive in the non-saturated markets of Eastern Europe, Turkey and Latin America, and its largest overseas investment was in Minas Gerais, in Brazil, operational from 1976. Muammar Gaddafi, the Libyan dictator, during the same year, contracted Fiat to build a bus and truck plant in Tripoli, and his government bought a 10 per cent stake in the Italian company at a price estimated to be three times market value. Fiat, with its poor cash flow, wanted the investment, but inevitably, and reasonably, critics questioned Gaddafi's motives. Fiat withdrew from selling its cars in the USA, during the 1980s, and closed its plants in Uruguay, Chile, Colombia and Argentina, but it kept its Brazil operation intact (Estapé-Triay, 1999; Tortella, 2000; Harrison, 1978).[80]

Pirelli, the well-known maker of tyres, rubber products and cables, could claim international leadership in management and research, and it resumed its internationalization from 1953 onwards, rapidly extending its presence across Western Europe, North America, Latin America and Australia. It expanded through sole ownership but often with joint ventures, and, as with Fiat, sold its expertise in Eastern Europe where it built turnkey factories. Olivetti invested in Britain in 1947, hoping to supply the Empire and Commonwealth too, later setting up in Spain, Argentina and Mexico, and it went to its largest market, the USA, in 1959, the year it produced Italy's first computer (Franko, 1976).[81]

Canada, Australia and international business

During the Second World War, British investment in Canada retreated, while US companies advanced: the result was 11.5 per cent of Canada's inward FDI coming from Britain, but 84 per cent from the economic giant to the south. Canada shared with the nations of Western Europe the distinction of being developed, and US manufacturers – among them Ford, General Motors, Chrysler, IBM, Heinz, Kellogg and Kimberly-Clark – had established subsidiaries, mostly in highly industrialized Ontario. But for tariffs, import quotas and content regulations, their larger and more efficient factories in the USA could have supplied the consumers of their northern neighbour. Trade

Table 4.12 *Foreign and US investment in Canada by industry sector (%)*

	Foreign investment 1957	US investment 1957	US investment 1968
Petroleum and natural gas	75		54
Mining and smelting	56	46	54
Railways	30	11	
Manufacturing	50	39	44

Source: Easterbrook and Aitken (1988); Wilkins (1974).

restrictions were, as a result, strongly associated with the country's rapid industrialization since the 1920s. As well as providing tax concessions and subsidized sites for investors, Canada had the advantage of being politically secure, and for US businesses it was linguistically and (arguably to a lesser extent) culturally familiar. But, for investors, the country's main attraction was its minerals and natural resources (Table 4.12). The local ownership of oil, gas, pulp and paper, mining, and especially the extraction of iron and titanium – and the local ownership of manufacturing activities linked to the resource sectors – fell throughout the 1950s.

If we look for explanations, it was not a shortage of capital, since Canada's savings and overseas investments rose. Instead, as discoveries revealed the scale of Canada's mineral resources, US businesses moved to secure their raw material needs, and vertical integration was pronounced. Manufacturer Kimberly-Clark could usefully integrate vertically, starting up pulp production in 1948 for its Ontario tissue factory. Canada's trade became dependent on its south-bound exports, and US duties on fully or partially manufactured items left it dependent on the trade in commodities. Although Canadian opinion was suspicious of economic integration, or 'Continentalism', expressing an anxiety about genuine economic sovereignty, there was no viable alternative. So Canada remained open to foreign investment, and, as it hoped to improve its own access to the USA's huge market, its own tariff levels fell over time. During 1948–58, some 57 per cent of Canada's exports went to the USA (compared to about one third before the war); two thirds of its imports came from the USA in 1950, reaching in later years a peak of nearly three quarters; and, it is important to remember, one fifth of US exports went to Canada by 1958 (Easterbrook and Aitken, 1988).

Canada was part of a post-war global trend that took utilities into public ownership, during and after the Second World War: by 1975, only 18 per cent of Canada's electricity was privately generated, and, despite exceptions such as the Niagara Falls Company, US involvement inevitably fell away (Levitt, 1970). Otherwise, television and insurance, from the 1950s, and banks and newspapers, from the 1960s, were amongst the few restrictions on inward FDI. Although Europe replaced Canada as the favourite destination of US capital, Canada continued to be the country with the largest stock of its outward FDI. After the Second World War, the USA switched from exporting to importing copper, zinc and lead; domestic iron ore was depleted; and the new technology of nuclear power needed the uranium to be found just across the border (Wilkins, 1974). The Kennecott Copper Company, in 1946, discovered iron ore and the world's largest deposit of titanium in Quebec-Labrador, a region rich in minerals; two years later, it established the Quebec Iron and Titanium Corporation with the New Jersey Zinc Corporation, which had been conducting its own competitive surveys.[82] Most US steel firms bought mines in Canada, and, together, came to own 74 per cent of its iron ore production. Five of them – Republic Steel, National Steel, Armco Steel, Youngstown Sheet and Tube, and Wheeling Steel – created the Iron Ore Company of Canada, which began shipments in 1954. Steel firms did not, typically, control mines overseas, and preferred, globally, to contract some four fifths of their needs. But US investors saw the risks of investing across the border as near zero, and geographical distances were small: as a result, they chose, in this one case, economic integration over bartering in international commodity markets.

Canada was host to 49 per cent of all US mining FDI by 1970, compared to 29 per cent in 1929 (Cobbe, 1979; Brown and McKern, 1987; Wilkins, 1974). Forced out of Spain, the Rio Tinto Company, in 1955, invested in the uranium mines of Canada's Elliot Lake district, along with those in Western Australia. As the merged Rio Tinto Zinc, after 1962, amongst the many international acquisitions that followed were Canada's mining firm Lornex Copper and specialist metal maker Atlas Steels. Discoveries by Jersey Standard's Imperial Oil in Alberta, in 1947, turned Canada into a major producer and exporter of oil and gas. Some 75 per cent of Canada's petroleum and gas sector was foreign-owned as early as 1957, compared to 56 per cent for mining and smelting, 50 per cent for manufacturing, and 30 per cent for railways. By 1968, 54 per cent of its petroleum-gas and its mining-smelter sectors were US-owned, and 44 per cent of the manufacturing (Easterbrook and Aitken, 1988; Wilkins, 1974). Jersey Standard's Alberta Oil, during 1970, made further important offshore finds in the western Arctic. Canada was host to 13 per cent of US FDI oil assets in 1950, and 24 per cent twenty years later (Wilkins, 1974). Over 78 per cent of oil and gas production was foreign-controlled by 1973, and this stark fact, the decade's rising oil prices, and fears about economic security brought Pierre Trudeau's second Liberal government to introduce its National Energy Programme in 1980.

Ford's personnel, from its home base in Detroit, could look across the river which divided the USA and Canada and see their subsidiary in Walkerville, Ontario. The only rationale for its existence was Canada's trade restrictions. Ford's post-war policy was to transfer its management methods and proven competitive abilities to its overseas factories, through negotiations with local managers, but, to facilitate its strategy, it took full ownership of the Canadian business in 1949. The company next built a larger plant and a new subsidiary headquarters at Oakville, Toronto, completed in 1953, and opened an assembly plant, in 1967, at Talbotville.[83] Ford, GM and Chrysler wanted to integrate their Canadian and US operations fully, but could not do so until the signing in 1965 of the Automotive Products Trade Agreement, which lifted content regulations and all tariffs on assembled vehicles. The big three companies gained from greater returns to scale and enhanced cross-border vertical integration, and could view Canada and the USA as a single market. Chrysler, within two years, consequently, but very unusually, adopted a policy of wage equalization between the two countries. Closer daily operations meant that Ford's Canadian subsidiary became, by 1974, a full unit of the US parent. Canada wanted to improve production efficiency and southerly access for its exports, and obtained a promise from Ford, General Motors and Chrysler (all central to the economy of Ontario) that they would maintain overall levels of output and employment (Wilkins, 1974; Gallard, 2004).[84]

Canada's outward FDI was concentrated in public utilities, railways, farm implements, beverage manufacture and mining (Easterbrook, 1988), and, by 1967, amounted to 3.6 per cent of world FDI assets.

Separated from Alcoa in 1950, Alcan took an aggressive approach to the US market. Over the following decade, it supplied 90 per cent of the USA's aluminium imports, in the form of ingots, and it was prepared to cut the prices set by Alcoa in the USA, gaining, not surprisingly, the thanks of independent fabricators, and their support for lower tariffs. Rising local competition progressively cut Alcan's exports – being 21 per cent of the world total in 1954, but 13 per cent in 1969 – and it responded by founding fabricating plants in eleven countries. Similar reasoning led to acquisitions in the USA from 1963, and a subsidiary called Alcan Aluminum Corporation, incorporated in 1965, had within two years oversight of 12 plants in eight US states. Higher transportation and labour costs in Canada, and political pressures overseas persuaded Alcan to build primary smelters in Australia, Britain, Norway, India and Japan, and, in 1972, its foreign subsidiary capacity equalled that of the home company. It had an alumina refinery in Ireland, and bauxite mines in Brazil by 1980. Alcan's lack of presence in fabricated products meant that it did not own the higher margins for aerospace, autos and cans, as energy costs rose in the 1970s, when overall demand for its output fell markedly.[85] Massey Ferguson – the new name for the Massey-Harris company from 1959, and already in the USA – moved to make acquisitions in Britain: during the 1960s, it bought Standard Motor's tractor operations, a tractor engine business, and a manufacturer of construction equipment.[86]

As a wealthy economy attracting manufacturing investment, and as a country replete with natural resources, Australia holds comparison with Canada. Legal institutions and low risks of disappropriation helped attract FDI, and the English language could be no disadvantage. To promote industrialization at home, and to encourage FDI, Australia had similarly employed tariffs, import licensing, and content restrictions. Multinational investors in automobiles, oil, chemicals, branded goods and mining were all notable (Wilkins, 1974). The GM-Holden factory had been converted to war production, but, in its 1944 review of international policy, GM had confidence in Australia's domestic market. The government, on the return of peace, actively promoted the re-establishment of the industry and the manufacture of an Australian-designed car. The post-war dollar shortage, and therefore government preference for sterling purchases, supplied another reason for GM to invest further, and in 1946 thirty of its engineers left Detroit for

Australia. The subsidiary focused at first on vehicle bodies, but in 1948, a year in which it made only 112 vehicles, it launched the Holden. The car was inspired by the Chevrolet, and GM-Holden followed its first Australian launch with utility, sedan, and farm models.

GM-Holden invested heavily in its factories, raising the level of local content, and by 1954 it was selling 55,000 vehicles. It made models that achieved local iconic status: the firm had turned a jingle about four components of US identity – 'Baseball, Hot Dogs, Apple Pies and Chevrolet' – into something more fundamentally Australian – 'Football, Meat Pies, Kangaroos and Holden Cars'. GM-Holden began exporting, in 1954, to New Zealand, and by 1963 it was selling throughout South East Asia, Africa, the Middle East, the Pacific islands and the Caribbean. GM established an assembly plant in South Africa in 1959, where it made Holden models, and, during the 1970s, almost inevitably, it ran advertisements linking 'Braaivleis, Rugby, Sunny Skies and Chevrolet'. The development of the compact Gemini in Australia in cooperation with Isuzu, GM's Japanese affiliate, in 1975, illustrated rising levels of cross-border integration in the industry.[87] Ford, in the post-war period, made Australian variations of its British and Canadian models, but in 1960 launched the Falcon, supported by its new plant near Melbourne.[88]

The Standard-Vacuum Oil Company – or Stanvac, the Jersey Standard and Socony-Vacuum joint venture in East Asia – built a refinery in 1949, and Caltex – the Standard Oil of California and Texaco joint venture to market Saudi oil – did so in 1950 (Wilkins, 1974). Caltex joined with the Australian Motorists Petrol Company (Ampol), in 1947, to explore the Exmouth region of Western Australia, forming West Australian Petroleum (WAPET), which drilled its first well in 1953. They soon afterwards went to Barrow Island – the first civilians to do so after British atomic testing on nearby Monte Bellos Islands – and made a large discovery in 1964. In a further show of its major part in developing the Australian oil industry, WAPET found the first commercial quantities of natural gas, near Dongara, in 1961, and built a pipeline to Perth.[89] Both Union Oil Company of California (Unocal) and Philips made breakthroughs in Queensland (in 1964); Esso, in partnership with the Australian conglomerate and miner BHP, made a series of finds, some spectacular (1964–72); Aquitaine, too, established economically important gas and oil fields (1969–72).[90] As part of its new, post-Spain strategy of geographical and commodity diversification, RTC bought the Mary Kathleen uranium mine in 1955, and it controlled some 15 per cent of uranium oxide output by 1960.[91]

The Zinc Corporation merged with the Imperial Smelting Corporation, and, in 1949, formed the Consolidated Zinc Corporation (CNZ), which owned Consolidated Zinc Proprietary (CZP), founded as its Australian subsidiary, and other interests, such as New Broken Hill Consolidated. For practical reasons, operational control of CNZ's varied Australian interests was placed with CZP in 1951, and it had a major role in developing Queensland's vast bauxite lode, constituting perhaps one third of the world's resources, at Weipa on the Cape York Peninsula. To exploit this find fully, CZP looked for overseas capital and a partner experienced in such projects, and founded a joint venture, in 1956, with Kaiser, called the Commonwealth Aluminium Corporation (Comalco).

Rio Tinto Zinc (RTZ) – the union of RTC and CNZ in 1962 – transformed the CZP subsidiary into Conzinc Riotinto of Australia (CRA), and CRA took charge of the Australian businesses, while the official parent, RTZ, looked after the rest of the world. The Australian government forced CRA to export less bauxite ore to Japan and Europe, and to found a refinery, in 1963, with Kaiser and Pechiney, named Queensland Alumina (QAL), which Comalco supplied from Weipa. Comalco, with its command of supplies, in 1968 formed a consortium of European aluminium companies to build a refinery in Sardinia, and, in order to exploit local and cheap hydroelectric power, it established New Zealand Aluminium Smelters, in a partnership with Japanese producers and end-users. Alcoa of Australia, formed in 1961 between the US company and Australian mining firms, also became one of the local aluminium industry's leading enterprises.[92]

The Australian government lifted its restrictions on the export of iron ore, imposed to encourage industrialization at home, in 1960, and, two years later, with support from RTZ, CRA and Kaiser created Hammersley Holdings to exploit the Hammersley Range iron ore deposits, recently discovered in Western Australia. The need to develop this resource with overseas capital and know-how brought the change of policy. The impressive growth of the post-war Japanese steel industry provided the main justification for CRA's investment, as it made the export of iron ore from distant Australia economic. As RTZ generally traded separately from CRA, the parent company's shareholding in the subsidiary declined, and there were conflicts of interest between the two firms. CRA's commercial arrangements were highly complex for a combination of reasons: they highlighted the capital and technological intensity of mining, the critical international flow of expertise and finance, and the competing perspectives of involved parties as generated by the geographical distance between the ores, processing, and final markets.

Since CRA could not muster all the capital and technological know-how required, and since it was officially part of RTZ, Australian politicians could question whether its stewardship of world-significant resources was in the country's best interests. The same points might be directed to CRA, from 1966, when it formed Bougainville Copper in Papua New Guinea, where Australia's mandate – until self-government in 1973 and formal independence in 1975 – removed any investment risk.[93] Multinationals in building supplies and construction, which grew out of the country's advantages in minerals, continued to expand in the post-war period. With the benefits of fast economic growth in Australia, bringing industrialization and urbanization, Pioneer International Ltd went overseas, in 1961, with a concrete plant in Hong Kong, and, by 1980, it owned construction, building supply, quarrying, mining and asphalt interests in Asia, Africa, Israel and much of Europe. When it bought a plastics manufacturer in Australia, in 1967, it found itself the owner of tea and coffee plantations in Papua New Guinea. Ready Mix Concrete of Australia, having in 1952 bought up its RMC British counterpart, from which it had split before the war, rapidly expanded across Europe. It bought a concrete-making equipment manufacturer in Dusseldorf and the Taylor Woodrow construction business in Britain, but sold off the British RMC, in 1963, fearing that its management was becoming too independent-minded.[94]

Japan, trade and industrialization

For the US administration that ruled Japan after 1945, the family-owned zaibatsu conglomerates had been part of the nationalist military regime that had provoked war in the Pacific. GHQ was determined to replace the controlling families, and, with its imported US perspective on monopoly and antitrust, it ended the economic power of the groups by breaking them up into unconnected companies. The

Japanese government, from 1949, began to ease anti-monopoly regulations, and went further with the relaxation of rules after the Korean War, deeming the business groups as important to its post-war policy objectives. Former zaibatsu reconvened after 1954 as *kigyo shudan* (often called, mistakenly, *keiretsu*), this time looser groupings of independent businesses run by professional managers; other major *kigyo shudan* coalesced around major banks. By pooling capital and spreading commercial risks, they could assist bold plans in investment and manpower, as made at the Ministry of International Trade and Industry, to bring about Japan's rapid industrialization.

One new characteristic of the *kigyo shudan* was cross-shareholding amongst member firms, relieving executives of external shareholder pressure, and allowing them to focus on growth over profits. Post-war business groups contained insurance companies as well as house banks as sources of much-needed finance, plus trading enterprises that helped to secure and cheapen the price of raw materials and stabilize demand by buying and marketing finished products. Members could share commercial information, coordinate their business strategies, and jointly cooperate with government industrial policies. As well as being suspicious of the zaibatsu, GHQ had objected to the size and reach of the *sogo shosha*, or general trading companies. They had been the most internationalized of Japanese businesses, but military defeat had meant the loss of their overseas assets. GHQ split up the trading companies, and two important zaibatsu members were radically altered by the Holding Companies Liquidation Commission in 1947: Mitsui Bussan ended up as 233 separate enterprises, Mitsubishi Shoji as 139.

To re-establish their role as efficient multinationals involved in commodities and logistics, the Japanese trading companies had to re-acquire scale; re-create their overseas offices and commercial networks; and, crucially, obtain the flow of materials that would sustain Japan's economic recovery. The Mitsui Bussan sister companies, although separated, in reality remained in contact, and the largest of them, Nitto Warehousing Company and Daiichi Bussan, began the process of regrouping after 1951. The fall in demand after the Korean War, in 1953, necessitated rescues and mergers of the smaller traders created by the Americans. When Nitto and Daiichi joined together, in 1958, they refounded Mitsui & Co. and resurrected the name, one year afterwards. To meet in particular the demands of the heavy and chemicals industries, the merged business put in place procurement schemes that ensured reliable access to raw materials, including long-term contracts and the financing of resource developments overseas. Another of Mitsui's pivotal roles in Japan's post-war economic miracle was its importing of technology and equipment from North America and Europe, and its commitment to building export markets in every type of manufactured good, from cloth to ships. It involved itself, in the 1960s, in copper mining in Mexico, Chile, Canada and Australia, and, from 1971, it allied with three Japanese chemical firms and the National Iranian Oil Company (NIOC) to form the Iran Japan Petroleum Company. Divisions amongst the Japanese partners and disagreements with NIOC plagued the project from the outset, and, when the Iranian Revolution of 1979 and the Iran–Iraq War brought failure, the project exposed Japan's worst case of international business risk management and underlined the country's abiding anxiety for energy security.[95]

Several former Mitsubishi Shoji companies reunited in 1950, and they were allowed to use the *sogo shosha*'s famous name; further mergers, in 1954, created once again a business of worldwide scale. Mitsubishi Shoji, too, worked on liquid natural gas (LNG) production, with Shell and the Brunei government, from 1968, its first major overseas investment; it established, in 1969, Balikpapan Forest Industries in Indonesia; it bought Australian and Canadian iron-ore and coal mines from 1971; and it created joint ventures, producing salt with the Mexican government in California, developing tourism in Kenya, and marketing Mitsubishi cars with Chrysler in the USA. Mitsubishi Shoji anglicized its name to Mitsubishi Corporation in 1971, a statement of its intention to look more international.[96]

The Japanese government initiated a shipbuilding scheme, from 1947, which aided businesses such as Kawasaki Heavy Industries, although Japan was not allowed to pursue commercial ocean-going shipping until the San Francisco peace treaty came into effect, in 1952. Japanese shipping lines struggled, over the following decade, to make a profit, and the government used subsidies as an instrument to enforce mergers. In 1964, Nippon Yusen Kaisha (NYK) took over Mitsubishi Kaiun KK; Kawasaki Kisen Kaisha (K-Line) assumed control over Iino Kisen Kaisha; and rivals Osaka Shosen Kaisha (OSK) and Mitsui Steamship Co. (MS) formed Mitsui OSK Lines (MOL). The government also subsidized the change to containerization, and the shipping lines later benefited from government assistance to acquire special ships for importing oil and LNG and for the booming export in cars. The importance of government direction behind the securing of raw materials, technology and equipment, and the strategy of export-orientated industrialization, was further shown in 1968. MITI insisted that Nissho Company, the seventh-largest *sogo shosha*, absorb the failed Iwai & Co., the tenth-largest, founding Nissho Iwai as a result.[97]

There was a recurrence of government-directed rationalizaton in 1977, when C. Itoh was ordered to incorporate Ataka, a takeover again presented as a merger. SCAP, in 1949, had broken up the Daiken Company, spinning off the C. Itoh textile firm and turning its merchant division into an entirely separate enterprise. By the 1960s, in partnership with Mitsubishi Shoji, Nissho Iwai and local companies, C. Itoh trading company owned Australian nickel and cobalt mines for the manufacture of stainless steel by the Kawasaki and Nisshin companies.[98] Marubeni, too, came out of the Daiken Company, then diversified during the Korean War; after merging with a department store group, it was called Marubeni-Iida. MITI selected it to source the needs of the Yawata and Fuji steel companies, which merged in 1970 to create the world's largest steel business, Nippon Steel. Marubeni-Iida additionally supplied the nuclear, electronics and chemicals industries, and contracted military aircraft for Japan's defence forces. Through a merger, in 1965, with Totsu Company, it was officially appointed a *sogo shosha* – recognition of its status as a key instrument of growth and industrialization – and it changed its name to Marubeni Corporation in 1973.

In Japan's hidden political and business networks, traders provided early revelations of moral hazard: Marubeni found itself mired, during 1976, in the Lockheed bribery scandal, accused of paying politicians who might influence the fleet purchases of the state-owned All Nippon Airlines (ANA). Former prime minister Kokuei Tanaka was arrested, and the investigation into the airline manufacturer's doings went also to Indonesia, Italy and the Netherlands, where the well-connected Prince Bernhard was personally implicated.[99] Nissho Iwai appeared to repeat the format of the Lockheed scandal in 1979, this time on behalf of McDonnell Douglas and Boeing, leading to resignations and one ritual suicide at the trading company. By 1977, following Itoh's takeover of Ataka, the top nine *sogo shosha* still controlled over

80 per cent of Japan's trade, and could justifiably claim a major contribution to Japan's policy of export-orientated industrialization and
its post-war economic miracle.[100]

Tokyo Automobile Industries Company became known as Isuzu in
1949. Under licence from the Rootes Group, from 1953 it made the
Hillman Minx and subsequently, from 1961, its own car, the Bellel.
After five more years, it came under pressure from MITI, seeking to
limit the number of firms in each industry, to ally with Subaru or Fuji
Heavy Industries. Isuzu briefly allied with Mitsubishi Motors and then
Nissan, but, finally, in 1971, it signed a more permanent deal, not with
a Japanese partner, but with General Motors. The US multinational
soon took 34 per cent of the shares, and the flow in design and product
development went in both directions. The Isuzu Faster inspired the
Chevrolet LUV or pick-up truck, which appeared in 1972, first in the
USA and later in Latin America, while Opel's Kadett transmuted into
Izusu's Gemini, launched in 1974, and into Buick's Opel, for the US
market. With the help of GM's international networks, the Japanese
company's exports grew from 0.7 to over 35 per cent of its production,
in the short span of 1973 to 1976.[101]

Many Japanese *kaisha* had created the leadership in management,
products and technology (often combining low price and rising quality) that could be a foundation for future multinational investment.
Fujitsu Fanuc (Fuji Automatic Numerical Control) – a wholly owned
subsidiary of Fujitsu spun off as a separate enterprise in 1972 – dominated the factory automation business in Japan, and, in 1975, licensed
its technology to Pratt & Whitney, the US aerospace engineering company, and to Siemens, which also took a shareholding in the Japanese
firm.[102] Others used their experience and expertise to take contracts
for turnkey factories. Furukawa Aluminium Company – founded in
1959 with technical assistance from Alcoa – built two such plants in
Romania during 1966, and Nippon Seiko set up ball-bearing factories
for local producers in Czechoslovakia, Pakistan, Poland and Bulgaria
between 1967 and 1972.[103]

We know, furthermore, that the engineering conglomerate Hitachi
Zosen built a chemical fertilizer plant for the Gujarat State Fertiliser
Company of India, in 1957, in a record thirty-three months,[104] and
that Furukawa Aluminium announced its international expansion in
civil engineering by laying a high-voltage cable from Tehran to the
Caspian Sea in 1978.[105] The construction company Kajima – with its

expertise in earthquake technologies – took up the challenges of overseas projects throughout Asia in the 1960s before, in the decade that
followed, undertaking major and diplomatically sensitive contracts
in East Berlin, and entering the USA. Japan's rapid industrialization
and urbanization created construction and engineering companies with
experience of managing large projects.[106] Change in Korea had similar
and especially early effects: Hyundai Heavy Industries gained its first
overseas project with a highway in Thailand, in 1965, and became an
important player in construction projects in the Middle East.[107]

Within Japanese manufacturing, Fuji Photo Firm continued to compete with Kodak and AGFA-Gevaert in developed markets with
exports, yet, from 1971, established itself in Brazil, Korea and Indonesia, whilst Ricoh founded an assembly plant for its photocopiers,
during 1973, in California.[108] Under the regional cooperation and
war liability clauses of its peace treaty, Japan organized commercial,
government and assistance loans to fund the building of Korea's first
integrated steel plant, the Pohang Iron and Steel Company (POSCO),
by 1968; the plant was planned and built by a consortium of Mitsubishi
Heavy Industries, Nippon-Kokan and the Nippon Steel Corporation. POSCO, in its turn, during 1978, helped with the founding of
Taiwan's Chinese Steel Corporation.[109] While preferring for the time
being to export to the developed markets of Western Europe and North
America, setting up sales offices, Toyota did establish its first overseas
operation in 1958, an assembly plant in Brazil, and then two more in
South Africa, in 1964, and Ghana, in 1969, in part as responses to
government pressure.

Fuller FDI strategies followed the examples of multinational appren-
ticeship, encouraged by the rising value of the yen and by the relaxing
of government controls on outward flows of capital in 1971. Nippon
Seiko – adopting a strategy of providing enhanced customer service
in its export markets – founded its first overseas factory in São Paulo
in 1970, another in Michigan in 1973, and one in Peterlee, Scotland,
in 1976.[110] Japan's second-largest bearing maker, NTN Corporation,
was similarly manufacturing in the USA, and additionally in Canada
and Germany, by 1980.[111] Kawasaki Steel Corporation founded a
joint venture in Brazil with Italy's Finsider and a local company,
Siderbrás, in 1974, the same year in which Matsushita established
an electric relay firm in Germany and an automation control business
in the USA. Sony – building its reputation in the electronics industry

as an innovator – opened its first US plant in 1971, and another in South Wales, in the UK, by 1974.[112] The take-off in Japanese FDI and, therefore, in Japanese manufacturing FDI occurred, nonetheless, during the 1980s, when governments in the USA and Western Europe imposed quotas and tariffs that threatened the overseas markets so successfully won through exports. Therefore, before the take-off, some 66 per cent of Japanese FDI could be found in developing countries, against 27 per cent by US multinationals and 20 per cent by those from Britain (Kojima, 1978).

Box 4.1 Economic development, trade and the multinational

It is no coincidence that Japanese theorists, looking at the experience of their own country, put forward a number of new perspectives on multinational enterprise, which could also be applied to Korea, China and developing countries generally. Kojima and Ozawa both emphasize the government policy and macro-economic influences on the nature of multinational activity, as opposed to beginning with the firm and its internal capabilities. Their ideas can be linked to ideas on late development or the developmental state, in which government plays a determinant role in industrialization in order to create competitive companies and to secure investments in technology, education and infrastructure. Kojima and Ozawa, furthermore, directly link the needs of the economy (the search for raw materials, industrial components, or machinery) with early stages of multinational activity; as the home economy goes through further stages of development, it is able to produce firms with the capabilities for FDI.

Kojima questions the dominant analysis of multinational strategies and competencies. Japan during a period of rapid industrialization lacked raw materials, and an early objective of outward FDI was to obtain natural resources. Government policy effectively prevented foreign-owned multinationals from operating in Japan, and, until the 1970s, it restricted overseas investment not directed towards the raw materials or components needed for industrialization and exports. Japanese manufacturing firms preferred to draw upon their home-based advantages in suppliers, labour skills or bank finance, and to engage in trade. Only the raising of duties and import quotas by the USA and by West European governments in the

1980s turned Japanese manufacturers away from their export orienta-
tion towards FDI. Their multinational strategies were those of protecting
and following their trade (Kojima, 1985).

Ozawa agrees with the macro-economic focus, with the attention paid
to government policy, and with the trade-motivated nature of Japanese
FDI. He observes, too, that exports and FDI are reflective of stages of economic development. As an industrializing nation, Japan needed to obtain
raw materials; expand its exports; limit competition from advanced
economies in its home market; and develop its own capabilities. Its
overseas trade was at first based on low-cost, labour-intensive and low-
technology products. The extraction of natural resources, trading companies, and industrial components determined FDI outflows. As labour
and other costs in Japan grew, bigger margin and high-technology manufacturing became the basis of Japanese competitiveness and exports,
and firms in labour-intensive sectors had an incentive to become multinationals in low-cost nations. There is, therefore, an emphasis on home-
country factors. The internal capabilities of firms and multinationals are
embedded in a national economic model composed of a developmental state, export-orientated industrialization, close bank–industry relations, business networks and partnerships, and long-term investment
in production systems, technology and human resources. Raw material
shortages and then changing domestic costs affected FDI approaches.
Once Japanese firms had advanced ownership advantages, they undertook FDI in order to maximize sales revenues and to accelerate the
upgrading of home operations (Kojima and Ozawa, 1984; Ozawa, 1989;
Ozawa, 1991).

Japanese firms built competitive capabilities in their domestic market, behind protective walls, and moved from exports to FDI once faced
with protective duties and quotas in developed markets. Nation states
and stages of economic development, as well as multinationals, are part
of the story. Wells draws attention to multinationals from developing
countries and their possibilities. Both the search for natural resources
and technology, and limited opportunities in the home market might
stimulate outward FDI, despite a shortage of domestic capital. During
the 1980s, however, the circumvention of trade restrictions and the protection of export markets were the usual main reasons. Multinationals
from developing nations would not have O-advantages, as outlined in
the OLI model, in technology or management systems, but they might
succeed where FDI was small in relation to home country activities and
where overseas investment complemented export trade in terms of raw
materials, components or distribution (Wells, 1983).

Trading companies and colonialism's legacy

With its trading surplus, Switzerland allowed free convertibility of its currency in the post-war decades, and it continued to be a favoured location for finance companies. It specialized in US dollar transactions, and vied with London to be number two, after New York, in the making of foreign loans. Light-touch regulation, secrecy, low taxes, and the potential for deals attracted foreign investors, and American Express Company and First National City Bank joined firms already there, such as Paribas, Crédit Lyonnais and Lloyds. Conditions in Switzerland acted as a magnet for international finance, but, arguably, encouraged its own banks to stay at home and not to improve their weak representation overseas (Cassis, 2006). They also made this land-locked country a prime location for trading companies. At least 30 per cent and maybe as much as 60 per cent of the world's grain transactions were conducted within its borders by 1980, and it was a global venue for cotton and textile commodities. Cargill moved its European operation, Tradax, to Switzerland, in 1956, and Andre & Cie ran a global operation from its Lausanne headquarters. Marc Rich, a US citizen, in 1974 founded his eponymous firm in the Zug canton, drawn by low taxes and low scrutiny of his trades in metals and oil (the business later evolved into Glencore). Rich was accused of ignoring the international boycott imposed on South Africa's apartheid regime, and of swapping weapons for Iranian oil during the hostage crisis of 1979–80, when fifty-two US citizens were held captive in Tehran.[113]

The post-war acceleration in trade offered opportunities for trading companies, at least in principle. Since much of that growth was commerce between developed economies, however, British traders predominantly located in the developing world were not well placed. The beneficiaries of a different era, and a disappearing international system being replaced by another, many of them did not have the resources or inclination to evolve. The end of colonialism in Asia and Africa undermined the foundations on which many of them had constructed their businesses. The governments of developing countries – frequently former colonies – wanted to control the production and sale of the local commodities, the very mainstay of their economies. They had a panoply of options – the promotion of local businesses, state marketing and export companies, nationalization, import substitution policies, exchange controls, taxation, and the revision of natural resource concessions – with which to curtail the influence of foreign traders.

Each case of decolonization had its own particularities. The policies of states that emerged out of the British Empire affected companies from the old imperial power in a variety of ways. At one extreme, the multinationals that decided to stay in racist South Africa received favourable treatment; at another extreme, as reminders of an imperial past and as holders of vital national assets, British companies generally confronted either sequestration or stage-by-stage retreat. The subsidiaries of Netherlands firms – simply because they were so highly concentrated in one new nation, Indonesia – were ultimately sequestrated. Not surprisingly, given the political and armed turmoil in South East Asia during the post-war years, French businesses there withdrew; those in Africa seemed to have endured better in general than their British counterparts. Despite instability and rising bloodshed in Angola and Mozambique, multinationals hung on until revolution at home brought a practical end to the Portuguese empire, during 1974–5.

On independence in 1948, Burma's government took over the valuable teak forests that Wallace Brothers and Steels had lost during the Second World War. When the new military government adopted policies of full-scale nationalization and autarchy, in 1963, Steels was deprived of its remaining assets. Multinationals increasingly turned away from India in the post-war period. The heavier taxation imposed on private firms from independence in 1949 was highly inimical to British traders. A 1956 law limiting the number of managed companies per managing agency to ten was capped by another in 1967 that entirely abolished the management agency system: a lucrative source of income for foreign trading and investment houses was thus first squeezed and then ended. Agencies had been the organizational foundation of the coal mining and tea industries, in particular, and, in 1970, the coal industry was nationalized. Rupee devaluation was another concern for multinational investors. While foreign exchange laws in 1947 and 1957 had complicated dealings and remittances, the 1973 Foreign Exchange Regulation Act was a more direct attempt at boosting indigenous ownership, by enforcing restrictions on all firms that were 40 per cent or more foreign-controlled (Roy, 2006).

A few cases can illustrate how, at different junctures, the old imperial houses of India perceived the passing of an historical era: the Inchcape family began withdrawal, early in 1949, by selling assets to the Tata Group; local businesses similarly bought up Birds in 1961; Yule Catto sold its shares in Andrew Yule to the Indian government in 1969; and James Finlay completed the sale of its tea business, also to Tata, by 1976 (Jones, 2000). The loss of China as a market, and the decline in the Indian cotton trade hurt the Danish-owned Volkart, but the company proved able to reposition itself as a world cotton and coffee trader.[114]

Elsewhere, the Borneo Company declared, in 1953, its intention to shift from Asia to commercially safer territories. Guthries and Harrisons & Crosfield were able to retain their place in Malaysia's rubber business because their R&D helped to stay the threat from synthetics, and because of the large costs associated with the process of replanting. Along with Sime Darby, Boustead and, after its investments made from 1947 onwards, UAC, these two firms had extensive interests in palm oil, although Harrisons & Crosfield hedged its risks in Malaysia, in 1967, by investing in Papua New Guinea.[115] In 1971, following a series of violent protests, the government introduced its New Economic Policy, in favour of transferring wealth and business ownership to native Malays, and discriminating against the local Chinese and Indian populations (Turnbull, 1989). It wanted, furthermore, to reduce overseas influence: in 1976, the government bought a 10 per cent stake in Sime Darby, an enterprise in the engineroom of the Malaysian economy, and forced out all its British directors.[116] It likewise terminated British control over Guthries in 1981.[117]

Given UAC's important role in the economy of the African continent, it was not surprising that more than a dozen African governments frequently acquired ownership of its diverse operations, sometimes with full compensation, sometimes with compensation deferred. Unilever itself – with some 140,000 acres in Congo, during 1959, constituting the world's largest palm oil enterprise – retained its presence in that country, and the company, overall, made some 12 per cent of global output. UAC lost its grip on the processing, exporting and price-setting of African commodities, often to state-owned marketing boards, and it ceased, for example, to export products from Nigeria in 1961. Across the continent, UAC ceased to be a highly diversified conglomerate, and adopted the role of specialist importer and owner

of western-style stores (Fieldhouse, 1978). The risks of political instability, and currency and exchange controls encouraged divestments in
Latin America, and although firms like Gibbs, Balfour Williamson,
or Duncan Fox retained important assets, there were no new major
investments (Jones, 2000).

Although many British traders were sequestered and others entered
into long-term decline, there were notable stories of transformation
and expansion. Some traders continued in their role as investors and
guarantors in developing countries, although their involvement was
no longer fundamental to these economies. Wallace Brothers bought
plantations and ranches in many African countries between 1950 and
1954,[118] and Finlay acquired tea estates in Kenya and trading interests
in Rhodesia in 1956.[119] In some cases of manufacturing investment,
firms were mostly reacting to government pressure. Nigeria persuaded
UAC, a significant importer of autos, to found an assembly plant
in 1958, but the venture was never economic.[120] Import duties and
government policies led to Anglo-Thai being contracted to build an
assembly plant for Ford vehicles in 1960, which it sold to the US
manufacturer in 1970.[121] UAC, in 1961, joined Guinness in its joint
venture in Nigeria, then Guinness's second-largest overseas market,
and they repeated the project in Ghana in 1975. Despite the growing
political complexity of their historical host territories, traders could
still display commercial opportunism and a flair for deal making.[122]
Examples included department stores (UAC in Nigeria in 1958), phar-
macies (Holts in West Africa), the new Dubai port (Gray Mackenzie
in 1972), and support services for Brazil's offshore oil industry (an
Ocean Wilsons and Inchcape joint venture in 1978).

What British trading companies had to do was find new types of
business in new locations, and some of them managed to grow by
acquisition. The various private enterprises connected with the Inchcape family were consolidated, in 1958, into Inchcape & Company,
a business with 17 subsidiaries, where the majority or full control
of businesses replaced shared partnerships, overlapping ownership,
or contractual arrangements. Inchcape became public, with 25 per
cent of its shares on the London Stock Exchange, and it began to
acquire other traders: Borneo Company in 1967, Dodwell in 1972,
and the Anglo-Thai Corporation in 1976. It purchased, too, assets in
Britain, notably the car dealership Mann Egerton in 1973. Inchcape –
once a grouping of shipping agencies, trading firms, tea plantations

and Indian textile manufacturers – became a British general trad-ing company with a large automobile distribution business.[123] Swire and Jardine Matheson recovered successfully from the Pacific War. They further developed their extensive real estate, docks, transport, finance, hotels, and manufacturing assets in Hong Kong, but sought to be less reliant on a politically precarious and strategically vulnerable colony. Butterfield & Swire, from 1948, began its noted development of Cathay Pacific as a regional and international airline, and it made numerous acquisitions, including the Coca-Cola bottling plant supply-ing East Asia, in 1965, and trader James Finlay, in 1976. When the next generation of Swires took control of the family conglomerate, in 1972, their reorganization of the business led to its renaming, as John Swire & Sons Ltd, two years later.[124]

John Keswick returned to run Jardine Matheson after the Second World War. He tried to work with the Communists in Shanghai in 1950, but, with the outbreak of the Korean War, and once a trade embargo had been imposed on China, he had to write off the consider-able properties that had been nationalized. Jardine Matheson, which went public in 1961, expanded into shipping in Australia, and into sugar plantations in the Philippines and Hawaii. With the Communists in power in China, the two British-owned hongs, or Guangdong-based trading houses, had lost substantial parts of their business, but there were disturbing commercial trends too.[125] By the 1970s, for exam-ple, firms like Hawker-Siddeley could sell six jetliners to the Chinese directly and without the expertise of intermediaries. In Hong Kong, moreover, the Chinese hongs had developed into serious competitors of the commercial establishment. Yue-Kong Pao's World-Wide Ship-ping Group diversified into the Hongkong and Kowloon Wharf and Godown Company, and into Wheelock Marden's real estate, retail, ferries, shipping terminals and trams. Li Ka Shing's Cheung Kong Holdings was the first to buy up a British hong, Hutchinson Wham-poa, in 1979, which had another eclectic mix of real estate, retail, shipping terminals and insurance.[126]

From 1952 onwards, with political unrest in Guyana, the chairman of Booker Brothers, McConnell – John 'Jock' Campbell – looked for 'hedge-building' investments beyond the colony and the sugar busi-ness. The company took up loss-making ventures in engineering, but over the long term successfully concentrated on supermarkets, food production and agricultural consulting, in Trinidad, Britain, Canada,

Zambia and Malawi. When Guyana achieved its independence in 1966, it elected a Communist government, and the conglomerate sold up its plantation and other activities. The business adopted the simplified name of Booker, McConnell, in 1968 (later the Booker Group).[127]

From 1961, Roland 'Tiny' Rowland transformed the London and Rhodesia Mining and Land Company (Lonrho) into a sprawling conglomerate with worldwide interests but, above all, deep involvement in Africa. As well as being a business maverick, Rowland was secretive, hiding his German heritage and brief membership of the Hitler Youth, and his wartime detention as an enemy alien in the Isle of Man. He was determined to maintain a similar veil over his commercial transactions, and gained a reputation for opportunism and ruthlessness. His greatest skill was a talent for forming relationships with Africa's new rulers and political elite: the Malawi government, for example, commissioned the company to take on sugar refining and to meet the whole country's needs. Rowland's methods provoked a managerial power struggle within Lonrho, and British prime minister Edward Heath referred to the 'unpleasant and unacceptable face of capitalism', but Rowland remained firmly in charge of the business empire he had created.[128]

The strategy of investing in the security of the British home market was a key change in the strategy of many traders. Between them, Anglo-Thai, Guthries, Harrisons & Crosfield, Jardine Matheson, Holts, Inchcape, Dalgety, and Booker Brothers, McConnell gained footholds in chemicals, insurance, car dealing, wine, agriculture, retailing, supermarkets, pet food, timber merchants and anything else that might make a profit, but many of their acquisitions were quickly sold. After Britain, the secure and developed destination of Australia attracted a large portion of trader investments. The five largest British trading companies, in 1978, were Lonrho, Jardine Matheson, Swire and Inchcape – all of them autonomous – and UAC – separately managed, but a subsidiary of the European food giant Unilever.

A long list of famous British trading houses failed and lost their independence. The acquisition of the Borneo Company, Dodwell, Anglo-Thai and Finlay we have already noted. In addition, the Bank of London and South America, in 1960, bought Balfour Williamson, which had tried to diversify in Africa and Australasia. When Lloyds International took over BOLSA, in 1973, it sold Balfour Williamson's trading activities to Lonrho and Inchcape. Dalgety bought the associated Balfour Guthries, with its major lumber and poultry business in the USA, during 1970. By turning into the world's leading cotton trader, as pressures built in its commercial base of India, Ralli was unusual, as so many British-registered firms struggled to find a new destiny. It fell victim, nonetheless, to corporate raider Slater Walker in 1969, which sold it on to pulp and paper manufacturer Bowater three years later. The Hongkong Bank extended its reach to Latin America by gradually absorbing Gibbs, during 1972–80, carefully choosing a non-Jewish firm that would not threaten its ambitions in the Middle East. The Bank of England asked Standard Chartered to buy the failing Wallace Brothers, in 1977, to prevent a loss of confidence spreading through Britain's corporate sector (Jones, 2000).

Did Netherlands trading businesses – with a shared influential colonial past – undergo the same fate as their British counterparts and for the same reasons? After several years of warfare, an independent Indonesia was formed in 1949. The old trading firms returned, hoping the new government would value their capabilities and know-how, but they were aware of their need to explore new territories. Indonesia restricted imports and profit transfers, and gave preference to indigenous merchants. Internatio, Borsumij and Hagemeyer opened branches in the region, most obviously in Malaya and Australia, and began to look further overseas. Then, in 1957, all Netherlands capital in Indonesia was nationalized, and the managers were replaced. Internatio entered Kenya, Tanzania and Uganda in 1953, but in the next decade was working against the increasing current of African decolonization, controls on imports and profits, non-convertible currencies, and suspicion of enterprises with imperial histories. Hagemayer, from 1951, bought two Netherlands operations, one operating in West Africa (J. F. Sick & Co.), and one in Congo (L. E. Tels & Co.), but its peak of 22 per cent of subsidiary investments in Africa in 1962 fell to some 2 per cent by 1970. L. E. Tels was, in fact, an old East Indies business that had started up in the Congo in 1948. Borsumij began in the Congo, too, in 1952, and bought a firm with cross-African interests, Twentsche Overzee Handelmaatschappij, in 1955. It maintained the business, but rarely agreed any new investment capital.

There were two other means of coping with the post-war period's changed international political economy: rationalization, and investment in the home country. Geo. Wehry joined with Borsumij in 1961. Maintz & Co., which had developed public utilities in the East Indies, acquired a company in the Netherlands that provided technical services. Internatio bought a manufacturer of electrical components in 1968, and merged with Muller, a big player in mineral trading, transport and ports. By 1970, some 80 per cent of Internatio-Muller's investments were in Western Europe, and it set about divesting from Asia entirely. Hagemayer bought manufacturer after manufacturer, from 1965, including leatherware, kitchenware and cosmetics makers, so that 70 per cent of its assets were in Europe by 1970. The figure for Borsumij, in the same year, was 66 per cent, mostly in non-manufacturing businesses. The Netherlands traders had largely refocused in their home continent as diverse enterprises in manufacturing and distribution, but the economically turbulent 1970s exposed the long-term viability of many of these new investments. Hagemayer could not make its industrial subsidiaries profitable and would eventually close them all (Jonker and Sluyterman, 2005).

There is evidence that French trading companies began to resume their activities in Africa by the early 1950s; they included Maison Devès et Chaumet in Senegal, Sudan and Mali, and Daniel Ancel et Fils with its three branch offices and a coffee factory in the Ivory Coast. As countries gained their independence, and some of them sided with the Communist bloc, French traders tended to abandon commodity production and exports, and used their facilities and knowledge to expand imports. From 1950 onwards, International Harvester, Remington and Otis appointed Compagnie Française de l'Afrique Occidentale (CFAO) as their sole distributor, and the company specialized in the distribution of automobiles, as well as plastic products, and in supermarket chains in Africa and France. During the 1970s, it extended both its portfolio of interests and its reach into many parts of Europe and the USA.[129] Optorg – the textile group linked to Russia and Asia – bought Société de Haute Ogooué in 1947, and Establishments Ch. Peyrissac, a distributor of automobiles and industrial equipment, in 1955. From 1963, it pulled out of South East Asia, the centre of geopolitical turmoil, in favour of Africa.[130]

Hurt by the wartime disruption to international commerce, the grain trader Cargill diversified into manufacturing after 1945 through the purchase of animal feed and food processors in the USA. It set up Tradax in Belgium, in 1953, to represent its varied international interests and to sell grain throughout Europe, before deciding three years later to register the firm in Switzerland. Over the next two decades, it acquired a feed business and corn millers in the Netherlands, and a soya bean plant in Spain (Broehl, 1998). Cargill and Continental Grain were principal suppliers to the Soviet Union – signing deals with Exportkhleb, the state export agency, in 1964 and 1972 – because the country's collectivized system of farming continued to fail. During 1979, Continental Grain and a Thai conglomerate, Charoen Pokphand (CP), established Conti Chia Tai International (CCTI), near Shenzen, just as China was taking its first steps in economic and farm reform. The joint venture was the first major FDI in the People's Republic – accordingly registered as number '001' – as Beijing's government began to look for much-needed capital and the transformation of its feed industry.[131]

A few state-owned enterprises – prominently Exportkhleb, the Canadian Wheat Board, the Australian Wheat Board, and the Australian Barley Board – and the 'big five' private companies effectively controlled the international grain trade. Cargill, Continental (both from the USA), Louis Dreyfus (France), Bunge y Born (Argentina), Andre (Switzerland) and Toepfer (Germany) in the 1970s were responsible for 90 per cent of Europe's wheat exports and 96 per cent of those from the USA (Chalmin, 1987). Since state-owned grain marketing boards grew in number and influence in the post-war period, Louis Dreyfus strived to reduce its risk exposure and to expand through diversification: from 1969, it moved into a variety of commodity markets, including government bonds, and, from 1971, into commercial property management within the USA and Europe.[132]

One famous trader particularly illustrates a strategic retreat from traditional activities into manufacturing, as well as relocation from established countries of business. From the point that Peter Grace took over W. R. Grace in 1946, he worried about political and economic instability and anti-US feeling in Latin America. The firm's primary assets were southerly-bound steamship lines, sugar plantations and cotton mills in Peru and Chile, the Panagra airline joint venture with Pan Am, and the Grace National Bank. Family holdings overcame board-level resistance to transforming the business, and the firm went public, in 1953, to raise the capital needed. Attracted by the size of Du Pont's profits, Peter Grace organized the purchase of thirteen US chemical companies, inevitably making it one of the largest in the industry; investments in leisure, sports and retailing followed. He wanted also

to be the 'General Foods of Europe', buying a Netherlands chocolate manufacturer, a Danish ice cream maker and an Italian pasta
company. Grace then sold off its airline and banking interests. The
Peruvian Revolution of 1968 – installing a nationalist military government – brought about the forced public ownership of large sugar
plantations and some petroleum companies, mines and banks in the
year that followed; the events appeared to validate the redirection of
the trading firm he had inherited (Pike, 1967).

To achieve his ends, Peter Grace received the help of an old friend,
Friedrich Karl Flick. His father, Friedrich Flick, was the founder of
Flick Kommanditgesellschaft (KG) and a war criminal, convicted for
the use of wartime slave labour in his coal, steel and engineering conglomerate, who rebuilt his business empire and Germany's largest family business in the 1950s. His son sold a significant portion of Daimler
Benz to Deutsche Bank for $900m and wanted to avoid a large tax
liability by reinvesting the money. In 1976, he took by agreement a
30 per cent share in W. R. Grace, leaving the founding Grace family with a mere 3 per cent between them; Flick, busy with his business
empire in Europe, made a friend's agreement not to interfere in Grace's
management.[133]

Finance multinationals

Until the 1960s, much of the business conducted in the world's financial centres was confined by a national border. Between 1955 and
1962, for example, New York foreign issues came to $4.2bn, unim-
portant sums next to the $127bn for national purposes. The figure
was small, too, compared to the $98bn in economic and military aid
granted by the USA from 1945 to 1952, and, in general, governments
and the IMF undertook the largest cross-border capital movements.
Since France had nationalized its banks, after Liberation in 1944, in
order to further post-war recovery plans, the country was closed to foreign multinationals; similarly, the cartelization of domestic banking in
many countries until the 1970s squeezed out new competitors and
overseas entrants. Exchange controls and low currency convertibility
left few opportunities for cross-border financing, and December 1958
marked only the easing and not the end of controls across Europe. In
developed economies, therefore, multinational banking was a rarity,
particularly in the retail banking sector and in international service

markets, and most cross-border deals continued to rely on the historically well-established practice of correspondent banks (Cassis, 2006).
In this period, banking FDI went mostly into locations – such as Luxembourg, Switzerland or the Cayman Islands – that helped companies
avoid taxation and regulations, or into locations – such as London and
New York – that offered participation in global and capital markets.

The City of London, with its relative lack of regulation, quickly
acquired a unique international banking network. There were, by
1960, 80 foreign banks in London, a presence far above any other
financial centre, much of it trade-related, and sterling was still used in
half of the world's commerce. Exchange markets in rubber, tin, cocoa,
lead, zinc, copper, wool and coffee all reopened in London (Cassis,
2006). The overseas branches of British banks – 2,315 in 1938 – grew
in number to 3,612 by 1955, although three quarters of them were in
Australia, New Zealand and South Africa. Barclays Bank DCO had
997 overseas branches, while National City Bank from the USA had a
mere 55. Yet loss of empire, the long-term decline of sterling, and
comparatively slow domestic growth all disadvantageously affected
the prospects of Britain's banks, and they progressively lost out to US
competition. There were 8 US banks, with 124 overseas branches, in
1960, but 159, with 799 foreign branches, by 1980.

Citibank and Chase, typically and initially, followed clients as they
established or expanded their multinational operations, and began
to settle in major global financial centres, but direct involvement in
host economies, as opposed to conducting international transactions
in host economies, remained small-scale alongside their total activities.
Rising local competition and more restrictive regulations similarly cut
into the market share of British banks overseas. The merger of Union
Bank of Australia and Bank of Australasia, in 1951, was an example of British bank consolidation; the joining of the successor, ANZ
Bank, with English, Scottish and Australian (ES&A), in 1970, was the
country's biggest banking merger of the time, creating ANZ Banking Group. The business built a network in the Asia Pacific region,
including Hong Kong, one of the few remaining places where foreign
banks operated freely. When Australian government regulations effectively prohibited further British-owned mergers, they barred ANZ,
with a quarter of the nation's deposits, from the rapid growth available to its competitors. Foreign-owned banks, additionally, worked
with tougher liquidity conditions, and there were tensions between

the London headquarters and ANZ's local management, who ran the company. While ownership remained almost entirely British, the headquarters was moved to Australia in 1977. ANZ developed into one of the six groups that came to control British overseas banking, and others aimed to link their international operations with a City of London fast re-emerging as a leading centre of global finance (Jones, 1993).

Lloyds Bank International bought minority holdings in California and New Zealand, and National Westminister consolidated its French and Belgian branches into International Westminister Bank, which expanded in the 1970s across various locations, including the USA and Germany. Barclays amalgamated its various interests abroad in 1971, establishing Barclays Bank International, the only British overseas bank entirely owned by a parent firm. Despite entering markets in Canada, New York and California, it focused on developing countries and diversified into merchant banking and corporate finance (Jones, 1990).

French banks maintained the largest foreign branch network after London, and Paris was the world's third most important host – after London and New York – with 32 foreign branches and 41 representative offices. While most of France's financial sector came under government control, the Banque de Paris et des Pays-Bas (Paribas) and the *haute banque* were exceptions, since their main interests were overseas rather than domestic. The Banque Nationale pour le Commerce et l'Industrie (BNCI) in 1947 separated from its London branch so that it could form a partnership with local companies S. G. Warburg and Robert Benson. By the 1950s, BNCI could claim to own branches in London, as well as in France's dependencies and former colonies, and in developing countries where historically it had been active. It joined with Comptoir National d'Escompte de Paris to create Banque Nationale de Paris (BNP) in 1966, and took control of its London branch. Alongside its expanding activities in developing countries, BNP went to Tokyo in 1972, and by 1977 it had a presence in San Francisco, Chicago, Los Angeles, Newport Beach, Vancouver, Moscow, Düsseldorf, Stockholm and Amsterdam. It began a joint venture with Inchcape – called Compex – in which BNP gained contact with Inchcape's 450 subsidiaries and affiliates, and Inchcape likewise won a connection with BNP's branches in 65 countries.[134]

Crédit Lyonnais, in 1963, had 85 directly owned foreign branches and 113 others it owned through subsidiaries and associated banks. By

1972, it had entered Tokyo, Singapore, Sydney and New York, as well as several countries in Latin America, and it was the first western bank to set up business in the USSR, in Moscow.[135] The Allies, in 1948, had broken up Deutsche Bank into ten regional firms and stripped it of its worldwide holdings. These ten came together in 1952 to form three – Norddeutsche Bank, Rheinisch-Westfälische Bank and Suddeutsche Bank – and these three in turn merged in 1957 to resurrect Deutsche Bank. The strategist behind the reorganization, Herman J. Abs, was a key figure in West Germany's financial recovery, and Deutsche Bank started to re-create itself internationally in 1952. Dresdner Bank could quote 17 overseas branches by 1967, ahead of Deutsche with 11, and Commerzbank with 8. The big three German banks tended to favour complex cooperative ventures, with Luxembourg as a favoured location, but disappointing results encouraged the founding of directly owned subsidiaries. They had, by 1980, 74 overseas branches or subsidiaries, 64 representative offices and 26 investments.[136]

Not every Swedish multinational depended on their expertise in machinery and engineering products. Skandinaviska Enskilda Banken (ESB) founded FinansSkandic (UK) in London, to offer a full banking service to Swedish and international corporate clients. It also joined Bergen Bank, from Norway, and Union Bank, from Finland, in the Scandinavian Bank consortium, likewise based in the financial hub of London. These three and Privatbanken, from Denmark, formed Scandinavian Banking Partners to facilitate money transfers and cash management services in their own countries. ESB, incorporated in 1972, next founded or participated in subsidiary operations in Frankfurt, Luxembourg and Singapore, between 1976 and 1979.[137]

The country's largest bank, Svenska Handelsbanken – responding to the fact that international Swedish companies had to use the services of its foreign rivals – also went overseas by joining a consortium, made up of Danish, Norwegian and Finnish firms, which had a presence in London and Paris from 1970. It soon owned representative offices in Moscow (by 1974, as trade with the Soviet Union grew), in New York (in 1975, but dealing with trade transactions only), and in the lightly regulated tax haven of Luxembourg (by 1978).[138] The Swiss Bank Corporation, already international before the Second World War, organized representative offices worldwide after 1958, including Luxembourg and the Cayman Islands, mostly to serve Swiss multinationals.[139] The Union Bank of Switzerland was more inclined to carry out international deals at home, despite having representation in New York, and founding a London branch in 1967, but it did develop a securities business in the world's two biggest financial centres by the late 1970s.[140]

Despite unpromising conditions, and national restrictions on their activities, international bankers proved themselves inventive. One unanticipated consequence of governments regulating financial markets was the emergence of the Eurodollar. There was an abundance of dollars in international markets: the demand was stoked by low interest rates in the USA; by transfers to American multinational subsidiaries and military personnel in Europe; by US Federal domestic banking regulations that made it difficult for foreign firms to access dollars at their source; and by, in the 1970s, the growing power of the Organization of the Petroleum Exporting Countries (OPEC) and the volume of petrodollar transactions. Eastern Europe's Communist states were particularly unwilling to keep the dollars they held in the USA, and London dealers saw an opportunity to attract firms interested in dealing in non-sterling currencies. Compared to Paris or Frankfurt, market entry to London was easy and liquidity conditions were light.

While the City no longer supplied the world's capital, pre-eminence having shifted to New York, it was able to re-emerge as a global location for financial services. Launched in 1955, and growing rapidly after 1958, the Eurodollar market was not regulated by host governments, and it was unaffected by domestic cartel arrangements. Loan rates, it followed, were attractive. Eurobonds were for the same reasons a largely unregulated capital market. The London investment house Samuel Montagu issued the first Eurobond in 1963, on behalf of the Belgian government; Warburg was the second example of a Eurobond issuer, when it acted for Autostrade Italiane, still owned by the state holding company Istituto per la Ricostruzione Industriale (IRI), founded before the war by Mussolini. The Eurodollar brought Deutsche Bank back to London in 1976, having left as long ago as the First World War, and 328 foreign banks were doing business in London by 1979. French banks went into Eurocurrency dealings, and Lyonnais did so with Commerzbank, Banco di Roma and Banco Hispano. Tokyo, Singapore, Hong Kong, and offshore tax havens such as the Cayman Islands and Panama took their share of dollar transactions, and US banks responded to the lure of profits by establishing themselves in London and elsewhere (Cassis, 2006). The Eurodollar, having re-initiated a period of international capital movements, hinted at a future era of banking globalization and economic financialization. It encouraged, in addition, those with a talent for circumventing regulations, and seemingly (if ultimately fallaciously) supported the irrelevance of state regulation to long-term, stable financial services.

In order to protect the interests of policyholders, governments required insurance companies to hold reserves locally. From the perspective of the companies, these rules tied up capital and removed much of the gain from pooling and transferring funds across borders. Frequently, these solvency rules for foreign enterprises were tougher, and cartel agreements formed another competitive constraint, the markets in France, Germany and Japan being especially difficult for multinational entrants. In general, the regulatory barriers against the life sector were greater than the non-life business (Yoffie, 1993; Michie, 1992).

American International Underwriters, or AIU, re-entered Germany and Japan by selling insurance to US troops stationed there, and, in the post-war period, with local firms facing financial difficulties, it emerged as a Europe-wide dealer. The expansion of US businesses abroad – making in effect a 'home-foreign' market – gave the insurer further incentive. It founded holding companies in tax-friendly Bermuda to coordinate its diverse overseas life and non-life agencies, and by the end of the 1950s AIU could be found in 75 countries, despite each having its own regulations and characteristics. Its international holding company in life insurance, American International Reinsurance Co. Inc. (AIRCO), formed the American International Group (AIG) subsidiary in 1967. AIG became the vehicle for acquiring and coordinating the existing network of domestic and overseas companies, a process largely completed by 1970. AIU diversified further, selling for foreign companies in the USA, insuring oil and gas installations, or supplying risk management and pension fund services, and then consolidated these into four divisions. To simplify and tighten the group's managerial structure after a long period of continuous growth and eleven years of corporate reorganization, AIG absorbed its own parent in 1978.[141]

Several US insurers went north to Canada: Provident Life and Accident Insurance Company of America (in 1948), having found, as a business from Tennessee, regulations and registration in New York state more problematic to navigate;[142] Aetna Life and Casualty (1960),[143] John Hancock Mutual Life Insurance (1969),[144] and Mutual Life Insurance Company of New York (1971) [145] were further instances. The Combined International Corporation (later to be called Aon) also went to Canada and the other English-speaking markets of Britain, Australia and New Zealand in the 1960s. It tailored its products for differing countries, by, for example, focusing on income cover if (unlike the USA) governments already met the cost of medical expenses. Having gained international experience, it went to Germany and France in 1977.[146] The American Family Corporation took a bold initiative, in 1974, when it registered for business with Japan's Ministry of Finance. It succeeded by supplying unmet needs, such as cancer cover, and by managing the employee benefit plans of large corporations. It was clear about employing experienced or retired Japanese executives with vital personal networks and knowledge of the local industry, and their activities would generate two thirds of AFC's revenues.[147]

Combined International Corporation established itself in Japan in 1980. Continental Corporation preferred, between 1973 and 1976, to develop overseas revenues through minority holdings in established companies (in France, Germany and Latin America).[148] Marsh and McLennan Companies (MMC) did likewise from 1973 onwards (in France, Germany and Belgium), but its determination to join the Lloyds of London insurance market, by buying brokers C. T. Bowring in 1980, ended with a pyrrhic victory. When Bowring's management rejected its bid, MMC approached the broker's shareholders. It faced down British parliamentary opposition and public questioning over why the USA protected its insurance industry (restrictions had been placed on foreign firms in 1940). MMC got its prize, but much of the Bowring management, with their essential commercial contacts and knowledge, left.[149] Joint ventures, sharing the risks in developing or difficult markets, were another international strategy: the USA's Continental Insurance and British Royal Insurance combined in Iran, and, in 1973, Chubb & Son and First National City Corporation bought Companhia de Seguros Argos Fluminense in Brazil.[150]

Italian insurers had been early pioneers of international insurance. But the 1947 Peace Treaty between Italy and the victorious powers turned their property in Hungary, Romania and Bulgaria into compensation for the Soviet Union. The asset seizure significantly affected Assicurazioni Generali and Riunione Adriatica di Sicurtà (RAS). Throughout Eastern Europe, by 1948 the Communist parties that came to power nationalized foreign assets; Italian companies permanently lost, in addition, their smaller operations in the former colonies of Libya and Ethiopia. In total, fourteen subsidiaries were taken from Assicurazioni Generali which, still thinking ambitiously along the lines of international expansion, under Gino Baroncini's leadership, looked instead to Latin America. It bought control of Providencia in Argentina, and began trading in Brazil, Guatemala, Venezuela, Ecuador and Colombia. It resumed, in parallel, in Greece and the Middle East, and acquired South Africa's Standard General Insurance. In 1950, it took over Buffalo Insurance, and consequently gained a licence to trade in the USA. Through ownership of La Concorde and Erste Allgemeine, Assicurazioni Generale developed into the biggest foreign insurer in France and Austria. It forged a strategic alliance with Aetna, using differing strengths to grow business overseas. It began a process of rationalization during the 1970s, creating Generali France, Generali Belgium and Generali Lebensversicherung as local companies, in order to be compliant with local laws and regulations on the insurance sector.

The post-war division of Europe deprived RAS of one third of its former revenues: Czechoslovakia had once been its most important market outside Italy. The fall-out from the war created debate, too, over the future of Trieste – confirmed as part of Italy in 1954 – and so the firm moved its headquarters to Milan. It added Australian and Swiss subsidiaries to its international operations in 1960.[151] Allianz, like other German companies, found itself part of a diminished domestic market in 1945, and the Berlin Blockade of 1948 convinced it to transfer its headquarters to Munich and its life business to Stuttgart. With wealth and stability returning to Germany, it focused on its home economy, where its name became singularly identified amongst consumers with the insurance industry.[152]

Swiss firms too in the post-war period had to rebuild their international businesses. Winterthur Schweizerische Versicherungs-Gesellschaft bought, in 1950, the American Casualty Company, and transferred its existing clients in the USA to its new subsidiary (although it later sold the company on). It refounded a network of branches in Western Europe and made acquisitions in property and life insurance in Portugal, Belgium and Austria between 1958 and 1966. Schweizerische Ruckversicherungs-Gesellschaft (the Swiss Reinsurance Company, or, more commonly Swiss Re) abandoned its arrangements with a London associate in 1968, setting up its own company in its place, and it refounded Neue Holding as Schweizer Rück Holding AG as a means of expanding its business in Germany, taking the chance to impose a tighter international management structure.[153] Zurich Versicherungs-Gesellschaft – international since the nineteenth century – moved back to Germany, in 1969, through acquisition.[154]

The Netherlands Insurance Company – although already present in Belgium since before the war – sought to grow through acquisition, specifically buying up Australia's Associated National Insurance (1954), Canada's oldest insurer in the form of The Halifax (1956), and Commercial Life Insurance, also in Canada (1959). Indonesia, independent from 1949, nationalized all enterprises from the former imperial power, but Netherlands Insurance was able to return in 1972. The company merged with the Nationale Life Insurance Bank in 1963, creating Nationale-Nederlanden, which then bought businesses in England (1963), Norway (1964), Scotland (1968) and the USA (1979).[155] In France, the government nationalized thirty-four insurance firms in April 1946 and raised the barrier against inward FDI in the sector. Overseas, La Sequanaise gave up its Saigon office during 1952, as the conflict against France's continued colonization of Vietnam intensified, and President Gamal Abdel Nasser nationalized Egypt's insurance industry and the company's assets in 1956, along with the Suez Canal. L'Urbaine-Incendie was generating premiums in 64 countries by 1961, although its withdrawal from Algeria, which gained independence in 1962, was yet another confirmation of its enforced post-war exit from North Africa. It re-formed as Union des Assurances de Paris in 1968, intent on building a business in Francophone Africa, but it also acquired Commerce Group, in Canada, during 1977. Groupe Ancienne Mutuelle – the future AXA – was mostly domestically focused, but did, in 1955, enter the Francophone market of Quebec (Ruffat, Caloni and Laguerre, 1990).[156]

Post-war austerity in Britain, combined with cartel-like arrangements, left few growth opportunities for domestic insurance. Already a multinational, in 1959 Commercial Union bought the North British and Mercantile Insurance Company, chiefly for its assets in the USA; during the 1970s, it added Les Provinces Reunies in Belgium, and

Delta Lloyd in the Netherlands. Legal and General resumed international sales, after the war, in its established Dominion markets of
Australia, Canada and South Africa, and, from 1972, it adopted a
strategy of cooperative agreements with entrenched players in Europe
and Japan.[157] Prudential bought local insurers in Belgium during 1972,
and in Canada six years later.[158] Royal Insurance, which had extensive US sales, was amongst the few foreign companies, in 1975, to
receive an insurance licence from the Japanese government.[159] Since
the British insurance industry received half of its premiums from overseas – largely from fire, accident and maritime policies – it could
make the justified claim to be highly internationalized and a major
contributor to the country's depleting balance of payments (Cassis,
2006).

Japan was, by 1965, the world's fourth-largest insurance market,
after the USA, Britain and Canada, and the Ministry of Finance strictly
controlled competition and limited firms to particular products. The
large Japanese insurers generally re-joined the business groups broken
up by the US occupying administration, and re-formed as a network
of companies run by professional managers. Japan's marine and fire
companies, as another outcome of the war, had lost their offices and
business overseas. Yasuda Fire and Marine Insurance Company – a
wartime consolidation by government to help finance the conflict overseas – was again operating in foreign markets as early as 1949, making breakthroughs in Brazil (in 1959) and New York (1962), before
its overseas agencies multiplied in the 1970s.[160] Taisho Marine and
Fire Insurance Company (later, Mitsui Marine and Fire) responded, in
1955, to the striking growth of the Japanese merchant fleet by resuming
its international agency operations; having taken up auto insurance,
it invested in firms in Australia, New Zealand and South East Asia
during the 1960s.[161] The Tokio Marine and Fire Insurance Company
(a Mitsubishi group member) renewed direct underwriting in Britain
and the USA in 1956, and, affiliated with the Continental Insurance
Company, it expanded to a total of nineteen countries during 1964–75.
From 1971, the company was offering group benefit plans to Japanese
companies overseas, and taking minority stakes in a Brazilian general
insurer and a US life company.[162] Sumitomo Marine and Life Insurance Company, which forged a reciprocal agreement with Chubb &
Son in 1971, gaining a New York licence, built a worldwide agency
network.[163]

Service multinationals

International retailing was not as far developed as the manufacturing sector: restrictive trading practices, local planning restrictions and the distinctiveness of national markets all complicated the possibilities for expansion overseas. But some companies continued to make break-throughs (Godley, 2003). After the Second World War, Sears founded stores in Havana and Mexico City, and formed the Simpsons-Sears Ltd joint venture with the Hudson's Bay Company, in Canada, in 1952. The US retail giant acquired, also, assets in Franco's Spain, an undeveloped and troubled investment market (Hollander, 1970; Truitt, 1984).[164] Hudson's Bay, historically registered in London but with assets in Canada, and therefore technically a multinational, nat-uralized in 1970, when it moved its headquarters to Winnipeg.[165] As the world's largest and richest consumer market, US retailers pio-neered developments in chain stores and supermarkets, and Safeway embarked on a strategy of international acquisition, hoping to max-imize lessons from growth in its home market. It arrived in Britain, Australia and Germany (during 1962–3), and looked two decades later to Mexico and Saudi Arabia (Wilkins, 1974).[166] Woolworths created a remarkable success in Britain by 1970, by which time it owned over a thousand shops (Godley, 2003). Established in 1943 in Sweden, IKEA began with mail-order selling, but by 1958 it had developed its busi-ness model of low-price, designer-led flat-pack furniture to be bought at a giant store. It first crossed a border, in 1963, to Norway, followed by Denmark in 1969. It therefore began as a multinational by moving into geographically nearby markets, with which it was most familiar, The founder, Ingvar Kamprad, transferred the company headquarters to Copenhagen in 1973, as a more central location for Europe, and IKEA had founded stores in Germany, Switzerland, Austria, Australia, Canada, the Netherlands and Singapore by 1979.[167]

The French-owned Carrefour likewise developed a distinctive retail concept at home – opening, during 1963, its first out-of-town hyper-market offering one-stop convenience, huge variety and fresh produce, in the Paris suburb of Sainte-Geneviève-des-Bois – and it used joint ventures with local companies to facilitate and finance its internation-alization. It began in the neighbouring market of Belgium in 1969 (with Delhaize Frères-Le-Lion), going next to Switzerland (in partner-ship with Mercure), Britain (Wheatsheaf Investment), Italy (Italware) and Europe's other Mediterranean countries. When a law in France, in 1970, put the brakes on large store developments, it pushed Carrefour into seeking growth opportunities elsewhere. One specific gain from the joint venture strategy was to ensure that its overseas stores won over new clients with the marketing of fresh local foods, and it avoided exporting produce from France. Over time, and as it gained in knowledge and experience, Carrefour acquired full ownership and control of its international stores, and, in 1975 it opened its first hypermarkets in Brazil and Latin America.[168] The Netherlands clothing retailer C & A, Brenninkmeyer, or simply C&A, opened a Brooklyn outlet as early as 1948, and leapt in size in 1962 when it acquired Manhattan's well-known department store Ohrbach's, which had branches in Long Island, New Jersey and California.[169] Koninklijke Ahold, owners of the leading Netherlands supermarket chain, Albert Heijn, launched in the USA, in 1977, through a mix of acquisitions and joint ventures, and soon diversified with restaurants in Belgium and at home, and with holiday parks in West Germany.[170]

US hotel chains grew by standardizing price, accommodation and customer experience, and sought to transfer their commercial formula to foreign markets. Sheraton Hotels, for example, bought two Canadian chains, the Laurentian Hotel Company and Eppley, in 1949 (before itself being acquired by ITT in 1968),[171] and, along with rivals Holiday Inn, Inter-Continental and Hilton, it emerged worldwide. They frequently employed franchising, which shared the financing, but they had to hone the technique of writing and monitoring service contracts that successfully protected their brand name, business model and reputation. Increasing travel and tourism by US citizens was an initial spur, and Inter-Continental had a promotional link with Pan Am,[172] just as Hilton signed an agreement with TWA, although, in 1967, TWA ended up acquiring Hilton International.[173]

US restaurant chains showed a similar impulse to internationalize through franchising: the hamburger chain business McDonald's began overseas in 1967, funding joint ventures and licensing its name to local contractors, including, in 1971, its entry into the newly rich market of Japan.[174] J. Lyons, the owner of Britain's well-known tea rooms, on the other hand, perceived the potential of fast-food chains and bought its business model. It took up the rights to Wimpey Bar's international franchise, founded on the US original, in 1954. It established a global burger chain over twenty-three countries – including Europe, Australia,

South Africa, Thailand, Congo and Hong Kong – by 1970 (Hollander, 1970).

Within the leisure sector, there was a social revolution founded on rising living standards and mass international tourism. Gerard Blitz, a Belgian diamond cutter, and Gilbert Trigano founded Club Méditerranée in 1950, when they brought members of a holiday club to Majorca, where they were offered the chance to help with cleaning and cooking, and stayed under US Army surplus tents. Its holidays had the distinctive appeal of low cost and communal spirit, and its advertising sold images of sun-drenched hedonistic singles. It extended to Italy and Greece, and diversified into skiing in Switzerland. To finance further growth, the Rothschild Group, under Edmond de Rothschild, which already had hotel interests, became the largest shareholder in 1961, and within four years Club Méditerranée had 14 summer villages and 11 winter resorts. The firm had the novel idea of hiring a Soviet ship for holiday cruises, but a crew used to handling cargo did not prove customer-friendly. It did enter the cruise market again, this time more successfully, and from 1968 it was selling holidays in New York for travel to Guadeloupe, and running mountain resorts in North California and Colorado.[175]

There were few government barriers to multinational accounting services, but companies needed local, specialized knowledge of clients, laws and practices. Therefore, before 1939, a few accountancy firms had formed businesses under the same name in both the USA and Britain, but they remained independent and operationally separate. In the post-war period, international federations of accountancy partnerships came into prominence, using a single company name in many different countries. In most cases, these remained a combination of internationally recognizable names and associated local affiliates, since local regulations and established client relationships necessitated flexibility. Price Waterhouse created a separate international business in 1945, and Britain's Deloitte, Plender, Griffiths & Co., together with Haskins & Sells, from the USA, established in 1952 Deloitte Haskins & Sells, in order to facilitate their expansion in Latin America, Africa and Japan.[176] Cooper Brothers (from Britain), Lybrand, Ross Brothers and Montgomery (USA) and McDonald, Currie (Canada) created Coopers & Lybrand in 1957.[177] Then, in 1960, George Touche steered his various interests in Touche, Bailey, Niven & Smart (USA) and Ross (Britain and Canada) to form Touche Ross.

When expanding internationally, accountancy federations preferred to merge with existing local firms, bringing name changes or affiliate status, but they did create completely new businesses whenever necessary. Coopers & Lybrand, by 1975, was present in 73 countries, Price Waterhouse (from the USA) in 76, and Peat Marwick Mitchell (British) in 86. Arthur Anderson had a very particular international strategy: it ended its agreements with local firms in the 1950s, and then founded practices under its own name that promoted and emphasized the quality of its services.[178] Of the big eight 'world' accounting firms that emerged in the post-war period, only Arthur Young had fewer than 50 per cent of its partners working under its common name, and Arthur Anderson by contrast would reach the figure of 98 per cent of partners working under its common name (by 1982). Yet, because legislation in France protected the independence and name of local accountants, Arthur Anderson needed an association with Guy Barbier (retained until 1983) (Canderwick, 1989). While the American firm was unusually highly centralized, Touche Ross with its eclectic mix of merged firms – some utilizing its international name, others requiring a variation – and alliances with local partnerships was more typical. The large international accountants were predominantly Anglo-American. On the other hand, Klynveld Main Goerdler (KMG), founded in 1979, was an amalgamation of leading national firms in nine countries in North America, Australia and Europe. In forming the largest federated grouping, it did not adopt the world firm organization common amongst the big eight.[179]

Management consultants McKinsey opened its London operation in 1959 and had 17 offices in four continents by 1971.[180] This agency was especially identified with evangelizing US organizational best practice to European companies. As we have seen, to cope with the demands of mass production and marketing, American large-scale enterprises had built teams of professional managers, formed a strategic headquarters, and divided operational control amongst semi-autonomous divisions. This multidivisional structure, or M-form, spread quickly in Europe during the 1960s, although changing organizational structures became arguably an unquestioned obsession of corporate managements, with little impact on the realities of better products or marketing. Booz Allen Hamilton and accountants Touche Ross had founded management consultancies in Britain by 1960, and the Boston Consulting Group had offices in Britain, France, Germany and Japan by the end of the following decade (Jones, 2005). These management consultancies could offer and transfer across borders what they described as the 'best practice' management techniques, and they built an international reputation and name. They formed, nonetheless, a grouping of operationally separate national firms, which could meet the specific requirements of local clients (Aharoni, 1993).

When American businesses went overseas, their advertising agencies often followed; whenever a US multinational chose one agency for all their foreign operations, the advertiser internationalized rapidly. With their leading capabilities in market research and consumer psychology, plus experience of the world's biggest and richest consumer market, US advertising agencies were able, as a next step, to attract local clients. But, so long as national markets and their consumers differed, they needed to build host country knowledge of markets and promote native talent. By the end of the 1970s, US advertising agencies had offices in every non-Communist country excepting six (West, 1988). The British-born advertising executive David Ogilvy – who in 1948 established his New York firm Hewitt, Ogilvy, Benson & Mather – forged links with London firms Mather & Crowther and S. H. Benson. International cooperation through the personal connections between partners continued until 1964, when all three merged into Ogilvy & Mather.[181]

The engineering and construction business from Sweden Allmanna Svenska Elektriska Aktiebolaget (ASEA) struggled in the post-war years to keep up with the demand for its services. It broke into the US market in 1947, where it carried out large projects for the Tennessee Valley Authority and on the West Coast. After building the trains and infrastructure for Sweden's electric railway system, it had the capabilities to license, by 1975, its technology to General Electric, which had a contract with Amtrak. Swiss competitors Brown Boveri worked on government projects and on engineering and nuclear technologies, also in the Tennessee Valley, before taking up, during the 1970s, some of the large demand for infrastructure and oil projects in the Middle East and Africa.[182]

Capitalism and the Communist bloc

After the Second World War, ideological differences and international rivalries between former allies would create within Europe two separate political and economic spheres. The victory of Communist partisans brought the quick establishment of the Socialist Federal Republic of Yugoslavia, in November 1945, and the Soviet Union, with the help of local allies, exercised full control over the occupied zone of eastern Germany. Elsewhere in Eastern Europe, interim coalition governments assumed formal authority, but they were Communist-dominated. By the end of 1948, with the help of the Soviet Union, these national Communist parties had seized power in Eastern Europe, and they imposed state ownership on major industries within a year. Their objective was to create powerful economies through central planning and the exclusion of private enterprise. Shell, which had lost its Russian operations to the Bolshevik Revolution, suffered losses in Yugoslavia, Czechoslovakia and Hungary, but, more critically, the Romanian regime dissolved Astra Romano, whose oil wells had influenced the war strategies of Germany and the Allies (Sluyterman, Jonker, Howarth and Van Zanden, 2007). For the Soviet Union under Stalin, the desire of US companies to sell goods overseas and to buy up foreign firms was insidious, conceding the advantage of a rival superpower, but the founding of command economies and acts of nationalization choked off that prospect.

Comecon, a grouping of Communist economies set up in 1949, was another device for holding back US economic influence. A sense of shared diplomatic and political interests between the USA, Canada and Western Europe would create in the post-war period a stable and secure arena for trade and FDI, and multinationals, with an increasing surge from the manufacturing sector, adopted market-seeking strategies in these large and wealthy economies. Communism was, in theory, rooted in the principles of internationalism. The Soviet Union, Bulgaria, Romania, Czechoslovakia, Hungary and Poland were the original signatories to Comecon, and Albania and East Germany were soon added. The organization espoused cooperation rather than integration (for fear of copying the capitalist alienation of producers). But Soviet Union dominance cut across the declared principle of 'sovereign equality', and, in practice, the policies of Comecon member states remained for many years almost wholly autarchic. From 1954, following Stalin's death, the Soviet Union acknowledged the need for economic decentralization and for greater emphasis on the production of consumer goods, and its satellites, particularly Hungary and Czechoslovakia, made some progress in implementing reforms.

To make good the ideals of cross-border coordination, Comecon, in 1956, appointed ten standing committees. A number of multinational partnerships were formed after 1959, under the organization's new charter, mostly in the extraction of minerals and other natural resources, in heavy industries such as steel or chemicals, and in transportation. The result of intergovernmental agreements, the partnerships were largely the property of participating states, and government ministries financed and directly ran their activities. By the time of the cross-border ventures being formed, during 1959, other Communist countries had acquired observer status at the organization's meetings. In 1961, Khrushchev openly attacked Stalin's legacy and again called for economic renewal, founded on greater enterprise freedom and incentives. Again, while some East European countries attempted to take up the challenge, Poland and Romania remained hard-line in their commitment to traditional Communist ideology. Similarly, there was some attempt to address the failings of the Comecon ventures, during the 1960s, by allowing greater operational and profit responsibility, and encouraging fuller international integration of these state-owned enterprises. From 1971, under its new leadership of Brezhnev and Kosygin, and with the Cold War entering its period of détente, the Soviet Union began to allow imports that could assist its economic development, and it encouraged the use of Western technologies and methods. But its inefficient and centralized system largely prevented its enterprises from effecting change at home and from achieving the levels of international economic integration that might have acted as a catalyst. China and Albania, which split from the Soviet Union, had left Comecon by 1961, and the independently inclined Yugoslavia had a form of associate membership by 1964. Mongolia, Vietnam and Cuba were to become fully signed up by 1978. Yet this grouping of Communist countries never emulated the scale of capital flows, technology transfers and managerial integration witnessed amongst the capitalist economies of the North Atlantic (Gaddis, 1998).

The Tatabanya Coal Mines, in Hungary, and the Katowice Coal Mines, in Poland, formed a joint stock company called Haldex, which from 1959 sought to exploit an invention for reprocessing slag. Other examples were Interatominstrument (nuclear machinery makers), Intertekstilmash (textile machinery manufacturers) and Intersputnik (created, in 1972, to coordinate satellite communications). In all these cases, the aim was to exploit a technology that had a comparative advantage within the Communist bloc or in the Third World.[183] Comecon founded the International Bank for Economic Cooperation in 1964 and the International Investment Bank in 1970, both of them governed by a council, representing the participating governments. With their shortage of hard currency, trade by the Comecon countries relied substantially on barter, although these arrangements allowed the bloc, in the 1970s, to benefit from the Soviet development of its oilfields and the production of cheap fuel.

The Soviet Union continued to operate four overseas banks and insurance firms – founded in the interwar years – during the most difficult point of the Cold War, and Czechoslovakia, Hungary, Poland and China, too, retained banks in Western Europe. The Moscow Narodny Bank, for example, had branches in Paris, Luxembourg, Singapore and Beirut and, by the 1970s, the Foreign Trade Bank of the USSR controlled 1,520 offices in 100 nations, and the Bulgarian Foreign Trade Bank had over 1,000 branches. Inter-bloc trade brought much-needed foreign currency and technology, and called for Communist banks to be within the centres of financial capitalism, where they forged relations with Western firms and raised syndicated funds. Communist banks were active, too, in Eurodollar markets, because they preferred not to keep their dollar accounts in the USA. Energomashexport, a Soviet business engaged in the manufacture and supply of power engineering equipment, did have joint operations in neutral Finland, which maintained good relations with its powerful neighbour. Otherwise, the enterprise restricted its investments and projects to the Communist bloc or the Third World, working, where necessary, in partnership with pragmatic capitalists Brown Boveri.[184]

The State Union Institute for the Design of Metallurgical Plants (Gipromez), based in Moscow, built the steelworks at Bhilai and Bokaro, and the Soviet Union and Romania assisted with India's largest oil refineries at Barauni, Koyali and Mathura. Skoda, from Czechoslovakia, owned an assembly plant in India, in addition to those in Iran, Mexico and Turkey.[185] Communist countries, by 1962, owned some 50 businesses located in the capitalist world; by 1976, helped by policies of détente, the number had grown to some 700, two thirds of these in developed countries. Such enterprises, however, were mainly representative offices concerned with trade and finance rather than FDI, and had neither the strategic intent nor the organizational capabilities to establish overseas subsidiaries.

The flow of investment from West to East was hardly large in global terms, even if it outmatched that from East to West. Having liberated itself without the direct assistance of the Red Army, unlike the rest of Eastern Europe, Yugoslavia was refounded in June 1945 and proved able to determine its own post-war political and economic settlement. The Communists, led by Josip Broz Tito, had established a one-party state, the Federal People's Republic of Yugoslavia, by November. As an ally of the Soviet Union, it imposed a centralized economy, but in 1948 Tito openly split with Stalin on how Bulgaria and Albania might be included in a greater Yugoslav federation. Deep down, the dispute turned on the Soviet Union's refusal to treat Yugoslavia as an equal and ally, as opposed to a satellite. Fearing intervention, including an invasion, Tito looked to the West for economic assistance, which began to flow over the course of the next year. From this point, Yugoslavia began to diverge from the Soviet system: it declared the aims of market socialism, in June 1950, founded on worker self-management and on the decentralization of political powers to the constituent republics. The new arrangements – with the backing of Western aid – brought fast and continuous rates of economic growth.

The government armaments factory at Kragujevac had, for a brief period before the Second World War, assembled Chevrolet trucks, and, in a vote conducted in 1953, the plant workers at the Zavodi Crvena Zastava (Red Flag Institutes) voted to make automobiles again. To enable the switch to mass production and to raise product quality, the enterprise signed a deal to assemble Fiat cars, in 1954, under its own name. Zastava was exporting to Poland by 1965, and, some three years later, Fiat was in charge of its capacity expansion from 85,000 units per year to 130,000. When it first appeared, in 1962, the Zastava 750 (a version of the Fiat 600) relied on imported components; by 1969, the Fića, or little Fiat, as it was fondly called, used only domestically produced parts.[186] By 1963, as we have seen, Citroën also set up an assembly plant in Yugoslavia with Tomos to produce its 2CV (Gallard, 2004). Yugoslavia was a loose brick in the East–West divide, and both power blocs vied for influence. With the support of presidents Sukarno (from Indonesia), Nasser (Egypt) and Nkrumah (Ghana), and prime minister Nehru (India), Tito had been the architect of the Heads of State or Government of Non-Aligned Countries, later called the Non-Aligned Movement, which convened for the first time in Belgrade in 1961. The organization advocated a middle way between the Western and Communist blocs and supported the New International Economic Order proposals, made at the United Nations from 1974, to restructure the trade and investment balance between developed and developing nations, and to assert the control of sovereign nation states on multinational corporations (Gaddis, 1998).

The Soviet auto industry, in 1949, produced some 211,000 cars, and so had exceeded the level achieved before the war, but the wartime production miracles were not continued into peacetime. In 1958, the year before he boasted to Vice-President Nixon about the achievements of Communism, President Khrushchev criticized Moscow's Likhachev Automobile Factory for manufacturing the same number of trucks in 1958 as fourteen years before. There was recognition, too, that the whole industry had fallen behind in technology, the quality of components, and scale economies. When a group of greyer apparatchiks replaced the increasingly erratic Khrushchev, in October 1964, they set about stabilizing the position at home and abroad, by encouraging higher economic performance and meeting the consumer demand for goods. In that year, the historic deal struck by Exportkhleb, the Soviet Union's grain purchasing agency, to buy supplies from the USA and the world market was a highly visible acknowledgement that the Soviet Union's collective agrarian system was failing. The USA agreed to the deal, seeking to improve diplomatic relations, and easing trade restrictions. Exportkhleb, a symbol of Soviet planning, signed lucrative contracts with the capitalist trading firms Continental Grain and Cargill, and Hungary, too, began to import food produce. The transaction resonated with historical irony: Continental Grain could trace its origins to the First World War as a major exporter of grain from Imperial Russia, then Europe's breadbasket; it only transferred its headquarters from Belgium to the USA during the Second World War.[187]

Premier Alexei Kosygin was soon reiterating past criticism of vehicle manufacturing in the Soviet Union, and to build and develop the Volga Automobile Plant (AutoVAZ) the Soviet Union needed the assistance of Western multinationals (Holliday, 1979). Experienced in building turnkey plants overseas, Fiat was a very obvious choice. The objective was to establish a car factory on the banks of the Volga and to develop a city around this factory. The leader of the Italian Communist Party, the pro-Kremlin Palmiro Togliatti, had died on holiday in 1964 in Yalta, where he was also reportedly supporting the election of Leonid Brezhnev as General Secretary of the Soviet Communist Party and as

President of the USSR. He was, in tandem with his lobbying for Brezhnev, pivotal in securing the deal for Fiat, and Stavropol-on-Volga, where AutoVaz would be built, was renamed, in his honour, Tolyatti, a near enough approximation of his name in Russian. The agreement was signed in 1966, and the AutoVaz gained fame for making the USSR's people's car, the Lada, which appeared in 1970, its production employing some 110,000 people. Although originally made for Eastern bloc consumers, exports began in 1974, and the cheap, no-frills vehicle won over consumers in Western Europe and Canada. Exceptions included the USA, where trade bans were in force, and Italy itself, where Lada's Fiat copies could not compete directly with the originals. The Italians met extensive difficulties working within the Soviet system, over differing management styles and working practices, and over the interpretation of contracts and product licensing agreements. Its experience made investors reluctant to take on the Kama Truck Plant (KamAZ), built between 1969 and 1976, in Naberezhnye Chelny, Tatarstan, although there were support deals with firms such as Renault (Estapé-Triay, 1999; Tortella, 2000; Harrison, 1978).[188]

Poland's Communist government, in 1951, had founded the prosaically named Fabryka Samochodów Osobowych (FSO) – it means Factory for Passenger Automobiles – in Warsaw, on the banks of the Vistula, and at first it made Soviet cars under licence. Although hardliners retook control of policy, the government sought to quicken the pace of industrialization with Western help, as Poland was one of the least developed countries of the Eastern bloc. FSO, in 1965, signed a deal to make the Polski Fiat 125p, production beginning within two years (and the licensing agreement lasting until 1982) (Estapé-Triay, 1999; Tortella, 2000; Harrison, 1978).[189] With the support of Khrushchev, at this time, Bulgaria had purged most of its Stalinists; it, too, wanted to push its economy from agriculture towards industry. Balkankar, a State Production Cooperative, signed a deal with the Italian multinational to manufacture the Pirin-Fiat cars and to install a factory. Bulgaria's Export Trade Organizations would pay for the services and materials contracted by SPC Balkankar, through the bartering of exports. The deal proved to be brief, lasting only four years from 1967 to 1971. Poland and Fiat repeated the FSO experiment, with Fabryka Samochodów Małolitrażowych (FSM), based in Bielsko-Biala and Tychy, during 1973, making the Fiat 126p (the multinational later acquired the business, in 1991) (Estapé-Triay, 1999; Tortella, 2000; Harrison, 1978).[190]

When the Warsaw Pact approached the USA to hold a summit, in 1971, President Richard Nixon perceived the offer as an historic opportunity, which ended with limitations on nuclear and biological weapons, in 1972, and the founding of the Conference on Security and Cooperation in Europe, in 1975, as a forum for discussing political, economic and human rights issues. The Soviet Union's wheat crop failed in 1972, and state-owned farming could not produce enough animal feed to satisfy a growing demand for meat. Companies such as Continental Grain and Cargill, in 1972, entered into bigger and more profitable deals than those of seven years before. Collectivization would turn the two largest farming nations – the Soviet Union and China – into net importers of grain. Demands from the Soviet Union put an upward pressure on world grain prices, and led to claims that the traders were manipulating the market, dubbed the 'Great Grain Robbery'. International détente enabled the possibility of inward investment and technology transfer.[191]

PUK exploited its capabilities in metals, chemicals and pharmaceuticals with technical assistance contracts in the Third World and Yugoslavia, and added the Soviet Union to its overseas operations.[192] Yet, within the Soviet bloc, the benefits from international business did not easily materialize. The Ursus tractor factory in Poland, for example, could not utilize the technology it licensed from Massey Ferguson. Most Comecon countries found themselves indebted to the West, and capital flows fell as the spirit of détente faded and worldwide recession began in 1979. Multinationals had in any case remained cautious about investment across the Iron Curtain. Dow Chemicals, IBM, ITT, AEG Telefunken, ICI and Creusot-Loire were amongst the list of companies operating in the Soviet Union, with local partners, by 1980, yet the total inward FDI amounted only to some \$1bn (Wilcyznski, 1976; Holliday, 1979). The invasion of Afghanistan by Soviet troops, in late 1979, ended the détente period, and the West reacted by imposing a trade embargo.

Sovereignty versus property

There had been few instances of the forced nationalization of foreign enterprises before 1945: combatants had sequestrated enemy property during the First and Second World Wars; the Bolshevik Revolution of 1917 led to the end of private enterprise; after disputes about concession terms, royalties, or profit share, Bolivia, in 1937, and Mexico, in 1938, took control of their oil industries; Argentina expropriated nearly 40 per cent of American & Foreign Power's subsidiaries during 1943–5; and, in 1946, the Canadian-owned Mexican Tramways entered public ownership. Under the peace treaties, the defeated powers of Germany, Italy and Japan relinquished their overseas assets as war reparations. In the immediate post-war decades, however, forced divestments were relatively few and, on the whole, ultimately settled by agreement. Under the presidency of Juan Perón, elected in 1946 and committed to the cause of national economic independence, Argentina paid generously for the remaining British-owned railways. British companies resolved any disputes with India, Pakistan and Burma after 1947, and later with Malaysia. The Netherlands, similarly, came to terms with nationalizations in Indonesia from 1957 onwards.

Petrobras, in Brazil, controlled the country's oil assets, but continued to work with foreign multinationals to effect exploration, production and export. ITT, Rio Tinto and Ford felt that operational difficulties and discriminatory policies had effectively forced them out of Fascist Spain by 1954, although terms, however grudgingly accepted, were agreed. As the Soviet Union tightened its control of Eastern Europe, in 1947–8, it supplied one exception to this general pattern of post-war multinational and host-government agreement. China provided another. So, British-American Tobacco, by agreement with Chiang Kai-shek's Nationalist government, re-entered China, only to be wrong-footed by the victory of Mao Zedong's Communists in 1949. In return for its managerial personnel being released, in 1953, BAT signed over its assets to the new Chinese government, which began to sequestrate all private businesses.[193] Traders and investors Jardine Fleming and Butterfield and Swire also lost heavily in the new People's Republic (Encarnation, 1989; Fritsch and Franco, 1991).[194]

In the Cold War era, as illustrated by the cases of the Anglo-Iranian Oil Corporation and of United Fruit in Guatemala, during 1951 to 1954, Western governments and their multinationals showed themselves able and willing to protect the ownership and operations of overseas subsidiaries, through embargoes and covert interference in the politics of host countries. The motives of intervening governments were more geopolitical than economic, and the Suez Crisis, beginning with the nationalization of a vital waterway, marked a turning point, with host governments exercising the advantage of sovereignty over investors (Piquet, 2004). Events in Guinea, during 1959, and in Cuba, during 1960–1, seemed confirmation of changing realities (Safarian, 1993). In 1962, at the United Nations, the USA and the Soviet Union engaged in a diplomatic tussle over the principles of 'prompt, adequate and effective compensation' for nationalized property or 'the inalienable right of people and nations to the unobstructed execution of nationalization and expropriation'. The UN's General Assembly did adopt a resolution on the Permanent Sovereignty over Natural Resources, which called for appropriate compensation in accordance with the national state and international law, but recognized the principle of full state sovereignty, even if agreements freely entered into should be observed.

The Soviet Union – with so little outward FDI and wanting to discourage outside interference in its internal affairs – argued for the inalienable rights of nation states; the United States, while it was uneasy over the vagueness of the word 'appropriate' for compensation terms, had at this juncture few examples of appropriation. Mostly as a reaction to the Cuban Revolution and to the acquisition of ITT in Brazil, the US Congress passed the Hickenlooper Amendment, demanding the withdrawal of aid from countries nationalizing US companies without giving compensation within six months. Yet the provision was hardly ever used, and the State Department opposed its automatic use, preferring to apply it pragmatically and to secure room for negotiations with host governments (Sigmund, 1980). Legislation, in 1964, allowed claimants to seek compensation in US courts for expropriations overseas, although, whenever reasons of state intruded, the President could exercise a blocking waiver.

The Suez Canal crisis had shown how gunboats could not guarantee the return of sequestrated property. As the pace of nationalizations and host government interference in multinational subsidiaries quickened, investing countries and companies increasing accepted the principle of national sovereignty over ownership, while arguing for the principle of proper compensation. Beginning with Iraq's acquisition of mineral rights in 1961, oil-producing countries over the next decade or so took control away from the majors, a trend that culminated in Saudi Arabia's nationalization of the Arabian American Oil Company (Aramco), in 1976 (Wilkins, 1974; Safarian, 1993). Burma completed the removal of assets owned by firms from the old colonial power by 1963; Indonesia had done so by 1965 (Vickers, 2005). In 1966, the Republic of Congo (the future Zaïre) nationalized mining; Zambia followed in 1969 (Shillington, 2005). Peru began a policy of state ownership in 1968, and completed its policy by 1975 (Williamson, 1992). Some twenty countries signed up in 1966 to the International Centre for Settlement of Investment Disputes, under the auspices of the World Bank, with membership numbers reaching sixty within three years. In addition to the Court of Arbitration at the International Chamber of Commerce, it provided another forum for settling international investment cases. The aim was to establish a framework for settling disputes, rather than outcomes being decided case by case.

Chile acquired control of its copper mines from US multinationals, from 1969 to 1971, and, despite resentment over the terms, it was able to agree compensation. Cold War calculations, and the nationalization of telecommunications, and therefore ITT assets, induced covert action by the USA against the Allende government, and a military junta seized power in Chile in 1973 (Williamson, 1992; Wilkins, 1974; Sampson, 1973; Schoenberg, 1985). Mining and oil nationalizations were almost complete by 1976, as were a significant number in utilities. With the backing of the Communist bloc, capital-importing economies at the United Nations had, in 1972, won a motion declaring that the nationalization of foreign assets was an expression of political sovereignty. The US President, Richard Nixon, condemned the seizure of US assets as an unfair act against shareholders, and argued that such actions were in the long term self-defeating for developing countries. The Gonzalez Amendment, passed by the US Congress, declared that it would halt all World Bank and other international loans to offending nations, and legislation in 1974 allowed the imposing of sanctions. A vote, proposed by the developed economies, at the United Nations, to confirm the right of compensation for foreign investors was defeated (Sigmund, 1980).

The 1974 Trade Act empowered the imposition of sanctions on any state seizing US overseas assets. The State Department had identified 106 disputes with US multinationals in 39 countries, affecting $3.5bn out of the $25bn total American FDI in Asia, Africa and Latin America, almost all of it in minerals and natural resources. Multinationals, however, showed themselves to be pragmatic, and preferred to find means of cooperating with governments and even nationalizations in order to secure compensation or future business opportunities. Firms such as Rio Tinto Zinc and Kaiser Aluminum followed strategies of seeking state or local partners as a means of offsetting commercial risks,[195] although leading miners additionally switched as far as possible to investments in developed and politically favourable countries such as Australia or Canada, just as oil firms explored Alaska, Canada, or the North Sea (Safarian, 1993; Sigmund, 1980).

Developing countries, through the United Nations Conference on Trade and Development (UNCTAD), fashioned a set of proposals to replace the Bretton Woods system, and the General Assembly of the UN adopted the Declaration for the Establishment of a New International Economic Order (NEIO), in 1974. The agenda addressed how the South could participate in and benefit more from the global economy: stable and remunerative prices for raw materials and commodities, non-reciprocal changes in tariff regimes, unconditional economic and technological assistance, the unhindered right of primary producers to form international associations, freedom to nationalize or expropriate foreign property on favourable terms, and the right of sovereign nations to regulate and control multinational corporations. Some supporters of the NEIO perceived international trade and investment – given the dominance of the North, which had set the terms of the international economic system – as a zero-sum game that benefited the rich at the expense of the poor. To redress the balance, they argued for more state planning and greater limits on free markets. Liberated nations wanted, additionally, to tackle the historical wrongs of colonialism and contemporary concerns about foreign domination, and accordingly explained their slow progress in economic and social development. Defenders of the multinational argued that an international code drawn up by developing economies would be so radical that it would offer investing companies the security of the condemned prisoner (Leff, 1978). The Tokyo round of the General Agreement on Tariffs and Trade (GATT), from 1973 to 1979, witnessed the first major effort to change the global system. Although there were significant customs duty reductions by the world's nine major industrial markets, participants from all sides generally left the conference with more disappointment than a sense of achievement.

The activities of multinationals in the Third World, in decolonized Asia and Africa and in Latin America, frequently jarred with forces of nationalism or radicalism, with development policies founded on state direction or control of major economic assets, or with problems of governance and unstable polities and economies. Many states viewed foreign-owned operations as a challenge to national sovereignty and as a barrier to social justice; multinationals viewed restrictions and expropriations as contrary to free trade principles and international property rights. Unsurprisingly, decolonization brought reactions against former European rulers and their vested commercial interests, although, it is well to recall, some level of compensation was forthcoming. The 'dependency school' argued that investment by multinationals from developed nations was just an alternative means of maintaining dominance over a country, after the era of formal imperialism had been broken (Frank, 1969; Cardoso, 1972).

Small states were especially vulnerable, and a high export dependency on a single or small range of commodities similarly undermined autonomy. An 'interdependence school' contended that states and multinationals needed each other: firms looked for markets and commercial opportunities overseas, but needed security and clear governance structures; states, potentially, gained technology, management skills, investment, infrastructure, employment, exports and world market access (Stopford and Strange, 1991). In the era of the Cold War, Third World countries had in principle a choice of very different international partners and investors. In many cases, as shown by India, they showed a preference for socialist planning in conjunction with a wariness of foreign-owned companies. Clashes between a multinational and the host nation were, therefore, capable of acquiring an ideological edge, and cases, whether Iran, Guatemala, or Suez, grew in prominence once mixed with the geopolitical calculations and rivalries of competing nation states (McKern, 1993). Multinationals posed questions about the advantages of very different economic systems, and about the benefits of open trade and investment. Nor was the Communist or socialist model the only challenger to Western political economy. Japan illustrated a mix of state activism and markets – based on the notion that only government could initiate the process of industrialization and protect industries during their growth stage – and, when South Korea, Taiwan and Singapore in key respects followed this example, they fashioned a distinct Asian or developmental state model. Japan and then South Korea effectively barred inward FDI – to nurture indigenous companies – yet, as they were important Cold War allies, the USA continued to offer access to its technology and its home market.

Post-war Asia and Africa

Once the Second World War had bankrupted European empires, they began their long retreat from Asia and Africa. The government of liberated Burma, in 1948, took control of its forestry away from British trading firms, and later, in 1963, a military government embarked on policies of autarchy and the full nationalization of major industries, transferring the assets of foreign multinationals, including those of Burmah Oil. It is not possible to understand the strength of nationalism and the search for economic autonomy in post-war Burma without reckoning the resentment stoked by multinational investors during colonial rule. There was popular feeling too, not unjustified, that British profits from plantations, oil, mines and industries had not adequately benefited locals, and that much of the employment had been given to migrant labour. Because of the large demand for its products in the Indian subcontinent, and in the hope of protecting its sales there, the Schweppes tonic water company, from Britain, decided to invest in newly independent India.[196] The overall trend, however, was disengagement. Jawaharlal Nehru inherited Mahatma Gandhi's concern for village production and rural betterment, but, as India's first prime minister, from 1947 until his death in office in 1964, he added state-controlled heavy industry, electrification and infrastructure in a series of five-year plans, beginning in 1951. He was instinctively suspicious of inward investment by foreign-owned businesses. From the country's founding, heavier taxation on private firms, exchange controls, rupee devaluation, and discouragement of foreign ownership made overseas companies unwilling to sanction new investments in India. The coal industry was nationalized in 1970, and the 1973 Foreign Exchange Regulation Act (FERA) sought to boost the indigenous ownership of business by penalizing all firms that were 40 per cent or more foreign-controlled. From the date of independence onwards, as their position in a post-colonial country declined British trading companies had sold up to the Indian government and to local enterprises.

Despite operational and regulatory problems in India, Western manufacturers – Fiat, Pilkington, AKU, SKF, AB Atlas, Alcan and International Harvester amongst them – arrived. International Harvester, because of its small share of the Indian market, was willing to concede full ownership of its subsidiary. On the other hand, IBM was a very prominent example of a multinational that did not want to lose control over its subsidiary and its technological knowledge, and decided to exit India, in 1978, as a result of FERA. The Indian economic policy was statist and sympathetic to central planning, and, as a prominent member of the Non-Aligned Movement, it was a theatre for economic rivalry between the West and the Soviet Union. As we have seen, Gipromez, a Soviet agency, built steelworks in India; the Soviet Union and Romania assisted with the country's oil refineries, and Czechoslovakia's Skoda owned an assembly plant (Tomlinson, 1989; Fieldhouse, 1978; Encarnation, 1989; Lall, 1985). An independent India pressured American & Foreign Power to divest, and the company had exited by 1951. There were parallels in developed countries from 1946 to 1948: France, Austria, South Australia and West Germany all provided examples of rising public ownership and control of electricity. As for developing territories during the same years, Algeria declared nationalization, South Africa took over Victoria Falls and Transvaal Power, and Egypt adopted the principle of state ownership, meaning no new concession to foreign investors (Hausman, Hertner and Wilkins, 2008).

The Borneo Company began, from 1953, its withdrawal from Asia. In Malaysia, multinationals retained their place in rubber and palm oil, thanks to their access to capital and their control of technological knowledge, but the New Economic Policy, introduced in 1971, given its aim of favouring native Malays, was a clear signal for divestment (Turnbull, 1989). After several years of warfare, an independent Indonesia was formed in 1949. The Netherlands trading firms returned, but Indonesia restricted imports and profit transfers, and gave preference to indigenous merchants. Then, in 1957, Indonesia nationalized all Netherlands companies within its borders – about half of all the European country's overseas assets – and replaced their managers (Vickers, 2005). As we have seen, some Asia-based traders attempted to transfer their skills in commodities and developing economies to Africa: these included Wallace Brothers, Finlay and Internatio. Yet, on the whole, and over time, most British trading firms evolved into companies investing in a wide range of industries and services in their home economy, while those from the Netherlands tried to become, with mixed success, Europe-wide businesses (Jones, 2000; Jonker and Sluyterman, 2000; Sluyterman, 2003).

As in Asia, investment in Africa ran against an increasing current of decolonization. The Arab countries of North Africa, beginning with

Libya in 1951, gained their formal independence, and Ghana initiated the process for sub-Saharan Africa in 1957, with the pace greatly quickening across the continent in the 1960s. British, French and Netherlands banks, like their trading company counterparts, were in retreat. The colony of Hong Kong's fast growth and low tax, and its emergence as a financial centre favoured the Hongkong Bank, which continued to operate throughout East Asia. It bought up, in 1960, the British Bank of the Middle East, itself expanding in an oil-rich region. The ANZ Banking Group had an important presence in Asia, and Standard Chartered, formed from a merger in 1969, operated across Asia, Africa, Australia and Britain. Barclays had major interests in South Africa, and, after 1945, was able to extend its network across Africa (Jones, 1990). Yet new nation states were generally suspicious of enterprises with imperial histories, and, although they had now gained political sovereignty, they might perceive multinationals as a block on their economic independence. Multinationals felt disadvantaged against local or state companies, and increasingly had to deal with import, profit and currency controls on imports and profits.

During the post-war decades, global FDI flows shifted away from ventures in minerals, natural resources and utilities and towards manufacturing, reflecting market-seeking strategies by multinationals in rich and developed host nations: by 1966, the leading nations of the Organization for Economic Cooperation and Development (OECD) held only 22 per cent of their total manufacturing FDI assets, measured by value, in developing countries. The rich North continued to invest in the South and in the Middle East for their minerals, commodities and oil: by 1966, the OECD's FDI assets in less developed countries were 40 per cent in oil, 9 per cent in mining and smelting, and 27 per cent in manufacturing (Turner, 1970).

The USA was a key motor of the post-war international economy, and, as we have seen, much of the increase in FDI came from its manufacturing sector, flowing north to Canada and across the Atlantic to Europe. At an early point, the new economic and military superpower switched its backing for outward investment away from Europe as a destination to developing countries, with the aim of furthering its influence overseas and combating that of the Soviet Union, during the polarized Cold War conflict. The International Development Act of 1950, as we have seen, supported science and industry in developing countries, just as the Investment Guaranty Scheme, after 1951, was used to cover the additional risks of conflict, policy reversals, or expropriation in the Third World. The US government funded the Export-Import Bank for the same reasons, and negotiated international agreements that prohibited double taxation and discriminatory policies, although Third World countries in the 1960s began to view open trade and investment as a system that entrenched the economic hegemony of the West. The Internal Revenue Service offered multinationals credit for double taxation (Sigmund, 1980; Wilkins, 1974; Safarian, 1993), and it introduced special provisions for oil companies: the royalties paid for concessions overseas became, from 1950, tax-deductible, and allowed multinationals to raise the percentage of revenues going to the Saudi Arabian government from 12 to 50 per cent without affecting their corporate profits. They provided an incentive for US oil companies to maintain their involvement in Aramco, and, therefore, in one of the world's most important sources of oil (Sigmund, 1980).

Strategically, manufacturing multinationals gave much less priority to emerging economies, with their smaller markets and lower per capita incomes. US companies looked more often to Latin America, although, as we have seen, Coca-Cola evolved into a global brand. Kellogg built a factory in South Africa in 1948,[197] while S. C. Johnson owned, by 1968, subsidiaries across Africa and South East Asia.[198] Government pressure induced Pilkington, the glassmakers, to establish a plant in South Africa during 1951, and another in India three years later.[199] The British Oxygen Company (BOC), with a joint venture in South Africa, added further to the manufacturing, banking and mining interests of British and other multinationals.[200] Rather than being a safe haven for investors, however, apartheid South Africa in fact became a cauldron of internal civil protest and violence, and the focus of international outrage. From 1946 to 1957, new constitutional arrangements ensured that Nigeria exercised greater autonomy than previously; formal decolonization took place in 1960. Under pressure from the Nigerian government, the United Africa Company (UAC), an arm of Unilever, began the assembly of motor cars in 1958, and so protected an import and distribution business it had created.[201] Guinness, building on export sales, in the 1960s began production in Nigeria, Malaysia, Cameroon and Ghana, as well as Jamaica.[202]

Multinationals – mostly British and US – curtailed new capital injections in the Third World, but did not, during this period, divest. In the

1960s, the flow of British FDI began to switch to the European Economic Community and to Western Europe more generally. Michelin owned factories, by 1970, in Nigeria, Algeria and Vietnam,[203] and Pechiney founded an aluminium plant in Cameroon in 1954 and an alumina factory in Guinea, in 1960.[204] Mannesmann AG had established steel and tube mills in Turkey by 1955, while Volkswagen finished its Beetle in an assembly plant, as a result of state policy, in South Africa from 1950 onwards.[205] The service sector provided one interesting, if very atypical, case in the history of multinational enterprise. A frustrated IBM salesman, H. Ross Perot, in 1962 founded Electronic Data Systems Corporation (EDS), which went international, in 1976, with a Saudi university contract, and then with a major commission from the Iranian government to provide computer services and training. When payments due from Iran ceased, two years later, EDS suspended operations, and Perot ordered most of his employees home. When the two who remained were arrested, as part of the contract dispute, Perot hired a former Green Beret colonel to organize their rescue. Luckily, when pro-Ayatollah Khomeini protestors broke into their prison, during the Islamic Revolution of 1979, these employees simply walked out of their cells, and the rescue team had only to transport them home. General Motors would buy up EDS in 1984, and Perot gained a wider fame, in 1992 and 1996, as a third party, protest candidate for the US Presidency.[206]

Mineral diplomacy in Asia and Africa

Oil was the world's main source of energy, and an essential commodity of the chemical and materials industry. Demand was highest in the industrialized and wealthy West, with the spread of mass car ownership in the rich nations accentuating the economic and political sensitivity of oil prices, yet the richest sources of supply in the postwar decades were towards the equator and the southern hemisphere. It followed that the oil industry was both strategically vital to the world economy and by necessity highly international; there was, too, an inbuilt danger of global instability. Since exploration, extraction and distribution were capital intensive and technologically complex, large-scale Western multinationals dominated the oil industry outside the Communist bloc. These firms sought control over mineral rights or long-term concessions to undertake extraction, but host countries increasingly associated ownership of their natural resources with true national sovereignty, or challenged previously agreed royalty or taxation terms as unjust. Developing countries sought to review the concession agreements of oil multinationals, some of them settled under colonial regimes, or, seemingly, imposed by powerful multinationals on former weak or corrupt governments. Oil revenues provided, also, a ready means to sustain and validate the political and economic legitimacy of states, many of which lacked democratic credentials, or suffered from discernible failings in governance. Host governments, with their oversight of supplies, and multinationals, with their organizational, operational and distribution expertise, needed each other, but resentments against oil multinationals and the division of the spoils had the potential to boil over into political and diplomatic crises.

The oil business revealed a major vulnerability in the post-war golden age of the international economy. Iraq, Kuwait, Iran, Saudi Arabia and Venezuela founded the Organization of Petroleum Exporting Countries (OPEC) in Baghdad in 1960, and nine other states soon joined them. They had established a cartel that declared national sovereignty over natural resources, and strove to wrench control of oil supplies away from the multinationals. OPEC, with so many Arab members, reacted to US support for Israel during the Yom Kippur War of 1973 with an embargo that caused steep price increases and worldwide recession. Panic in the global oil markets after the Iranian Revolution of 1979 contributed to another economic downturn over the following three years. As their share of global production fell, and although they had no choice but to extract oil in developing nations, oil companies retained control of the final markets, and reduced their greater vulnerability and the costs of foreign exchange by moving their refining operations. In 1951, oil companies had conducted half of their refining in oil-producing areas, but by 1965 they had reduced this figure to 16 per cent (Chapman, 1991).

Unlike manufacturers, oil and mining firms had to go wherever the minerals lay in the ground, and these multinationals featured prominently in the economic, diplomatic and legal disputes with host nations. Even where a government was receptive to multinationals, it had to respond to domestic dissent or international events, or risk its own political legitimacy. The US multinationals – Socal, the Texas Company, Jersey Standard and Socony-Vacuum – that controlled the Arabian American Oil Company, or Aramco, had a stable working relationship with the Saudi royal family which ruled most of the Arabian Peninsula. The company was committed to non-interference in the country's affairs, and it briefed new managers on local cultural sensitivities in an effort to prevent misunderstandings. It built hospitals and schools, and awarded study scholarships in the USA. As the number of oil discoveries grew, the foreign presence of Aramco, its infrastructure and personnel numbers expanded. King Ibn Saud had seized power with the support of the Wahhabi sect, fundamentalist Sunni interpreters of Islam, and some of its adherents denounced this notable example of Western influence in a country that held stewardship of the holy sites at Mecca.

In 1950, fearing nationalization, Aramco conceded the king's demands for a greater profit share, agreeing to a 50–50 split (a precedent set, two years earlier, when Creole Petroleum, a Jersey Standard subsidiary, made concessions to a new Venezuelan government).[207] In any case, we have seen how Aramco convinced the US government to maintain its profit levels with a counterbalancing tax concession, and Washington recognized that continued privileged access to Saudi oil was in the national interest. The State Department was highly aware of a growing anti-American undertone in the dealings between the Saudis and Aramco, and fearfully speculated how the forces of nationalism and Communism would move the Middle East against the USA (Litvin, 2003).[208] Washington and the oil multinationals regarded Saudi Arabia as a vulnerable but friendly regime, yet followed a very different course in Iran when popular discontent there brought about the nationalization of a dominant multinational. In the early 1950s, at the height of US power overseas, its government and multinational companies proved able to defend their economic interests against the policies of sovereign states. One notorious example occurred in Iran; another took place in Guatemala.

Britain, in 1948–9, on behalf of the Anglo-Iranian Oil Corporation, had offered Iran revised terms for its operating concession and its effective monopoly of the country's output, but no agreement was possible. The Iranian government remained highly aggrieved by the royalty returns, by AIOC's failure to give it any say in the management of the business, and by wage disputes involving local workers. When Aramco agreed to a 50–50 profit share with Saudi Arabia, anger intensified, and the prime minister, Ali Razmara, resisting nationalist pressure, was assassinated. In 1951, the democratically elected Majlis appointed Mohammed Mossadegh as his replacement, voted unanimously for oil nationalization, putting aside 25 per cent of the profits to meet compensation claims, and founded the National Iranian Oil Company (NIOC). The AIOC refused to negotiate on the principle of national ownership over natural resources, or on a 50–50 profit share agreement that had taken Venezuela as its model. The British government, instead, pleaded its case at the International Criminal Court in The Hague, but lost.

Meanwhile, the world's largest oil multinationals from the USA, Britain, the Netherlands and France all combined, and, with their control of processing plants and final markets in developed countries, they blocked supplies from Iran. They had a mutual interest in protecting overseas assets and their control of oil prices, but events did, initially, reveal divisions amongst the Western powers. Since the Second World War, during which Britain and the Soviet Union had occupied Iran, the USA had opposed the restoration of European imperialism, especially in the strategically important Middle East. The USA was the world's largest user of oil, and saw colonialism and AIOC privileges in Iran as shoring up unfair competition. The USA supported a 50–50 profit split – its multinationals had accepted similar settlements in Venezuela and Saudi Arabia – but also urged the pragmatic recognition of nationalization. Needing support for the Korean War, it did not push strongly against Britain's rejection of changes to the concession terms. Then, the election of the Eisenhower administration hardened Cold War and anti-Soviet attitudes in Washington, and the USA and Britain, in 1953, through the Central Intelligence Agency and the Secret Intelligence Service, initiated policies of subversion. The planned coup in Iran initially failed, and the pro-Western Shah, Mohammad Reza Pahlavi, fled to Baghdad and subsequently to Rome. On his return, a second attempt succeeded, and he appointed a new government agreeable to a compromise settlement.[209]

Having bought assets in Iraq and Kuwait, AIOC had changed its name to British Petroleum (BP) during 1954, expressing its strategic wish not to be almost wholly reliant on Iran for its future. Yet public opinion in Iran was too strong to let back the renamed company on the old terms, and the other oil majors and the USA wanted, in any case, a revised concession. An international consortium, registered in the Netherlands, formed the Iranian Oil Participants Ltd (IOP): it consisted of BP (with a 40 per cent share), Gulf Oil (which ultimately merged with Socal to form Chevron), Shell, Compagnie Française des Pétroles (CFP, later transformed into Total), and the four Aramco partners. By accepting NIOC's ownership of the oil and facilities, and a 50–50 profit split, the IOP was given operational control, but continued to deny any Iranian oversight of the management or the accounts. The consortium and the British government also organized compensation for BP and its loss of monopoly (Bamberg, 1994; Bamberg, 2000; Sluyterman, Howarth, Jonker, and Van Zanden, 2007). Western governments and the oil multinationals defeated the national ownership of the country's oil resources, but the final settlement, in giving substantially more revenue to the Iranian government, was acknowledgement of new political realities (Penrose, 1968).

In Guatemala, during 1954, the USA had similarly carried out subversion and engineered a military coup: it was a brutal example of Cold War politics, and simultaneously secured the property interests of a multinational. Iran's economy had been particularly reliant on oil and the AIOC, just as Guatemala depended heavily on bananas and United Fruit. Political change and domestic instability meant risks for multinational investors, but companies might have greater bargaining power over developing and export-orientated economies and, in the case of Guatemala, over small countries. The events in Iran and Guatemala were not, it is well to remember, typical of state–multinational relations in the 1950s, even if they became infamous. They illustrated a high point of Western multinational enterprise influence, because companies from the industrialized world owned unmatched leads in management, finance and technology; they, similarly, gave concrete illustration of an apogee in US diplomatic and military power. The oil majors had acquired a stranglehold on both worldwide production and distribution, and acted in concert to reverse Iran's seizure of AIOC; United Fruit, undeniably, exercised a determining influence on the states of Central America, made infamous for their instability, corruption and injustice. Nonetheless, it was the willingness of the US and British governments to intervene – not the actions of the multinationals themselves – which decided the outcomes of events in 1954, which left a longstanding legacy on the politics and popular perceptions of Iran and Latin America (Williamson, 1992; May and Plaza, 1958; McCann, 1976).[210]

It had been Egypt's nationalization of the Suez Canal that had marked the beginning of a turning point in the power relationships between host countries and investing multinationals. In 1951, Mustafa el-Nahhas Pasha, his Wafd nationalist party having just won an election, revoked the 1936 treaty with Britain, which had formally recognized Egyptian sovereignty in return for troops being stationed at Suez. Attacks on the British garrison, on property and on the expatriate community were matched by civilian deaths and a threat to occupy Cairo, and King Farouk dismissed Nahhas Pasha as prime minister. The political situation was reversed, in 1952, by a military coup headed by General Muhammad Naguib, and by the creation of the Egyptian republic during the following year. Britain, with Anthony Eden as its Foreign Secretary, preferred at this stage to negotiate, terms being reached with Gamal Abdel Nasser, who had replaced Naguib as Chairman of the Revolutionary Council in 1954: British troops would leave Egypt in under two years, and Egypt would respect the freedom of navigation through the Suez Canal. Britain would retain majority ownership of the canal itself, still registered in France, for twenty-five years. The USA saw Egypt as a cornerstone of an anti-Soviet bloc in the Middle East – consequently, looking to the end of the colonial legacies of Britain and France – but overestimated the strength of its links with Cairo. Eden, now prime minister, frustrated Nasser's ambition to buy the weapons he needed for an attack on Israel, and Egypt bought aircraft, tanks and other equipment from the Soviet Union via Czechoslovakia instead. The politics of the situation were volatile and complex: the currents of impassioned anti-colonial feelings crossed those of anti-Israel aims, rivalry in the region for leadership of the Arab nations, and the Cold War clashes of rival superpowers.

After his election as President, in 1956, Nasser called for pan-Arab unity and accused the Saudi royal family of being slaves to Aramco and stooges of imperialism. The Soviet Union, under Khrushchev, was on a new diplomatic course of allying with non-aligned nations, and agreed to assist with the building of the Aswan Dam, vital to irrigating the Nile Valley and to Egypt's economic development. The USA, aggrieved by Nasser's recognition of the Soviet Union and China, and growing sceptical of the diplomatic returns from its aid, had refused, as had Britain and the World Bank. To secure the necessary funding, Nasser declared that he would nationalize the Suez Canal, in 1956, and prompted a combined military reaction from Britain, France and Israel, through a secret pact. But the USA, led by an incensed Eisenhower, and world opinion forced withdrawal of the occupying forces. The Suez Crisis had long-lasting implications for international politics, but, amongst those of multinational enterprise, the canal remained a foreign-owned asset nationalized without compensation. Egypt took all British and French FDI into state ownership in 1957. The Compagnie Universelle du Canal Maritime de Suez renamed itself Compagnie Financière de Suez, a holding company, which invested in French banking, water utilities and waste management, evolving into one of France's major businesses (Piquet, 2004; Hall and Lobina, 2013).

One year after becoming independent, in 1958, Guinea provided another example of nationalizations not being reversed, in land ownership and wholesale distribution, which were dominated by French interests. However, the new state saw itself as too economically vulnerable to appropriate the mining firms and banks (Shillington, 2005). Next, the victory of Fidel Castro in Cuba, during 1959–60, brought about the quick nationalization of foreign-owned assets. US companies had controlled some 37 per cent of Cuba's sugar crop, and there were extensive US interests in transport and energy utilities, fruit growing, hotels and leisure. Despite the weight which a nearby superpower could bring to bear on its small neighbour, US investors permanently lost their sugar and fruit estates, hotels and other leisure businesses (Safarian, 1993). The influence of Che Guevara and evolving alignment with the Soviet Union in the era of the Cold War encouraged Castro's commitment to communist ideology. But the perceived closeness of international investors to the corrupt Batista regime – with many in hotels and leisure being dubiously associated with Mafia criminal organizations – and the control foreign businesses had over the Cuban economy additionally pushed him towards radicalism.

The position of the seven oil majors and CFP began to weaken for two related reasons: firstly, developing countries gained success in imposing the state ownership of mineral rights or revising concession agreements, and multinational partners had to accept contract terms different to those at one time deemed acceptable; secondly, by being willing to offer better terms to producer countries, new competitors from the USA, Europe and Japan were already wearing down the production, processing and marketing oligopoly of more established concerns. It became cumulatively unrealistic for the USA or any other investing country to police every host economy, and oil multinationals step by step had to transform their ways of doing business. Emerging states posed problems for the seven oil majors and others with existing concessions, but gave opportunities to those companies more eager to offer host governments better terms, in pursuit of a commercial foothold.

The Italian government established Ente Nazionale Idrocarburi, or ENI, in 1953, making its former parent company, Azienda Generale Italiana Petroli, or Agip, its subsidiary. It additionally charged the new business with supplying the nation's energy and pioneering its general economic development. Enrico Mattei – a man who abandoned his support for Italian Fascism, joining the Christian Democrats, when Mussolini was driven from power – took charge of ENI. He was determined to break into the closed circle carefully guarded by the seven majors, and, as a result, as well as pioneering better terms for new developing states, he supported independence movements in the Third World. Another way in which ENI was ready to throw out the established rules of an international industry was an agreement it brokered with the Soviet Union, in 1958, despite protests from the USA and other NATO countries. Mattei declared that he always bought the cheapest oil available – so, Italy became the Soviet Union's largest export market for its oil – while Communism's leader country gained foreign currency or bartered for manufactured goods in return. The Italian company, by 1964, had secured enough supplies worldwide to sell to Bulgaria.

ENI, with a contract from Egypt's government, in 1955 had formed the International Egyptian Oil Company (Ieoc), and, within another year, had brought in Belgium's Petrofina as a partner. The Egyptian General Petroleum Corporation – founded in stages in 1956 and 1962, initially to issue exploration licences and subsequently to manage joint ventures – established the Gulf of Suez Petroleum Company (Gupco) with Standard Oil of Indiana and Petrobel in partnership with ENI-Petrofina's Ieoc. EGPC brought, also, another US independent, Phillips, to Egypt as a joint venture participant. After a period of restructuring the industry, in 1964 Egypt nationalized Anglo-Egyptian Oilfields, a Shell-BP owned joint venture. To enhance the capabilities of NIOC, Iran passed a law, in 1957, which allowed the company to enter into joint ventures for the exploration of areas not under IOP management. ENI-Agip manoeuvred quickly and was the first multinational to sign a deal, forming, with NIOC, the jointly owned Société Irano-Italienne des Pétroles (Sirip). To gain the business, Mattei made proposals that transformed the relationship between oil multinational and host country: ENI offered a partnership in the development of a country's natural resources, but often assumed the exploration costs and handed over three quarters of the financial returns, half in taxes and royalties, and the remaining quarter as a profit share. He had initiated what became known as ENI's '75/25 plan'.[211]

The Iranians followed the same approach with Iran Pan American Oil Company, owned equally by Standard Oil Company of Indiana and NIOC. By 1966, through political pressure and despite its 'victory' of twelve years before, the IOP had conceded some 25 per cent of the lands over which it had exploration rights, and this action enabled the Iranian government to sign service contracts with European multi-nationals and US independents, beginning with France's state-owned Entreprise de Recherches et d'Activités Pétrolières (ERAP, transforming, from 1976, into Elf Aquitaine and, later, Total), with nine such agreements being concluded by 1971.[212] NIOP won its own oil supplies through policies of joint ventures and licensing, yet the IOP still produced some 89 per cent of all Iranian oil exports. The Iranian business did have sufficient supplies to export to Eastern Europe, Africa and Asia, and, by 1969 to 1971, it had acquired the capabilities to move overseas, helping to develop refineries and a fertilizer plant in South Africa and India. NIOP took formal control of the consortium area in 1973 – although the result was endless disputes with the IOP, which had been given preferential purchasing rights – and Iran by this period had evolved into a principal founder of OPEC, constituted to shift economic power to host nations (Louis, 2007; Bamberg, 2000).[213]

After Iran, between 1958 and 1962 ENI used its 75/25 plan in Morocco, Libya, Sudan, Tunisia and Nigeria, and later, from 1963 to 1967, it signed deals with the Republic of Congo, Oman, Mexico, Saudi Arabia and Brazil, beginning usually with exploration contracts and subsequently bringing in joint ventures. It agreed with China, in 1979, to organize offshore exploration, just one year after that country had announced its period of reform and its opening up to the international economy. ENI established, furthermore, a series of refining and distribution agreements.[214]

With the support of the Japanese government, as its country's energy needs multiplied, the Japan Petroleum Trading Company was able to sign exploration agreements by offering Saudi Arabia and Kuwait favourable terms, during 1958 and 1959. It founded the Arabian Oil

Company, which made its first big discovery in 1960 and thereafter built production and refining capabilities.[215] With an oil embargo being one of the causes of the Pacific War, Japan had historically been excluded from the Middle East, and had lost the Dutch East Indies as its major supply source.

In Libya, the founding of the Libyan General Petroleum Corporation (Lipetco) placed oil revenues under government control in 1968, leading to contracts with ENI-Agip as well as ERAP, Société Nationale des Pétroles d'Aquitaine (or SNPA, which also merged into Elf Aquitaine and then into Total), Ashland Oil and Refining (a US independent), and also a major, Royal Dutch Shell. The new republican government, led by Colonel Gaddafi, changed Lipetco's name to the Libyan National Oil Company (NOC) in 1970. The new organization concentrated on production-sharing agreements with ENI, majors and independents, and asked multinationals to bear the risks of exploration.[216]

A cartel of multinationals – AIOC, Shell, CFP, Standard Jersey and Socony-Vacuum – had historically controlled the British-registered Iraq Petroleum Company and, therefore, the country's oil production. These multinationals had resisted any efforts to allow Iraqi investment and participation in IPC, and, although British occupation of the country had ended in 1947, the restoration of the pro-Western Hashemite monarchy had simplified the imperial exit, and in theory safeguarded foreign economic interests that remained. The government did, in 1952, in what were described as friendly negotiations, gain a 50–50 agreement with IPC, modelled on that of Aramco, but, as in Egypt, the military coup of 1958 transformed the political scenario. Given the dependence of Iraq on oil, nationalist dissent was inevitably focused on the multinational's monopoly and vast land holdings, portraying its role in the country as both feudal and imperialist; on the other side, the government needed the technical and managerial assistance given by the oil multinationals through IPC to ensure production took place.

By 1960, Abd al-Karim Qasim, Iraq's new leader, was demanding 20 per cent of IPC and 55 per cent of its annual profits, but, buoyed by diplomatic intervention from Washington and London, the multinational did not feel the need to concede. When world demand fell, in 1961, the owning firms asked their Iraqi subsidiary to accept a lower price for its supplies and, as popular anger grew, the government reacted by nationalizing almost all of the concession areas.

Unlike the case of Iran ten years earlier, the international oil industry decided to accept the decision: political and diplomatic realities had moved on, but, in any case, IPC still controlled production. The nationalist and socialist Ba'ath party, already part of the government, organized a coup in 1963, inevitably stirring allegations that the USA had engineered the replacement of Qasim. In fact, the new regime founded the Iraq National Oil Company (INOC) in the following year and gave the state-owned company exclusive rights to develop oil. For a while, it worked with IPC, but, during 1967, the year of the Six Day War between Israel and neighbouring Arab countries, Iraq brought in Soviet expertise to the Rumaila oilfield, and what followed, from 1969 to 1972, were a series of treaties on technical assistance and finance for the oil industry, hydroelectric power generation, mining, and river navigation. In 1970 the Iraqi government was confident enough of INOC's capabilities to demand 20 per cent of IPC's ownership and more direct control of its operations. By this juncture, IPC knew it had to make concessions, but the Ba'athist government lost interest in a compromise, and transferred the multinational's assets to INOC in 1972 (Brown, 1979; Sluyterman, Howarth, Jonker and Van Zanden, 2007).

Events in Syria had parallels. In a reaction to the occupation of Suez, its government signed a pact with the Soviet Union, and in 1958 it merged with Egypt to create the United Arab Republic. The union existed essentially on paper only, but, when Syria ceded in 1961, it created, within two years, enough instability to put its version of the Ba'ath party in control, eventually bringing Hafez al-Assad to power. Syria nationalized its oil assets, discovered by US and West German firms, during 1964, and brought the two fields on stream with Soviet assistance. The country did not admit foreign contractors before 1974, when a Romanian company accepted a production-sharing concession, with the first Western capitalist business, a Shell subsidiary, winning an exploration agreement in 1977.

Britain and France, which administered Libya until 1951, supported the appointment of King Idris as the country's only monarch. Major oil discoveries, from 1959 onwards, gave the new nation a strong financial base, and Idris's government granted concessions to multinationals, ultimately through the Libyan General Petroleum Corporation (Lipetco). Yet clan rivalries, pan-Arabism inspired by Nasser, opposition to pro-Western policies, anti-Israel protests, and nationalist and revolutionary movements all undermined the solidity of Idris's rule, and in 1969 a military coup, led by Muammar Gaddafi, easily established a republic. The new government, during the following year, saw the removal of British bases alongside the planned withdrawal of US forces, the nationalization of all assets belonging to the old colonial power of Italy, the signing of the Tripoli Agreement that increased revenues from investing multinationals, and the creation of the Libyan National Oil Company (Linoco). Gaddafi's Revolutionary Council began to apply its declared socialist principles with the takeover of operations owned by BP and Phillips during 1971–2, and then announced the full- or part-nationalization of oil companies and concessions in 1973. Linoco subsequently made production-sharing, refining and drilling deals with companies such as Occidental Petroleum, Phillips (US independents), Exxon-Esso, Mobil, SNPA, CFP and ENI. From 1974, all production revenues were divided 85–15 onshore and 81–19 offshore in favour of Linoco. Despite needing the contribution of multinationals, the trend was towards full nationalization: Libya brought the Socal-Texaco joint venture Amoseas, Amoco, Hunt Oil, Atlantic Richfield, Shell, BP, Exxon-Esso, Phillips and Mobil-Gelsenberg, by 1979, into full state ownership.[217]

After a bloody conflict with France, Algeria achieved political sovereignty in 1962, but reliance on oil multinationals and exports to France jeopardized its economic independence. The Franco-Algerian Oil Agreement of 1965 provided for greater local involvement and the right to 55 per cent of oil revenues from the French companies that dominated production. The Société Nationale pour la Recherche, la Production, le Transport, la Transformation et la Commercialisation des Hydrocarbures (Sonatrach), founded by the government in 1963 and renamed in 1966, took control of the Esso and Mobil subsidiaries and over half of Getty Oil, as well as nationalizing all distribution and refining, between 1967 and 1969. As relations with France worsened, Algeria nationalized all remaining oilfields, in 1971, and assumed a 51 per cent share of all operating multinational subsidiaries. France initially responded with an embargo on Algerian oil, but, ultimately, both CFP and Elf Aquitaine accepted the new conditions.[218]

Diplomatic events and domestic pressures affected relations with investors even in nations that remained highly friendly to the West, and hurried oil companies in their search for supplies outside the Middle East. The Arab–Israeli War of 1967 had led to an oil embargo as a protest against the policies of many Western countries, and King Faisal had denounced all countries supporting Israel as aggressors. Sheik Ahmed Zaki Yamani, as Saudi Minister for Oil and Natural Resources, did not at this point favour nationalization, given Aramco's reliance on the expertise of the multinationals, but he persuaded OPEC to declare that each government should require a 'reasonable participation' in its own oil industry. Like other foreign firms in Saudi Arabia, in 1972 Aramco accepted 25 per cent Saudi government ownership, set to rise to 51 per cent by 1983. Fearing nationalization or a revolution, the company saw itself as being in a weak position.

During the 1973 Arab–Israeli crisis, King Faisal pointed out to Aramco that Saudi Arabia was one of the few Arab nations friendly to US interests, and thought that the company had influence over policy in Washington. Aramco campaigned amongst US corporations for an even-handed approach to the Arab–Israeli conflict but had small impact, and the subsequent oil shock showed the economic price to be paid for regional instability. Nearby Kuwait and Qatar announced, in 1974, that they would take 60 per cent ownership of foreign oil concessions, and Saudi Arabia decided, in 1976, on full control of its fields. Unlike other cases, there was no sudden expulsion, and relations continued through operating concessions, training, and distribution arrangements (formal control of all oil operations occurred, in 1988, with the establishing of the Saudi Aramco Oil Company).[219] Nigeria, on the other hand, continued to rely heavily on BP and Shell, and it was exporting oil from 1958 onwards, discoveries there offering replacements for oilfields lost elsewhere in the world. Despite competition from Mobil and Gulf Oil, BP and Shell still controlled some 70 per cent of production by 1966, although the Nigerian government began to change the contract terms and revenue settlements in the following year.[220]

The central strategic issue facing oil companies – the need to extract supplies from developing nations undergoing rapid political change – applied to mining enterprises, too. As in the case of oil, international mining was controlled by a small number of multinationals. It was technologically and organizationally complex, and extensive financial resources were needed to support capital-intensive operations, long investment horizons, and worldwide marketing. The risks were high, and failed ventures left enterprises with non-transferable assets. As colonial regimes gave way to new sovereign states, miners had to learn new operating skills and to fashion political connections. While control over mineral assets was removed or eroded, managerial and technological know-how, vertical links along the commodity and production chains, and access to Western markets, as in the case of oil, continued to give mining companies bargaining power (Schmitz, 1986).

Nationhood brought challenges to old colonial companies, but potentially opportunities for others. Ghana led the process of independence in sub-Saharan Africa, in 1957, and its first President, Kwame Nkrumah, was socialist in outlook but internationally Non-Aligned. He sought to plan Ghana's economic development and industrialization, in order to secure its economic sovereignty. As well as promoting agriculture and cocoa exports, and opening up bauxite and gold deposits, the government conceived two ambitious and interconnected schemes: the construction of the Akosombo hydroelectric dam across the Volta to provide irrigation and electricity, and the creation of an integrated aluminium industry. Overseas lenders did not see the hydroelectric project as viable without guarantees from a large user of energy, and most metal-making companies withdrew until only two were left. Kaiser Aluminum and Chemical agreed to take a 90 per cent holding in the Volta Aluminium Company Limited (VALCO), in partnership with another US firm, Reynolds, which held the remaining 10 per cent, and, in doing so, had to agree to pay for a minimum level of electricity, whether actually used or not, over a period of thirty years.[221] The Kennedy administration in the USA had facilitated the deal, giving a demonstrable example of support for the first black African nation, but the commercial judgement belonged to the two US companies, looking for sources of bauxite. VALCO, founded in 1964, was producing aluminium within three years, but, by this point, Nkrumah had been ousted from power (Wolfgang, Kuyper and Candolle, 1995).[222] One reason was his increasing authoritarianism, but another was overspending on uneconomic capital projects and rising national debt, and the new government began a programme of selling state assets.

In Malaysia and Indonesia, multinational miners lost their control of world tin production, which they shared with Bolivian producers, which were nationalized in 1952. Seven copper firms, during the 1950s, accounted for some 60–70 per cent of the metal sold. Steel producers had historically preferred to use local ores, but, as well as entering

Canada, US companies went to Latin America and Africa in search of new supplies. Both Bethlehem Steel and Republic Steel invested in Liberia, from where they exported the raw material (Rodrik, 1982; Cobbe, 1979; Hennart, 1986; Wilkins, 1974; McKern, 1976; Brown and McKern, 1987).

Rio Tinto Zinc, on its formation in 1962, owned diamond mines in South Africa, copper deposits in South Africa and Uganda, and uranium assets in Papua New Guinea and Namibia. Both Kaiser Aluminum and RTZ followed strategies of partnerships with other multinational investors, which shared the commercial risks, and with host governments, which reduced the political risks and facilitated operations. Despite its almost complete ownership of VALCO, Kaiser usually looked for a 25–30 per cent share. Dependence on the extracting, processing and distribution skills of multinationals meant that forced divestments of mining multinationals were few (Shafer, 1983). The Republic of Congo did impose state ownership on the Société Générale de Belgique's mining operations, in 1966, because the company was a domineering influence on its economy, in addition to being a colonial legacy. Zambia did the same to US- and British-owned copper mines, in 1969, and converted the assets owned by the Roan Selection Trust and the Anglo-American Corporation into Zambia Consolidated Copper Mines (ZCCM), as much an instrument of social as economic development. It was in Chile that, during the 1970s, the nationalization of the copper industry brought about global diplomatic and political repercussions (Turner, 1970).

Post-war Latin America

Bolivia and Mexico had, as we have already noted, nationalized their oil industries before the Second World War; Mexico had acquired US- and Canadian-owned tram, water and power utilities; and Argentina, soon after the return to peace, had paid generously for its British-owned railways. In the decades following the Second World War, risks of political instability, and currency and exchange restrictions encouraged trading firms to divest from Latin America; while some stayed, there were no new major investments in a region where, historically, they had once been prime movers (Greenhill and Miller, 1998; Hunt, 1951). One policy pattern amongst Latin American states – as in Asia and Africa – was a growing determination to exert ownership or control over their natural resources. Through a coup, in 1945, the popularly supported Acción Democrática took power in Venezuela – then the world's largest oil producer after the USA and the Soviet Union – and, over the next three years, it was remarkable for organizing the country's first democratic and clean elections. Venezuelan regimes had been increasing oil taxes since before the Second World War, but the new government decided on what was seen at the time as a bold initiative: during 1948, the country's Congress decreed a 50–50 share of oil revenues, setting, as events in the Middle East soon proved, a global benchmark for agreements between host nations and multinationals.

The increased flow of funds supported Venezuelan government attempts at educational and land reform, but much of it went to patronage, and support by the military and the middle classes for Acción Democrática ebbed, resulting in a yet another coup, in 1948. The story had a delayed denouement, because some of the ousted figures returned to government after ten years, and Juan Pablo Pérez Alfonso, who had introduced the 50–50 share throughout the industry, was a key figure, as energy minister, in the formation of OPEC. Creole Petroleum, a Standard Jersey subsidiary, was Venezuela's most important oil business; indeed, during the 1950s the subsidiary frequently accounted for nearly 40 per cent of the multinational's revenues. It oversaw exploration, production, refining and distribution, and its infrastructure, power plants, transport systems, sewage treatment, schools, hospitals, housing and mess halls gave the business a very visible part in the lives of Venezuelans. Creole Petroleum in this decade used some 2,200 expatriates, but (as political pressures grew) it was prepared to train local personnel, so that these numbers fell to some 200 by the time of the oil industry's nationalization. Venezuela halted all grants of concessions and founded the Corporación Venezolana de Petróleo (CVP), to compete with multinationals and to gain know-how, during 1959–60; it announced, in 1971, that mineral rights would revert to the state at the end of each concession; in the following year, it laid out plans to acquire the industry. The transfer, despite disputes over the value of assets, occurred smoothly in 1976. Petróleos de Venezuela SA (PDVSA) absorbed Creole Petroleum and other multinational subsidiaries, but could offer willing foreign companies lucrative contracts (Coronel, 1983; Petras, Morley and Smith, 1977; Philip, 1982).[223]

For the post-war decades, Guatemala serves, after Iran, as the most conspicuous and notorious case of multinational business interfering in political processes and in pursuit of its own interests. Again, as in the Iranian case, the circumstances of Cold War rivalry and the fact that the USA was at the high point of its international power made a contribution to the events and their outcome. Jacobo Árbenz Guzmán, elected as president from 1951, pledged to make Guatemala into a modern state, and prioritized land reform. He wanted, also, to reduce the country's dependence on overseas markets and multinational enterprises. Bananas accounted for half the country's exports, and, as well as being the nation's biggest landowner, United Fruit dominated banana production and transportation; critics cited frequent breaches of the eight-hour-day legislation, the capping of wages, and poor working and living conditions.

United Fruit, through personal, and even familial, connections, had direct links to the State Department and the CIA. Thomas Dudley Cabot, who had served as the State Department's Director of the Office of International Security Affairs, was a director and shareholder in United Fruit. The CIA Director, Walter Bedell Smith, became Under-secretary of State in the Eisenhower administration, and, through both roles, was directly involved in the planning and execution of a coup against Árbenz, before leaving office for a position with the multinational. The Secretary of State, John Foster Dulles, had once been a partner in a law firm with the multinational as a major client, and his brother Allen Dulles – Smith's successor as Director of the CIA – had formerly served on the company's board of trustees. Spruille Braden, recently Assistant Secretary of State for Western Hemisphere Affairs, had retired from public life to be a paid lobbyist for United Fruit, and would play a major part in organizing the attack from Honduras against Árbenz.

The USA, which in the Cold War era regarded Central America as its backyard, formed the view that Árbenz's government was Soviet-influenced, a view apparently confirmed when it took a shipment of arms from Czechoslovakia. United Fruit was keen to establish that link in the minds of Americans with a short film it produced entitled *Why the Kremlin Hates Bananas*. Inspired by its recent success in Iran, the USA issued a tough statement about the property rights of investors, funded rebels via Honduras, and, in 1954, engineered a successful military coup. Ernesto 'Che' Guevara recounts in his *Motorcycle Diaries*, recording his early 1950s journeys across Latin America, how working and living conditions at the Anaconda and Kennecott mines at Chuquicamata, in Chile, had helped bring about his political radicalization, and he had arrived in Guatemala, before the coup, in order to give direct support to Árbenz. His travels through Central America had made him aware of the United Fruit 'octopus', but his application for a medical internship with the company suggests that his political outlook had not yet fully hardened. He was a front-line witness to the events: subsequently arguing that American political and economic imperialism had overthrown Latin America's first democratic reformist government, he concluded that only an armed popular uprising could bring about change. It was a view he communicated to Fidel Castro in 1955, when they met in Mexico City as fellow exiles and revolutionaries.

Despite land reform in Guatemala being abandoned, United Fruit thought it a prudent policy, over the next three years, to sell land to local producers and farmers. But it operated in a country in which violence remained commonplace, and living standards and the median age remained amongst the lowest in the world. As United Brands, a name adopted in 1970, we know that the company bribed the Honduran government to lower the export tax on bananas (moreover, it subsequently evolved into Chiquita). The counterargument to the record of United Fruit is that, in order to effect its business in a developing region, it had been Central America's biggest investor in commodities, railways, roads, ports, swamp drainage, workers' housing, schools and medical services, whilst organizing a major export industry that created jobs, foreign exchange, and by local standards high wages (Bucheli, 2005; Chapman, 2007; Dosal, 1993; MacCameron, 1983; Williamson, 1992; Wilkins, 1974; Safarian, 1993).[224]

In Brazil, President Getúlio Vargas, the former dictator who was democratically returned to power in 1951, continued his policies of developmentalism, economic nationalism, and state-owned enterprise, with the founding of Petroleo Brasileiro, or Petrobras, in 1953. The new company exercised formal monopoly, while granting concessions and continuing to work with oil multinationals. In Peru, the power of International Petroleum Company (IPC) was a continuous source of domestic political tension, as was the role of ITT. In 1969, the military regime of President Juan Velasco Alvarado used the International Petroleum Company, a Jersey Standard subsidiary, to found the state-owned Petróleos del Perú (Petroperú), taking over in addition several banks and mining firms (Williamson, 1992; Wilkins, 1974). The Southern Peru Copper Corporation – founded by ASARCO and Cerro de Pasco Corporation in 1952, and involving Phelps Dodge and Newmont Mining Corporation by 1955, all of them being US firms – had the right to develop the Toquepala copper deposit in return for giving 30 per cent of net profits to the government. In their search for new sources of iron ore, in the 1950s, Bethlehem Steel had invested in Chile and Venezuela, and US Steel, too, established mines in Venezuela (Cobbe, 1979; Wilkins, 1974; McKern, 1976; Brown and McKern, 1987).

The Export-Import Bank, a US agency supportive of trade and investment in developing countries, helped to provide some of the initial funding, and Southern Peru Copper built a railway and a coastal processing plant for exports to ASARCO's refineries in Baltimore and Belgium. The company was entitled to make a recovery on its initial investment, but soon entered into an enduring dispute over payment levels and their calculation, commissioning an advertising campaign to point out that it was Peru's largest payer of income tax. So long as the large Cuajone copper mine deposits needed to be developed, along with railways, roads and aqueducts, the company held the upper hand, although the military government that came to power in 1968 did increase the tax on profits to 47.5 per cent, rising to 54.5 per cent once the company's investment had been recovered. By 1975, nonetheless, there were 29 acts of expropriation, involving 47 foreign companies, by a Peruvian government set on a policy of economic nationalism (Hausman, Hertner and Wilkins, 2008).

Before the Second World War, Bolivia had turned a Standard Jersey subsidiary into the nationalized Yacimientos Petrolíferos Fiscales Bolivianos (YPFB), but in 1951 it began to invite back oil multinationals interested in bidding for concessions. The Revolutionary Nationalist Movement (MNR) came to power in 1952 and initiated the twelve years of the Bolivian National Revolution, meaning universal suffrage, land reform and schools, but beginning with the nationalization of the country's largest mines, whose owners were amongst their most determined opponents. Amongst those taken into state ownership was the Patiño Mines, founded by Simón Iturri Patiño, the 'Andean Rockefeller', with mining or refining interests in Chile, Britain, Germany and Malaysia. It was said that his son, who had opposed organized labour in the company mines, assisted the successful military coup of 1964, which created a series of unstable juntas (Klein, 2003; Williams, 1992; YPFB, 2011).

The only prominently successful oil enterprise in Bolivia was the Bolivian Gulf Company, part of Gulf Oil, which made a number of successful strikes around Santa Cruz from 1956 onwards. As well as selling domestically, it exported to the USA and Argentina, via a pipeline to the Chilean port of Arica. Bolivian Gulf was ultimately nationalized, during 1969, when the President, General Alfredo Ovando Candía, in a diplomatic surprise, forged relations with Cuba, Romania and the Soviet Union as alternative sources of economic and technical assistance (Klein, 2003).[225] If we consider outcomes, however, Bolivia's attempts during the 1970s to attract new FDI generally failed. The burning of a General Motors building in Uruguay, in 1969, became a very visual example of widespread anti-American feelings throughout Latin America (Turner, 1970).

Argentina's part-acquisition of American & Foreign Power operations, during 1943–5, and the takeover of Sofina's Mexico Tramways, during 1946, gave a hint of future trends. Two municipalizations – one involving American & Foreign Power in Cali, Colombia, in 1947, and another affecting Sofina's Compañia Hispano-Americana de Electricidad, in Rosario, Argentina, to take place by 1952 – re-emphasized the lessons. Disputes over prices and suspicion of profiteering – whether well grounded or not – inclined governments and localities to prefer indigenous ownership. While still digesting the acquisition of British railways, the Perón administration threatened to nationalize the Sofina-CHADE subsidiary in Argentina and placed limits on remittances, with American & Foreign, the country's biggest overseas investor, willing, by 1950, to sell up.[226]

In Brazil, as profits shrank and inflation took its toll, the US company became equally receptive to an offer from the government. State-sponsored projects, some funded by the World Bank, as against FDI, emerged as the norm for building new supply capacity in Latin America. Nonetheless, in 1956, four holding companies – American & Foreign Power; Brazilian Traction, Light and Power Company; International Power Company; and the Mexican Light and Power Company – still owned enterprises in fourteen countries in the region, and produced and distributed some third of its electricity. Furthermore, the Switzerland-based Motor-Columbus and Brown Boveri, in partnership

with British interests, retained their ownership of Lima Light; mining multinationals, including Anaconda and Kennecott in Chile, and
Southern Peru Copper, were major producers and users of electricity.
Estimates are tricky, but foreign multinationals may have been responsible for around two thirds of electricity generation in Latin America.
The years after 1958 brought transformation for utility multinationals, which took the view, despite growth in demand, that higher taxes,
price controls, inflation, and restrictions on remittances made government acquisition with compensation attractive.

During 1958–9, Argentina bought out American & Foreign Power,
Motor-Columbus and, despite a bitter argument over bribery and corruption, CHADE. In Cuba, American & Foreign naively invested heavily, but lost all its assets, larger than those in Argentina, by 1959 to
Castro's Communist revolution. American & Foreign and Sofina's
Mexican Light and Power, whose market share had fallen from 60 to
33 per cent, had sold up to the Mexican government by 1960, and once
Canadian International Power, the successor to International Power,
had agreed terms for Monterey Railway, Light and Power in 1962, all
of Mexico's giant utility multinationals had left. In Colombia, the government acquired the remaining assets of American & Foreign in 1961;
in Venezuela, in 1964, a private firm bought the multinational's subsidiary, and Canadian International Power's concessions simply came
to an end in 1973 and 1976, the year of that country's oil nationalizations; in Chile, the state agreed to pay compensation for acquisition, in 1965, so long as American & Foreign reinvested the money
locally.

Brazil, from 1959 to 1961, witnessed the appropriation of power
utilities by three of its constituent states; by 1962, the federal government had established Eletrobrás, Latin America's largest generating
and distribution business, as one component of its three-year economic plan. The government agreed to American & Foreign's request,
during the following year, to buy whatever assets remained to the
multinational. By the time of these events (in fact, from 1961), a representative of the labour movement, João Belchior Marques Goulart,
had become president and won a reputation for radicalism in Brazilian political history, with an agenda of land, education and electoral
reform. Compensation for American & Foreign, however, only materialized after the 1964 military coup had made Humberto de Alen-
car Castelo Branco president, and then on condition the money was

reinvested in the Brazilian economy. Despite the commercial and political risks, the Canadian-owned Brazilian Traction decided to stay at first, but, as Brascan, finally relented in 1979. Peru, implementing a series of nationalizations, had ended foreign ownership of Lima Light in 1972 (Hausman, Hertner and Wilkins, 2008).

Although the majority of FDI to Latin America was concentrated in the natural resources sector and secondly in utilities, manufacturers, most obviously those from the USA, showed an increasing interest in its markets. The tyre manufacturer Goodyear established itself throughout the region after the Second World War, and Caterpillar had opened a subsidiary in Brazil by 1956.[227] Pechiney took stakes in aluminium fabrication companies in Argentina and Brazil in 1947–8,[228] and the big three of the German chemicals industry re-established themselves in Latin America, sometimes, ironically, purchasing companies they had lost during the Second World War. Bayer acquired Quimicas Unidas, in Mexico, during 1952, and thereafter bought back Allianca Commerciale de Anilinas, in Brazil.[229] Mannesmann AG, by 1955, had established a steel mill in Brazil, and Companhia Siderurgica Mannesmann evolved into a group of companies, active throughout Latin America and engaged in high-grade steels, industrial machinery, compressors, excavators, control systems, mining and trading.[230] H. J. Heinz went to Venezuela, while Kellogg built a factory in Mexico, in 1951.[231]

General Foods – whose brands Maxwell House (coffee), Birds Eye (frozen foods), Jell-O and others had high recognition – was, by the 1960s, a worldwide food giant, with subsidiaries in Latin America alongside those in developed countries.[232] S. C. Johnson – the maker of Johnson's Wax, Glade air freshener and Pledge spray polish – owned, by 1968, subsidiaries across the region.[233] By 1970, Ericsson had added subsidiaries in Brazil and Mexico to its international operations, as had Michelin.[234] General Motors had opened its Caracas plant, in Venezuela, as early as 1948, and Ford began production in Brazil and restarted in Argentina, in 1957.[235] Seven auto multinationals could be found in Mexico, in 1947, when the government introduced its first set of local content regulations, in order to hasten the process of industrialization. Mexico imposed price controls on vehicles during 1951, and the multinationals attempted to maintain profits through production quotas. When a 60 per cent local content rule was announced, coming into effect in 1964, five companies – Mercedes-Benz,

Fiat, Citroën, Peugeot and Volvo – decided to exit. However, General Motors, Ford, Chrysler, American Motors, Renault and Volkswagen all stayed (Wilkins and Hill, 1964).

As a result of pressure from governments, Volkswagen had built assembly plants for the Beetle, so suited to developing markets, in South Africa (1950), Brazil (1953) and Mexico (1967).[236] In Brazil, while the post-war presidency of Eurico Gaspar Dutra, from 1946, and that of re-elected former dictator Getúlio Dornelles Vargas, from 1951, expressed policies of 'developmentalism', supporting the nationalization of natural resources, it adopted a friendly approach to foreign direct investment. By 1956, Brazil imposed high tariffs and currency restrictions on imported foreign cars, and imposed local content rules of 35–50 per cent on vehicles; these rose to 90–96 per cent by 1961. Most firms were reluctant to undertake FDI, despite government pressure and the size of the Brazilian market, but Volkswagen saw an opportunity. It opened its subsidiary as an assembly operation, in 1953, expanding in 1957 in response to government policy, and also selling 20 per cent of the shares in its plant as a means of shoring up local acceptance and support of the government.

VW, with its Beetle, established itself as Brazil's number one maker of cars. By 1968, eight automobile multinationals were assembling in Brazil, looking for a share of the country's populous markets. But the penalizing rates of inflation and unstable economic conditions during this period were inevitably negatives for foreign investors, as was the 1962 law limiting remittances, passed by the left-wing President João Goulart, and implications could be drawn from the enforced nationalization of utility subsidiaries. The military government that seized power in 1964 continued to welcome FDI, and Fiat, the Italian automobile producer, made its largest investment in Minas Gerais, in Brazil, operational from 1976. By this time, Ford and GM, having recognized the importance of the country's large and protected market, had emerged as the second- and third-largest producers. Brazil, by 1980, was exporting 15 per cent of its automobile output, in the main to other Latin American countries. VW had begun exporting to Mexico by 1954 and began production locally in a joint venture with Chrysler during 1961. It was the building of the Puebla plant, six years later, which enabled the company to establish the Beetle as a popular choice of Mexican motorists (Williamson, 1992; Fritsch and Franco, 1991; Wilkins and Hill, 1964).[237]

Compared to tram and electricity utilities, telecommunications created the greater diplomatic controversies, thanks, in part, to the aggressive responses of ITT under the iron rule of its president and CEO, Harold Geneen. Under Goulart's presidency, in 1963 Brazil took an ITT subsidiary into public ownership in the comparatively rich state of Rio Grande do Sul. Goulart saw himself as a successor to Vargas in the struggle to rid Brazil of foreign domination. In Washington, both the Kennedy and Johnson administrations came to distrust his left-wing views, Peronist-style popularism, and the presence of Communists in his government, and Brazil's resumption of diplomatic relations with the Soviet bloc and his opposition to sanctions against Cuba confirmed their suspicions. Goulart also imposed restrictions on the remittances of multinationals. Geneen, at ITT, feared the expropriation of Brazil's national telephone business, another ITT subsidiary, and lobbied furiously for all US aid to be halted in any country compulsorily taking over a multinational, repudiating a contract, or imposing discriminatory taxes or regulations. Kennedy believed that any such amendment would merely inflame nationalism in the Third World, and he mediated a settlement between ITT and the Brazilian government. Attention next turned to A. M. Hanna Company, which dug iron ore, much of it going to the US's National Steel Corporation, which, in turn, supplied Chrysler. Both A. M. Hanna and ITT had contacts in the CIA – Geneen was a friend of its director, John McClone – and the CIA helped organize the 1964 coup. The dictatorship remained welcoming to FDI and fortuitously enjoyed an economic boom; the military retained power for some twenty-one years. McClone, after he had resigned from the CIA, gained employment with ITT.

The utility's record in Latin America was not convincing: it was making losses, generally retrenching, and closing its component factories in Brazil and Argentina, and governments concluded that the multinational was failing their economies. Chile, in 1965, agreed to acquire some 49 per cent of ITT's subsidiary within five years, so long as the network was expanded. The multinational accepted Peru's wish, expressed in 1970, to own 50 per cent of its local utility, and Argentina announced the nationalization of the entire communications sector. ITT's hard-line policies towards host governments in Latin America – including involvement in covert operations – could not halt step-by-step withdrawal and loss of its major overseas investment. Profitability abroad, too, was being squeezed. Under Geneen, in the 1960s, ITT bought some 300 companies in an attempt to diversify from telephone communications: Sheraton Hotels, Wonder Bread maker Continental Baking and Avis car rental were amongst the famous international brands it acquired. Sheraton, on its takeover in 1968, had hotels in Caracas, Puerto Rico and Jamaica.[238]

In 1969, Chile bought 51 per cent of the Chuquicamata and El Salvador copper mines owned by the USA's Anaconda Copper Company, and a majority of the Kennecott Copper Corporation's El Teniente, the world's largest underground copper project. For a reformist government, the measure was a necessity: copper provided 80 per cent of the national income. Aware of the possibility of enforced and full nationalization, Kennecott had been reducing its exposure in Chile for a decade and did not oppose the government's involvement in El Teniente. Anaconda, on the other hand, had continued to invest heavily, and was set to be badly hit by unfolding events. The purchases were, nonetheless, accepted as negotiated nationalizations, through which the country consolidated its hold on the production and export of a vital mineral resource. The Chilean government preferred negotiation to allow the necessary accumulation of managerial and technical knowledge, but its critics, often from the political left, accused it of paying too much and of bowing to American imperialism. The outright nationalization of remaining overseas involvement in the copper business without compensation was an issue during the 1970 election, and the new Socialist president, Salvador Allende, was committed to the policy.

Chile's government fully nationalized the whole copper industry in 1971, and, following the examples of Brazil and Argentina, it additionally took control of telecommunications, including ITT's Chilean Telephone Company (Chiltelco), because it saw the multinational as failing the needs of Latin American economies. Compensation for the recent nationalized copper mines was agreed, in 1972, despite disputes over historical excessive profits and whether, consequently, the final settlement should be reduced. Not all the payments materialized, though the Overseas Private Investment Corporation (OPIC), a US government agency, had insured Kennecott's investment and covered most of that company's losses. Public spending and US financial pressure exacerbated the economic crisis, high inflation rates, growing political instability and widespread strikes. Harold Geneen, at ITT, formed a committee to destabilize the Chilean government, and some evidence suggests that the company helped in the funding of the coup that toppled the Allende government in 1973. The State Department and the CIA, weighing the Cold War implications, helped to install a military junta led by General Augusto Pinochet Ugarte, who became infamously associated with the suppression and torture of opponents. He followed a highly free-market policy, but, although compensation for ITT was forthcoming, its failings meant that it had to remain part of Chile's public sector (Williamson, 1992; Wilkins, 1974; Sampson, 1973; Schoenberg, 1985; Safarian, 1993).[239]

Multinationals: 1948 to 1980

After 1948, the international economy gradually re-emerged from the Second World War and its immediate aftermath, and became a catalyst for growth in global output. The USA's post-war economic, techno-logical and military hegemony enabled it to determine the framework of the post-war international economy, while the era of European imperialism came to an end. The Bretton Woods institutions, the IMF and World Bank, were a reaction to the economic disintegration of the 1930s, and they were charged with assisting trade imbalances, financing reconstruction, and preventing competitive devaluations. The USA's commitment to free trade was initially curtailed, but the General Agreement on Tariffs and Trade began the process of lower-ing export barriers, and negotiations in 1964–7 achieved major break-throughs. Western governments over time, therefore, adopted policies of free trade and stable exchange rates.

The Cold War set the geographical boundaries of the international economy and the flows of FDI. The Communist bloc was separated from the international economy and had its own system of trade, often resting on barter. Multinationals had no strategic presence in the Soviet Union, Eastern Europe and China, or in other, smaller economies that went Communist, including North Korea, Laos, Cuba and Viet-nam. What evolved, principally in the West, was a highly dynamic but strictly demarcated international economy. FDI and trade con-tacts were, therefore, reflective of Cold War alliances, as well as the capabilities of investing multinationals.

A Cold War international political economy of superpower rivalry fitted uneasily with the remnants of a political economy founded on imperialism. The USA formally opposed European imperialism, which it saw as excluding its businesses. Yet, as it assumed leadership of the

West, it would frequently find itself siding with autocratic governments against nationalist, liberation or radical movements, most controversially in Indochina and Latin America, but in Asia and Africa too. The property rights of foreign-owned companies, especially when they played a critical role in their host economy, or controlled the country's mineral rights and natural resources, could jar against a new nation's sense of sovereignty. From the late 1960s onwards, states looked for a new international economic order to replace the dominance of the USA and the West more generally in output, trade and FDI. The multinationals retained leverage over Third World countries because of their control over management, technology, capital and market access, but could not, even with the support of their governments, ultimately resist acts of nationalization or regulation. They had to acquire new techniques and skills to operate in politically, economically and geographically challenging locations.

US loans and investments supported the reconstruction of Western Europe, where rising living standards and consumption demonstrated the superiority of free markets and democracy, and strengthened the North Atlantic alliance. Flows of manufacturing FDI grew, largely destined for Western Europe and Canada. US companies – because of their competitive lead in management, capital, technology, products and marketing – were at the forefront of these developments. Their motives were market seeking, and multinationals mainly replicated their home-grown capabilities in overseas subsidiaries, albeit on a smaller scale. Initially, they tended to produce for the national market in which they were located. Manufacturing FDI by developed home economies in developed host economies had precedents as far back as the period before the First World War, and the 1920s had proved favourable for US automobile makers and the producers of rubber and branded food, drink and household goods.

The rapid expansion of chemical, computing and office machinery multinationals in the post-war period revealed the breadth of US capabilities and competitiveness. The lifting of capital and currency controls, after 1958, facilitated both US investment in Europe and investment by European firms in their home continent. By the late 1960s and as economic conditions worsened in the 1970s, multinationals in Europe sought to rationalize, and to manufacture products regionally rather than for each individual national market. On the other side of the Atlantic, the more that the US and Canadian economies integrated, the more multinationals treated the two countries as one market. US and Western oil and mining companies had established, before the Second World War, strong footholds in developing countries, but the favourable concession and operating terms they had assumed in a previous era came increasingly under attack from Third World nations.

The US multinational – with its strong ownership capabilities and advanced technology, developed by a market-seeking parent firm in its home economy and transferred to a subsidiary as a smaller version of itself, and doing so within an integrated internalizing hierarchy – seems to have set the model that framed the ideas of the first theorists of FDI in the 1960s. As we have seen, the multinational has, historically, adopted a range of strategies and came in a variety of organizational forms, because of differences between industries and host economies, and because the international political economy has changed its structure over time.

US interests in bananas, coffee, cocoa, railways and ports dominated the economies and politics of Central America. As former colonies gained their independence, European trading companies were on the retreat, proving the importance of the governmental support they had once enjoyed. But, generally speaking, the governments of new nations and multinationals were able to come to terms, however grudgingly conceded. Until the late 1960s, forced and uncompensated divestments were few.

The USA's global power reached its peak in the 1950s, and Cold War rivalry and the defeat of Communism largely determined its policies overseas. Inevitably, economic interests made up part of the calculation. In the cases of Guatemala and Iran, the USA was able to force the reversal of nationalizations. The fiasco of the Suez Crisis did not mark a clear turning point, but it was symbolic for developing countries seeking greater control over their resources. Events in Chile mixed multinational investments and Cold War fears, and showed the continuing strength of US power, but at the same time the Vietnam war highlighted its limitations. After the late 1960s, the incidence of forced divestments in the Middle East, Africa and Latin America increased markedly.

The Cold War was more fiercely fought in the Third World than in Europe, but, at the ground level, anti-imperialism, nationalism, radicalism, and the control over economic resources mixed with matters of superpower rivalry and the interests of foreign multinationals. With the sanction of UN resolutions, national sovereignty and government policy were given precedence over international property rights. In the Third World, the USA found itself supporting authoritarian regimes against liberation movements. Nationalizations were concentrated in minerals, oil, natural resources generally, essential infrastructure, and utilities. On the other hand, political acts did not always change the economic realities that many developing economies continued to face in their need for the capital, technology and management that multi-nationals controlled.

5 | *Global economics?: 1980–2012*

International economy phase IV?

By the end of the 1980s, commentators had invented a new vogue word: 'globalization'. The international convergence of politics, business and culture, it was argued, had the power to transform human existence. Events overseas could no longer take place in 'a far-off country'. As countries became, economically speaking, more markedly interdependent, national governments assumed the 'inevitability' of cross-border trade and finance being liberalized. The fall of the Berlin Wall in 1989 opened up Eastern Europe, Russia and Central Asia to international business, and policy changes in China increasingly drew a country that had espoused autarky into the global economy.

Foreign direct investment and trade expanded even more rapidly throughout the 1990s, and 'globalization' became, in popular usage, associated with the growing reach and seemingly unchecked activities of multinational enterprises. These ever-bigger businesses took greater responsibility for the cross-border movement of commodities and manufactures, and invented complex, more integrated cross-border management systems and operational practices. The scale and spread of their undertakings, it was argued, forced the international convergence of business systems, work methods, spending patterns, government policy and, ultimately, cultural values. Globalization meant, for many, expectations of regular air travel; it introduced new media technologies and sources of information; it transformed consumer expectations and home life, and symbolized the continuous growth of demand and big business; it affected the daily work of the New York banker, the Bangalore software engineer and the Shenzen factory operative.

Phase I of the global economy – approximately from the 1840s to 1914 – was marked by dynamic growth in trade and FDI; investment by leading industrialized economies in primary products and in developing and undeveloped territories was prominent; multinationals in trade-related and commodity-seeking activities took a lead in international business activities; and imperialism underpinned much of the international economic system and the flow of FDI. Following more than thirty years of world wars, economic depression and trade barriers, phase III of the global economy – approximately from 1950 – was marked by the return of trade and FDI as dynamic sources of growth; outside the Communist bloc, by the long-term lowering of tariff and investment controls; investment by leading industrialized economies markedly in manufacturing and in developed economies; and, lastly, the dominance of large-scale multinationals, with market-seeking strategies, based on the transfer of human, financial and technological resources to overseas subsidiaries they directly owned and controlled.

To what extent were the years after 1980 a continuation or a break with post-war trends? There were more examples of MNEs acting more regionally and even globally in their commercial interests, and becoming less dependent on revenues from their home nation market. FDI began a switch away from the richest nations and towards emerging economies, and was boosted by the further lowering of government controls. Investors looked to the many opportunities provided by privatizations in the West, but in the Soviet Union and its East European satellites too. Of great historical significance, too, was the breakthrough by businesses from emerging economies into the lists of the world's top companies. International services grew markedly in relation to manufacturing, in a reversal of past trends.

Did the changes justify the claims not of mere 'internationalization' but of 'globalization'? The transformation of once-Communist countries and their inclusion in the international economic system were, undoubtedly, important events in world history. There was, additionally, rapid economic growth, greatly improved living standards, and the rise of competitive businesses and major multinationals within industrializing and transition economies, rebalancing diplomatic, military and economic power away from the West. After the Asian Crisis of 1997, the leading G7 nations – comprising the USA, Canada, Germany, France, Italy, Britain and Japan – concluded that only a larger grouping could secure international financial stability. Consequently, a G20 composed of nineteen major economies and the European Union and representing some four fifths of world GDP was established in December 1999. Alongside resource-rich successes such as Russia, Brazil, or

Indonesia, the manufacturing industries of China and South Korea had become core components of the global economy. With the great recession taking hold after 2008, the G20 achieved a new status. Its member nations accounted for some 90 per cent of global output, and 80 per cent of world trade. Representing about two thirds of the world's population, the G20 had another strong claim to credibility, but actions did not fulfil the expectations of its press releases, and the group lacked a permanent secretariat. Nonetheless, was not the G20's existence demonstration of a different international trading and investment system emerging, in which both long-established industrial nations and newly emerged economies were substantial players?

Some patterns remained the same. Not every nation was visibly benefiting from the mix of globalization and growth, and the gap between the gainers (growing in number) and the rest widened. In 1870, the average per capita income in the world's seventeen richest nations was 2.4 times those of the others; by 1990, the same group was 4.5 times wealthier (Pritchett, 1997). Large regional differences and income disparities within rising economic powers such as China, India, Brazil, or South Africa remained, and highlighted the uneven impact of growth and globalization within countries as well as between them. China, with over 1.3 billion people in 2011, might potentially overtake the USA as the world's largest economy, but Americans continued to enjoy living standards eight times greater (World Bank, 2012). Although firms from emerging and transition nations built international competitive advantages and invested worldwide, those from the USA, Western Europe and Japan continued to dominate lists of top multinationals. Although shifts in the structure of the international economy were historically profound, they were also partial.

Global trends

Since trade re-emerged as a source of economic change, the period 1950 to 1973 could with some legitimacy be labelled the 'Golden Age'. Aggregate trends thereafter were not so impressive: following exchange rate instability and rising commodity prices there were sharp downturns in the business cycle (bringing the two recessions of 1979–83 and 1989–92) and the Asian Crisis of 1997 (disrupting the world's fastest-growing region). The long-term rise in merchandise exports could not equal those of the 1960s (Table 5.1). Yet trade did continue

Table 5.1 *Merchandise export growth, 1960–2006: average annual (%)*

1960–9	8.6
1970–9	5.0
1980–9	4.0
1990–9	6.5
2000–6	5.5

Sources: GATT, International Trade, 1989–1990, 1990; WTO (2000, 2001, 2007).

Table 5.2 *Average annual change (%) in exports, world GDP, FDI flows, and FDI stock, 1986–2006*

	1986–90	1991–5	1996–9	2000–6
Exports of goods and non-factor services	15.4	8.6	1.9	6.0
World GDP	11.7	6.3	0.7	3.0
Outward FDI flows	26.2	16.3	37.0	9.2*
Outward FDI stock	20.5	10.8	16.4	14.6*

* FDI flow and stock figures are for 2001–5 only.
Sources: WTO (2007); UNCTAD (2007, 2010).

as a generator of growth, most prominently in the recovery after 1983 and in the longer upswing after 1992. Increases in the years 1984 and 1988 matched those of the post-war decades, and 1994, 1995, 1997 and 2000 especially turned in historically remarkable results. As trade grew faster than world GDP, the global economy continued to become more interconnected (Table 5.2) (WTO, 2007, 2008).

Europe maintained its percentage of world exported merchandise, buoyed by the strength of cross-border traffic within the European Union, while the relative importance of North America declined. In Asia, Japan's performance had peaked by the early 1990s, but China transformed itself into a global workshop, and other countries throughout the region pursued export-orientated industrialization. North America and Western Europe were responsible for 66 per cent of merchandise exports in 1990, but their share had fallen to

Table 5.3 *World merchandise exports, 1983–2006: region and selected country*

	1983	1993	2003	2006
World ($USbn)	1,838	3,676	7,376	11,783
By percentage				
North America	16.8	18.0	15.8	14.2
USA	11.2	12.6	9.8	8.8
South and Central America	4.4	3.0	3.0	3.6
Europe	43.5	45.4	45.9	42.1
EU	31.5	37.4	42.4	38.5
Germany	9.2	10.3	10.2	9.4
CIS			2.6	3.6
Africa	4.5	2.5	2.4	3.1
Middle East	6.8	3.5	4.1	5.5
Asia	19.1	26.1	26.2	27.8
China	1.2	2.5	5.9	8.2
Japan	8.0	9.9	6.4	5.5
Australia and New Zealand	1.4	1.4	1.2	1.2

Source: WTO (2010).

some 40 per cent by 2006. The three regions of North America, Western Europe and East Asia, on the other hand, together produced over 79 per cent of merchandise exports in 1983, and 84 per cent in 2006. Other parts of the world, such as Latin America, fell back relatively speaking; their trade, nonetheless, expanded in real terms (Table 5.3). Asia was the largest decade-by-decade winner, and some 80 per cent of Asian exports in 2006 were in manufactures, while the Middle East, the Commonwealth of Independent States and Africa had a two thirds bias towards fuels and mined minerals.

Germany, through its specialization in high-value-added manufactures, acquired the position of leading merchandise exporter from the USA in 2003. But the most spectacular change at the very top of the table was the entry of China, pushing out Italy, with which it also competed directly in industries such as clothing. It subsequently overtook Japan in 2004, the USA in 2008, and finally Germany in 2009, achieving poll position. Yet all the G7 nations could still be found amongst the nine largest merchandise exporters (IMF, 2009; UNCTAD, 2010). Commercial service exports rose faster than merchandise at the end of

Table 5.4 *Growth of commercial
service exports per person (%),
1990–2009*

1990–5	8.0
1995–2000	5.0
2000–9	9.0

Source: WTO (2009).

the 1990s, and significantly more quickly after 2000 (tables 5.1 and
5.4). Since Asian countries took a larger and larger share of manufactures, developed economies relied more on the sale of commercial
services. The US was consistently the largest service exporter, and the
UK performed well after 1993 to become second. China, in 2007,
replaced Italy in position number 6. Trade in commercial services was
highly concentrated within Europe, with 50 per cent of the world total,
and the EU alone accounting for 25 per cent. Asia and North America
had 29 and 15 per cent respectively (tables 5.4 and 5.5) (WTO, 2001,
2007, 2010).

By 1980, despite the international economy experiencing three
decades of expansion, the value of FDI stock remained smaller in
proportion to the world economy than before the First World War.
Then, from 1984 to 1987, global outflows of FDI tripled, and they
grew by a further 20 per cent in both the years that followed. The
potential of this FDI surge was compared – in its ability to encourage
economic growth and higher living standards, and in its potential for
transforming business systems and technological knowledge – to the
dynamic effects of trade growth between 1950 and 1973. Exports had
grown faster in the post-war period than output, and trade between
nations made them increasingly interdependent; FDI accelerated more
than exports and output from the mid 1980s, making the production of
goods and services reliant on cross-border coordination and organization, and making nations more interdependent in qualitatively different
ways. Five major investing countries – Japan, the USA, Britain, Germany and France – maintained their 70 per cent share of FDI outflows,
and the contribution of developed economies as a group increased to
over 81 per cent. Japan, by the end of the 1980s, was the bold new
entrant, when an appreciating yen and protectionism in the USA and

Table 5.5 *Largest exporters of merchandise and commercial services, rank, country, and %, 1990–2006*

Merchandise				
1990	1993	2000	2003	2006
1 USA (14.6)	USA (12.0)	USA (11.3)	Germany (9.9)	Germany (9.2)
2 Germany (12.2)	Germany (10.1)	Germany (8.7)	USA (9.6)	USA (8.5)
3 Japan (8.4)	Japan (9.7)	Japan (7.5)	Japan (6.2)	China (8.0)
4 France (6.3)	France (5.6)	France (4.7)	China (5.8)	Japan (5.3)
5 UK (5.4)	UK (4.9)	UK (4.5)	France (5.2)	France (4.1)
6 Italy (5.0)	Italy (4.9)	China (3.9)	UK (4.0)	UK (3.7)
Total (51.9)	Total (47.2)	Total (40.6)	Total (40.7)	Total (38.8)

Commercial services				
1990	1993	2000	2003	2006
1 USA (17.0)	USA (17.7)	USA (19.1)	USA (15.5)	USA (14.3)
2 France (8.5)	France (7.9)	UK (7.0)	UK (8.5)	UK (8.3)
3 UK (6.8)	UK (6.1)	France (5.7)	Germany (6.4)	Germany (6.7)
4 Germany (6.6)	Germany (6.0)	Germany (5.6)	France (5.5)	France (4.5)
5 Italy (6.2)	Italy (5.5)	Japan (4.8)	Japan (3.9)	Japan (4.1)
6 Japan (5.3)	Japan (5.5)	Italy (4.0)	Italy (3.9)	Italy (3.5)
Total (50.4)	Total (48.7)	Total (46.2)	Total (43.7)	Total (41.4)

Hong Kong is assessed on its exports as opposed to re-exports, and so is not included in the above data of the top 6.
Source: WTO (2000, 2010).

the European Union forced its major manufacturers to adapt their highly successful export policies (Table 5.6) (UNCTAD, 1991).

The rapid expansion of FDI flows continued during 1992 to 2008, multiplying eightfold, unlike world trade at 1.5 times, and output by 1.45 times. Following three years of robust performance, it peaked at a phenomenal 40 per cent increase for the year 2000, and remained historically high in the decade that followed (Table 5.2) (WTO, 2010; UNCTAD, 1991). Given the new scale and advantages of FDI, the sales

Table 5.6 *World GDP, merchandise exports, service exports, and outward FDI stock, 1983–2003*

	1983	1993	2003	2006
(i) $USbn in current terms				
World GDP	12,344	25,363	37,501	49,536
World merchandise exports	1,848	3,780	7,561	11,783
World service exports	383	998	1,897	2,755
Total exports	2,230	4,777	9,458	14,538
(ii) Ratios				
Merchandise/export total	82.9	79.1	80.0	81.0
Service/export total	17.1	20.9	20.0	19.0
World exports/GDP	18.1	18.9	25.2	29.3

Source: WTO (2000, 2007, 2010); UNCTAD (1991, 2000, 2010).

of all foreign-owned affiliates grew faster than world exports from the 1980s onwards, and, by 2000, they had become 2.2 times larger (Table 5.7). By 2007, there were an estimated 79,000 MNEs, operating some 790,000 overseas subsidiaries and employing 82 million people (UNCTAD, 2008).

For Global Economy IV, and unlike the other periods, we have a plethora of FDI statistics, thanks largely to the work of United Nations agencies. Yet inconsistencies remain, due to revisions of previous data, and, most notably, because variations in recording methods generate large differences between inward and outward FDI totals. We can, nonetheless, indicate both the trends and their scale. So, when outward FDI stock (expressed as a ratio of world output) finally overtook the level gained during the First Global Economy, it was an historical milestone: the figure by 1990 was 9.4 per cent, nearing but still not beating the latest estimate of 11.1 per cent by 1914, with 1993 finally recording 11.3. It was the unprecedented surge in FDI during the 1990s that propelled the world GDP ratio to 18.7 by 2000, and the even more dramatic developments of the 2000s would create by 2009 a figure of 34.5 (Table 5.7) (UNCTAD, 2006; WTO, 2010). According to a revised long-term series, the value of global outward FDI stock, some $524bn in current terms in 1980, then $1,791bn in 1990, reached $6,471bn in 2000, climbing subsequently to $10,672bn for 2005 (Table 5.8). The United Nations Conference on Trade and

Table 5.7 *Foreign direct investment, 1990–2009, US$bn, 1,000s employees, and %*

	1982	1990	2000	2005	2009
FDI inflows $bn	59	208	1,271	986	1,114
FDI outflows $bn	28	241	1,150	893	1,101
Inward FDI stock $bn	647	2,082	6,314	11,525	17,743
Outward FDI stock $bn	600	2,087	5,976	12,417	18,982
Cross-border mergers and acquisitions $bn		151	1,144	716	250
Sales foreign affiliates $bn	2,620	6,026	15,680	21,721	29,298
Gross product foreign affiliates $bn	646	1,477	3,167	4,327	5,812
Assets foreign affiliates $bn	2,108	5,938	21,102	49,252	77,057
Exports foreign affiliates $bn	647	1,498	3,572	4,319	5,186
Employment foreign affiliates (thousands)	19,537	24,476	45,587	57,799	79,825
World GDP $bn	10,899	22,121	31,895	45,273	55,005
World gross fixed capital formation (GFCF) $bn	2,397	5,099	6,466	9,833	12,404
World exports of goods and services $bn	2,247	4,414	7,036	12,954	15,716
% outward FDI stock / world GDP	5.5	9.4	18.7	27.4	34.5
% FDI inflows / GFCF	2.5	4.1	19.7	10.0	9.0
% affiliate product / world GDP	5.9	6.7	9.9	9.6	10.6

Source: UNCTAD, *World Investment Report* (2001, 2006, 2010).

Development (UNCTAD) records even more impressive trends and totals of $18,892bn for 2009 and $21,288bn for 2010. The developed economies attracted the greater share of inward FDI flows during the 1980s, but the 1990s and 2000s saw developing economies close the gap in total FDI stock (Table 5.9). Inward FDI flows accounted for a quickly rising share of capital formation in host economies, pointing to the role of multinationals as keepers and transmitters of finance, technology and management (Table 5.7).

Multinational affiliates – excluding therefore the major contribution of parent companies in their home economies – accounted for one third

Table 5.8 *Outward stock of FDI by major home countries and regions, 1980–2005 ($bn)*

	1980	1990	2000	2005
Developed economies	507.4	1642.2	5578.3	9271.8
European Union	213.0	810.3	3050.1	5475.0
UK	80.4	229.3	897.8	1238.0
France	23.6	110.1	445.1	853.2
Germany	43.1	151.6	541.9	967.3
Belgium and Luxembourg	6.0	40.6	179.8	386.3
Netherlands	42.1	106.9	305.5	641.3
Spain	1.9	15.7	167.7	381.3
Italy	7.3	60.2	180.3	293.5
Sweden	3.7	50.7	123.2	202.8
Other Western Europe	22.1	77.0	593.0	769.3
Switzerland	21.5	66.1	229.7	394.8
Norway	0.6	10.9	362.6	365.1
North America	244.0	515.3	1553.9	2450.6
USA	220.2	430.5	1316.2	2051.3
Canada	23.8	84.8	237.6	399.4
Other developed economies	28.3	239.5	381.4	576.9
Japan	19.6	201.4	278.4	386.6
Australia	2.3	30.5	85.4	159.2
Developing economies	16.5	148.7	871.0	1273.6
Asia				
Hong Kong, China	0.1	11.9	388.4	470.5
Singapore	3.7	7.8	56.8	110.9
Taiwan, China	0.1	30.4	66.7	97.3
China		4.5	27.8	46.3
Malaysia	0.2	2.7	22.9	44.5
Republic of Korea	0.1	2.3	26.8	36.5
Indonesia		0.1	6.9	13.7
India	0.2	0.1	1.9	9.6
Turkey		1.2	3.7	8.1
Africa				
South Africa	0.6	15.0	32.3	38.5
Latin America				
Brazil	0.6	41.0	51.9	71.6

Table 5.8 (*cont.*)

	1980	1990	2000	2005
Mexico	0.2	2.7	8.3	28.0
Argentina	6.1	6.1	21.1	22.6
Chile		0.2	11.2	21.3
Russian Federation			20.1	120.4
EU 10 new member states	0.3	0.9	5.2	26.5
World	523.9	1,791.1	6,471.4	10,671.9

Source: Dunning and Lundan (2008); UNCTAD (2001).

of world exports by the 1990s. MNEs – parent and subsidiary alike – had by 2000 some two thirds of merchandise and service exports, much of it in intra-firm trade. This intra-firm trade – cross-border activities organized by MNE management between directly owned plants and offices – expanded in importance, from 20 per cent of international commerce to about 40 per cent by 2000 (WTO, 2010). The upward trend in the sales, value added and exports of the foreign affiliates owned by multinationals can be seen, and shows that more multi-nationals became more international and less a predominantly home country enterprise with added foreign subsidiaries (Table 5.7). Such impressive measures do not include the complex international networks of contracted suppliers and associated businesses increasingly coordinated and determined by MNEs, and requiring new strategies and forms of organization.

Continuity is noteworthy too. In 1980, the USA had some 42 per cent of outward FDI stock, the top five investing nations some 89 per cent, and all the developed economies 97 per cent. The relative importance of the USA, as world leader, and the G7 fell after 2000, but developed nations as a defined group in 2010 still accounted for 82 per cent. The shift went to East Asia mainly, and also to South East Asia, which together gained some 7.5 per cent between 1990 and 2010. During these two decades, the share of the developed economies fell by 10.8 (Table 5.10). In 2008, MNEs from the USA, Western and Northern Europe, Japan and Australia occupied 92 places in the top 100 non-financial international businesses; five countries – the USA, France, Britain, Germany and Japan – could claim 70 between them.

Table 5.9 *Inward stock of FDI by major home countries and regions,*
1980–2005 ($bn)

	1980	1990	2000	2005
Developed economies	374.9	1,418.9	3,976.2	7,117.1
European Union	185.7	768.2	2,179.7	4,499.1
UK	63.0	203.9	438.6	816.7
France	22.9	86.8	259.8	600.8
Germany	36.6	111.2	271.6	502.8
Belgium and Luxembourg	7.3	58.4	195.2	492.3
Netherlands	19.2	68.7	243.7	463.4
Spain	5.1	65.9	156.3	367.7
Italy	8.9	60.0	121.2	219.9
Ireland	3.7	56.5	127.1	211.2
EU 10 new member states		2.5	97.7	273.9
Other Western Europe	15.1	47.0	118.1	232.2
Switzerland	8.5	34.2	86.8	172.5
North America	137.2	507.8	1,469.6	1,982.6
US	83.0	394.9	1,256.9	1,625.7
Canada	54.2	112.8	212.7	356.9
Other developed economies	37.0	95.9	208.8	403.2
Japan	3.3	9.9	50.3	100.9
Australia	13.2	73.6	111.1	210.9
Developing economies	240.8	370.3	1756.5	2757.0
Asia and the Pacific	174.5	193.8	1066.4	1555.1
Hong Kong, China	138.8	45.1	455.5	533.0
Singapore	6.2	30.5	112.6	186.9
Taiwan, China	2.4	9.7	17.6	41.9
China	6.3	20.7	193.3	317.9
Malaysia	5.2	10.3	52.7	47.8
Republic of Korea	1.1	5.2	37.5	63.2
Indonesia	10.3	8.9	24.8	21.1
India	1.2	1.7	17.5	45.3
Turkey	0.1	11.2	19.2	42.2
Vietnam		1.7	20.6	31.1
Africa	16.2	58.4	151.0	264.5
South Africa		9.2	43.4	69.4
Nigeria	2.4	8.5	23.8	34.8
Egypt	2.3	11.0	18.3	28.9
Latin America and the Caribbean	50.0	118.1	539.0	937.4

Table 5.9 (*cont.*)

	1980	1990	2000	2005
Brazil	17.5	37.2	103.0	201.2
Mexico	9.0	10.1	45.8	73.6
Argentina	5.3	8.8	67.6	55.2
Chile	0.9	10.1	45.8	73.6
South East Europe and CIS			70.3	255.7
Russian Federation			32.2	132.5
World	615.8	1789.3	5802.9	10129.7

Source: Dunning and Lundan (2008).

The developed economies had all of the top 50 financial multinationals, and the five leading nations had a total of 24 (UNCTAD, 2009). While the challenge from multinationals from developing and transition economies was set to grow, those headquartered in the developed world continued to dominate for the moment in the assets, sales and employees of foreign affiliates (tables 5.11 and 5.12).

During the 1980s, with its economic miracle under way, East Asia absorbed much of the increases in FDI, while trends in Latin America declined. Investment in developing countries went predominantly to those undergoing industrialization or possessing natural resources. Egypt and Nigeria, as oil producers, accounted for 86 per cent of FDI flows to Africa. Amounts to developing countries did increase (US$12.5bn in 1980–4 and US$22.4bn in 1985–9), but developed locations retained by far the greater pulling power (UNCTAD, 1991). Policy changes transformed the reach of MNE activities in the 1990s: China's economic isolation ended step by step, with the Communists still very much in control, but collapse and realignment exposed the Soviet bloc to the disruptive forces of the global marketplace. The new international political economy created a category of 'transition economies', and later 'developing and transition economies', or DTEs, to contrast with the 'developed' world. Western multinationals looked to China's huge domestic market, its role as an export platform, and its low labour costs, transferring, from 1979 to 2000, some $346bn (Huang and Yu, 2012) (tables 5.9 and 5.10).

Investors, on the other hand, remained wary of a Russia associated with unclear legal rights, political interference, corruption, inflation,

Table 5.10 *FDI stock, 1990–2010 (%)*

	Outward			Inward		
	1990	2000	2010	1990	2000	2010
Developed economies	93.1	88.9	82.3	75.2	75.9	65.3
G7	75.0	72.3	55.9	54.6	57.3	38.3
Western and Northern Europe	42.3	47.2	49.1	38.9	32.8	39.8
European Union	38.7	43.9	43.8	36.6	31.2	36.0
France	5.4	11.6	7.5	4.7	5.3	5.3
Germany	7.2	6.8	7.0	5.3	3.7	3.5
Italy	2.9	2.3	2.3	2.9	1.6	1.8
Netherlands	5.1	3.8	4.4	3.3	3.3	3.1
UK	10.9	11.3	8.3	9.8	5.9	5.7
USA	34.9	33.8	23.7	25.9	37.4	18.0
Canada	4.0	3.0	3.0	5.4	2.9	2.9
Japan	9.6	3.5	4.1	0.5	0.7	1.1
Australia, Bermuda, Israel, and New Zealand	2.1	1.4	2.4	4.5	2.2	3.4
Developing economies	6.9	10.8	15.4	24.8	23.3	31.1
Africa	1.0	0.6	0.6	2.9	2.1	2.9
Latin America and Caribbean	2.8	2.6	3.6	5.3	6.7	9.0
Brazil	2.0	0.7	0.9	1.8	1.6	2.5
Asia and Oceania	3.2	7.6	11.2	16.6	14.4	19.2
East Asia	1.9	6.3	7.8	11.6	9.6	9.9
China	0.2	0.4	1.5	1.0	2.6	3.0
Hong Kong, China	0.6	4.9	4.6	9.7	6.1	5.7
South East Asia	0.5	1.1	2.1	3.1	3.6	4.9
South Asia	0.02	0.04	0.5	0.3	0.4	1.4
India	0.006	0.03	0.5	0.1	0.2	1.0
West Asia	0.4	0.2	0.8	1.5	0.8	3.0
South East Europe and CIS	n/a	0.3	2.3	n/a	0.8	3.6
Russian Federation	n/a	0.3	2.1	n/a	0.4	2.2

Source: UNCTAD (2011).

and competition from government-controlled monopolies. Shadowy dealings exaggerated inward flows, as much of it quickly exited, and even the official figures for per capita FDI were well below the CIS average. The position improved only from 2003, more markedly so

Table 5.11 *Assets and sales of foreign affiliates headquartered in developed economies and in DTEs, 1995 and 2005, as % of world trade*

	Assets		Sales	
	1995	2008	1995	2008
Developed economies	98.9	92.0	98.7	90.9
European Union	27.9	40.4	37.7	40.9
USA	55.5	29.5	28.0	29.1
Japan	8.8	13.3	27.8	13.9
DTEs	1.1	8.0	1.3	9.1
Asian economies	1.0	6.6	1.1	7.6

Source: UNCTAD (2010).

after 2006, with the flotation of state enterprises in banking and the liberalization of electricity generation contributing to the relative boom in inward investment.[1] The 'transition economies' of the CIS and South East Europe moved from effectively zero to less than a 1 per cent share, by 2000, still minuscule in world terms. The impact on certain sectors and on industrially advanced countries in Eastern Europe was far-reaching, however, as ultimately was investment in energy-rich Kazakhstan. Inward FDI stocks in the CIS and Eastern Europe constituted 3.6 per cent of the global total by 2010 (tables 5.9 and 5.10) (UNCTAD, 2006).

FDI flows to the non-developed world rose from 17.4 per cent annually (1985–90) to 35–40 per cent (1995–2000), before receding to above 30 per cent (2004–8). Asia continued to take much of the gain, with China being second only to the USA as a destination in the late 1990s; within Latin America, Brazil and Mexico were the important choices of investors (UNCTAD, 2009). The demand for natural resources, industrializing economies, low costs and greater political stability caught the attention of MNEs. By 2009, DTEs were hosts to about half of inward FDI flows, although the bulk still gravitated to the most successful countries amongst them (WTO, 2010). The developed world's share of inward FDI stock fell from about 75 to 65 per cent between 1990 and 2010 (tables 5.9 and 5.10).

The manufacturing MNEs that had been at the forefront of FDI in the post-war decades had shown a preference for wholly owned subsidiaries and frequently greenfield investments, and concern for direct control of their management and therefore the firm's

Table 5.12 *Assets, sales, employment and TNI of foreign affiliates headquartered in developed and developing economies*

	100 largest TNCs	100 largest TNCs from DTEs
Assets (US$bn)		
Foreign affiliates	6,172	907
Total	10,760	2,680
%	57	34
Sales (US$bn)		
Foreign affiliates	5,173	997
Total	8,354	2,240
%	62	45
Employees (1,000s)		
Foreign affiliates	8,905	2,652
Total	15,408	6,779
%	58	39
Transnationality (TNI) Index		
Developed economies	63.4	
European Union	67.6	
USA	58.1	
UK	75.5	
Japan	50.0	
DTEs	50.7	

TNI: weighted index of assets, sales and employees in foreign-owned affiliates as percentage of company totals. DTE: developing and transition economies.
Source: UNCTAD (2010).

proprietary knowledge. For the post-1980 period, across all sectors, strategies tended to embrace joint venture and strategic alliances, as vehicles for sharing the costs of R&D, production or marketing. Another crucial trend in the entry-mode strategies of MNEs was the pursuit of cross-border mergers and acquisitions (M&A). The lowering of investment barriers and a worldwide spate of privatizations supplied the needed mix of opportunity and incentive. M&A allowed MNEs to respond to intensifying international competition by enabling rapid and global expansion; it accelerated the international consolidation and restructuring of industries, plus the capture of technology, cost or infrastructure advantages available in overseas locations. Contrary to strategies of market-seeking through nationally orientated subsidiaries, utilizing capabilities transferred from the parent company, it empowered asset-seeking policies and the purchase of capabilities in R&D, production, or marketing (UNCTAD, 2001).

The statisticians at the UN did not bother to record cross-border M&A in the early 1980s, but did note totals of $151bn in 1990, rising in the late 1990s to a peak, and reaching $1,144bn in 2000: what, in perspective, had been some 41 per cent of all outward FDI climbed to a near absolute 99.5 per cent, before falling away to almost 23 per cent by 2009 (Table 5.7). There were 114 so-called 'megadeals' of above $1bn in 1999; 175 in 2000; and, by 2008, over $3bn was the measure of an M&A megadeal, with some 73 being recorded. During the height of M&A activity, the telecommunications and automobile industries achieved prominence, as did transactions within the EU and the stimulating framework of its Single Market. M&A tended, also, to involve the flow of funds from developed nations to other developed locations (UNCTAD, 2001, 2006, 2009).

One new feature of cross-border M&A in the late 1990s was the involvement of private equity and related firms, benefiting from a combination of low interest rates and international financial integration. Their five-to-ten-year investment horizons – implying financial engineering and asset stripping – raised policy issues for host-country governments. The influence of private equity faded with the drop in fund-raising and leveraged buy-outs, after 2000, and especially after the 2008 crisis, but some of the slack was taken up by sovereign wealth funds (SWFs). Of the $65bn accumulated in FDI by SWFs between 1987 and 2008, $57bn occurred after 2005; 70 per cent of this total stock went to services and utilities, and only 17 and 13 per cent to manufacturing and the primary sector respectively. There were 50 recorded SWFs from 40 countries by 2008, including the Kuwait Investment Authority (founded in 1953), Singapore's Temasek Holdings (1974), Norway's Government Pension Fund (1990) and the China Investment Corporation (2007). They tended to be cautious, long-term investors, but the control of economic assets by foreign governments posed even bigger dilemmas for host countries than private equity funds (UNCTAD, 2006, 2009, 2010).

Global governance

The biggest change in the governance of the international economic system was the founding of the World Trade Organization (WTO) in

January 1995. Although tariffs overall had continued their long-term downward trend (UNCTAD, 2006), developments after 1980 had put the old GATT arrangements under stress. By 1986, for example, Voluntary Export Restraints affected some 16 per cent of imports to industrialized countries. Japanese companies had succeeded as exporters and international investors, but the Japanese home market was perceived as closed. Trading blocs lowered barriers internally, but the EU looked like a fortress to the outside world. The USA contrasted its open market with discriminatory policies abroad, arguing it suffered from trade deficits and unemployment as a result. Agreement to establish the WTO was reached during GATT's Uruguay round of negotiations, from 1986 to 1993. The name World Trade Organization harked back to the UN's Havana Conference of 1948, when, despite the urging of the USA, participating nations decided not to outlaw discriminatory trade controls.

The new organization's task was to lower barriers hindering cross-border commerce and investment, and to establish and enforce more consistent rules of conduct. It was decided to scrap many tariffs on manufactures and to lower the rest, so that duties on imported manufactures fell to their lowest level in post-war history.[2] The lifting of textile barriers benefited developing economies, as did limited reductions on agricultural subsidies. Developed nations welcomed the first-ever General Agreement on Trade in Services (GATS), despite important opt-outs for developing nations and most service sectors. On the insistence of the USA, Trade-Related Aspects of Intellectual Property Rights (TRIPS) extended protection for patents, copyright and trademarks, fundamental to success in the high-tech industries, branded goods or entertainment software associated with developed economies. Within ten years, WTO members had to enforce patents and copyright for 20 and 50 years respectively. Critically, whenever competitors fell into dispute, members could now appeal to a binding court of arbitration at the WTO with powers to impose fines or sanctions (Rugman and Brewer, 2001).

At least in principle, states agreed not to discriminate between the trade and investment activities of indigenous and foreign enterprise. One outcome was Trade Related Investment Measures (TRIMS): it brought stricter limits on local content regulations, and on export targets set for foreign firms as a balancing of any components they imported. Nonetheless, the USA, the EU, Japan and Canada had preferred a comprehensive agreement on investment, prohibiting technology transfer requirements, controls on foreign exchange, curbs on the transfer of profits, and expropriation to the past, but accepted for the time being a watered-down TRIMS instead (Rugman and Brewer, 2001).

The WTO and its charter had sidetracked three controversies – the protection and subsidizing of agriculture, the safeguarding of intellectual property, and restrictions on FDI and the operations of foreign-owned subsidiaries – and they were all included for discussion in the Doha trade negotiations, begun in 2001 (UNCTAD, 2010). Arguments over quotas, investment controls, or intellectual property revealed differing national interests, and emphasized (broadly speaking) the lead in high-tech products, branded goods, and services held by the West and Japan versus concern for low-cost manufacturing and the production of raw materials by the others. While firms from developed nations, through their competitive advantages, generally benefited from the liberalization of trade and investment, developing nations strove to protect their nascent manufacturing. The WTO contained, by 2010, 154 member states, representing some 97 per cent of world trade (UNCTAD, 2010).

In allowing the WTO to decide trade disputes, nations gained more effective governance of the international economy, but bargained a portion of their sovereignty in return. Not surprisingly, nationalists, conservatives, believers in economic planning, and globalization critics generally viewed this new super-national power with suspicion. The WTO constituted only one symbol of globalization and nation state decline. The IMF was a lender of last resort for governments but, in the 1990s, its intervention came with prescriptions of trade and market liberalization, lower government spending, and privatization. Many condemned the shock therapy administered to Russia, and questioned the IMF's role in Asia and the developing world (Stiglitz, 2002).

In the minds of conspiracy theorists, the United Nations might, bizarrely, be a plot to secure world government, and sinister cliques such as the Bilderberg Group or the World Economic Forum, which met in Davos every January, might secretly run world affairs. Less paranoid commentators could make the point that global NGOs such as the WTO or the IMF had detracted (for better or worse) from the sovereignty of nation states, as had the International Organization for Standardization, or the International Criminal Court at The Hague.

All four organizations, interestingly, dated back to the Second World War or earlier, not the new era of globalization. It was the sheer scale and benefits of trade and FDI – expanding since 1950, and accelerating noticeably since 1980 and more so since 1990 – that determined the policy options of any single nation state. For some writers, exaggerating real trends, nation states that had appeared in the nineteenth century had come to the end of their historical cycle, and footloose multinationals were representative of the new coming force in world affairs (Ohmae, 1999).

Could MNEs command the resources and coercive powers of nation states? Where they operated, they usually required or benefited from the cooperation or support of governments. It was nation states that set the policies of the IMF, the World Bank, the WTO and the United Nations, even if the results of diplomatic compromise were frustrating. The more powerful states and the larger economies could still influence the international economy, and mould the policies of global NGOs. The US or the EU mustered powerful trade delegations at the WTO, and continued by right to hold the top posts at the IMF and World Bank. Moreover, most Asian nations that had successfully industrialized had done so by combining international economic engagement with strong and interventionist governments. As before in history, it was frequently the relationship between international business, on one side, and developing economies and small states, on the other, that caused the majority of controversies. It was too easy to exaggerate the power of the multinational, and yet it was a fact that some 500 firms and their executives were responsible, by 2000, for over half of the world's trade and approximately four fifths of outward FDI (UNCTAD, 2001). Their role in domestic economies and politics and their place in the international system had grown markedly at the turn of the twentieth century. It was not world domination, but it was tangible power.

There remained no single or consistently applied global system of rules for FDI. The World Bank and the IMF introduced, in 1991, guidelines on the rights and obligations of international business. Yet they built upon the primacy of national sovereignty, and did not define principles of international law and adjudication. The core idea was that host governments should treat indigenous and foreign companies equally, and that disputes between host governments and MNEs would be settled in national courts or through some agreed mechanism. The code stressed the positive impact of multinational investment and open borders, and the need for regulatory stability and investor confidence, but the governments of developing nations remained suspicious of the implications. The developed economies, dissatisfied with TRIMS, under the umbrella of the WTO, refloated the original plan as the Multilateral Agreement on Investment (MAI), and, from its founding in 1994, the North American Free Trade Area (NAFTA) provided an example of its precepts in action. But India and Malaysia, amongst others, voted against any further discussions on the liberalizing of FDI. By prioritizing non-discrimination for foreign multinationals, many nations saw the MAI as a bill of rights for companies, undermining in effect their political and economic sovereignty. When the opposition of developing economies strengthened, supporters abandoned the proposal in 1998. The USA felt, for example, that too many exceptions had been introduced, allowing, for example, special taxes on multinationals, and, in the interests of local cultures, limits on foreign television programmes and music (Rugman and Brewster, 2001; WTO, 2008). In sum, the developed economies failed to appoint the WTO as world guardian of overseas investment in addition to its responsibilities for trade.

Regional blocs continued to evolve, and also raised parallel arguments about national sovereignty and the costs of intensifying international competition. NAFTA began with the USA and Canada in 1989, and included Mexico by 1994: it liberalized cross-border commerce and FDI, and covered services and intellectual property in addition to merchandise. In 1993, the European Economic Community acquired the political and institutional dimensions of the European Union, and the European Single Market came into existence. The euro was introduced during in the following year. Attempts to imitate the EU in Latin America, even to a limited extent, were not so successful. The customs union envisaged by the Andean Pact (re-established in 1990) and then the Andean Community (1997) did not effectively materialize until 2003. There were five members: Bolivia, Ecuador, Peru, Colombia and Venezuela. Mercosur, which began in 1988 as an agreement between Brazil and Argentina, included Paraguay and Uruguay by 1990. Although trade between members boomed, a full customs union proved elusive. With tariffs as high as 70 per cent for those outside the agreement, the four countries involved were inefficiently producing cars, buses, agricultural equipment and other goods that they could only sell to each other. Venezuela, in 2006, left the Andean Community to join Mercosur.

The English-speaking Caribbean Community (Caricom) repeatedly failed to fulfil its declaration of economic union from 1984, and its fifteen members decided to reformulate themselves as the Caribbean Single Market and Economy (CSME) in 2006. The East African Community was likewise refounded in 2001, but made small headway with its agenda of customs union and political federation. The USA did, in 2005, sign the Central America Free Trade Agreement (CAFTA) with Costa Rica, El Salvador, Guatemala, Honduras, Nicaragua and the Dominican Republic. In Miami, in 1994, a Free Trade Area of the Americas was proposed, but foundered over US insistence on the safeguarding of intellectual property rights and lower manufacturing tariffs, while Brazil and Argentina wanted an end to agricultural protection in the USA. ASEAN's member states created the ASEAN Free Trade Area (AFTA) in 1992, but full agreement on tariff reductions took until 2003. Even then, many of its signatories continued to favour forms of protectionism and insisted on a wide range of exceptions. In 2010, on the other hand, its ten members signed an agreement with China that lifted tariffs on 90 per cent of traded goods.[3] Only NAFTA and the EU had detailed codes on the equal rights of international investors.

It is estimated that some 90 per cent of the 2,600 changes made by national governments to their FDI laws and regulations between 1992 and 2008 would have encouraged foreign investment (UNCTAD, 2009). An analysis of 102 new government measures, for 2009, revealed that some 30 per cent of them had tightened regulations on FDI, the highest ratio since 1992, and nationalizations had taken place in Venezuela and Bolivia. Yet the majority were more reflective of post-1980 trends, by opening closed sectors, privatizing state-owned businesses, ending monopolies, and allowing land acquisitions. There were 5,939 operative International Investment Agreements (IAAs) between nation states by 2009, covering technical issues such as double taxation, and outlining dispute procedures between host governments and multinationals. The majority of cases occurred in developing and transition economies. Some of them, it was noted, had begun to question and reject the International Centre for Settlement of Investment Disputes (ICSID), founded by the World Bank to remove non-commercial risks and to free the flow of private overseas investment. The ever-rising need for overseas capital and know-how in developing and transition economies had reawakened arguments about protecting natural resources and strategic industries in a world of powerful multinationals (UNCTAD, 2010).

Global services

An information systems cluster with global reach, which emerged around Bangalore, in India, starkly demonstrated the increasing participation of developing economies in cross-border commerce, and the expanding importance of commercial services. Another striking phenomenon was the new speed of communications and business transactions, thanks to a technological revolution in information systems. Government investment in research facilities, most obviously in the Indian Institute of Science and in aerospace and electronics projects, stimulated growth in the city and its surrounding region, and, by the 1980s, India was producing 150,000 computer engineers every year. Low labour costs and high levels of proficiency in English added to the set of international advantages on which 'India's Silicon Valley' was built. Texas Instruments was the first multinational to recognize Bangalore's assets, establishing a research laboratory there in 1985.[4] Indian firms moved quickly from working with foreign companies to selling basic software services and maintenance, and then on to direct competition with Western firms for programming projects and consultancy services. One of these was Wipro, a highly diverse business group, once best known for cooking oils and other consumer goods. When IBM left India, which had introduced foreign ownership restrictions, Wipro took its chance and entered IT production in 1980.[5] Another success story was Infosys Technologies Ltd, founded one year later.[6]

The worldwide web from the 1990s created a global software factory, in which programmes could be written in the USA and tested in Bangalore, and maintenance checks could be conducted from overseas. The time difference, far from being a problem, was a boon: work could be carried out overnight ready for the beginning of office hours the next day. Infosys soon showed its ambitions by opening an overseas branch in 1987, and by the end of the 1990s it had nine offices in the USA and four elsewhere. North America at this point was generating 82 per cent of its revenues, from a client list of over 200 companies; India generated only 3 per cent. Infosys was the first Indian firm, in 1999, to register on a US stock exchange, NASDAQ, where it could raise the capital to fund growth and acquisitions. In the following year, it bought the Massachusetts-based EC Cubed, an application provider for business-to-business e-commerce, and the Hong Kong office, opened in 2000, was Infosys's first move into the Asia Pacific region.[7] A few large firms accounted for India's software exports, and foreign-owned firms held only one fifth of this trade in 1999 (UNCTAD, 2002). By 2011, as in the case of Infosys, Wipro had emerged as a multiple service provider, listed in New York as well as in India, and employing 100,000 people across 55 countries.[8]

Microsoft entered India in 1990, its headquarters in New Delhi well placed for contracts with the government, and it established an R&D centre in Hyderabad.[9] IBM had fallen behind technologically in the 1980s, and, with its mainframe business collapsing, it began to record enormous losses. In 1991, 'Big Blue' declared its intention to be, within three years, a world-class supplier of technological services to corporations. The company returned to India in 1992, one year after the ownership rules for foreign companies had been relaxed, in a joint venture with the Tata business group; it fully acquired the subsidiary in 1999. By 2007, IBM had invested some $2bn in India. IBM Global Services (IGS) – formally established in 1996, within the company's new and more commercially flexible holding company structure – offered consultancy on supply chain management, finance, customer relationships, and outsourcing, as well as IT and software solutions. The strategy was to integrate, through IGS, the company's numerous divisions and resources into a coordinated full-package, large-scale solutions provider. In 2001, for the first time in IBM's history, services generated more sales than hardware, and employed 46 per cent of its international workforce (UNCTAD, 1991).[10]

No single factor could explain the lead role that services took in multinational business developments: the mix of reasons included technology, government policies, and long-term shifts in the make-up of advanced economies and in spending patterns. In the decade after 1980, micro-electronics and communications technology breakthroughs inspired a new sphere of business and information services. Governments, of the developed economies particularly, revised their protectionist policies in air transportation, telecommunications, utilities, banking and insurance. Internationalization quickened in advertising, management consultancy, hotels and distribution, when previously they had lagged behind other sectors. It was no longer possible to advocate FDI in manufacturing and natural resources, and inconsistently deny its benefits to the tertiary sector. Those firms with a leadership in products, technology, systems, people, or finance were given the chance to transform slow-moving domestic markets. The prospect of a Single Market freed trade and investment in services and banking, and notably incentivized European multinationals (UNCTAD, 2006; WTO, 2010).

Although it did not have general oversight over multinational investment, the WTO did broker a deal, in February 1997, which established rules of open and fair competition in telecommunications. The 68 signatory nations comprised 90 per cent of the world market, and the USA, the EU and Japan had deregulated the industry by the next year. A WTO agreement on financial services and banking, to be implemented from March 1999, involved 102 countries and covered 95 per cent of the sector's global revenues. The USA and the EU ended all commercial barriers to outside investors, and many Asian nations made noteworthy concessions (UNCTAD, 2010). Manufacturing amounted to a falling proportion of output in developed nations, and their high discretionary incomes, large markets and liberalized regulatory regimes encouraged cross-border investment in the tertiary sector (UNCTAD, 1991). Finally, companies further embraced strategies of outsourcing and offshoring, and they looked to wherever in the world operations, human resources, costs or capital were most favourable (UNCTAD, 2006; WTO, 2010).

Since services had been one quarter of outward FDI stock in the 1970s, it followed that they offered the greatest growth opportunities: services rose to just under half of the total by 1990, and to some two thirds by 2005. The share of manufacturing, therefore, fell from 44 to 26 per cent between 1990 and 2005, primary production from 9 to 6 per cent. The role of developing economies in service sector outward FDI did grow – between 1990 and 2005, from 1.4 to 11.7 per cent – but companies from developed nations very evidently remained dominant. Over 70 per cent of all these activities were in the category of 'intermediate', namely finance and business services, although telecommunications, utilities and infrastructure all showed large increases. As commerce in commodities and goods was important to their growth or industrialization, developing economies were more inclined to invest in trade or trade-related services. Some 84 per cent of FDI stock was located, by the mid 1980s, in developed countries, compared to 75 per cent for FDI stock generally (UNCTAD, 1991). The locus of investment and activity shifted slightly to developing and transition economies after 1990, but the advanced economies still retained nearly 77 per cent of the total by 2010. As well as trade and trade-related services, construction and tourism made up a significant proportion of service inward FDI flows to developing nations (Table 5.13).

One other general trend is noteworthy. Services accounted for 40 per cent of all international M&A in the late 1980s, and 63 per cent by 2005, with deals in banking, finance, telecommunications and utilities to the fore. Strategies overall were market-seeking, since services often had to be provided locally. The overseas subsidiaries of US service multinationals made 84 per cent of their sales locally, in 2001, compared to 61 per cent for US manufacturers. On average, for 2003, service MNEs had a trans-nationality index of 20 per cent, while manufacturing with its complex cross-border production and marketing chains achieved some 40 per cent. Approximately 10 per cent of global services were traded; in the case of manufacturing, 50 per cent. Overseas investment in services could, furthermore, be neatly combined with local capital through franchising, management contracts and partnerships. While FDI in hotels or water distribution, like that in manufacturing, concerned tangible assets, services were more likely to depend for their success on intangible assets, such as knowledge, soft technologies, managerial organization, or experience. Such knowhow and procedures could be codified in management contracts for franchisees or partners, specifying performance conditions and quality control. Such non-equity deals were commonplace in hotels, restaurants, car rental, retailing, accounting, and legal and professional services (UNCTAD, 2004, 2006; WTO, 2007).

Trade and transport

Not every industry could embrace global liberalization: while banking, energy and telecommunications changed dramatically, airlines looked trapped in the past. In 2003, the International Air Transport Association, or IATA, representing 273 airlines, called for freedom from sixty years of government control. The Single Market discontinued foreign ownership restrictions within the EU, and open skies agreements, most

Table 5.13 *World outward FDI stock by sector and industry, and world inward FDI stock by sector, 1990 and 2005 ($m and %)*

	World outward FDI stock		
	1990		
	Developed economies	Developing economies	World
Primary	161,564	2,219	163,783
% primary FDI total	98.7	1.3	100.0
% world FDI total			9.0
agriculture, forestry, fishing	5,245	319	5,564
mining, quarrying, petroleum	156,319	1,900	158,219
Manufacturing	793,573	6,452	800,025
% manufacturing FDI total	99.2	0.8	100.0
% world FDI total			44.1
food, beverage, tobacco	75,603	446	76,049
textiles, clothing, leather	19,550	191	19,741
chemicals, chemical products	150,917	810	151,727
metal, metal products	66,350	87	66,437
machinery, equipment	42,040	22	42,063
electricals and electronics	97,505	1,040	98,545
motor vehicles, transportation	60,255	10	60,265
Services	834,927	11,623	846,550
% of services FDI total	98.6	1.4	100.00
% world FDI total			46.6
electricity, gas, water	9,618		9,618
construction	18,242	169	18,410
finance	399,951	7,230	407,180
business activities	55,111	1,310	56,421
Unspecified	4,139	716	4,855
% world FDI total			0.3
Total	1,794,203	21,010	1,815,213
% world FDI total	98.9	1.1	100.0

	2005			
	Developed economies	Developing economies	SE Europe & CIS	World
Primary	584,093	35,365	neg.	619,458
% primary FDI total	94.3	5.7		100.0
% world FDI total				5.9

(*cont.*)

Table 5.13 (*cont.*)

| | 2005 | | | |
	Developed economies	Developing economies	SE Europe & CIS	World
agriculture, forestry, fishing	4,256	1,575	87	5,918
mining, quarrying, petroleum	577,362	33,791	neg.	610,176
Manufacturing	2,655,294	117,426	1,562	2,774,282
% manufacturing FDI total	95.7	4.2	0.1	100
% world FDI total				26.2
food, beverage, tobacco	298,755	2,510	178	301,442
textiles, clothing, leather	132,192	3,264	1	135,458
chemicals, chemical products	559,999	3,568	892	564,458
metal, metal products	266,304	1,538	247	268,090
machinery, equipment	108,933	513	3	109,450
electricals and electronics	240,602	9,036	3	249,641
motor vehicles, transportation	427,360	1,305	52	428,717
Services	6,264,020	830,740	802	7,095,562
% services FDI total	88.3	11.7	(0.01)	100.0
% world FDI total				67.1
electricity, gas, water	96,465	6,814	440	103,718
construction	73,133	8,668	neg.	81,095
finance	2,208,900	176,692	211	2,385,803
business activities	2,127,245	454,253	563	2,582,061
Unspecified	68,670	21,538	179	90,387
% world FDI total				0.8
Total	9,572,077	1,005,069	2,543	10,579,689
% world FDI total	90.5	9.5	(0.02)	100.0

Table 5.13 (*cont.*)

	World inward FDI stock		
	1990		
	Developed economies	Developing economies	Total
Primary	139,013	27,847	166,860
% primary FDI total	83.3	16.7	100.0
% world FDI total			9.4
Manufacturing	584,069	144,996	729,065
% manufacturing FDI total	80.1	19.9	100.0
% world FDI total			41.0
Services	713,721	155,123	868,844
% services FDI total	82.2	17.8	100.0
% world FDI total			48.8
Unspecified	9,662	4,767	14,429
% world FDI total			0.8
Total	1,446,465	332,733	1,779,198
% world FDI total	81.3	18.7	100.0

	2005			
	Developed economies	Developing economies	SE Europe & CIS	Total
Primary	551,202	201,559	37,717	790,478
% primary FDI total	69.7	25.5	4.8	100.0
% world FDI total				7.9
Manufacturing	2,196,968	716,624	61,927	2,975,519
% manufacturing FDI total	73.8	24.1	2.1	100.0
% world FDI total				29.6
Services	4,683,574	1,339,574	87,484	6,110,632
% services FDI total	76.7	21.9	1.4	100.0
% world FDI total				60.8
Unspecified	114,311	48,668	8,230	171,209
% world FDI total				1.7
Total	7,546,055	2,306,425	195,358	10,047,838
% world FDI total	75.1	23.0	1.9	100.0

Source: UNCTAD (2007).

notably that between the USA and EU, in 2007, ended limitations on landing rights. The USA kept its maximum of 25 per cent foreign control, with the most liberal states – Australia, Kenya, New Zealand, or Peru – going no further than 49 per cent of foreign equity. While airlines linked their future to operational freedom and restructuring, a complex system of bilateral agreements gave preferential landing rights to national flag-carriers, and complicated mergers and changes of ownership. Privatizations, from the mid 1980s, had already turned 'national flag-carrier' into an outmoded concept. Yet when Air France and KLM amalgamated (in 2004), and British Airways and Iberia did likewise (2011), they had to make complex arrangements to protect the national identities of each business. US domestic flights remained closed to inward investors, unlike the EU, where low-cost Ryanair and Easyjet added to cross-border competitiveness and consumer choice (WTO, 2006).[11]

Trade and transport services inevitably grew in line with cross-border commerce (WTO, 2010; UNCTAD, 2006). A small number of specialist firms continued to dominate world trade in grain, sugar, coffee, cotton and metals. Many commodity-producing nations remained reliant upon large traders: Cargill continued to be Argentina's biggest agribusiness exporter, in 2011, and owned its largest soya-, wheat- and corn-processing plants, in a country where food processing was the main industry.[12] But British trading firms, which had once spanned Asia and Africa, were in retreat. Inchcape – heir to several British traders, each of significance – was a European *sogo shosha*, and had three main areas of business in the 1980s: insurance and shipping, distribution, and investments in tea, timber and other natural resources. After 1998, following the Asian Crisis, it concentrated on its profitable international motor delivery business – which had a lucrative deal with Toyota – and jettisoned much of its portfolio.[13] Harrisons & Crosfield left Malaysia between 1982 and 1989, and Indonesia in 1994, seeing only a poor future in tropical commodities. It became the speciality chemicals maker Elementis, in 1997.[14] Yule Catto transformed into a speciality chemicals and building products producer;[15] Boustead into a speciality engineering manufacturer;[16] Booker McConnell into a food and grocery business, located mainly in Britain and North America;[17] and UAC Nigeria passed into local ownership (Biersteker, 1987; Fieldhouse, 1994).

On the other hand Lonrho, with its ruthless executive 'Tiny' Rowland, proved adept at building good relations with African governments, receiving credit in Mozambique and the Sudan for negotiating ceasefires, but linked to bribery and corruption back home in Britain. The company acquired labyrinthine and diverse interests in North America, Europe and Asia, and new management, in 1998, refocused the company into agribusiness, transport, infrastructure and hotels under the Lonrho name and into the mining business called Lonmin.[18] The Swire Group similarly reinvented itself in a rapidly changing Asia. It benefited from China's economic reform after 1978, often working in close cooperation with the state-owned China International Trust and Investment Corporation (CITIC). Swire had the expertise to introduce ICI, Carlsberg, Tate & Lyle and Coca-Cola, by the end of the 1990s, to China, and it acquired extensive property interests in China's major cities. It purchased Dragon Air and Air Hong Kong, and welcomed the state-owned Air China as a partner in Cathay Pacific. In 2000, it bought James Findlay traders, based in India and Africa, and the Steamships Trading Company, an Australian enterprise with commodity, transport and manufacturing concerns throughout Papua New Guinea.

Diverse investors looked for partners with knowledge and contacts in Asia, and, consequently, Jardine Matheson embraced diversification. It co-founded Jardine Schindler, its first industrial joint venture in China, as early as 1980. Across Asia, it built franchises with 7–11, Pizza Hut, Starbucks and IKEA. It established supermarkets such as Hero, in Indonesia, and, from 1996, founded the Mandarin Oriental international hotel chain in London. It added insurance dealing at Lloyds of London, while the private equity fund manager Jardine Rothschild Asia Capital combined Jardine Matheson's regional expertise with Rothschild's banking skills in 2006–7.[19]

Marc Rich & Co. AG moved from transport and marketing into farming, mining, smelting, refining and processing, beginning its transformation by investing in a US smelter in 1987, and taking control of a Peruvian zinc and lead mine during the following year. The USA pursued Marc Rich, the founder, for tax evasion and dealings with Iran, until President Clinton controversially issued a presidential pardon in 1991. The global trader Trafigura was founded from a group of Marc Rich companies spun off in 1993. During the following year, huge losses in zinc trading led to the firm's restructuring, the new name of Glencore, and the appointment of a management which included CEO Ivan Glasenberg. Glencore was called 'the most important company you have never heard of': it was, by 2010, the world's largest commodity trader, processing some 60 per cent of tradable zinc, plus 50 per cent of tradable copper, and owning production facilities all over the world.

Floated in 2011, Glencore International immediately joined the FTSE 100, and made executives and major investors into multi-billionaires. The company had adopted a well-funded investment approach, working upstream from its trading relationships, and focusing on a controlling equity interest. In Colombia, a subsidiary was implicated in the massacre of Wuyuu Indians, and bribery allegations emerged over its complex acquisition of Katanga Mining in Democratic Republic of the Congo. It lost substantial mining and processing enterprises, including a large smelter complex, in Bolivia to nationalization imposed in 2007 (WTO, 2006).[20]

Japanese general traders, a main pillar of their country's export-orientated industrialization, were well placed to take advantage of Asian growth. They were, however, encountering major challenges, and beginning the search for a new business model (UNCTAD, 1994, 1998). Manufacturers such as Toyota or Sony could now equal the traders' knowledge of foreign markets, and, as their export markets grew, they needed their own strong presence overseas. When new competitors, usually Asian, challenged the *sogo shosha* for their bulk merchandise trade, they frequently had advantages in costs and privileged market access. The end of Japan's fast growth era, from 1990, hurt general traders whose fortunes were tied to the country's import–export trade. With little scope for growth at home, the *sogo shosha* needed to foster business worldwide, and abandoned their traditions of a fully comprehensive service and maximum sales for the profit-testing of every commercial activity. They became more involved in business solutions, consultancy, project management, IT, communications, venture capital, investments, and technology acquisition, as well as logistics and chain management.

Using its organizational competencies in human resources, market knowledge, commercial experience, global information networks, and finance, Mitsubishi Corporation stressed its unique global combination of logistics, capital and marketing. From 1998, it refocused the company on high-performing transactions. Further strategic plans in 2000 and 2003 consolidated Mitsubishi Corporation into six profit-orientated business groups and granted its regional headquarters overseas greater autonomy over business decisions and the employment of local talent. By 2005, trading brought only 14 per cent of the company's income, financing 12 per cent, and investments a significant 74 per cent. Amongst a highly diverse portfolio, by 2011, were Princes branded foods in the UK; Lawson's convenience stores in Japan; in China, Dalian Nisshin Oil Mills, a partnership with other Japanese companies, and JinLing (Tianjin) Logistics Company, in collaboration with local firms; and, from 1994, a share of the huge oil and liquid gas project Sakhalin II, the first international joint venture of its kind in Russia.

Mitsubishi Corporation's great rival, Mitsui & Co., similarly in the 1980s began the move into advanced business services, and cut low-profit contracts. As well as being involved in Sakhalin II, it utilized its global networks to build a high-speed railway in Taiwan during the 1990s, in partnership with Mitsubishi Heavy Industries.[21] The largest *sogo shosha* continued to deal with a highly diverse range of products, up to 30,000; in 2000, 18 of them alone still handled 62 per cent of Japan's imports and 37 per cent of its exports. Amongst the world's 17 largest traders, 10 were Japanese (Gabel and Bruner, 2003). Four *sogo shosha* could be found, moreover, in the list of the world's top 100 non-financial MNEs for 2008, measured by overseas assets; of these four, Mitsubishi was the largest, in 32nd place, followed by Mitsui & Co., Sumitomo Corporation and Marubeni (UNCTAD, 2009).

Unlike the *sogo shosha*, Korean trading companies were not independent but owned by family-owned business groups, or *chaebol*. To help them secure the resources needed for industrialization, the government appointed and assisted official trading enterprises. By the 1980s, Hyundai Corporation owned coal interests in Australia and oil sources in Yemen. Like the *sogo shosha*, their competitive advantages were their commercial networks and an ability to seize varied opportunities (Colpan, Hikino and Lincoln, 2012). By 1990, for example, Hyundai had completed the Bekasi Industrial Complex, in Indonesia, and in 2005 it founded Qingdao Hyundai Shipbuilding in China. It joined with sister company Hyundai Heavy Industries, in 2009, to evolve into a comprehensive business solutions provider.[22] From 1996, Samsung Corporation had worked closely with Samsung Engineering and

Construction for similar reasons, covering logistics, engineering, out-sourcing and finance.[23]

Korea's Hanjin Shipping Company took its place amongst the world's top ten shipping and transport businesses by following a low-cost strategy, as did rivals Evergreen and Yang Ming, from Taiwan. As well as by achieving low costs, shipping lines succeeded by establishing overseas offices and investing in container, oil, LNG or dry bulk termi-nals worldwide.[24] Another challenger was Orient Overseas Container Line (OOCL), based in Hong Kong, whose close relations with the People's Republic of China culminated in its owner, Tung Chee Hwa, being appointed the former colony's first chief executive, in 1997.[25] Hutchinson Whampoa had interests in trading, wholesaling, retail-ing and ports by 1980, and in Felixstowe docks from 1991. Cheung Kong Infrastructure Holdings had been a significant shareholder in Hutchinson Whampoa since 1979, and took control in the same year as Hong Kong's sovereignty was transferred, becoming in addition the first Chinese company to assume ownership of a British-style 'hong' (WTO, 2010). Its owner-founder, Li Ka-Shing, was the richest man in Asia and one of the region's most prominent business figures. Western shipping lines struggled to cope with the competitive pressures and from the 1980s adopted the tactic of reflagging and employing foreign seamen, as did Japan's K-Line and NYK.[26] When P&O and Royal Nedlloyd joined, in 1997, it was the first major merger in a frag-mented and cost-sensitive industry. After the Danish group Maersk had acquired P&O Nedlloyd, in 2005, it became the world's largest carrier, but did not keep its share of global trade.[27] China Ocean Ship-ping Company (Cosco) – a state-owned business, rising to be the 80th largest non-financial MNE by 2008 – was a corporate measure of a quickening shift in global economics. By 2010, it operated some 800 ships and 32 terminals, working from 1,600 ports in 160 countries and offering chartering and marine engineering services in addition to carrying.[28]

Banks, deregulation and the global market

Multinational banking had several noted characteristics and dimen-sions by 1980: large banks with overseas offices because they had followed their clients abroad; foreign loans, predominantly to gov-ernments; the super-national Eurodollar market; cross-border services and trade finance; and the remnants of foreign-owned retail banks, their role in national economies declining, and ironically so, given the turnaround in events to come. It was from the 1980s onwards – as regulatory barriers fell and technological change transformed their industry – that financial MNEs became a driving force of the international economy. The USA had already abandoned exchange controls limiting capital outflows in 1974, but the new free-market British government surprised the City of London and set an international trend by doing the same in 1979. Most West European countries liberalized overseas investment from 1988 to 1990, and Switzerland, Germany and Japan had freed capital inflows by the end of the decade (Cassis, 2006).

The deregulation of financial markets took longer, but the 'Big Bang' of 1986 in the London Stock Exchange, quickly attracting business from other financial centres, also inspired imitation elsewhere. It brought – like the 1975 reforms in New York – an end to restrictive practices such as fixed brokerage commissions. But it was London's combination of liberalized markets and IT investments that revolutionized the speed, competitiveness and scale of financial transactions. Banks could now acquire stockbrokers, and further legislation in the same year broke down the distinction in Britain between banks (offering clearing accounts) and building societies (providing mortgages). Companies, in short, could supply any financial product, or all of them. As well as facilitating capital flows, the Single Market in Europe liberalized finance industry investment, in the hope of creating globally competitive companies and offering consumers cheaper services.

The USA – although early to remove stock exchange restrictions – was slow in easing its extensive domestic banking regulations. There was some loosening in the late 1980s and again from 1994 onwards. When the Federal Reserve agreed to the merger of Citicorp and the insurers Travelers, which owned investment bankers Salomon Brothers and Smith Barney, it created the world's largest financial business, renamed Citigroup. The union of retail banking, insurance, and investment banking once condoned turned the Glass-Steagall Act – which had deemed such links as causes of economic instability – into a dead letter, and the USA repealed the legislation in the next year, 1999.[29] Foreign exchange transactions – recorded as $60bn a day in 1982 – were $1,880bn in 2004. Alongside the process of internationalization, the sale of derivatives – through which traders could speculate on the future value of an asset, or spread their risks – was the most striking development of late twentieth-century financial markets, and grew to $3,450bn in 1991 and on to $184,000bn in 2004.

Financial services, once seen as a back-up to the 'real' economy, morphed into dynamic sources of wealth in their own right, and New York, London, Tokyo, Frankfurt, Paris, Zurich, Hong Kong and many others all vied to be the spaces to which a rapidly internationalizing industry might gravitate. London gained top place for cross-border transactions, most prominently foreign exchange and loans, but the power of the US economy made New York the largest financial centre, with a very substantial lead in capital markets. On the other hand, Chicago had a larger trade in derivatives than its rival on the Hudson. London boasted the greatest number of overseas-owned banks and representative offices, yet most of London's merchant banks – once the City's aristocracy – were bought up by foreign institutions, leading to talk of a 'Wimbledon effect', in which London might organize the world's best tournament but did so on behalf of the foreign players that habitually won the prizes (Cassis, 2006). All of the 50 most international financial MNEs, by 2008, originated from developed economies. The USA and UK, with large financial sectors, had seven and six companies in the list, with three each from Canada and Japan, and 31 from the rest of Europe (UNCTAD 2009).

While J. P. Morgan waited for deregulation in the USA, it traded in Eurobonds and became a leader in cross-border corporate mergers, such as SmithKline Beckman with Britain's Beecham Group, in 1989. But it suffered large losses lending to Latin American governments during the debt crisis that began with Mexico from 1982 onwards. The Federal Reserve granted J. P. Morgan a limited investment bank licence, a return to its historical roots, in 1989; once Glass-Steagall had been consigned to the past, a decade later, it evolved into a truly global bank that incorporated wealth management, institutional asset management and private equity, as well as investment banking. Chase Manhattan, by contrast, had reacted to its 1980s losses by scaling back internationally. Then, in the new era of deregulation, it bought the Robert Fleming investment bank in Britain, and it agreed to the major merger that created the worldwide financial powerhouse J. P. Morgan Chase.[30]

Citicorp could claim 90 overseas operations by the end of the 1980s, but decided thereafter to focus on fast-growing markets. Involvement in the smuggling of illegal funds, in Mexico, suggested that governance lagged behind expansion, and the purchase of Banco Confia, in 1998, revealed inadequate due diligence overseas since it associated the company with the laundering of drug money. The union of Citicorp-Travelers created what *The Economist* called 'a global financial supermarket', despite contravening Federal law for a year, and Citigroup was the first company in the USA to register as a financial holding company trading across a wide portfolio. The acquisition of Associates First Capital Corporation, in 2000, introduced it to the US sub-prime credit market, and Citigroup absorbed the British investment bank Schroders in 2001, the year of its then largest overseas purchase, Grupo Financiero Banamex-Accival in Mexico. It established retail operations in Russia and China after 2002, and it emerged as the world's number one issuer of credit cards and, by 2008, as the largest service multinational. Scandals continued in the wake of its progress: it paid fines, in 2002, for producing research that hyped the shares of clients, and, like Morgan Chase, it was a main Enron banker, restructuring the energy trader's toppling stack of loans, and consequently hiding them from shareholders.[31]

The international bank able to attract the greatest controversy, however, was Goldman Sachs, and the crisis of 2008–9 fuelled a list of accusations. The bank, it was said, put together and sold complex debt packages (the subsequently infamous 'collaterized debt obligations', or CDOs) as investments, while systematically burying the risks from view. Goldman Sachs participated in 'short-selling', in which they sold future options on these hollow packages, in the knowledge that it could profit by buying them, in actuality, at a later date once their value had fallen. Although implicated in the questionable practices that had brought down AIG, Goldman Sachs benefited as a creditor from the US government's need to rescue the insurer. Overseas, it was revealed in 2010 that the firm had used its expertise to mask the Greek government's looming bankruptcy, notoriously inventing a commercial index that showed the soundness of Greece's public finances. Conspiracy theorists worried about Goldman Sachs's influence over the US government. Undoubtedly, when two former chief executives served as US Secretary to the Treasury, in 1995–9 and 2006–9 respectively, they could only confuse the supposedly clear role of poacher (that is, the bank) with that of gamekeeper (or policymaker and regulator) (Cohan, 2011).[32]

Banks and international business strategy

Largely reliant on its British home market, where competition was intensifying in the 1980s, Barclays looked to diversification and overseas expansion. It divested its 148-year-old subsidiary in apartheid South Africa in 1986, responding finally to worldwide opinion and political pressure, and losses explained its phased withdrawal from the USA between 1987 and 1996. Having bought investment banks in London to benefit from the 'Big Bang', it acquired others in Germany and France in 1990, and concentrated on the European Single Market to replace its retreat from Africa and other locations deemed too risky. It did return to a liberated South Africa – buying, in 2006, the Absa Group, the largest consumer bank there – and two years later it snapped up the investment banking and trading businesses of the bankrupt Lehman Brothers in the USA, Canada and Latin America. It rejected a British government bail-out in 2008, but the slow take-up of its rights issue ended with Sumitomo Mitsui Banking Corporation, the China Development Bank and the Qatar Investment Authority as influential shareholders (UNCTAD, 2010).[33]

Like Barclays, Standard Chartered was unprepared for the intensifying competition of the 1980s. Its Asian heartland was performing poorly, and it had focused on commercial banking while its clients preferred international firms providing comprehensive services. It followed Barclays out of South Africa in 1987, and it adopted a new strategy of growing in consumer, corporate and institutional banking in Asia, Latin America and the Middle East's emerging markets.[34] The Hongkong Bank, while extending its activities in mainland China and Hong Kong, looked in the 1980s principally to developed economies for its transformation, acquiring Marine Midland Bank in the USA by 1987, and, by 1992, Midland Bank with its UK high street presence and European branch network. It transferred its headquarters from Hong Kong to London in 1991, re-incorporating as HSBC Holdings plc, and over the next decade diversified in the USA and entered Latin America.[35]

Deutsche Bank became a gauge with which to measure the impact of globalization on the banking sector. It had a pivotal part in Germany's post-war economic miracle: highly regulated and risk-averse banks supplied long-term finance to firms, and nationwide businesses such as Deutsche Bank were intricately engaged in the success of their corporate clients by sitting on their supervisory boards. Germany resisted the shareholder pressures and the financial engineering of the Anglo-American economies: market capitalization represented 30 per cent of GNP in 1996, compared to 130 per cent for Britain. Despite the creation of the European Central Bank in Frankfurt, entrenched practices continued to provide a block on any substantive change in Germany (Cassis, 2006). Overseas, however, Deutsche Bank could embrace the global financial zeitgeist. It bought up renowned investment bankers Morgan Grenfell in London in 1984, then McLean McCarthy in Toronto in 1988 and Bankers Trust in the USA in 1999. From 1986, it acquired in stages the Eurasbank Consortium, active in twelve Asian countries, renaming it Deutsche Bank (Asia), and it purchased retail operations in Western Europe. In the 1990s, it furthered the transformation of international politics and economics by positioning itself in Eastern Europe and Russia. By the end of the millennium, Deutsche Bank made more profits from overseas investment banking than from commercial and retail banking in Germany. International in scope and interests, it was listed on Wall Street in 2001. It gained, too, the public notoriety and criticism of other global finance firms, just like that symbol of 'no-holds-barred' US capitalism Goldman Sachs: it was a major player in the US housing bubble from 2004; it marketed ultimately worthless debt packages; it profited from their short-selling; and it received Federal money from the salvage of AIG.[36]

Global ambition took hold of many European banks. Société Générale, privatized in France in 1987, established itself worldwide from 1999, simultaneously diversifying into investments, securities, asset management and derivatives. In January 2008, revelations of losses of $7.2bn by one of its traders shook confidence in the company, and it needed the US government to cover its $11bn losses with AIG.[37] The Swiss banks – once content to attract business to Switzerland with its tax advantages and traditions of secrecy – sought to make up lost ground. Credit Suisse, in 1997, decided to become a truly global company. The Swiss Bank Corporation, having declared an end in 1993 to its historically cautious business principles, bought up Brinson Partners asset management in Chicago, investment bankers S. G. Warburg in London, and Dillon Read in New York between 1995 and 1997. Despite the Union Bank of Switzerland making tentative international steps, shareholder criticism of its conservative management, in 1998, brought about its merger with SBC, creating UBS. But globalization revealed dangers in this case too. UBS could offer its overseas clientele the benefits of Swiss bank accounts, but be charged, in 2008, with helping US citizens avoid their taxes. It lost calamitously in the US sub-prime property market – some $50bn – in 2008–9, surviving only thanks to a Swiss government bail-out. It introduced tighter capital-ization rules and corporate governance, yet a rogue trader in London racked up $2bn of losses. Its chief executive, Oswald Grubel, resigned, signalling a return to less risky forms of banking.[38]

Deregulation in the Netherlands, in the 1980s, had the intention of globalizing the financial sector and creating larger, more competitive companies: the 1991 merger that founded ABN AMRO was one result of the policy. Its strategy of being a full-service international financial business failed, and manoeuvrings by the TCI hedge fund triggered its corporate collapse. The consortium that defeated Barclay's offer to buy ABN AMRO effected history's biggest bank takeover, and divided the assets.[39] Santander gained Banco Real in Brazil and Banca Anton-veneta in Italy. The Benelux operations went to Fortis, and the whole-sale and Asian businesses to RBS. The expansion-minded directors at RBS – a team rooted in Edinburgh before they grew global – dismissed the usual caution of due diligence during an acquisition, and, as the 2008–9 crisis deepened, the company caught a deadly virus from ABN AMRO. Their strategic overreach ended with the British government as the owner of RBS. The Netherlands, Belgian and Luxembourg gov-ernments similarly acquired shares in Fortis. The Belgian government was able to sell its piece of Fortis to BNP Paribas, but only after local investors, some of whom had lost their life savings, objected to the terms of the deal by throwing coins and shoes at the management during a shareholders' meeting (WTO, 2006).[40]

Banking, regional patterns and acquisitions

For Spain, EU membership in 1986 and the promise of the Single Market were vital tools for transforming the domestic economy. Mod-ernization meant, in addition, reform of a protected, highly regulated industry, and mergers: 'Given the importance of the financial sector,' said Pedro Toledo Ugarte, Banco de Vizcaya's chairman, 'every coun-try wants some of the institutions which compete worldwide to be made up of and managed by its own people. We all know that this requires management, technologies and, without doubt, a minimum size.' Banco de Vizcaya and Banco de Bilbao, therefore, united into BBV in 1988. Spanish banks had a lengthy historical presence in Latin America, but BBV and rival Santander launched into rapid growth by acquisition there from 1995, bringing far-reaching change to the region's finance sector, especially in Mexico and Brazil (UNCTAD, 2001).

Falling margins at home motivated BBV's expansionary rivalry with Santander in Latin America, where returns were contrastingly high. Some of the purchases came through privatizations, such as Banco Continental in Peru, and BBV Bancomer was Mexico's leading bank when it was incorporated in 2000. At home, and at the same time, BBV joined Argentaria Caja Postal y Banco Hipotecario, itself a merged enterprise, to form Grupo BBVA, and the next four years brought full control over all subsidiaries, which were stamped with the new BBVA logo.[41] By 2006, as well as diversifying into pension funds in Argentina, mortgages in Mexico, and into vehicle financing in Chile, BBVA had bought Valley Bank in California, and the Texas-based Laredo National Bank, which catered for the US Hispanic market. Alongside assets in Latin America, Santander had an important European presence too, having bought banks in Germany and Portugal by 1990, and, between 2004 and 2008, three large building societies in the UK, becoming that country's third-largest holder of retail deposits. From 2004–9, it took full control of Sovereign Bancorp, in the USA.[42]

Strategies were regional, as well as global, most apparently in preparing for or responding to the European Single Market. Danske Bank emerged from the restructuring of Denmark's fragmented banking industry, in 1990, and felt the need to acquire internationally or be acquired internationally. It concentrated on pan-Nordic acquisitions, then entered the Balkan countries, and secured a foothold in the major centres of London and New York. By 2000, there were five major banks operating across the Scandinavia–Baltic region.[43] The Skandinaviska Enskilda Bank grew and diversified internationally, and had some 670 branches, by 2009, as well as securities businesses in the major financial capitals (UNCTAD, 2010).[44] FDI levels in the financial sector across Eastern Europe and the Balkans were small compared to those in manufacturing and trade, but the impact was dramatic and immediate on bankrupt businesses neglected during the Communist era. MNEs brought managerial know-how and technology, as well as capital, and foreign affiliates easily outperformed local companies

(UNCTAD, 1995). By 2005, over 97 per cent of banks' assets in Slovakia and 94 per cent of those in the Czech Republic were foreign-owned, mostly by Austrian, Italian, Belgian, German and French firms (Barisitz, 2006). In the Balkans, by 2008, some 90 per cent of banking assets were foreign-owned. Unicredito, after 1999, could be found in twenty-two European countries, and had 5,000 branches in Central and Eastern Europe alone (UNCTAD, 2010).

Canadian banks had tended to invest in their giant neighbour. Nonetheless, the Bank of Nova Scotia – frequently called Scotiabank – led globalization of the Canadian banking sector, usually through minority holdings in established businesses, acquiring in the 1990s assets in Latin America and Asia (UNCTAD, 1995). When Standard Chartered left South Africa in 1987, it sold up to local investors, and, with the end of apartheid, the Standard Bank Group bought up banks significant to the economies of Uganda and Nigeria. In 2007, the state-owned Industrial and Commercial Bank of China bought a 20 per cent stake in the Standard Bank Group to assist the financing of China's economic diplomacy and search for raw materials in Africa, as well as its rapidly growing trade. It gained two seats on the board, and, with the Bank of China, China Development Bank and CITIC Bank, lent $1bn to Standard. The South African bank was present in 16 African nations by 2011 and, through acquisitions, in 14 other locations worldwide, notably with a two-thirds ownership of Standard Urdu in Turkey and about one third of Troika, Russia's second-biggest investment bank. When China Investment Corporation bought a stake in the US investment firm Blackstone, falling share values immediately proved it a bad investment. Blackstone did, nonetheless, help China Development Bank buy part of Barclays Bank, also well-connected in Africa (Nwankwo and Ibeh, 2014).[45]

Japan's business model was at its zenith in the 1980s: its manufacturing companies were establishing themselves as leading multinationals, and its banks began to emerge internationally. Sanwa Bank stated its simple strategy: to be the world's top bank. Mitsubishi Bank and Dai-ichi Kangyo Bank entered the USA in their quest to be international full-service financial firms. When the Japanese economic bubble burst, in 1990, the Japanese banks' capital melted away, and they retreated internationally. Tokyo's own 'Big Bang', in 1994–7, was an attempt to mend its declining influence: it implemented deregulation, breaking down competitive barriers between financial services, ended any remaining exchange controls, and envisaged a more internationalized financial industry (Cassis, 2006). It initiated a series of mergers leading to the emergence of 'mega-banks' better able to compete globally, including Bank of Tokyo Mitsubishi, in 1996, and a succession of further amalgamations to create Mitsubishi UFJ Financial Group, in 2005, as the world's largest bank by assets, and, in 2008, the world's 38th financial multinational. Its decision to invest in Morgan Stanley, acquiring over one fifth of its shares, restored confidence in the US investment bank's viability and highlighted how Japanese banks had passed through the worst and recapitalized themselves, ready for a more international role.[46] The securities and investment firm Nomura was regarded as setting the pace of internationalization for Japanese banks in the 1990s, in its practices and through worldwide operations.[47] Its rival, Daiwa, worked with Sumitomo Mitsui from 2001 to 2010, before preferring to act independently, aiming to be a leader in Asia, while Nikko had become part of Salmon Brothers and subsequently Citigroup in 2008.[48]

With the lifting of restrictions on cross-border capital flows, on foreign ownership, and on full-service companies, mergers and acquisitions had become a viable international business strategy in all sectors of finance, and fuelled the rapid growth in the size and cross-border reach of financial MNEs. Some 63 per cent of the sums used in M&A were incurred in the service sector. The two largest international acquisitions were Abbey National in Britain (by Santander) and John Hancock in the the USA (by Manulife Financial). Another prominent deal was the purchase of Bayerische Hypo- und Vereinsbank (BHV) and Bank of Austria Creditanstalt by Unicredito. Standard Chartered bought Korea First Bank, following the Asian crisis and market liberalization in Korea after 1997, and Barclays took ABSA in South Africa.

Some banks – like the Metropolitan Banking and Trust Company, from the Philippines, or United Overseas Bank Ltd, from Singapore – were less known internationally, but could claim to be global in scope (UNCTAD, 2006). MBTC grew through joint ventures with investors in the Philippines – including Toyota, Sumitomo Mitsui Banking Corporation and AXA – before establishing 32 overseas offices throughout East Asia and entering the USA, Spain and Italy. UOB gained a network of 500 offices in 19 countries in Asia Pacific, Western Europe and North America (UNCTAD, 2010).[49] The extensive liberalization and the privatization of financial services, and the internationalization, acquisition and rapid growth of firms contributed to the 2008–9 crisis, and ended, ironically, with many banks being state-owned. Profits had been privatized, but losses had to be nationalized. In the USA, Lehman Brothers was bankrupted, and Merrill Lynch was sold to Bank of America. The Federal government recapitalized and became a major shareholder of Bear Stearns, Wells Fargo and Citigroup. In Britain, HBOS was sold to Lloyds TSB, which imitated RBS over ABN AMRO by failing in the normal precautions of due diligence, becoming as a result a bankrupted publicly owned business. The French and Belgian governments had to act jointly in order to rescue Dexia, in 2011, from its global risk exposure (WTO, 2006).[50]

Insurance

AIG was already highly internationalized by 1980, and had formed joint ventures with East European state-owned firms even before the fall of the Berlin Wall. By 1992, it could claim to be the first and second foreign insurer to receive a licence in Japan and Korea respectively, and its shares were listed in London, Paris and Zurich. It had diversified, buying Switzerland's Uberseebank, and it was the first insurer to enter China since the 1949 revolution. Its Financial Services Group, by 1994, dealt with currency, derivatives, brokering, investments and aircraft leasing. AIG agreed with the Tata Group to sell life and non-life policies in India, which had opened up its insurance markets to private and multinational investment in 1995. AIG controlled some 70 per cent of life insurance premiums in Chile and Argentina, and non-US revenues reached over 50 per cent of the total. The Federal Reserve issued a warrant to acquire 80 per cent of AIG's equity in the autumn of 2008, when the sale of credit default swaps, a market in which third parties could trade and bet on risks they did not directly bear, brought about the company's collapse. AIG became liable when these risks materialized during the financial crisis, and Société Générale, Deutsche Bank, Goldman Sachs and Merrill Lynch gained as creditors from the ensuing flow of tax dollars (Pearson, 2010).[51]

The world's largest insurance multinational in 2008 was Allianz; AIG had slipped to 13th. Allianz bought up the market leaders in France and Italy in the 1980s, and it entered Hungary, the first Communist country to reform, in 1989, declaring its intention to expand eastwards, and controversially buying a privatized state company with a monopoly position in the former East Germany. Foreign firms transformed the Hungarian insurance industry in less than three years, and some 97 per cent of its firms held international equity. Most East European countries abolished inward investment restrictions in insurance, which brought much-needed capital, management skills and technology, although Russia maintained its barriers (UNCTAD, 1995). Allianz bought the Fireman's Fund Insurance Company because the USA was essential to its global strategy. The architect of the company's transformation was Wolfgang Schieren, as CEO and then chairman, from 1971 until 1996. Allianz was the most powerful institution in the German capital market, and the company's large domestic resources funded an ambitious series of overseas acquisitions. For Schieren, Allianz was a German institution that had to embrace globalization and Anglo-American business practices, and he was driven, also, by his bitter rivalry with Deutsche Bank.

Overseas markets supplied 45 per cent of Allianz's premiums by 1991, and board meetings came to be conducted in English. The company formed, as required, a joint venture in China, in 1998, called Allianz Dazhong, and bought both insurance and banking interests in an economically wounded South Korea. Diversification beyond insurance – acquiring US investment and asset management businesses – marked a strategic turning point, and in taking over Dresdner Bank in 2001, Allianz turned itself into a 'German Citigroup'. Although consolidation and withdrawal soon followed years of expansion, and Dresdner was sold to Commerzbank in 2009, Allianz still retained 700 firms spread across more than 70 countries.[52] Like AIG and Allianz, Zurich Financial Services' operations – in Europe, North America, Latin America, Asia and Australia by 1998 – were global.[53]

Market liberalization, the collapse of Communism, and the European Single Market all contributed to the internationalization of insurance firms from the late 1980s. Once almost wholly linked to its domestic market, Assicurizioni Generali began its transformation through a joint venture with a state-owned Hungarian business, in 1989, and embarked on purchases across the European Community, the USA and Asia. In Europe, with the end of highly controlled national financial markets, it created a regional organization and replaced the autonomy of subsidiaries.[54] It was Claude Beacute – called, in his native France, 'the cowboy of insurance' – who ensured the domestic growth and internationalization of Groupe Unies Mutuelle, in 1985 re-christened AXA, a meaningless palindrome that could be pronounced in any language. AXA evolved into a diversified provider of financial services, pensions and health care.[55]

A series of mergers, from 1998 to 2002, created Aviva, a Europe-focused financial group.[56] Canada's Manulife Financial went to the USA, Indonesia, Japan and China from 1984 to 1996. The Mutual Life Assurance Society – Old Mutual – emerged from its South African home base to establish its presence in developed markets. Although present in the UK from 1986, the end of apartheid in 1994 allowed rapid growth and diversification outside South Africa. By 2001, it could be found in the USA, Canada, India, Kenya, Namibia, Botswana and Zimbabwe, and its purchase of Skandia, in 2006, added several European and Latin American countries to its portfolio.[57]

Leisure and retailing

Starbucks was a child of the international economy. Following his time in Italy, the marketing director, Howard Schultz, wanted to replicate in the USA the coffee house experience, conceiving the coffee house as a welcoming 'third destination' between home and office. The company's international expansion began in Japan in 1996, and by 2003 it had some 500 outlets throughout the Pacific Rim. Starbucks launched itself in Europe in 2002, hoping to break into the continent's deep coffee culture. A fundamental feature of its success was the licensed franchise, which minimized capital and monitoring costs, and maximized the commitment of local investors. A contract set out the design concept and quality standards; managers and employees underwent training courses; and the company supplied the core products. Starbucks guarded its reputation by buying and promoting fair trade coffee, and by 2011 it had over 17,000 shops in 55 countries.[58]

Other powerful symbols of Americana and globalizing consumer tastes were the burger chain McDonald's, KFC and Pizza Hut. Such companies, nonetheless, had to adjust their fare to local tastes. Jollibee, from the Philippines, took McDonald's as its model, but came to the conclusion that the US firm's fare was far too standardized. It used spices to make its beefburgers sweeter, introduced pineapple burgers,

and offered rice to its Asian clientele. By the mid 1980s, it had outlets in Indonesia, and followed Filipino guest workers to the Middle
East. It broke into the USA by 2000, and thereafter founded over a
hundred stores in China selling indigenous fast food under the name
of Yonghe.[59]

The US retailer Wal-Mart began its international journey in 1991
with a joint venture in Mexico. It bought up Woolco in Canada,
Wertkauf and Interspar hypermarkets in Germany, Asda in the UK,
and Seiyu in Japan between 1994 and 2006. In China, Wal-Mart found
itself in breach of labelling and labour laws, and low wages and working conditions in its Bangladeshi and Chinese suppliers generated bad
publicity for a business depicted as a price-cutting leviathan.[60] Wal-
Mart was listed as the world's biggest retailer, and Metro AG as the
second. The third, their British rival, Tesco, went international in 1994,
in Hungary. In Eastern Europe and Asia, it preferred a strategy of joint
venture with players well established in markets of high-growth potential, gradually working towards majority or full ownership. It evolved
an international business strategy of securing the talents and commitment of employees in acquired companies, while transferring its global
capabilities in logistics, IT and customer relations.[61]

GAP opened its first store outside North America in London in
1987, and joined the trail to China in 2010. Millard 'Mickey' Drexler,
from 1983, transformed the company into a brand as well as a multiple outlet.[62] Another clothing chain, the Spanish Zara, began its
multinational progress next door, in Portugal, in 1988, moving soon
afterwards to the USA and France, and purchasing Massimo Dutti
in 1995. It established a presence in over seventy countries, principally across Europe, aiming for high, designer quality at affordable
prices. Industry commentators talked of its innovative style in logistics
and design, and most notably in the reduction of lead times, in what
founder Amancio Ortega called 'instant fashions', through a comput-
erized adaptation of Toyota's just-in-time system. Zara was a Spanish
success story in the era of globalization, and public flotation of the
company, in 2001, propelled Ortega into becoming Spain's richest citizen.[63] Japanese retailers – Seven & I Holdings, owner of Ito-Yokada
and Aeon – expanded within Asia, but remained highly reliant on their
home market. The most impressive entrant was Uniqlo, which took
GAP as its model and shared Zara's mix of good design, high quality,
low price and fast logistics. It leveraged a global production network in

India, Bangladesh and China, while Zara continued to make in Spain and elsewhere in Europe, or alternatively on Europe's periphery, and it also advertised its shops and brand. Uniqlo opened its first store in Tokyo in 1984, going international in London and Shanghai by 2002, and ultimately operating in 10 overseas countries by 2012. Success, according to Forbes, made founder and president Tadashi Yanai the wealthiest person in Japan.[64]

Telecommunications, media and utilities

Vodafone began as a 1991 spin-off from British electronics firm Racal, and became one of the world's most important service multinationals. Its strategy was to engage in aggressive acquisition and expansion, and the purchases of Air Touch in the USA, in 1999, and the German firm Mannesman, in 2000, were transitional. The Mannesman acquisition – at $112bn – was at the time the largest in corporate history, although the EU forced the sale of its Orange subsidiary to France Telecom. By 2010, Vodaphone could claim 370m customers in 30 countries: over one third of these customers were in India, while Egypt, Germany, Italy, Britain and Spain were numerically important. From 2008 to 2010, Vodaphone attracted controversy for using a Luxembourg holding company to avoid taxation, with the bizarre agreement of Britain's customs and revenue authorities, and it was accused of shutting down Egypt's mobile phone network in January 2011 under the orders of the Mubarak regime, which was seeking to disrupt communications between pro-democracy protestors during the Arab Spring.[65] The Compagnie Générale des Eaux, after 1980, morphed into an international water, waste management, energy, transport, construction, property, entertainment and media conglomerate called Vivendi by 1998. The ambitious expansion of the late 1990s proved disastrous, however, and it subsequently sold assets and spun off the Veolia water and waste management company to emerge focused on mass media and telecommunications.[66]

News Corporation, a holding company formally founded in 1979, developed into the world's second-largest media business, owning newspapers, publishing, film studios and television stations, and providing telephone and internet services. Its main owner, Rupert Murdoch, once an Australian, famously became a US citizen to overcome a regulatory hurdle blocking his acquisition of Fox Broadcasting. He defeated the British print unions to revolutionize work methods and technology in the newspaper industry, and, after launching Britain's first satellite broadcaster, BSkyB, gained an effective monopoly of British pay-per-view television. With Hutchinson Whampoa and Cheung Kong Holdings, News Corporation founded STAR TV, Asia's satellite service. When the BBC news annoyed China's government, in 1994, it was excluded from STAR's coverage. News Corporation's HarperCollins published a complimentary biography of Deng Xiaoping, but dropped plans to publish the memoirs of Chris Patten, Hong Kong's last governor, whose capacity for blunt talking was not well regarded in Beijing.[67] In Britain, News Corporation's newspapers gained an unprecedented influence over the governments of prime ministers Blair, Brown and Cameron, until the 2011 revelations that it had illegally hacked the mobile phone of a murdered schoolgirl turned its name toxic (WTO, 2006).

A 1989 European directive opened up national telecommunications markets and ended monopolies within four years. The Hong Kong conglomerate Hutchinson Whampoa launched Orange mobile services in Britain during 1994, selling it to Mannesman five years later (UNCTAD, 2010).[68] To meet the new challenges of a deregulated market, France Telecom was founded out of a government department in 1993. With no French-style accents in its official name, the company projected itself as international, and, after taking Orange, in 2000, it made further acquisitions in Europe. One of these was Telekomunikacja Polska, the largest act of FDI at the time in Eastern Europe, where foreign-owned operators came to dominate cellular phone networks (UNCTAD, 2001). The French government held only a minority holding in France Telecom by 2004. The company gained deep footholds in Francophone Africa, but bought a 51 per cent stake in Kenya Telkom in a joint venture with the government in 2007.[69] Deutsche Telekom, like France Telecom, emerged out of the state sector, in 1996. It obtained direct and indirect holdings throughout Eastern Europe – in Hungary, Slovakia, Croatia, Macedonia, Montenegro, Romania, Bulgaria and Albania – and in Greece's OTE and Cosmote. By building its T-Mobile and T-system brand, half of Deutsche Telekom's revenues came from outside Germany by 2010.[70] Telefonica – part privatized in 1995 and later fully so – developed or acquired brands such as O2, vivo, terra, and movistar. By 2011, it had 190m customers in Latin America, re-emphasizing the importance of

Spanish investment in the region, as against the 57m it had signed up in Europe. Although first buying equity in Argentina, Brazil and Peru, it fulfilled its long-term strategy of full ownership (UNCTAD, 2001).[71]

Italy's Ente Nazionale per l'Energia Electtrica (Enel) created WIND Telcommunicazioni in 1998, and commissioned France Telecom and Deutsche Telekom as the operators. By 2006, WIND was bought in stages by the Orascom Group, an Egyptian conglomerate, which also made acquisitions in Greece and Canada. Nonetheless, its strategy was to pursue undeveloped markets, expanding in Africa and South Asia, and, as critics made public, it built networks for the brutal dictators of Iraq and North Korea. WIND merged with VimpelCom, Russia's second-largest mobile phone operator, in 2010 to found the world's sixth-largest telephony business.[72] In Africa, the telecommunications sector was at the forefront of intra-continental FDI, and 52m mobile users in 2003 had risen to 400m by 2010. Basic technology and pre-paid cards helped expand the customer base, but so did innovative software that facilitated local access to social and other media. Alongside France Telecom and Vodafone, MTN from South Africa claimed to be the largest mobile services provider by 2007, present across the continent (UNCTAD, 2010).[73]

The Sudanese-born Mo Ibrahim, in 1998, established MSI-Cellular Investments, later called Celtel, and it had 24m customers in 14 African countries by 2005, the year in which Kuwait-based Mobile Telecommunications Company (or MTC) made Ibrahim a billionaire by purchasing the company he had founded. He used his fortune to found the Mo Ibrahim Foundation, which awarded a good governance prize to African leaders, and published a governance index for Africa, hoping to improve the lives of the continent's citizens. Celtel had grown successfully with its One Network, which had allowed free cross-border roaming. MTC became Zain in 2010, and, one year later, sold its African operations to Bharti Airtel, part of the group founded by Sunil Bharti Mittal, using its dominance of services in India as a base to sell telephony in 20 South Asian and African countries.[74]

Another characteristic of the new global economy of the 1990s was FDI in electricity, gas and water utilities, not seen for a century. To prepare for its entry into the European Community, Spain abandoned protectionism and merged public and privatized electricity concerns into Empresa Nacional de Electricidad, or the Endesa group. Shares in the new business were available by 1988, including an offering in New

York. With its transformed corporate status, it moved into Latin America, acquiring generators Electricidad de Argentina and Tejo Energia, and distributors Edenor, in 1992–3.[75] International M&A brought about the widespread restructuring of electricity generation in Latin America (UNCTAD, 2001).

Economic liberalization led to examples of intra-regional FDI, too. The authoritarian Pinochet government, with its fundamentalist belief in free markets, had established the privatized utility Enersis, which, from 1992 to 1997, under a democratic Chile, acquired an Argentine generator, entered Peru and Colombia, and joined with the Endesa group to acquire distributors in Rio de Janeiro. The Spanish company had been investing in Enersis since 1989, and took majority control during 1997–9. It was fully private by 1998, and selling its shares on Santiago's stock exchange two years later. When Endesa bought Société Nationale d'Électricité et de Thermique, or SNET, in 2004, it stirred criticism and resentment by shedding 30 per cent of the workforce (UNCTAD, 2006). In Argentina, through its Edesur subsidiary, Endesa fell into a dispute with the government over 'dollarization' arrangements and pricing, leading the president to accuse the company of deliberately orchestrating blackouts.[76] The French company EDF had the same issues, taking its case to the International Court for the Settlement of Investment Disputes, but selling its distributor in Mendoza province, in 2004 (PSIRU, 2004). Compagnie Financière de Suez was another French company to exit Argentina. Tractabel, Suez's energy division, also claimed it faced unfair competition from state enterprises in Brazil, and halted further investment, while AES – a US-registered business focused on overseas investments, over half of them in Latin America and the rest in Europe, Asia and Africa – shut down its generators in the Dominican Republic until the government paid its debts.

The Argentinian government accused Repsol of failing to invest in its subsidiary, with the result that, in 2010, the country became a net importer of energy; Repsol, which had become the majority owner of the formerly state-owned YPF in 1999, replied that it was government policies that inhibited further investment, including the development of the newly discovered Vaca Muerta oilfield. As the dispute intensified, the government declared a policy of 'energy sovereignty' and began the process of renationalization. Cynics argued that Repsol was glad to be rid of a troublesome asset, and that Argentina remained reliant on the expertise of other multinationals for the foreseeable future while holding to policies perceived as unfriendly to investors (UNCTAD, 2006).[77] In the era of globalization, Latin America continued to provide examples of the principles of national sovereignty and international property rights in conflict. Venezuela and Bolivia offered radical challenges to the global consensus of the twenty-first century.

Britain had begun the privatization of its electricity industry in 1990, and the process of acquisition and control by foreign multinationals. The European Union's planned introduction of a single market in electricity similarly ended protectionism and had big implications for cross-border investment. But France, with its state-owned monopoly intricately associated with its nuclear generation programme and national energy security, delayed preparations. Despite protests, President Chirac and Chancellor Kohl cut a deal to phase in the single market three years later than planned. When the still-protected Electricité de France (EDF) bought London Electricity in Britain's deregulated industry, aggrieved feelings intensified. EDF had acquired international experience in the previous decade, completing engineering projects in Francophone Africa and China, and exporting spare capacity to France's European neighbours. During the 1990s, it was involved, often with local partners, in generation and distribution operations in Sweden, Italy, Brazil, the USA and Argentina, and made further acquisitions in Britain. The Cheung Kong group acquired EDF's distribution and non-regulatory activities in the UK in 2010 (PSIRU, 2004).

Gaz de France (GDF) was another public company that wanted to sell its expertise overseas, and by 2001 it was involved in the international exploration, production and distribution of gas, in Germany, Mexico, the Netherlands and elsewhere, and had joint projects with state companies in Algeria, Malaysia and Lithuania. GDF merged, in 2008, with Compagnie Financière de Suez, which owned worldwide interests in energy and in water processing and distribution. When GDF bought International Power in the UK, in 2010, it gained the acquired firm's operations in the USA, Australia, the Middle East and Indonesia, and became the world's largest utility concern, active in 70 countries.[78]

Europe-wide liberalization of electricity markets brought part-privatization to Enel in 1999, and, forced to sell assets at home in water, real estate and telecommunications, by 2004, it looked abroad instead: it bought a renewable energy firm in the USA and Canada, acquired a Spanish generator and distributor, and built transmission lines in Brazil.[79] Two former state businesses – VIAG and Veba – in 2000 transformed into E-On, taking its name from *aeon*, Greek for eternity. It then seized opportunities overseas: beginning with Power-Gen in the UK, and moving on to Sweden, the USA, Eastern Europe, and, in partnership with OGK-4 and Gazprom, in Russia. Enel won a battle with E-On to buy Endesa, in 2007, with the German company being compensated with the chance to acquire some of Enel's French, Italian and Spanish companies. It left the Italian multinational, in 2008, in twenty-two countries, spanning nuclear, clean coal and renewables.[80] Germany's RWE, once a regional generator, diversified and internationalized, after 1981, into mining, chemicals, engineering, gas, water and electricity.[81]

Battle for resources and oil

As services expanded, the relative importance of international business in primary goods continued to fall: in 1990, it amounted to about 9 per cent of all outward FDI stock; by 2005, less than 6 per cent. Oil and mining took up almost all of this investment, with the rest going to agriculture, forest and fishing. The primary industry FDI stock owned by firms from developed economies declined, but only from nearly 99 per cent to a still very dominant 94. The location of extractive activities changed more than its ownership. Over 80 per cent of cross-border investments in primary goods in 1990 could be found within developed economies, yet declined to nearly 70 per cent by 2005 (Table 5.13). Market liberalization and privatizations by developing nations, and the dramatic transition of the Communist bloc were major causes of this geographical shift. In addition to policy changes, and the new era of international relations, rising commodity values from the 1980s onwards altered the calculations of risk versus reward in emerging economies. Since countries became more open to international business, inward FDI in the primary sector doubled in real terms between 1990 and 2000, and rose by half again to 2005. Nonetheless, in the oil business, for reasons of political necessity, multinationals disinterred new sources in developed territories, such as the North Sea or the Gulf of Mexico.

Primary products had led FDI in the nineteenth and early twentieth centuries – European and North America multinationals undertaking projects in the southern hemisphere – and no other sector had such a close association with imperialism or such a chequered history. With post-war decolonization, governments of newly founded states assumed sovereignty over their mineral rights and nationalized their extractive industries. Alongside an ideological preference for public enterprise was a perception that multinationals had brought exploitation, not development. For sure, the demands of the international economy and the socio-economic needs of poor countries were not by necessity harmonious, and the ability of governments to negotiate and to benefit from their engagement with multinationals rested on various factors – mainly the relative bargaining power and authority of states, but additionally their administrative competence and corruption levels.

Multinationals sought access to the geographical source of raw materials, and states required access to the multinationals' capital, technology, managerial know-how and international marketing networks. Those countries with weak production capabilities were more likely to rely on cross-border investment, just as those with small home economies would tend to produce for the world market. In capital-intensive activities, the local employment effects might not be substantial, and, within undeveloped economies, oil and mining companies might continue to rely on overseas equipment and suppliers rather than on stimulating small-scale business nearby. Multinationals could, nonetheless, bring about improved infrastructure – whether in roads, ports, power generation, or water supply – since these supported their own commercial activities, or formed part of the overall agreement, sometimes involving the investing country's government as well as the host's.

Many energy-rich states had continued to reduce the role of multinational affiliates after 1980. It was estimated, in 2005, that developing countries held 84 per cent of global oil reserves, and transition economies another 10 per cent; the figures for gas were 59 and 31 per cent. More specifically, oil and gas equalled nearly 98 per cent of Nigeria and Algeria's export values, 89 per cent in the case of Saudi Arabia, and over 83 per cent for Venezuela (UNCTAD, 2007). There were no multinational affiliates in Saudi Arabia, Kuwait and Mexico, and foreign companies were responsible overall for 11 per cent of oil and gas production in transition economies, and 19 per cent in developing nations.

Yet sub-Saharan Africa remained reliant on multinationals, which managed 57 per cent of production there. Globally, foreign-owned subsidiaries supplied 22 per cent of oil and gas output. The three largest oil producers were state-owned enterprises – Saudi Aramco, Gazprom and the National Iranian – as were half of the 50 biggest oil companies. Saudi Aramco, with privileged access to its home country's reserves, produced twice as much as ExxonMobil, the largest oil major. Levels of transnationality, therefore, formed a dividing line in the industry. So, nationally sponsored companies operated, in most cases, almost exclusively within their borders, while the privately owned multinationals, mostly from developed countries, found half their supplies overseas. Multinationals had to offer or sell their competencies, in technology, production, or distribution, to the sovereign owners of mineral rights. They faced increasing international competition from developing and transition economies: Chinese enterprises such as CNOOC, CNPC and Sinopec throughout Asia and Africa, Petrobras across Latin America, or Petronas in South East Asia (UNCTAD, 2007).

The oil majors

How did the oil majors, having lost their control of global production and now challenged in distribution and marketing, cope with decades of rapid global transformation? Political change and a wave of nationalizations from the 1970s onwards put a company that had staked its whole policy on access to Middle East oil – British Petroleum – into a strategic spin. Discoveries in the North Sea and Alaska, nonetheless, developed the engineering and operational prowess it needed to extract oil from remote and deepwater locations. To refine and distribute its growing Alaskan flows, the company bought a stake in Standard Oil of Ohio (Sohio), fully incorporated, from 1987, into BP America. The British government then sold off its remaining share in the parent business, sparking, ironically, the particular interest of the state-owned Kuwait Investment Office until any influential stake was blocked on grounds of national economic security.

After a decade in which BP had diversified into animal feed, coal and copper, the company after 1990 looked to its traditional strengths in exploration, production, refining, distribution and chemicals. It strove to become less bureaucratic – pushing decision making downwards to operational levels, and away from headquarters committees – and to emerge consequently as leaner and more competitive. It formed strategic partnerships as a means of cutting costs, merging its European refining and marketing with Mobil, and founding a joint venture with Shanghai Petrochemical Company to supply Asia. One key officer involved in the resulting impressive growth in profits was John Browne, who took charge in 1995. He pushed through a series of acquisitions – unprecedented for the industry as well as for the company – taking on Amoco (once Standard Oil of America), ARCO (Atlantic Richfield) and Burmah-Castrol, and searching out reserves in Russia, the Gulf of Mexico, North America, Azerbaijan and Indonesia.

Browne was widely acclaimed as Britain's most admired executive, but his personal fate and that of BP soon afterwards starkly illustrated the changing fortunes of international business. By 1994, the company had joined Amoco and state enterprises from Azerbaijan, Russia and Turkey to establish the Azerbaijan International Mining Company, which explored the vast resources of the Caspian Sea, and, three years later, it took a minority holding in Russia's Sidanko. It merged its Russian interests, in 2003, with a consortium of three oligarchs to form the country's third-largest oil producer, TNK-BP. The oligarchs quickly took the view that Bob Dudley, the subsidiary's president and a BP man, was too steeped in the British multinational's interests, and, as he concluded, their influence with the authorities led to the sustained harassment of staff. He tried to manage TNK-BP from a secret location for five months, but finally left the company in 2008. Observers drew parallels with Sakhalin II: during 2005–6, a strict interpretation of environmental regulations struck at its operational viability and forced Shell and its Japanese partners to give control to Gazprom, a state-owned business.

On the other side of the world, an explosion at a Texas City refinery killed 15 people and injured 180, and critics blamed BP's poor safety record on its fixation with cost-cutting and rapid growth. The incident shook Browne's professional reputation. After perjuring himself, in 2007 – in an injunction taken out against a British newspaper – he resigned as BP's leader. The Deepwater Horizon explosion, in April 2010, left 11 people dead, discharging crude from the sea floor into the Gulf of Mexico. Although BP was the majority owner of the Macondo oilfield, it was a US firm, Transocean Ltd, that had operated the rig at fault, and Halliburton, the service company, too was implicated. It was BP's image in the USA and worldwide that was hurt, however, and the environmental damage was incalculable.

The multinational replaced its chief executive, Tony Hayward – made to look inept and uncaring by the intense media scrutiny – and appointed Dudley, fortuitously a US citizen, as his replacement. He hoped to move the company forward through a joint venture with the state-controlled Rosneft, to extract oil from the Arctic shelf, and he had seemingly obtained the support of Igor Sechin, Rosneft chairman and deputy prime minister to Vladimir Putin. Yet BP's established oligarch partners had not gone away: they claimed that TNK-BP contractually represented all BP's Russian interests, and court action initiated a further spate of official harassment. Rosneft took the chance from this delay to sign the Arctic exploration deal with ExxonMobil, expecting, it was said, concessions in Texas and the Gulf in return. These unhappy events highlighted for international investors the Russian Federation's uncertain legal and institutional environment, but BP, heavily committed to a country with vast energy resources, had a very tricky dilemma and no easy strategic answer, except, finally, exit.[82]

The cost of searching new fields; exploration and production at the technological frontier; years of negotiating with governments over mineral rights; competition with state-owned enterprises; oversupply and falls in crude prices, brought about a peak in oil industry mergers during 1998–2002. There were BP's deals with Amoco, ARCO and Burmah-Castrol. Also, Exxon joined with Mobil in 1999 and Chevron with Texaco in 2001. Total-CFP bought Petrofina (1999), and merged with Elf Aquitaine to emerge as Total Fina Elf (2001). Conoco, decoupled from Du Pont (1998), linked up with Phillips (2002). Only Shell – of the great oil multinationals – decided against merger or major acquisitions.[83] In the 1990s, it had sought to improve its performance by integrating its highly diverse global business, most obviously in upstream exploration and production, and it reduced the independence of national subsidiaries, including Shell Oil, still perceived locally as wholly American. When it was revealed to be exaggerating its oil reserves, and inflating therefore its balance sheet, the company fell into a corporate crisis.

To improve external accountability and internal procedures, Shell ended its twin Anglo-Dutch structure, and, in 2005, created a reorganized and unified enterprise called Royal Dutch Shell plc, with its primary listing on the London Stock Exchange, and its operational headquarters in The Hague. More significant to wider public opinion than an accounting malpractice were accusations of widespread pollution and uncontrolled gas flaring in the Niger Delta. The government of Nigeria, in 1995, had hanged Ken Saro-Wiwa and eight other Ogoni tribe leaders who opposed damage to their homeland and civil rights abuses. Campaigners such as Amnesty International saw Shell as exercising a strong influence over a government associated with corruption, and the company found itself involved in protracted legal cases in London and The Hague.[84]

Although Mobil lost control over Middle East oil reserves, it adeptly built strong relationships with the Saudi ruling family, and invested in Aramco. By the 1980s, it had a strong presence in Nigeria and the Asia Pacific. The Exxon Company and Imperial Oil continued to manage the USA and Canada respectively. Until BP's Gulf disaster, the crash of the *Exxon Valdez* in Alaska's environmentally vulnerable Prince William Sound, in 1989, was the industry's most notorious oil spill, and became a negative symbol of 'big corporate'. During the 1990s, Mobil developed new fields in Russia, Central Asia, Venezuela and Africa, and the merged ExxonMobil, as the world's largest oil business, gained a reputation as an efficient and cost-conscious global behemoth.[85] Socal, once the Saudi government had nationalized Aramco, on which it had been almost wholly dependent, sought to diversify at home and make acquisitions overseas. It bought Gulf Oil, with its assets in Mexico, the North Sea and Canada, and it made a major breakthrough, as Chevron, with its Kazakh government joint venture, to develop the Tengiz oilfield, in 1993. Its acquisition of Texaco, in 2001, allowed the new ChevronTexaco, or, from 2005, the Chevron Corporation to compete with the largest oil firms of ExxonMobil, BP and Shell.[86]

The Compagnie Française des Pétroles changed its name to Total-CFP in 1985, hoping to capitalize on the greater public recognition of its best-known brand. Through the 1990s, it aimed to transform a bureaucratic culture, and secured sources of supply outside the Middle East. It also simplified its name to Total in 1997 – lost in the complexity of subsequent mergers, but reinstated in 2003. The new man in charge, Thierry Desmarest, with the support of the French government, took the bold step of signing a deal with Iran, the first foreign company to do so since the 1979 Revolution. While Total faced fewer competitors in politically difficult locations, it risked sanctions by other countries, and, just days before the signing, sold all its US refining and marketing businesses. The acquisition of the Belgium-based Petrofina reinforced Total's distribution across Europe, and it bought Elf Aquitaine, boosting global exploration, often through joint ventures.[87]

ENI, smaller in scale and resources than the majors, strategically positioned itself as a firm that would work in countries in which others were excluded. In the 1980s, it was still an Italian state agency used to bail out failed private-sector firms. Its part-privatization, in 1992, was a first step towards becoming a commercially orientated multinational, and it began to sell non-core assets, such as newspapers and its fresh flowers business. It signed operational and partnership agreements, during the 1990s, in Kazakhstan, China, Russia, Egypt, Azerbaijan, and, in 1999, cooperating with Total, in Iran. Despite showing some interest in Elf, it did not join the industry mega-mergers after 1998, but it did buy mid-sized British Borneo in 2000, followed by UK-based Lasmo, with reserves in the North Sea, the Asia Pacific and Latin America. While the Italian state reduced its holdings in ENI to 30 per cent, it retained a controlling golden share.[88]

The North Sea oil boom – unsurprisingly – was pivotal to the history of Statoil, and the Norwegian government gave the company control of mineral rights within its territorial waters. Statoil was the country's largest firm – worth some 10 per cent of national GDP – and, with its experience of this strong domestic base, it made its first foreign acquisition in 1985 with a British distribution and petrochemicals enterprise. It followed with purchases in its 'locale', in Denmark and Germany, and then joined with BP to explore more globally. Operating, often in joint ventures, in Europe, Asia, Africa and Russia, it was part-privatized in 2001, beginning a change that its CEO, Olav Fjell, said was needed to create a more competitive company responding to worldwide trends, EU deregulation, and Norway's maturing fields. Its dealings with state-owned NIOC in Iran brought accusations of bribery back home and a crisis in corporate governance, beginning with its offices being raided and ending in resignations of its officials.[89]

Developing-economy oil companies

Overseas investment projects by state-owned enterprises, with monopoly domestic control, commonly focused on market-seeking investment, with Aramco's part ownership of a Fujian refinery providing one clear example. Some used their position at home to evolve capabilities that could be exploited elsewhere, frequently in regional or developing economies. When the Malaysian government founded Petronas, a primary motive was national political and social stability. It charged the state-owned oil producer with improving the employment and economic opportunities of native Malays, or *bumiputra*, which it saw as disadvantaged relative to the Chinese and Indian minorities. Petronas, supervising the country's oil reserves, signed production-sharing contracts with foreign investors, and hoped to learn from their capabilities and technology. Its first excursion overseas was a Myanmar joint venture in 1990, followed by Vietnam, and another joint venture with the China National Offshore Oil Corp and Chevron to explore Liaodong Bay. By 2002, it had built pipelines in Pakistan and from Chad to Cameroon, and it could be found in Gabon, Cameroon, Niger, Egypt, Yemen and Indonesia.[90]

The government of resource-rich Brazil, during the 1980s, saw in state-owned Petrobras a powerful means of stimulating its faltering economy, but moved to perceiving it as a vehicle for internationalization and liberalization. The company lost its control over Brazilian oil production in 1997, when its government and other Latin American governments agreed to open their borders and markets to foreign companies: so, from 2003 onwards, it bought Perez Companc (PECOM) Energia in Argentina, and founded operations in Bolivia, Peru, Paraguay and Chile. Despite projects in Asia and Africa, Petrobras's overseas investments were predominantly Latin American. When, in 2006, the socialist President Evo Morales nationalized Bolivia's energy sector, it was an unusual rejection of global policy trends. His fellow socialist and president Hugo Chavez, in Venezuela, had enforced minority ownership on oil multinationals in joint ventures, but ostensibly continued to welcome foreign companies. Morales sent in the army to occupy the country's multinational-owned oilfields, including those of Petrobras, which alone accounted for 18 per cent of his country's GDP. The Brazilian government very reluctantly accepted the sequestration, when Petrobras was promised some future profits from its lost assets. Multinationals such as Shell or Portugal's Galp Energia participated with Petrobras in the continuous discovery of megafields off the coasts of Rio de Janeiro and São Paulo, which allowed Brazil to achieve the important national goal of self-sufficiency.[91]

ONGC Videsh Limited (OVL) – founded in 1989 as a subsidiary of India's state-owned Oil and Natural Gas Corporation (ONGC) – began by developing Iranian oilfields, but its breakthrough occurred in 1992 in Vietnam in partnership with BP and Petro-Vietnam. It could be found in 15 countries by 2011.[92] Lukoil, privatized after 1994 and taking Western companies as its business model, used its key position in the Russian energy industry to develop capabilities for exploration and production overseas. From 2004, the company explored fields in Iraq jointly with ConocoPhillips, and could be found in some 30 countries, although most of its overseas investment could be found in Central Asia. ConocoPhillips, needing connected partners in Russia, took a growing stake in Lukoil. Gazprom produced in Asia, Iraq and Nigeria through joint ventures, and built transnational pipelines to sell its domestic output. The Russian state could apply through Gazprom economic pressure on energy-dependent neighbours, such as Ukraine, split between those favouring pro-Russian and those favouring pro-Western alignment. Throughout Europe, despite US criticism, countries had gambled on cheap supplies from the east, yet increasingly sought reassurances about Gazprom's commercial independence, while considering other long-term options (UNCTAD, 2006, 2010).[93]

The spread of industrialization worldwide and, most observably, the rise of China heightened anxieties about the contrast of endless demand versus finite materials. The search for resources became inevitably mixed with matters of international diplomacy. China's outward FDI, rising since its post-1978 economic reforms at home, took off noticeably from 2003 onwards. If we exclude Chinese FDI to Hong Kong, that going to Asia in 2008 was some 8.9 per cent of the total; so, Africa was, with 9.8 per cent, China's most important investment destination, and a supplier of essential raw materials. Four state-owned oil companies were to be found amongst the country's eight biggest MNEs, by overseas assets, and the importance of oil, mining, commodities, and trading businesses in the top 40 list indicated a concern for accessing raw materials.

Extractive industries accounted for 48 per cent of China's outward FDI flow in 2005. For a developing nation, such as China, with notable success in manufacturing and exports, these were wholly expected findings. With their willingness to work in economically and politically difficult locations, Chinese MNEs possessed an advantage that compensated them for any shortfalls, measured against internationally long-established firms, in management and technology. Committed support from government and easy finance from state-owned banks offered extra counterweights, and mineral concessions in Africa were often as much agreements between China and host governments as commercial projects. Chinese companies could offer a combination of mature technologies and low manpower costs, although this latter advantage limited the local employment effects of their investments. An estimated 750,000 Chinese workers may have been temporarily relocated to Africa between 1999 and 2008 on oil, mining and infrastructure projects (UNCTAD, 2007; WTO, 2006).[94]

CNPC went multinational in 1993, when it signed a service contract for Peru's Talara oilfield, then another for Muglad in Sudan. The company was heavily involved in the development of Central Asia: it bought, for example, control of Kazakhstan's Aktobe Oil Company in 1997, and it purchased the Alberta-registered PetroKazakhstan for $4.2bn, in 2005 the biggest overseas acquisition of any Chinese company, although it sold a minority stake to the state-owned KazMunaiGaz in the face of local opposition. CNPC partnered Lukoil in Uzbekistan and BP in Iraq's Rumaila oilfield, and could operate in Iran when sanctions had forced Western firms to withdraw. Sudan supplied 5–7 per cent of China's oil by 2011, for which China agreed to complete a hydroelectric project, railways and the president's palace. Finance for the Merowe Dam allowed Sudan to bypass the multilateral Nile Basin Initiative for the equitable and peaceful development of regional water resources. China–Africa trade, some $12m per year in the 1980s, reached approximately $50bn by 2006.[95]

The intricacies of Chinese oil diplomacy in developing Africa had parallels in ENI's investments in Libya: the energy company agreed, in 2006, with the government and the National Oil Corporation to train graduates and to build a port, a desalination plant, a hospital and housing, along the Gulf of Sidra. The personal diplomacy of prime minister Berlusconi and Libyan dictator Gaddafi led ultimately to the 2008 'friendship treaty', which included compensation for thirty years of colonization, part of which was construction of a 1,700km highway linking the Tunisian and Egyptian borders.[96] In Brazil, raw material exports paid for imported Chinese manufactures, and Sinopec bought

40 per cent of Repsol YPF's Brazilian subsidary.[97] On the other hand, Chinese oil and mining companies avoided the political and competitive difficulties of investing in Russia, where agriculture and fisheries formed the largest element of Chinese FDI (UNCTAD, 2006).

The attempt by CNOOC to buy the Unocal (Union Oil Company of California) highlighted the strategic importance of energy assets and their centrality to the diplomatic calculations of the USA and China in an increasingly bipolar world. Unocal had gained notoriety in the 1980s for its links with US intelligence services and for acting as a conduit to the Taliban when they took control of Afghanistan in the 1990s. By 1995, firms like Levi Strauss had already left the repressive Myanmar, but Unocal took a stake in the country in partnership with Total. In 2005, when Unocal's human rights record in Mynamar was under investigation, the US House of Representatives voted against CNOOC's move, eventually blocked by President George W. Bush, allowing therefore Chevron to acquire the company instead. Congressmen cited reasons of national security, but were responding to widespread public opposition, while the Chinese perceived unjustified political opposition and protectionism. Chevron finally took its chance and bought Unocal (UNCTAD, 2006, 2007).

Mining, competition and politics

In the oil industry, developing countries allowed multinationals access through joint ventures, concessions, service contracts and production sharing agreements. In 2007, such PSAs were the foundation for about 50 per cent of contracts in developing countries, which needed multinational involvement but wanted a mechanism to the secure economic benefits from production. Concessions and joint ventures, nonetheless, were dominant in Algeria, Kazakhstan, the Russian Federation and Venezuela. Contracts usually covered issues of royalties and tax, frequently local content regulations or the training of locals, the role of state-owned enterprises, and increasingly human rights or environmental issues. In the mining industry, concessions were the most common mode, and contracts would commonly cover rules on disputes, the employment of local employees, royalties and taxation. The geographical distribution of minerals influenced the risks and operational demands of multinationals. Copper production, for example, was divided between developed countries (43 per cent of the total), Latin America and the Caribbean (21 per cent), and south-eastern Europe and the CIS (21 per cent). Consumption was indicative of changes in the structure of the world economy: while the developed nations' demand for copper fell from 64 to 46 per cent between 1995 and 2005, that of developing Asia grew phenomenally, from 28 to 42 per cent (UNCTAD, 2006, 2010).

While state-owned enterprises in developing and transition economies had continued to dominate oil and gas production, the situation in mining was reversed. In the 1990s, high debt levels and poorly performing state-owned enterprises necessitated policy changes, and world levels of FDI in mining as well as investment in developing economies grew (UNCTAD, 2010). By 2005, state-owned enterprises extracted only 14 per cent of metallic ores, and, out of the twenty-five largest mining firms, fifteen originated from developed nations. The top two were BHP Billiton and Rio Tinto, while the fourth-largest was Anglo American. The third-largest, from Brazil, was called Companhia Vale do Rio Doce, or, in English, the poetic-sounding Sweet Valley River Company: on the other hand, it was not a multinational until its overseas purchases in 2005–6. Three other firms amongst the top twenty-five miners – Codelco (Chile), Alrose (Russian Federation) and KGHM Polska Mledz (Poland), all state-owned – were not multinationals. Chile was the world's largest copper producer, in 2005, representing some 45 per cent of its exports. The top four miners were engaged in a wide range of mining activities, but the fifth, Codelco, was essentially a copper business. The top ten miners accounted for some 33 per cent of non-energy minerals, and the top ten copper miners provided some 58 per cent of copper ores. They increased, in addition, their control over refining between 1995 and 2000. So, by 2005, the top twenty mining companies owned some 40–60 per cent of refining capacity in aluminium, copper and zinc, plus 80 per cent in nickel. Rio Tinto, located in ten countries, was the most international mining business, followed by Anglo American, AngloGold Ashanti and Glencore (UNCTAD, 2007).

RTZ (Rio Tinto Zinc) grew through acquisitions and mergers, buying operations in 15 countries from 1989 onwards, most prominently BP Minerals and, therefore, also the Kennecott Corporation. It merged, in 1995, with CRA Group to create the world's largest mining firm, renaming itself as Rio Tinto plc two years later. It looked to new opportunities and sales in Asia and particularly in China, but the acquisition of aluminium maker Alcan left it with a debt burden that dragged the industry into commercial and diplomatic complications.[98] As Rio Tinto choked on the scale of the Alcan deal, rival BHP Billiton manoeuvred for a takeover that would have created a global iron ore duopoly with Brazil's Vale (formerly CVRD).

Fearing a rise in commodity prices and for its own economic security, the Chinese government sought to scupper the deal through an alternative pairing of Rio Tinto with the state-owned aluminium company Chinalco, financially backed by four state banks. Seeing a chance to increase sales and to buy political protection in China, Rio Tinto's management opened negotiations over an increased 18 per cent holding by Chinalco and two board seats. In Australia, disquiet over the loss of national assets and over China's rise as a regional power stoked public opinion, and BHP Billiton lobbied the government to block the deal. Rio Tinto's shareholders too rebelled against its management, and in June 2009, within hours of the Chinalco deal's collapse, Rio Tinto and BHP Billiton had announced a merger of their iron ore interests in Western Australia.[99] The Australian government was satisfied – glad to have dodged the diplomatic repercussions of intervening – but it did block a bid by another state-owned enterprise, China Minmetals Company, to buy OZ Minerals, whose copper and gold mines were located near a military installation (WTO, 2006).

For Chinalco, these events were a lesson in the speed and ruthlessness of multinational enterprise; they generated resentment in China, Rio Tinto's largest market, where the company was accused of offering smaller discounts than it offered to other customers overseas. Within a month, the Chinese authorities had arrested four of its employees, one an Australian national leading negotiations on iron ore prices, for corruption and espionage(WTO, 2006).[100] Chinalco, nonetheless, continued to be Rio Tinto's biggest shareholder, and they had strong mutual interests. In 2010, they jointly initiated a project in Simandou, Guinea, potentially one of the world's most important sources of iron ore. Rio Tinto had the advanced technological, business and marketing capabilities, while the Guinea government favoured China's participation, which brought significant infrastructure and transport spin-offs. Guinea was dependent on commodity exports, with its bauxite, alumina, gold and diamonds making up nearly 90 per cent of the totals by 2005 (UNCTAD, 2007).[101]

BHP Billiton had been created by a 2001 merger. BHP was Australian in origin, and it had grown internationally, from 1985, by acquisitions in Africa, Utah (from General Electric), Canada, South America (including the huge Escondida mine in Chile) and Papua New Guinea (for gold and copper). By 1996, overseas activities formed 70 per cent of its revenues. Billiton, owned by Shell until 1994, then added mining and refining interests in Brazil, Panama, Canada, Australia and other locations, entering Yunnan in China through joint venture deals in 2001. When executives left BHP Billiton, in 2001, to take over Sudelektra, they set out to build through a strategy of acquisition a large, diverse mining business. To achieve their ambitions, they created Xstrata, which by 2011 was present in some thirty countries, the world's largest exporter of thermal coal and the biggest producer of ferrochrome, while being also a global player in coking, copper, nickel and zinc.[102] Xstrata shared its top management with commodity producer and trader Glencore International, from 2006, with both firms having their headquarters in the Swiss canton of Zug. Glencore took a major holding in Xstrata, leading to takeover in 2012. Glencore had an expertise and leadership in the international coordination of smelting and refining, giving it influence over the distribution of end products and commodity prices (UNCTAD, 2005).[103]

The Anglo American Corporation commanded a central place in the history of South Africa, and was closely associated with the apartheid regime. In the era before liberation, sanctions prevented AAC investing overseas, except for diamond mining in Botswana, through its De Beers subsidiary. The company's shares and those of affiliates, including large holdings in Barclays National Bank and South African Breweries, accounted for 25 per cent of the South African stock market. Ernest Oppenheimer and his son Harry declared against democratic majority rule, and, while they did favour a relaxation of the resented labour and settlement laws, these were reforms that would have helped AAC create, amongst its mostly black employees, a more stable, less transitory workforce. When the 1992 all-white referendum accepted free elections, AAC feared nationalization, and set out to protect its interests by acquiring assets overseas and internationally transferring ownership of its South African companies. Its Luxembourg-registered subsidiary, Minorco, had already expanded in the USA and Canada, and from 1993 it assumed formal ownership of all non-African, non-diamond assets. When AAC and Minorco merged, in 1998, Anglo

American plc was established in London as a British company. Under a new generation of managers, which took over from 2000, the company initiated worldwide acquisitions in Africa, Latin America, Alaska and Australia.[104]

The largest mining firm from a developing country – CVRD – carried responsibility for supporting the Brazilian economy. It took the lead, in the 1980s, in the Grand Carajas project, effectively administering large parts of the impoverished northern region of Para, its mining operations participating in internationally funded developments in power generation, clean water resources, transport, and basic infrastructure. Foreign multinationals were reluctant to be directly involved, although RTZ, AAC and BP Minerals did give financial and technical support. The project, moreover, attracted opposition from environmentalists and Amazonian tribes that lost their lands and way of life. CVRD's part privatization, in 1997, was a signal that it would focus in future on its core mining business and expand its non-ferrous operations. When, some 12 per cent government-owned, it bought nickel miner Canico Resources in 2005, and, more significantly, Canada's second-largest mining business, Inco, in 2006, it became a multinational. It also purchased coal miner AMCI Holdings in Australia during 2007, and it had interests in Chile and Peru, as well as in Asia and Africa (UNCTAD, 2007).[105]

The Chinese government linked the securing of raw materials in Africa with direct aid. A multi-billion-dollar infrastructure agreement secured copper concessions in Mashamba West and Dikuluwe, once Congo's government had eased out Katanga Mining. China signed a contract worth $6 billion to build roads, railways, hospitals, health centres and universities. Gabon signed an iron ore deal in return for electricity plants, railways and ports, using Chinese workers, just as Guinea was motivated by the Chinalco–RTZ deal. In Zambia, a joint venture between China Nonferrous Metals and Yunnan Copper Group built the Chambishi Copper Smelter, establishing finishing processes on the African continent, and reinforcing China's regional commercial hold. Wage disputes at Chambishi and with the Mineworkers Union of Zambia (MUZ) suggested that Chinese companies paid less well than other multinationals and brought about intervention from the government.

There was a reminder of the non-economic complications of multi-national enterprise in 2011, when Chinese companies appeared to be associated with the ruling party that lost the general election, and the victors had long campaigned against their operating conditions and low wages. China promoted its African Policy – bringing much-needed economic development – primarily through bilateral, government-to-government, secretive agreements. A hydroelectricity project in Ghana, Senegal transport and infrastructure, Uganda's Naguru hospital and a national defence college in Zimbabwe were only a few examples of trade-and-aid for natural resources, frequently providing international contracts for Chinese construction firms and their workers. The recapitalization of the failing Zambia China Mulungushi Textiles Company, and investments in the Henan Haode Mozambique Industrial Park, a textile and clothing industry in Marracuene district, were rarer examples of Chinese FDI building industrial capacity in Africa. China's FDI stock, $49m in 1990, grew to $588m by 2003, but to $9.2bn by 2009. Despite the publicity generated, the latest figure was just a little more than 2 per cent of China's outward FDI stock, and a little under 2 per cent of Africa's inward FDI stock (WTO, 2006).[106]

Manufacturing trends and global value chains

The decline of manufacturing as a share of all outward FDI assets was a characteristic of the fourth phase of the Global Economy: it declined from over 44 per cent in 1990, to some 26 per cent by 2005. Real dollar totals in manufacturing, of course, tracked the growth of global business. Multinationals from the developed economies – once accounting for almost all of this investment – still held nearly 96 per cent of total assets by the end of this period. Chemicals and chemical products maintained its role as the lead sector, though electricals and electronics fell back to fifth place, directly supplanted at number two by motor vehicles and transportation. The food, beverages and tobacco, and the metals and metal products sectors maintained their prominent position, as did, further down the rankings, machinery and equipment, and textiles, clothing and leather. As with services and natural resources, there was some shift, too, in the location of manufacturing assets: the percentage found in developing economies increased from nearly 20 to over 24 between 1990 and 2005 (Table 5.9).

The 1980s were the decade of Japanese multinationals, when their surging investments in the USA and the European Community sought to defend sales threatened by rising tariffs and stricter import quotas.

It proved possible to be too successful at exporting. Japan's outward FDI levels had formerly been low – mainly to secure raw materials or key components – and it took less favourable trade policies in Japanese multinationals' major export markets to bring about a change in international business strategy and their conversion into global multinationals. By 1988, Japan had overtaken the European Community and the USA as the largest supplier of outward FDI flows (UNCTAD, 1991). Toyota, Sony and Panasonic became important multinationals, as well as owners of international brands. Moreover, new Japanese manufacturing affiliates overseas brought with them the management and production techniques that had made them such highly successful exporters, and Western firms tried to restore their dwindling competitive position by imitating them (with mixed results). Their methods had acquired the reputation of global best practice. Japan was home to eight of the top fifty non-financial multinational enterprises, as ranked by assets, in 1992, seven in manufacturing, one in trading; it could claim eight manufacturers and six trading companies in the top 100 by 1998, although some sliding down the table rankings was an early hint that their comparative competitiveness had already peaked (UNCTAD, 2002).

Worldwide, of the top 100 non-financial transnational corporations in 2008, measured by assets, 54 were involved in manufacturing, but many were also diverse and providing various services. The largest manufacturing multinational, and consequently the largest international electrical and electronic equipment maker, was the USA's General Electric. Next were Toyota (Japan), Arcelor-Mittal (formally Luxembourg, with a controlling firm of Indian origin), Volkswagen (Germany) and Anheuser-Busch Inbev (Netherlands). The USA had 12 entrants, followed by Germany with 8 and France with 7. Britain could claim 6, although their number included SAB Miller (South African in origin) and Unilever (in reality, Anglo-Dutch). Japanese multinationals at this point accounted for 5, as did Switzerland, continuing to maintain an international presence significantly above the relative weight of its economy. There were 7 other European companies in the list and 1 from Israel. Only 3 came from developing countries: Samsung Electronics, Hyundai (both being Korean) and Cemex (from Mexico) (UNCTAD, 2010).

The period was one of considerable change in the location, organization and strategies of international manufacturing. Trade barriers explained the need for Japanese multinational enterprises to establish factories in Europe and North America, in the 1980s, but many reasons induced them to stay and deepen their investment. After 1994, signatories to the WTO agreed to the phasing-out of all voluntary export agreements, as used by European and US governments to restrain imports from Asia. All multinationals with plants in their major markets could achieve a better understanding of consumers, improve product customization, hire local managerial or technical talent, and seek rising returns to scale, as sources of competitive advantage (UNCTAD, 2002). Furthermore, the ending of exchange controls and foreign ownership restrictions in developed economies and, overall, their easing in developing nations opened up investment opportunities for manufacturing FDI. Governments, once wary of competition from investing multinationals, now looked positively on their potential to boost technology, management, employment and exports, as well as the stock of capital. The reform of the Communist bloc was, in particular, a momentous turning point in geopolitics and the international economy. Industrialization continued to spread to a greater number of countries, and offered more bases for low-wage and low-cost manufacture. Multinationals built plants in eastern Europe and shipped goods westwards, just as, within NAFTA, international businesses positioned themselves south of the Mexico–USA border (UNCTAD, 2006).

One estimate is that the pool of global labour quadrupled in 1985–2005, mostly after 1990. The share of unskilled workers in the national wealth of the USA, Europe and Japan fell, and that of skilled workers rose. Globalization, it was contended, had exported their jobs to developing countries, and left industry in the developed nations to compete in the long term through technology and education (IMF, 2007). The simple bipolar international division of labour of an earlier era – between manufacturing nations versus commodity producers – gave place to a tripartite scenario, which separated high-value, high-tech production from low-cost, labour-intensive output, and separated them from commodity producers. Furthermore, manufacturers could now exploit the very different advantages of locations for different stages of production: the availability of cheap labour favoured assembly operation, technological resources suited knowledge-intensive processes, and good infrastructure facilitated trade and exports. The largest multinational enterprises found that they had to utilize the resources of locations all over the world, as well as to compete for every major market.

FDI and the relocation of production serviced greater returns to scale and efficiencies for each production stage, and created complex cross-border value chains. International manufacturers moved from being multinational, in the sense that similar nation-based subsidiaries largely met the demands of local markets, to being more obviously transnational, with vertically separated operations and globally orientated factories, in which the coordination of cross-border transactions became as important a source of competitive advantage as other internal capabilities such as R&D or branding. A subsidiary or a location's 'fit within the global value chain' became a fundamental strategic consideration. Japanese subsidiaries in Malaysia might make components assembled in Japan for export to the USA, or Japanese factories in Eastern Europe or Turkey, combining low costs with nearness to final markets, supplied the richer countries of Western Europe.

A Taiwanese business, Foxconn, bringing its capital and international connections to China, and benefiting from cultural familiarity, established the huge plant in Shenzen that met the design and product requirements of the US's high-tech and design phenomenon Apple. Globalization brought the globalization of markets, products and brands, and the globalization of production through international value chains. As investment and ownership regulations fell away, international mergers and acquisitions increased the possibilities of FDI for developing and developed economies alike, especially where state-owned businesses were privatized. Multinational enterprises no longer had to evolve the capabilities that would allow them to compete successfully overseas, but could buy firms with the technological, managerial or market knowledge they required. Asset-seeking strategies, nonetheless, especially appealed to the so-called 'dragon multinationals' from emerging economies that began to use FDI as means of upgrading, improving their performance in their home economy, or closing more quickly the gap with competitors from developed economies.

Global business organization

There was early recognition of both the impact of Japanese manufacturing multinationals and the emergence of 'regional' and 'global production networks'. Some 77 per cent of the sales to Japan made by Japanese-owned plants in Asia were components for a parent company, in 1987, while the figures for sales to Japanese-owned plants in the USA and the European Community were over 50 per cent. Within the EC, Japanese firms were still developing their production networks, and intra-firm transactions were some 19 per cent of affiliate sales, low compared to US subsidiaries at 50 per cent (UNCTAD, 1991). In general, the lowering of trade barriers, improved transport, and the technological revolution in communications inspired a greater range of corporate arrangements for the international organization of production, with consequences for the ownership and management of subsidiaries.

Once, manufacturing multinationals had preferred equity ownership and direct ownership of their overseas subsidiaries, in order to safeguard product and managerial knowledge, and to facilitate the effective transfer of capabilities, usually from the parent company. Now, instead, they showed greater inclination to adopt licensing, franchising, subcontracting, or strategic alliances, and other collaborative arrangements that supported outsourcing and offshoring in competitive locations. Organizationally, multinational enterprises adopted a flagship model, in which production and not just support services could be externalized, so long as companies exerted authority through the setting of technical, quality or delivery standards, and retained control of key processes or the brand. They had to tackle, as a result, the considerable challenges of coordinating between cultural, institutional, political and geographical distances. Where multinational enterprises resorted to offshoring and outsourcing, they could focus on those parts of the global value chain that maximized competitive advantage, control, or value-added, most likely involving R&D, product definition, marketing, or branding (UNCTAD, 2002).

Duplicate factories had suited a scenario of trade barriers and highly differentiated national markets, but increasingly made less sense. During the 1990s, Procter & Gamble closed some thirty plants, laying off 13,000 employees, and, in 2005, it tore up its organizational model of a parent company supervising overseas national or regional satellites in favour of seven global business units.[107] Worldwide product divisions tended to replace business organizations based on a dominant parent company in its home economy with an international division overseeing overseas subsidiaries. Rather than overseas subsidiaries being reliant on capabilities transferred from the parent, their management might assume a global role within the whole multinational, often utilizing the technological, cost, infrastructure or other advantage of the affiliate's location. HP Singapore, in the 1980s, progressed from making components to exporting calculators and ink-jet printers worldwide and then to their design and product development.[108] Nonetheless, the tensions between the geographical aspects of business organization – international, regional and national – and the product and function dimensions remained, even in matrix solutions which seemingly gave equal weight to all three aspects (Bartlett and Ghoshal, 1989).

The internationality of a multinational was related to levels of intra-firm trade, which required scale economies and the rationalization of world capacity. In 1970, the intra-firm trade in manufactures amounted to 20 per cent of the total, and climbed, in 2000, to 40 per cent (Mathews, 2002). Since multinationals increasingly organized and coordinated the flow of exports and imports, the role of multinationals in the global economy became even more pronounced. Trade in parts and components assumed a greater portion of world exports, and international production chains were built on the intra-firm division of labour. For the top twenty exporting nations, in non-resource-based manufacturing, foreign affiliates were responsible overall for 30 per cent of their trade: Hungary led with an 80 per cent figure, followed by Estonia (60 per cent), then China and Costa Rica (both 50 per cent), and Malaysia, Canada and the Netherlands (some 44–45 per cent) (UNCTAD, 2002). Trade liberalization, invoking the invisible hand of the international market, brought in actuality the visible hand of international management and intra-firm coordination.

The spread of industrialization, growing living standards, and the growth of manufacturing FDI outside the North Atlantic axis facilitated changes in the location and organization of global production. Labour cost reduction and other forms of efficiency-seeking became principal objectives for manufacturing multinationals investing overseas, when production in their developed-economy home base turned uneconomic. Strategic choices led to differences in the organization of production chains between industries and individual companies. In automobiles, semi-conductors and steel, mergers and acquisitions partnered globalization, and production stages were split between different countries, allowing scale and exploiting the cost, technological or logistical advantages of each location. On the other hand, the transport of its comparatively heavy products and protectionist-minded governments ensured that its output was more regional than in the more highly globalized case of electronics. By 2002, the top ten auto companies owned three quarters of total world production. Toyota employed a mixture of directly owned subsidiaries, those undertaking the most modern or the final stages of manufacture, and a multi-tiered network of formally independent subcontractors. It had three plants in the USA and one in Canada; five in Europe; one each in Australia and South Africa; three in Latin America; and eight in Asia, including joint ventures Tianjin Toyota Motor Company in China, Toyota Kirloskar in India, and PT Toyota-Astar in Indonesia. The company operated regional production networks in the heart of its major markets, but utilized, too, low-cost sites in Mexico to serve the USA, and in Turkey and the Czech Republic to supply Western Europe (UNCTAD, 2002).[109]

General Motors, Ford, DaimlerChrysler, Nissan and Volkswagen – in addition to Toyota – could be found in Mexico. Volkswagen, as early as 1989, made the decision to consolidate all its North American operations, and it modernized its Puebla plant to supply the rich markets to the north and to act as a global engine factory. Eventually, the multinational closed its US operations, and the Puebla plant exported the Beetle worldwide. The signing of NAFTA, in 1994, and the Mexico–EU trade agreement, in 2000, confirmed the soundness of the policy. VW owned the third-largest foreign-owned factory in Latin America and, overall, overseas revenues moved from 36 per cent of group sales to 61 per cent, the highest of any automobile multinational (UNCTAD, 2002). Production might be regionalized, too: the Golf was predominantly a European car, just as Toyota had designed and manufactured the Yaris in Europe for sale to Europeans (UNCTAD, 2010).[110]

The largest semiconductor multinational, by 2002, was Intel, with one quarter of global sales and owning 13 fabrication plants and 11 assembly-and-testing sites in seven countries. Its international production system continued to rely on equity affiliates for R&D and specialized production stages, but used outsourcing for most other activities. China, South East Asia and Costa Rica acted as low-cost sites for semiconductors, while Korea, Ireland and Israel offered high-tech locations. Compared to US electronics manufacturers, Japanese firms tended to internalize a greater number of production stages, as well as strategic functions such as R&D. Rapid technological change, short product cycles, and privatizations drove competition in the global telecommunications industry, and the boom of the late 1990s was followed by a sharp downturn and overcapacity. Ericsson, the biggest telecommunications firm in 2000, cut the number of its plants from some 70 to fewer than 10 and resorted more extensively to outsourcing. The company retained control of manufacturing, innovation and design, but moved everything else to non-equity plants, while Cisco exited manufacturing entirely (UNCTAD, 2002). Founded by Taiwanese immigrant William Wang, the Californian firm Vizio, held some 22 per cent of the US flat-screen market by 2010. It succeeded by selling through large-scale outlets, such as Costco, but additionally exploited global value chains by contracting in South Korea, China and Mexico, employing only a hundred or so employees in design, sales and customer service in the USA. Japanese companies, such as Sony and Hitachi, responded to the new global realities by leaving the USA for Asian-made components assembled at factories in Mexico (*Business Week*, 2010–13; *New York Times*, 2010–11).[111]

Clothing was marked by low entry barriers, larger numbers of producers, and relatively small factories. It accounted for 20 per cent of all low-tech, non-resource-based manufacture in 2000. Success in garments rested on knowledge of fast-moving market trends, and production remained flexible and small-scale. The contracting out of production gave cost advantages, but design, scheduling and transportation came under the tightening control of multiple retailers in the developed economies and specialized contract manufacturers coordinating a global network on their behalf (UNCTAD, 2002). Contract suppliers outside the USA made almost all of Nike's apparel by 2009, and factories in Vietnam, China and Indonesia supplied some 74 per cent of its footwear (UNCTAD, 2011). From an early stage, however, as early as 1996, ethical campaigners revealed the dangers of international subcontracting when Nike became associated with poor pay and unhealthy working conditions in Vietnam and elsewhere. Levi Strauss's contractors were found to be working 1,200 Chinese and Filipino women for 72 hours a week in guarded compounds, and the company pulled out of China when instances of child labour and forced work breached the guidelines established after previous revelations.[112]

By 2003, Levi Strauss – an American icon – had shifted all its production to Latin America and Asia. Garments, footwear, toys and housewares were organized by buyer-driven commodity chains in which retailers, brand-name merchandizers and trading companies oversaw decentralized production networks mainly in emerging markets. On the other hand, fashion-orientated retailers and the makers of designer products could still source in locations such as France and Italy. Most production networks used a mix of interfirm and intra-firm transactions; those in automobiles, aircraft, electrical machinery and computers were producer-driven chains; those in clothing and shoes were buyer-driven by large retailers and brand-name merchandizers (Gereffi, 1994).

The growing scale and incidence of cross-border production chains and outsourcing strategies meant that contract manufacturers grew in size and underpinned the workings of the global economy. In the USA, the owner of Victoria's Secrets and La Senza, Limited Brands, oversaw what it called a 'global network of relationships, resources and support personnel'; its subsidiary, Mast Industries, by 2000 formed one of the clothing industry's largest contract manufacturers, managing 400 factories in 37 countries, mostly in Asia, and coordinating over 600 associates. In other cases, supply and contract companies used their links with multinationals to extend their services and to evolve themselves into complex multinationals. Li & Fung, from Hong Kong, began as a regional sourcing agent but evolved into a full-package provider that involved, first, design, product development and quality control, as well as contracting and logistics, and, subsequently, complete control of seasonal fashion portfolios for large retailers. The firm indirectly employed some 1.5 million people for 700 customers in the USA and EU, not directly owning factories abroad on its own account, but instead sharing risks with network partners in over forty countries (UNCTAD, 2002).

The world's largest contract electronics manufacturer, by revenue, in 2009 was Foxconn, employing 611,000 people in its main production bases of Malaysia, Vietnam and the Czech Republic, but, most notably, China. Taiwanese-owned businesses provided five of the top ten electronics contractors, including, as we have noted before, Apple and Amazon. Flextronics, from Singapore, with some 160,000 employees in thirty countries and eight directly owned factories, was Foxconn's biggest competitor. It took over much of Motorola's mobile phone production, and all of Ericsson's, by offering scale, volume flexibility and shared capital risk. Both Foxconn and Flextronics were amongst

China's biggest multinational exporters. At the head of contracting in auto parts was the Denso Corporation, present in 33 countries, whose most important customer was Toyota, taking some 30 per cent of total sales. It generated over 42 per cent of its revenues outside its home country of Japan, but was beaten by the figure of 76 per cent achieved by Robert Bosch outside Germany (UNCTAD, 2002, 2011). ENGTEK, headquartered in Penang, Malaysia, was an example of a regional contract supplier, making marine engines, and growing through its links with multinational enterprises (UNCTAD, 2002).

A complex chain of mergers and acquisitions, between 1994 and 2004, transformed the pharmaceutical industry: amongst many others, Ciba-Geigy and Sandoz united into Novartis; Zeneca acquired Swedish Astra, forming Astra Zeneca; Smith Kline Beckman and the Beecham Group made Smith Kline Beecham, and subsequently joined the merged Glaxo Wellcome to create GSK; Hoechst and Rhone-Poulenc merged into Aventis, in turn purchased by the merged Sanofi-Synthelabo, renamed Sanofi Aventis in 2004, and more simply Sanofi in 2011.[113]

After a decade in which changes in Japan's patent laws had led to rapidly rising expenditure on R&D, its pharmaceutical companies looked to recoup the costs through expansion overseas. Takeda's breakthroughs in antibiotics made licensing agreements possible, and, by 1983, it had arrangements with twenty companies, most prominently Abbott Laboratories in the USA. This strategic link led to a joint venture, two years later, and Takeda established a fully owned factory in the USA too in 1985. It repeated the use of strategic partnerships in the USA, from 1995, including a deal with SmithKline Beecham, and linked up with Denmark's Novo Nordisk, plus manufacturing in Ireland, and forming national marketing companies worldwide. To push its interests in the USA, it set up Takeda America Holdings Inc. with the aim of developing beyond its strategic partnerships; from 2000, it established R&D centres in the USA and the UK, and, from 2008, in Singapore, merging these facilities with those in Japan to create one global R&D function.[114] While needing research units in the USA, Hikma Pharmaceuticals, from Jordan, was the type of firm that could utilize a combination of licensing agreements and cost advantages, in this case manufacturing both regionally in two Arab countries and in Portugal (UNCTAD, 2006).

Box 5.1 Emerging-economy multinationals

Mathews proposed a theory of multinational enterprises from emerging or post-Communist transition economies – given the name *dragon multinationals* – which varied from traditional models he saw based on companies from the developed world. He noted that, unlike established multinationals, they did not possess competitive or ownership advantages but had to hone organizational learning abilities. He put forward an LLL model: *linkage* is the ability to connect with partners to acquire resources and assets available overseas; *leverage* involves using networks or interfirm linkages to access these resources and assets; and *learning* means gaining from the knowledge and advantages they access internationally. The key difference was that multinationals no longer needed to develop ownership advantages in their home economy to overcome the disadvantage of operating in foreign markets; now, multinationals could form strategic alliances or purchase companies overseas to acquire ownership advantages in order to be more competitive in their home or host economies (Mathews, 2002; Goldstein, 2007).

Dragon multinationals

As we have seen, much of the investment from emerging nations was related closely to the demands of industrialization and economic development: given the speed and the scale of its transformation, China needed access to the world's raw materials, and its oil and mining companies had a powerful impact on the balance of power in international business and politics. Although state ownership was common in resource multinationals from emergent economies, history had shown how governments of developed countries had also involved themselves in questions of national economic security. Nonetheless, the arrival of multinational enterprises from emerging economies with regional and international scope was a new factor. Most notably in the manufacturing sector, they broke the link between advanced national economic development, the subsequent emergence of companies with strong competitive capabilities, and successful multinational expansion. Market liberalization meant that it was easier for multinationals to overcome the problem of being foreign, and that it was easier to engage in international mergers and acquisitions with which to buy leading firms and their assets.

Manufacturing firms following market-seeking strategies had founded greenfield factories or joint ventures, and, with the rise in cross-border production and the broadening choice of worldwide locations for operations, they became motivated by efficiency seeking. International M&A, especially from the 1990s, enabled asset seeking or asset augmenting, the purchase of a firm for its technology, managerial knowledge, design function, brand, or some other capability. Previously, ideas in international business had portrayed companies as honing competitive advantages (predominantly in developed economies) and using the capabilities they owned to overcome the difficulties of being a foreign firm overseas. Now, on the contrary, companies could become multinationals in order to acquire needed capabilities to compete more effectively in either their home or international markets. Instead of capabilities being transferred from the parent to the subsidiary's host economy, they were transferred from subsidiary to the parent's home economy. In the case of developing economies, multinational investment was no longer the culmination of economic development but a means of jumping stages of economic development. The strategy of these multinationals was to build links and alliances, learning organizationally from the interaction, and, if advantageous, eventually acquiring their partner (UNCTAD, 2006).

The entry of dragon multinationals – those from emerging economies – was an indicator of change in the world economy, once almost entirely associated with the trade and investment activities of the North America, West Europe and Japan triad. It is fair to add that most multinational enterprises from developing and transition nations remained small alongside those from developed nations, but many did achieve international prominence, notably Korean enterprises from the 1990s onwards (encouraged by government policies of *segyewha* or 'international openness') and their Chinese rivals after 2000 (under Beijing's 'go global' slogan). At the turn of the century, the most international non-financial multinational enterprise from a developing country was Hong Kong's Hutchinson Whampoa, with Cemex and LG Electronics in second and third place. *Fortune 500* listed 19 multinational enterprises from the developing and transition economies in 1990 and 47 in 2005.

As well as showing a high level of state ownership, with many also being privatized firms, much of the investment originating from

Africa, Latin America and the CIS could be accounted for by companies from South Africa, Brazil and Mexico and the Russian Federation respectively. Multinational enterprises from Asia – those from China, Hong Kong, Korea, Taiwan, Singapore, Malaysia and Thailand – were regionally very significant, and further advanced in their cross-border scope and capabilities than their Latin American counterparts. Russian FDI was largely in the resource industries. Of the 100 largest multinational enterprises from developing and transition economies, 77 were Asian. Overall, they showed a bias towards automobiles, chemicals, steel, electronics, energy, construction, transport and finance. Some 28 per cent of the 82,000 multinational enterprises in 2008 were from developing or transition economies, compared to 10 per cent in 1992 (UNCTAD, 2002, 2006, 2010).

Multinational enterprises from developing and transition economies possessed advantages in production process capabilities and costs, and relied on networks and strategic alliances, government finance, or diplomatic support as compensating factors against those with advanced technologies or brands. Yet Acer, Huawei, Samsung Electronics, Hyundai-Kia, Infosys and Wipro could claim to be industry leaders. Leading Korean firms had tended to follow the 'traditional' FDI pattern of building capabilities in production methods and, latterly, in R&D and design, and using these capabilities to establish operations overseas. Many suffered setbacks in the 1990s, as their capabilities and brand recognition proved inadequate to the task. The Daewoo conglomerate, bankrupted, was broken up, but Samsung Electronics, LG Electronics, Hyundai-Kia and others emerged ultimately as global successes.

Posco, the state-owned steel maker privatized in 2000, responded to rising wage costs in Korea by investing overseas. It founded numerous joint ventures in China, including by 2006 the country's first fully integrated stainless steel mill in Jiangsu province, incorporating processes from iron ore smelting to cold rolling. Controversies over malpractice amongst local officials, forest damage, and the impact on local people, however, held up the development of an integrated steel plant in India's Orissa state (UNCTAD, 2007).[115] Mittal Steel grew rapidly through acquisitions after 1992 – in Germany, the USA, Canada and France, as well as Kazakhstan, eastern Europe, the Balkans and Mexico – buying up unprofitable or privatized businesses. It invested, too, in a China joint venture. The company set the pace for globalizing and consolidating the steel industry, and took over Arcelor – itself a merger of European makers with transcontinental interests – in 2006, creating ArcelorMittal, the world's largest steel maker. It continued to expand, notably in Latin America, and its securing of mining operations in Liberia and Brazil underlined the global integration of production as an objective. Acquisition propelled the Indian conglomerate Tata into international steel manufacture, when it beat Brazil's Companhia Siderurgica Nacional (CSN) in a takeover battle for the Anglo-Dutch business Corus in 2007. When it sold on its new assets, in Teesside, Britain, to Sahaviriya Steel Industries (SSI), in 2011, it allowed the Thai firm to undertake its first main venture overseas (UNCTAD, 2006, 2007).[116]

From China, Haier and Lenovo in the USA and TCL in France provided clear examples of acquisitions being motivated by upgrading (WIR, 2006). By 2005, Haier controlled 13 factories in Iran, Malaysia, the Philippines and the USA, and 6 overseas design centres (UNCTAD, 2006). Acer progressed from contractor to building its own global computer brand through a complex network of cross-border strategic alliances and directly owned facilities. Taiwanese companies appeared particularly adept at operating international financial and production networks as a source of competitive advantage, without a hierarchical system of parent company and divisional management.[117] Arcelik, part of the Koc group from Turkey, undertook acquisitions in Romania, Germany, Austria and the UK, adding established names such as Grundig to its own Beko range. In the USA, it bought a stake in Ubicom, and sourced the chips it produced for smart household devices. Overall, by 2006, it owned 12 foreign affiliates (UNCTAD, 2006).

Cemex was an early Latin American success. Gaining experience in its own region, then in South East Asia and Egypt, it bought and turned around two failing firms in Spain. The purchase of Southland, in Texas, USA, in 2000, and RMC, in Britain, in 2005 turned it into a big player in developed markets, where it offered its speciality quick-drying cement and prompt delivery.[118] In Latin America, conditions for dragon multinationals improved after 2003. Government policies had consolidated the largest and oldest business groups, sometimes privatizing them. Once products of the uncompetitive import substitution period, they were exposed to competition and encouraged to go overseas. Some Mexican and Brazilian businesses, notably, moved beyond Latin America and into the developed economies (UNCTAD, 2010). By 2002, the Brazilian engineering and energy conglomerate Construtora Norberto Odebrecht, as well as undertaking projects in the USA and Argentina, owned non-residential construction businesses in the linguistically familiar countries of Portugal and Mozambique, where it was one of the country's largest employers. Embraer, a Brazilian maker of small commercial and military aircraft, privatized in 1994, founded a joint venture in China in 2004.

By 2003, South African Breweries had 108 breweries in 24 nations, employing some 31,000 people, becoming the fourth-largest brewer by volume. With the ending of apartheid, it began as a regional investor in Africa, but soon looked to large developing markets, such as China and the CIS, where the penetration of multinational enterprises was low. SAB accrued skills working in abnormal markets, overcoming problems in basic infrastructure, and in using mechanization and management to cut costs for price-sensitive consumers. It broke into the USA by buying Miller Brewing in 2002, and bought brewers in Colombia and Peru in 2006. As beer customers tended to remain loyal to national brands, SAB adopted an acquisition, market-seeking, multi-domestic strategy (UNCTAD, 2002, 2006, 2010).

Many dragon multinationals had important regional roles, not global presence. Singapore Technologies Telemedia (STT) had, from 2002, a presence in Britain, the USA and Latin America, but was overwhelmingly a leading information-communications company in South East Asia, where it looked for cross-border synergies and local market access. The Brazilian bus and coach manufacturer Marcopolo operated in Argentina and Mexico, and Malaysia's AIC Corporation, a diversified auto parts, IT and plastics business, invested in Singapore, China and Thailand. Integrated Microelectronics Inc. (IMI), from the Philippines, carried out contract manufacturing in Singapore and China, willing to acquire firms whose assets could raise its productivity, and establishing an R&D unit in the USA (UNCTAD, 2006).

Multinationals: 1980 to 2010

During the period 1870–1914, there was a comparatively limited link between the ownership and competitive advantages developed by a parent multinational firm in its home economy, and its subsequent ability to establish a successful subsidiary overseas. Undoubtedly, the multinational formally registered in its country of origin – for legal reasons and because it needed access to capital – and it would send leading figures or partners abroad to take charge of companies that quite typically only operated outside the home economy. The organizational form adopted – networks of firms, partnerships and contracts – was reflective of this strategy. The important role of service businesses, in trade and finance, also explains the structure of international business, since their success rested on building external networks and making deals in the location of their activities, not on the transplanting of internal capabilities in technology or production management. Similarly, extractive multinationals, in mining and oil, had to conduct their core activity wherever the minerals were to be found, and the same logic applied to all those processing and shipping natural resources.

Nonetheless, business logic is a partial answer, and the realities of imperial control supported the substantial investments made in colonies, as did diplomatic influence and military pressure on China, Egypt and the Central American republics. The location of FDI – in which territories in Latin America, Asia or Africa were drawn, through a succession of dramatic historical events, commercially and politically into the international system – helps to explain the development of multinational enterprises. There were plentiful examples of manufacturers transferring capabilities for reasons of market seeking in more developed economies, but resource-seeking and export-related strategies by traders, finance and miners dominated in this period.

The First World War inevitably disrupted the international economy, and temporary tariffs frequently turned out to be permanent. Economies such as Australia or Japan used import controls to encourage inward FDI and to promote their industrialization. We tend to look at the period after 1914 as a series of events leading to higher levels of economic catastrophe, global conflict and widespread destruction. The wish, in the 1920s, was for a return as much as possible to the conditions prevailing before the First World War, including, with adjustments for new industrializing countries, free trade. Contemporaries could not have predicted the consequences of the Great Depression, or the unprecedented death toll of the Second World War.

There were, consequently, prominent examples of manufacturing FDI by US companies in Canada, and by US and European companies in Europe, designed to protect exports or to expand sales overseas.

Elsewhere imperialism did not come to an end, but actually reached its high point in the 1920s, often dressed up as League of Nations mandates. The trade-related and resource-seeking motives of multinationals in undeveloped territories, therefore, persisted, although they faced new problems from the unstable or falling price of commodities. These multinationals continued to enjoy favourable operating terms. Even in countries in which imperial governments responded to nationalist pressures with measures of self-government, such as Iraq and Egypt, or in new nations such as Saudi Arabia, oil multinationals took the chance to secure long-term and highly advantageous concession terms. The origin of the multinational and its transferable capabilities had greater strategic importance in manufacturing FDI, but, for trading and natural resources, geographical location combined with political influence or control was more fundamental.

With the wave of manufacturing FDI in the immediate post-1945 decades, largely in Western Europe and Canada, the lead of US companies in management, capital, technology, products and marketing explains their particular success. As much as possible, they mainly replicated home-grown capabilities in overseas subsidiaries intended to serve their host market economies. In other sectors, the politics and economics of the location acquired greater and increasing resonance. In a period of decolonization, government-owned or indigenous firms replaced the trades and banks tainted with imperialism. The extractive industries retained their command of technology, business organization and market access, but their importance to host economies and their historically favourable terms clashed with the growing sense of sovereignty.

The Cold War set the framework of the international political economy, with US management and technology used to bolster allies in Western Europe, Japan, South Korea and Taiwan. In the Third World, the USA had a dislike of European imperialism, broken in any case by the cost of the Second World War, but it found itself supporting authoritarian regimes against nationalist liberation movements. The decision by OPEC to increase the price of crude oil grew out of the difficult history of multinationals in their members' territories, and impelled two severe economic crises in 1973–5 and 1979–81 that significantly disrupted the international economy (if not to the extent of the 1930s crisis).

How did the expansion of the international economy, from the 1980s, and more especially from the 1990s, differ from the previous period? The increase in FDI outstripped the growth in trade and became a generator of economic growth globally. Indeed, the grip of major multinationals on trade – in the cross-border interactions of their numerous subsidiaries, or through complex networks of contracted suppliers – tightened. The levels of service FDI grew markedly, proportionately at the expense of manufacturing and primary goods. With governments relaxing capital and currency controls, multinationals swung to strategies of international mergers and acquisitions, away from greenfield entry, and they were enabled to adopt the asset seeking of technologies, brands and products as a tool for enhancing their own capabilities. Asset seeking had an obvious appeal to emerging-market multinationals, but became commonplace for developed-market multinationals also. With the further spread of industrialization, notably to low-cost countries, multinationals had more opportunities for efficiency seeking by offshoring production in locations with cheaper labour and lower overheads.

Manufacturers moved from a preference for equity ownership and the managerial control of overseas subsidiaries to a mix of full equity, partial equity, strategic partners, and networks of contracted suppliers and distributors (in a way that had parallels with multinational business organization in the nineteenth century). While previously designated as multinationals by reason of equity in foreign plants, they became more internationalized in the sense that the production of goods evolved into a cross-border process through the creation of global value chains. The locus of investment flows shifted from the developed economies to developing economies (again, for the first time since the nineteenth century). Finally, multinationals with their origins in developing or transition economies began to make their mark regionally, and, in increasing cases, globally.

All of these changes constituted a difference with the international economy of the post-war decades, and were far-reaching enough to justify the term Global Economy IV. But, if we look back further in history, then only the rise of emerging-country multinationals was without any meaningful precedents, although the scale of the cross-border production organization is noteworthy. The term 'globalization' was used to explain and even justify almost every trend in economics, society and politics, but the forces of change, rather than being 'new', had a deep history, even if no time could be exactly like another.

Globalization as an inevitable trend envisaged the declining away of the nation state or governments, but it was government policies, of course, that made the trend possible, and government policies could be reversed. In trade and investment negotiations, the governments of major economies continued to exercise greater influence on the structure of the international economy, and, in developing and transition economies, experienced multinationals continued to appreciate the importance of good relations with the local government. Developing economies with strong governments – as shown frequently in Asia – were able to engage better in the international economy and to negotiate better with multinationals than those emerging economies – as exampled in Africa – with weak governments. For developing economies, openness to global forces was only a partial policy solution to their economic progress.

Maybe what the crisis of 2008 demonstrated was not the uselessness of regulation in an age of globalization, but the need for new or even stronger forms of regulation. The fallout from the 'Great Recession' suggested that history is chaotic and full of unexpected events, and that the search for overall explanations and long-term patterns in the development of the multinational enterprise and the context in which it operates is – as is the search for overarching explanations in history – a project with an inbuilt failure mechanism. Multinationals have certainly adopted a diversity of strategies and organizational forms, due to differences between industries, the varied operating demands of host economies, and changes in the structure of the international political economy. The globalization commentary, since the 1990s, has tended to exaggerate the power of multinational companies and to downplay the role of nation states. Over time, the multinational has undertaken the route of continuous change, in defiance of the search for long-term or underlying explanations of its reasons to exist, and seemingly in order to contradict the work of theorists. As a result, it needs to be studied historically, and, to understand its impact on the modern world, and its interactions with home and host governments, placed where appropriate at the centre of world affairs.

Conclusion: International business in time

What might be said to distinguish international business from business generally? And how did some of the key features that specifically distinguish international business change over time? Even with a broad and detailed survey, looking at the impact of the multinational through world trends and particular events, it is only possible to focus on some of its dimensions, inevitably downplaying others. Nonetheless, the first key differentiating factor to consider for international business, identifying it as a subject in its own right, is the actions and policies of host governments, or their ability and power to manage relationships with multinationals and, potentially, with the multinationals' home governments. In assessing any case, the strength and standing of a host government, the stability and coherence of its institutions, the size of the country, the scale of its own security and economic resources are additionally relevant.

In the years between 1870 and 1914, or, if preferred, Global Economy I, Asian polities commonly found themselves poorly equipped to cope with the economic changes and policy demands brought by multinationals that originated, for the most part, in Europe. The history of a nineteenth-century Africa divided by and shared out amongst European states – justified by claims of respecting the rights of local polities and indigenous peoples by formally seeking their 'agreement' – makes the point even more strongly.

As transnational contact grew and the search for the 'normalization' of trade and investment relations intensified, there was the heightened possibility of the second differentiating factor in international business, the representation or involvement of a multinational's home government. In the context of the period, the transnational forces of traders and investors brought the risk of direct and visible intervention. It would be incorrect to see the foreign policies of interventionist governments as merely determined by the interests of multinationals and

merchants: in some cases, consideration of these interests was inciden-
tal, although never wholly inconsequential, while sometimes they were
at the very centre of events.

As we have noted, the British government commonly intervened in
Asia and Africa with reluctance, in response to border instability overseas, domestic political pressures, or the complex game of major power
rivalries, and it weighed the dangers of becoming overstretched militarily and economically. The German government, certainly under the
chancellorship of Bismarck, could similarly interpret the activities of its
own ambitious international entrepreneurs in undeveloped territories
as creating dangerous situations over which they might lose control.
Yet, throughout South East Asia and West Africa, and in Egypt or Iran,
the influence of commercial considerations on the foreign policies of
governments was easily discernable. The Anglo-Persian Oil Company
and Deutsche Bank are just two prominent examples of multinationals
that evolved into trusted agents of government policy.

Britain's power over any specific state or territory constitutes only
part of its international impact between 1870 and 1914. As the leading
industrial and military state of the time, and as the principal source of
overseas capital, Britain set the framework for an international system
based on free markets and political and legal liberalism – however
imperfectly applied – and it led the unprecedented spread of imperialism. The policy agenda it was able to set in both politics and economics helped colonizer and colonized to justify their situation. The
ruling elites of Latin America could accept foreign multinationals and
governments as progressive forces, while directly benefiting from the
export commodity trades, investments and loans that the multinationals could organize.

The willingness and ability of European powers to impose imperialist rule throughout Asia and Africa created favorable conditions for
the operations of multinationals. Colonization removed the risks from
political change or civil unrest, while, as in the cases of Siam, China,
or Japan, all of whom remained formally independent, Western countries forced acceptance of trade treaties, commercial codes, and even
extraterritoriality that gave guarantees and even preference. Despite
successive military and diplomatic humiliations, China proved too
large or too powerful a country to control effectively, with routine out-
bursts of violence against foreign influence, and multinationals needed
alliances with local businesses to penetrate its populous market. Japan

was able to form, in the late nineteenth century, a strong central state, and it was this factor, over time, that gave it the ability to negotiate and deal with foreign multinationals and their governments. As a result, the Japanese government was able to promote Japanese trading companies that could challenge the control of foreign traders on its exports and imports, and to begin the process of founding indigenous industrial concerns.

Multinationals cannot assume so central a role in international affairs but for a third differentiating factor in international business: they possess capabilities in management, technology, or finance that they have the ability to transfer transnationally from their home economies or to develop transnationally in an overseas location. In many cases, it was the possession of these capabilities that bestowed on multinationals their bargaining power over host governments and overseas territories, which needed access to the know-how or resources controlled by foreign businesses. In some cases, the importance of a multinational gave it leverage over its own home government – notably in precious minerals, oil, or strategic waterways across Egypt or Panama – or at least consideration at the highest level.

Unlike the chartered companies of the mercantile era, multinationals in the nineteenth century expected commercial rivalry and had to demonstrate their capabilities. They brought economic development, infrastructure, employment, exports, capital, expertise and technology, leaving aside the issues, explored elsewhere, about who benefited the most or who suffered from the speed and the scale of a transformation simultaneously occurring globally and locally. In the system of the late nineteenth century, the capabilities of multinationals were commonly not incubated at home, within a successful parent company, and then transferred overseas. Companies were often created and registered in the home country, but the operational capabilities were first developed overseas (though, critically, key personal were sent abroad, utilizing their experience and facilitating the formation of international personal and organizational networks). Host location was important during this period in determining the flow of FDI, which showed a bias towards extracting minerals, growing plantation crops, trading or finance services, or the building and running of utilities. For free-standing companies, strongly related to the imperial project and to resource-based investments, access in the home country to capital was fundamental.

The relationship between companies and highly differing levels of home and host country economic development is the fourth differentiating factor for international businesses. The large gap between Europe and much of the southern hemisphere clearly underpinned the imperialist nature of the international political economy, and explains the extensive influence of British, US, European and Canadian businesses in Latin America. Variations in economic development led to flows of capital, technology and know-how southwards, and to the need for investments in infrastructure and utilities.

The pronounced division between industrialized nations and the rest helped to create states and colonies that provided the raw materials and natural resources mostly destined for export. The dominance of a small number of leading economies – notably Britain, the USA, France, Germany, the Netherlands and, more latterly, Japan – over global output, trade, overseas capital, and the FDI organized by multinationals was set and remained intact until the 1990s.

One final differentiating factor is the access or control that a multinational possesses over the final market or over established networks of cross-border supplies, distribution, production, or finance. For host economies, frequently dependent on exported commodities, or on specific stages in the production process, the issue is vital. In the context of the period 1870 to 1914, it was especially pertinent, since the control of final markets and international networks was linked closely to the trade-related and resource-seeking composition of FDI, and, by extension, to the differing levels of economic development between the industrialized and the rest.

Furthermore, trading-, finance- and service-orientated multinationals embraced a cross-border form of organization based on networks of contracted firms, interlocking partnerships, and equity shares because they suited the nature of their operations and added to their competitive success. These choices were not a stopping point towards the highly integrated and managerially coordinated form of multinational enterprise identified in the 1960s, following a wave of FDI by US manufacturers in Western Europe, Canada and other developed nations. They were a central component of the pre-1914 international economy, just as they would be revived as a major part of multinational business strategy in the post-1980 phase.

To what extent did the factors specifically characteristic of international business change between the beginning of the First World War, in 1914, and the resetting of the international economic framework from 1948? One problem with any assessment is the strong argument that these dates, in terms of trends in the international economy, possess little coherence as a period. The year 1929 is a more convincing watershed (just as the 1970s would make a break with the strong internationalizing trends of the immediate post-war decades and the revival of the 1980s).

There is, too, the view that the period between the First World War and the Second was in essence a gap between the first international economy of the nineteenth century and its return in the 1950s, or, in other words, the international economy had simply gone into reverse for some thirty years. Through examination of the case evidence, we know that this is too simple an interpretation. For example, imperialist economic relations continued, and Britain and France gained territorially from the First World War. Imperialism determined the origins of the oil industry of the Middle East (as well as the US challenge to European control).

On the other hand, war from 1914 onwards did bring about the first recorded sequestrations of foreign assets, permanent in the case of Germany and its allies, and for all companies with operations in what became the Soviet Union. Governments introduced exchange controls and tariffs, many of which were not revoked with the return of peace. The only danger, historically, is to think that the disruption to international economic and trading relations as a result of the First World War was irreversible. The interwar period proved unfavourable to established trading and finance multinationals, but there were new and profitable opportunities, such as rubber and tin, and the 1920s were a decade marked by a strong trend in manufacturing FDI. Finally, world trade recovered by the end of that decade from the fall it had experienced since 1914. With regard to trends in home nation policy, imperialist governments maintained or increased their control or influence over large parts of the world's territory – to the advantage of their multinationals – and the USA's position in the Americas and globally grew.

Nonetheless, there were trends in host state environments that differentiated the interwar period, or more exactly the years after the Wall Street Crash of 1929, from the earlier generation. In Latin America, the more democratic, radical and nationalist agenda followed by governments led, ultimately, to nationalizations in Bolivia and Mexico during the 1930s, and in Argentina during the 1940s. Many of the efforts made by multinationals, in oil, mining and utilities, to assuage governments and local popular opinion in the region failed. World-wide, while tariffs and import quotas might favour inward FDI, currency and exchange controls undermined the rationale and pointed out the risks (as, of course, did the global fall in prices, output and demand).

In Europe, notably Germany, and in Japan, governments imposed discriminatory policies intended to enforce or encourage the indige-nous ownership of industry. Nazi Germany recognized the usefulness of many multinationals within its borders, but, with the Nazis' rule over an important and highly developed economy well established, Germany could curtail the operations of foreign subsidiaries and even extend control over them. Multinationals attempted to minimize the impact, with some successes in the late 1930s, but they had to rely, with diminishing returns, on persuasion. Nor were they able to halt Japan's determination to establish local control over its industry, noticeable after the invasion of Manchuria, in 1931, and strongly applied after the beginning of its Pacific War, in 1937.

By contrast, the power of multinationals and their capabilities to shape governments in Central America and Venezuela was notable. In Saudi Arabia, Kuwait, Iraq, or Iran, by the 1930s, multination-als had to accommodate domestic political sensitivities, but, critically, could still obtain concession and operating terms that allowed high returns and minimum interference. At its stage of economic develop-ment, Japan relied on the transfer of management and technology, and, where necessary, it was willing to maintain joint ventures with foreign enterprises. Australia used tariffs and other measures to encourage the multinational investment it needed. But the fact of imperialism throughout Asia and Africa inevitably limited the impact or relevance of host nation policy changes on FDI.

Despite the growth of manufacturing FDI in developed countries, developing nations and territories still accounted for the large major-ity of multinational business assets. Given the differences in levels of economic development, multinationals maintained their far-reaching capabilities in management, technology and finance, and, crucially, their sway over final markets in the developed world and over cross-border supply, distribution, finance, and production networks.

It is not surprising that the decades which saw two global conflicts and the Great Depression – that is, Global Economy II – saw cross-currents and changes in government policy and economic trends. After the First World War and the post-war slump, between 1914 and 1921, there were positive trends in growth and attempts to restore the lost policy framework for the international economy. From 1931, once the full implications of the Great Depression had been realized, nation states abandoned the nineteenth-century beliefs in free trade, fixed exchange rates, and non-intervention in commercial affairs.

In the post-war world, the ideological differences between powerful military blocs set the geographical dimensions and characteristics of Global Economy III. What fundamentally characterized the period, dating from 1948 to 1980, was the leadership of the USA militarily, diplomatically and economically. The USA became the main provider of overseas capital and FDI at the same time as it reached the height of its global power, as well as being the main recipient of investment. It had the means to influence host governments, and it advocated and gained from the opening up of national markets and expanding free trade arrangements. As with Britain in the nineteenth century, the USA set the framework of the international economy, while simultaneously pursuing its own interests in individual instances.

Multinational investment extended the influence of the USA in host countries, demonstrated the country's material success and countered socialist and communist alternatives. The other side of the home-country influence and power exercised by the USA from the 1950s onwards was European imperialism reaching its point of retreat. Despite this critical change in international political economy, British and Netherlands multinationals were able to compete effectively in the post-war decades, as did companies from the small economies of Switzerland and Sweden, while French and German FDI revived from the 1960s.

Transatlantic economic relations accounted for a large portion of the world economy. European nations became the locales for US FDI, and they were on the whole accepting, despite many of them formally having the means to impede the strategies of multinationals. Part of the explanation was that the governments of Western Europe linked their long-term economic fortunes to intra-regional trade and invest-ment and to creating a continental market to rival that of the USA.

After independence, former colonies challenged the roles trading and finance multinationals, headquartered in Europe, exercised over their economies, ultimately through forced sale or nationalization (compensation was usually forthcoming, even if the final terms rarely achieved consensus).

In the Third World – that is, neither the developed West nor its Communist rivals – US military, diplomatic and economic power could fit uneasily with the nationalist and socialist agenda of host nations. The USA, in the 1950s, revealed its ability to determine the political and economic fortunes of independent states. The politics of the Cold War and superpower rivalry mainly motivated US policy, and could override the concerns and requirements of multinationals. Nevertheless, in Guatemala and Iran, as in other examples, foreign policy and multinational business interests coincided. There is evidence to suggest that, at times, multinationals had influence at the highest level in the determination of policy.

From the 1960s, it was evident that host governments in developing economies were curtailing the power of multinationals and their home governments, and that, in the long term, companies needed to build relations and joint interests with them. Yet the difficulties of resolving disputes over the property rights of multinationals and the sovereign rights of nation states would continue to cause successive instances of international tension. Manufacturing FDI tended to involve the transfer of internal capabilities in management and technology, in pursuit of a market-seeking strategy, with a subsidiary intended mainly for a single host market (although Europe did provide examples of regionalization in Europe as early as the late 1960s).

The advanced capabilities of US multinationals – most prominently in the surge of manufacturing FDI, mostly destined for Canada and Western Europe – were pronounced. The economic advantage of the USA made even the developed nations of Europe gainers from the transatlantic transfer of loans, technology, management methods and FDI. The extractive sector also required the transfer of multinational capabilities and resources, often in developing economies. US and Western multinationals generally continued to control final markets and cross-border networks, and, as a result, they retained their dominance of the international oil and mining industries, despite Third World nations revising their concession terms and frequently taking production into state hands. Governments, despite acting against foreign-owned subsidiaries, including acts of nationalization, over the long term could seek some form of cooperation with multinationals possessed of important capabilities and resources.

After the economic crises of the 1970s, the international economy recovered, gradually at first in the 1980s, and at an accelerating pace in the 1990s. How did the five factors – the power of home nation states and their willingness to act, the policies of host economies, levels of economic development, the internal capabilities of multinationals, and influence over final markets and cross-border networks – change and justify descriptions of Global Economy IV?

The dominance of the G7 nations – the USA, Canada, Germany, France, Italy, Britain, and Japan – over world trade and as the home nations of outward FDI remained intact at the beginning of Global Economy IV, but the international political economy soon acquired a more multilateral aspect in the ownership of economic assets and through supranational institutions such as the World Trade Organization or the G20. As economic growth and industrialization spread to a greater number of countries, the power of countries that had traditionally been recipients of multinational management know-how, technology and finance grew. They emerged, in addition, as the home bases of regional and even global international business, frequently owned and allied to their government (and called dragon multinationals). Former members of the Communist bloc joined the international economy, at first absorbing large amounts of FDI, and finally evolving into international investors, with China becoming a major economic power. The lowering of host government regulations on finance and trade and trends of 'globalization' induced exaggerated claims about the decline of the nation state.

Regarding varying economic levels or roles, there was an approximate division between nations with advanced manufacturing and a service bias, those with low-cost manufacturing, and less developed countries still benefiting the least from worldwide trends, plus some whose status depended on their ownership of natural resources and energy. Given shifts in global production, trade and investment, established multinationals, usually from Western nations or Japan, could not count so much on their control of final markets. Multinationals, moreover, had to invest more in local subsidiaries and their management in order to maintain their role in individual host economies, and they had to pay greater attention to the emerging markets that were expanding faster than the developed world.

Nonetheless, multinationals increased their control over cross-border value chains of supply, distribution, finance and production, and, through these, proved adept at utilizing national locations with differing competitive advantages and levels of economic development. Across these complex networks, they employed a mix of equity control, alliances, partnerships and contracts, different in character to the organizational trends of the immediate post-war decades when multinationals had preferred more direct supervision within a managerial hierarchy. The approach of the 1990s was resonant of the international networks so familiar to the trading, finance and utility multinationals of the nineteenth century. As a consequence, while enhancing their ability to manage greater degrees of uncertainty, modern multinationals could control or influence ever greater concentrations of capabilities in management, technology and capital, with which to maintain their competitive lead, and to negotiate with host governments that sought to attract the assets they owned.

Notes

2 Empires of business: 1870–1914

1 Jardine Matheson: University Library, Cambridge University, Jardine Matheson, Correspondence, 1820–1914, and Miscellaneous Papers; Jardine, Skinner, Calcutta Office, 1843–73, and Correspondence.

2 Cowasjee: Cowasjee Group, August 2009, 'Our history'. Russell & Co.: Baker Library, Harvard Business School, Letter Books, 1842–91.

3 Jardine Matheson: University Library, Cambridge University, Jardine Matheson, Correspondence, 1820–1914, and Miscellaneous Papers; Jardine, Skinner, Calcutta Office, 1843–73, and Correspondence.

4 Hudson's Bay Company: Archives of Manitoba, 'Brief history'.

5 Gibbs & Sons: London Metropolitan Archives, Branch Correspondence 1822–1914.

6 Siemens: Minutes of Meetings, Reports, and Business Correspondence; Marconi, Minutes Books, Correspondence, 1863–1919.

7 Eastern Telegraph Company: Marconi Archive, Evidence to Lord Balfour's Committee, 1899–1905.

8 Ralli Brothers: London Metropolitan Archives, Business Papers 1822–1914; 'Historical notes, 1902–52'.

9 Suez: Centre des Archives du Monde du Travail, October 2009, Correspondence; Statutes; F. de Lesseps Papers, 1854–1901.

10 Deutsche Bank: Annual Reports 1870–1914; Deutsche Überseeische Bank, 1886–1914; Deutsch-Asiatische Bank, 1889–1914.

11 Volkart Brothers Winterthur: E. D. & F. Man, August 2009, 'History of Volcafe'.

12 Dodwell, Carlill: London Metropolitan Archives, Dodwell & Company, Private Notebooks of G. B. Dodwell, 1891–1914.

13 Russell & Co.: Baker Library, Harvard Business School, Letter Books, 1842–91.

14 Jardine Matheson: University Library, Cambridge University, Jardine Matheson, Correspondence, 1820–1914, and Miscellaneous Papers; Jardine, Skinner, Calcutta Office, 1843–73, and Correspondence.

15 Dent & Co.: HSBC Archives, Branch Correspondence, 1867; Jardine Matheson, Correspondence, 1820–1914.

16 Swire group: School of Oriental and African Studies, London Office Correspondence; Organization Papers, 1867–1914; Butterfield, Swire collection; 'Swire: our story'.

17 Dodwell, Carlill: London Metropolitan Archives, Dodwell & Company, Private Notebooks of G. B. Dodwell, 1891–1914.

18 T. D. Findlay & Son: Glasgow University, Administrative Records; 'A short history of T. D. Findlay & Sons: East Asian Markets, 1839–51'. Irrawaddy Flotilla Company: Glasgow University, 'A short history of T. D. Findlay & Sons: East Asian Markets, 1839–51'.

19 T. D. Findlay & Son: Glasgow University, Administrative Records; 'A short history of T. D. Findlay & Sons: East Asian Markets, 1839–51'.

20 Dunlop: London Metropolitan Archives, Annual Reports 1901–14.

21 Sime-Darby: July 2009, 'A short history of Sime Darby'.

22 East Asiatic Company: Odense University Studies in History and Social Sciences, vol. 164, 'The life memoirs of Hon State Councilor H. N Andersen', 1993.

23 British North Borneo Company: School of Oriental and African Studies, Reports; Press Cuttings, 1880–1914.

24 Dent & Co.: HSBC Archives, Branch Correspondence, 1867; Jardine Matheson, Correspondence, 1820–1914.

25 Jardine Matheson: University Library, Cambridge University, Jardine Matheson, Correspondence, 1820–1914, and Miscellaneous Papers; Jardine, Skinner, Calcutta Office, 1843–73, and Correspondence. Swire group: School of Oriental and African Studies, London Office Correspondence; Organization Papers, 1867–1914; Butterfield, Swire collection; 'Swire: our story'.

26 W. R. Grace & Co.: Columbia University, Archival Collections, Correspondence; Annual Reports 1854–1915.

27 Liebeg's Extract of Meat: Unilever, 'Our history'.

28 M. Guggenheim's Sons: Guggenheim Partners, June 2009. 'Guggenheim: heritage of success'.

29 Amalgamated Copper Mining Company: Anaconda Copper, Annual Report 1915, BP-ARCO.

30 Kennecott Mines Corporation: Annual Reports 1906, 1918, Rio Tinto Group.

31 ASARCO: Annual Reports 1918, 1919.

32 Canadian Copper Company: Legislative Assembly of Ontario, Mineral Production of Ontario, 1912.

33 Du Pont: Hagley Museum, Du Pont Collection, 'Notes on Du Pont history'.

34 United Fruit: Chiquita, United Fruit Annual Reports 1900, 1913, 1919.

35 Ibid. Elders and Fyffes: 'Fyffes: our story', June 2009.

36 Royal Niger Company: Unilever archives, 'History of the United Africa Company'; Reports and correspondence, 1888–1930.

37 East African Company: 'Carl Peters', *Encyclopaedia Britannica*, 1911.

38 Imperial British East Asian Company: London Metropolitan Archives, Smith, Mackenzie, Operational Records 1886–1914.

39 Unilever: 'Our history', September 2009.

40 Banque d'Outremer: Belgian State Archives, 'Archives of the Banque d'Outremer: history'.

41 Companhia Agrícola de Cazengo: 'Milestones in BNU history', Banco Nacional Ultramarino.

42 Companhia de Moçambique: 'About the Group', Grupo Entreposto.

43 Banque Imperiale Ottomane: Ottoman Bank Archives and Research Centre, 'History of the Bank'; E., Eldem, 'A 135-year-old treasure: glimpses from the past in the Ottoman Bank Archives', 1997.

44 Lewis and Marks: Sammy Marks Museum, 'Sammy Marks: the uncrowned king of the Transvaal'.

45 British South Africa Company: National Archives, Colonial Office, BSAC Government Gazette, 1894–1923; Administration of Territories of BSAC.

46 HSBC: records, HSBC archives, and company information, September 2009; 'HSBC's history'.

47 Société Générale de Belgique: GDF Suez, 'GDF Suez history'; 'Société Générale de Belgique', 1922.

48 Compagnie Lyonnaise l'Indo-Chinoise: Credit Agricole Corporate and Investment Bank, Credit Agricole, Group Historical Archives.

49 Mitsubishi Corporation: 'Mitsubishi Corporation: a history'; 'Mitsubishi Corporation and the Japanese economy'.

50 Dodwell, Carlill: London Metropolitan Archives, Dodwell & Company, Private Notebooks of G. B. Dodwell, 1891–1914.

51 Mitsubishi Corporation: 'Mitsubishi Corporation: a history'; 'Mitsubishi Corporation and the Japanese economy'.

52 Nichimen: enquiry to Sojitz Corporation, September 2009, 'Historical study of Sojitz Corporation and its predecessors'.

53 Suez: Centre des Archives du Monde du Travail, October 2009, Correspondence; Statutes; F. de Lesseps Papers, 1854–1901.

54 British South Africa Company: National Archives, Colonial Office, BSAC Government Gazette, 1894–1923; Administration of Territories of BSAC.

55 Pauling: National Archives, Colonial Office, Administration of Territories of BSAC. showing BASC interests.

56 Bayer: Bayer Company Archives, September 2009, 'Milestones in Bayer's history'; 'Bayer – a fascinating story'; 'Becoming an international company. 1881–1914'.
57 BASF: September 2009, 'BASF historical milestones'.
58 Siemens: Minutes of Meetings, Reports, and Business Correspondence; Marconi, Minutes Books, Correspondence, 1863–1919.
59 AFA: enquiry to VARTA, October 2009, 'History of VARTA'.
60 'Mannesman AG History', *International Directory of Company Histories*, 2001.
61 'Metallgesellschaft', *International Directory of Company Histories*, 1997; *Financial Times*, 9 February 1999.
62 General Electric: 'Our company: our history'; Annual Reports 1894, 1900, 1903, 1918.
63 Western Electric: archives, 'Western Electric – a brief history'; Annual Reports 1900, 1913.
64 Ibid.
65 NEC: 'NEC Corporation: the first 80 years', 1984.
66 Ericsson: 'Ericsson – the facts'; 'Our corporate story'.
67 Otis: 'Otis history'.
68 American Radiator: Annual Reports 1907, 1914; , 'The history of American Standard', October 2009.
69 Eastman Kodak: 'History of Kodak', September 2009.
70 NCR: 'Timeline and history'; S. C. Allyn, 'My half century with NCR', 1967.
71 Dodwell, Carlill: London Metropolitan Archives, Dodwell & Company, Private Notebooks of G. B. Dodwell, 1891–1914.
72 Cameron Brothers: BAT, 'British American Tobacco – our history'.
73 J. & P. Coats: Glasgow University Archives, Minute books 1880–1914; Letterbooks and correspondence 1868–1914.
74 Dunlop: London Metropolitan Archives, Annual Reports 1901–14.
75 Pirelli: Pirelli Foundation, October 2010, 'Pirelli overseas'; Minutes of Partners' Meetings, 1900–14.
76 'Kraft Jacobs Suchard', *International Directory of Company Histories*, 1999.

3 The reverse gear?: 1914–1948

1 Goodyear: University of Akron, Annual Report 1919.
2 Unilever: 'Our history', September 2009.
3 Siemens: 'Siemens history'; 'Our history in 51 countries'.
4 Fiat: April 2010, 'History'.
5 Goodyear: University of Akron, Annual Report 1919.

6 Michelin: April 2010, 'The history of Michelin'.
7 Commonwealth Shipping Line: Australian National Maritime Museum, September 2010.
8 RCA: 'On the shoulders of giants: 1924 to 1946 – the GE story', 1979; 'Radio Company of America', *Encyclopedia Britannica*, 15th edn, 2010.
9 Anglo-German Brewery Company: 'Tsingtao Brewery Group', *International Directory of Company Histories*, 2003; Asahi, 'Asahi Group's history'. Dai-Nippon Brewery: Sapporo Holdings Ltd, February 2010, 'The history of Sapporo Breweries'.
10 BASF: March 2010, 'Historical milestones'.
11 Institute of Electrical and Electronic Engineers: Report on the Safeguarding of Industries, 1926.
12 ICI: British Dyestuffs Corporation, Annual Reports 1920, 1925; *Hansard*, 2 July 1919.
13 Siemens Brothers: Marconi Archives, Minutes Books, Correspondence, 1863–1919.
14 Deutsche Bank: Historical Archive of Deutsche Bank, Annual Reports 1920–48; Head Office 1920–45; Deutsche Überseeische Bank, 1920–45.
15 Ibid.
16 Bayer: September 2009, 'Milestones in Bayer's history'; 'Bayer – a fascinating story'.
17 Merck & Co.: 'Business heritage', April 2010.
18 Bayer: 'Milestones in Bayer's history', September 2009 ; 'Bayer – a fascinating story'. Sterling Drug: Smithsonian Institute, 'Sterling Drug, Inc.', April 2010.
19 'Milestones in Bayer's history', September 2009 ; 'Bayer – a fascinating story'. Grasselli Dyestuffs Corporation: Annual Reports 1923, 1929.
20 Renault: 'Renault SA', *International Directory of Company Histories*, 1999.
21 Ericsson: 'The history of Ericsson', October 2009.
22 Sandoz: Novartis, May 2010, 'Sandoz history'.
23 Ciba-Geigy: Novartis, 'Geigy, Ciba and Sandoz, 1758–1970', June 2010.
24 Hoffman La Roche: 'Roche milestones', May 2010; '1896–1996: Highlights in the history of an international Basel company', *Roche Magazine*, January 1996.
25 Nestlé: 'Nestlé history', 1975.
26 Unilever: 'Our history', September 2009; Unilever Hindustan India, 'Our history'; 'Research report: Unilever Brazil', 2006; 'Unilever Thai Trading Ltd'; PT Unilever Indonesia, 'Over seventy years going forward with Unilever Indonesia'.

27 Deutsche Erdöl-Aktiengesellschaft: BP Archives, Warwick University, Anglo-Persian, Annual Reports 1919, 1928; RWE, 'The chronicle of RWE DEA since 1899'.

28 Deutsche Bank: Historical Archive of Deutsche Bank, Annual Reports 1920–48; Head Office 1920–45; Deutsche Uberseeische Bank, 1920–45.

29 Royal Dutch Shell: interviews strategy and research departments, March 2009, and 'Shell Global: our history', May 2010.

30 BP: Warwick University, Anglo-Persian Oil Company, Annual Reports 1918, 1924, 1929; BP, 'History of BP'.

31 Royal Dutch Shell: interviews strategy and research departments, March 2009, and 'Shell Global: our history', May 2010. Jersey Standard: Annual Reports 1919, 1922, 1929.

32 Jersey Standard: Annual Reports 1919, 1922, 1929.

33 Royal Dutch Shell: interviews strategy and research departments, March 2009, and 'Shell Global: our history', May 2010.

34 Ibid.

35 General Motors: Annual Reports 1918–1948; 'History and heritage'; GM Holden, 'Holden history'; 'A history of General Motors in Canada', *Globe and Mail*, 22 June 2013; 'Opel – history and heritage'.

36 Chrysler: 'Chrysler history', March 2010; 'T. J. Richards Bodybuilders – Chrysler Australia', National Motor Museum, Australia.

37 Ford: 'Ford Motor Car Company history'; Annual Reports 1925–39; University of Windsor Archives, Ford Motor Company of Canada Ltd, 1904–71.

38 Krupp: Krupp Historical Archive, Krupps steel works and headquarters, reports.

39 Siemens Brothers: Marconi Archives, Minutes Books, Correspondence, 1863–1919.

40 Ford: 'Ford Motor Car Company history'; Annual Reports 1925–39; University of Windsor Archives, Ford Motor Company of Canada Ltd, 1904–71.

41 Amtorg: 'Stealing America's know how', *American Mercury*, 74: 75–84 (February 1952); 'American–Soviet trade relations', *Russian Review*, Autumn 1943.

42 GAZ: GAZ UK, 'History'; US Department of State, Washington: American Consul, Riga, 7 December 1932, to the Department of State. 'Memorandum on the plant "Autostroy", near Gorki (Nizhni Novgorod), Russia', in Records of the Department of State relating to Internal Affairs of the Soviet Union, 1930–1939.

43 Fiat: April 2010, 'History'.

44 Simca: company information.

45 Warwick University, Morris Motors, Directors Records, 1931; Austin Motors, Annual Report 1930, 1935, 1938.
46 Mitsui Mining, 'History'.
47 Firestone: Annual Report 1919.
48 BF Goodrich: Annual Reports 1917, 1920, 1924.
49 Goodyear, University of Akron, Annual Reports 1926–36; Goodyear, 'History by year'; 'Goodyear history'.
50 Pirelli Foundation, October 2010, 'Pirelli overseas'.
51 Michelin: April 2010, 'The history of Michelin'.
52 Dunlop: London Metropolitan Archives, Annual Reports 1914–48.
53 Ibid.
54 Seiberling Rubber Company: Annual Reports 1929, 1933, 1938.
55 Du Pont: Annual Reports 1919, 1929, 1938.
56 International Harvester: 'International Harvester Co. – a timeline', Navistar International, November 2010; C. Wendel, '150 years of International Harvester', 2004.
57 Caterpillar: 'Company history'; '33 years in the Russian market', November 2010; Annual Report 1938.
58 Gipromez: Plekanov Russian University of Economics.
59 Siemens: 'Siemens history'; 'Our history in 51 countries'.
60 C. Illies: 'History, 1859–2010', August 2010.
61 Krupp Historical Archive, Krupps steel works and headquarters, reports.
62 Dr C. Otto & Co.: Thyseen Krupp, Otto & Company papers, October 2010; Thyssen Krupp Industrial Solutions, News, November 2011, 'Thyssen Krupp acquires Otto Corporation in Japan'. Heinrich Koppers: Thyssen Krupp, October 2010, Heinrich Koppers, 1891–1980, reports.
63 Siemens: 'Siemens history'; 'Our history in 51 countries'.
64 NEC: 'NEC Corporation: the first 80 years', 1984. ITT: 'History of ITT', May 2010; Annual Reports 1933–40, 1945, 1948.
65 'The history of Ericsson', October 2009.
66 ITT: 'History of ITT, May 2010; Annual Reports 1933–40, 1945, 1948.
67 Metal Box: Nampak, South Africa, 'Nampak's history'; *Times of India*, Dec.–January 2001.
68 Ciba-Geigy: Novartis, 'Geigy, Ciba and Sandoz, 1758–1970', June 2010. ICI: British Dyestuffs Corporation, Annual Reports 1920, 1925; *Hansard*, 2 July 1919.
69 ICI: British Dyestuffs Corporation, Annual Reports 1920, 1925; *Hansard*, 2 July 1919.
70 Unilever: 'Our history', September 2009; Unilever Hindustan India, 'Our history'; 'Research Report: Unilever Brazil', 2006; 'Unilever Thai Trading Ltd'; PT Unilever Indonesia, 'Over seventy years going forward with Unilever Indonesia'.

71 Distillers: Diageo Archives, 'Timeline', October 2010. Seagram: Western University, Business Archives, 'Distillers Corporation Seagrams Limited'.
72 Nestlé: 'Nestlé history', 1975.
73 Heinz: Annual Reports 1935, 1938; 'Heinz story'.
74 Quaker Oats Company: 'Quaker history', September 2010.
75 Ingredion: Corn Products, 'History: a rich legacy'.
76 Kellogg: 'A historical overview', September 2010.
77 Nestlé: 'Nestlé history', 1975.
78 Swedish Match: 'Company history', August 2010.
79 W. R. Grace & Co.: Columbia University, Archival Collections, Correspondence; Annual Reports 1920–39.
80 Optorg: 'A long history of distribution in Africa', September 2010.
81 CFAO: Groupe CFAO, 'Group history', September 2010.
82 Paribas: 'History of the group', BNP Paribas, May 2010.
83 AIG: 'Our 90 year history', May 2010.
84 Pan Am: 'A brief history of Pan Am, April 2010.
85 British Airways: 'Explore our past', May 2010; Quantas, 'The Quantas story'.
86 Du Pont: Annual Reports 1919, 1929, 1938.
87 Firestone: Annual Report 1919.
88 Goodyear, University of Akron, Annual Reports 1926–36; Goodyear, 'History by year'; 'Goodyear history'.
89 Ford: 'Ford Motor Car Company history'; Annual Reports 1925–39; University of Windsor Archives, Ford Motor Company of Canada Ltd, 1904–71.
90 Michelin: April 2010, 'The history of Michelin'.
91 Unilever: 'Our history', September 2009.
92 Union Minière du Haut-Katanga: Umicore, 'A short history', June 2010.
93 Sime Darby: 'A short history of Sime Darby', June 2010.
94 LTC: Malaysian Mining Corporation, 'Timeline', June 2010.
95 ASARCO: 'Company history', August 2009; Annual Reports 1922, 1929.
96 Alcoa-Alcan: Alcoa Records Centre, 'Histories of the manufacturing properties of the Aluminum Company of America, affiliated companies, and defense corporation plants'; 'Alcoa history'.
97 BP: Warwick University, Anglo-Persian Oil Company, Annual Reports 1918, 1924, 1929; BP, 'History of BP'.
98 Royal Dutch Shell: interviews strategy and research departments, March 2009, and 'Shell Global: our history', May 2010.
99 Iraq Petroleum Company: International Petroleum Cartel, Federal Trade Commission (Washington, DC, 1952), 'Joint control through common

ownership – the Iraq Petroleum Co., Ltd'; US Dept of State, Office of the Historian, Red Line Agreement, http://history.state.gov/milestones/ 1921–1936/red-line.

100 YPF: 'YPF and the return of national sovereignty', *Argentina Independent*, 18 April 2012; Repsol, 'Our history', April 2012.

101 Royal Dutch Shell: interviews strategy and research departments, March 2009, and 'Shell Global: our history', May 2010. Creole Petroleum: Jersey Standard, Annual Reports 1928, 1938. Venezuela: 'Creole Petroleum: good neighbour', *Time*, 19 December 1955. Jersey Standard: Annual Reports 1919, 1922, 1929.

102 ITT: 'History of ITT, May 2010; Annual Reports 1933–40, 1945, 1948.

103 Goodyear: University of Akron, Annual Report 1919.

104 Michelin: April 2010, 'The history of Michelin'.

105 Ford: 'Ford Motor Car Company history'; Annual Reports 1925–39; University of Windsor Archives, Ford Motor Company of Canada Ltd, 1904–71.

106 Michelin: April 2010, 'The history of Michelin Group'; 'Where we have been: North America'.

107 Ford: 'Ford Motor Car Company history'; Annual Reports 1925–39; University of Windsor Archives, Ford Motor Company of Canada Ltd, 1904–71.

108 Fiat: April 2010, 'History'; SEAT, '60 years of history'.

109 General Motors: Annual Reports 1918–48; 'History and heritage'; GM Holden, 'Holden history'; 'A history of General Motors in Canada', *Globe and Mail*, 22 June 2013; 'Opel – history and heritage'.

110 Unilever: 'Our history', September 2009; Annual Reports 1948, 1960, 1970; P. Rijkens, 'Trade and walking: neglected memoirs, 1888–1965', 1965; Rijkens, 'Large companies in development', 1961; W. F. Lichtenauer, 'Rijkens, Paul Carl (1888–1965)', *Biographical Dictionary of the Netherlands*, 2000.

111 Nestlé: 'Nestlé history', 1995.

112 Ford: 'Ford Motor Car Company history'; Annual Reports 1925–39; University of Windsor Archives, Ford Motor Company of Canada Ltd, 1904–71.

113 General Motors: Annual Reports 1918–48; 'History and heritage'; GM Holden, 'Holden history'; 'A history of General Motors in Canada', *Globe and Mail*, 22 June 2013; 'Opel – history and heritage'.

114 Ibid. Sterling Drug: Smithsonian Institute, 'Sterling Drug, Inc.', April 2010. J. P. Morgan Chase: company information, September 2010, 'History of JP Morgan Chase: 200 years of leadership in banking'.

115 Jersey Standard: Annual Reports 1919, 1922, 1929.

116 ITT: 'History of ITT, May 2010; Annual Reports 1933–40, 1945, 1948.

117 Ford: 'Ford Motor Car Company history'; Annual Reports 1925–39; University of Windsor Archives, Ford Motor Company of Canada Ltd, 1904–71.

118 Coca-Cola: 'History of Coca-Cola', September 2010; *New Statesman*, 3, 17, 24 May 2004.

119 Unilever: 'Our history', September 2009.

120 Credit Suisse: 'Credit Suisse – our history', September 2010; *Economist*, articles July–September 1998.

121 Nissan: 'A short history of Nissan Motor Company', May 2010.

122 Isuzu: 'Isuzu: a legendary history', June 2010.

123 Toyota: 'History of Toyota', April 2010.

124 Ibid.

125 Isuzu: 'Isuzu: a legendary history', June 2010.

126 Fujitsu: 'History of Fujitsu', March 2010; 'Company history', 1989.

127 Toshiba: 'Toshiba history', May 2010.

128 Mitsui Mining, 'History'.

129 Nissan: 'A short history of Nissan Motor Company', May 2010.

130 Mitsui Mining: 'History'.

131 Goodyear, University of Akron, Annual Reports 1926–36; Goodyear, 'History by year'; 'Goodyear history'.

132 Deutsche Erdöl-Aktiengesellschaft: BP Archives, Warwick University, Anglo-Persian, Annual Report 1919, 1928; RWE, 'The chronicle of RWE DEA since 1899'.

133 Saudi Aramco: 'Saudi Aramco – our history', February 2011.

134 Unilever: 'Our history', September 2009.

135 Nestlé: 'Nestlé history', 1975.

136 Coca-Cola: 'History of Coca-Cola', September 2010; *New Statesman*, 3, 17, 24 May 2004.

137 Sterling Drug: Smithsonian Institute, 'Sterling Drug, Inc.', April 2010.

138 ITT: 'History of ITT, May 2010; Annual Reports 1933–40, 1945, 1948.

139 Coca-Cola: 'History of Coca-Cola', September 2010; *New Statesman*, 3, 17, 24 May 2004.

140 ITT: 'History of ITT, May 2010; Annual Reports 1933–40, 1945, 1948.

141 Jersey Standard: Annual Reports 1948–51.

142 Credit Suisse: 'Credit Suisse – our history', September 2010; *Economist*, July–September 1998. UBS: 'History of UBS: more than 150 years of interesting stories', June 2010; *Economist*, 2, 7 July 1998.

143 Bank of International Settlements: *Daily Telegraph*, June–July 2013.

144 Siemens: 'Siemens history'; 'Our history in 51 countries'; G. Siemens, 'History of the House of Siemens', 1957.

145 General Motors: Annual Reports 1918–48; 'History and heritage'; GM Holden, 'Holden history'; 'A history of General Motors in Canada', *Globe and Mail*, 22 June 2013; 'Opel – history and heritage'. Ford: 'Ford Motor Car Company history'; Annual Reports 1925–39; University of Windsor Archives, Ford Motor Company of Canada Ltd, 1904–71.

146 General Motors: Annual Reports 1918–48; 'History and heritage'; GM Holden, 'Holden history'; 'A history of General Motors in Canada', *Globe and Mail*, 22 June 2013; 'Opel – history and heritage'.

147 Firestone: Annual Report 1919.

148 Goodyear: University of Akron, Annual Report 1919.

149 General Motors: Annual Reports 1918–48; 'History and heritage'; GM Holden, 'Holden history'; 'A history of General Motors in Canada', *Globe and Mail*, 22 June 2013; 'Opel – history and heritage'.

150 Ibid. Ford: 'Ford Motor Car Company history'; Annual Reports 1925–39; University of Windsor Archives, Ford Motor Company of Canada Ltd, 1904–71.

151 Ford: 'Ford Motor Car Company history'; Annual Reports 1925–39; University of Windsor Archives, Ford Motor Company of Canada Ltd, 1904–71.

152 Krupp Historical Archive, Krupps steel works and headquarters, reports.

153 Ford: 'Ford Motor Car Company history'; Annual Reports 1925–39; University of Windsor Archives, Ford Motor Company of Canada Ltd, 1904–71.

154 Fiat: April 2010, 'History'.

155 Deutsche Bank: Historical Archive of Deutsche Bank, Annual Reports 1920–48; Head Office 1920–45; Deutsche Überseeische Bank, 1920–45.

4 Cold War and the new international economic order: 1948–1980

1 General Motors: Annual Reports 1948–63; 'GM – History and heritage'; GM Holden, 'Holden history'; 'A history of General Motors in Canada', *Globe and Mail*, 22 June 2013; 'Opel – history and heritage'.

2 Ibid.

3 Ibid.

4 Ibid.

 5 Ford: 'Ford Motor Car Company history'; Annual Reports 1954–80; University of Windsor Archives, Ford Motor Company of Canada Ltd, 1904–71.
 6 Ibid.
 7 Ibid.
 8 Ibid.
 9 Chrysler: Annual Reports 1958, 1964, 1968.
10 Jersey Standard: Annual Reports 1948–51.
11 Ibid.
12 Chevron: 'People, partnership and performance since 1879', May 2012.
13 Dow Chemical: 'Our company history', March 2011; Annual Reports 1960, 1973.
14 Allied Chemicals: Honeywell, Inc., 'Honeywell history'.
15 National Lead: Harvard Business School, Lehman Brothers Collection, National Lead Company; 'A new look at National Lead', *Financial World*, 11 September 1963.
16 Du Pont: Hagley Museum, Du Pont Collection, 'Notes on Du Pont history'. Du Pont: Annual Reports 1952, 1958, 1963, 1970.
17 IBM: April 2011, 'Chronological history of IBM'.
18 Honeywell: 'Honeywell History', March 2011; 'The first 100 years, Minneapolis', 1985.
19 Ibid.
20 NCR: 'Timeline and history'; S. C. Allyn, 'My half century with NCR', 1967.
21 Hewlett-Packard: 'HP history', March 2011.
22 ITT: 'History of ITT', May 2010, Annual Reports 1960–73.
23 Goodyear: Annual Reports 1956, 1957; Goodyear, 'History by year'; 'Goodyear history', housed at University of Akron.
24 Caterpillar: 'Company history', November 2010; Annual Reports 1956, 1960.
25 Rank Xerox: Xerox Corporation, 'Making history for more than 100 years', March 2011.
26 Fuji Xerox: 'Corporate history', March 2011.
27 General Electric: August 2009, 'Our company: our history'; Annual Reports 1960, 1973.
28 Coca-Cola: 'History of Coca-Cola', September 2010; 'The chronicle of Coca-Cola, since 1886'.
29 Pepsi Cola: 'Pepsi – 100 years', 1997; 'How Pepsi won the cola wars', 1976.
30 Heinz: 'Heinz story', September 2010.
31 Campbell's: 'History of the Campbell Soup Company', June 2011; 'The Campbell story'.

32 General Foods: Harvard Business School, Lehman Brothers Collection, General Foods; Kraft General Foods Archives, 'A chronological history of Kraft General Foods', 1994.

33 Bestfoods: *Forbes*, 5 October 1987; *Wall Street Journal*, 16 February, 17 October 1997; *Journal of Commerce & Commercial*, 10 June 1996; *Fortune*, 22 October 1990; Ingredion, Corn Products, 'History: a rich legacy'.

34 S. C. Johnson: 'S. C. Johnson – a family company', April 2011.

35 Kimberly-Clark: 'Historical journey', April 2011.

36 Fujitsu: March 2010, 'History of Fujitsu'; 'Company history', 1989.

37 Alcoa-Alcan: Alcoa Records Centre, 'Histories of the manufacturing properties of the Aluminum Company of America, affiliated companies, and defense corporation plants'; 'Alcoa history'; *Hansard*, 15, 25 April 1958, 18, 30 January 1959.

38 Chrysler: Annual Reports 1958, 1964, 1968.

39 Goodyear: Annual Reports 1956, 1957; Goodyear, 'History by year'; 'Goodyear history', at University of Akron.

40 BAT: 'British American Tobacco – our history', August 2011.

41 ICI: 'Imperial Chemical Industries', *International Directory of Company Histories*, 2003.

42 BOC: 'British Oxygen Company', *International Directory of Company Histories*, 1999.

43 Bowater: Bowater-Scott, Grace's Guide, 2013.

44 GKN: 'An exceptional story', August 2011; *Financial Times*, 10 August 1989, 5, 23 August 1996; *Economist*, 16 September 2000; *Management Today*, October 1984; GKN, 'Brief history of Guest, Keen & Nettlefolds', 1980; *Director*, 10 March 1988.

45 Pilkington: Pilkington/Nippon Sheet Glass, September 2011, 'Pilkington history, 1950–1999'.

46 Rio Tinto: Rio Tinto Alcan, August 2009, 'Company history timeline'; RTZ-CRA, 'United for growth', Rio Tinto Review, 2006.

47 BP: Warwick University, Anglo-Persian Oil Company, Annual Reports 1960, 1973, 1980; BP, 'History of BP'.

48 Royal Dutch Shell: 'Shell Global: our history', May 2010; 'The Americanization of Shell: the beginnings and early years of Shell Oil Company in the United States', 1972; 'Shell Oil Company: a story of achievement', 1984; '75 years serving America', 1987.

49 Unilever: Unilever: 'Our history', September 2009; Annual Reports 1948, 1960, 1970. The Hague: Institution for Dutch History: P. Rijkens, 'Trade and walking: neglected memoirs, 1888–1965', 1965; Rijkens, 'Large companies in development', 1961. W. F. Lichtenauer, 'Rijkens, Paul Carl (1888–1965)', *Biographical Dictionary of the Netherlands*, 2000.

50 Philips: 'The history of Philips', October 2011; 'Our heritage'; *Forbes*, 15 July 1969, 14 April 1980.

51 Heineken: 'Heineken: our history', October 2011.

52 Nestlé: 'Nestlé history', 1995.

53 Kraft: Harvard Business School, Lehman Brothers Collection, General Foods; Kraft General Foods Archives, 'A chronological history of Kraft General Foods', 1994; 'Kraft Jacobs Suchard', *International Directory of Company Histories*, 1999.

54 Ciba-Geigy: Novartis, 'Geigy, Ciba and Sandoz, 1758–1970', June 2010.

55 Sandoz: Novartis, May 2010, 'Sandoz history'.

56 SAAB: 'A history of high technology', September 2011.

57 Ericsson: 'Ericsson – the facts'; 'Our corporate story', October 2009.

58 Electrolux: 'Founding an international company'; 'Elektrolux becomes Electrolux', September 2011.

59 ABS Separator: 'History of Alfa Laval', September 2011.

60 Dyno Industrier: 'Dyno Industrier: history', October 2011.

61 Sofina: 'Historical outline', October 2011.

62 Renault: 'Renault SA', *International Directory of Company Histories*, 1999.

63 Michelin: April 2010, 'The history of Michelin Group'; 'Where we have been: North America'.

64 Groupe Danone: 'Danone: 40 years of a unique trajectory', September 2011.

65 PUK: 'Pechiney', *International Directory of Company Histories*, 2002; *Economist*, 18 April 1981; 'Ugine SA', *International Directory of Company Histories*, 1999.

66 Schlumberger: 'Our history', May 2009.

67 Airbus Industrie: 'The success story of Airbus', September 2011.

68 *Der Spiegel*, 9 December 1964, 27 January 1965, 25 April 1966; Deutsche BP: F. Förster, 'Geschichte der Deutschen BP 1904–1979', 1980.

69 Villeroy and Boch: 'Three centuries of craftsmanship', October 2011.

70 Bayer Company Archives, September 2009, 'Milestones in Bayer's history'; 'Bayer – a fascinating story'; 'Expansion of foreign business, 1974–88'.

71 Ibid.

72 Hoechst: 'Hoechst AG', *International Directory of Company Histories*, 1997.

73 'Mannesman AG history', *International Directory of Company Histories*, 2001.

74 Siemens: 'Siemens history'; 'Our history in 51 countries'; G. Siemens, 'History of the House of Siemens', 1957.

75 AEG: AEG-Telefunken, '50 Jahre AEG, als Manuskript gedruckt', 1956; G. Hautsch, 'Das Imperium AEG-Telefunken, ein multinationaler Konzern', 1979.
76 Volkswagen: 'Volkswagen chronicle: becoming a global player', Corporate Archives, 2008; 'Group history', 2009.
77 Continental: 'History, 1871–2001', November 2009.
78 'MAN Chronicle, 1750–2012', January 2013.
79 Fiat: April 2010, 'History'; SEAT, '60 years of history'.
80 Ibid.
81 Pirelli Foundation, October 2010, 'Pirelli overseas'.
82 Kennecott Mines Corporation: Annual Reports 1950, 1973, Rio Tinto Group.
83 Ford: 'Ford Motor Car Company history'; Annual Reports 1954–80; University of Windsor Archives, Ford Motor Company of Canada Ltd, 1904–71.
84 Ibid. General Motors: Annual Reports 1948–63; 'GM – history and heritage'; GM Holden, 'Holden history'; 'A history of General Motors in Canada', *Globe and Mail*, 22 June 2013; 'Opel – history and heritage'. Chrysler: Annual Reports 1958, 1964, 1968.
85 Alcan: 'Alcan Aluminum Ltd', *International Directory of Company Histories*, 2000; P. Farin and G. G. Reibsamen, 'Aluminium: profile of an industry', 1969.
86 Massey-Ferguson: 'Massey-Ferguson: Our history', January 2011.
87 GM Holden: General Motors, 'History and heritage'; GM Holden, 'Holden history', June 2013.
88 Ford: 'Ford Motor Car Company history'; Annual Reports 1954–1980; University of Windsor Archives, Ford Motor Company of Canada Ltd, 1904–71.
89 Chevron: 'People, partnership and performance since 1879', May 2012.
90 Jersey Standard Annual Reports 1948–51.
91 Rio Tinto: Rio Tinto Alcan, August 2009, 'Company history timeline'; RTZ-CRA, 'United for growth', *Rio Tinto Review*, 2006.
92 Ibid.
93 Ibid.
94 RMC: 'RMC Group plc', *International Directory of Company Histories*, 2000.
95 Mitsui & Co.: 'History of Mitsui & Company Ltd', June 2009.
96 Mitsubishi Corporation: June 2009, 'Mitsubishi Corporation: a history'; 'Mitsubishi Corporation and the Japanese economy'.
97 NYK; 'NYK history', September 2009; Nissho Iwai KK, *International Directory of Company Histories*, 1988.
98 C. Itoh: 'Itochu history', September 2009.

99 Marubeni: 'Our history from 1842'.
100 NYK: 'NYK history', September 2009; Nissho Iwai KK, *International Directory of Company Histories*, 1988.
101 GM-Isuzu: March 2010, 'Isuzu: a legendary history'.
102 Fujitsu: March 2010, 'History of Fujitsu'; 'Company history', 1989.
103 Furukawa Electric: 'The history of Furukawa Co. Ltd', July 2011.
104 Hitachi: 'Hitachi history, 1910–2011', February 2012.
105 Furukawa Electric: 'The history of Furukawa Co. Ltd', July 2011.
106 Hitachi: 'Hitachi history, 1910–2011', February 2012.
107 Hyundai Heavy Industries: 'History: 1974–2011', November 2012.
108 POSCO: 'History of POSCO, 1965–2009', November 2012.
109 Nippon Seiko: 'History of Nippon Seiko', typescript, n.d.
110 Ibid.
111 NTN Corporation: 'Revolution in motion: corporate history', September 2012.
112 Kawasaki Steel: 'History of KHI, 1878–2010'.
113 Glencore: Marc Rich, profile, *Observer*, 13 May 2013.
114 Volkart Brothers Winterthur: E. D. & F. Man, August 2009, 'History of Volcafe'.
115 Harrisons & Crosfield: London Metropolitan Archives, 'Administrative/biographical history'; Elementis plc, 'History of a business', May 2013; Sime Darby, Sime Darby World. Harrisons & Crosfield Timeline.
116 Sime Darby: 'A short history of Sime Darby', June 2010; 'Sime Darby Berhad', *International Directory of Company Histories*, 2001.
117 Guthries: SOAS archives, and company information, June 2010; Guthries GTS, 'Corporate history'.
118 Wallace Brothers: Guildhall Library, 'Wallace Brothers: Elephants, East African plantations and Rangoon forests', July 2010; London Metropolitan Archives, Wallace Brothers, 'Administrative/biographical history'; London Metropolitan Archives, 'Wallace Brothers (Holdings) Ltd: Wallace and Adam'.
119 James Finlay: Glasgow University, Managers' Letters; Administrative Records, 1948–64; Finlays, 'History and company overview'.
120 United Africa Company of Nigeria: www.uacnplc.com/company/history.htm.
121 Anglo-Thai: www.ford.co.th/en/about/corporate/ford-thailand.
122 United Africa Company of Nigeria: www.uacnplc.com/company/history.htm.
123 Inchcape: company information, March 2009, 'History, 1840–2000'.
124 Swire group: School of Oriental and African Studies, London Office Correspondence; Organization Papers; 'Swire: our story'.

125 Jardine Matheson: 'Jardines – 175 years of looking to the future', 2007.

126 Cheung Kong Holdings: Cheung Hong/Hutchinson Whompoa, June 2013; 'Milestones, 1828–2013'.

127 Booker McConnell: Booker Group, 'A history'; *Guyana Times International*, 31 August 2012.

128 Lonrho: 'Lonrho: a history'; *Forbes*, 21, 27 March 1998; *Economist*, 26 December 1992.

129 CFAO: Groupe CFAO, 'Group history', September 2010.

130 Optorg: 'A long history of distribution in Africa', September 2010.

131 Continental Grain: 'History and heritage: timeline', September 2012.

132 Dreyfus: 'Louis Dreyfus Groupe', *International Directory of Company Histories*, 2004.

133 W. R. Grace & Co.: 'A story of innovation and change'; 'W. R. Grace', *International Directory of Company Histories*, 2003.

134 BNP Paribas: 'History of the Group', May 2010.

135 Credit Lyonnais: 'Credit Lyonnais', *International Directory of Company Histories*, 2000.

136 Deutsche Bank: Historical Archive of Deutsche Bank, 'Deutsche Bank 1870–2010'; *Economist*, 22 June 1991.

137 SEB: 'Skandinaviska Enskilda Banken, *International Directory of Company Histories*, 2004.

138 Svenska Handelsbanken: 'History of Svenska Handelsbanken', 2012.

139 Swiss Bank Corporation: 'Credit Suisse – our history', September 2010.

140 UBS: 'History of UBS: more than 150 years of interesting stories'.

141 AIG: 'Our 90 years of history', May 2010.

142 Provident Life and Accident Insurance Company of America: 'History of Unum Provident', *International Directory of Company Histories*, 2003.

143 Aetna Life and Casualty: 'Aeta Inc.', *International Directory of Company Histories*, 2003.

144 John Hancock Mutual Life: 'American Financial Corporation', *International Directory of Company Histories*, 2003.

145 Mutual Life Insurance Company of New York, *International Directory of Company Histories*, 2003.

146 Aon: *International Directory of Company Histories*, 2003.

147 American Family Corporation: *International Directory of Company Histories*, 2003.

148 Continental Corporation: *International Directory of Company Histories*, 2003.

149 March and McLennan Companies: *International Directory of Company Histories*, 2003; 'About Marsh and McLennan companies'.

150 Continental Corporation: *International Directory of Company Histories*, 2003. Chubb & Son: *International Directory of Company Histories*, 2003.
151 Assicurazioni Generali: Generali Group, 'Generali's history', August 2012.
152 Allianz AG: 'History of Allianz', 1890–2009.
153 Swiss Re: company information, May 2010.
154 Zurich Versicherungs-Gesellschaft: company information, June 2010.
155 Nationale-Nederlanden: www.nn-group.com/Who-we-are.htm, September 2010.
156 AXA: 'History, 1817–2010', June 2012; UAP: 'Union des Assurance de Paris', *International Directory of Company Histories*, 1991.
157 Commercial Union: 'Commercial Union', *International Directory of Company Histories*, 1996; 'Legal and General', *International Directory of Company Histories*, 1999.
158 Prudential: 'Prudential plc', *International Directory of Company Histories*, 2003.
159 Royal Insurance: 'Royal Insurance Holdings', *International Directory of Company Histories*, 1991.
160 Yasuda Fire and Marine: *International Directory of Company Histories*, 1991.
161 Mitsui Marine and Fire: *International Directory of Company Histories*, 1991.
162 Tokio Marine and Fire: *International Directory of Company Histories*, 1991.
163 Sumitomo Marine and Fire: *International Directory of Company Histories*, 1991.
164 Sears Archives, 'History of Sears', July 2012.
165 Hudson's Bay Company: Archives of Manitoba, 'Brief history'.
166 Safeway: Annual Reports 1961, 1966.
167 IKEA: 'IKEA's history', January 2012.
168 Carrefour: 'Carrefour Group history', January 2012.
169 C&A: 'C&A – a success story', March 2012.
170 Koninklijke Ahold: 'Ahold: the 2nd half of the 20th century', September 2010.
171 Sheraton Hotels: Sheraton-Starwood Hotels, 'Sheraton's history, 1937–2008', December 2012.
172 Intercontinential Hotels: 'The IHG story', December 2012.
173 Hilton Hotels: 'Our history: 1910–2010', December 2012.
174 McDonald's: 'McDonald Corporation', *International Directory of Company Histories*, 2003.
175 Club Mediterranée: 'Club Med's history since 1950', June 2012.

176 Deloitte: 'A century of exceeding expectations', June 2012.
177 Coopers and Lybrand: 'Pricewaterhouse Coopers', *International Directory of Company Histories*, 1999.
178 Arthur Andersen: 'Arthur Andersen's fall from grace is a sad tale of greed and miscues', *Wall Street Journal*, 7 June 2002; 'Arthur Andersen', *International Directory of Company Histories*, 2005.
179 KPMG: 'KPMG International', *International Directory of Company Histories*, 2000.
180 McKinsey: 'About our history', July 2012.
181 Ogilvy and Mather: History of Advertising Trust, 'Ogilvy history', June 2012.
182 Asea Brown Boveri: 'ABB history', September 2012; *Economist*, 6 January 1996. EDS: *Chicago Tribune*, 9 July 1992.
183 Skoda UK: 'History of Skoda over 100 years'.
184 Energomashexport: Corporation: www.emeco.ru/en/about/, May 2011.
185 Gipromez: www.gipromez.com.ua/history_en.php, June 2011.
186 Zastava: Fiat, April 2010, 'History'.
187 Exportkhleb: 'Cargill', *International Directory of Company Histories*, 2001
188 Fiat: April 2010, 'History'; SEAT, '60 years of history'.
189 FSO: Fiat, April 2012; Fiat: April 2010, 'History'; SEAT, '60 years of history'.
190 Ibid.
191 Continental Grain: 'History and heritage: timeline', September 2012.
192 PUK: 'Pechiney', *International Directory of Company Histories*, 2002; *Economist*, 18 April 1981; 'Ugine SA', *International Directory of Company Histories*, 1999.
193 BAT: 'British American Tobacco – our history', August 2011.
194 Jardine Matheson: 'Jardines – 175 years of looking to the future', 2007. Swire group: School of Oriental and African Studies, London Office Correspondence; Organization Papers; 'Swire: our story'.
195 Rio Tinto: Rio Tinto Alcan, August 2009, 'Company history timeline'; RTZ-CRA, 'United for growth', Rio Tinto Review, 2006. Kaiser Aluminum: 'Kaiser Aluminum and Chemical Corporation', *International Directory of Company Histories*, 1991.
196 *New York Times*, 15 November 1964.
197 Kellogg: 'A historical overview', September 2010.
198 Kimberley Clarke: 'Historical journey', April 2011.
199 Pilkington: Pilkington/Nippon Sheet Glass, September 2011, 'Pilkington history, 1950–1999'.

200 BOC: 'British Oxygen Company', *International Directory of Company Histories*, 1999.
201 United Africa Company of Nigeria: www.uacnplc.com/company/history.htm.
202 Guinness: 'Diageo plc', *International Directory of Company Histories*, 1999.
203 Michelin: April 2010, 'The history of Michelin Group'; 'Where we have been: North America'.
204 PUK: 'Pechiney', *International Directory of Company Histories*, 2002; *Economist*, 18 April 1981; 'Ugine SA', *International Directory of Company Histories*, 1999.
205 Mannesman: 'Mannesman AG history', *International Directory of Company Histories*, 2001. Volkswagen: 'Volkswagen chronicle: becoming a global player', Corporate Archives, 2008; 'Group history', 2009.
206 EDS: *Chicago Tribune*, 9 July 1992.
207 Jersey Standard: Annual Reports 1948–51.
208 Saudi Aramco: 'Saudi Aramco – our history', February 2011.
209 BP: Warwick University, Anglo-Persian Oil Company, Annual Reports 1960, 1973, 1980; BP, 'History of BP'.
210 United Fruit: 'Chiquita Brands International', *International Directory of Company Histories*, 1999.
211 ENI: 'The history of a company', August 2012; *Time*, 29 November 1954, 22 July 1961, 2 November 1962.
212 Total: 'A major energy operator for over a century', September 2012.
213 Warwick University, Anglo-Persian Oil Company, Annual Reports 1950–53, 1960, 1970, 1980; BP, 'History of BP'; *New York Times*, August 1953.
214 ENI: 'The history of a company', August 2012; *Time*, 29 November 1954, 22 July 1961, 2 November 1962.
215 Japan Petroleum: 'History of Mitsui & Company Ltd', June 2009.
216 Libyan National Oil Company: 'National Oil Corporation', *International Directory of Company Histories*, 2004; ENI: 'The history of a company', August 2012.
217 Ibid.
218 Total: 'A major energy operator for over a century', September 2012.
219 Saudi Aramco: 'Saudi Aramco – our history', February 2011.
220 Royal Dutch Shell: 'Shell Global: our history', May 2010; 'The Americanization of Shell: the beginnings and early years of Shell Oil Company in the United States', 1972; 'Shell Oil Company: a story of achievement', 1984; '75 years serving America', 1987.

221 'Kaiser Aluminum and Chemical Corporation', *International Directory of Company Histories*, 1991.

222 *New York Times*, 15 November 1964.

223 Jersey Standard: Annual Reports 1948–51.

224 United Fruit: 'Chiquita Brands International', *International Directory of Company Histories*, 1999.

225 Gulf Oil: 'History of a company', August 2012.

226 Sofina: 'Historical outline', October 2011.

227 Goodyear: Annual Reports 1956, 1957; Goodyear, 'History by year'; 'Goodyear history', at University of Akron. Caterpillar, 'Company history', November 2010; Annual Reports 1956, 1960.

228 PUK: 'Pechiney', *International Directory of Company Histories*, 2002; *Economist*, 18 April 1981; 'Ugine SA', *International Directory of Company Histories*, 1999.

229 Bayer Company Archives, September 2009, 'Milestones in Bayer's history'; 'Bayer – a fascinating story'; 'Expansion of foreign business, 1974–88'.

230 Mannesman: 'Mannesman AG history', *International Directory of Company Histories*, 2001.

231 'Heinz story', September 2010. Kellogg: 'A historical overview', September 2010.

232 General Foods: Harvard Business School, Lehman Brothers Collection, General Foods; Kraft General Foods Archives, 'A chronological history of Kraft General Foods', 1994.

233 S. C. Johnson, 'S. C. Johnson – a family company', April 2011.

234 Ericsson: 'Ericsson – the facts'; 'Our corporate story', October 2009. Michelin: April 2010, 'The history of Michelin Group'; 'Where we have been: North America'.

235 General Motors: Annual Reports 1948–63; 'GM – history and heritage'; GM Holden, 'Holden history'; 'A history of General Motors in Canada', *Globe and Mail*, 22 June 2013; 'Opel – history and heritage'. Ford: 'Ford Motor Car Company history'; Annual Reports 1954–80; University of Windsor Archives, Ford Motor Company of Canada Ltd, 1904–71.

236 Volkswagen: 'Volkswagen chronicle: becoming a global player', Corporate Archives, 2008; 'Group history', 2009.

237 Ibid.

238 ITT: 'History of ITT', May 2010, May 2010, Annual Reports 1960–73.

239 Ibid. Kennecott Mines Corporation: Annual Reports 1950, 1973, Rio Tinto Group. Anaconda: Annual Reports 1950, 1973, BP-ARCO.

5 Global economics?: 1980–2012

1 *Wall Street Journal*, 11 January 2006, 19 June 2009. European Union, Directorate-General for Economic and Financial Affairs (ECFIN), Country Focus, January 2008.

2 *Economist*, 31 August 2000.

3 *Financial Times*, 19 September 1991, 8 October 1998, 1 January 2010.

4 Texas Instruments: company information, June 2013.

5 Wipro: www.wipro.com, June 2013; *Economic Times*, 'Wipro – a history', 17 November 2012.

6 Infosys Technologies: www.infosys.com/about/Pages/history.aspx, May 2013; 'N. R. Narayana Murthy', *Business Week*, 3 July 2000.

7 Ibid.

8 Wipro: www.wipro.com, June 2013; 'Wipro – a history', *Economic Times*, 17 November 2012.

9 Microsoft: www.microsoft.com/en-in/about/about_microsoft/microsoft-in-india.aspx, September 2013.

10 IBM: enquiry to the company, April 2011, 'Chronological history of IBM'; 'History of IBM Global Services'.

11 IATA *Annual Review*, 2003–11.

12 Cargill: www.cargill.com/company/history/index.jsp, January 2010.

13 Inchcape: www.inchcape.com/, March 2009; 'History, 1840–2000'.

14 Elementis: http://elementis-specialties.com/, March 2013; *Financial Times*, 25 October 2007.

15 Yule Catto: www.synthomer.com/, http://ssl.e-catto.com/yulecatto/site.nsf/page!openform&page=abouthomeeurope, April 2013.

16 Boustead: Boustead Singapore, www.boustead.sg/about_us/company_history.asp, April 2012; Affin Investment Bank, Boustead Holdings, July 2012; 'Company history'.

17 Booker McConnell: Booker Group, www.bookergroup.com/, September 2012.

18 Lonrho: www.lonrho.com/, October 2012. Lonmin: www.lonmin.com, October 2012.

19 Swire group: www.swire.com/en/index.php, March 2009; 'Swire: our story'.

20 Glencore: *Guardian*, 19 May 2011, 2 December 2012; *Sunday Times*, 14 October 2012. www.bbc.com/news/17702487, BBC News, 16 April 2012.

21 Mitsubishi Corporation: interview Mitsubishi economic advisor, February 2009; enquiry to company, June 2009, 'Mitsubishi Corporation and the Japanese economy'. Royal Dutch Shell: interviews, March 2009, and 'Shell Global: Our history', May 2010.

22 Hyundai Corporation: www.hyundaicorp.com/en, June 2013.

23 Samsung Corporation: www.samsungcnt.com/EN/cnt/index.do, June 2013.
24 www.hanjin.com/hanjin, July 2013. www.evergreen-line.com/, July 2013. www.yangming.com/english/ASP/index.asp, July 2013.
25 OCCL: www.oocl.com/eng/aboutoocl/companyprofile/ooclhistory/Pages/default.aspx, August 2013.
26 K-Line: www.kline.co.jp/en/corporate/history/index.html, August 2013. NYK: www.nykline.co.jp/english/profile/about/history.htm, June 2013.
27 Maersk: www.maersk.com/Aboutus, July 2013.
28 Cosco: http://en.cosco.com/col/col771/index.html, October 2013.
29 Citigroup: www.citigroup.com/citi/, March 2013.
30 Morgan Chase: www.jpmorganchase.com/, March 2013.
31 Citigroup: www.citigroup.com/citi/, March 2013; *Economist*, 31 August 2000.
32 Goldman Sachs: www.goldmansachs.com/, February 2013; *Washington Post*, 16 March 2012.
33 Barclays: www.barclays.co.uk/, 11 March 2013; BBC News, 27 June 2012.
34 Standard Chartered: www.sc.com/, March 2013; *Wall Street Journal*, 8 August 2012.
35 HSBC: www.hsbc.com/, September 2009; HSBC, 'HSBC's history'.
36 Deutsche Bank: www.db.com/index_e.htm, March 2010; 'Deutsche Bank 1870–2010'; *Wall Street Journal*, 3 August 2009; BBC News, 12 June 2012, 6 February 2013.
37 Société Générale: GDF Suez, June 2009, www.societegenerale.fr/; *New York Times*, 5 October 2010.
38 UBS: www.ubs.com/, June 2010; UBS, 'History of UBS: 150 years of interesting stories'; BBC News, 31 October 2012; *Wall Street Journal*, 18 June 2010, 26 August 2010; *Financial Times*, 19 September 1991, 8 October 1998, 1 January 2010.
39 ABN AMRO: www.abnamro.nl/en, June 2013; Annual Report 2011; *Economist*, 15 July 2008.
40 Ibid.
41 BBVA: www.bbva.com.es, June 2013; 'History of BBVA, 1857–2011'.
42 Santander: www.santander.com, July 2013; BBC News, 27 May 2009; 'More than a century of history, 1857–2013'.
43 Danske Bank: www.danskebank.com, August 2013.
44 Skandinaviska Enskilda Bank: www.seb.se, November 2010.
45 Standard Bank Group: www.standardbank.com, June 2013; 'Standard Bank Group: historical overview', 2009. Bank of China: interviews, sales manager, director research department, March 2013; *Forbes*, 4 June 2011.

46 Mitsubishi UFJ Financial Group: www.mufg.com/english, April 2010.

47 Nomura: www.nomura.com, March 2010.

48 Daiwa: interviews chairman and research director, February 2010; 'Overview of Daiwa Securities', January 2010; www.daiwa.com.

49 MBTC: /www.metrobank.com.ph.

50 *Financial Times*, 19 September 1991, 8 October 1998, 1 January 2010.

51 AIG: www.aig.com/_3171_441789.html May 2010; 'Our 90 years of history'.

52 Allianz AG: www.allianz.com/en/about_us, June 2011; 'History of Allianz Australia'; 'History of Allianz', 1890–2009. *Der Zeit*, 7, 29 June 2009.

53 Zurich Financial Services: www.zurich.com/, April 2013.

54 Assicurazioni Generali: www.generali.com/Generali-Group.

55 AXA: www.axa.com/en/group/, June 2012; BBC News, 14 June 2006; Annual Report 2010.

56 Aviva: www.aviva.com/, January 2012.

57 Manulife Financial: www.manulife.com/, March 2012; 'Global company factsheet', May 2012; 'Manulife Financial – milestones'.

58 *Business Week*, October 2012; www.starbucks.com/, April 2012; *Wall Street Journal*, 11 January 2006, 19 June 2009.

59 Jollibee: www.jollibee.com.ph/, June 2010.

60 Wal-Mart: www.walmart.com, May 2013; *Washington Monthly*, April 2006; BBC News, 31 July 2006, 23 December 2012; *Washington Post*, June 2008.

61 Tesco: interview general manager Korea, March 2008; www.tesco.com/, September 2011.

62 GAP: www.gap.com/, May 2013.

63 Zara: www.zara.com, June 2013; *Business Week*, 4 April 2006; *Bloomberg*, 12 November 2006; www.businessweek.com/stories/2006–09–03/fashion-conquistador.

64 Uniqlo: www.uniqlo.com/, January 2013; *New York Times*, 30 November 2006; www.forbes.com/profile/tadashi-yanai/.

65 Vodafone: www.vodafone.com, December 2011; 'Racal's key milestones'; *Financial Times*, 26 July 2011; http://investing.businessweek.com/research/stocks/private/snapshot.asp?privcapId=4702685; BBC News, 11 February 2000.

66 Vivendi: www.vivendi.com/home/, March 2010. Veolia: www.veolia.com/home/, March 2010.

67 News Corporation: www.newscorp.com/, May 2013; *Guardian*, 13 July 2011; BBC News, 26 June 2012; *Guardian*, 13 July 2011.

68 Hutchinson Whompoa: interview European strategy manager, March 2010; www.hutchison-whampoa.com/en/global/home.php.

69 France Telecom: www.orange.com/en/home, November 2011.
70 Deutsche Telecom: www.telekom.com/, December 2011.
71 Telefonica: www.telefonica.es/, September 2011.
72 Orascom/WIND: company information, June 2013; BBC News, 1 August 2002; *Guardian*, 2 February 2010.
73 MTN: www.mtn.com/MTNGROUP/About/Pages/History.aspx, July 2013.
74 Zain: www.zain.com/, June 2013.
75 Endesa: www.endesa.com/en/aboutEndesa/ourOrganisation/Home, August 2013.
76 Edesur: www.edesur.com.ar/index.aspx, August 2013.
77 GDF Suez: www.gdfsuez.com/; *Economist*, 8 September 2005, 27 October 2005; Reuters, 27 August 2010.
78 Ibid.
79 Enel: www.enel.com/en-GB/group/about_us/history/, August 2013.
80 E-On: www.eon.com/en/about-us/profile/history.html, June 2013; *Guardian*, 9 April 2001; *Economist*, 8 August 2002.
81 RWE: www.rwe.com/web/cms/en/9134/rwe/about-rwe/profile/history/, September 2013.
82 BP: www.bp.com/en/global/corporate/about-bp/our-history/history-of-bp/late-century.html; www.bp.com/en/global/corporate/about-bp/our-history/history-of-bp/new-millennium.html; reports in *New York Times*, August 2010; BBC News, August 2008, June, 2010, October 2010, March 2013; *Fortune*, March 2013; BBC News, February 2013; *Daily Telegraph*, May 2007.
83 Fortune Global 500 (2001): *Fortune*, 7 May 2001; *Economist*, 31 August 2000.
84 Royal Dutch Shell: www.shell.com/, interviews with headquarters staff, March 2009; *Guardian*, 26 May 2009; BBC News, 30 January 2013.
85 ExxonMobil: http://corporate.exxonmobil.com/, May 2010; *Financial Times*, 6 June 2008.
86 Chevron: www.chevron.com/about/history/, May 2010.
87 Total: interview, February 2012, with former corporate affairs executive; www.total.com/en/corporate-profile/thumbnail/history, September 2012; *Business Week*, 24 January 2010.
88 ENI: www.eni.com/en_IT/company/history/our-history.page, August 2012; *Financial Times*, 28 May 2001, October 2004.
89 Statoil: www.statoil.com/en/about/history/pages/default3.aspx, May 2013; BBC News, 11 June 2004; Bloomberg, 4 October 2006.
90 Petronas: www.petronas.com.my/about-us/Pages/default.aspx, June 2009; www.saudiaramco.com/en/home/news/latest-news/2009.

91 Petrobras: www.petrobras.com/en/about-us/our-history/, May 2013; *New York Times*, 28 May 2006; BBC News, 2 May 2006.
92 ONGC Videsh Ltd: www.ongcindia.com/wps/wcm/connect/ongcindia/ Home/Company/History/, August 2013.
93 Lukoil: www.lukoil.com/new/history/2014, August 2013; *Financial Times*, 28 July 2010.
94 *Financial Times*, 19 September 1991, 8 October 1998, 1 January 2010.
95 CNPC: interview, June 2012; http://classic.cnpc.com.cn/en/?COLLCC =3732474836&, June 2013; *Financial Times*, 23 June 2010; *Bloomberg*, 6 March 2013; *Guardian*, 25 June 2009, 7 January 2011.
96 ENI: www.eni.com/en_IT/company/history/our-history.page, August 2012; *Financial Times*, 28 May 2001, October 2004.
97 Repsol YPF: www.repsol.com/es_en/corporacion/conocer-repsol/ perspectiva_historica/, May 2013; *Economist*, 15 July 2013.
98 Rio Tinto Alcan: www.riotinto.com/aboutus/history-4705.aspx, August 2009.
99 BHP Billiton: www.bhpbilliton.com/home/aboutus/ourcompany/ Pages/ourHistory.aspx, January 2013; Reuters, 30 July 2009; *Wall Street Journal*, 17 June 2009.
100 *New York Times*, 29 March 2010; BBC News, 17 March 2010, 29 July 2010.
101 Xinhua News Agency, 24 April 2012. *Economist*, 31 August 2000.
102 BHP Billiton: www.bhpbilliton.com/home/aboutus/ourcompany/ Pages/ourHistory.aspx, January 2013; Reuters, 30 July 2009; *Wall Street Journal*, 17 June 2009.
103 Glencore: *Guardian*, 19 May 2011, 2 December 2012; *Sunday Times*, 14 October 2012, 18 November 2012.
104 Anglo-American: www.angloamerican.com/about/history.aspx, May 2013; *Financial Times*, 12 December 2012; *Guardian*, 26 March 2003.
105 CVRD: Vale, www.vale.com/brasil/en/pages/search-results.aspx?k= history; www.vale.com/canada/EN/aboutvale/book-our-history/Pages/ default.aspx, June 2013; *Economist*, 27 March 1999, 4 September 2010.
106 *Financial Times*, 19 September 1991, 8 October 1998, 1 January 2010. Reports in the *Financial Times*, July 2012, June 2013; *New Yorker*, June 2013; *Guardian*, November 2011; *Economist*, April 2011; *Guardian*, June 2006, October 2012. www.bbc.com/news/17702487, BBC News, 16 April 2012. China, Ministry of Finance, Annual Report on the Chinese Outward Investment, 2009.
107 Procter & Gamble: www.pg.com/en_US/company/global_structure_ operations/, May 2013; *Business Week*, 1 February 2013.

108 Hewlett-Packard: www.hp.com/sg/en/campaign/ebc/experience.html, March 2011.

109 Toyota: interview European executives, March 2010; www.toyota-global.com/company/history_of_toyota/, May 2010.

110 Ibid.

111 Vizio: http://store.vizio.com/about/, November 2010.

112 *New York Times*, 29 March 2010; BBC News, 17 May 2010, 29 July 2010.

113 www.novartis.com/about-novartis/company-history/, June 2010. www.astrazeneca.com/About-Us/History, November 2012. www.gsk.com/about-us/our-history.html, March 2012. http://en.sanofi.com/our_company/history/history.aspx. March 2012.

114 Takeda: www.takeda.com/company/history/, March 2012; JETRO, Newsletter, February 2012.

115 POSCO: www.poscoenc.com/english/about/history.asp, November 2012.

116 Mittal, http://corporate.arcelormittal.com/who-we-are/our-history, September 2012.

117 Acer: www.acer-group.com/public/The_Group/overview.htm, September 2012; *Taipei Times*, 1 June 2002, 8 June 2003; ACER Annual Report 2008.

118 Cemex: www.cemex.com/AboutUs/History.aspx, June 2010.

Bibliography

Abel, C., and Lewis, C., eds., 1985. *Latin America, Economic Imperialism and the State* (London: Athlone Press).

Abelhauser, W., Hippel, W. Van, Johnson, J. A., and Stokes, R. G., 2004. *German Industry and Global Enterprise: BASF: The History of a Company* (Cambridge University Press).

Aharoni, Y., ed., 1993. *Coalitions and Competition: The Globalization of Professional Business Services* (London: Routledge).

Alejandro, C. D., 1970. *Essays in the Economic History of the Argentine Republic* (Yale University Press).

Alfaro, L., and Rodriguez-Clare, A., 2004. 'Multinationals and linkages: an empirical investigation', *Economia*.

Allen, G. C., and Donnithorne, A. G., 1954. *Western Enterprise in Far Eastern Economic Development* (1954, reprinted London: Routledge, 2003).

    1957. *Western Enterprise in Indonesia and Malaysia* (reprinted London: Routledge, 2003).

Amatori, F., and Jones, G., 2003. *Business History around the World* (Cambridge University Press).

Andaya, B. W., and Andaya, L. Y., 1982. *A History of Malaysia* (Basingstoke: Palgrave).

Ando, K., 2004. *Japanese Multinationals in Europe* (Basingstoke: Edward Elgar).

Anstey, V., 1929. *The Trade of the Indian Ocean* (London: Longmans, Green).

Armstrong, C., and Nelles, H. V., 1988. *Southern Exposure: Canadian Promoters in Latin America and the Caribbean, 1896–1945* (University of Toronto Press).

Ashworth, W., 1964. *A Short History of the International Economy 1850–1950* (London: Longmans).

Ayala, C., 1999. *American Sugar Kingdom: The Plantation Economy of the Spanish Caribbean, 1889–1934* (Chapel Hill: University of North Carolina Press).

Bagchi, A. K., 1972. *Private Investment in India, 1900–39* (Cambridge University Press).

Baker, W. J., 1988. *The History of the Marconi Company* (London: Methuen).

Bamberg, J. H., 1994. *The History of the British Petroleum Company*, vol. II (Cambridge University Press).

2000. *British Petroleum and Global Oil, 1950–1975: The Challenge of Nationalism* (Cambridge University Press).

Barisitz, S., 2006. 'Banking transformation (1989–2006) in Central and Eastern Europe'. Oesterreichische Nationalbank Working Paper.

Barjot, D., 1988. *From Tournon to Tancarville: The Contribution of French Civil Engineering to Suspension Bridge Construction, 1824–1959* (London: Taylor and Francis).

Barnett, P. G., 1943. 'The Chinese in Southeastern Asia and the Philippines', *Annals of the American Academy of Political and Social Science*, vol. 226.

Barnett Smith, G., 1893. *The Life and Enterprises of Ferdinand de Lesseps* (London: W. H. Allen).

Bartlett, C. A., and Ghoshal, S., 1989. *Managing across Borders* (Cambridge, MA: Harvard Business Press).

Battilossi, S., and Cassis, Y., eds., 2002. *European Banks and the American Challenge: Competition and Cooperation in International Banking under Bretton Woods* (Oxford University Press).

Bayly, C. A., 2004. *The Birth of the Modern World, 1780–1914* (Oxford: Blackwell).

Beamish, P. W., Delois, A., and Makino, S., eds., 2001. *Japanese Subsidiaries in the New Global Economy* (Basingstoke: Edward Elgar).

Beasley, W. G., 1963. *The Modern History of Japan* (Orlando: Harcourt).

1972. *The Meiji Restoration* (Stanford University Press).

1987. *Japanese Imperialism, 1894–1945* (Oxford University Press).

Beaton, K., 1957. *Enterprise in Oil: A History of Shell in the United States* (New York: Appleton Century Crofts).

Beaud, C., 1986. 'Investments and profits in the International Schneider Group, 1894–1943', in A. Teichova, M. Levy-Leboyer, and H. Nussbaum, eds., *Multinational Enterprise in Historical Perspective* (Cambridge University Press).

Beaver, P., 1976. *Yes! We Have Some: The Story of Fyffes* (Stevenage: Publication for Companies).

Bebbington, T., 1998. *50 Years of Holden* (Sydney: Australian Publishing).

Behrman, J. N., and Fischer, W. A., 1980. 'Overseas R&D activities of transnational companies', *Thunderbird International Business Review*, vol. 22, no. 3, 15–17.

Behrman, J. N., and Grosse, R. E., 1990. *International Business and Governments* (New York: McGraw-Hill).

Belanger, J., 1999. *Being Local Worldwide: ABB and the Challenge of Global Management* (New York: Cornell University Press).

Bellak, C., 1997. 'Austrian manufacturing MNEs: long-term perspectives', *Business History*, 39.

Bideleux, R., and Jeffries, I., 1998. *A History of Eastern Europe: Crisis and Change* (London: Routledge).

Biersteker, T. J., 1987. *Multinationals, the State, and Control of the Nigerian Economy* (Princeton University Press).

Black, E., 2012. *IBM and the Holocaust: The Strategic Alliance Between Nazi Germany and America's Most Powerful Corporation* (Dialog Press).

Blake, R., 2000. *Jardine Matheson: Traders of the Far East* (London: Orion Press).

Blight, J. G., and Lang, J. M., 2004. *The Fog of War: Lessons from the Life of Robert S. McNamara* (Lanham, MD: Rowman and Littlefield).

Boehl, W. G., 1992. *Cargill: Trading the World's Grain* (Hanover, NH: University Press of New England).

Bolle, J., 1968. *Solvay* (Brussels: Weissenbruch).

Bonin, H., ed., 2002. *Transnational Companies (19th–20th Centuries)* (Paris: Plage).

Bonin, H., Lung. Y., and Tolliday, S., 2003. *Ford: 1903–2003: The European History*, 2 vols. (Paris: Plage).

Bordo, M. D., Taylor, A. M., and Williamson, J. G., 2003. *Globalization in Historical Perspective* (University of Chicago Press).

Borscheid, P., 1990. *100 Jahre Allianz 1890–1990* (Munich: AG Allianz).

Borscheid, P., and Haueter, N. V., eds., 2012. *World Insurance: The Evolution of a Global Risk Network* (Oxford University Press).

Borscheid, P., and Pearson, R., eds., 2007. *Internationalisation and Globalisation of the Insurance Industry in the 19th and 20th Centuries* (Marburg: Philipps University).

Bosson, R., and Varon, B., 1977. *The Mining Industry and Developing Countries* (Oxford University Press).

Bostock, F., and Jones, G., 1989. 'British business in Iran, 1860s–1970s', in R. P. T. Davenport-Hines and G. Jones, eds., *British Business in Asia since 1860* (Cambridge University Press).

  1994. 'Foreign multinationals in British manufacturing, 1850–1962', *Business History*, 36.

Bowen, H. V., Lincoln, M., and Rigby, N., 2002. *The Worlds of the East India Company* (Cambridge University Press).

Brass, T., 1999. *Towards a Comparative Political Economy of Unfree Labour: Cases and Debates* (London: Frank Cass).

Braudel, F., 1996 (1949). *The Mediterranean and the Mediterranean World in the Age of Philip II* (University of California Press).

Brech, M., and Sharp, M., 1984. *Inward Investment: Policy Options for the United Kingdom* (London: Routledge and Kegan Paul).

Broehl, W. G., 1998. *Cargill: Going Global* (NH: Dartmouth College Press).

Brown, I., 2011. 'Tracing Burma's economic failure to its colonial influence', *Business History Review*, vol. 85.

Brown, J., and Knight, A., 1992. *The Mexican Petroleum Industry in the 20th Century* (Austin: University of Texas Press).

Brown, M., and McKern, B., 1987. *Aluminium, Copper and Steel in Developing Countries* (Paris: OECD).

Brown, R., 1994. *Capital and Entrepreneurship in South East Asia* (New York: St Martin's Press).

2000. *Chinese Big Business and the Wealth of Nations* (Basingstoke: Palgrave).

Brown, S. R., 1979. 'The transfer of technology to China in the nineteenth century: the role of foreign direct investment', *Journal of Economic History*, 39.

Brown Boveri, 1966. *75 Years of Brown Boveri: 1891–1966* (Baden: Brown Boveri).

Brunschwig, H., 1970. 'Politique et économie dans l'empire français d'Afrique Noire 1870–1914', *Journal of African History*, no. 11, 401–17.

Bucheli, M., 2005. *Bananas and Business: The United Fruit Company in Colombia, 1899–2000* (New York University Press).

2010. 'Multinational corporations, business groups, and economic nationalism: Standard Oil (New Jersey), Royal Dutch-Shell, and energy politics in Chile 1913–2005', *Enterprise and Society*, 11.

Buckley, P. J., and Casson, M., 1976. *The Future of Multinational Enterprise* (London: Macmillan).

1985. *The Economic Theory of Multinational Enterprise* (London: Macmillan).

Buckley, P., and Roberts, B., 1982. *European Direct Investment in the USA before World War I* (London: Macmillan).

Bussiere., E., 1983. 'The interests of the Banque de l'Union Parisienne in Czechoslovakia, Hungary, and the Balkans, 1919–30', in Teichova, A., and Cottrell, P. L., eds., *International Businesss and Central Europe, 1918–1939* (London: Palgrave Macmillan).

Butler, L. J., 2000. 'Capitalism and nationalism at the end of empire: state and business in decolonising Egypt, Nigeria and Kenya, 1945–1963', *Journal of African History*, 41.

2007. *Copper Empire: Mining and the Colonial State in Northern Rhodesia, c.1930–64* (Basingstoke: Palgrave Macmillan).

Cailluet, L., 1999. 'Nation states as providers of capability: French industry overseas, 1950–1965', *European Yearbook of Business History*, 2.

Cain, P., and Hopkins, A. G., 1993. *British Imperialism: Crisis and Deconstruction, 1914–1990* (London: Routledge).

Calvo., A., 2008. 'State, firms and technology: the rise of multinational telecommunications companies: ITT and the Compañía Telefónica Nacional de España, 1924–1945', *Business History*, vol. 50.

Cameron, R., and Bovykin, V. I., 1991. *International Banking, 1870–1914* (New York: Oxford University Press).

Campbell-Kelly, M., 1990. *ICL: A Business and Technical History* (Oxford: Clarendon Press).

Cantwell, J. A., 1989. *Technological Innovation and Multinational Enterprise* (Oxford: Blackwell).

Cardoso, F. H., 1972. 'Dependent capitalist development in Latin America', *New Left Review*, I/74, July–August.

Cardoso, F. H., and Faletto, E., 1979. *Dependency and Development in Latin America* (Oakland: University of California Press).

Carlos, A., and Kruse, J., 1996. 'The decline of the Royal African Company: fringe firms and the role of the charter', *Economic History Review*, 49.

Carlos, A., and Nicholas, S., 1988. 'Giants of an earlier capitalism: the chartered trading companies as modern multinationals', *Business History Review*, 62.

Carr, E. H., 1962. *What Is History?* (Cambridge University Press).

Carstensen, F., 1984. *American Enterprise in Foreign Markets: Singer and International Harvester in Imperial Russia* (Chapel Hill: University of North Carolina Press).

Cassell, C. A., 1970. *Liberia: The History of the First African Republic* (London: Foutainhead).

Cassis, Y., 2006. *Capitals of Capital: a History of International Financial Centres, 1780–2005* (Cambridge University Press).

Casson, M., 1983. *The Growth of International Business* (London: George Allen and Unwin).

1986. *Multinationals and World Trade* (London: Routledge).

1994. 'Institutional diversity in overseas enterprise: explaining the free-standing company', *Business History*, 36.

Caves, R. E., 1982. *Multinational Enterprise and Economic Analysis* (Cambridge University Press).

Cerretano, V., 2012. 'European cartels, European multinationals and economic de-globalization: insights from the rayon industry, c.1900–1939', *Business History*, 54.

Chalmin, P., 1987. 'The rise of international trading companies in Europe in the nineteenth century', in S. Yonekawa and H. Yoshihara, eds., *Business History of General Trading Companies* (Tokyo University Press).

    1990. *The Making of a Sugar Giant: Tate and Lyle, 1859–1989* (London: Routledge).

Chamberlain, M. E., 1999. *The Scramble for Africa* (Essex: Pearson).

Chan, Y. K., 2006. *Business Expansion and Structural Change in Pre-war China: Liu Hongsheng and his Enterprises, 1920–37* (Hong Kong University Press).

Chandler, A. D., 1962. *Strategy and Structure: Chapters in the History of the American Industrial Enterprise* (Cambridge, MA: MIT Press).

    1977. *The Visible Hand: The Managerial Revolution in American Business* (Cambridge, MA: Harvard University Press).

    1980. 'The growth of the transnational industrial firm in the United States and the United Kingdom: a comparative analysis', *Economic History Review*.

    1990. *Scale and Scope: the Dynamics of Industrial Capitalism* (Cambridge, MA: Harvard University Press).

Chandler, A. D., Amatori, F., and Hikino, T., eds., 1997. *Big Business and the Wealth of Nations* (Cambridge University Press).

Chandler, A. D., and Mazlish, B., eds., 1997. *Leviathans: Multinational Corporations and the New Global History* (Cambridge University Press).

Channon, D. F., 1973. *The Strategy and Structure of British Enterprise* (Basingstoke: Palgrave Macmillan).

Chapman, K., 1991. *The International Petrochemical Industry* (Oxford: Blackwell).

Chapman, P., 2007. *Bananas: How the United Fruit Company Shaped the World* (New York: Canongate).

Chapman, S. D., 1985. 'British-based investment groups before 1914', *Economic History Review*, 38.

    1987. 'Investment groups in India and South Africa', *Economic History Review*, 40.

    1992. *Merchant Enterprise in Britain* (Cambridge University Press).

Chaudhari, K. N., ed., 1971. *The Economic Development of India under the East India Company, 1814–1858* (Cambridge University Press).

    1978. *The Trading World of Asia and the English East India Company, 1660–1760* (Cambridge University Press).

Cheape, C., 1999. 'Not politicians but sound businessmen: Norton and Company and the Third Reich', *Business History Review*, 73.

Chen, E. Y. K., ed., 1994. *Technology Transfer to Developing Countries* (London: Routledge).

Cheng, L., 1937. *The Chinese Railways: Past and Present* (Shanghai: China United Press).

Cheong, W. E., 1979. *Mandarins and Merchants* (London: Taylor & Francis).

Chew, E. C. T., and Lee, E., eds., 1991. *A History of Singapore* (Oxford University Press).

Chick, M., ed., 1990. *Governments, Industries and Markets* (Basingstoke: Edward Elgar).

Child, J., Faulkner, D., and Pitkethly, R., 2000. *The Management of International Acquisitions* (Oxford University Press).

Cho, D. S., 1984. 'The anatomy of the Korean general trading company', *Journal of Business Research*, 12.

1987. *The General Trading Company* (Lexington Books).

Church, R., 1986. 'The effects of American multinationals in the British motor industry, 1911–1983', in A. Teichova, M. Levy-Leboyer, and H. Nussbaum, eds., *Multinational Enterprises in Historical Perspective* (Cambridge University Press).

Clarence-Smith, W. G., and Topik, S., eds., 2003. *The Global Coffee Economy in Africa, Asia and Latin America, 1500–1989* (New York: Cambridge University Press).

Clark, C., 2012. *The Sleepwalkers: How Europe Went To War in 1914* (New York: HarperCollins).

Clayton, L. A., 1985. *Grace. W. Grace & Co. The Formative Years: 1850–1930* (Erie, PA: Jameson Books).

Cleveland, H. V. B., and Huertas, T. F., 1985. *Citibank, 1812–1970* (Cambridge, MA: Harvard University Press).

Coase, R. H., 1937. 'The nature of the firm', *Economica*, vol. 4.

Cobbe, J. H., 1979. *Governments and Mining Companies in Developing Countries* (Boulder, CO: Westview Press).

Cochran, S. G., 1980. *Big Business in China: Sino-Foreign Rivalry in the Cigarette Industry, 1890–1930* (Cambridge, MA: Harvard University Press).

2000. *Encountering Chinese Networks: Western, Japanese, and Chinese Corporations in China, 1880–1937* (University of California Press).

Cohan, W. D., 2011. *Money and Power: How Goldman Sachs Came to Rule the World* (New York: Doubleday).

Coleman, D. C., 1969. *Courtaulds: An Economic and Social History*, vols. i–ii (Oxford: Clarendon Press).

1980. *Courtaulds: An Economic and Social History*, vol. iii (Oxford: Clarendon Press).

Colijn, H., 1927. *World Economic Conference of 1927* (Geneva: League of Nations).

Colpan, A. M., Hikino, T., and Lincoln, J. R., eds., 2012. *The Oxford Handbook of Business Groups* (Oxford University Press).

Corley, T. A. B., 1983. *A History of the Burmah Oil Company, 1886–1924* (London: Heinemann).

1986. *A History of the Burmah Oil Company, 1924–1966* (London: Heinemann).

1994. 'Britain's overseas investments in 1914 revisited', *Business History*, 36.

Coronel, G., 1983. *The Nationalization of the Venezuelan Oil Industry* (Lexington, MA: Lexington Books).

Cox, H., 2000. *The Global Cigarette: Origins and Evolution of British American Tobacco, 1880–1945* (Oxford University Press).

Cray, E., 1980. *Chrome Colossus: General Motors and Its Times* (New York: McGraw-Hill).

Crisp, O., 1976. *Studies in the Russian Economy before 1914* (London: Macmillan).

Croce, B., 1941. *History as the Study of Liberty* (London: Allen & Unwin).

Crouzet, F., 1982. *The Victorian Economy* (London: Routledge).

Däbritz, W., 1931. *Fünfzig Jahre Metallgesellschaft 1881–1931* (Frankfurt am Main: Metallgesellschaft).

Dalton, G., 1965. 'History, politics, and economic development in Liberia', *Journal of Economic History*, 25.

Darwin, J., 2009. *The Empire Project: The Rise and Fall of the British World System 1830–1970* (Cambridge University Press).

Dassbach, C. H. A. C., 1989. *Global Enterprises in the World Economy* (New York: Garland).

Daunton, M. J., 1989. 'Firm and family in the City of London in the nineteenth century: the case of F. G. Dalgety', *Economic History Review*, vol. 42.

Davenport-Hines, R. P. T., 1986. 'Vickers as a multinational before 1945', in G. Jones, ed., *British Multinationals: Origins, Management and Performance* (London: Gower).

Davenport-Hines, R. P. T., and Jones, G., 1989. *British Business in Asia since 1860* (Cambridge University Press).

Davenport-Hines, R. P. T., and Slinn, J., 1992. *Glaxo: A History to 1962* (Cambridge University Press).

Davidson, B., 1969. *Africa in History* (New York: Simon & Schuster).

Davies, P. N., 1973. *The Trade Makers: Elder Dempster in West Africa, 1852–1972* (London: Allen & Unwin).

1977. 'The impact of the expatriate shipping lines on the economic development of British West Africa', *Business History*, 19.

1990. *Fyffes and the Banana: musa sapientum: A Centenary History, 1888–1998* (London: Athlone Press).

Davies, R. B., 1976. *Peacefully Working to Conquer the World: Singer Sewing Machines in Foreign Markets, 1854–1920* (New York: Arno Press).

Davis, L. E., and Huttenback, R. A., 1986. *Mammon and the Pursuit of Empire: the Political Economy of British Imperialism, 1860–1912* (Cambridge University Press).

De Guevara, C., and Miller, R., 1999. *Business History in Latin America: The Experience of Seven Countries* (Liverpool University Press).

Deloitte, Plender, Griffiths & Co., 1958. *Deloitte & Co., 1845–1956* (London, privately published).

Devos, G., 1993. 'Agfa-Gevaert and Belgian multinational enterprise', in G. Jones and H. G. Schroter, eds., *The Rise of Multinationals in Continental Europe* (Aldershot: Edward Elgar).

Dick, H., Houben, V. J. H., Lindblad, J. T., and Wie., T. K., 2002. *The Emergence of a National Economy: An Economic History of Indonesia, 1800–2000* (National University of Singapore Press).

Dicken, P., 2003. *Global Shift* (London: Sage).

Dierikx, M., 1991. 'Struggle for prominence: clashing Dutch and British interests on the colonial air routes, 1918-1942', *Journal of Contemporary History*, 26, 333–51.

Dosal, P. J., 1993. *Doing Business with Dictators: A Political History of United Fruit in Guatemala, 1899–1944* (Wilmington: Scholarly Resources).

Drabble, J. H., 1991. *Malayan Rubber: The Interwar Years* (Oxford University Press).

Drabble, J. H., and Drake, P. J., 1981. 'The British agency houses in Malaysia: survival in a changing world', *Journal of South East Asian Studies*, 12.

Dunca, J. S., 1937. 'British railways in Argentina', *Political Science Quarterly*, 52.

Dunn, Walter S., 1995. *The Soviet Economy and the Red Army, 1930–1945* (New York: Praeger).

Dunning, J. H., 1958. *American Investment in British Manufacturing Industry* (London: Allen & Unwin).

   1993 *Multinational Enterprises and the Global Economy* (Wokingham: Addison-Wesley).

Dunning, J. H., and Houston, T., 1976. *UK Industry Abroad* (New York: Financial Times).

Dunning. J. H., Kogut, B., and Blomstrom, M., 1990. *Globalization of Firms and the Competitiveness of Nations* (Lund: Institute of Economic Research).

Dunning, J. H., and Lundan, S., 2008. *Multinational Enterprises and the Global Economy* (Aldershot: Edward Elgar).

Dyer, H., 1904. *Dai Nippon: The Britain of the East, London* (Glasgow: Blackie and Son).

Dymock, Eric, 1997. *Saab: Half a Century of Achievement, 1947–1997* (Newbury Park, CA: Haynes North America).

Eakin, M. C., 1989. *British Enterprise in Brazil* (Durham, NC: Duke University Press).

Easterbrook, W. T., and Aitken, H. G. J., 1988. *Canadian Economic History* (University of Toronto Press).

Edelstein, M., 1982. *Overseas Investment in the Age of High Imperialism: The United Kingdom, 1850–1914* (New York: Columbia University Press).

Edlin, C., 1992. *Philippe Suchard (1797–1884): Schokoladefabrikant und Sozialpionier* (Zurich: Verein für Wirtschaftshistorische Studien).

Edwards, T., and Ferner, A., 2002. 'The renewed "American challenge": a review of employment practice in US multinationals', *Industrial Relations Journal*, vol. 33.

Egelhof, W. G., 1982. 'Strategy and structure in multinational corporations – an informational approach', *Administrative Science Quarterly*, vol. 27.

1984. 'Patterns of control in US, UK and European multinational corporations', *Journal of International Business Studies*, vol. 15, no. 2, 73–83.

Eggers-Lurat, A., 1993. 'The Danes in Siam: their involvement in establishing the Siam Commercial Bank Ltd. at the end of the last century', *Journal of the Siam Society*, vol. 81, Pt 2, 131–40.

EIU (Economic Intelligence Unit), 2006. *World Investment Prospects in 2010: Boom or Backlash?* (London: EIU).

Emmer, P. C., ed., 1986. *Colonialism and Migration: Indentured Labour before and after Slavery* (Dordrecht: Springer).

Encarnation, D. J., 1989. *Dislodging Multinationals: Industry's Strategy in Historical Perspective* (Ithaca, NY: Cornell University Press).

Enderwick, P., 2013. *Multinational Business and Labour* (London: Routledge).

ed., 1989. *Multinational Service Firms* (London: Routledge).

Enri, P., 1979. *The Basel Marriage: History of the Ciba–Geigy Merger* (Zurich: Neue Zürcher Zeitung).

Estape-Triay, S., 1998. 'Economic nationalism, state intervention, and foreign multinationals: the case of the Spanish Ford subsidiary, 1936–1954'. Paper presented to the European Business History Association conference.

1999. 'State and industry in the '40s: the Spanish automobile industry'. Paper presented to the European Business History Association, Rotterdam, 24–26 September.

Evans, P. B., 1979. *Dependent Development: The Alliance of Multinational, State and Local Capital in Brazil* (Princeton University Press).

Evans, R. J., 2001. *Lying About Hitler: History, Holocaust, and the David Irving Trial* (New York: Basic Books).

2005. *In Defence of History* (London: Granta Books).

Ewans, M., 2002. *European Atrocity, African Catastrophe: Leopold II, the Congo Free State and Its Aftermath* (London: Routledge).

Ewell, J., 1999. *Venezuela and the US: from Monroe's Hemisphere to Petroleum's Empire* (University of Georgia Press).

Fairbank, J. K. and Liu, K.-C., eds., 1980. *The Cambridge History of China*. vol. 2: *Late Ch'ing, 1800–1911* (Cambridge University Press).

Falkus, M., 1989. 'Early British business in Thailand', in R. P. T. Davenport-Hines and G. Jones, *British Business in Asia since 1860* (Cambridge University Press).

Farnie, D. A., 1979. *The English Cotton Industry and the World Market, 1815–1896* (Oxford University Press).

Feinstein, C., 1990. 'Britain's overseas investments in 1913', *Economic History Review*, 43.

Feinstein, C. H., 2005. *An Economic History of South Africa* (Cambridge University Press).

Feldenkirchen, W., 2000. *Siemens, from Workshop to Global Player* (Columbus: Ohio State University Press).

Feldman, M. P., 1989. 'FDI and spillovers in the Swiss manufacturing industry: interaction effects between spillover mechanisms and domestic absorptive capacities', in M. P. Feldman and G. D. Santangelo eds., *New Perspectives in International Business Research* (Progress in International Business Research, vol. III) (Emerald Group Publishing), pp. 263–87.

Fenton-O'Creevy, M., Gooderham, P. N., and Nordhaug, O., 2005. 'Diffusion of HRM to Europe and the role of US MNCs', *Management Revue* 16 (1), 5.

Ferguson, N., 1998. *The World's Banker: The History of the House of Rothschild* (London: Weidenfield and Nicolson).

2011. *Civilization: The West and the Rest* (London: Penguin).

Ferrier, R. W., 1982. *The History of the British Petroleum Company*, vol. 1 (Cambridge University Press).

Fieldhouse, D. K., 1965. *Colonial Empires: A Comparative Survey from the 18th Century* (New York: Delacorte Press).

1978. *Unilever Overseas* (London: Croom Helm).

1994. *Merchant Capital and Economic Decolonization: The United Africa Company, 1929–87* (Oxford University Press).

2006. *Western Imperialism in the Middle East, 1914–1958* (Oxford University Press).

Finch, M. H. J., 1985. 'British imperialism in Uruguay: the public utility companies and the British state, 1900–1939', in C. Abel and C. M. Lewis, eds., *Latin America, Economic Imperialism and the State* (London: Athlone Press).

Finlay & Co. Ltd, 1951. *James Finlay & Co. Ltd* (Glasgow: Jackson, Son & Company).

Fitzgerald, R., 1995. *Rowntree and the Marketing Revolution, 1862–1969* (Cambridge University Press).

2009. 'Marketing and distribution', in G. Jones and J. Zeitlin eds., *Oxford Handbook of Business History* (New York: Oxford University Press).

Forbes, N., 2000. *Doing Business with the Nazis: Britains's Financial and Economic Relations with Germany 1931–39* (London: Routledge).

Forbes-Munro, J., 1998. 'From regional trade to global shipping: Mackinnon, Mackenzie & Co. within the Mackinnon Enterprise Network', in G. Jones, *The Multinational Traders* (London: Routledge).

Foreman-Peck, J., 1994. *A History of the World Economy: International Economic Relations since 1850* (Harlow: Financial Times/Pearson).

Frank, A. G., 1969. *Latin America: Underdevelopment or Revolution* (New York: Monthly Review Press).

Franko, L., 1976. *The European Multinationals* (Stamford, CT: Greyford Publishers).

French, D., 1991. *The US Tire Industry* (Boston, MA: G. K. Hall).

Friedenson, P., 1986. 'The growth of multinational activities in the French motor industry, 1890–1979', in P. Hertner and G. Jones, eds., *Multinationals: Theory and History* (Farnham: Ashgate).

Friedman, T., 2005. *The World Is Flat: A Brief History of the World Twenty Years From Now* (New York: Farrar, Straus and Giroux).

Fritsch, W., and Franco, G., 1991. *Foreign Direct Investment in Brazil: Its Impact on Industrial Restructuring* (Paris: OECD).

Fritz, M. and Karlsson, B., 2007. *SKF: A Global History: 1907–2007* (Stockholm: Informationsförlaget).

Fruin, W. M., 1992. *The Japanese Enterprise System: Competitive Strategies and Cooperative Structures* (Oxford University Press).

2002. *Japanese Enterprise System: Competitive Strategies and Cooperative Structures* (Oxford University Press).

Fuji Xerox, 1994. *Three Decades of Fuji Xerox, 1962–1992* (privately published).

Gabel, M., and Bruner, H., 2003. *Global, Inc.: An Atlas of the Multinational Corporation* (New York: New Press).

Gaddis, J. L., 1998. *Now We Know: Rethinking Cold War History* (Oxford University Press).

Gales, B. P., and Sluyterman, K. E., 1993. 'Outward bound: the rise of the Dutch multinationals', in G. Jones and H. Schroter, eds., *The Rise of Multinationals in Continental Europe* (Aldershot: Edward Elgar).

Galey, J., 1979. 'Industrialist in the wilderness: Henry Ford's Amazon venture', *Journal of Interamerican Studies and World Affairs*, 21.

Gall, L., Feldman, Gerald D., James, Harold, and Holtfrerich, Carl-Ludwig, 1995. *The Deutsche Bank 1870–1995* (Princeton University Press).

Gallard, Philippe, 2004. *À l'assaut du monde: L'aventure Peugeot-Citroën* (Paris: F. Bourin).

Garfield, S., 2001. *Mauve* (New York: Norton).

Garretson, F. C., 1958. *History of the Royal Dutch*, 4 vols. (privately published).

Gereffi, G., 1994. *Commodity Chains and Global Capitalism* (Westport, CT: Praeger).

Gerschenkron, A., 1965. *Economic Backwardness in Economic Development* (Cambridge, MA: Belknap).

Geyl, P., 1955. *Debates with Historians* (Groningen: Wolters).

Giddens, A., 1999. *Runaway World: How Globalization Is Shaping our Lives* (London: Profile Books).

Giebelhaus, A. W., 1994. 'The pause that refreshed the world: the evolution of Coca Cola's global marketing strategy', in Jones, G., and Morgan, N. J., eds., *Adding Value: Brands and Marketing in Food and Drink* (London: Routledge).

Gillespie, R. W., 1972. 'The policies of England, France and Germany as recipients of foreign direct investment', in F. Machlup, W. S. Salant, and L. Tarshis, eds., *International Mobility and Movement of Capital* (New York: Columbia University Press).

Gimbel, P. J., 1990. *Science, Technology and Reparations: Exploitation and Plunder in Postwar Germany* (Stanford University Press).

Glaser-Smith, E., 1994. 'Foreign trade strategies of I.G. Farben after World War I', *Business and Economic History*, vol. 23.

Godley, A. C., 1999. 'Pioneering foreign direct investment in British manufacturing', *Business History Review*, 73.

　2003. 'Foreign multinationals and innovation in British retailing, 1850–1962', *Business History*, 45.

Goldstein, A., 2007. *Multinational Companies from Emerging Economies: Composition, Conceptualization and Direction in the Global Economy* (Basingstoke: Palgrave).

Gondola, C. D., 2002. *The History of Congo* (Westport, CT: Greenwood Press).

Gonjo, Y., 1993. *Banque Coloniale ou Banque d'Affaires. La Banque de l'Indochine sous la IIIe Republique* (Paris: IGDPE).

Goodman, J. B., 1993. 'Insurance domestic regulation and international service competition', in D. B. Yoffie, ed., *Beyond Free Trade: Firms, Governments and Global Competition* (Boston, MA: Harvard University Press).

Gordon, A., 2003. *A Modern History of Japan: From Tokugawa Times to the Present* (Oxford University Press).

Graham, R., 1968. *Britain and the Onset of Modernization in Brazil, 1850–1914* (Cambridge University Press).

Grandin, G., 2009. *Fordlandia: The Rise and Fall of Henry Ford's Forgotten Jungle City* (New York: Picador).

Gray, J., 1998. *False Dawn: The Delusions of Global Capitalism* (London: Granta).

Greenhill, R., and Miller, R., 1998. 'British trading companies in South America after 1914', in G. Jones, eds., *The Multinational Traders* (London: Routledge), pp. 102–27.

Guex, S., ed., 1998. *Switzerland and the Great Powers, 1914–1945* (Geneva: University of Geneva Centre of International Economic History).

Gupta, B., 1997. 'Collusion in the Indian tea industry in the Great Depression: an analysis of panel data', *Explorations in Economic History* 34, no. 2: 155–73.

Haikio, M., 2002. *Nokia: The Inside Story* (New Jersey: Prentice Hall).

Hall, D., and Lobina, E., 2012. *The Birth, Growth and Decline of Multinational Water Companies*. Public Services International Research Unit Report (May).

Hamilton, A., 1791. *Report on Manufactures*, cited in Church, John, *The Works of Alexander Hamilton: Miscellanies, 1789–1795* (John F. Trow, 1850).

Harcourt, F., 1981. 'The P&O Company: flagships of imperialism', in Palmer, S. and Williams, G., eds. *Chartered and Unchartered Waters* (London: National Maritime Museum).

Harlaftis, G., 1996. *A History of Greek-owned Shipping: The Making of an International Tramp Fleet, 1830 to the Present Day* (London: Taylor and Francis).

Harrison, P., and George, S., 1983. *L'Empire Nestlé* (Lausanne: Centre Europe-Tiers Monde Pierre-Marcel Favre).

Harrison, R. J., 1978. *Economic History of Modern Spain* (Manchester University Press).

Harvey, C., 1981. *The Rio Tinto Company: An Economic History of a Leading International Mining Concern, 1873–1954* (Penzance: Alison Hodge).

Harvey, C. E., and Press, J., 1990. 'The City and international mining, 1870–1914', *Business History*, 32, 98–119.

Harvey, C. E., and Taylor, P., 1987. 'Mineral wealth and foreign direct investment in Spain, 1851–1913', *Economic History Review*, 60.

Hatton, T. J., and Williamson, J. G., 1998. *The Age of Mass Migration* (Oxford University Press).

Hausman, W. J., Hertner, P., and Wilkins, M., 2008. *Global Electrification: Multinational Enterprise and International Finance in the History of Light and Power, 1878–2007* (Cambridge University Press).

Heaton, M. W., 2008. *A History of Nigeria* (Cambridge University Press).

Heer, J., 1966. *World Events, 1866–1966: The First Hundred Years of Nestlé* (privately published).

1991. *Nestlé 125 years (1866–1991)* (Vevey: Nestlé).

Held, D., McGrew A., Goldblatt, D., and Perraton, J., 1999. *Global Transformations: Politics, Economics, and Culture* (New Jersey: Wiley).

Hennart, J.-F., 1982. *A Theory of Multinational Enterprise* (Ann Arbor: University of Michigan Press).

1986. 'The tin industry', in M. Casson, ed., *Multinationals and World Trade* (London: Allen and Unwin).

1994. 'Free-standing firms and the internationalization of markets for financial capital: a response to Casson', *Business History*, 36.

Hertner, P., and Jones, G., 1986. *Multinationals: Theory and History* (Farnham: Ashgate).

Hidy, R. W., and Hidy, M. E., 1955. *Pioneering in Big Business: The History of the Standard Oil Company (New Jersey), 1882–1911* (New York: Harper).

Hobsbawm, E., 1989. *The Age of Empire, 1875–1914* (London: Abacus).

1998. *On History* (New York: New Press).

2003. *The Age of Extremes: The Short Twentieth Century, 1914–1991* (London: Abacus).

Hobson, J. A., 1902. *Imperialism* (London: J. Nisbet).

Hochschild, A., 1988. *King Leopold's Ghost* (Boston, MA: Houghton Mifflin).

1998. *King Leopold's Ghost : A Story of Greed, Terror, and Heroism in Colonial Africa* (London: Pan Macmillan).

Hodges, M., 1974. *Multinational Corporations and National Government* (Oxford: Saxon House).

Hoesel, R. van, 1999. *New Multinational Enterprises from Korea and Taiwan: Beyond Export-Led Growth* (London: Routledge).

Hoesel, R. van, and Narula, R., 1999. *Multinational Enterprises from the Netherlands* (London: Routledge).

Hollander, S., 1970. *Multinational Retailing* (University of Michigan Press).

Holliday, G. D., 1979. *Technology and East West Trade* (Santa Monica: Rand).

Hood, J., 2004. *John Brown Engineering: Power Contractors to the World* (privately published).

Hood, N., and Young, S., 1979. *The Economics of Multinational Enterprise* (Aldershot: Palgrave).

Hopkins, A.G., 1980. 'Property rights and empire building: Britain's annexation of Lagos', *Journal of Economic History*, 40.

Huang, Y., and Yu, M., 2012. *China's New Role in the World Economy* (New York: Routledge).

Hudson's Bay Company, 1934. *Hudson's Bay Company: A Brief History* (privately published).

Huff, W. G., 1994. *The Economic Growth of Singapore: Trade and Development in the Twentieth Century* (Cambridge University Press).

Humes, S., 1993. *Managing the Multinational* (New Jersey: Prentice Hall).

Hunt, W., 1951. *Heirs of Great Adventure: History of Balfour, Williamson and Son*, vol. 1: *1852–1901* (London: Jarold & Son).

Hyde, F. E., and Harris, J. R., 1956. *Blue Funnel: A History of Alfred Holt & Co. of Liverpool from 1865 to 1914* (Liverpool University Press).

Hymer, S., 1960. 'The international operations of national firms: a study of direct foreign investment'. PhD thesis, MIT.

Iggers, G. C., and Powell, J. M., 1973. *Leopold von Ranke and the Shaping of the Historical Discipline* (New York: Syracuse University Press).

IMF, various years. *World Economic Outlook* (Washington DC: World Bank).

Innes, D., 1984. *Anglo American and the Rise of Modern South Africa* (New York: Monthly Review Press).

James, H., 2004. *The Nazi Dictatorship and the Deutsche Bank* (Cambridge University Press).

Jeffreys, D., 2008. *Aspirin: the Remarkable Story of a Wonder Drug* (New York: Bloomsbury Publishing).

Jones, C., 1987. *International Business in the Nineteenth Century* (University of Chicago Press).

Jones, G., 1981. *The State and Emergence of the British Oil Industry* (Basingstoke: Palgrave Macmillan).

　1986a. *Banking and Empire in Iran* (Cambridge University Press).

　1986b. *British Multinationals: Origins, Management and Performance* (London: Gower).

1987. 'The Imperial Bank of Iran and Iranian economic development, 1890–1952', *Business and Economic History*, 16.

1988. 'Foreign multinationals and British industry before 1945', *Economic History Review*, 41.

ed., 1990. *Banks as Multinationals* (New York: Routledge).

1993. *British Multinational Banking, 1830–1990* (Oxford: Clarendon Press).

1996. *The Evolution of Modern Business: An Introduction* (London: Routledge).

ed., 1998a. *The Multinational Traders* (London: Routledge).

1998b. 'Multinational cross-investment between Switzerland and Britain, 1914–1945', in S. Guex, ed., *Switzerland and the Great Powers, 1914–1945* (University of Geneva Centre of International Economic History).

2000. *Merchants to Multinationals* (Oxford University Press).

2005a. *Multinationals and Global Capitalism: From the Nineteenth to the Twenty-First Century* (Oxford University Press).

2005b. *Renewing Unilever: Transformation and Tradition* (Oxford University Press).

Jones, G., and Bostock, F., 1996.'US multinationals in British manufacturing before 1962', *Business History Review*, 70.

Jones, G., and Galvez-Munoz, L., eds., 2001. *Foreign Multinationals in the United States* (London: Routledge).

Jones, G., and Khanna, T., 2006. 'Bringing history (back) into international business', *Journal of International Business Studies*, 37.

Jones, G., and Schroter, H., eds., 1993. *The Rise of Multinationals in Continental Europe* (Aldershot: Edward Elgar).

Jones, G., and Trebilcock, C., 1982. 'Russian industry and British business, 1910–30: oil and armaments', *Journal of European Economic History*, 11.

Jones, S., 1986. *Two Centuries of Overseas Trading: Origins and Growth of the Inchcape Group* (Basingstoke: Palgrave Macmillan).

Jonker, J., and Sluyterman, K. E., 2005. *At Home on the World Markets: Dutch International Trading Companies between the Wars from the 16th Century to the Present* (Montreal: McGill Queen's University Press).

Karnow, S., 1994. *Vietnam: A History* (London: Penguin).

Kawabe, N., 1987. 'Development of overseas operations by general trading companies, 1868–1945', in S. Yonekawa and H. Yoshihara, eds., *Business History of General Trading Companies* (Tokyo University Press).

1989. 'Japanese business in the United States before the Second World War: the case of Mitsui and Mitsubishi', in A. Teichova, M. Levy-Leboyer, and H. Nussbaum, eds., *Historical Studies in International Corporate Businesss* (Cambridge University Press).

Kenwood, A. G., and Lougheed, A. L., 1992. *The Growth of the International Economy, 1820–1990* (London: Taylor and Francis).

1999. *Growth of the International Economy 1820–2000: An Introductory Text* (London: Routledge).

Kershaw, I., 2004. *Making Friends with Hitler. Lord Londonderry and Britain's Road to War* (London: Allen Lane).

Keswick, M., 1982. *The Thistle and the Jade* (London: Frances Lincoln).

Keynes, J. M., 1919. *The Economic Consequences of the Peace* (New York: Harcourt, Brace & Co.).

1936. *General Theory of Employment, Interest and Money* (New York: Harcourt, Brace & Co.).

Kindleberger, C. P., 1960. *American Business Abroad* (New Haven: Yale University Press).

ed., 1970. *The International Corporation* (Cambridge, MA: MIT Press).

King, F. H. H., King, C. E., and King, D. J. S., 1987–8. *The History of the Hong Kong and Shanghai Banking Corporation*, 4 vols. (Cambridge University Press).

Kinzer, S., 2006. *Overthrow: America's Century of Regime Change from Hawaii to Iraq* (New York: Macmillan).

Kipping, M., and Engwall, L., eds., 2003. *Management Consulting: Emergence and Dynamics of a Knowledge Industry* (Oxford University Press).

Kirchner, W., 1981. 'Russian tariffs and foreign industries before 1914: the German entrepreneur's perspective', *Journal of Economic History*, vol. 41.

Kirkpatrick, C., and Mixson, F., 1961. 'Transnational corporations and economic development', *Journal of Modern African Studies*, vol. 1.

Klein, H. S., 1965. 'The creation of the Patino tin empire', *Inter-American Economic Affairs*, 19.

2003. *A Concise History of Bolivia* (Cambridge University Press).

Kobrak, C., 2002. *National Cultures and International Competition: The Experience of Schering AG, 1851–1950* (Cambridge University Press).

2007. *Banking on Global Markets: Deutsche Bank and the US, 1870 to the Present* (Cambridge University Press).

Kogut, B., and Parkinson, D., 1993. 'The diffusion of American organizing principles to Europe', in B. Kogut, ed., *Country Competitiveness, Technology and the Organization of Work* (Oxford University Press).

Kojima, K., 1978. *Direct Foreign Investment: A Japanese Model of Multinational Business Operations* (London: Croom Helm).

1985. 'Japanese and American direct investment in Asia: a comparative analysis', *Hitotsubashi Journal of Economics*, 26: 1–35.

Kojima, K., and Ozawa, T., 1984. *Japan's General Trading Companies: Merchants of Economic Development* (Paris: OECD).

Kudo, A., 1994. 'IG Farben in Japan: the transfer of technology and managerial skills', *Business History*, 36.

Kudo, A., and Hara, T., 1992. *International Cartels in Business History* (Tokyo University Press).

Kumar, N., ed., 1980. *Transnational Enterprises: Their Impact on Third World Societies and Cultures* (Boulder: Westview Press).

Kumar, N., 2012. *India's Emerging Multinationals* (London: Routledge).

Kuwahara, T., 1990. 'Trends in research on overseas expansion by Japanese enterprises prior to World War 2', *Japanese Yearbook on Business History*, vol. 7.

Kuznets, S., 1966. *Modern Economic Growth: Rate, Structure and Spread* (New Haven: Yale University Press).

Lai, C. K., 1994. 'China Merchants' Steam Navigation Company, 1872–1902 ', *Journal of Economic History*, vol. 54.

Lall., S., 1985. *Multinationals, Technology and Exports* (London: Macmillan).

   ed., 1993. *Transnational Corporations and Economic Development* (London: Routledge).

Lall, S., and Streeten, P., 1977. *Foreign Investment, Transnationals and Developing Countries* (Boulder: Westview).

Lange, O., 1971. 'Denmark in China, 1839–42: a pawn in a British game', *Scandinavia Economic History Review*, 65.

Langlois, R. N., 1989. *Microelectronics: An Industry in Transition* (London: Unwin).

Lanthier, P., 1989. 'Multinationals and the French electrical industry, 1889–1940', in A. Teichova, M. Levy-Leboyer, and H. Nussabaum, eds., *Historical Studies in International Corporate Business* (Cambridge University Press).

Larsen, L., 2000. 'Seizing the opportunities: Chinese merchants in Korea, 1876–1910', *Chinese Business History*, vol. 7.

Larson, H. M., 1971. *New Horizons: History of Standard Oil Company, 1927–50* (New York: Harper and Row).

Lasker, B., 1946. 'The role of the Chinese in the Netherlands East Indies', *Far Eastern Quarterly*.

Laux, J., 1992. *European Automobile Industry* (Boston, MA: Twayne).

LeFevour, E., 1971. *Western Enterprise in Late Ch'ing China* (Cambridge, MA: Harvard University Press).

Leff, N., 1978. 'Multinationals in a Hostile World', *The Wharton Magazine* (Summer, 1978).

Lenin, V. I., 1916. *Imperialism: the Highest Stage of Capitalism* (reprinted Moscow: Progress Books, 1963).

Leonard, T. M., 2011. *The History of Honduras* (Westport, CT: Greenwood).

Levitt, K., 1970. *Silent Surrender: The Multinational Corporation in Canada* (Montreal: McGill Queen's University Press).

Lewis, C., 1983a. *British Railways in Argentina, 1857–1914* (London: Athlone Press).

1983b. 'The financing of railway development in Latin America, 1850–1914', *Ibero-Amerikanisches Archiv*, 9.

1985. 'Railways and industrialization: Argentina and Brazil, 1870–1929', in C. Abel, and C. M. Lewis, eds., *Latin America, Economic Imperialism and the State* (London: Athlone Press).

Lewis, C., and Shlotterbeck, K. T., 1938. *America's Stake in International Investments* (New York: Arno Press).

Lewis, W. A., 1978. *Theory of Economic Growth* (Homewood, IL: Richard D. Irown).

Lief, A., 1951. *The Firestone Story: a History of the Firestone Tire and Rubber Co.* (New York: Whittlesea House).

Lin, C., 1937. *The Chinese Railways: Past and Present* (Shanghai: China United Press).

Lin, M. H., 2001. 'Overseas Chinese merchants and multiple nationality: a means for reducing commercial risk, 1895–1935', *Modern Asian Studies*, 35.

Linder, M., 1994. *Projecting Capitalism : a History of the Internationalization of the Construction Industry* (Westport, CT: Greenwood).

Lippman, W., 1947. *The Cold War* (New York: Harper).

Lipson, C., 1985. 'Bankers' dilemmas: private cooperation in rescheduling sovereign debts', *World Politics*, vol. 38, no. 1.

List, F., 1841. *The National System of Political Economy* (reprinted London: Longmans, Green, 1909).

Little, D. J., 1979. 'Twenty years of turmoil: ITT, the State Department, and Spain, 1924–1944', *Business History Review*, 53.

Litvin, D., 2003. *Empires of Profit* (Knutsford, Cheshire: Texere).

Liu, K. C., 1962. *Anglo-American Rivalry in China, 1862–74* (Cambridge, MA: Harvard University Press).

Lombard, D., and Aubin, J., 2000. *Asian Merchants and Businessmen in the Indian Ocean and the China Sea* (Oxford University Press).

Longhurst, H., 1956. *The Borneo Story: The First 100 Years* (London: Newman Neame).

Lopes, T., 2006. *Global Brands: The Evolution of Multinationals in Alcoholic Beverages* (Cambridge University Press).

Lottman, H., 2003. *The Michelin Men: Driving an Empire* (London: I. B. Tauris).

Louis, W. R., 2007. *Ends of British Imperialism: The Scramble for Empire, Suez, and Decolonization* (London: I. B. Tauris).

Lundstrom, R., 1986a. 'Banks and early Swedish multinationals', in A. Teichova, M. Levy-Leboyer, and H. Nussbaum, eds., *Multinational Entreprise in Historical Perspective* (Cambridge University Press).

1986b. 'Swedish multinational growth before 1930', in P. Hertner and G. Jones, eds., *Multinationals: Theory and History* (Farnham, Surrey: Ashgate).

Lyttleton, O., Lord Chandos, 1962. *Memoirs* (London: Bodley Head).

MacCameron, R., 1983. *Bananas, Labor and Politics in Honduras, 1954–1963* (New York: Syracuse University Press).

MacIntyre, B., 2004. *Josiah the Great* (New York: Harper Collins).

Maddison, A., 1999. *Monitoring the World Economy* (Paris: OECD).

2007. *Contours of the World Economy 1–2030: Essays in Macroeconomic History* (Oxford University Press).

Maizels, A., 1963. *Industrial Growth and World Trade* (New York: Cambridge University Press).

Maljers, F. A., 1992. 'Inside Unilever: the evolving transnational company', *Harvard Business Review*, September–October, 46–51.

Marriner, S., and Hyde, F. E., 1967. *The Senior: John Samuel Swire, 1825–1898* (Liverpool University Press).

Marshall, A., 1959. *Principles of Economics* (London: Macmillan).

Marx, K., and Engels, F., 1948. *The Communist Manifesto* (republished Moscow: Progress Publishers, 1969).

Mason, M., 1987. 'Foreign direct investment and Japanese economic development, 1899–1931', *Business and Economic History*, 16.

1990. 'With reservations: pre-war Japan as host to Western Electric and ITT', in T. Yuzawa, and M. Udagawa, eds., *Foreign Business in Japan before World War II* (Tokyo University Press).

Mathews, J. A., 2002. *Dragon Multinationals: A New Model for Global Growth* (Oxford University Press).

Matsusaka, Y. T., 2003. *The Making of Japanese Manchuria, 1904–1932* (Cambridge, MA: Harvard University Press).

Matthews, R. C. O., Feinstein, C. H., and Odling-Smee, J. C., 1982. *British Economic Growth, 1856–1873* (Stanford University Press).

Maude, W., 1958. *Merchants and Bankers: A Brief History of Anthony Gibbs and Sons and its Associated Houses' Business during 150 Years, 1808–1958* (London, privately published).

Maurer, N., 2011. 'The empire struck back: sanctions and compensation in the Mexican oil expropriation of 1938', *Journal of Economic History*, vol. 71.

Maxcy, G., 1981. *The Multinational Motor Industry* (London: Routledge).

May, S., and Plaza, G., 1958. *The United Fruit Company in Latin America* (London: Forgotten Books).

McCabe, I. B., Harlaftis, G., and Minoglou, I. P., 2005. *Diaspora Entrepreneurial Networks: Five Centuries of History* (New York: Berg).

McCann, T. P., 1976. *An American Company: The Tragedy of United Fruit* (New York: Random House).

McCreary, E. A., 1964. *The Americanization of Europe;: The Impact of Americans and American Business on the Uncommon Market* (New Jersey: Wiley).

McCullough, D., 1977. *The Path Between the Seas: The Creation of the Panama Canal, 1870–1914* (New York: Simon and Schuster).

McDonald, J., 2002. *A Ghost's Memoir: The Making of Alfred P. Sloan's 'My Years with General Motors'* (Cambridge, MA: MIT Press).

McDowell, D., 1988. *The Light: Brazilian Traction, Light and Power Company Limited, 1899–1945* (University of Toronto Press).

McKay, J. P., 1970. *Pioneers for Profit: Foreign Entrepreneurship and Russian Industrialisation, 1885–1913* (University of Chicago Press).

McKern, B., 1976. *Multinational Enterprise and Natural Resources* (McGraw-Hill).

McKern, R. B., ed., 1993. *Transnational Corporations and the Exploitation of Natural Resources* (London: Routledge).

McMillan, J., 1989. *The Dunlop Story: The Life, Death and Rebirth of a Multinational* (London: Weidenfield and Nicolson).

McNeil, W. H., 1963. *The Rise of the West* (University of Chicago Press).

Mejcher, H., 1989. 'Banking and the German oil industry, 1890–1939', in R. W. Ferrier and A. Fursenko, eds., *Oil in the World Economy* (London: Routledge).

Melby, E. D. K., 1981. *Oil and the International System: the Case of France, 1918–1969* (New York: Arno Press).

Meredith, D., and Dyster, B., 1999. *Australia in the Global Economy* (Cambridge University Press).

Merret, D., 1985. *ANZ Bank: History of the Australia and New Zealnd Bank* (London: Allen & Unwin).

Meuleau, M., 1990. *Des Pionniers en Extrême-Orient: Histoire de la Banque de l'Indochine, 1875–1975* (Paris: Fayard).

Meyer, L., 1977. *Mexico and the United States in the Oil Controversy, 1917–42* (Austin: University of Texas Press).

Meyer, M. C., and Sherman, W. L., 1987. *The Course of Mexican History* (Oxford University Press).

Michie, R., 1992. *The City of London* (Basingstoke: Palgrave Macmillan).

Miller, M. B., 2012. *Europe and the Maritime World: A Twentieth Century History* (Cambridge University Press).

Miller, R., 1982. 'Small business in the Peruvian oil industry: Lobitos Oilfields Limited before 1914', *Business History Review*, 56.

1993. *Britain and Latin America in the 19th and 20th Centuries* (London: Longman).

Milward, A., and Saul, S. B., 1978. *The Development of the Economies of Continental Europe, 1850–1914* (London: Allen & Unwin).

Minami, R., 1987. *Power Revolution in the Industrialization of Japan* (Oxford University Press).

Minoglou, I. P., 1998. 'The Greek merchant house of the Russian Black Sea. A 19th century example of a Traders' Coalition', *International Journal of Maritime History*, vol. 9.

Minoglou, I. P., and Louri, H., 1997. 'Diaspora entrepreneurial networks of the Black Sea and Greece, 1870–1917', *Journal of European Economic History*, vol. 28.

Mirza, H., 1986. *Multinationals and the Growth of the Singapore Economy* (New York: St Martin's Press).

Miyoshi, N., 2004. *Henry Dyer: Pioneer of Education in Japan* (Tokyo: Global Oriental).

Modig, H., 1979. *Swedish Match Interests in British India during the Inter-war Years* (Stockholm: Liberfohl).

Monopolies and Mergers Commission (1982). *BTR* (London: HMSO).

Montenegro, A., 1993. 'The development of Pirelli as an Italian multinational, 1872–1992', in G. Jones and H. Schroter, eds., *The Rise of Multinationals in Continental Europe* (Aldershot: Edward Elgar).

Morgan Rees, J., 1922. *Trusts in British Industry 1914–1921* (Kitchener, Ontario: Batoche Books).

Munro, J. F., 1981. 'Monopolists and speculators: British investment in West African rubber, 1905–1914', *Journal of African History*, 22.

1987. 'Shipping subsidies and railway guarantees: William McKinnon, Eastern Africa and the Indian Ocean, 1860–93', *Journal of African History*, 28.

Myint-U, T., 2001. *The Making of Modern Burma* (Cambridge University Press).

Nagakawa, K., ed., 1977. *Strategy and Structure of Big Business* (Tokyo University Press).

Navin, T. R., 1978. *Copper Mining and Management* (University of Arizona Press).

Nehmer, S., 2013. *Ford, General Motors and the Nazis: Marxist Myths about Production, Patriotism and Philosophies* (Bloomington, IN: Author House).

Neil-Tomlinson, B., 1998. 'The Nyassa Chartered Company: 1891–1929', *Journal of African History*, vol. 1, 109–28.

Nevins, A., and Hill, F. E., 1954. *Ford: The Times, the Man, the Company* (New York: Scribner).

1957. *Ford: Expansion and Challenge 1915–1933* (New York: Scribner).

1963. *Ford: Decline and Rebirth 1933–1962* (New York: Scribner).

Nicholas, S., 1982. 'British multinational investment before 1939', *Journal of European Economic History*, 11.

1983. 'Agency contracts, institutional modes, and the transition to foreign direct investment by British manufacturing multinationals before 1935', *Journal of Economic History*, 43.

North, D. C., *Institutions, Institutional Change and Economic Performance* (Cambridge University Press, 1990).

Nwankwo, S., and Ibeh, K., eds., 2014. *The Routledge Companion to Business in Africa* (London: Routledge).

O'Creevy, M. F., 2002. 'Diffusion of HRM to Europe and the Role of US MNCs', *Management Revue*, vol. 13.

Odagiri, H., 1996. *Technology and Industrial Development in Japan* (Oxford University Press).

Ohmae, K., 1995. *The End of the Nation-State: the Rise of Regional Economies* (New York: Free Press).

1999. *The Borderless World: Power and Strategy in the Interlinked Economy* (New York: HarperCollins).

Okochi, A., and Inoue, T., eds., 1984. *Overseas Business Activities* (Tokyo University Press).

Oonk, G., 2000. *The Karimjee Jivanjee Family: Merchant Princes of East Africa, 1800–2000* (Amsterdam University Press).

Osterhammel, J., 1989. 'British business in China, 1860s–1950s', in R. Davenport-Hines and G. Jones, eds., *British Business in Asia since 1860* (Cambridge University Press).

Ozawa, T., 1989. *Recycling Japan's Surpluses for Developing Countries* (Paris: OECD).

1991. 'Japan in a new phase of MNCism and industrial upgrading: functional integration of trade, growth and FDI', *Journal of World Trade*, 25 (1): 43–60.

Paige, J. M., 1997. *Coffee and Power: Revolution and the Rise of Democracy in Central America* (Cambridge, MA: Harvard University Press).

Paquet, G., ed., 1972. *The Multinational Firm and the National State* (New York: Collier Macmillan).

Partnoy, F., 2008. *The Match King: Ivar Kreuger. The Financial Genius behind a Century of Wall St Scandals* (New York: Public Affairs).

Paterson, D. G., 1976. *British Direct Investment in Canada, 1890–1914* (Toronto University Press).

Patrikeff, F., and Shukman, H., 2007. *Railways and the Russo-Japanese War: Transporting War* (New York: M. E. Sharpe).

Pearson, R., 2010. *The Development of International Insurance* (London: Pickering and Chatto).

Penrose, E., 1959. *The Theory of the Growth of the Firm* (Oxford University Press).

1968. *The Large International Firm in Developing Countries: The International Petroleum Industry* (New York: Praeger).

Perez, T., 1998. *Multinational Enterprises and Technological Spillovers* (London: Taylor and Francis).

Perras, A., 2004. *Carl Peters and German Imperialism 1856–1918. A Political Biography* (Oxford University Press).

Petras, J. E., Morley, M., and Smith, S., 1977. *The Nationalization of Venezuelan Oil* (New York: Praeger).

Philip, G., 1982. *Oil and Politics in Latin America: Nationalist Movements and State Companies* (Cambridge University Press).

Pike, F. B., 1967. *The Modern History of Peru* (New York: Praeger).

Piquet, C., 2004. 'The Suez Company's concession in Egypt, 1854–1956: modern infrastructure and local economic development', *Enterprise and Society*, 5.

Pitelis, C. N., 2009. 'International business at 50 – a semi-celebration, challenges and ways ahead', *Academy of International Business Insights*, vol. 9.

Platt, D. C. M., 1972. *Latin America and British Trade, 1806–1914* (New York: Barnes and Noble).

ed., 1977. *Business Imperialism, 1840–1930: An Inquiry Based on British Experience in Latin America* (Oxford: Clarendon).

1980. 'British portfolio investment before 1870: some doubts', *Economic History Review*, 33.

1986. *Britain's Investment Overseas on the Eve of the First World War* (New York: St Martin's Press).

Pohl, H., 1989. 'The Steaua Romana and the Deutsche Bank (1903–1920)', *Studies on Economic and Monetary Problems and on Banking History*, 24.

Pointon, A. C., 1964. *The Bombay Burmah Trading Corporation Limited, 1863–1963* (Southampton: Millbrook Books).

Pollard, S., 1985. 'Capital exports, 1870–1914: harmful or beneficial?', *Economic History Review*, 38.

1997. *The International Economy since 1945* (London: Routledge).

Pomfret, R., 1993. *The Economic Development of Canada* (London: Methuen).

Ponting, C., 2000. *World History: A New Perspective* (London: Pimlico).

Powell, J., 1956. *The Mexican Petroleum Industry, 1938–1950* (Berkeley: University of California Press).

Pozzi, D., 2010. 'Entrepreneurship and capabilities in a "beginner" oil multinational: the case of ENI', *Business History Review*, vol. 84.

Pritchett, L., 1997. 'Divergence, big time', *Journal of Economic Perspectives*, 11.

PSIRU, 2004. *La electricidad en América Latina* (London: Public Services International Research Unit).

Pugh, M., 2006. *Hurrah for the Blackshirts* (London: Pimlico).

Purcell, W. R., 1966. 'The development of Japan's trading company network in Australia, 1890–1941', *Australian Economic History Review*, 21.

Ramachandran, N., 1963. *Foreign Plantation Investment in Ceylon* (Central Bank of Ceylon).

Raphael, L., 1973. *The Cape-to-Cairo Dream* (New York: Columbia University Press).

Ray, I., 1999. *The French East India Company and the Trade of the Indian Ocean* (New Delhi: Munshiram Manoharlal).

Ray R. K., 1979. *Industrialisation in India* (Oxford University Press).

Read, R., 1983. 'The growth and structure of multinationals in the banana export trade', in M. Casson, ed., *The Growth of International Business* (London: George Allen & Unwin).

1986a. 'The banana industry: oligopoly and barriers to entry', in M. Casson, ed., *Multinationals and World Trade* (Farnham: Ashgate).

1986b. 'The copper industry', in M. Casson, ed., *Multinationals and World Trade* (Farnham: Ashgate).

Reader, W. J., 1970. *Imperial Chemical Industries: A History*, vol. I (Oxford University Press).

1975. *Imperial Chemical Industries: A History*, vol. II (Oxford University Press).

1976. *Metal Box: A History* (London: Heinemann).

Reed, P. M., 1958. 'Standard Oil in Indonesia, 1898–1928', *Business History Review*, 32.

Regalsky, A. M., 1989. 'Foreign local capital, local interests and railway development in Argentina: French investments in railways, 1900–1914', *Journal of Latin American Studies*, 21.

Reich, L. S., 1992. 'General Electric and the world cartelization of electric lamps', in A. Kudo and T. Hara, eds., *International Cartels in Business History* (Tokyo University Press).

Remer, C. F., 1933. *Foreign Investment in China* (New York: Macmillan).

Reynolds, J., 1997. *André Citroën: The Man and the Motor Cars* (Basingstoke: Palgrave Macmillan).

Rippy, J. F., 1959. *British Investments in Latin America, 1822–1949* (Oxford University Press).

Rippy, M., 1972. *Oil and the Mexican Revolution* (Leiden: E. J. Brill).

Roberts, R., 1992. *Schroders, Merchants and Bankers* (London: Macmillan).

Rodrik, D., 1982. 'Changing patterns of ownership and integration in the international bauxite-aluminium industry', in Jones, L. P., ed., *Public Enterprise in Less Developed Countries* (Cambridge University Press).

Rothstein, M., 1963. 'A British firm on the American West Coast, 1869–1914', *Business History Review*, vol. 37, no. 4, 392–415.

Roy, T., 2006. *The Economic History of India 1857–1947* (Oxford University Press).

Rugman, A. M., 2005. *The Regional Multinationals: MNEs and 'Global' Strategic Management* (Cambridge University Press).

Rugman, A. M., and Brewer, T., eds., 2001. *The Oxford Handbook of International Business* (Oxford University Press).

Ruffat, M., Caloni, E. V., and Laguerre, B., 1990. *L'UAP et l'histoire de l'assurance* (Paris: Maison des Sciences de l'Homme).

Sachs, J. D., 2005. *The End of Poverty: How We Can Make It Happen in Our Lifetime* (London: Penguin).

Safarian, A. E., 1993. *Multinational Enterprise and Public Policy* (Basingstoke: Edward Elgar).

Sakamoto, M., 1990. 'Diversification: the case of Mitsui Bussan', in S. Yonekawa, ed., *General Trading Companies: A Comparative and Historical Study* (United Nations University Press).

Sampson, A., 1973. *The Sovereign State of ITT* (Hodder and Stoughton).
 1991. *The Seven Sisters: The Great Oil Companies and the World They Shaped* (New York: Viking Press).

Saunders, K., 1984. *Indentured Labour in the British Empire, 1834–1920* (London: Croom Helm).

Saunier, P.-Y., 2013. *Transnational History* (Palgrave Macmillan).

Sauvant, K. P., and Mallampally, P., 1993. *Transnational Corporations in Services* (Basingstoke: Edward Elgar).

Sauvant, P., Pradham, J. P., Chatterjeee, A., and Harley, B., eds., 2010. *The Rise of Indian Multinationals: Perspectives on Indian Outward Foreign Direct Investment* (New York: Macmillan).

Savary, J., 1984. *French Multinationals* (Aldershot: Palgrave Macmillan).

Scherer, F. M., 1980. *Industrial Market Structure and Economic Performance* (Chicago: Rand McNally).

Schmitz, C., 1979. *World Non-Ferrous Metal Production and Prices, 1700–1976* (London: Routledge).
 1986. 'The rise of big business in the world copper industry, 1870–1930', *Economic History Review*, 39.
 ed., 1995. *Big Business in Mining and Petroleum* (Basingstoke: Edward Elgar).

Schoenberg, R. J., 1985. *Geneen* (New York: W. W. Norton).

Schroter, H., 1988. 'Risk and control in multinational enterprise: German businesses in Scandanavia, 1918–1939', *Business History Review*, 62.

1990. 'Cartels as a form of concentration in industry: the example of the international dyestuffs cartel from 1927 to 1939', *German Yearbook on Business History 1998*.

1993a. 'Continuity and change: German multinationals since 1850', in G. Jones and H. Schroter, eds., *The Rise of Multinationals in Continental Europe* (Basingstoke: Edward Elgar).

1993b. 'Swiss multinational enterprise in historical perspective', in G. Jones and H. G. Schroter, eds., *The Rise of Multinationals in Continental Europe* (Basingstoke: Edward Elgar).

2005. *Americanization of the European Economy* (Dordrecht: Springer).

Schults, R. L., 1972. *Crusader in Babylon: W. T. Stead and the Pall Mall Gazette* (Lincoln: University of Nebraska Press).

Scobie, R., 1971. *Argentina: A City and a Nation* (Oxford University Press).

Sebag-Montefiore, S., 2007. *Young Stalin* (London: Weidenfield and Nicolson).

Servan-Schreiber, J.-J., 1968. *The American Challenge* (London: Hamish Hamilton).

Service, R. J., 1997. *A History of 20th Century Russia* (Harvard University Press).

Shafer, M., 1983. 'Capturing the mineral multinationals: advantage or disadvantage?', *International Organization*. vol. 11.

Shapiro, H., 1994. *Engines of Growth: The State and Transnational Auto Companies in Brazil* (Cambridge University Press).

Shelp. R. K., ed., 1984. *Service Industries and Economic Development* (New York: Praeger).

Shillington, K., 2005. *A History of Africa* (Basingstoke: Edward Elgar).

Shimokawa, K., 1994. *The Japanese Automobile Industry: A Business History* (Atlantic Highlands, NJ: AthlonePress).

Sigmund, P. E., 1980. *Multinationals in Latin America: The Politics of Nationalization* (University of Wisconsin Press).

Sloan, A. P., 1964. *My Years with General Motors* (New York: Doubleday).

Sluglett, P., 2007. *Britain in Iraq: Contriving King and Country, 1914–1932* (New York: Columbia University Press).

Sluyterman, K. E., 1994. 'From licensor to multinational enterprise: the small Dutch firm Oce-van der Grinten in the international world, 1920–66', *Business History*, 34.

2003. *Dutch Enterprise in the Twentieth Century* (London: Routledge).

Sluyterman, K., Howarth, S., Jonker, S., and Van Zanden, J. L., 2007. *A History of Royal Dutch Shell*, 4 vols. (Oxford University Press).

Smith, A., 1776. *An Inquiry into the Nature and Causes of the Wealth of Nations* (London).

Smith, C., McSweeney, B., and Fitzgerald, R., 2008. *Remaking Management: Neither Global Nor National* (Oxford University Press).

Smith, D. N., and Wells Jr, L. T., 1975. *Negotiating Third World Mineral Agreements: Promises as Prologue* (Cambridge, MA: Ballinger Publishing Company).

Smith, G. D., 1988. *From Monopoly to Competition: the Transformation of Alcoa, 1886–1996* (Cambridge University Press).

Smith, J. K., 1982. 'National goals, industry structure and corporate strategies: chemical cartels between the wars', in A. Kudo and T. Hara, eds., *International Cartels in Business History* (Tokyo University Press).

Smith, J. W., 1987. *Sojourners in Search of Freedom: the Settlement of Liberia of Black Americans* (Lanham, MD: University of America Press).

Sobel, R., 2003. *ITT: The Management of Opportunity* (Frederick, MD: Beard Books).

Southard, F. A., 1931. *American Industry in Europe* (Boston, MA: Houghton Mifflin).

Spar, D. L., 1994. *The Cooperative Edge: The Internal Politics of International Cartels* (Ithaca, NY: Cornell University Press).

Spender, J. A., 1930. *Weetman Pearson, First Viscount Cowdray, 1856–1927* (London: Cassell).

Spero, J. E., and Hart, J., 1997. *The Politics of Economic International Relations* (London: Routledge Chapman Hall).

Stead, W. T., 1902. *Americanization of the World* (London: Horace Markley).

Stern, F., 1973. *The Varieties of History from Voltaire to the Present* (London: Macmillan).

Stiglitz, J. E., 2002. *Globalization and Its Discontents* (New York: Norton).

Stocking, G. W., and Watkins, M. W., 1946. *Cartels in Action: Case Studies in International Business Diplomacy* (New York: Twentieth Century Fund).

Stone, I., 1977. 'British Direct and Portfolio Investment in Latin America before 1914', *Journal of Economic History*, vol. 37.

Stopford, J. M., 1974. 'The origins of British-based multinational manufacturing enterprise', *Business History Review*, vol. 48.

Stopford, J. M., and Dunning, J. H., 1983. *Multinationals, Company Performance and Global Trends* (Basingstoke: Palgrave Macmillan).

Stopford, J. M., and Strange, S., 1991. *Rival States, Rival Firms* (Cambridge University Press).

Stopford, J. M., and Wells, L. T., 1972. *Managing the Multinational Enterprise* (New York: Basic Books).

Strange, R., 1993. *Japanese Manufacturing Investments in Europe* (London: Routledge).

Sugiyama, S., 1987. 'A British trading firm in the Far East: John Swire & Sons, 1867–1914', in S. Yonekawa and H. Yoshihara, eds., *Business History of General Trading Companies* (Tokyo University Press).

Sutton, A. C., 1968. *Western Technology and Soviet Economic Development, 1945–65* (Stanford University Press).

Suzuki, T., 1990. 'Post-war development of general trading companies', in S. Yonekawa, ed., *General Trading Companies* (Tokyo University Press).

Sverdberg, P., 1978. 'The portfolio-direct composition of private foreign investments in 1914 revisited', *Economic Journal*, 88.

Swedenborg, B., 1979. *The Multinational Operations of Swedish Firms* (Stockholm: Almqvist & Wiksell).

Sweet, G., and Knowlton, E. H., 1956. *The Resurgent Years, 1911–1927* (New York: Harper).

Tamaki, N., 1990. 'The Yokohama Specie Bank: a multinational in the Japanese business interest, 1879–1931', in G. Jones, ed., *Banks as Multinationals* (New York: Routledge).

Tarbell, M., 2009. *The History of the Standard Oil Company* (Minneapolis: Harvey).

Tate, D. J. M., 1996. *The RGA History of the Plantation Industry in the Malay Peninsula* (New York: Oxford University Press).

Taylor, A. J. P., 1963. *The Struggle for Mastery in Europe, 1848–1918* (Oxford University Press).

1984. *A Personal History* (New York: Atheneum).

Taylor, G. D., and Baskerville, P. A., 1994. *A Concise History of Business in China* (Hong Kong University Press).

Taylor, G. D., and Sudnik, P. E., 1984. *Du Pont and the International Chemical Industry* (Boston, MA: Twayne).

Teichova, A., and Cottrell, P. L., eds., 1983. *International Businesss and Central Europe, 1918–1939* (Boston, MA: Twayne).

Teichova, A., Levy-Leboyer, M., and Nussbaum, H., eds., 1986a. *Historical Studies in International Corporate Business* (New York: Cambridge University Press).

eds., 1986b. *Multinational Enterprise in Historical Perspective* (Cambridge University Press).

Thoburn, J., 1977. *Primary Commodity Exports and Economic Development* (London: Wiley).

1981. *Multinationals, Mining and Development: A Study of the Tin Industry* (London: Gower).

Tilly, R., 1993. 'The internationalization of West German banks, 1945–87', in G. Jones and H. Schroter, eds., *The Rise of Multinationals in Continental Europe* (Basingstoke: Edward Elgar).

Tinker, H., 1974. *A New System of Slavery: The Export of Indian Labour Overseas, 1830–1920* (Oxford University Press).

Tolentino, P. E. E., 1993. *Technological Innovation and Third World Multinationals* (London: Routledge).

Tomlinson, B. R., 1978. 'Foreign private investment in India, 1920–1950', *Modern Asian Studies*, vol. 12, 605–30.

1981. 'Colonial firms and the decline of colonialism in eastern India, 1914–1947', *Modern Asian Studies*, vol. 15.

1989. *The Economy of Modern India, 1860–1970* (Cambridge University Press).

Topik, S. C., and Wells, A., eds., 1998. *The Second Conquest of Latin America: Coffee, Henequen, and Oil during the Export Boom, 1850–1930* (Austin: University of Texas Press).

Tortella, G., 2000. *The Development of Modern Spain: An Economic History of the Nineteenth and Twentieth Centuries* (Cambridge, MA: Harvard University Press).

Toynbee, A. J., 1934–61. *A Study of History* (reprinted Oxford University Press, 1987).

Trebilcock, C., 1977. *The Vickers Brothers* (London: Europa).

Truitt, N. S., 1984. 'Mass merchandising and economic development: Sears, Roebuck and Co. in Mexico and Peru', in R. K. Shelp, ed., *Service Industries and Economic Development* (New York: Praeger).

Turnbull, M., 1989. *A History of Malaysia, Singapore and Brunei* (London: Allen & Unwin).

Turner, H. A., 2005. *General Motors and the Nazis: The Struggle for Control of Opel, Europe's Biggest Carmaker* (New Haven, CT: Yale University Press).

Turner, L., 1970. *Invisible Empires: Multinational Companies and the Modern World* (New York, Harcourt Brace).

Turrell, R., and van Helten, J.-J., 1986. 'The Rothschilds, the exploration company and mining finance', *Business History*, 28.

Udagawa, M., 1990. 'Business management and foreign-affiliated companies in Japan before World War II', in T. Yuzawa and M. Udagawa, eds., *Foreign Business in Japan before World War II* (Tokyo University Press).

UNCTAD, various years. *World Investment Report* (Geneva: UNCTAD).

Van der Putten, F.-P., 2001. *Corporate Behaviour and Political Risk: Dutch Companies in China, 1903–1941* (Leiden: CNWS Publications).

Van der Wee, H., 1991. *Prosperity and Upheaval: World Economy, 1945–80* (New York: Viking).

Van Hoesel, R., 1997. *Beyond Export-Led Growth: The Emergence of New Multinational Enterprises from Korea and Taiwan* (London: Routledge).

Vaughn-Thomas, W., 1984. *Dalgety: The Romance of a Business* (London: Welland).

Vaupel, J. W, and Curhan, J. P., 1969. *The Making of Multinational Enterprise: A Sourcebook of Tables Based on a Study of 187 Major US Manufacturing Corporations* (Cambridge, MA: Harvard University Press).

Venn, F., 1986. *Oil Diplomacy in the Twentieth Century* (Palgrave Macmillan).

Vernon, R., 1966. 'International investment and international trade in the product cycle', *Quarterly Journal of Economics*, vol. 95.

1971. *Sovereignty at Bay* (London: Longman).

Vickers, A., 2005. *A History of Modern Indonesia* (New York: Cambridge University Press).

Wainwright, D., ed., 1969. *Brooke Bond: A Hundred Years* (privately published).

Walker, T. W., 2011. *Nicaragua: Living in the Shadow of the Eagle* (Boulder: Westview Press).

Wallerstein, I. M., 1974–2011. *The Modern World System*, 4 vols. (Oakland: University of California Press).

Waters, M., 1995. *Globalization* (London: Taylor and Francis).

Weber, M., 1903–4. *The Protestant Ethic and the Spirit of Capitalism* (reprinted London: Routledge, 1992).

Weiher, S. von, and Goetzeler, H., 1984. *The Siemens Company: Its Historical Role in the Progress of Electrical Engineering 1847–1980: A Contribution to the History of the Electrical Industry* (Publicis MCD Werbeagentur Verlag).

Wells, H. G., 2010. *Outline of History* (1920, reprinted Vancouver, BC: Read Books).

Wells, L. T., 1983. *Third World Multinationals* (Cambridge, MA: MIT Press).

Wendel, C. H., 1992. *150 Years of International Harvester* (Sarasota, FL: Crestline Publishing).

Wessel, H. A., 1997. 'Mannesmann in Great Britain 1888–1936: an investment dependent on politics and the market', *Journal of European Economic History*, 26 (2), 399–410.

West, D. C., 1988. 'Multinational competition in the British advertising agency business, 1936–1987', *Business History Review*, 62.

White, C., 1986. 'Ford in Russia: in pursuit of the chimerical market', *Business History*, 28.

Whitney, G. W. R., 1985. *General Electric and the Origins of US Industrial Research* (New York: Columbia University Press).

Wilcynski, J., 1976. *The Multinationals and East–West Relations* (London: Macmillan).

Wilkins, M., 1970. *The Emergence of Multinational Enterprise: American Business Abroad from the Colonial Era to 1914* (Cambridge, MA: Harvard University Press).

   1974. *The Maturing of Multinational Enterprise: American Business Abroad from 1914 to 1970* (Cambridge, MA: Harvard University Press).

   1977. 'Modern European economic history and the multinationals', *Journal of European Economic History*, vol. 6.

   1986a. 'The history of European multinationals: a new look', *Journal of European Economic History*, 15.

   1986b. 'Japanese multinational enterprise before 1914', *Business History Review*, 60.

   1988a. 'European and North American multinationals, 1870–1914: comparisons and contrasts', *Business History*, 30.

   1988b. 'The free standing company, 1870–1914', *Economic History Review*, 61.

   1989. *The History of Foreign Investment in the United States before 1914* (Harvard University Press).

   1990. 'Japanese multinationals in the United States: continuity and change, 1879–1990', *Business History Review*, 64.

   1993. 'French multinationals in the United States: an historical perspective', *Enterprises et Histoire*, 3.

   1994. 'Comparative hosts', *Business History*, 36.

   2004. *The History of Foreign Investment in the United States 1914–1945* (Cambridge, MA: Harvard University Press).

   2005. 'Europe and home and host to multinational enterprise', in H. G. Schroter, ed., *The European Enterprise: Historical Investigation into a Future Species* (New York: Springer).

   2009. 'Multinational enterprise in insurance: an historical overview', *Business History*, 51.

Wilkins, M., and Hill, F., 1964. *American Business Abroad: Ford on Six Continents* (Detroit, MI: Wayne State University).

Wilkins, M., and Schroter, H., eds., 1998. *The Free-Standing Company in the World Economy, 1830–1996* (Oxford University Press).

Williams, E. E., 1896. *Made in Germany* (London: Heinemann).

Williams, S., 2005. *Olga's Story* (London: Penguin).

Williamson, E., 1992. *Penguin History of Latin America* (London: Penguin).

Williamson, O. E., 1975. *Markets and Hierarchies: Analysis and Antitrust Implications* (New York: Macmillan).

Wilson, C., 1954. *A History of Unilever: A Story of Economic Growth and Social Change*, 2 vols. (London: Cassell).

   1968. *A History of Unilever*, vol. III (London: Cassell).

Wilson, M. W., 1947. *Empire in Green and Gold: The Story of the American Banana Trade* (New York: H. Holt).

Wolfgang, P., de Kuyper, J.-Q. and de Candolle, B., 1995. *Arbitration and Renegotiation of International Investment Agreements* (Kluwer Law International).

Wolmar, C., 2009. *Blood, Iron and Gold: How the Railway Changed the World Forever* (New York: Public Affairs Press).

World Bank, various years. *Statistics* (Washington, DC: World Bank).

Wray, W. D., 1984. *Mitsubishi and the NYK, 1870–1914* (London: Routledge).

Wright, W. R., 1974. *British-Owned Railways in Argentina* (Austin: University of Texas Press).

WTO, various years (not 2006). *International Trade Statistics* (Geneva: World Trade Organization).

WTO, 2006. *Air Transport and the GATS* (Geneva: World Trade Organization).

Wurms, C., 1993. *Business, Politics and International Relations* (Cambridge University Press).

Wutzberg, C. E., 1986. *Raffles of the Eastern Isles* (London: Hodder and Stoughton).

Wyatt, D., 2003. *Thailand: A Short History* (New Haven: Yale University Press).

Yacob, S., 2003. 'Beyond borders: Ford in Malaya 1926–1957', *Business and Economic History*, vol. 32.

   2009. 'Ford's investment in colonial Malaya, 1926–1957', *Business History Review*, vol. 77.

Yamashita, S., ed., 1991. *The Transfer of Japanese Technology and Management to the ASEAN Countries* (University of Tokyo Press).

Yamazaki, H., 1987. 'The logic of general trading companies in Japan', in S. Yonekawa and H. Yoshihara, eds., *Business History of Trading Companies* (University of Tokyo Press).

Yang, D., 2010. *Technology of Empire: Telecommunications and Japanese Expansion in Asia, 1883–1945* (Cambridge, MA: Harvard University Press).

Yasamuro, K., 1984. 'The contribution of sogo shosha to the multination-alization of Japanese industrial enterprises in historical perspective', in A. Okochi and T. Inoue, eds. *Overseas Business Activities* (University of Tokyo Press).

Yen, C. H., 1982. 'Overseas Chinese and Late Ch'ing economic moderniza-tion', *Modern Asian Studies*, vol. 16.

Yergin, D., 1992. *The Prize: The Epic Quest for Oil, Money, and Power* (New York: Free Press).

Yoffie, D., 1993. *Beyond Free Trade: Firms, Governments and Global Com-petition* (Cambridge, MA: Harvard Business School Press).

Yonekawa, S., ed., 1990. *General Trading Companies: A Comparative and Historical Study* (Tokyo University Press).

Yonekawa, S., and Yoshihara, H., eds., 1987. *Business History of General Trading Companies* (Tokyo University Press).

Young, L., 1999. *Japan's Total Empire: Manchuria and the Culture of Wartime Imperialism* (University of California Press).

YPFB, 2011. 'Historical background to the rise of MAS, 1952–2005', in Pearce, A., ed., *Eva Morales and the Movemento al Socialismo in Bolivia* (London: Institute of the Americas).

Yuzawa, T., and Udagawa, M., 1990. *Foreign Business in Japan before World War II* (Tokyo University Press).

Zhongli, Z., Zengrian, C., and Xinrong, Y., 1995. *The Swire Group in Old China* (Shanghai People's Publishing House).

Zurwicki, L., 1979. *Multinational Enterprises in the West and East* (New York: Springer).

Index

Index 607

United Engineering and Foundry
Company, 196
United Fruit Co., 89–93, 167, 218–20,
222, 240, 255, 377, 390, 402–3,
512, 530, 541, 546, 558–9
United Kingdom, 54–5, 68, 162–3,
175, 186, 269–71, 273, 278, 280–1,
283, 285, 306–7, 313–14, 316, 344,
420–1, 424, 428, 430, 447, 450,
452, 455, 460–1, 466–7, 473, 491,
495, 516, 529, 546
United Nations, 264–5, 378, 414,
431–2
United Nations Conference on Trade
and Development (UNCTAD), 380,
418, 423
United Overseas Bank Ltd, 457
United States of America, 1, 3, 8, 12,
16–17, 20, 25–9, 34–8, 40–3, 45–8,
50–5, 57, 59, 61, 64, 68–70, 73–5,
79, 81–3, 85–93, 99, 102, 104–6,
108–11, 113, 115, 118–20, 122–5,
127–41, 143–5, 148, 151, 154–6,
158–9, 161–74, 176–86, 188–97,
199–210, 213–19, 221–6, 228–34,
237–8, 240–51, 253, 255, 257–314,
316–25, 327–40, 342–4, 346, 349,
352–7, 359–70, 372, 374–6, 378–9,
381, 384–94, 396–414, 417,
419–22, 424–5, 427–30, 432,
434–40, 444–5, 449–62, 465–7,
470–5, 477, 480, 482–6, 488–91,
494–8, 504–5, 507–9, 514, 516,
519, 523, 527, 536, 539, 542–9,
553–5, 559, 561, 563, 565–6,
569–71
United Telephone Company, 124
United Traders Ltd, 207
University of Strathclyde, 112
Unocal (Union Oil Company of
California), 336, 477
Unternehmergeschaft, 125
Urals, 195
uranium, 309, 333, 400
urbanization, 24, 43, 60, 151, 157,
338, 343
Uriburu, J. F., 226
Uruguay, 104, 107, 111, 124, 126,
225, 242, 247, 331, 405, 432, 435,
549

Usinor steel, 266
Utah, 480
utilities, 29, 50–1, 55, 58, 60–1, 104,
109, 124, 126, 129, 151, 159, 212,
214, 218, 256–7, 274, 290, 307,
319, 333–4, 353, 379, 384, 392,
400, 406–7, 409, 414, 431, 438–40,
464, 503–4, 506
Uzbekistan, 476

VGF, 169, 205
Vaccaro Brothers, 91
Vale, 478–9, 536
Valencia, 283
Valletta, V., 189, 252, 330
Valley Bank, 455
Valley of Mexico, 124
Valparaíso, 41, 85, 131
Van Den Bergh, 78, 136, 173, 206
Van Stolk, 58
Van Zeeland, Paul, 312
Vancouver, 70, 357, 569
Vansittart, R., 234
Vargas, President Getúlio, 403, 408–9
Vauxhall Motors, 181–3, 233, 249,
278–9, 281
Vega Rumänische Petroleum
Raffinerie, 173
Velasco Alvarado, President Juan,
403
Venezuela, 88–9, 106, 120, 176, 226,
292, 362, 387–9, 401, 404, 406–7,
435–6, 466, 468, 472, 474, 477,
506, 519, 545, 548, 562
Veolia, 462, 534
Vereinigte Elektrizitäts und Bergwerks
Aktiengesellschaft (VEBA), 326
Vereinigte Glanzstoff, 314
Vereinigte Kugellagerfabriken, 210
Versailles Treaty, 168, 170–1, 187–8
VIAG, 467
Vichy, 247, 252
Vickers, 80, 176, 195, 249, 311, 383,
545, 568, 569
Victor Company of Japan (JVC), 167
Victor Talking Machine, 167
Victoria, Australia, 126, 134, 184
Victoria, Queen, 74, 97, 120
Victoria Falls & Transvaal Power Co.
Ltd, 126, 383